CHEROKEE RENASCENCE IN THE NEW REPUBLIC

I can see my native country, rising
from the ashes of her degradation . . . and taking
her seat with the nations of the earth.

Buck Watie (Elias Boudinot), 1826

CHEROKEE RENASCENCE IN THE NEW REPUBLIC

WILLIAM G. McLOUGHLIN

PRINCETON UNIVERSITY PRESS

PRINCETON, NEW JERSEY

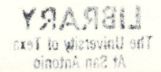

This book is dedicated
to
CRAIG ELLIOTT
and
PETER GRENIER,
two nice guys

CONTENTS

ix

CONTENTS

ILLUSTRATIONS

TABLES

ACKNOWLEDGMENTS

During the ten-year course of researching and writing this book, I have run up numerous debts to people who have given me their generous help along the way. First I wish to acknowledge gratefully the financial assistance of the National Endowment for the Humanities, the American Council of Learned Societies, and the Newberry Library for fellowships and scholarships. Then I want to thank the many librarians and archivists who have been of invaluable help in tracking down materials: Dan McPike and Marie E. Keene of the Gilcrease Institute, Tulsa, Oklahoma; Bill Towner and John Aubrey of the Newberry Library, Chicago; Rella Looney and Louise Cooke of the Oklahoma Historical Society, Oklahoma City; Marty Shaw of the Houghton Library, Harvard University; George Stevenson of the North Carolina State Archives, Raleigh; the staff of the Cherokee Library, Cherokee History Museum, Qualla, North Carolina; Mary Creech and Elizabeth Marx of the Moravian Archives, Winston-Salem, North Carolina; Lother Madeheim of the Moravian Archives, Bethlehem, Pennsylvania; Jack D. Haley of the Western Historical Collections of the University of Oklahoma, Norman; Elma S. Kurtz of the Atlanta Historical Society, Atlanta; Marilyn Bell and Dawnene Matheny of the Tennessee State Library and Archives, Nashville; Pat Bryant of the Secretary of State's Office, Atlanta; Dean R. Kirkwood of the American Baptist Foreign Missionary Society, Valley Forge, Pennsylvania; William H. Brackney of the American Baptist Historical Society, Rochester, New York; Janet S. Fireman and John M. Cahoon of the Natural History Museum of Los Angeles County, Los Angeles; and David A. Jonah, Dorothy Day, and Janet Draper of the Brown University Library, Providence.

I also wish to thank numerous scholars in the field of Native American history whose works I have cited and particularly those who have gone out of their way to provide me with specific answers to queries: Thurman Wilkins, Douglas C. Wilms, Edwin A. Miles, A. D. Lester, Theda Perdue, Walter H. Conser, Jr., Michael Coleman, Dwight Heath, and Robert F. Berkhofer, Jr. I want especially to thank Mary E. Young for her comments on the manuscript.

And finally, as always, I wish to express my deepest thanks to my wife, Virginia W. McLoughlin, whose assistance has been constant and whose judgments always sensible.

PREFACE

This is a study of the rise of romantic nationalism in America, told in terms of the struggle of the Cherokee people to accept the promise of equal citizenship in the new nation.

Hector St. John de Crèvecoeur had asked in 1783, as the United States was born into nationhood, "What then is the American, this new man?" He answered his question in prophetic terms: "He is either an European or the descendant of an European." The Founding Fathers, however, had a different view. For them an American was a rational, civilized, more or less Christian citizen who was committed to republican ideology and to the rising greatness of the United States. George Washington held out the promise of full and equal citizenship to the Indians within America's boundaries. The first Congresses implemented this promise by passing legislation to provide aid that would enable these "savages" to become civilized, Christianized farmer-citizens. Thomas Jefferson continued the promise; "We shall all be Americans," he told the western Indians, and to that end intermarriage was encouraged and federal assistance continued through the first six presidential administrations. "The Indian," Jefferson wrote, "is the equal of the European in mind and body." Jefferson, a true apostle of the Enlightenment, believed in the unity of the human race; he wrote that it was a self-evident principle that "all men are created equal." It was the accepted scientific view of his day. Adam and Eve were the progenitors of all humankind; skin color was only an environmental accident.

Yet between 1783 and the end of the Cherokees' remarkable effort to become civilized and Christianized citizens fifty years later, something drastic happened to the self-image of white Americans. Scientists abandoned the Enlightenment view of the unity of the human race and concluded, with revisionist scientific backing, that there was a hierarchy of races. Not surprisingly, they found the new race of Americans (with their presumed Anglo-Saxon heritage) superior to all others.

This shift in the definition of what it meant to be an American has generally been described in terms of the transition in Western culture from the world view of the Enlightenment to the world view of Romanticism.

Literary historians have long noted that American writers (chiefly on the eastern seaboard) romanticized the Indian into a noble, but disappearing, savage to cover up the dramatic diminution of the ideal of American-ness from an all-inclusive to a particularistic definition. By 1833, "the Indian" was a race apart. Many historians have explained the shift in terms of "western expansion" or "the land greed" of the frontiersman and the land speculator eager to make excuses for stealing the Indian's land. Some have even argued that no great change took place in Indian policy. The effort to remove the Indians from the eastern Mississippi Valley to the west, they claim, was consistent with the original Indian policy; it marked only a change in strategy—a recognition that, for the good of the Indians (because of Indian cultural persistence and the inveterate anti-Indian prejudice of the white frontiersmen), they needed more time to become truly civilized and Christianized. These explanations are inadequate.

A tremendous cultural reorientation took place in America between 1783 and 1833. White Americans drastically revised their views of nature, the supernatural, and human nature. In the process a very different kind of national outlook developed. The removal of the Indians to the west was not simply an incident in this cultural transformation; it was an integral part of it. The changing attitude toward the Indian's place in the new nation was essentially a redefinition of what it meant to be an American; to study what happened to the Indians is to study what happened to white Americans in these years.

In redefining God during the Second Great Awakening (theologically described as the shift from Calvinism and deism to Evangelical Arminianism), Americans also redefined how He worked, which is to say how they thought about man's place in the universe and America's role in human history. The shift from Calvinistic or Enlightenment determinism included the belief that man had free will, that he and God were partners, and that God had chosen the Americans as a special people with a special mission to save the world and bring on the millennium.

The nineteenth-century missionary impulse to perfect the world by converting everyone in it became so ethnocentric that it embodied a patriotic zeal to exclude lesser breeds from more than spiritual salvation. In popular thought, God had chosen the white, Anglo-Saxon, Protestant Americans to save the world. As the voice of the people became the voice of God (a view the Founding Fathers doubted but that Jacksonian democrats voiced freely by 1833), it became important to define the "people" in terms particularly favorable to a romantic nationalism. Americans discovered who they were by deciding who they were not, and those who were deciding were not black Africans or red Indians; this was a white man's country led by special kinds of Europeans who had the innate potential to fit the mold now called "American." The republican ideology ceased to be universal and became exclusionary.

The Cherokees did not think of themselves as a nation in 1776 or in 1789. They were a people united by language, customs, and kinship. They had fought not to establish the new American nation but to prevent its independence. Nor had they been consulted about the first Indian policy of the United States. However, many Cherokees came to accept the generous promises of that policy to a conquered and "unenlightened" people, for the policy granted them respect, hope, and the promise of equal participation. Realizing after their defeat in 1794 that their greatly diminished territory necessitated a transition from a hunting to a farming economy, the Cherokees accepted the "civilizing" policy set for them, at least to the extent that survival depended on agriculture rather than on the fur trade. A few of their leaders, especially those of mixed (Indian-white) ancestry, pressed eagerly forward in this effort. From 1794 to 1815 the Cherokees did their best to adapt to their new situation. Even after the great disappointments following their decision to join General Jackson against the British, the Creeks, and Tecumseh in the War of 1812, they continued to hope that the original promises would be kept. However, they became increasingly aware of the shifting mood of white America. As early as 1816 some Western governors were saying that if the Indians were given citizenship, their status would only be that of freed slaves; after all, were they not a savage, pagan, people of color?

From 1815 to 1833 the people of the United States wrestled with the conflict between their original commitment to integrate Indians and their desire to expand and exploit the land the Indians occupied. At the same time, the Indians wrestled with the question of their own identity and future. With unerring logic, they concluded that national identity rested upon a cultural heritage imbedded in history, language, culture, and a distinct and identifiable "homeland." They too became romantic nationalists, stressing their differences from other people. After all, they had a perfect model of evolving nationhood before them. When they thought about this, they realized that they had a far better claim to ethnic identity and nationhood than the motley, polyglot European peoples who had come to the New World.

Ironically, however, the concept of tribal sovereignty that the Cherokees evolved shared much of the ideology of the individual sovereign states of the Union. States' rights and the bitter conflict over federal supremacy also reached its first peak in the 1820s. The white frontiersmen therefore argued that the Indian nations were trying to establish "imperia in imperia," nations within the states of the Union. The federal treaty power, which had sustained the integrity of Indian nations, became the bulwark of Indian sovereignty at the very time that states' rights became the bulwark of the new program of Indian removal. Western politicians claimed that Indian nationalism derived from the backwardness of a savage people too lazy, ignorant, or simple to adopt civilized ways. In fact, the most sophisticated of Cherokee mixed bloods, as well as the growing ethnic identity of the full bloods, sustained their growing nationalism. Furthermore, awareness of the racial and ethnocentric paternalism developing among even the most benevolent white philanthropists forced the Cherokees to struggle to retain their sovereignty and their land. The Cherokees were at least as "progressive" in this respect as white romantic nationalists. The evidence indicates that the white Americans reversed their view of the Indian's potential before the Indians altered their commitment to the policy of civilization and integration.

By 1827 the Cherokees had learned so well the ideology of their conquerors that they were able to use it against them. If Americans fought for freedom in order to assert government by the consent of the governed, so should the Indians. If the Constitution made treaties "the supreme law of the land," the states had no control over Indian affairs. If treaties "guaranteed" them the right to hold their land and to refuse its sale, then Indian sovereignty was inviolable. Furthermore, by treaties and under the Trade and Intercourse Acts of Congress, the federal government (in return for Indian nonviolence) promised to use its army to protect the boundaries of the Indian nations from all intrusions.

The Cherokees, adopting their own written constitution (after a convention elected by their citizens) in 1827—a constitution modeled directly on that of the United States in its republican ideology—seized the initiative for sovereignty from the states'-rights theorists who surrounded them. In the critical years from 1827 to 1833, Cherokee sovereignty, states' rights, and American nationalism moved in the same direction. With the election in 1828 of a western, populist Indian-fighter to the Presidency, white Americans faced the necessity of reconciling the conflicting impulses of their own destiny. It was no accident that the nullification crisis over the tariff in 1828 coincided with the constitutional crisis over "the Indian question," raised by Georgia's effort that same year to assert its sovereign jurisdiction over the Cherokee Nation. The ability of the Cherokees to hire the most influential jurists and lawyers to plead cases for them in the United States Supreme Court and to arouse intense popular lobbying in Congress on their behalf indicates that more was at stake than the plight of 15,000 "savages."

Two other important features of Cherokee history unite their struggle with that of the United States: slavery and Christianity. The Cherokees were slaveholders; their laws and constitution upheld the institution of chattel slavery. Their land was suitable for growing cotton and, as the slaves among them increased from 583 in 1809 to over 1,500 by 1833, they developed a "black code" relegating Africans to precisely the same status they had in the slaveholding states surrounding the Cherokee Nation. The Cherokees knew they could not be an abolitionist nation in the heart of the Deep South. They also knew that they could not expect equality for themselves if they gave equality to Africans.

The growing influence of white missionaries also links the rise of Cherokee nationalism with the rise of white American nationalism. By the 1820s white Americans considered the United States not only "a white man's country" but "a Christian nation." It had been argued that Indians, being pagans, were not fit for equal citizenship; in white courts (where all their civil and criminal trials involving whites were tried) Indians were denied the right to testify in their own defense. Yet by 1828 Christianity had made such rapid strides in the conversion of Cherokees to Protestantism that many of the missionaries in the Cherokee Nation (Methodists, Baptists, Moravians, Presbyterians, and Congregationalists) were prepared to state that the Cherokee Nation was as Christian in spirit and practice as most of the white communities surrounding it. And could one Christian people treat another as contemptuously as frontier whites wished to treat these Indians?

Having become farmers, having learned to read, dress, talk, vote, and worship like white Americans, the Cherokees became the focal point of this dramatic American confrontation between ideals and practicality, between laws and prejudice, between constitutional principles and the will of the majority, between Christian principle and secular materialism. The rhetoric was equal to the occasion on both sides. But in this study I have tried to get beneath the rhetoric to the reality, at least as far as the cultural historian can. The great Cherokee renascence of 1794–1833 was the rebirth of that people in the image of the United States, yet with a difference.

Providence, Rhode Island   William G. McLoughlin

ABBREVIATIONS

The following abbreviations will be used in the footnotes:

ABCFM
: Papers of the American Board of Commissioners for Foreign Missions. These are indexed by name in the Houghton Library, Harvard University.

ASP I, ASP II
: *American State Papers: Indian Affairs*, vols. I and II, *Documents, Legislative and Executive of the Congress of the United States*, edited by Walter Lowrie, Walter S. Franklin, and Matthew St. Clair Clarke (Washington, D.C.: Gales and Seaton, 1832, 1834).

BFMB
: Baptist Foreign Mission Board (later Baptist Mission Union) Papers, American Baptist Historical Society, Rochester, New York. These consist of "letters sent" and "letters received," arranged by tribe or nation and ordered alphabetically by the names of the missionaries.

Brainerd Journal
: The official journal kept by the missionaries of the ABCFM at Brainerd Mission in the Cherokee Nation. Entries are not attributed to any single individual. This journal is located with the ABCFM Papers at Houghton Library, Harvard University.

Cherokee Laws
: *The Laws of the Cherokee Nation* (Tahlequah, Cherokee Nation, 1852).

MAB
: Moravian Archives, Bethlehem, Pennsylvania

MAS
: Moravian Archives, Salem (Winston-Salem), North Carolina

Payne Papers
: John Howard Payne Papers, Newberry Library, Chicago. I have given the volume and pages for the typescript rather than for the originals, although the typescripts are not always accurate and should be checked against the originals.

GOVERNMENT MICROFILM

The government microfilm series cited most frequently in this volume fall into two groups: those from the Bureau of Indian Affairs, Record Group 75, and those from the Office of the Secretary of War, Record Group 107.

M-15 Bureau of Indian Affairs, RG 75: Letters Sent by the Secretary of War Relating to Indians Affairs, 1800–1824. (Letterbooks, paginated.)

M-21   Bureau of Indian Affairs, RG 75: Letters Sent by the Office of Indian Affairs, 1824–1832. (Letterbooks, paginated.)

M-22   Office of the Secretary of War, RG 107: Register of Letters Received, Main Series, 1800–1870. (Frame numbers given as #1341, etc.)

M-208 Bureau of Indian Affairs, RG 75: Records of the Cherokee Indian Agency, Tennessee, 1801–1835. (Arranged by date; no pagination, no frame numbers.)

M-221 Office of the Secretary of War, RG 107: Letters Received by the Secretary of War, Main Series, 1801–1870. (Frame numbers given.)

M-222 Office of the Secretary of War, RG 107: Letters Received by the Secretary of War (Unregistered), 1789–1861. (Frame numbers given.)

M-234 Bureau of Indian Affairs, RG 75: Letters Received by the Office of Indian Affairs, 1824–1881. (Frame numbers given.)

M-271 Bureau of Indian Affairs, RG 75: Letters Received by the Secretary of War Relating to Indian Affairs, 1800–1823. (Frame numbers given.)

M-668 Bureau of Indian Affairs, RG 75: Ratified Indian Treaties. (Frame numbers given.)

CHEROKEE
RENASCENCE
IN THE NEW
REPUBLIC

ONE

CHANGING CHEROKEE WAYS,
1690–1790

*My people cannot live independent of the English. . . . The clothes we
wear we cannot make ourselves. They are made for us. We use their
ammunition with which to kill deer. We cannot make our own guns.
Every necessary of life we must have from the white people.* —Chief
Skiagunsta to the governor of South Carolina, 1745

*Game is going fast away from us. We must plant corn and raise cattle,
and we desire you to assist us. . . . In former times we bought of the
trader['s] goods cheap; we could then clothe our women and children,
but now game is scarce and goods dear.* —Chief Eskaqua to George
Washington, 1792

B y 1790 the Cherokees were no longer sure of their place in the universe. Not only had they suffered many bloody and devastating de-
feats in battle during the previous fifteen years, but ever since their first
regular contact with Europeans in the 1690s they had gradually lost touch
with important aspects of their old way of life. At first, they voluntarily
accepted the fascinating and useful technology that the Spanish, French,
and English offered them in exchange for deerskins and furs. Then they
became, in effect, the employees of the fur traders who established regular markets for larger and larger catches each year. Soon they fell victim
to the white man's diseases, against which neither their own health de-
fenses nor the practices of their priest/doctors were able to save them. Although they were one of the largest tribes east of the Mississippi in 1690,
their population decreased by more than half by 1740—from over 20,000
to less than 10,000. As the tide of English settlement moved irresistibly
inland, frequent disputes took place that were resolved by forcing the
Cherokees to yield more and more of their territory. By 1776, they had
ceded 50,000 square miles, some of it hunting areas they had shared with
other tribes. During the American Revolution, as defeat followed defeat,
their cultural framework suffered shocks that further undermined its
cohesion and order. Thousands of their people were driven from their
homes and forced to resettle further inland. By 1790, the Cherokees had

lost their ability to sustain the proper relationship between themselves and their environment. The world of spirits that protected (and plagued) them did not respond to their prayers, rituals, and ceremonies as it had in earlier times. Forces beyond their reckoning and control continually overwhelmed them. Harmony was their highest social and religious value, yet the sense of living in harmony among themselves as well as with nature and the spirit world seemed to have been lost. Disorder was everywhere—between old chiefs and young chiefs, between one town and another, between parents and children, between man and the retreating animals. Somehow they had lost control of their destiny as a people. Whether this was permanent or simply a temporary disorientation they could not tell.

Before the white man came there had been a clearly established pattern and structure to their lives, sustained by age-old customs, rituals, beliefs, ceremonies, and symbols guiding the rightful and eternal order of things. After 1690, what had seemed at first to be miraculous blessings, brought from afar by white men in their great white-sailed ships, had become a curse. Once the Cherokees had proudly defined their name, Ani-Yun-wiya, to mean "the real people" or "the principal people." By 1790 they seemed a ruined people. In order to appreciate the remarkable renascence of the Cherokee people from 1794 to 1833, it is first necessary to understand the shocks suffered by their culture in the century from 1690 to 1790. Some of these occurred gradually, such as their entanglement in the market economy and political wars of the expanding empires of western Europe. Some of them came in swift and repeated blows, such as smallpox epidemics and border wars. Cultural shock reached its most desolating stage in the quarter century after 1776. The Cherokees fought on the side of the losers—first the British, then the Spanish—in the struggle for control of the New World.[1]

When the Cherokees began to obtain guns in large numbers from the English colonists of Virginia and the Carolinas (probably by the 1690s), they inaugurated the first phase in the radical transformation of their traditional way of life—the transition from a stable, hunting-gathering-farming society with a subsistence economy and an internally oriented, communal order to a mobile, free-trade, market economy with heavy reliance on European trade goods and alliances.[2] This transformation began

---

[1] See Gary C. Goodwin, *Cherokees in Transition* (Chicago: University of Chicago, Dept. of Geography, 1977), pp. 105–149, for a good description of the ecological reasons for this cultural disorder.

[2] The best anthropological studies of Cherokee society in the eighteenth century are Charles M. Hudson, *The Southeastern Indians* (Knoxville: University of Tennessee Press, 1976); James Mooney, "Myths of the Cherokees," Smithsonian Institution, Bureau of American Ethnology *19th Annual Report, 1897–98*, part 1 (Washington, D.C.: Govern-

TABLE 1

Fur Shipments to England from South Carolina, 1700–1715

Type of Skin	Number Shipped	Type of Skin	Number Shipped
Dressed deerskins	718,719	Moose hides	1,365
Undressed deerskins	164,267	Wildcat skins	848
Beaver pelts	9,841	Black fox belts	283
Fox pelts	8,159	Elk skins	41
Raccoon skins	3,615		
Otter skins	2,035	Total	909,173

SOURCE: Gary C. Goodwin, *Cherokees in Transition* (Chicago: Department of Geography, University of Chicago, 1977), p. 96.

voluntarily as the Cherokees eagerly sought guns to assist them in their wars with neighboring Indian tribes, tribes that might have been barriers and allies against the European invasion but whose previous enmity seemed more threatening. With guns, the Cherokees could kill deer more easily; with deerskins, they could enter regular trading relations with the English to the east of them, the Spanish to the south, and the French to the southwest. By obtaining more guns, steel traps, sharp knives, and hatchets, the Cherokees enlarged their participation in the fur trade. By 1725 it had become the central feature of their lives. As they became skillful with guns and traps, they rapidly depleted the game around them and had to spend more time hunting farther west, impinging upon the domains of other tribes. A good Indian hunter could sell fifty or more dressed deerskins a year; by 1750, the Cherokees alone were selling 25,000 a year (see table 1).

As the occupation of the men changed, so did the lives of their families. Women welcomed manufactured goods that made their lives easier— iron, brass, and tinware to cook in; machine-woven cloth and blankets to replace dressed deer- and bearskins. They learned to use steel needles, scissors, and thread rather than bone needles, sinew, and buckskin; the ancient arts of firing clay pottery, making bone tools, and weaving fiber mats were neglected.[3] By the 1790s some women were cooking pork and

ment Printing Office, 1900); Fred O. Gearing, *Priests and Warriors*, American Anthropological Association Memoir 93 (Menasha, Wis.: American Anthropological Association, 1962); the most useful historical sources for eighteenth-century Cherokee life are Henry T. Malone, *Cherokees of the Old South* (Athens: University of Georgia Press, 1956) and David H. Corkran, *The Cherokee Frontier, 1740–1762* (Norman: University of Oklahoma Press, 1962).

[3] On changing agricultural and settlement patterns among the Cherokees in the eighteenth century see Goodwin, *Cherokees in Transition*, and Douglas C. Wilms, "Cherokee Settlement Patterns," *Southeastern Geographer* 14 (1974):46–53.

TABLE 2

Fur Trade Exchange Rates, Charleston, South Carolina, 1716

Item Traded For	Deerskins Required	Item Traded For	Deerskins Required
Gun	35	Narrow Hoe	3
Broadcloth coat, laced	30	Hatchet	3
Half-thick coat	20	Half thicks (per yard)	3
Pistol	20	Red girdle	2
White Duffield blanket	16	Bullets (30)	1
Calico petticoat	14	Knife	1
Stroud (per yard)	8	Scissors	1
Shirt	5	Flints (12)	1
Axe	5	Steel (to strike flint)	1
Broad Hoe	5	Strings of beads (2)	1

SOURCE: Gary C. Goodwin, *Cherokees in Transition* (Chicago: Department of Geography, University of Chicago, 1977), p. 96.

NOTE: In one hunting season a good hunter might get 50 deerskins.

beef and making butter and cheese from cow's milk, had learned to grow and spin cotton, and were starting to weave their own cloth on European looms. With heavy steel axes Cherokee men built different styles of houses and boats. With more efficient hoes, shovels, and mattocks and eventually with horses, cattle, hogs, and plows, the Cherokees developed a more intensive form of agriculture, an increasing reliance upon domestic livestock, and a new diet. From Europeans they had also acquired new fruits and vegetables—potatoes, watermelons, peaches, and apples. They replaced their older ornamentation of wampum, carved bone, dyed porcupine needles, and feathers with colored beads, mirrors, and glass obtained from the traders, though Cherokee silversmiths continued to make fine silver ornaments. Iron pipes to smoke tobacco replaced soapstone pipes; the carvers who had sculpted bird and animal figures on the pipes gave up this art.

Although manufactured goods brought greater efficiency and new decorative arts, they also brought increasing Cherokee dependence upon the traders who supplied them (see table 2). A Cherokee chief in 1745 pleaded with the authorities in Charlestown, South Carolina, to reopen trading with them that had been cut off because of murders by Indians along the frontier: "My people cannot live independent of the English. . . . The clothes we wear we cannot make ourselves. They are made for us. We use their ammunition with which to kill deer. We cannot make our own guns. Every necessary of life we must have from the white people."[4] As all the

[4] This statement by Chief Skiagunsta is quoted in Corkran, *Cherokee Frontier*, p. 14.

Indian tribes east of the Mississippi obtained guns, alliances with Europeans were necessary to obtain replacements—more lead, flints, powder, parts—or else each tribe would be at the mercy of its enemies. Guns brought a new and more terrible form of warfare; the Europeans taught the Indians about massive attacks to exterminate enemy forces and expropriate large tracts of land. Before they realized the significance of it, the Cherokees had helped to wipe out the Yemassees, Tuscaroras, Catawbas, and Uchees (Yuchis) who had stood between them and the white coastal settlements. The Cherokees felt secure from white invasion because their towns were located 150 to 200 miles or more from the Atlantic Coast, some across the Appalachians. Yet by 1721 they had to make the first cession of their own land to the English in South Carolina; by 1790, they had lost forever thousands of square miles and many former town sites. With the admission of Tennessee to the Union in 1792 and Kentucky in 1796, the Cherokees had whites on every side—the Spanish were in Florida and French settlements were moving up the Mississippi from New Orleans to St. Louis.

The Cherokees were an Iroquoian people, different in language and customs from the Muskogee peoples among whom they lived (the Creeks to the south of them, the Choctaws and Chickasaws to the southwest, the Seminoles in Florida; see map, p. 8). Centuries before the English came to North America, the Cherokees had been driven south, out of the Iroquoian area north of the Ohio River, probably after years of warfare with the Delawares.[5] By 1700, they had been established for several centuries in the southernmost part of the Appalachians in a region that was later to become the states of West Virginia, North and South Carolina, Kentucky, Tennessee, Georgia, and Alabama. The territory over which the Cherokees claimed hegemony in the eighteenth century was almost 350 miles from east to west and 300 miles from north to south, including all the land between the Ohio and Tennessee rivers and from the Blue Ridge mountains through the middle of Tennessee. Most of the western area was hunting ground that they shared with other tribes—the area that became Kentucky (their upper hunting ground) and the area from the Cumberland River to the Tennessee River (their lower hunting ground). Cherokee settlements covered roughly 15,000 square miles from western South Carolina to what is now northeastern Tennessee; they centered in the Great Smoky Mountains that now separate North Carolina from Tennessee.

The best estimates of Cherokee population in 1700 place it at roughly

[5] On the Iroquoian origin of the Cherokees see James Mooney, *Historical Sketch of the Cherokee* (Chicago: Aldine Publishing Co., 1975), pp. 3–8.

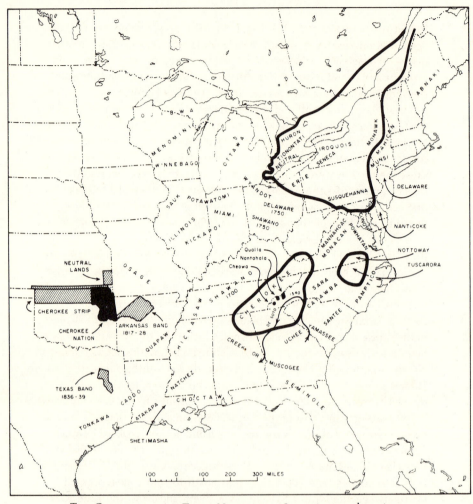

THE CHEROKEES AND THEIR NEIGHBORS. Iroquoian peoples prior to European settlement are shown by the wide lines. Those described in the text as the "western Cherokees" lived from 1794 to 1828 in the area shown by hachure and designated as the "Arkansas band." The area occupied by the Cherokee Nation from 1838 to 1906 and the areas occupied today by those Cherokees who resisted removal are shown in black. From James Mooney, *Historical Sketch of the Cherokee* (Chicago: Aldine Publishing Co., 1975), p. 2.

20,000 individuals or about 4,000 families. These families were divided into sixty or more settlements, called towns or villages by the English, usually of 300 to 400 acres and containing an average of about 300 to 350 persons. Each town had a large council house, a ceremonial square, and from 20 to 200 square, stick-and-wattle houses covered with bark; some towns were surrounded by a palisade of upright logs. The towns were clustered into five distinct regions on both sides of the Appalachian Ridge, along the banks of rivers flowing down the eastern slopes of the Appalachians into the Atlantic Ocean and down the western slopes into the upper Tennessee River. The cluster known in 1700 as the Lower Towns, closest to the English settlements, was on the Chattooga, Tugaloo, and Keowee rivers (the upper branches of the Savannah River) in what is now the western tip of South Carolina. To the northwest of these towns, in western North Carolina, were the Out Towns of the Tuckaseegree River, the Middle Towns along the uppermost reaches of the Little Tennessee, and the Valley Towns along the upper Hiwassee, the Valley, and the Notley rivers. Beyond these to the northwest were the Overhill Towns to the west of the Unicoi range of the Great Smoky Mountains on the Little Tennessee, Tellico, and lower Hiwassee rivers in what is now the northeastern tip of Tennessee. Beyond the Overhill Towns, between the Ohio and Tennessee rivers, lay the great hunting ground that they shared with the Chickasaws, Creeks, Iroquois, and Shawnees.

The Cherokees were a tall, athletic, and handsome people, whose posture, stamina, physique, and good looks were universally admired by the Europeans. They were taller than most Europeans, hardier, and better athletes. Oval-headed and olive-colored, they did not have the high cheekbones and Roman noses of the Plains Indians. Men and women usually tatooed their faces, arms, and bodies; they also wore silver arm bands, earrings, and nose ornaments. The men shaved their faces and heads, except for a small topknot; this they bound with silver or wampum and decorated with tufts of feathers for ceremonial occasions. For war and ceremonies the men also colored their faces with stripes and circles of red, black, ochre, and blue earthen pigments.

Prior to 1700 the Cherokees had lived a sedentary life that was balanced between hunting, agriculture, war, and ceremonial activities. Every town had a communal garden in which women, children, and old men cultivated three kinds of maize (corn), several types of beans (chiefly lima and kidney), various kinds of melon and squash, and Indian tobacco. The land was held in common and food was shared from a town granary, where hundreds of bushels were stored in cribs from harvest to harvest. In addition, each family had a truck garden near its house. By 1700 they were planting sweet potatoes, watermelons, and starting peach and apple orchards with seed acquired from the Spaniards. Their rivers and lakes provided fish, eels, crawfish, and mussels; in the spring and summer they gathered twelve varieties of wild berries (primarily blackberries, raspberries, and strawberries) and in the fall they gathered ten kinds of nuts and seeds (especially pecans, chestnuts, acorns, and sunflower seeds).[6] Meat was dried and salted; dried fruits were also preserved.

Hunting was done by the able-bodied men in the fall and winter. Their chief game was deer, elk, moose, buffalo, and bear. They also caught woodchucks, rabbits, and chipmunks as well as turkeys, partridges, and pigeons. They shot heavy game with bows and arrows or trapped it in snares; the lighter game, especially birds, was killed with blowguns. Clothing and moccasins were made from deerskins; the implements for planting and cultivation from shoulder bones, sharpened stones, and pointed sticks. Corn and nuts were crushed by stone pestles in hollowed-out log mortars. The women wove mats and skirts from bark, reeds, and fibers and baked pottery from clay. Skilled craftsmen sculpted figures on soapstone pipes, worked silver into ornaments, and made wampum from shells.

Families were kept small, averaging three children. Mothers regularly practiced abortion and infanticide; brain-damaged or deformed infants were seldom allowed to live. The hospitality ethic required sharing family food and supplies, no matter how meager, with anyone who came to the door or asked to stay overnight. Occasionally an early or late frost, a prolonged drought, insect plagues, floods, or hailstorms might ruin a crop and cause food shortages. At these times their priests (shamans, medicine men) performed ceremonial prayers and dances to alleviate the disaster and extra effort was put into hunting, fishing, and foraging.

The Cherokees had no centralized political system in the eighteenth century. Each town was self-sufficient and self-governing. Men and women could speak in the town council meetings, which chose and could demote the chiefs or headmen in each town. The town councils did not make laws by majority vote, for the Cherokees lived by well-established, unwritten customs. Council meetings resolved problems within the unwritten law or dealt with wars and alliances; decisions were reached by consensus, usually after prolonged discussion over many days. Until the English began to dominate their trade and alliances, there was no tribal chief or tribal council.[7] Towns might act totally independent of each other. The Cherokees were an ethnic nation, but not a nation-state. There were, however, "Mother Towns" and "Sacred Towns" (called by some "Towns of Refuge"), whose chiefs were held in somewhat higher esteem. National councils were occasionally called in the eighteenth century to deal with major problems of war, peace, or trade alliance that concerned

---

[6] See Goodwin, *Cherokees in Transition*, and Wilms, "Cherokee Settlement Patterns," on Cherokee agricultural patterns and land use.

[7] The best study of Cherokee tribal leadership in the eighteenth century is Gearing, *Priests and Warriors*.

all the towns. Everyone could attend and speak at national councils as in town councils. Tribal decisions were not binding on the towns. No national or town authorities were empowered to maintain a police or court system; the councils exercised no coercive power over individuals. Custom and public opinion sufficed to maintain order. Usually war parties were combinations of towns retaliating against an enemy raid that had killed some of their relatives. In times of war the "red" or "war chiefs" assumed power; in peacetime the old men of the town (the "white" or "peace chiefs") took charge. A town might have from five to seven headmen with various counselors.

What tribal unity existed came in part from the common customs and language but more essentially derived from the clan kinship system. There were at least three (and probably more) distinct tribal dialects, one of which replaced *l* sounds with *r* sounds, and thus made "Tsa-la-gi" (Cherokee) into "Tsa-ra-gi" or the town "Ustanali" into "Ustanary."[8] Seven matrilineal, exogamous clans (sometimes called "tribes" or "families") to which all Cherokees belonged provided the basic cohesion and social infrastructure of the nation. Each clan had its own totemic name (Bird Clan, Deer Clan, Wolf Clan, etc.). They governed marriages, provided protection for members, regulated incest and homicide, and provided a matrilineal kinship system that ordered family life and inheritance. Members of all seven clans inhabited each town, and thus clan unity transcended town self-government and kinship united all the towns. Every town council house had seven sides and people seated themselves by clan at council meetings, even though this separated wives from husbands and children from fathers. No one could marry someone of his or her own clan. When a traveling Cherokee entered another town, his first concern was to find the members of his own clan for hospitality and protection.[9]

The great ideal of the Cherokees' social order was harmony in town affairs, personal relations, and tribal business, as well as in their relationship to nature and to the supernatural. If a Cherokee could not agree with a carefully worked-out consensus in a town council, he withdrew from that activity; he did not form an opposition movement. He might be scorned for refusing to go along with the group, but he was not punished. There was no such concept as treason, even for those who refused to join in a war. The desire to obtain as complete a consensus as possible often

[8] On the various Cherokee dialects see Mooney, *Historical Sketch*, pp. 16–17.

[9] On Cherokee clan structure and its fundamental role in sustaining the unity and order of Cherokee life see Hudson, *Southeastern Indians*, pp. 184–96; John Philip Reid, *A Law of Blood* (New York: New York University Press, 1970) and Rennard Strickland, *Fire and Spirits* (Norman: University of Oklahoma Press, 1975).

meant that no decision at all could be reached. Quarreling was avoided and slights or injuries were ended by efforts to forget bad thoughts on both sides and replace them with good thoughts. An annual "purification" ceremony was dedicated to wiping the slate clean of all disagreements and to seeking harmony with the spirits who governed the universe.

Social order was maintained by clearly understood and faithfully carried out responsibilities of kinship, respect, honor, and mutuality that were taught to children from birth. Public ridicule, disdain, or ostracism were the only forces employed to keep down dissidence, but these were extremely powerful given the high value placed upon not disturbing the public harmony. The Cherokees knew that there was a distinct spiritual order in the world that must also be sustained. Offenses against spiritual order brought penalties to the individual concerned, to his clan, and to his town. Punishment of spiritual offenses, however, was inflicted by the spirit world and not by the chiefs of the community. A man who did not participate in town festivals or who broke taboos might be socially scorned or ostracized until he had purged himself, but his punishment would come when the offended spirits sent sickness or misfortune to him or his family. Socially unacceptable actions (lying, stealing, failing to respect the chiefs or one's elders, refusing to grant hospitality) caused offenders to be held up to scorn and ridicule. Sometimes the offender received a sarcastically appropriate name and was shunned until he altered his behavior and made amends. Such public disgrace was hard to bear; few risked it. Children were taught that their self-interest should give way to the will of the community.

The clan was the only body granted coercive authority, and only in cases of homicide or incest (i.e., marriage within the clan). As an extended family the clan had the duty to avenge or seek restitution for loss by death (whether by malice or accident) of any of its members. The purpose of clan retaliation was not punitive but rather to equalize the balance of things and to overcome the disorder brought by premature death. The obligation to avenge homicide fell upon the closest related male relative on the mother's side (an older brother of the deceased or his mother's brother). If the murderer could not be found, retribution could be taken upon a clan relative of the murderer. Known as "the law of blood" or "blood revenge," this process was so clear, so well defined, that its execution required no court and no police. Homicide was a private, not a public, act. When the murderer was killed by the injured clan, his relatives took no counteraction. The deaths were thus balanced; order was restored; the debt was paid. Often murderers simply gave themselves up, so certain was the death sentence to be inflicted. An older brother or uncle who failed to carry out vengeance was held in the highest contempt. The Cherokees believed that after death the spirits of the dead went to live in a similar but better world. This afterworld was located in the west, where the sun set. However, the aggrieved spirit of a murdered man, whose relatives had not yet avenged his death, might continue in this world and cause misfortune to fall upon the delinquent clan members.

Murder by a member of another tribe or by a European also called for retaliation to restore the balance. The clan members of the person murdered were the first to volunteer for a war party against the guilty tribe. In this case other Cherokees were encouraged to join in taking vengeance. But for theft, injury, assault, or rape, there was no form of corporal punishment, only community disdain. Rape was extremely uncommon because sexual permissiveness was so pervasive from the advent of puberty. Women were not considered the private property of their husbands. A husband might punish his wife for adultery but it was more common simply to leave her. Likewise, a woman could put her husband out of her house for adultery, or for any reason, to end her relationship with him. Marriage, though usually honored for long periods if not for life, was never considered permanently binding on either party. The Cherokee word for husband meant literally, "the man I am living with." Marriage sometimes followed an elaborate ritual (including the exchanging of venison by the man for corn by the woman).[10] Nor was monogamy prescribed. Sometimes a man might marry two or even three sisters at the same time. Divorce was simple and often unilateral. Because of the matrilineal clan system, separated mothers, with their children, could always count upon their mothers, brothers, and sisters to support them. Furthermore, at marriage the husband came to live in the wife's town, where she was near the care and protection of her family. When a husband left or was put out, the wife kept their home, their children, and any property of her own; the husband returned to his town.

The penalty for clan incest was death, as was the penalty for witchcraft. The clan killed the incestuous member; the bewitched person or persons killed the witch (after consulting a priest, who had to confirm that the offender was a witch).[11] Witches were perennial troublemakers whose failure to live in harmony with their fellow townspeople indicated that they were malevolent and, as such, in league with evil spirits. Unless such per-

[10] On marriage ceremonies see Hudson, *Southeastern Indians*, pp. 196–202, and William H. Gilbert, Jr., "The Eastern Cherokees," Smithsonian Institution, Bureau of American Ethnology *Bulletin* 133 (Washington, D.C.: Government Printing Office, 1943), pp. 169–414.

[11] On witchcraft see Raymond D. Fogelson, "An Analysis of Cherokee Sorcery and Witchcraft" in *Four Centuries of Southern Indians*, ed. Charles M. Hudson (Athens: University of Georgia Press, 1975), pp. 113–31.

sons were killed, the town would continue to live in disorder and confusion.

Although Europeans, finding no written law, courts, or police system among the Cherokees, concluded that there were no laws among the Indian tribes, the unwritten laws were clearly understood and faithfully carried out. The Cherokee belief system imposed both a rigid personal morality and an intense communal ethic. It integrated their lives into a clear, cohesive, and meaningful order.

Similarly, European observers often said that the Cherokees had no religious system because no churches, shrines, idols, or state-supported priesthood were found. But the Cherokees led a life full of ritual, ceremony, myth, and symbol. In their cosmology, the earth was a flat, circular disc suspended from the stone dome of heaven at the four cardinal points of the compass and resting upon a vast and deep body of water.[12] Above the dome of the earth was the Upper World of benevolent, guiding spirits; below the earth was the Under World of malevolent spirits. Wicked spirits crept from the Under World onto the earth through caves, springs, and deep lakes. When they caused trouble, the priest/doctors of the nation, called "ado-ni-sgi," (sometimes men, sometimes women), were asked to call upon the powerful spirit of the Upper World to counter the evil activities and restore order again. The necessary harmony between the human and animal world could easily get out of balance. Sickness was the most obvious sign of this. For a man, sickness usually indicated that he had, when hunting, failed to ask forgiveness before killing an animal and thus caused the spirit of that animal to avenge itself upon him. Every animal inflicted its own special sickness. For a woman, sickness was usually ascribed to breaking some taboo of female impurity. Fortunately, the plant world was friendly toward the human world. The adonisgi were skilled in the proper herbal remedies to be applied to the sick in conjunction with ritual prayers and dances involving the aid of the proper superior animal spirit. Medical treatment consisted of giving or applying the proper herb and then, after the ritual song or prayer, literally removing (often by sucking it out) the intruding source of the pain that was gnawing or poking at the inner parts of the sick person. Europeans who observed this process described it as "conjuring" and spoke of the medicine men as "conjurors" because they would often produce a small, sharp stone or stick after their ceremonies that they said they had removed from the sick person—the cause of his or her pain.

Failure to perform the required religious duties toward the spirit world

[12] On Cherokee cosmology see James Mooney, "The Sacred Formulas of the Cherokees," Smithsonian Institution, Bureau of American Ethnology *7th Annual Report, 1885–86* (Washington, D.C.: Government Printing Office, 1891).

would also disturb the balance between man and the elements. Droughts or windstorms that harmed the crops indicated some failure in the community to fulfill spiritual obligations. Likewise, deaths or injuries in a war party could be attributed to the omission of some purification rite by a warrior, to his commission of some offense (such as failure to maintain sexual abstinence before going on the warpath), or to the failure of the war party's leader to heed some warning dream or omen. Even sporting events (surrogates for war), such as the important Cherokee ball play (an early form of lacrosse played with web-ended sticks), required intense spiritual preparation and purification (including sexual abstinence and a scratching ceremony to purify the blood) for each player prior to every game.[13]

Cherokee life was hedged with spiritual significance in every respect. All dreams were important omens. There was no secular area of life free from spiritual meaning; sports, war, hunting, agriculture, family, town, and tribal affairs were all woven together into a unified pattern of religious rules and connections involving harmony with the world above, the world below, and the world around them. Furthermore, all the physical aspects of their environment—rivers, caves, springs, mountain tops, lightning-scarred trees—were imbued with spiritual significance. The sun and moon were sources of spiritual power, as were thunder and wind. Fire was important for home and town life. Tobacco smoke was particularly associated with creating a harmonious atmosphere between man and nature or for discussions of political affairs.

To sustain their spiritual harmony with the world of nature (which itself was supernatural), the Cherokees not only performed daily personal prayers and rituals but also engaged in a series of festivals and rites closely linked to the agricultural seasons. The headmen and priests set the dates for these communal celebrations at the time of the new year, the first green grass, the first harvest of green corn, the final fall harvest, the end of the year, the purification ceremony (when personal grievances were set aside and forgotten), and the lighting of the new fires in each house. All-night dances accompanied these ceremonies, in which both women and men participated, to the music of drums, flutes, and gourd or tortoise-shell rattles. Singing and prayer, chanting and smoking, and drinking special (but not alcoholic) concoctions were all part of these ceremonies. At the annual purification festival, which started the new year after the harvest was in the corn cribs, the whole town went into the nearest running water. The newly fallen leaves gave the water a healthful me-

---

[13] See James Mooney, "The Cherokee Ball Play," *American Anthropologist*, o.s., 3 (1890):105–132.

dicinal quality; as the priest chanted the sacred formula, the people removed their old clothes to let them float away, dipped themselves four times in the river, facing each of the cardinal points of the compass, and then emerged to don new clothes and start with a clean heart and friendship toward their neighbors, having made peace with each other and with the spirit world.[14]

Into this carefully balanced world of man, animals, seasons, sun, moon, plants, spirits, water, fire, wind, and smoke came the white invaders from Europe. They moved steadily westward from the Atlantic shoreline and the fertile tidewater areas, up the rivers and into the Piedmont and mountain valley areas, hunting for game, cutting timber, grazing cattle, looking for mineral deposits, and starting farms wherever the land was fertile. The Cherokees had first met the white man in 1540, when Hernando De Soto's expedition passed through their territory in its search for the seven cities of gold. De Soto's men rode horses, wore armor, carried guns, and used African and Indian slaves as burden bearers. The Cherokees met other explorers in the seventeenth century. At one time the Spanish in Florida sent miners to dig for gold along streams at the eastern edge of the Cherokee nation. In 1634 the Cherokees first met the British who settled in Virginia. But not until the 1690s did they come into regular contact with the closer British settlements in South Carolina.

The British, failing to find gold, turned to the cultivation of tobacco. For this they needed land and labor, both of which they tried to acquire from the nearest Indians. As early as 1693, a group of Cherokee chiefs came to Charleston to complain that the neighboring Catawbas, Savannas, and Congarees had been capturing Cherokees and selling them to the colonists as slaves.[15] The English kept up this practice for thirty years but finally had to abandon it. Unless shipped to the West Indies, Indian slaves too easily escaped back to the woods, often taking runaway African slaves with them. Furthermore, the increasingly lucrative fur trade made it necessary to remain on good terms with the Indians. Next to tobacco and timber, the most important sources of income for the British colonies were furs and hides.

Game was plentiful and the European trade goods were greatly desired by the Cherokees. It was hard to imagine that within one man's lifetime the game would be depleted and the white man would be pushing the Indians off their land. By 1714 white traders were making annual trading trips to the Cherokee towns. Some settled in them and raised mixed-

---

[14] On purification rituals and other ceremonies see Hudson, *Southeastern Cherokees*, pp. 317–75.

[15] See Theda Perdue, *Slavery and the Evolution of Cherokee Society, 1540–1866* (Knoxville: University of Tennessee Press, 1979).

blood families. The traders encouraged the Cherokees to spend less and less time in ceremonies and town affairs and more and more time hunting for profitable beaver, otter, fox, and bear furs or deer, elk, and moose hides. By 1740, there were 150 traders buying up the Cherokees' pelts and furs by the thousands each spring.

Tribes as far from the coast as the Cherokees had the choice of trading with the English on the Atlantic, the Spanish on the Gulf, or the French on the Mississippi. They learned how to play off one European nation against another by threatening to switch trade and alliances in order to obtain higher prices for their labor or more guns. But in general the English were the most important European people. They were more easily accessible, had more traders, more and better goods, and usually were the most threatening to Cherokee security. Alliances, however, required tribal unity. Europeans wanted to bargain with heads of state whose agreements would bind the whole nation. Finding that the Cherokees had no such national chief or political unity, the English tried to create a "King" to unite them. In 1721, the Governor of South Carolina met with thirty-seven Cherokee chiefs and persuaded them to make Chief Wrose-tawasatow their "King."[16] In 1730, Sir Alexander Cumming helped the Cherokees to designate a chief named Moytoy as "Emperor." In later years a succession of chiefs were assumed by the English (and later by white Americans) to speak for the nation: Old Hop in the 1740s; Atta-kullaculla (The Little Carpenter) in the 1760s, Oconostota in the 1770s, Old Tassell, Little Turkey, and Hanging Maw (Scoloscuta) in the 1780s. On two occasions groups of Cherokee chiefs were taken to England to meet the British King and to be impressed with the might of his empire. Most of these were war chiefs, because the Cherokees experienced fewer and fewer periods of peace as the century wore on. As war and hunting came to dominate their lives, the quality of harmony and balance in communal life became harder to sustain. European aggressiveness forced the Cherokee into a more aggressive style of life in the eighteenth century. But not being a united nation at the time, they were never able to wield the power that they might have.

European diseases caused more Cherokee deaths than all of the border raids and Indian wars. Smallpox, typhus, whooping cough, and measles were hitherto unknown in America and the Cherokees had neither built up immunities nor found cures. The remedies tried by their medicine men often simply hastened the death of the victims. This failure of their doctor/priests tended to erode faith in them and their rituals. After a particularly devastating epidemic of smallpox in 1738–1739, which was re-

---

[16] Mooney, *Historical Sketch*, p. 24.

ported to have killed almost half of the Cherokees, tribal animosity against the priests resulted in what seems to have been a repudiation of them and their methods, perhaps even their assassination. Some generations later, the Cherokees spoke of a former priestly hierarchy that had existed in olden times but of which no remnants were left. The adonisgi who performed similar roles after 1790 were said to be of a different and lesser order.[17] The fact that European doctors were able to prevent or cure many of these diseases led some Cherokees to argue that the white man's understanding of the spirit world and his power to apply that knowledge to prevent death were greater than those of the Indian. But whether the white man's medicine and religion were meant for the use of the red man remained unclear. Many Indians concluded that the Great Spirit had ordained total separation between the two people and that what worked for one would not work for the other.

In the eighteenth century, friction occurred more and more frequently between Cherokees and white traders, who filled the Indians with rum or brandy and then cheated them of their winter's catch. By 1755, so many Cherokees had become angry at the truculent behavior of the British that they became more friendly toward the French and Spanish. Neither of these nations was planting settlers on their land; France and Spain were primarily interested in sustaining the fur trade.[18]

When war broke out between the French and the British in 1755, the Cherokees at first honored their alliance with England, but after several unprovoked assaults upon them by Carolina frontiersmen in 1760, some Cherokees switched sides. For two years fierce warfare took place in the Cherokee Nation. Large armies of English frontiersmen invaded Cherokee towns, burning the houses and granaries, laying waste to crops, and slaughtering men, women, and children. Over a dozen of the Cherokee Lower and Middle Towns nearest to the Carolinas were destroyed in 1760–1761. The frontier settlers used the occasion to try to drive the Cherokees west of the Appalachians. The Cherokees were not sufficiently united or well armed to defend themselves and the French did not provide adequate support. In 1761, the Cherokees made peace on the Englishmen's terms.

When the French gave up the war with Britain in 1763, leaving the British in control of the upper Mississippi Valley, the King of England tried to halt the westward expansion of the American colonists by a royal proclamation that forbade any settlements beyond the Appalachian

---

[17] Mooney, *Historical Sketch*, p. 26.

[18] On the impact of the fur trade upon the Cherokees see Goodwin, *Cherokees in Transition*, pp. 96–106, and John Philip Reid, *A Better Kind of Hatchet* (University Park: Pennsylvania State University Press, 1976).

Ridge. The British surveyed the ridge line from Maine to Georgia and established superintendents among the western Indians to sustain the fur trade, uphold the King's rule, and keep the peace. Two of the assistant superintendents came to live among the Cherokees: Alexander Cameron in the North Carolina mountains and John McDonald along the Tennessee River near what is now Chattanooga. But the King could not stop the westward thrust of white farmers and land speculators who were always seeking more and better land. In the late 1760s Daniel Boone led hundreds of families through the Cumberland Gap into what later became Kentucky and Tennessee, where the Cherokees had many towns and some of their best hunting grounds. As these settlers cleared trees and depleted the game upon which the Indian hunters depended for their livelihood, further animosities developed and hostilities occurred. East of the Appalachians the Cherokees agreed to part with thousands of square miles of their land in 1768, 1770, and 1773, as the colonists moved farther into the Piedmont and Blue Ridge Mountains region. Then, in 1775, a group of Kentucky settlers, led by Richard Henderson, persuaded a handful of the chiefs (led by Attakullaculla and Oconostota) to sell them, for a cabin full of trade goods, the whole upper half of their hunting grounds, including almost all of what is now the State of Kentucky and the Cumberland Valley. Henderson's Purchase of 27,000 square miles was illegal under both tribal and English law. The chiefs involved later said that they thought they were only renting the land. But the Cherokees were never able to get it back, and perhaps the chiefs knew that it was not entirely the property of their people but also of the Shawnees and Iroquois who hunted there.

The war that broke out between the unruly colonists and the King in 1776 found the Cherokees on the side of the King. Eager for an excuse to strike back at the white colonists, the Cherokees launched a series of devastating border raids in the summer of 1776 in the Carolinas, Georgia, and eastern Tennessee (on the Watauga and Holston settlements). The frontiersmen soon raised large armies to retaliate. The King and his Indian superintendents were unable to provide either the arms or the military assistance to support their Cherokee allies. Once again dozens of Indian towns east of the Appalachian Ridge were subject to fire and slaughter. In addition, the settlers in what became Kentucky and Tennessee attacked the towns west of the Appalachians. Several thousand Cherokees became homeless, fleeing further to the southwest. Their chiefs were forced to sign treaties with the eastern states of the new American nation in 1777, ceding over 8,000 more square miles. This time the land ceded was not unsettled hunting ground but the site of some of their oldest towns, in which their people had lived for centuries. They were totally expelled from Virginia and lost all but a tiny tract in South Carolina; their territory in North Carolina and what is now Tennessee was cut in half. In 1783 Georgia forced the Cherokees to cede 1,650 square miles near the Chattahoochee River where the Cherokee Nation bordered on the Creek Nation.

Many of the chiefs and warriors were angered not only by the fraudulent cession made to Henderson by the old chiefs in 1775 but also by the quick peace signed with the revolutionaries by these same chiefs in 1777. A group of the intransigent chiefs, led by Dragging Canoe, The Glass, Bloody Fellow, Tolluntuskee, Fool Charles, The Badger, Will Webber, Will Elders, Doublehead, Pumpkin Boy, Unacata, and John Watts gathered together the warriors who were still willing to fight and the displaced families from the eastern part of the nation. They moved to the far southwestern area of the nation, on land shared with the Creeks and Chickasaws. Here they founded a series of new towns along the Tennessee River between Chickamauga and Muscle Shoals, mostly in what is now northern Alabama. They were called the Chickamauga, or Lower Towns, partly because so many of the Cherokees who moved there came from the old Lower Towns in South Carolina and partly because these towns were lower down the Tennessee River from the old Overhill town region north of the Hiwassee River. The King's agent, John McDonald, and his son-in law, Daniel Ross, lived among them and encouraged them to keep up the war. Scores of adventurous colonists loyal to the King fled from their homes in the colonies to settle in the Chickamauga towns. Many of these white Loyalists married Cherokees and later played a large part in Cherokee history—John Rogers, John Walker, John McLemore, John Fields, John Thompson, John D. Chisolm, John McIntosh, Edward Adair, Edward Gunter, Arthur Coody, Richard Taylor, and William Shorey. Once married to Cherokees, they were considered full members of the tribe or "Cherokee countrymen." They assisted Dragging Canoe in his guerrilla warfare against those seeking independence from England and some Loyalists donned buckskins and war paint to participate in the continual raids along the frontier for the next seventeen years. They were joined in this border warfare by Creek warriors to the south and Shawnees to the north. The white revolutionary patriots settled in Watauga and Transylvania (in what became eastern Tennessee) as well as on the western borders of Georgia and the Carolinas bore the brunt of this warfare and never forgot their hatred and distrust of "the savages." As in most guerrilla wars, no quarter was given on either side; men, women, and children were shot, hacked, scalped, burned, and taken captive. The bitter enmity long outlasted the war.[19]

[19] Detailed accounts of the Cherokee border warfare from 1780 to 1794 can be found in

When the King made peace with the colonists in 1783, his peace treaty contained no provisions to rescue the Indians and their Loyalist "countrymen" from the vengeance of the colonial frontiersmen. Many of the Cherokees remained at war for another decade. Freed from fighting the King's armies, the American frontiersmen now turned their full force against the Cherokees, Creeks, and Shawnees. In Tennessee and Kentucky these militiamen ravaged the western Cherokee towns and forced more land cessions in 1783–1784. Finally, the Continental Congress, having persuaded the new states that it should take charge of Indian affairs, made the first national treaty for the United States with the Cherokees in 1785 at Hopewell. The Treaty of Hopewell was unique in several ways: first, it accepted the Cherokee version of their current boundaries even though many whites had already settled within those boundaries; second, it gave the Cherokees permission to evict any whites who were within their boundaries; third, it proposed to try to evict some of those whites who were located on the French Broad and Holston rivers (on the borders of what are now North Carolina and Tennessee). In effect the new American nation agreed to protect what was left of Cherokee territory from land-hungry citizens and to allow the Indians to maintain their own tribal self-government.

In exchange for peace, the Cherokees made a series of crucial concessions in 1785. They agreed that "the United States, in congress assembled, shall have the sole and exclusive right of regulating the trade with the Indians and managing all their affairs in such manner as they think proper." They conceded that "all traders" should have "liberty to go to any of the tribes or towns of the Cherokees to trade with them." The Cherokees were to "give notice" of any designs by other tribes "against the peace, trade or interest of the United States." The Cherokees acknowledged themselves "to be under the protection of the United States," and agreed that any robbery, murder, or assault involving whites (or whites and Cherokees) within the Cherokee boundaries was to be tried and "punished according to the ordinances of the United States." The United States was permitted "to send a deputy of their choice" to reside among the Cherokees as the agent of the United States. And, finally, the Cherokees agreed to give up "the idea of retaliation" or blood revenge against whites who murdered Cherokees and to leave justice in such cases to the white authorities.

Many of the harassed Cherokees were happy in 1785 to have their land under the protection of the federal government and to be freed from dealing with frontier leaders in each of the states. The federal government

John P. Brown, *Old Frontiers* (Kingsport, Tenn.: Southern Publishers, 1938) and Robert S. Cotterill, *The Southern Indians* (Norman: University of Oklahoma Press, 1954).

seemed to them to express a generous, even-handed view of Indian relations, unlike the vindictive westerners. Assuming that the federal government was superior in power to the states, the Cherokees expected that their boundaries would be secure. They were especially eager to have the government eject the many whites who had settled upon the French Broad and Holston rivers. They did not realize how weak the federal government was and how sensitive it was toward the feelings of its western citizens. Nor did they realize that many whites assumed that the clause in Article 8 of this treaty giving the United States the right to manage "all their [Cherokee] affairs in such manner as they think proper" meant that the Cherokee had lost all sovereign rights and become merely "tenants at will" to the white men who had conquered them.

The Continental Congress proved to be a weak reed upon which to hang their hopes. In the first place, neither Georgia nor North Carolina had yet given up its western land to the United States and therefore most of the Cherokee territory was still technically under the jurisdiction of these states. Before North Carolina yielded its western land (ultimately the State of Tennessee) in 1790, it allocated thousands of square miles there (much of it within Cherokee territory) to its Revolutionary War veterans as bounties for their war service. When North Carolina yielded this Tennessee area to Congress it stipulated that these bounty rights were to be protected and, whenever land on which bounties had been given was ceded by the Cherokees, the bounty land was to revert to the veterans or their heirs or assigns. Before Georgia yielded its western land to Congress in 1802 (ultimately to become the states of Alabama and Mississippi) the state legislature sold off millions of acres of Choctaw, Creek, Chickasaw, and Cherokee land to various land-speculating companies (notably the Yazoo fraud tracts). Georgia agreed to allow the federal government to buy out the land-speculating companies in exchange for Georgia's turning this whole area over to the federal government. However, in the famous "Georgia Compact" that Thomas Jefferson made with Georgia in 1802 to seal the bargain, the President agreed that the federal government would extinguish all Indian claims to land within the limits of Georgia as soon as reasonably possible and return that land to Georgia.[20]

The inability of Congress after 1785 to compel North Carolina to eject its citizens from farms they had established within the Cherokee boundaries on the French Broad and Holston rivers led the Chickamauga Cherokees, under Dragging Canoe and Bloody Fellow, to repudiate the Hope-

---

[20] The "Georgia Compact" of 1802 is discussed in *Cherokee Removal: The 'William Penn' Essays and Other Writings by Jeremiah Evarts*, ed. Francis Paul Prucha (Knoxville: University of Tennessee Press, 1981), pp. 156–61.

well treaty. With their Creek and Shawnee allies, they continued to attack whites who had settled anywhere in Kentucky and Tennessee as well as those on the Cherokee border in Georgia. The Upper Town Cherokees (those who lived in the towns that wished to abide by the treaty), led by Old Tassell, Little Turkey, and Hanging Maw, tried to restrain the Lower Town warriors. Not being able to do so, they suffered from invasions of frontier armies who made little distinction between the friendly and the unfriendly Indians around them. The federal government stood by ineffectually as this frontier phase of the Revolution continued for nine years after the Treaty of Hopewell, with considerable losses on both sides.

After the thirteen original states of the Union adopted a new Constitution in 1789 and inaugurated George Washington as their President, he and his Secretary of War, the New Englander Henry Knox, tried their best to compel the North Carolinians in eastern Tennessee to move outside the bounds of the Cherokee Nation, but by then these frontiersmen were in rebellion against North Carolina. They had created a new state, called Franklin, centered in the area under dispute with the Cherokees. The Franklinites, led by men like John Sevier and James Robertson, were determined to drive all Indians from their area (later the State of Tennessee). In defiance both of North Carolina officials and the new President, these westerners not only continued to expand their settlements on Cherokee land but to wage their own form of guerrilla warfare against the Cherokees. Claiming that the Upper Towns, though ostensibly friendly, were in fact aiding and abetting the Chickamauga Cherokees in the Lower Towns, these frontier fighters in 1788 murdered a group of Upper Town chiefs led by Old Tassell who came to bargain with them under a flag of truce; in 1792 they seriously wounded his successor, Hanging Maw, and killed his wife, although Hanging Maw was at peace. These assassinations led many Upper Town warriors to migrate south to join the Chickamaugans in the Lower Towns and to continue the effort to thrust the whites back across the Appalachians.

In 1791, after North Carolina had ceded the Tennessee area to the federal government, President Washington tried to obtain peace in the area. That year the Treaty of Holston asked the Cherokees to yield the land in eastern Tennessee from which the government could not expel the whites; the President said that in exchange for this he would guarantee that the remainder of their land would be kept free from intruders. Washington left the negotiation of the treaty to Governor William Blount of Tennessee Territory. Blount, like most western politicians, was eager to obtain as much land from the Indians as possible to satisfy the intruders who were his constituents. He was also heavily engaged in land speculation that would net him handsome profits from the treaty. The chiefs summoned to the council at Holston in July 1791 were astounded when Blount told them that the government could not live up to its treaty at Hopewell to "solemnly guarantee forever" the boundaries arranged at that time. Instead of removing the whites who had intruded, Blount asked the Cherokee to cede 4,157 square miles of land on the French Broad and Holston rivers for an annuity of one thousand dollars. The chiefs, led by Bloody Fellow, objected strenuously. Blount said that there was no other solution and that without such a cession friction would continue on that frontier. He threatened them with dire consequences if they did not yield. Reluctantly the chiefs agreed. Blount then ran the boundary when no Cherokees were present, in their opinion running it to his advantage.[21] Washington was embarrassed by Blount's actions; he later agreed when Bloody Fellow came to see him in Philadelphia to increase the annuity to $1,500 and to require Blount to remove some intruders who were still within the new line. But Blount could not, or would not, do this and the bloody warfare continued. Dragging Canoe died in 1792 and John Watts, Bloody Fellow, and Doublehead succeeded him as leaders of the Chickamaugans.

The Upper Towns considered the Treaty of Holston to have superseded the Treaty of Hopewell and were pleased that it seemed to restore Cherokee sovereignty. Although Article 3 stated that "the United States shall have the sole and exclusive right of regulating their trade" it now omitted the phrase saying the United States could manage "all their affairs in such manner as they think fit." The fact that the United States purchased this cession from them indicated, they believed, that they were not tenants at will but full owners of their land. Not only were they again solemnly guaranteed "all their lands not herein ceded" but they retained internal self-government under their own chiefs and councils. Under Article 14, the United States agreed to "furnish gratuitously, the said nation with useful implements of husbandry" in order that they "may be led to a greater degree of civilization and to become herdsmen and cultivators instead of remaining in a state of hunters." From this the Cherokees assumed that they were to be accepted as part of the Union, with their own guaranteed borders and government and with direct assistance toward improving their condition so as to become useful citizens of the republic. Furthermore, the treaty allowed the Cherokees to punish and evict any citizens of the United States who trespassed on their land and it stipulated

---

[21] On the boundary of the Treaty of Holston see Charles C. Royce, *The Cherokee Nation of Indians, 1887* (reprint, Chicago: Aldine Publishing Co., 1975), pp. 34–42.

that no white citizen could "go into the Cherokee country without a passport." White citizens who committed crimes against Cherokees and Cherokees who committed crimes against whites were still to be tried in the white man's courts. The Cherokees agreed to set aside land for a federal agent to live on and to grant a right of way through their nation for the Cumberland Road connecting Knoxville with Philadelphia to the east and Nashville to the west.

The United States delayed in making its final survey of the cession of 1791 until more whites had settled in areas within the new Cherokee boundaries. The Chickamaugans were still determined to drive the whites out of their hunting lands. They saw no reason to believe that the Upper Town chiefs had done any more for the nation in 1791 than they had in 1785. In 1792, McDonald and the Lower Towns made an alliance with the Spanish, and the guerrilla war went on, aided by supplies from Spanish Florida. But it was hopeless. The Cherokees' long war with the United States finally ended in November 1794, after the defeat of John Watts and Bloody Fellow in a series of destructive attacks upon the Lower Towns by Colonel James Ore of Tennessee. Furthermore, the Spanish had stopped assisting the Chickamaugans due to Napoleon's invasion of their country. In the area north of the Ohio River, General Anthony Wayne defeated the Northwestern Indian Confederacy of Miamis, Ottawas, and Shawnees (aided by a contingent of one hundred Cherokees) at the Battle of Fallen Timbers in 1794, thus depriving the Chickamaugans of Shawnee assistance. The treaty made by the Lower Towns in 1794 merely confirmed their acquiescence in the treaty of 1791. In February 1795, George Washington told Congress: "Hostilities with the Cherokees have ceased and there is a pleasing prospect of permanent peace with that nation."[22]

Between 1776 and 1794 the Cherokees had reached a critical junction in their history. Their population was barely ten thousand; three-fourths of the land they had once considered theirs was closed to them (see table 3, chronology of treaties, and maps of territorial losses and land cessions); over half of their towns were destroyed and ceded to the United States; those who lived in those towns had to move into what was left of the nation and start over again. Precisely how much independence was left to them as a people was unclear. Although they continued to follow their traditional patterns as much as possible, they found it increasingly difficult to make a living. The fur trade upon which they had depended for

---

[22] *American State Papers: Indian Affairs*, vols. I and II, *Documents, Legislative and Executive of the Congress of the United States*, ed. Walter Lowrie, Walter S. Franklin, and Matthew St. Clair Clarke (Washington, D.C.: Gales and Seaton, 1832, 1834), vol. I, p. 51. Hereafter abbreviated as ASP I and II.

TABLE 3
Cherokee Land Cessions, 1721–1806

	Year	Colony/State	Area (sq. mi.)		Total Area per Cession (sq. mi.)
1.	1721	S.C.	2,623		2,623
2.	1755	S.C.	8,635		8,635
3.	1768	Va.	850		850
4.	1770	Va.	4,500		
		W. Va.	4,300		9,050
		Ky.	250		
5.	1772	W. Va.	437		
		Ky.	10,135		10,917
		Va.	345		
6.	1773	Ga.	1,050		1,050
7.	1775 "Henderson's Purchase"	Ky.	22,600		
		Va.	1,800		27,050
		Tenn.	2,650		
8.	1777	S.C.	2,051		
9.	1777	N.C.	4,414	6,174	8,225
		Tenn.	1,760		
10.	1783	Ga.	1,650		1,650
11.	1785	N.C.	550		
		Tenn.	4,914		6,381
		Ky.	917		
12.	1791	Tenn.	3,435		
		N.C.	722		4,157
13.	1798	Tenn.	952		1,539
		N.C.	587		
14.	1804 "Wafford's Tract"	Ga.	135		135
15.	1805	Ky.	1,086		8,118
		Tenn.	7,032		
16.	1806	Tenn.	1¼		1¼
		Tenn.	5,269		6,871
		Ala.	1,602		
	Total				97,252¼

SOURCE: Charles C. Royce, *The Cherokee Nation of Indians* (reprint, Chicago: Aldine Publishing Co., 1975), p. 256.

almost a century was now so small that the hunters had to stay out longer and travel further each winter to make a good catch. Their old hunting grounds were filling up with white hunters and often with illegal white squatters. The federal government had promised in 1791 to help them make a living as herdsmen and farmers, but the Cherokees knew little about the kind of horse-and-plow farming needed to support a family, nor did Indian wives know how to be farmers' wives. The Cherokees

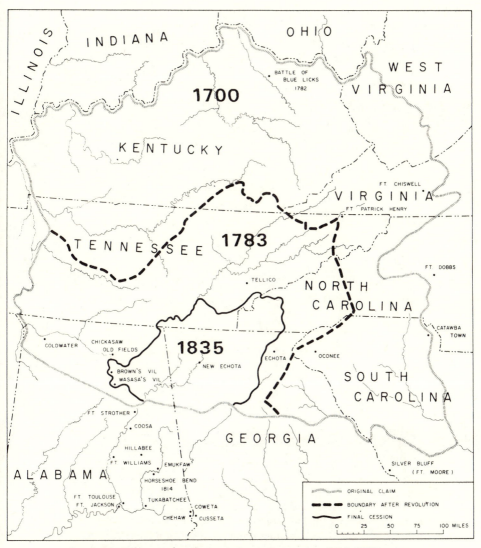

CHEROKEE TERRITORIAL LOSSES, IN THE PERIODS 1700–1783 AND 1783–1819. In 1838 the Cherokees were forcibly removed from the area marked 1835 as a result of the fraudulent Treaty of New Echota in 1835. From James Mooney, *Historical Sketch of the Cherokee* (Chicago: Aldine Publishing Co., 1975), p. 10, with additions.

seemed unable, even in peace, to regain the stability, harmony, and order they had known in the past. Nor were their religious ceremonies any longer able to give them a sense of control over their destiny. They now lived on a different part of their land from that of their ancestors. Their

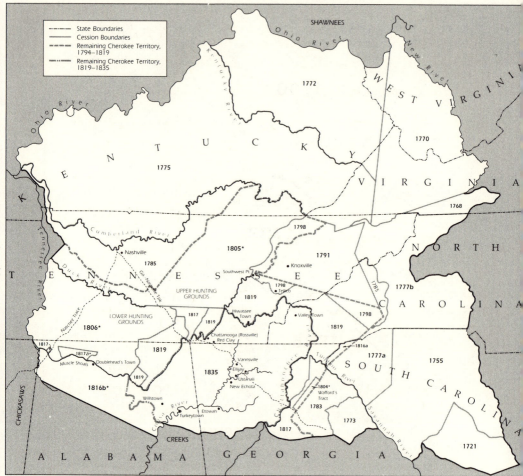

CHEROKEE LAND CESSIONS, 1721–1835. The years shown correspond to the treaties listed in the accompanying chronology. The starred years mark cessions discussed in detail in the text: Wafford's Tract (1804); the upper hunting grounds (1805); the lower hunting grounds (1806); the land taken from the Cherokees in 1814 by the Creek Treaty, returned in March 1816, and then fraudulently ceded back to the U.S. (1816b); and the tract given to Doublehead for a model town in 1806 and taken back by the U.S. in 1817 (1817a). Based on maps in Charles C. Royce, *The Cherokee Nation of Indians* (Chicago: Aldine Publishing Co., 1975); prepared by Lisa Tingey Davis.

28

CHRONOLOGY OF TREATIES WITH THE CHEROKEES, 1721–1835
The land ceded in each treaty is shown in the accompanying map,
where the cessions are dated as in the first column below.

Colonial Period

1721	Treaty of 1721 with Gov. Nicholson of South Carolina
1755	Treaty of November 24, 1755, with Gov. Glenn of South Carolina
1768	Treaty of October 14, 1768, with J. Stuart, British Supt. of Indian Affairs
1770	Treaty of October 18, 1770, at Lochaber, South Carolina
1772	Treaty of October 1772 with the governor of Virginia
1773	Treaty of June 1, 1773, with J. Stuart, British Supt. of Indian Affairs
1775	Treaty of March 17, 1775, with Richard Henderson and others
1777a	Treaty of May 20, 1777, with South Carolina and Georgia
1777b	Treaty of July 20, 1777, with Virginia and North Carolina
1783	Treaty of May 31, 1783, with Georgia

Federal Period (all treaties made with the United States)

1785	Treaty of November 28, 1785
1791	Treaty of July 2, 1791
1798	Treaty of October 2, 1798
1804	Treaty of October 24, 1804 (Wafford's Tract)
1805	Treaty of October 25, 1805 (upper hunting grounds)
1805	Treaty of October 27, 1805 (covered small area, not distinguished on map)
1806	Treaty of January 7, 1806 (lower hunting grounds)
1816a	Treaty of March 22, 1816
1816b	Treaty of September 14, 1816 (area taken from Cherokees in 1814 by the Creek Treaty, returned in March 1816, and then fraudulently ceded back to the U.S. in this treaty)
1817, 1817a	Treaty of July 8, 1817 (1817a is tract given to Doublehead by Jefferson on January 7, 1806, for a model town and ceded back to the U.S. in 1817)
1819	Treaty of February 27, 1819
1835	Fraudulent treaty of December 29, 1835

Adapted from Charles C. Royce, *The Cherokee Nation of Indians* (Chicago: Aldine Pub. Co., 1975), p. 256.

center of population had moved almost one hundred miles south and west of the towns they had surrendered since 1775 (see map of settlement areas). Their young men were no longer to be trained to be warriors and hunting was becoming less and less profitable. They could not return to the way they had lived before the white man came, nor did they feel able to become farmers as their conquerors expected them to do.

Equally important, the values of subsistence farming were individualistic. The Europeans expected men and women to be guided by self-inter-

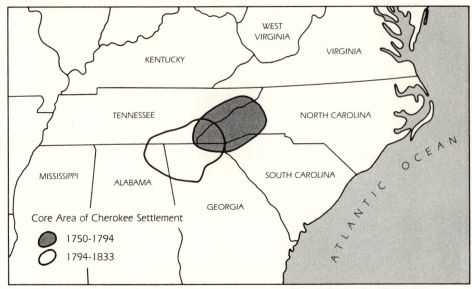

CHEROKEE SETTLEMENT AREAS BEFORE AND AFTER 1794. Between 1775 and 1794 the demographic center of Cherokee population shifted 100 miles to the southwest. Scale: 5/8″ = 100 mi. Map prepared by Lisa Tingey Davis; based on map in Goodwin, *Cherokees in Transition*.

est, putting themselves and their family first and striving always to acquire more goods, more land, and more personal wealth. The white men loved competition, but the Cherokee way of life honored subjugation of the self to the good of the clan and the community. In the past, a man's few worldly goods were placed beside him in his grave—his bow, his pipe, his medicine bag. But as Cherokees acquired property of more value, too many relatives had uses for his gun, his axes, his knives, his horse and bridle, his cattle. Already, much of the ritual centered around burial and mourning for the dead had been curtailed because so many died quickly in the wars and epidemics, and the living had to flee before invading white men. Much of their ceremonial life was related to hunting and war or concerned with sustaining communal harmony. If they dispersed to become farmers, they would have to give these up. Of what use now were the Scalp Dance, the War Dance, the Buffalo Dance, the Eagle Dance? It is true that new ceremonies might arise or old ones be adapted, but they would have to deal with a different ordering of life. For example, in the 1750s the Cherokees began to practice a new ceremony called the Booger Dance. In it the dancers wore elaborate false faces portraying horrifying spirit figures; they shouted and frightened the children. Some say it was designed to scare the young into obedience, but others believe it grew out

30

of the pervasive fears of death and destruction wrought by white invaders.[23] It seemed to teach that there was a new kind of disorder loose in their world. Demons from outside the Cherokee cosmogony were almost impossible to exorcise.

On the other hand, many whites had come to live among them and had fought with them as allies. Numerous Tories had joined them in the war against the American colonists after 1776; some deserters from the ranks of the French and Spanish had become intermarried "countrymen." Their children did not speak Cherokee or know Cherokee customs. These white men and their foreign-speaking, European-dressed children, when grown, proved helpful in certain ways. They understood the language and customs of whites and provided useful knowledge as well as serving as interpreters for the Cherokee leaders. However, many of the whites who fled to Cherokee towns were outlaws, renegades, bankrupts, and confidence men, eager to take advantage of Cherokee hospitality and of their women but indifferent to the Cherokee Nation in its troubles. These white men were not part of any clan; a few were adopted into a clan, but not many. White husbands did not respect the Cherokee customs regarding the right of the wife to her own property, her right to her house and children, her right to live in her own town near her kin; they refused to accept the matrilineal practices of inheritance. On the whole, the white men and many of their children were as much trouble as help in these years. Moreover, the children of mixed ancestry tended to marry their own kind, to raise their children as whites did, and to perpetuate a social group separate from the rest of the nation.

Another disturbing element after 1794 was the increasing number of African slaves and freedmen coming into the nation. Early in the eighteenth century the British colonists had made it plain that they did not intend to let the Indians on their borders harbor runaway slaves. In large parts of the southeast, the combined total of Indians and slaves had outnumbered the whites. There was always fear that these "colored peoples," feeling oppressed, might join forces against the whites who mistreated them. Fortunately for the Europeans, the Cherokees had little use for slave labor in the eighteenth century and were happy to accept the large rewards that the whites offered for the return of runaway slaves. By 1794 there were about one hundred blacks living among the Cherokees. Some of these had been captured from whites as the booty of raiding parties during the guerrilla wars. Some were runaways. Others were freed blacks who preferred to live among a people who did not as yet discrimi-

---

[23] On the Booger Dance see Hudson, *Southeastern Indians* and Goodwin, *Cherokees in Transition*, p. 143.

nate against them, letting them intermarry and live as equals. But most blacks in the nation were owned by white traders, Loyalists, and other whites who had brought them with them as slaves.[24] Because there were few laws and no taxes and because land was free within the nation to all "countrymen," the Cherokee Nation was an ideal place for a white man to start a farm or a plantation and gain a stake for himself. Cherokees of mixed ancestry saw the value of slave labor in an agrarian, staple-crop system. For full-blood Cherokees who could afford slaves, it was easier to let them do the heavy labor of a farm (a task traditionally assigned to women). As the Cherokees were forced to become farmers to survive, they naturally followed the pattern set by the white Southerners around them. Eventually they had to face the problem of being a multiracial nation. Could one be a black man and also be a Cherokee? Could persons of mixed black-and-Cherokee or black-and-white ancestry be Cherokees? In the states surrounding the Cherokee Nation the prejudices against color, whether black or red, made this question particularly difficult for the Cherokees to solve using their traditional principles.

Life in 1794 was far different from life in 1694. Confusion in their culture made it hard for the older generation to fulfill their roles as leaders, teachers, and guides for the young. So much that had been true for parents and grandparents simply was not applicable to the lives of the rising generation. Cultural persistence was powerful; most tried to retain the old patterns as best they could once peace was attained. But it seemed unlikely that they could ever return wholly to the old ways. A new, and as yet unspecified, way of life had to be found to fit their new circumstances. Somehow they had to revitalize their culture by combining old ways with new ones or by finding Cherokee versions of white ways. In the struggle to survive, the Cherokees did develop new patterns for life, but only after fifteen years of intense social and political crisis that at times amounted to civil war.

[24] See Theda Perdue, *Slavery and Cherokee Society*, pp. 50–56.

TWO

DISORIENTATION AND RESTRUCTURING,
1794–1810

The day will soon come when you will unite yourselves with us, join in our great councils, and form a people with us, and we shall all be Americans; you will mix with us by marriage; your blood will run in our veins and will spread with us over this great continent. —Thomas Jefferson to the western Indians, 1808

When peace finally came to the Cherokees in 1794, they were beset with problems. Although ostensibly united under Chief Little Turkey, they were still politically divided between the Lower Towns and the Upper Towns, each with its own regional chiefs and councils. They were also divided in many other ways. The older generation tried its best to sustain the old ways; the intermarried whites and Cherokees of mixed white-Cherokee ancestry were eager to try new ways. The young were caught between two worlds. The priests and medicine men tried to preserve the orderly relations between man and nature, but the old ways and the old belief system did not correspond with their new circumstances. They were still rebuilding old towns and starting new ones. The able-bodied men went out every fall to spend the winter in what was left of the hunting ground between the Tennessee and Cumberland rivers but were unable to find enough furs and skins to purchase all they needed for their families. The women, old men, and children continued to cultivate communal gardens, but with more people squeezed onto less land they often did not grow a large enough crop to carry them from harvest to harvest. They still celebrated some of their old festivals—the Green Corn Dance for thanksgiving, the purification ritual, the lighting of the new fire at the start of the new year, but other ceremonies died away. The biggest social occasions were the ball plays, where young men could still demonstrate their physical daring, stamina, and skill, but much of the religious content had gone out of these occasions. They often became scenes of drunkenness, gambling, brawling, and quarreling. Everything seemed out of joint.

For its own reasons the federal government tried to bring some order and conciliation to the frontier region. The United States needed a stable situation in the west and hoped to win the 250,000 Indians there into peaceful cooperation to control the Mississippi Valley. Resident federal agents were sent to each tribe in the 1790s to help them shift from the declining fur trade to intensive agriculture. There were eighty-five different tribes living in the area between the Appalachian Ridge and the Mississippi River. By treaty they still owned most of the land in that area. However, the British in Canada, the French on the lower Mississippi, and the Spanish in Florida continued to maintain their influence in the valley. The new American nation was not sufficiently wealthy to support the kind of army such a vast region needed for national security. Common sense dictated that the government, though it had temporarily defeated the Indians, should do its best to remain on good terms with them. More than that, it seemed wise to find some way to unite the interests of the Indians with those of the United States. The obvious means for this were commercial trading ties, intermarriage, and economic assistance to convert the Indians into yeoman farmers. Promises of citizenship and integration into the future destiny of the United States also seemed a wise and generous approach to "the Indian question."

By 1794 the white population west of the Appalachians in 1796 was larger than that of the Indians. Many frontiersman wished to drive all of the Indians across the Mississippi even if it meant further war. But the new nation could not afford that choice. "It is highly probable," said Secretary of War Knox in 1789, "that by a conciliatory system the expense of managing the said Indians and attaching them to the United States for the ensuing period of fifty years, may on an average cost $15,000 annually" whereas "a system of coercion and oppression pursued from time to time for the same period . . . would probably amount to a much greater sum of money."[1] One of the first orders of business in Washington's administration was to establish a clear set of policies to guide the nation's relations with the Indians. From the Indians the Americans wanted two things—peace and land. The fur trade was to be replaced by trade in agricultural products, livestock, and the manufactured goods necessary to a farming community. Peace was to be preserved by helping the Indians to acculturate.

The policy that Knox and Washington presented to Congress in 1789 and that guided white-Indian relations from 1789 to 1833 was based on the assumption that the Indians could and should be civilized to the point of becoming "incorporated" or integrated as equal citizens on the land where they were now to become farmers. Although many westerners

[1] ASP I, 13.

disliked various aspects of this policy, it was designed to assuage the white settlers' problems as much, or more, than those of the Indians. Having no alternative to it, the white westerners sullenly accepted it, but only as long as the promise of an increasing amount of Indian land being placed in the hands of white settlers was met by the federal government.

Federal Indian policy in Washington's administration consisted of five interlocking parts. First, the Indians were to be considered owners of the land on which they currently lived (within their existing treaty boundaries) and no part of it was to be taken from them without their consent. As Knox put it to Washington: "The Indians being the prior occupants, possess the right to soil. It cannot be taken from them unless by their free consent. . . . To dispossess them in any other principle would be a gross violation of the fundamental laws of nature, and of that distributive justice which is the glory of a nation." Knox even went so far as to say that the Indian tribes should be regarded as "independent nations" and "ought to be considered as foreign nations." Assuming that "the Indians possess the rights to all their territory," he added, "they should not be divested thereof but in consequence of open treaties made under the authority of the United States."[2]

Second, the federal agents who were to reside in each Indian nation in the future were to act as the liaison between the chiefs and the federal government. They were to "attach" the Indians "to the interests of the United States" and to assure them of the President's constant "desire to better the situation of the Indians in all respects."[3] The agent was also to protect the Indian boundaries by "prohibiting the citizens [of the United States] from intruding on the Indian lands"; he was to obtain permission from the Secretary of War whenever necessary to employ the United States army troops at the nearest frontier garrison for that purpose. In addition to resident agents of the War Department, the government established trading posts (or factories) in the larger Indian nations. A factor or manager for the trading post was paid by the government in order to provide the Indians with a place to sell their furs and skins at reasonable prices or to exchange them for well-made tools for farming so that they would not be at the mercy of unscrupulous white traders. In addition, as the Indians became farmers, the trading post extended them credit with which to purchase seed, hoes, horses, plows, and other farm implements. "Trade," as one western political leader put it, "is the great lever by which to direct the policy and conduct of the Indian tribes."[4] Agents and factors were to encourage the Indians to divide up their tribal property to

---

[2] ASP I, 13, 53, 61.

[3] ASP I, 247.

[4] ASP II, 78. See also ASP II, 26–28 and ASP I, 684.

give each family a tract of its own, in order to make it independent and self-reliant: "Were it possible to introduce among the Indian tribes a love for exclusive property" (or property owned "in severalty" rather than in common), said Knox, "it would be a happy commencement of the business" of civilizing them. "The civilization of the Indians" was, in the long run, the primary goal of the government agents.[5] To this end, Congress was to appropriate funds for the "tools of husbandry and domestic manufactures" that the agent would then freely distribute among the Indians—plows, axes, mattocks for the men; spinning wheels, cards, and looms for the women. The resident agent was also to use federal funds to hire skilled workmen—blacksmiths, carpenters, weavers, tinsmiths, coopers—to teach the Indians the skills they needed to become self-sufficient. Finally, the agent was to keep peace between the Indians and the whites and to see to it that criminal acts by whites against Indians or vice versa were prosecuted in the nearest state or federal court.

Third, Washington's policy stipulated that no Indian tribe was to make any treaty or trade alliance with any nation other than the United States and that no state or private citizen in the United States was to make treaties with Indians: "The general sovereignty [i.e., the federal government] must possess the right of making all treaties," Knox told Washington, because "the independent nations and tribes of Indians ought to be considered as foreign nations, not as the subjects of any particular States."[6] Fourth, "missionaries of excellent moral character should be appointed to reside in their nation who should be well supplied with all the implements of husbandry and the necessary stock for a [model] farm" in order to establish vocational training schools, where Indian boys would learn to be farmers and artisans and Indian girls would learn to sew, weave, cook, make butter and cheese while at the same time they were all learning to read, write, and do arithmetic.

Fifth, in exchange for these various forms of "management," "assistance," "benevolence," and "enlightenment," the Indians were to cede, from time to time, such land that they were not cultivating. For these cessions of their "excess land," the federal government would provide cash or trade goods for their further economic development. The regular sale of their unused land would thus become the basic means of capital funding for the Indian nations, enabling them to build roads, bridges, ferries, mills, and the other elements of a market economy that individuals alone could not provide. Money from land sales would go into the national treasury of each tribe and be administered under its own chiefs and coun-

[5] ASP I, 53.
[6] Ibid.

cils. "As the population [of white Americans] shall increase," Knox said, "and approach the Indian boundaries, game will be diminished and new purchases [of Indian land] made for small considerations. This has been, and probably will be the inevitable consequence of cultivation."[7] Eventually, the Indians would become self-supporting yeoman farmers and no longer need government aid. Once they understood the principles of agriculture, stock raising, and trade, they would no longer want their old hunting land. Gradually, over a generation or two, they would acquire the same characteristic mode of life as the white settlers and would imperceptibly merge into the advancing white frontier as equal citizens.

Thomas Jefferson, like all other Presidents from 1789 to 1828, faithfully carried out this policy and summarized its expected consequences in a talk he gave to a group of Indians in Washington, D.C., in 1808:

Let me entreat you, therefore, on the lands now given you to begin to give every man a farm; let him enclose it, cultivate it, build a warm house on it, and when he dies, let it belong to his wife and children after him. Nothing is so easy as to learn to cultivate the earth; all your women understand it, and to make it easier, we are always ready to teach you how to make plows, hoes, and necessary utensils. If the men will take the labor of the earth from the women, they will learn to spin and weave and to clothe their families. . . . When once you have property, you will want laws and magistrates to protect your property and person. . . . You will find that our laws are good for this purpose; you will wish to live under them, you will unite yourselves with us, join in our great councils and form one people with us, and we shall all be Americans; you will mix with us by marriage, your blood will run in our veins, and will spread with us over this great continent.[8]

To implement this "civilization program," Congress passed a series of laws governing "Trade and Intercourse with the Indians," the first of which came in 1790. The act was subsequently renewed and amended in 1793, 1796, 1802, and 1822. These acts incorporated all of the essential features of the policy that Knox and Washington had recommended in 1789. However, it was not until 1792 that the first agents were appointed and Congress appropriated $15,000 annually to provide economic assistance to the Indians, and not until 1795 was the program of Indian trading posts put into effect. Congress took no steps until 1819 to provide money for the education of Indian children. It had assumed that private missionary agencies would undertake this out of their spiritual commitment to Christianizing the Indians. However, missionary activity among the southeastern Indians was very slow in starting and extensive missionary

[7] ASP I, 13, 53.
[8] Quoted in Saul K. Padover, *Thomas Jefferson on Democracy* (New York: Mentor, New American Library, Appleton-Century Co., 1939), pp. 106–107.

work did not enter into Indian life there until after 1817. The first phase of Cherokee acculturation from 1794 to 1817 was consequently secular.

The first Trade and Intercourse Act in 1790 prohibited any state or private party from making treaties with any Indian nation, established a system for licensing white traders, and required that whites accused of crimes in Indian nations be tried in the federal courts (a later act, in 1802, changed this to allow any state court to try such cases). The second Trade and Intercourse Act authorized the War Department to make "presents" to the Indians to assist them in becoming farmers, herdsmen, and housewives; this law also authorized the army garrison nearest to any Indian nation to be used to remove white intruders from that nation. The law establishing Indian trading posts in 1795 created funds to regulate trade and commerce with the Indians through the establishment of federal factories and factors. A law in 1796 placed more stringent limits on intruders into Indian nations. Finally, the Trade and Intercourse Act of 1802 made it illegal for whites to introduce spirituous liquor into any Indian nation. This act, modified slightly in 1822, remained in force until 1834.[9]

The Trade and Intercourse Acts and the Factory or Trading Post Laws provided only the broad outlines of Indian policy. Much depended upon the political climate of each administration and upon the ability and character of the resident agents. Although Knox assumed that the Indians had sovereignty over their land and also the right of internal self-government, clearly there were many ambiguous elements in the policy. Just as the states of the Union were not certain of how much sovereignty they retained under the Constitution, so the Indian states never knew exactly how much sovereignty they retained under their treaties and the Trade and Intercourse Acts. How far, for example, could an Indian nation go in refusing to grant land to the federal government? If it failed to follow the guidelines for civilization—perhaps by refusing to divide its land in severalty—did it thereby abrogate other aspects of the program—say, federal economic assistance? Did the right of Congress to control interstate commerce mean that navigable waters through Indian nations were automatically open to all traffic? Did Congress have to ask for and pay for the right to construct federal turnpikes through Indian nations? Could canals, and later railways, be constructed through Indian nations without their permission? How much right did white police agencies on the Indian borders have to enter the nation in search of criminals such as horse, cattle, or slave thieves, runaway slaves, debtors, or murderers? If the federal

[9] The best discussions of American Indian policy are by Francis Paul Prucha. See his *American Indian Policy in the Formative Years* (Cambridge: Harvard University Press, 1962) and *The Great Father: The United States Government and the American Indians*, 2 vols. (Lincoln: University of Nebraska Press, 1984).

agent could license white traders, could Indian councils eject them anyway? Could an Indian nation refuse to admit missionaries or, having admitted them, eject them? Could they admit and eject all whites who came to pursue some trade—blacksmith, schoolteacher, millwright, carpenter, sharecropper, gambler? Could an Indian nation levy taxes on its own people and upon whites who lived or worked in the nation, such as traders? Did Indian nations have the right to exploit their own natural resources—timber, salines, saltpeter, gold, silver, minerals? Could the relatives of a white man enter the nation to claim his property when he died? Could they do so even if he left an Indian wife? Could the Indians continue to practice infanticide and to execute witches? Could an Indian nation abolish slavery and become a haven for runaway slaves? And, more important for the ultimate fulfillment of the integration program, when did an Indian become "civilized"? How did he or she attain equal citizenship? Was citizenship only available when a whole nation was somehow judged to have reached the appropriate level, or could individual Indians be given citizenship as they attained certain proficiencies? And what was equal citizenship? Under the federal system, everyone had two kinds of citizenship, state and federal. The federal government might grant full and equal citizenship to a person, yet the state in which he lived was entitled under the Constitution to set its own standards for voting and other privileges (holding office, attending schools, serving in the militia, testifying in court). Suppose the southern or western states did not agree with Knox, Jefferson, and most educated easterners that the Indian was potentially the full equivalent of the white man in mind and body? Did state or federal authority define the rights of Indians who became citizens?

Ultimately the Cherokee people raised all of these difficult questions as they tried to come to terms with their new circumstances. To their surprise and confusion, no consistent answers were given to most of them, either by their various federal agents, the various Presidents and Secretaries of War, the leading politicians, or by the voting public in the United States. To find their way under the aegis of the Indian policy of the United States, the Cherokees had to chart their own path and apply their own political solutions. But before they could do that, they had to decide among themselves what direction they wished to move in. The federal agents on the whole did their best to help them solve their problems, but the initiative rested with the Cherokee people.

The first federal agent sent to the Cherokees was Leonard Shaw, a recent graduate of Princeton University who came to live among them in 1792. Shaw proved to be most unusual. He had been reminded in his commission from the War Department that differences in skin color in no way indicated any fundamental difference between white and red men:

"The difference between civilized and savage modes of life is so great as, upon first view, almost leads to the conclusion that the earth is peopled with races of men possessing distinct primary qualities; but upon closer inspection this will appear fallacious, and that the immense differences arise from education and habits."[10] Shaw took this seriously, and soon after arriving in the nation he married a Cherokee. His primary task was to put an end to the guerrilla war and prevent any more of the Upper Town (friendly) Cherokees from joining the Chickamauga guerrillas who had refused to abide by the treaty of 1791. John Watts, with the aid of the British agent John McDonald, had aligned his guerrillas with a confederacy of Creeks, Choctaws, and Chickasaws who were still eager to carry on the war against the white Americans. These Indians made a treaty in 1792 with Arturo O'Neill, the Governor of Spanish West Florida, to provide them with arms and ammunition. Watts and his warriors were meeting at Willstown, west of Lookout Mountain, to plan the war when Shaw reached the Upper Town capital at Ustanali, east of Lookout Mountain. Little Turkey was at this time the ostensible chief of all the Cherokees. He was trying to maintain the peace agreed upon at Holston in 1791, but he had no control over the Lower Towns. Watts felt that the United States had been dishonest in that treaty because it had not removed the white intruders from within the Cherokee boundary on the French Broad and Holston rivers. In the instructions to Shaw, the War Department said that he must "infuse into all the Indians the uprightness of the views of the President of the United States and his desire to better the situation of the Indians in all respects. . . . You will fully and frequently inculcate the purity of the conduct of the General Government to the hostile Indians" and try to "make a firm peace with the said Indians." But how could Shaw tell them that the President was powerless to assert federal authority over the stubborn frontiersmen of the Tennessee— North Carolina border who saw their safety and future at stake? Nonetheless, until peace was obtained, Shaw was instructed to tell the Cherokees that "their young men, being constrained to join one side or the other . . . should join ours in preference to that of the hostile Indians." Moreover, since the Indian conflict north of the Ohio River was coming to a head, it was "of high importance that the Southern Indians should be prevented from joining the Indians north of the Ohio." Over this Shaw had no control whatever, and Watts's guerrillas continued to work closely with the Shawnees in the north. Shaw was also told to "learn their language" (an order that not a single agent ever followed out), to "collect materials for a history of all the Southern Tribes," and to "teach them

[10] ASP I, 247.

agriculture and such useful arts as you may know or can acquire." Above all, he was to keep in close touch with Governor William Blount of Tennessee Territory, who was the federal Superintendent of Indian Affairs south of the Ohio River.[11]

Shaw found it almost impossible to achieve any of his goals. He could not stop the guerrilla war in Tennessee nor even keep a group of white, frontier Indian-haters from entering the Cherokee town of Chota and trying to kill the friendly chief, Hanging Maw. During his two frustrating years among the Cherokees, Shaw watched helplessly as the people of Tennessee took their own measures to stop Watts and the Lower Town warriors. Governor Blount, Shaw's superior, convinced the President that matters were best left in the hands of frontier militia, who were experienced Indian fighters. Shaw discovered that Blount was heavily engaged in land speculations and was hoping that the defeat of the Cherokee guerrillas would force further land cessions from which he expected to profit. Blount and his friends were already profiting from the land ceded at Holston in 1791.[12]

Shaw, having allied himself by marriage to the Cherokees and having thereby become a "countryman," frankly warned the Cherokee chiefs to trust nothing that Blount told them because Blount's private interests were in conflict with his public trust. At a council of chiefs from the Lower Towns early in 1793, Shaw told John Watts not to try to negotiate with Blount about the intruders still within the line surveyed by Blount after the treaty of 1791. Watts should instead go directly to the President or Secretary of War, for Blount was "only a servant of the United States." Furthermore, according to James Carey, Shaw's interpretor, Shaw told Watts that "he ought not to mind Governor Blount or his letters; that they had better apply to Congress, for he knew that the United States, as soon as they had heard rightly how Governor Blount had wronged them out of their lands, he was satisfied they would restore them to the Indians again and send commissioners to run the line to their liking. 'If you go to Blount, you will be as far from getting your lands as ever. . . . Observe how much better the Lower Creeks are treated than you are; that is because they have a good man to do for them; that is more than you have got. . . . See how much Governor Blount has run the lines without your knowledge or [your] being present. . . . I will no longer be controlled by him. I will go to Congress and recover your lands for you, to the old line.' " Hearing this, John Watts grasped Shaw by the arm, saying, "Your offering is good to us, and we wish you to go to Congress and do

[11] Ibid.
[12] Royce, *Cherokee Nation of Indians*, pp. 41–45.

it for us . . . if you do that for us, we will then take you by the hand as a brother forever." Shaw told the Chickamaugans to maintain peace for seventy-five days until he went to Congress to rectify Blount's false treaty line. He also said that "if he did not get that line, he would return to them and share the same fate with them," since he was their country-man. He said "he would keep nothing hid from them and would join them in protecting their country" from the rapacious western land spec-ulators. Watts gave Shaw his word that no further acts of warfare against the whites would take place until he tried to accomplish this peaceful res-olution of the problem. Shaw then returned to Ustanali and persuaded the chiefs of the Upper Towns to agree to what he had worked out with Watts. Carey, however, who had been Shaw's interpreter through all this, was loyal to Blount. With a handful of Upper Town chiefs, Carey went to Blount in Knoxville and revealed that Shaw was trying to under-mine his authority. Carey said that the chiefs he trusted most (The King Fisher, Captain Dick, The Old Prince, and George Miller) preferred to work with Governor Blount as this would be "more advantageous to their nation."[13]

Blount thereupon explained Shaw's insubordination to the Secretary of War, adding to the charge of "great want of prudence" that of habitual "inebriety."[14] Shaw was replaced in 1794 by John McKee, who left all im-portant decisions to Blount and former Franklinite James Robertson.[15] Shaw's experience epitomized the three-way struggle between the Cher-okees, the westerners, and the federal authorities that made Cherokee re-vitalization so difficult over the next forty years. The goals and motives of these three groups were frequently at odds. Blount was elected to the United States Senate in 1796, but he was expelled from his seat when the Senate learned that he had plotted to undermine United States authority in the west. He and Carey had entered into a scheme with another nation (not named in the records) for this purpose; in effect, Blount was guilty of treason. Two Loyalists who had become Cherokee countrymen, John Rogers and John D. Chisholm, were involved with him in the plot.[16]

After Blount was relieved of the superintendency, President Washing-ton appointed Benjamin Hawkins, a former Senator from North Caro-lina; his title was "Principal Temporary Agent for Indian Affairs South of the Ohio." Hawkins in turn appointed Silas Dinsmoor as his assistant.

[13] ASP I, 437, 440–41.
[14] ASP I, 436. Malone, *Cherokees of the Old South*, pp. 37–38.
[15] Malone, *Cherokees of the Old South*, p. 38; ASP I, 531.
[16] Merrit B. Pound, *Benjamin Hawkins, Indian Agent* (Athens: University of Georgia Press, 1951), pp. 126–28. Blount was clearly plotting with the British. Rogers and Chisholm were to play important parts in Cherokee affairs in subsequent years, as was Blount's son, Willie.

Hawkins went to live among the Creeks; Dinsmoor resided among the Cherokees. These agents made the first significant efforts to persuade the Creeks and Cherokees to abandon hunting for farming. They distributed plows, spinning wheels, cotton cards and looms at government expense and employed white women to teach spinning and weaving to Indian women. Hawkins reported in 1796 that the Cherokee women were rapidly taking up the planting of cotton and were eager to learn how to spin it into thread and then to weave the thread into cloth. However, both men found that Indian males were reluctant to become tillers of the soil. In Cherokee myth and tradition, that task was always assigned to women. The men therefore continued to try to make a living from the fur trade. Every October most of them left for the hunting ground in northern Alabama and Middle Tennessee. Some of the hunting parties ranged as far west as Arkansas in search of the dwindling game. Yet every spring the hunters returned with smaller and smaller catches. Although the government had established a trading post among the Cherokees at Tellico Garrison in 1795, Cherokee hunters often preferred to trade with private traders, who went out to meet them as they came back. These traders sometimes offered better prices; they also provided whiskey, which the government trader was forbidden to do. The quality of trade goods was better at the government post, but the cost of transporting them from Baltimore and Philadelphia made the prices high.

Dinsmoor was an able and conscientious agent who did his best to help the Cherokees adjust to a new way of life. He was particularly concerned with the continual friction between the Cherokees and the frontier whites. These quarrels frequently ended in murders and, despite treaties to the contrary, the brother or uncle of the murdered Cherokee retaliated against the white murderer or his kin. Whites, many of them Scotch-Irish, held a similar code of family revenge. "Peace is the general talk of this country," Dinsmoor said in 1795, "and I believe it is really the desire of the Cherokees to bury the hatchet and not shed any more blood. Would to God the frontier people were of the same mind."[17] Part of the difficulty stemmed from the fact that the Creeks continued to make occasional raids on white communities in Tennessee and traveled through Cherokee territory on these occasions. "The Whites say," Dinsmoor reported, "they cannot distinguish between the Cherokees and Creeks, and I believe it would not be transgressing the bounds of Charity to say they do not wish to distinguish." Even if all Indians did not look the same, they were all "savages" who had probably participated in assaults on whites;

[17] Silas Dinsmoor to David Henley, March 18, 1795, Ayer Collection, Newberry Library, Chicago, Ill.

all Indians were therefore equally deserving of death. Some weeks later Dinsmoor wrote that the Cherokees were uneasy over the continued hostility: "Two of their people were killed a short time since by a scout from South Carolina for stealing horses. The honest people among them consider it as just, and the headmen have prevailed on the relations to accept white beads and not take satisfaction [retaliation]. The stealing of horses will, I fear, continue while the white people encourage them to it by purchasing them. The licensed traders at Tuskeega [in South Carolina] have lately purchased some horses knowing them to have been stolen from the frontiers of Georgia."[18]

To try to solve these problems, Dinsmoor and Hawkins together managed to persuade the Cherokee national council to take two major steps in 1797 toward centralizing political authority in the name of order and stability. One concerned limitations on clan revenge, the other the establishment of a police force. In the social confusion of that period there were also frequent quarrels among the Cherokees themselves that resulted in assault and death. By Cherokee tradition, killing in self-defense or by accident (during a drunken brawl, for example) did not exempt the murderer from the law of blood; a life must be given for a life lost. But times were different now. The Cherokees had already conceded in the Treaties of Hopewell and Holston that murders committed by whites would be settled in white courts under the white man's jurisdiction. In 1797 Dinsmoor and Hawkins persuaded the Cherokee (and the Creek) council to modify this tradition still further. Clan revenge served no useful purpose any longer, they said; it only added to social tensions when clans took revenge for accidental death. The council agreed, and voted that henceforth clans could retaliate only when a murder resulted from malice aforethought—a major concession to the Anglo-Saxon concept of individual responsibility. Hawkins explained the council's decision to the Secretary of War: "The Cherokees are giving proofs of their approximation to the customs of well-regulated societies; they did, in full council, in my presence, pronounce, after solemn deliberation, as law, that any person who should kill another accidentally should not suffer for it, but be acquitted; that to constitute a crime, there should be malice and an intention to kill."[19]

Hawkins did not explain what kind of judicial process would sort out the facts to "acquit" the defendant and save him from clan revenge; it may have been done by the clan elders or it may have been done by the council. In addition, at this same council, the Cherokees took the first ma-

---

[18] Silas Dinsmoor to David Henley, July 8, 1795, ibid.
[19] Quoted in Rennard Strickland, *Fire and the Spirits*, p. 57. For an excellent analysis of the Cherokee practice of clan revenge see Reid, *A Law of Blood*.

jor step toward creating a national system of law enforcement and punishing of crimes not associated with clan revenge. "They at the same time gave up, of their own motion," Hawkins said, "the names of the great rogues in the nation, as well as those of their neighborhood, and appointed some warriors expressly to assist the chiefs in preventing stealing and in carrying their stipulations with us into effect."[20] Several issues were involved. First, by "stipulation with us," Hawkins referred to the fact that treaty clauses required repayment from tribal funds of $60 per stolen horse when a white could prove that his horse had been stolen by a Cherokee. By "giving us the names" of those Cherokees known to be horse thieves, the council was admitting the collective responsibility of the tribe for such crimes and asserting a new form of national authority. In the past, the nation had sometimes accepted responsibility for the murder of a white or for the return of stolen or runaway slaves. But this occurred only under extreme duress in order to avoid massive white retaliation. By the law of 1797, the nation assumed responsibility for routine maintenance of law and order; in effect, it established a system of internal policing for crimes that tribal law had previously ignored. Hawkins did not explain the kind or form of punishments but presumably it was by whipping. This adoption of the concept of centralized tribal authorization for the protection of private property and the administration of physical coercion upon individuals was a significant step in Cherokee political centralization and judicial restructuring. However, it was seen as an emergency measure and faltered badly over the next decade. The Cherokees as a whole were by no means ready to accept all its implications.

Another hesitant step in this direction was taken in 1799 when the federal government and the Cherokee council jointly created a regular, paid police force. In 1797, ad hoc agents of law enforcement were appointed by the council to seize and punish specific individuals for specific crimes, such as known horse thieves. In 1799, the police force became a standing body, acting to maintain order on its own initiative. This action was instigated by Major Thomas Lewis, who replaced Dinsmoor as federal agent to the Cherokees in 1798. Lewis persuaded the War Department to let him use agency funds to pay for mounted Cherokee police, known as "the lighthorse regulators" or the Lighthorse. Lewis proposed that there should be fourteen regulators appointed by the council; the federal government would pay the wages for half of these, the Cherokees would pay for the other half.[21] The law of 1797 had failed to stem the tide

[20] Strickland, *Fire and the Spirits*, p. 57. Hawkins also persuaded the Creeks to institute a similar police system.

[21] The Glass to Return J. Meigs, June 30, 1801, M-15, reel 1, p. 72. Glass referred to it as

of horse stealing and more strenuous measures were needed. Two years later, however, in 1801, President Jefferson discontinued payment of the government's share of wages to the Cherokee regulators and thereafter policing became sporadic. From time to time Cherokee chiefs in various parts of the nation sought to reconstitute the force, but until 1808 the tribal council took no steps to do this. The Cherokees were demonstrating their reluctance to alter their traditional system of law and order; they did not like corporal punishment and they preferred decentralized town government. Such drastic changes had to come slowly.

Lewis also helped the federal government respond to a request by the State of Tennessee asking the federal government to obtain more land for its settlers. Tennessee's legislature told President John Adams that in its opinion the Indians were only "tenants at will" on their land, and it was the will of Tennessee that these tenants give up a large part of their hunting ground to satisfy the needs of white farmers. Adams appointed treaty commissioners and Congress appropriated funds to treat with the Cherokees; the commissioners hoped to obtain several million acres in Middle Tennessee. The negotiations took place in July 1798 at Tellico. The Cherokees flatly refused to sell any of their land. The government refused to take no for an answer; the commissioners returned to the nation in the fall and after much bickering they managed to obtain 90,000 acres in eastern Tennessee and 376,000 acres in western North Carolina, but the hunting ground remained intact. The Cherokees received $5,000 in cash and an addition of $1,000 to their perpetual annuity for these 1,644 square miles.[22]

In 1799 the first missionaries applied for a plot of land on which to establish a permanent station among the Cherokees. They were Moravians (or United Brethren) from Salem, North Carolina, a small evangelical Protestant group originally from Germany. The mission board's agents arrived from Salem in October to find that the able-bodied Cherokee males were all out on the hunting ground for the winter. Lewis told the missionaries to return the following fall; during the ensuing year he worked hard to persuade the chiefs of the advantages of a mission. When the Moravians returned in September 1800, Lewis arranged to have them speak through an interpreter to the council. The council asked whether the school the missionaries promised to start would provide free room, board, and clothing for the students. The Moravians said they did not expect to provide these, and the council rejected their offer. The missionaries were about to return to North Carolina, but Lewis persuaded them

---

the "mounted Indian Patrole." See also M-208, November 20, 1802, and December 3, 1802, for other references to this first system of mounted police among the Cherokees.

[22] Royce, *Cherokee Nation of Indians*, pp. 46–55.

to stay a week and try again. Finally, on October 6, several chiefs of the Upper Towns agreed to let the Moravians start a mission station near the house of James Vann in Springplace, Georgia. The mission opened in the spring of 1801, but it ran into trouble two years later when the chiefs discovered that the Moravians had no intention of opening a school until they had first converted a group of Cherokee parents to Christianity who would agree to come to live at the mission station, start farms, and place their children at a day school there.[23]

Meanwhile Lewis left his post under a cloud early in 1801. Apparently he had succumbed to the same problem that Blount alleged against Shaw, an addiction to alcohol. A revealing insight into the politics of patronage in the appointment of Indian agents was provided by Benjamin Hawkins. He made the statement in 1802 during a talk to the Creek council in order to explain the difference between John Adams's commitment to the policy of Indian civilization and that of Thomas Jefferson:

The President, Mr. Adams, who was the predecessor of the present President, he, although a great man and a good man, began to believe that the experiment for civilization could not be carried into effect; that the plan itself was ideal [but impractical]. He began to give it up by withdrawing his confidence from those entrusted with its execution. Your enemies [the frontier whites] by misrepresentation, induced him to turn out Mr. Dinsmoor, one of the best men in the Indian department—sober, prudent and very attentive to the duties of his appointment—and to replace him by quite another sort of man—one, as the Cherokees informed you and me, more attentive to his bottle and woman than to their interest. And serious attempts were made to lessen my standing with him . . . because I was an enemy to those speculative [i.e., land speculation] views of your enemies. In this state of things, Mr. Jefferson came into office. . . . He has kept me in; he has re-animated the plan for bettering your condition; he placed Colonel Meigs, an honest and estimable man, among the Cherokees; he has sought for and sent Mr. Dinsmoor to the Choctaws.[24]

Return J. Meigs, a Connecticut veteran of the Revolution and ardent Jeffersonian, became the federal Cherokee agent in June 1801, when he was sixty-one years old. Honest and efficient, he remained in that post until his death at eighty-three in 1823. Meigs found the Cherokees still in considerable disarray and still suffering from the problems of violent white intruders, murderous brawls, bloody retaliations, and constant horse stealing. Like previous agents, Meigs discovered that much of their

---

[23] William G. McLoughlin, *Cherokees and Missionaries, 1789–1839* (New Haven: Yale University Press, 1984), pp. 13–53, and Edmund Schwarze, *History of the Moravian Missions among the Southern Indian Tribes of the United States* (Bethlehem, Penn.: Times Publishing Co., 1923), pp. 43–55.

[24] ASP I, 677.

difficulty derived from the hostility of whites on the Cherokee borders. The frontiersmen did not want the Cherokees to remain where they were and become integrated; they considered Indians incapable of rising to equal citizenship. The Cherokees found that they were held in such low esteem by most frontier whites that they began to doubt whether there was any hope for peaceful coexistence with such people. In particular, the program for civilizing and educating the Indians annoyed the westerners; they feared that once the Indians became farmers, they would never get rid of them. "There are some [whites]," Meigs said, "that would not spend a dollar towards their improvement."[25]

The hatred frontier whites had developed for the Indians during the war years was now tinged with contempt. The frontiersmen considered the Indians to be either simple, backward, ignorant, and lazy or else untrustworthy, wily, volatile, and thieving. A drunken Indian was considered prone to violence and a poor Indian prone to lying, begging, and stealing. Many eastern visitors noted that frontier whites thought of Indians as little better than animals and were as ready to rid the country of them as they were to wipe out bears and wolves. The terms "barbarian," "savage," and "heathen," were meant to convey the opposite of civilized, Christian, and rational. One early missionary noted: "My residence and extensive acquaintance in Tennessee has given me an opportunity to converse much respecting the Indians, and I hope to remove some of the prejudices against them. But you cannot conceive the state of feelings [against them] even among professors [of religion]."[26] He also wrote: "The sentiment very generally prevails among the white people near the southern tribes . . . that the Indian is by nature radically different from all other men and that his difference presents an insurmountable barrier to his civilization."[27]

If the frontiersmen considered Indians scarcely human, many Cherokees concluded from their experience that the white frontiersmen were the offscouring of the human race. Many of them accepted the view that the two races were never meant to intermingle. "Many of the Cherokees," Meigs discovered, "think that they are not derived from the same stock as whites, that they are favorites of the great spirit, and that he never intended they should live the laborious lives of whites."[28] Meigs believed that Indians were potentially capable of civilization, if only they

---

[25] Return J. Meigs to Valentine Geiger, June 6, 1806, M-208.

[26] Cyrus Kingsbury to S. A. Worcester, November 28, 1916, Papers of the American Board of Commissioners for Foreign Missions, Houghton Library, Harvard University, Cambridge, Mass. Hereafter abbreviated as ABCFM.

[27] Cyrus Kingsbury to S. A. Worcester, July 3, 1818, ABCFM.

[28] Return J. Meigs to Benjamin Hawkins, February 13, 1805, M-208.

could overcome their inveterate dislike of the hard labor involved in sub-sistence farming; he responded to their polygenetic concept of the sepa-rate creations of different colors of people by noting that "these ideas, if allowed to have practical effect, would undoubtedly finally opperate [to] their extinction."[29] He considered it his duty to rescue the Cherokees from their low opinion of themselves, to convince them that they were capable of achieving all that whites could achieve, and thereby to persuade the frontier whites that Indians deserved respect, assistance, encourage-ment, and equal citizenship. This proved to be a far more difficult task than he anticipated in 1801.

The inability of the Cherokees to control either the murderous friction between whites and Indians or horse stealing was a significant part of their social and cultural confusion. Both Cherokees and whites were guilty of violent behavior when they met, but as the French traveler, the Duke de LaRochefoucauld, noted after touring the southern frontier in the 1790s, "although these people [the southeastern Indians] are held in aversion and endeavours are made to drive them beyond the Mississippi, yet it is allowed on all hands that in the continual quarrels which they have with the people on the boundaries, the latter are in the wrong four times out of five."[30] Furthermore, despite their efforts, the Cherokee chiefs were unable to stamp out the age-old practice of clan retaliation. Ultimately, Meigs had to develop his own solutions to the issue; he was forced to an alternative because he was unable to procure justice for the Cherokees in the frontier courts.

The problem of white aggression and Cherokee retaliation was com-plex, and at the turn of the century the Cherokees felt angry, frustrated, and desolate about it. The problem can best be described in terms of four murder cases that Meigs had to cope with in 1802. The first took place on April 21 in the Tennessee region of the Cherokee border. Two white horse thieves named Richmond and Irwin tried to take a horse from a Cherokee though they had no claim to it. The Cherokee resisted. The whites, according to Meigs's information, put "two bullets thro' his head" and took the horse. Colonel Henry McKinney of Tennessee, who investigated this affair for the War Department, wrote that there was no doubt that "the killing [of] the Indian was a Wanton, unprovoked mur-der." The whites in the vicinity were "much alarmed" by the act "and some of them are moving away" for fear of Cherokee retaliation by the clansmen of the murdered Cherokee. Meigs recommended restraint on the part of the Cherokees and tried to have the murderers prosecuted by

[29] Ibid.
[30] Quoted in the Papers of John Howard Payne, IX:105, Newberry Library, Chicago. Hereafter abbreviated as Payne Papers.

Tennessee authorities. He discovered that friends of Richmond and Irwin were willing to swear that the murder was justified because the Indian was riding a stolen horse. Meigs had evidence that this was not true. A jury of inquest was held and reported that "the Indian was murdered" and "all the circumstances . . . go to prove that Richmond and Irwin killed the Indian without provocation." Nevertheless, since there were no witnesses, the State of Tennessee would not proceed with the case.[31] Meigs warned the Secretary of War that if such murderers were not punished, they might "involve us in the horrors of an Indian war," but the Secretary did not pursue the matter. The Cherokee chiefs had restrained the murdered man's relatives on the false hope that Meigs could obtain punishment of the murderers by the white man's courts.[32]

The second incident took place a month later, in May 1802, on the Georgia border of the Cherokee Nation. Here, the agent learned from James Vann, "an Indian, happening to come into the Settlements . . . in a drunken frolic, came to a Plantation where he behaved shockingly. In his Rage he threw a child into the fire but happily the Child crawled out and is likely to do well. A young woman, who happened in his way, he killed with a Mattuck, splitting therewith her face from the forehead to the chin. . . . the Man of the House . . . took his Gun, loaded her with Nails, for wants of Bullets, and shot the Indian dead." Vann, the most influential Cherokee chief living in this vicinity told Meigs, "the Indian certainly got what he deserved for his horrid deed," but he could not promise that there would be no clan revenge nor could he help expressing fear that the incident would "breed further trouble" among the whites, who might be goaded to additional retaliation against the Cherokees.[33]

Two months after this, on July 2, a Cherokee named "The Goose" (or Sammy Goose) was killed in Tennessee by Barefoot Runion, a white man. Runion said the killing was an accident, and the chiefs in the council accepted his story. To avoid trouble, another council held in August "wrote off" the death and forbade Goose's clan relations to take revenge. Nevertheless, Ca-tah-coo-kee (or Dirt Bottle), his uncle, believed that Goose's spirit required vengeance. With four or five other kinsmen, Ca-tah-coo-kee went to Sevier County, where Runion lived, and on September 8 killed Runion's son Travenor with a tomahawk. A woman of the family was also killed in the fray. The whites in the vicinity were "much alarmed," Meigs reported, not knowing who else might be caught in this

[31] Captain Sampson Williams to Governor Archibald Roane, May 9, 1802, M-208; Colonel Henry McKinney to Governor Archibald Roane, May 14, 1802, M-208; Return J. Meigs to Henry Dearborn, June 6, 1802, M-208.

[32] Return J. Meigs to Henry Dearborn, June 19, 1802, M-208.

[33] James Vann to Return J. Meigs, May 3, 1802, M-208.

feud. Some of them wished to gather a posse and go after Ca-tah-coo-kee and his companions. One of them wrote to Meigs that "if the United States is Bound to keep up the Cherokee Nation in an Annual Salary [annuity], those who were the Avowed Enemies of the United States in their Struggle for Independence, and Good Citizens who have Suffered in the Defence of their Right and their Country, Must Now Submit to the Laws of that Nation, I mean the Cherokee Nation, Executed on them [blood revenge] with Impunity," then matters had come to a dangerous pass.[34] When Ca-tah-coo-kee returned home, the council, under prodding from Meigs, agreed to arrest him and turn him over to the white authorities in Tennessee. However, fearing that a lynch mob might hang him, the council insisted that he be placed in the United States army garrison jail in Hiwassee until his trial. When the trial took place, Ca-tah-coo-kee explained his position in terms of the tradition of clan retaliation, but the court took no cognizance of it, and he was hanged.[35]

The fourth case that year took place in North Carolina in September, when a group of Cherokees took vengeance upon the son of a white man who had murdered a member of their clan. This time the council refused to give up the murderer. As they told the agent, "the number of their people that have been killed by whites and for which no punishment has ever taken place" was now so large that the burden rested upon the white authorities and the War Department to fulfill its side of the treaty stipulation before it asked the Cherokees to execute another of their own people. Although the Cherokee council easily identified and apprehended its murderers, the council could see no evidence that the whites ever punished one of their own murderers.[36] Meigs had to report frankly to the Secretary of War that their observation was correct.

Two years later, Meigs wrote to Governor John Sevier of Tennessee

[34] Colonel Samuel Wear to Return J. Meigs, September 27, 1802, M-208.

[35] Return J. Meigs to William Davis, July 27, 1802, M-208; Return J. Meigs to Colonel Samuel Wear, September 21, 1802, M-208; Colonel Samuel Wear to Return J. Meigs, September 27, 1802, M-208; Cherokee Council to Return J. Meigs, November 17, 1802, M-208.

[36] Return J. Meigs to Henry Dearborn, October 5, 1802, M-208. Meigs reported that the white man had killed the Indian on July 27 in Tennessee and the chiefs had tried to hold back his relatives from clan revenge, but when no legal action was taken against the murderer by September 8, "a small party of Indians watched the House of the Whiteman who had killed the Indian, with a view to kill him, but not finding him, they killed his son, a young man about sixteen years old. It has been with difficulty the white people in that quarter were restrained from going against the Indians. Gov. Roane has exerted himself to keep peace." Meigs said he would ask the Council to turn over the murderer. See reply of the Cherokee Council to Return J. Meigs, April 20, 1803, M-208. In December 1802 Meigs looked into the murder of a Cherokee supposedly killed by a white man, only to find that he was killed by another Indian; see "Examination into the death of an Indian," December 22, 1802, M-208.

51

that there had been additional murders of Cherokees by whites but that so far, during his five years among the Cherokees, he had not been able to obtain the punishment of a single white man for the murder of an Indian.[37] The Cherokees blamed the federal government for this. Several years later the chiefs complained, Meigs reported, that "they have eight lives standing against us; their language is that we owe them eight lives. This I have no doubt is true. But as no proof but that of Indians can be adduced, the murderers could not be convicted and never will."[38]

The reason for this state of affairs was obvious. Even when a white murderer was brought to trial, white juries would not convict one of their neighbors of killing an Indian. In 1813, Colonel Meigs prosecuted four separate cases against whites for the murder of Cherokees; "all," he reported, "failed of producing punishment."[39] A second reason preventing the conviction of whites was that western and southern state courts would not allow Indians to testify as witnesses. "The state of the Indians is a deplorable one in this respect," Meigs said in 1812. "We arraign them as moral agents, charge them with crimes that cannot be committed without including an idea that they are, like ourselves [morally responsible], at the same time, we exclude them from all the advantages of beings capable of moral or religious conceptions; their testimony on oath is not admissable."[40] The Cherokee agent gave credit to the judges for trying to be fair, but they had no choice in the matter:

It is a fact that they [Indians] cannot have justice done to them in the courts of law. The judges are just and liberal . . . as far as related to distributive justice, and would deal out rewards and punishments to all men without being influenced by the accidental difference of the colour of the skin, but a jury impaneled in the frontier Counties dare not bring in a Verdict to take the life of a citizen for Killing an Indian. The Indians are . . . condemned and executed on the testimony of any white citizen of common character and understanding when at the same time a white man can kill an Indian in the presence of 100 Indians and the testimony of these hundred Indians to the fact amounts to nothing and the man will be acquitted.[41]

Long before this, the Secretary of War had proposed a solution that indicated the tendency of the government to reduce all conflicts to monetary terms. In 1802, fearing that the Cherokees would use the failure of white courts to uphold Article 8 of the Treaty of Holston as an excuse for

---

[37] Return J. Meigs to John Sevier, February 23, 1804, M-208.
[38] Meigs's memorandum listing eight deaths of Cherokees for which no murderer had been tried, March 19, 1812, M-208.
[39] Return J. Meigs to Governor Willie Blount, February 11, 1813, M-208.
[40] Return J. Meigs, memorandum, March 19, 1812, M-208.
[41] Return J. Meigs to William Eustis, April 6, 1812, M-208.

not making further cessions of land and rights of way desired by the government, Secretary of War Henry Dearborn proposed to all Indian agents among the southeastern Indians that they "endeavor to settle the disputes" by other means such as a "pecuniary compensation" to be paid to "the family or friends of the deceased."[42] It was left to the agents to set "such pecuniary satisfaction as in your judgment may be acceptable and proper." Dearborn suggested that a figure of "from one hundred to two hundred dollars for each man or woman actually murdered by white citizens" ought to suffice. Of course, the Indians were told that "the compensation is not intended to operate as an acquittal of the murderers," and the agents were to continue to try to prosecute them.[43]

When the Cherokee agent first suggested this option to the chiefs, they spurned it.[44] They were not interested in financial compensation; they wished the whites to indicate respect for Indians, and they expected the federal government to uphold its treaty obligations and to deal justly with them. After repeated failures to obtain justice, and fearing that the clans might continue to insist on their own form of revenge, the chiefs finally gave in. After 1803 murders were paid for at the rate of $100 to $200 each. The Cherokees continued to keep a strict account of the whites' lives "owed to them," because the unavenged spirits of the murdered Cherokees were not at rest. The clan relatives accepted the government payments but felt very uneasy about it. Many Cherokees held their chiefs to blame for their inability to force compliance with treaty guarantees in this respect. Others simply became angry and resentful over the failure of their efforts to cooperate with white officials.

Murder was only the most egregious form of abuse of Cherokees by whites. The agents were constantly being informed of assaults, stabbings, thefts, frauds, and breaches of contract. Unable to obtain legal redress for any of these civil claims in the state courts, the War Department itself had to pick up the bill in order to mollify the Indians. When the department began to complain of the enormous sums required for this purpose every year, the Cherokee agent provided documentary evidence of the cases.

The nature of these kinds of claims cannot be equitably determined by strictly adhering to the law of evidence. The Indians can't give legal testimony and by means of this disability the whites have an advantage; but by attending carefully

[42] Henry Dearborn to Silas Dinsmoor, May 18, 1802, M-15, reel 1, p. 213; Henry Dearborn to Return J. Meigs, May 30, 1803, M-208.

[43] Henry Dearborn to Return J. Meigs, May 30, 1803, M-208; Henry Dearborn to Return J. Meigs, May 30, 1803, M-15, reel 1, p. 352; Henry Dearborn to Silas Dinsmoor, January 7, 1804, M-15, reel 1, p. 417.

[44] Return J. Meigs to Henry Dearborn, April 22, 1805, M-208. See also reply of Council to Return J. Meigs, April 20, 1803, M-208; Return J. Meigs to Henry Dearborn, May 4, 1803, M-208.

to all the circumstances and to the character of the parties, justice can be done to the claimant, for altho' the claims may be just, the parties, especially the Indians, cannot support their rights and some characters of each party cannot be credited; but by care here we can, with few exceptions, make equitable decisions.[45]

In effect, the Indians had to depend upon the skill and fairness of the federal agents to "support their rights," and hope that the War Department would honor his judgments. The agent was their judge and jury, their only source of justice. On the other hand, the department was very strict in its insistence that the claims of whites against Cherokees should be paid out of Indian annuities. The agent was thus also judge and jury for white claimants against Cherokees who did not pay debts, committed thefts, committed injuries, or failed to fulfill contracts. Just as the United States Treasury bore the penalties for individual injustices by whites toward Indians on the frontier, so the Cherokees' treasury bore the penalties for the individual crimes of their citizens toward whites. It was hardly a way to teach the Cherokees the American belief in individual responsibility and self-reliance. Furthermore, the necessity of relying upon the good will of the agent to redress their grievances and disputes with whites did little to build up their sense of self-worth. Prior to their defeat in battle, the Cherokees had been a proud and independent people. Now they were reduced to the status of children asking their parents for help. Their council was powerless to render order or justice against whites. Agent Meigs tried to explain to a friend why, after all the government was trying to do to raise up the Indians, they still harbored "prejudices" against whites: "It does not arise from pride, as our [prejudices against them] do; it arises in the Indian from his humble conception of himself and of his fate from the discovery he makes that we look down on him as an inferior race of beings."[46] The agent did not mean simple racial prejudice; he meant that whites considered the Indian to be incompetent to fend for himself. The Indian was treated as a woman, a child, a ward, or a mental incompetent under white civil and criminal law of the time.

In addition, the Cherokees were well aware of the racial component to this treatment. In the southern states the only other "race of beings" placed in a similar childlike, dependent position vis-à-vis whites was the African. To many southeastern whites, the Indian was "a red nigger." Even the most distinguished leaders of the Cherokee tribe, men of wealth and respect (some of them with white ancestry) among their own people, were subject to continual indignities when they faced white men. Chief Richard Brown, son of a white trader and a Cherokee woman, was head-

---

[45] Return J. Meigs to Jenkin Whiteside, February 22, 1810, M-208.
[46] Return J. Meigs to Samuel Trott, August 3, 1817, M-208.

man in his town and a leading figure in Cherokee affairs. One day, he and some friends were searching for a stolen horse along the western border of the nation in what is now Alabama but was then part of Mississippi Territory. They found the horse in the possession of a white man, but he would not return it to them. Unwilling to resort to force, Brown wrote to the agent for help: "We have found a horse belonging to an Indian near Dittoes Landing or near Huntsville. We cannot recover him without aid. The oath of an Indian is not known by your laws. Decide in some way to give us our right. Are we considered as negroes who cannot support our claims?"[47] The situation was galling to Brown, who owned black slaves himself. Where was the Indian to fit in this evolving social order?

As the younger Indians came of age and saw their chiefs, grandparents, parents, and friends continually abused and cheated, they sought ways to express their anger. There was a direct relationship between the loss of Indian self-esteem after 1794 and the rise of horse stealing, cattle rustling, and other forms of criminal activity. The most satisfying way to "get even" with the whites was to steal their property. This not only satisfied vengeance but brought quick profits. More important, it was a surrogate for war. It required many of the same skills—daring, courage, self-discipline, planning, endurance. It also produced a sense of a camaraderie and loyalty among those who took dangerous risks together. Horse stealing was a group enterprise and the gangs that engaged in it regularly were known as "pony clubs." They had their own chiefs, their own rules, their own professional code and secrets. Out of the chaos of their old system, these men created a different sort of organization and discipline. Success in these activities brought back a sense of self-respect and perhaps even won the respect of other angry Cherokees.

The excuse for stealing was made very clearly: "The Indians steal horses from the white people and the white people steal their land; this is their way of expressing it," Meigs said.[48] Located on the frontier, where horses often served as money, it was not hard to dispose of stolen horses; the thieves would take them from Georgia settlers on their eastern boundaries, run them through the nation, and sell them in Alabama or Tennessee on their western boundary. The agent told the Secretary of War in 1807: "The number of horses carried thro' and into this country is almost incredible—from Georgia, both the Carolinas, and Kentucky." He then explained the economic reasons for this. "A considerable part of the land purchased in this country [the white frontier] is paid for in horses; they serve as a kind of currency for this purpose all over this

---

[47] Richard Brown to Return J. Meigs, June 21, 1811, M-208.
[48] Return J. Meigs to Henry Dearborn, February 9, 1801, M-208.

western country and hence arises the facility with which they are stolen by Indians and others."[49] In former times, all Cherokees held stealing of any kind in abhorrence; now the chiefs often winked at it and a few accepted some of the profits from it. The prevalence of Indian horse stealing made it difficult for honest chiefs to complain about whites who stole horses from Indians, but because Indian horses were notably thin and stringy, there was more profit for Indian thieves. Proven thefts were costly to the tribal treasury, but many of the younger Cherokees saw no virtue in a treasury designed to make them into farmers to walk all day behind a plow. The struggle between the lawless thieves and those who supported a lighthorse patrol to catch and punish them added to the divisions within the nation in these years. The agents took the view that horse stealing arose because the hunting was too poor to support the able-bodied men and their families. Their answer to it was to speed up the process of "civilizing" the hunters.

Faced with the pervasive breakdown of law, order, and authority in the years 1794 to 1810, the Cherokees had several options. There were some who simply gave up the effort to make any sense of life. These tried to escape by constant intoxication; they helped to provide the basis for the frontier stereotype of the drunken Indian and the myth that something in the Indians' physiology made them particularly susceptible to "fire water."[50] A second alternative for the frustrated and despondent was to emigrate west, to leave a chaotic cultural order and try to start over again far away from the white man. How many Cherokees took this option it is hard to say; hundreds certainly did so. In 1782, the first known emigrants crossed the Mississippi River to live in Spanish territory after receiving permission from the Spanish governor to settle there. After 1795 there was a stream of emigration to the part of Spanish territory that became Arkansas, particularly along the St. Francis River. Later emigrants went four hundred miles up the Arkansas River to Dardanelles Rock. By 1807, when the federal government decided to encourage Cherokee emigration, there were three to four hundred Cherokees living in Arkansas between the Arkansas and White rivers. This was an area their hunters had come to know well after 1794 as the game diminished in the east. However, it was also inhabited by other tribes, notably the Osages and the Quapaws who looked upon the Cherokee emigrants as invaders. Agent Meigs reported warfare between the Cherokees and the Osages in 1805–1807 and President Jefferson did his best to discourage it. But many

---

[49] ASP I, 265; Return J. Meigs to Henry Dearborn, December 19, 1807, M-208.

[50] See Dwight Heath, "Alcohol Use among Northern American Indians," *Research Advances in Alcohol and Drug Problems*, vol. 7, ed. Reginald G. Smart et al. (New York: Plenum Press, 1983), pp. 343–95.

Cherokees preferred the traditional activities of hunting and warfare that they knew well to the uncertain and frustrating life of a farmer.

A third alternative for many Cherokees was to withdraw to the most remote regions of the Cherokee Nation, the high hills and hidden valleys of the Great Smoky Mountains of western North Carolina. Others withdrew to the southern part of the nation on the border shared with the Creeks, where they seldom saw whites. In the Great Smokies life was difficult, but here the old customs could be continued, English was seldom spoken, and the festivals of the changing agricultural seasons were honored. There was a tendency among those who moved to these outlying areas of the nation to believe in the myth of racial separatism. The Great Spirit had not meant the red man to adopt the white man's ways and cease to be a Cherokee. In these areas, the Cherokees adopted from white culture only the minimum they needed to survive.

About three thousand Cherokees lived in the Great Smokies after 1794, in the area known as the Overhill or Valley Towns. Another three thousand lived in the Lower Town area near the Creeks and Chickasaws and along the Etowah River. The federal agent took little interest in these areas. He preferred to deal with those of mixed ancestry who spoke English and who offered a convenient bridge between the old ways and the new. The federal agency (or agent's headquarters) and the government factory were located until 1807 in the extreme northwestern tip of the nation at Southwest Point, Tennessee, along the Cumberland Road. It was an area where contact with whites was constant; the federal agent and the factor felt more secure here. The army garrison was located at Tellico Blockhouse only a few miles to the east.

In the years 1794 to 1810, rigid boundaries and diminishing freedom hemmed in the Cherokees, while internal divisions prevented unity. For the majority, none of the three forms of withdrawal seemed appropriate. To end their confusion they had to find ways to accommodate old traditions to new circumstances. They had to keep what was important from their heritage and yet graft onto it those aspects of the government's civilization program that would bring order to their lives and a new kind of economic and political security. But what parts of the older order could and should be held on to and what should be abandoned? Though desperately in need of social and political reintegration, the Cherokees found the federal Indian policy too alien. It had no roots in their culture or experience. In essence, it demanded obliteration of their past. To preserve their coherence and identity as a people the Cherokees would have to find their own way out of disorder, their own leaders, and their own will to survive as a people.

THREE

STARTING FARMS AND DEBATING
THE AUGUSTA-NASHVILLE
ROAD, 1799–1804

To fix the precise point where Barbarity terminates and when Civilization begins is perhaps impossible. But without the Knowledge of tillers [of the soil] civilization can hardly be said to exist. —Agent Return J. Meigs to the Cherokees, 1803

Additional presents may be made [to certain chiefs] for the purpose, but at all events, we must have a road. —Secretary of War Henry Dearborn to the Cherokee agent, 1803

By 1800 the federal government's paternalistic Indian policy was well under way. It was helping the Cherokees to become farmers with one hand and arranging for them to give up their old hunting ground with the other. The Cherokees were dubious about both aspects of this program.

The relentless quest of the federal government to obtain Cherokee land required a united response, but the Cherokees were as divided in their attitude toward land cessions as they were in their response to becoming farmers. The regional division between the Upper and Lower Towns became more pronounced. The Lower Towns tended to dominate tribal affairs. Theirs was the region south of the Hiwassee River along the Tennessee River; their towns stretched from the Conasauga and Ustanali (Oostanaulah) rivers in western Georgia, across Lookout Mountain, to the western edge of what became Alabama (where the Cherokee Nation bordered on the Chickasaw Nation) and from the Hiwassee River south to the northern border of the Creek Nation. Popular support was stronger for the war chiefs of the Lower Towns (also called the Chickamauga or River Towns) because of their stubborn defense of the nation up until 1794, but these chiefs seemed to have no clear policy. Most of them encouraged the nation to continue hunting and the fur trade economy; a few of the most influential, however, had concluded by 1800 that this was no longer feasible.

The Upper Towns were themselves politically divided. Those living in the Great Smoky Mountains of North Carolina, along the headwaters of the Hiwassee and Little Tennessee rivers (sometimes called the Overhill Towns) were among the most conservative in the nation. Their land was not suited to intensive or staple-crop farming and their isolation allowed them to sustain their old ways with less interference from whites. The part of the Upper Towns located in northwestern Georgia between the Chattahoochee and Connesauga rivers was filled with Cherokees who had been forced out of towns further east when their land was ceded to the states of South Carolina and Georgia. These uprooted people were confused, disorganized, and discouraged; their chiefs had little influence in council. The leadership of the Upper Towns rested with chiefs located in eastern Tennessee, north of the Hiwassee River. The towns here were among the oldest and most venerable in the nation, but they were also in closest contact with the whites. The chiefs in this area lacked the prestige of those in the Lower Towns because of their early capitulation to the whites in 1777 and their reluctance to fight afterward. It proved easy for the federal agent to follow a policy of divide and conquer among these various regional factions and he generally found the Lower Town chiefs more pliable.

Flattery, gifts, bribes (called "inducements" by officials in Washington), and favors (such as extended credit at the federal trading post) gave the agent important tools for winning support for land cessions or road rights. The Cherokees, accustomed to a system of decentralized town government and traditionally committed to consensus decision making, were ill-equipped to stand up to the federal pressures for immediate action. The agent pressed for a system of majority rule, arguing that the chiefs in council were delegated to act for the nation. The Cherokees had always believed that neither individuals nor towns were necessarily bound by actions of tribal councils. Furthermore, councils were supposed to act openly, in the presence of all the people; a general acquiescence was required to cede tribal land. The federal government, however, insisted upon quick and binding decisions. Between 1794 and 1810 the Cherokees had to work out a new political and economic system to cope with their precarious situation. Tradition was inadequate to their exigencies.

Although the Cherokee Nation was ostensibly united after 1794 under Little Turkey (and, after his death in 1802, under Black Fox), the major decisions for Cherokee affairs were at first made by a small group of Lower Town war chiefs with whom Little Turkey and Black Fox were associated. The Lower Town chiefs had not only earned the respect of the average Cherokee but of the United States as well. They had also gained the attention of federal authorities because of their strategic location in the western and southern parts of the nation. Here, allied with the

Creeks, they had access to Spanish, British, and French agents. Predominantly full bloods of great shrewdness and tenacity, the Lower Town warrior chiefs were led by John Watts until his death in 1802, but essentially they acted as an oligarchy that included chiefs Doublehead, Bloody Fellow, Little Turkey, Will Elders, The Glass, Dick Justice, Old Cabin, Turtle at Home, Pathkiller, Kategiskee, Tolluntuskee, Tuskegitehee, Black Fox, and Young Watts. With them were allied several influential whites (British agents or Loyalists) who had married into the nation, fought against the colonists, and provided links with British and Spanish traders: John D. Chisholm and John Rogers (who had conspired with Governor William Blount) and John McDonald, John Walker, William Thorp, and Daniel Ross (Loyalists who had little allegiance to the new American nation but who wished to protect the wealth they had acquired through trade). The Cherokees were convinced that under the leadership of the Lower Town chiefs the nation could expect stout resistance to white pressures for land cessions and firm insistence upon Cherokee treaty rights and self-government. In this they proved mistaken.

Because of the importance of the Lower Town region, Governor Blount had been annoyed when Leonard Shaw decided to settle at the town of Ustanali (east of the Oostanaulah River), where the Upper Towns held their regional councils. Blount wanted Shaw to settle in Willstown near the western end of Lookout Mountain, site of the regional councils of the Lower Towns. In 1801, Return J. Meigs gave a large American flag to the Lower Town chiefs to fly over their council house in Willstown. Meigs regularly attended the Lower Town councils and assigned his assistant, Major William S. Lovely, to attend the Upper Town councils. Only later did Meigs agree to provide an American flag to the Ustanali council house. He told the Secretary of War that Willstown was the most important town in the nation, and he directed the bulk of the government's economic and technical assistance to this region. The Upper Town chiefs, especially those in the Overhill Towns or Valley Towns of North Carolina (who seldom attended councils at Ustanali or Willstown because they had their own regional councils), ultimately complained to President Jefferson about Meigs's favoritism toward the Lower Towns.[1]

In 1794, Doublehead, who had been chosen "Speaker" for the nation, made a favorable impression upon the Cherokees by personally confronting President Washington in Philadelphia. Speaking, he said, with "the voice of the whole nation," Doublehead protested that the annual payment of $1,500 that the federal government had granted to the Cherokees in 1792 was too small a consideration for the large cession of land they

---

[1] Mooney, *Historical Sketch*, pp. 72–73.

60

had yielded in 1791 to appease Governor Blount and the frontier whites in eastern Tennessee: "The land is very valuable to the United States," Doublehead told Washington, and the needs of the Cherokees to rehabilitate their country, now that peace was at hand, were very great. Washington and Secretary of War Henry Knox, eager to placate the Lower Town warriors and secure lasting peace, agreed to raise the Cherokee annuity to $5,000 a year. In addition, they permitted Doublehead to pick out $2,000 worth of trade goods while he was in Philadelphia, which he took back with him. An army escort was provided for his triumphal return.[2] A chief of such boldness and self-assurance seemed well suited to speak for the nation in its years of readjustment. As it turned out, Doublehead used his influence primarily to aid the Lower Towns.

Two years earlier another Lower Town chief, Eskaqua (Bloody Fellow), had gone to Philadelphia to remind the President that in the treaty of 1791 the Cherokees had been promised economic assistance for their improvement: "The treaty mentions ploughs, horses, cattle and other things for a farm; this is what we want. Game is going fast away from us. We must plant corn and raise cattle, and we desire you to assist us. . . . We wish you to attend to this point. In former times we bought of the trader's goods cheap; we could then clothe our women and Children; but now game is scarce and good dear; we cannot live comfortably. We desire the United States to regulate this matter."[3] Congress voted to provide sufficient funds for such economic assistance in 1792.

Although Bloody Fellow, Doublehead, and Little Turkey seemed eager to promote a new system of farming and "domestic manufactures," the Cherokee Nation as a whole was still hoping to maintain the fur trade as the basis of its economy. When Benjamin Hawkins came to the nation in 1796, he found few Cherokees engaged in farming and most of these were of mixed white-and-Cherokee ancestry. When Silas Dinsmoor first broached the total abandonment of hunting to the national council in 1796 and suggested self-subsistent farming, "he was unanimously laughed at by the Council for attempting to introduce white people's habits among the Indians who were created to pursue the chase."[4] Nevertheless, Dinsmoor persisted in this aim as did his successors, Thomas Lewis and Return J. Meigs. The transition proved far more difficult than expected. Ten years after the peace of 1794, every able-bodied Cherokee still spent the winter in the hunting ground while every spring the women in the towns did the planting. But, as Eskaqua recognized, hunting was yielding smaller and smaller results each year. In 1801, The Badger's Son

[2] Royce, *Cherokee Nation of Indians*, p. 44.
[3] Malone, *Cherokees of the Old South*, p. 51.
[4] John Ridge to Albert Gallatin, Payne Papers, VIII:113.

complained to Meigs that white hunters were destroying their game and robbing their traps in Tennessee.[5] Meigs told the War Department that Cherokee hunters in Tennessee had been reduced to catching only small game—"raccoons, foxes and wildcats"—for whose pelts they received just fifty or twenty-five cents.[6] He blamed the rise in horse stealing upon the poor hunting and urged the Cherokees to sell their worn-out hunting ground and use the income to buy livestock and supplies to start farms: "That land is of no use to them [he wrote in 1805]; there is not a single family [living] on it and the hunting is poor. Yet those of an idle disposition spend much time rambling there and often return with a stolen horse" [in order to have something worth selling]. "In fact," he went on, their old hunting ground "is only a nursery of savage habits and operates against civilization which is much impeded by their holding such immense tracts of wilderness."[7] But it was only in part their antipathy to "civilization" and "the white man's ways" that led the Cherokee to cling to hunting. To become horse-and-plow farmers required skills they did not have, and bad harvests would put their families in jeopardy of starving.

Cherokee men found it harder than Cherokee women to try new ways. Women were closer to the daily problems of providing food and clothing for their families. Iron hoes and mattocks made cultivation easier for them; brass pots, tin kettles, sharp knives, and blankets had become necessities. When the federal agents promised to show the women how to grow, spin, and weave cotton to make the cloth that their husbands' hunting income could no longer provide, they were willing to try it. Cotton growing began among the Cherokees in the 1790s in those areas with good soil. It grew readily and the agents provided cotton combs to extract the seeds and card or comb out the fibers. They gave them spinning wheels and looms and hired teachers to show the women how to spin cotton into thread and to weave cloth. Cherokee women learned these skills quickly and were enthusiastic about their ability to provide the cloth, and hence clothing, for their families. As hunters lost status as providers, their womenfolk gained it. Probably some Cherokees shared the view of the Creek men who told Benjamin Hawkins that they objected to his teaching their women to spin and weave because "if the women can clothe themselves they will be proud and not obedient to their husbands."[8] In a

[5] Badger's Son to Return J. Meigs, September 7, 1801, M-208; George of Valley Town to Return J. Meigs, December 4, 1801, M-208; Return J. Meigs to Dearborn, December 7, 1801, M-208.

[6] ASP I, 676.

[7] Return J. Meigs to Benjamin Hawkins, February 13, 1805, M-208.

[8] Pound, *Benjamin Hawkins*, p. 114. See also Mary E. Young, "Women, Civilization, and The Indian Question," in *Clio Was a Woman: Studies in the History of American*

matrilineal society the status of women was already strong, however, and these new skills for women made it stronger. Soon the women's demands for cards, combs, wheels, and looms exceeded the ability of the agents to supply them. By 1801 Meigs reported to the Secretary of War: "The applications for wheels, cards and looms, etc. are numerous . . . they raise considerable quantities of Cotton for their own use. I have not hitherto been able to supply half the number who apply; they say they have Cotton and cannot work it for want of wheels, cards, etc."[9] A year later, he reported: "The raising and manufacturing of Cotton is all done by Indian Women; they find their conditions so much bettered by this improvement that they apply for wheels, cards, etc. with great earnestness." They were disappointed that the agent's supplies were so quickly exhausted each year.[10] In July 1801, he said he had been "informed that there was 32 pieces of Cloth wove in Doublehead's Town within 14 months past." In September he reported that "the Bold Hunter, a Cherokee Chief, has made six Looms for weaving Cotton Cloth—has five spinners in his family . . . [who] made ninety yards of Cotton Cloth from Cotton of his own raising."[11] Asking the Secretary of War to increase the quantity of tools for the Cherokees, Meigs wrote in 1802: "I have mentioned the need for more Wheels and cards than I have done at any other Quarter of the years because the Indians have, almost all of them, Cotton in hand and say they cannot work it for want of the wheels and cards. . . . It appears to me from the present temper of the Indians that the raising of Cotton and sheep and manufacturing of these articles may be easily carried to a very considerable extent and thereby civilization even amongst those who have been strongly attached to the hunting life."[12]

A story began to circulate at this time about a hunter who returned with his small catch one year to discover that his wife and daughters had woven "with so much assiduity as to make more cloth in value than the Chief's hunt of six months amounted to. He was astonished, and came to the agent with a smile, accusing him for making his wife and daughters better hunters [providers] than he and requested to be furnished with a plough and went to work on his farm."[13] It was a Horatio Alger folk tale designed and promulgated by those in favor of acculturation to make the transition from the old ways to the new seem easier than it really was.

Women, ed. Mabel E. Deutrich and Virgina C. Purdy (Washington, D.C.: Howard University Press, 1980), pp. 98–110.

[9] Return J. Meigs to Henry Dearborn, December 7, 1801, M-208.

[10] Return J. Meigs, "Journal," August [no day], 1802, M-208; see also Return J. Meigs to Henry Dearborn, January 1, 1803, M-208.

[11] Return J. Meigs, "Journal," July 6, 1801, September [no day], 1801, M-208.

[12] Return J. Meigs to Henry Dearborn, January 11, 1802, M-208.

[13] Payne Papers VIII:114.

Although the federal agents provided sheep to the Cherokees after 1794 to try to persuade the women to spin and weave wool, this was never as popular as cotton. Sheep were difficult to care for, though some did it. Gradually Cherokee craftsmen with woodworking skills began to make looms and spinning wheels to supplement those provided by the government as well as making and repairing the wooden parts of plows. For many Cherokee males the transition from hunting to farming began with raising cattle and horses. Women who raised hogs, chickens, geese, and milk cows learned at the same time to manufacture cheese and butter from milk. Hitherto the Cherokees had taken little interest in horses and cows. They hunted and fought on foot. Cattle ("the white man's buffalo") were troublesome to keep out of the corn and tiresome to milk daily. The Cherokees had learned by 1794 to like pork; hogs could be allowed to run wild and pork was easier to salt and store than beef. But when the deer became scarce and their carcasses had to be carried long distance, raising horses to carry burdens and cattle for meat and hides became necessary. By 1800 some Cherokees were regularly taking droves of cattle, hogs, and geese into the white settlements for sale or barter. Livestock sales provided a cash income to replace the bartering of pelts and skins. Cowhide also served many of the same purposes as deerskin. Beef cattle sold for ten dollars a head; horses for forty to sixty dollars. "The raising of Cattle and making of Cloth," said Meigs in 1801, "are their principle objects; they are not fond of expanding their tillage, but it must increase for their hunting is fast failing them."[14] Some of the more enterprising Cherokees, like James Vann, Daniel Ross, Samuel Riley, and William Shorey, would buy up cattle from nearby families until they had a herd large enough to make it worth driving to a large city like Charleston, Augusta, or Knoxville for sale. These early Cherokee traders were usually whites (married to Cherokee women) or mixed bloods (whose fathers were white) who spoke English and were able to barter successfully with whites.

Cherokee men did not rush to "expand their tillage" both because farming was not a role for men and because it was a new and different way of life. For families to leave their towns and move out to start homesteads ran counter to the communal ethic and the village life the Cherokee had always lived. Cherokees were gregarious. The women worked in groups; the men hunted and waged war together; the whole town joined in ceremonial activities. When the men were not hunting, they met regularly at the town council house to settle local problems; they repaired their implements or prepared for ball plays together. The agents spoke repeatedly

[14] Return J. Meigs to Henry Dearborn, December 7, 1801, M-208.

of the "slothful habits" or "indolence" of the Indian males, who allowed their women to toil in the hot sun while they sat in the shade, telling stories, and laughing together with other men. "From the soil they derived a scanty supply of corn, barely enough to furnish them with gah-no-ha-nah [the staple Indian cornmeal], and this was obtained by the labor of women and grey-headed men, for custom would have it that it was disgraceful for a young man to be seen with a hoe in his hand."[15] Plowing in the fields, said Meigs in 1808, "is painful and, in the idea of most of them, dishonorable."[16]

It was also risky. Those Cherokee men who first decided to brave the opprobrium of their peers and become farmers often failed miserably at it. They had never plowed fields before and they did not know precisely how or when to plant in deep furrows. They did not always choose the right soil or understand the need to fertilize or rotate crops. Moreover, it was expensive to buy good plow horses, a harness, and horsecollars, to build a stable, and to pay for constant horseshoeing. The federal government tried to provide plows and to hire blacksmiths to work here and there in the nation but, as with spinning wheels, looms, spinners, and weavers, it could not supply enough of them. The government did not supply experienced farmers to teach the science of farming; this was supposed to come naturally—just plow, plant, cultivate, and harvest. But it was not so simple.

Light plows required only one horse; heavier plows required two. The plows donated by the government were light plows with an iron moldboard attached to the wooden plowshare. Only a blacksmith could repair or replace the moldboard.[17] Insecure about their ability to be competent farmers but confident of their skill as hunters, Cherokee men hoped that better hoes and mattocks would enable their wives to improve their garden plots while they continued to provide furs and hides to barter for other necessities. Self-subsistent farmers needed many skills that the Cherokees had yet to learn. Even if a crop of corn yielded a surplus, it was not easy to find a market in which to sell it or to calculate the right market price for it.

Obtaining farmland, however, was no problem. Under the system of tribal ownership of the land any tract not occupied was available to any Cherokee (or Cherokee "countryman") who wanted it. By 1805 there was little alternative to farming, though it was hard to abandon their village life. Wives had to follow their husbands away from their clan rela-

---

[15] *Cherokee Phoenix*, January 21, 1829.

[16] Return J. Meigs to Henry Dearborn, June 3, 1808, M-208.

[17] Return J. Meigs to Henry Dearborn, October 10, 1802, M-208; Return J. Meigs to Henry Dearborn, February 25, 1804, M-208.

tions to live in isolated cabins. Children lost touch with their grandparents, aunts, and uncles who told them ancient stories and taught them traditional customs. Once they had left the town to farm, men had less time for council affairs, festivals, dances, and ballgames. Women no longer met each other daily to share their problems and their work or to seek help from each other in the chores of childbearing, childrearing, and sickness. The ritual taboos of female purification fell away. After 1805 the widely dispersed farms, with nuclear families, marked the beginning of the end of Cherokee communal life in the townhouse and the ceremonial square. People still came together for major religious celebrations, like the Green Corn Dance or for a ballplay, as frontier whites came together for camp meetings, husking bees, and house raisings, but daily life became centered upon the conjugal family. There was more emphasis upon self-reliance and individualism. A new ethic evolved for both men and women as private rights and profits replaced clan and town duties. Federal agents told the Cherokees that the self-discipline of hard work and the routinization of life would make them more prosperous, happy, and secure, but as Meigs reported, the Cherokees at first thought "our enjoyments cost more than they are worth."[18] Cherokee pleasures had always come from daily social activities; the white man's satisfaction came from accumulating material goods for his family. The white man believed in personal achievement and delayed gratification; the Cherokees lived for the community and the enjoyment each day could bring.

It required dire necessity and the example of respectable chiefs to persuade the Cherokees to take up the new way of life. In many respects, the chiefs were better able to make the change. They had special relationships with the agent and were able to make personal requests to him for credit at the factory or for government technical assistance. In 1801 Little Turkey, Principal Chief of the nation, gave up going on the winter hunt because he was too old. Deciding to become a farmer, he wrote (through a scribe) to the federal agent: "I am under necessity of acquainting you that my family is at a great loss for the want of knowing how to spin and weave. There is a certain Absolom Harriby lives in Pine Log [a nearby town] which is a wheel maker by trade and his wife learns the Indians how to weave. I can assure you we are in great want of them in this part to instruct us, and I shall take it as a Singular favour if you will send him into these parts; wheels and cards we are lacking. We have made a fine crop of cotton this year but for the want of utensils it does us no good." Little Turkey wanted these women's utensils "as quick as possible." "For my part," he went on, "I want . . . two shovel-plough moles [molds],

18 Return J. Meigs to Benjamin Hawkins, February 13, 1805, M-208.

twelve sheep, six mattocks, two pair Clivesses [clevises], single coalter [colter], twelve weeding hoes, six club axes. Be so good as to send these to me . . . as I wish to goe by the directions of the President and likewise yourself [and take up farming]."[19]

As other local chiefs made similar decisions, the onus of spending one's life behind a plow became more acceptable to Indian men; farming became sensible and respectable. With farming came the need for fencing and for new buildings—barns, stables, corn cribs, pig pens. Buildings required wood sawed into planks at sawmills. As the Cherokees grew more corn, they wanted gristmills to grind it. As they grew more cotton, they wanted cotton gins to remove the seeds. When the government requested a new right of way for a road or a new cession of land, the chiefs began to stipulate as part of the bargain that the government build these new mills for them. And the government provided them, though never as many as requested. The chiefs in whose towns the mills were built began to grow wealthy and to buy black slaves to extend their fields and tend their livestock. White men who married Cherokees enjoyed the opportunity to become the owners of large plantations; land cost them nothing and they paid no taxes. Mixed-blood Cherokees who spoke English began to adopt the life style of surrounding white farmers. Gradually the Cherokees developed a landed elite and a small group of shopkeepers and entrepreneurs formed a kind of bourgeoisie. Eventually these persons would become as influential as the war chiefs in decision making.

But the transition was slow and uneven. Even the best of farmers often failed to reap the harvest for which they worked so hard. Natural catastrophes were frequent and whole sections of the nation suffered when a drought, flood, hailstorms, or early frost destroyed the crops. In March 1804, the chiefs from Doublehead's town near Muscle Shoals (Doublehead, Kattegiskee, Pathkiller, Sequeechy, and Jucutul or The Seed) sent Meigs a letter that began, "we are like to perish for Bread. We have by Industrey failed the Last year to make Bread, not owing to Indolence but oweing to the hand of the great Spirit above—not sending us Rain—to witt, the Droth." There were 121 Indians and 15 white men in the town. The chiefs said they would starve unless the agent sent them enough corn to provide food until the harvest. "We are all at this place working hard and Inlarging our farms and [we] stands in great Kneed of plows and mattocks to grub our ground." They had been given tools, but they are "nearly worn out by so many using them. Our women are Raising cotton and spinning and is in great need of [new] wheels." The community needed emergency assistance: "Now, our great frend, father and Brother,

[19] Little Turkey to Return J. Meigs, December 23, 1801, M-208.

we are looking up to the great Spirit above to protect and lengthen your Days and Incline your hart to Relieve us." The letter also asked for "garden seeds" of cabbage, lettuce, mustard, onions, "collet," parsnips, carrots, "Parcelay, Sparrowgrass," turnips, sage, and wormwood. A new kind of diet was developing with truck gardening.[20]

The "starving times" (in 1804, 1807, 1811) alternated with epidemics of smallpox (1806, 1817, 1824) and other diseases that kept many Cherokees in an almost chronic state of emergency. Like any frontier community, the transformation of the wilderness into farmland required more than hard work; a great deal of luck was needed as well as continual access to capital or credit. When Washington and Knox worked out their policy in 1789 they had not realized how difficult the "civilization" of the Indians would be nor how expensive the technical assistance offered would become. Meigs sent three hundred bushels of corn to Doublehead's town in 1804 to help them through their shortage, but he kept track of such favors. When the next treaty negotiations took place he did not hesitate to remind the chiefs of how much they owed to the benevolent support of their Great Father in Washington. There was no hospitality ethic, no "free lunch," in the capitalist system. Meigs reported in June 1801 that during the first eighteen months of his agency, "I distributed 13 Mattocks, 58 plough irons, 44 Corn hoes, 204 pairs cotton cards, 215 spinning wheels, 28 [cotton] Reels, 4 looms, 53 sheep." The next year he distributed (in addition to dozens of brass pots, tin kettles, blankets, cards, hats, rolls of thread, yards of calico cloth, needles, and scissors) "60 plough irons, 112 small axes, 150 corn hoes." Part of this was paid for by the government and part by the Cherokees out of their annuity. Supplies were also provided on credit at the government trading post or on credit extended by white and Cherokee merchants. In increasing numbers the Cherokees left their villages between 1794 and 1810, gave up large-scale hunting for furs and skins, built log cabins, chopped down trees, dug up the stumps, plowed fields, and adopted the lives of husbandmen and farmers' wives.

In this "civilization" process, the Lower Towns received the most help from the government, but the Upper Towns in the Tennessee area used their government assistance more wisely. The Overhill Towns in North Carolina and the southernmost towns along the Creek border received the least assistance and remained the poorest parts of the nation. This was in part because the soil was poorer in the mountain areas but also because the people in these outlying districts were the most reluctant to acculturate. It was also apparent that families in which the father was white and

---

[20] Doublehead and others to Return J. Meigs, March 27, 1804, M-208. When those who signed a letter or other document are listed in the text, their names are spelled as in the original. An alternate spelling is sometimes noted.

the mother Cherokee or in which both parents were of mixed ancestry and spoke English made the transition more easily than full-blood families. The framers of America's Indian policy and the Presidents and agents who carried it out always thought of intermarriage between Indians and whites as one of the keys to rapid acculturation. Intermarried whites, especially males, tended to bring up their children to act and think like whites. Their success as farmers or entrepreneurs set the tone for the "civilization" process. The agents worked most closely with those who spoke English. Many of the influential chiefs went into partnership with white "countrymen," as Doublehead did with John D. Chisholm. Those of mixed ancestry constituted a higher proportion of the chiefs, moreover, because their skills enabled them to deal most effectively with white officials.[21] Return J. Meigs attributed most of the "progressive" leadership in the nation to these mixed bloods: "The Cherokees are making considerable improvement and are becoming more and more attached to the habits of a civilized life [he wrote in 1805]. Those of the mixed Blood are at least one half in number of the nation, and they are attached to the pursuits of husbandry and domestic manufactures and will eventually become an acquisition of useful people to the U. States [when integrated]."[22]

Meigs overestimated the number of mixed-blood Cherokees; the mixed bloods at this time probably constituted less than 15 percent of the Cherokee population. He was misled because he lived in an area where there were more such persons and because these were the Cherokees who most often came to talk with him. The full bloods (whom he called "the real Indians") stayed by themselves, eschewing contact with whites. A year later, Meigs reiterated his point to the Secretary of War. The mixed bloods "are almost without exception in favor of improvements and have very much thrown off the savage manners and habits. But those of the real Indians still hug the savage manners and habits and are unwilling to give [up] the pleasure of the shade and idleness."[23] Meigs feared that there was something rooted in the nature of the full bloods that made them incapable of acculturating. "It seems as if the Graver of time had fixed the savage character so deeply in the native Indians, I mean those who have arrived at manhood, that it cannot be effaced: but where the blood is mixed with the whites, in every grade of it, there is an apparent disposition leaning toward civilization, and this disposition is in proportion to its distance from the original stock."[24]

Part of the solution was to promote intermarriage and thus to infuse

[21] See Malone, *Cherokees of the Old South*, pp. 53–55.
[22] Return J. Meigs to Henry Dearborn, August 4, 1805, M-208.
[23] Return J. Meigs to Henry Dearborn, July 27, 1805, M-208.
[24] Return J. Meigs to Benjamin Hawkins, February 13, 1805, M-208.

"backward" savage blood with "progressive" white blood (blood in this case being a metaphor for training and habits); the other part was to concentrate upon training the young. "It cannot be expected that the adult real Indian will alter his habits but in a partial degree, but by their Intermarriages with the half Blood and with the whites" this obstacle would be overcome and "the real Indian will disappear."[25] They would disappear in two ways: their habits would become like those of whites and their skin color would lighten. "The Children that are coming up, especially those of the mixed Blood, and they compose a considerable part of the whole, may be brought to such a stage of improvement as to become an acquisition of useful citizens."[26]

Meigs once told a traditionalist Cherokee who held Meigs's encouragement of intermarriage against him: "You say I encouraged marriages between white men and Cherokee women; I always have and shall do it." It was for their own good, "because your women are industrious and because I conceive that by this measure civilization is faster advanced than in any other way." He conspicuously omitted encouraging the marriage of white women to Indian men because he assumed that husbands would play the major role in setting family standards. Believing that nurture and not nature was to blame for Cherokee "backwardness," he said he "always considered the whole human race as brothers."[27] Ethnocentrism, however, led him, as it led many later observers, to assume that white blood in Indian veins constituted some kind of beneficial change in Indian outlook and behavior.

Although most Cherokees had no racial objections to the intermarriage of whites and Indians, many held the similarly ethnocentric view that the Great Spirit had established a distinctly different way of life for Indians and for whites. However, when Meigs spoke of "the original stock" of the two races and when the Cherokees said that "they are not derived from the same stock as the whites," the line between ethnocentrism and polygenesis became blurred. It all depended on when and why the Great Spirit made men of different colors and whether he permanently "fixed" their habits and attitudes toward life.

Because those who provided the example and set the pattern of Cherokee acculturation were usually whites (or descendants of whites) who followed the agricultural and social patterns of the southern part of the United States, the Cherokees farmed by southern standards. They chose crops that naturally flourished in the climate; they adopted a staple- or cash-crop system; and they employed slave labor as soon as they could

[25] Return J. Meigs to Henry Dearborn, August 4, 1805, M-208.
[26] Return J. Meigs to Benjamin Hawkins, February 13, 1805, M-208.
[27] Return J. Meigs to Chiefs Chulio and Sour Mush, March 14, 1808, M-208.

70

afford it. In the 1790s there were probably fewer than 100 slaves in the nation, but according to a census or "statistical table" that Meigs commissioned in 1808, there were by that time 583 black slaves in the Cherokee Nation. Some of the wealthier Cherokees, like James Vann, Doublehead, Charles Hicks, Samuel Riley, and John McDonald, owned ten or more; Vann was said to have owned almost 100. The vast majority of Cherokees owned none. But those who owned them set the norm for the new entrepreneurial class, just as the large cotton planters did in southern white society. For the Cherokee bourgeoisie, slave ownership was a source of inheritable wealth and, with slaves, the size of a farm or plantation that a man could pass on to his children would naturally be larger (even though technically he did not own the land). Acculturation to private property and the accumulation of goods led toward a patrilineal system of inheritance just as it did toward a nuclear, self-sufficient family life.

To encourage the Indians to divide up their land in severalty, the federal agents constantly pushed them to sell their "unused" land. Once the Indians saw the benefits of self-subsistent yeoman farming, the federal government believed, they would have no more use for tribal ownership of the land. They would have become individual commercial farmers, speculators, and entrepreneurs, eager to buy and sell land as they did their cash crops, livestock, or slaves to increase their incomes. During these transitional years, however, the Cherokees feared the loss of their hunting land, for it was a fundamental tie to their traditional pattern of life. "They have a long time since resolved not to part with any more land," Meigs told the War Department in 1803; "there is not a man in the nation who dares advocate it; it is said that it would endanger his life."[28] Their status as a people depended upon their being a landholding nation; land was the only real source of wealth and power they had left. United on their land, they could bargain as a nation for the assistance of the federal government against the unfriendly frontiersmen; without their land, each Cherokee would find himself in an unequal contest with the white man. Those of mixed ancestry and wealth might fend for themselves, but the great bulk of the nation could not. Meigs deplored the fact that "the real Indians . . . have the ascendancy in public transactions" because by the sheer weight of numbers they were able to prevent the "more progressive" chiefs from acting out of their own private or class interests.[29] Meigs saw the reluctance of the full bloods to embrace the sale of their lands as "timidity." They did not trust individual competition or

[28] Return J. Meigs to Henry Dearborn, May 4, 1803, M-208.
[29] Return J. Meigs to Henry Dearborn, July 27, 1805, M-208.

71

self-interest to benefit the whole. Progress, Meigs believed, offered them prosperity, individual freedom, and economic mobility, but most Cherokees felt that progress, as he defined it, would add to their insecurity, detract from their freedom, and obliterate their ethnic identity.

Cherokee "timidity," as Meigs described it, was like that of children who were fearful of assuming the responsibilities of adulthood. It was necessary, he believed, "to wean them from their savage ways," which constituted the childhood of the human race. "I would hope," he said in 1806, "to do away [with] every custom inconsistent with civilized life. . . . I hope that time will come when they will look back with wonder that they had so long continued [in their irrational, backward ways]."[30] Unable to interest them in ceding land for the moment, Meigs concentrated upon encouraging them to admit skilled white artisans, mechanics, farmers, traders, and millwrights into the nation to show them how to develop their land and its resources; he encouraged them to establish schools and to build roads and utilize waterways in order to promote trade.

Although the Trade and Intercourse Acts empowered the federal agents to license white traders, it left up to the Indians themselves the extent to which they would encourage white artisans to enter their nation. Meigs found that the "progressive" chiefs were ready to take advantage of the skills these white men would bring but that the full bloods saw whites as potential sources of friction. They were quite aware that the profits a white man could make from the Indians were so small that only some kind of speculation would attract them. Most of the artisans, blacksmiths, school teachers, and sharecroppers who came to live among the Cherokees were men too incompetent or unreliable to make a living in white society. Many others were debtors and renegades seeking refuge from state law enforcement agencies.

The Cherokees were equally suspicious of missionaries, as the Moravians found. Prior to 1794 the Cherokees had had no use for missionaries or for schools. Occasionally itinerant preachers had come through, but their theology was incomprehensible. In 1758–1759 a Presbyterian minister named John Martin began coming from North Carolina to preach to certain villages, but after patiently hearing him out for several weeks the Cherokees asked him to leave because "he had so long plagued them with that they no ways understood" or cared to understand.[31] Their decision to admit the Moravians in 1800 stemmed from the desire of certain mixed-blood chiefs to have schools for their children and because it seemed that the white man might at last be prepared to share with them

[30] Return J. Meigs to Valentine Geiger, June 6, 1806, M-208.
[31] Malone, *Cherokees of the Old South*, p. 96.

some of the complex knowledge that he had learned from "the Great Book." The Cherokees thought of the Bible as the source of all the white man's wisdom and skills. When the Moravians had promised to teach them all that was in "the Great Book," one old chief, Arcowee of Chota, said "I believe that you have been inspired by the Great Spirit to be willing to come and to teach us" from "the great book from which they [the Cherokees] can learn all things."[32] The Cherokees were also impressed that the missionaries did not appear to share the hostility and contempt for Indians that most frontier whites did. Kulsatahee of Hiwassee Town talked to the Moravian agents in 1799 and explained modestly that the Cherokees "are indeed very stupid [dull] and clumsy" when it came to learning the new ideas of the whites. However, they were willing to learn, he said, provided the Moravians did not share the view that "we Indians are too evil and bad to become good people and that we are too unclean and brown [red-skinned]." He was pleased when the Moravians answered, "we love all people, no matter what their color," and he was delighted when they added that the Great Spirit also made no distinctions because of color.[33] From what Arcowee and Kulsatahee said, it appeared that Cherokee full bloods were ready to learn from the whites as long as whites treated them as equals and were prepared to share their knowledge as brothers. Moreover, the Moravians were pacifists and they had never taken part in any military activities against Indians.

The Moravians had got off to a bad start, however, as noted above. The council admitted them "on trial" in 1800 and gave them two years to start a boarding school. James Vann, an Upper Town chief, gave them his protection and helped them purchase the buildings of a farmer near Vann's home in Springplace, Georgia. Vann was the son of a well-to-do white trader who had established a store at Diamond Hill in northwestern Georgia. He married a Cherokee and left his fortune to his mixed-blood son. James Vann proved a shrewd trader and in the 1790s rapidly expanded his father's holdings, building a gristmill, operating a ferry over the Connesauga River, purchasing black slaves to expand his farm, and opening a second trading post near Huntsville, Alabama. By 1800 Vann was perhaps the wealthiest man in the Cherokee Nation, and under his protection the Moravian mission at Springplace was secure. However, as an Upper Town chief, Vann was not one of the inner group who directed the nation's affairs. His protection would have been adequate, nevertheless, had

---

[32] The conversation of the two Moravian missionaries, Abraham Steiner and Frederic de Schweinitz, with Chiefs Arcowee and Kulsatahee are in their account of their trip to the Cherokee Nation in October, 1799. See the Moravian Missionary records in the Moravian Archives, Bethlehem, Pennsylvania (hereafter abbreviated MAB).

[33] Ibid.

the Moravians done what the Cherokees expected them to do. Difficulties arose because the missionaries believed that Christianization must precede civilization; that is, they believed there could be no school until the parents of Cherokee children had become Christians and were committed to giving them a Christian education. Agents Meigs and Lovely thought the Moravians had got things backwards, and so did the Cherokees.

The Moravians began preaching at Springplace in the early summer of 1801. Having no interpreter, they preached in English; among themselves they spoke German. At first a few Cherokees came to hear them, but these soon gave up and their principal auditors on Sunday mornings turned out to be Vann's black slaves, most of whom understood some English. Three years went by. The Moravians made no converts (black or red), formed no church, and of course started no school. The Cherokee council had kept a careful eye on them and concluded that they had failed to keep their promise. The council withdrew its permission for the mission and instructed Meigs to tell the Moravians to leave.[34]

Meigs had already decided that the Moravian approach was wrongheaded and inadequate. In December 1802, he had proposed a different plan for Cherokee education to the Secretary of War: "There is reason to fear that without the diffusion amongst them of knowledge of letters, the object to save them from extinction will not be obtained." He was, he said, "sensible that to establish and support schools amongst these people would be expensive," and that "the present expense in supplying them with the implements of husbandry and manufactures and domestics and supporting Agents and Interpreters is a great expense[;] more cannot be expected from the United States." His solution was to persuade the Cherokees to develop their own endowment to support a school system. "Let them sell land to the amount of 200,000 dollars, the simple interest will be 12,000 dollars. This will support 30 school masters at 400 dollars each. . . . I know they will object to it"—but he felt that it was necessary for their own good and that the government must persist in the effort to make the Indians transform their excessive landholdings into funds for capital and public improvements.[35] Meigs's plan depended upon persuading the Cherokees to part with their hunting ground, but it was doomed to failure. Few Cherokees were prepared to sell their land to teach their children to become like white men.

Then, in the summer of 1803, an enterprising Presbyterian minister in eastern Tennessee, Gideon Blackburn, came to the council with a third educational proposal. Blackburn had come to Maryville, Tennessee, just

[34] Schwarze, *History of the Moravian Missions*, pp. 75-79.
[35] Return J. Meigs to Henry Dearborn, December 28, 1802, M-208.

north of the Cherokee border, as a young man and had served as chaplain with the Tennessee militia during the last bloody days of the guerrilla war in the early 1790s. After the Cherokee defeat, Blackburn felt moved to extend to them the blessings of civilization and to restore good feelings between the white and red man. His small frontier congregation was too poor to support a missionary effort and his denomination could give him only a few hundred dollars. Blackburn therefore went directly to President Jefferson and persuaded him to provide $300 in supplies (to be deducted from the budget of the Cherokee agency). Then, with the President's endorsement, he toured eastern Presbyterian churches, raising money for his philanthropic enterprise until he thought he had enough to begin.[36]

When he explained his plan to the council in October 1803, the chiefs were initially cool. Their experiment with the Moravians had miscarried. Blackburn explained that his plan was totally different. He believed that civilization should precede (or at least be concomitant with) Christianization. He did not want to preach or build churches. He would simply provide free schooling taught by secular school teachers. All he asked was permission to construct some schoolhouses. He promised to send "three or four school masters each of whom will take 25 to 30 Children to be fed and cloathed at the expense of their [the Presbyterian missionary] society." Blackburn's role would be simply that of supervisor; he would remain pastor of his congregation in nearby Maryville. Meigs gave Blackburn his full support, as did most of the white countrymen and mixed-blood leaders who lived in the Upper Towns of eastern Tennessee where Blackburn planned to start his schools. He received particular help from the McDonald, Ross, Fields, Hicks, Adair, Brown, Bell, and Riley families who lived between Hiwassee Town and Chickamauga to the east of the Tennessee River.

After considerable debate, the council decided to let Blackburn go ahead. The first school opened on the Hiwassee River in February 1804, after Meigs provided carpenters to build a dormitory and blankets for the children. Because many of the students already spoke some English (coming from homes in which their fathers spoke it), they proved apt pupils. About twenty-five could be accommodated at the Hiwassee School, and its success led Blackburn to open a second school in March 1806, eighteen miles to the south, on Sale Creek, on the plantation of Richard Fields.[37] The first was a boarding school; the second, a day school. Funds were never sufficient to open the other schools Blackburn had planned,

[36] On Blackburn's mission see McLoughlin, *Cherokees and Missionaries*, pp. 54–81.
[37] Gideon Blackburn to Henry Dearborn, October 31, 1806, M-222, roll 2, #0757.

but his enthusiasm was great and he lost no opportunity to publicize his work. It has been claimed that over the seven years during which his schools operated, Blackburn taught 300–400 Cherokees to speak English. The figure is inflated, though he doubtless improved the English of the children from mixed-blood families.

The Cherokees soon discovered that the Presbyterian curriculum included considerable Christian training; the children were taught to read from the Bible and catechism, to say Christian prayers daily, and to sing Christian hymns. They were forbidden to speak Cherokee. The schoolmasters and their wives were ardent Christians; they also did their best to teach the children how to dress, eat, and behave according to the manners of whites. Mixed-blood parents had no objection to any of this, but full-blood parents were less pleased. Few full bloods attended; the schoolmasters spoke no Cherokee and had to rely on their students to translate. Blackburn was convinced that the sooner the Cherokees abandoned their language, the better.

Meanwhile the Moravians, faced with ejection and with Blackburn's competition, finally grudgingly consented to open a small boarding school for seven students in 1804 (even though none of their parents was Christian). They limited the school to males and hoped to train first the children of influential chiefs, who would set an example for others. Unable to speak Cherokee or to afford interpreters, they too ended up teaching mostly the children of mixed-blood parents. Neither the Moravians nor the Presbyterians had any initial success in converting Cherokee adults to Christianity; no mission church existed in the nation until 1818. The decision to admit the Moravians and Presbyterians as school teachers was neither as important as the agent hoped nor as pernicious as the conservative Cherokees feared. The instruction was chiefly of use to those mixed-blood parents already committed to rapid acculturation, but even these were reluctant to have their children stay too long at the schools. As a rule they wished their offspring simply to learn enough to assist their parents in correspondence or business dealings with whites. Blackburn was so angry at the readiness of the parents to remove their children before they had become truly proficient in English that he persuaded the council to rule that parents who withdrew their children before their program was completed would have to forfeit the clothes, books, blankets, and other items given to them by the school.

Although most Cherokees came to accept the missionaries as "good men"—meaning that they were not trying to take their land or to cheat them—the fact that they were so few, so moralistic, and essentially apolitical meant that they were not particularly important figures in Cherokee acculturation prior to 1819. Faced with difficult problems of political and economic adjustment, the Cherokee leaders gave primary attention to the levers of power within the United States. In the early years of the century the Cherokees' primary controversy with the federal authorities arose over the constant demands that rights of way be granted through the nation for roads, turnpikes, and waterways to connect the white settlements. In 1798 the nation had been forced to allow the Cumberland Road to be built through its northern section, and a year later President Adams made plans to construct a federal turnpike from Athens, Georgia, northwest to Knoxville and Nashville. This road would run through the very center of the nation, introducing a constant flow of white traffic in both directions and consequently increasing the chances for conflict, theft, violence, and murder between Indians and whites. In their determined effort to prevent the building of "the Georgia Road," the Cherokees learned how difficult it was to say no to requests by their Father in Washington.

John Adams left office before he could press the Cherokees for this right of way, but Thomas Jefferson at once took it up. Not only did Jefferson believe roads were necessary in the region to promote settlement and trade, but he considered them of prime military importance. The conspiracies of William A. Bowles, Aaron Burr, and James Wilkinson in these years pointed to the threat from adventurers willing to make arrangements with the British, Spanish, or French. Even after the Louisiana Purchase in 1803, the Mississippi Valley was not at all securely in the hands of the United States. Jefferson and his Secretary of War, Henry Dearborn, ably assisted by Return J. Meigs, left no stone unturned between 1801 and 1803 to cajole and, ultimately, to compel the Cherokees to grant the roadway the government wanted. It took the government three years and four separate treaty negotiations (as well as numerous bribes or "inducements") before the matter received serious consideration. So intense did the antagonisms within the Cherokee Nation become that when James Vann purchased a wagon in anticipation of the road, the council assumed he had been bribed to support the measure and expelled (or "broke") him from his place as a chief.[38]

The government's efforts to obtain a right of way for the Georgia Road started in 1799 as part of a much larger project. Congress appropriated $25,000 that year to hold treaty negotiations with a number of southern tribes in order to obtain land and road rights from them. Adams said the sum was too small to be effective and in 1800 Congress added another $15,000. When Jefferson came into office in March 1801, he instructed his Secretary of War to pursue the project. From the Cherokees the gov-

[38] Brainerd Journal, November 9, 1819, ABCFM.

ernment now sought not only a road from Augusta (or Athens), Georgia, to Nashville (with a fork going to Knoxville) through the eastern half of their nation (the Upper Town region) but also a road from Nashville to Natchez (along the "Natchez Trace") through the western area of the nation (the Lower Town region). In addition, the people of Tennessee and Kentucky wanted the Cherokees to cede the northern half of their hunting ground, consisting of 1,100 square miles in Kentucky and 7,000 square miles in Tennessee. For this land the federal government offered them $5,000 in cash or trade goods plus an addition of $1,000 per year to their perpetual annuity (which now stood at $5,000). In June 1801, Jefferson commissioned three men to carry out this work: General James Wilkinson, Benjamin Hawkins, and Andrew Pickens (later changed to William R. Davie). He instructed them that if they could not obtain all of the land desired, they should get as much as they could at a commensurate reduction in price. They were to stress the need for the roads.[39]

The Cherokees, though not yet as adept as they would soon become at monitoring the debates in Congress or reading the newspapers to foresee what was in store for them, nevertheless were well aware by 1801 that negotiations for a land cession were about to start. They knew because whenever this happened, a flock of land speculators began to travel through the area to be ceded seeking the best spots for future purchase; in addition, swarms of frontier whites invaded these areas in order to obtain preemption rights by squatting on the land before it was sold. While Jefferson and Dearborn were still working out the details of the proposed negotiations, the chiefs of twenty-six of the Upper Towns met at a regional council at Ustanali to make demands of their own upon the government in March 1801. They were particularly concerned over a group of Georgians, known as Wafford's settlers, who had moved into an area between the Oconee River and Currahee Mountain (in northern Georgia). Colonel James D. Wafford had encouraged this settlement, believing that this land had been ceded by the Cherokees in 1785, though in fact it was within the boundaries guaranteed to the Cherokees in the Treaty of Hopewell. The government had delayed surveying that boundary until 1798, by which time Wafford's settlers had already built cabins and started farms. Jefferson agreed with the Governor of Georgia to request a cession of this tract but mistakenly started negotiations with the Creeks to obtain it. The Creeks said the land belonged to the Cherokees, so Jef-

[39] On the origin of the conflict over Wafford's Tract see Royce, *Cherokee Nation of Indians*, pp. 55–65, and ASP I, 650–51. On Governor Tatnall's actions on behalf of Wafford's settlers, see Josiah Tatnall to President Jefferson, July 20, 1802, M-208. For the Cherokees' reaction see Cherokee Council at Oostenali (Ustanali) to Return J. Meigs, March 20, 1801, M-208.

ferson added its acquisition to the tasks of his treaty commissioners.[40] The government felt responsible for the error made by Wafford and his friends because of its failure to run the survey quickly. The Cherokees, however, had been complaining for years about these intruders. By 1801 there were over fifty families at Wafford's settlement. They occupied an area of 100 square miles and were determined to keep it (with the full support of the politicians of Georgia).[41]

The council at Ustanali sent a strongly worded message to Colonel Thomas Butler, commander of the United States Army garrison at Tellico Blockhouse, "to keep the white people of[f] their encroachments on our lands." The settlers "near the Currahee Mountain" had first attempted "to offer goods for our land," the council said, and when these were refused, they "threaten" now that "they will make war with us." "The mother earth has been Divided" in this area by treaties, "one part [to the] whites and the other to the red people where those present [at Ustanali] have been raised from their infancy to the years of manhood and that ground must ever be dear to they [the] Chiefs." By treaty the government had the duty "to suppress all bad doings on both sides." It appeared that "the white people will not mind the Talks of the United States, but the red people minds the language of the chiefs of the Cherokee nation." The chiefs noted that the federal agent, Thomas Lewis, had promised to look into this matter, but nothing had been done about it; "had the Transgression been Committed by [one of] our people, you would have taken him long before this time. The beloved men [the President and Secretary of War] of the united States Calls the red people their Children; the father ought to protect their Childrens rights." "We wish you will send a body of soldiers to remove the Inhabitant[s] on the Currahee mountain." In addition, the chiefs at Ustanali mentioned the question of roads through their nation—a matter that Colonel Wafford and his settlers were very much interested in because they hoped to market their produce in Knoxville or at the United States garrison and agency along the proposed road to Nashville. "We have no disposition to encourage they [that] Travellers should pass through our lands as there is roads enough among the white settlements to go around" our territory.[42]

Because Major Lewis was "more attentive to his bottle and his woman" than to his official duties and because Colonel Butler refused to remove Wafford's settlers without express orders from Washington, the Cherokees sent a delegation to Washington headed by The Glass (a prominent chief of the Lower Towns) to speak directly with Dearborn about this and

[40] ASP I, 648–49, 656–57; Royce, *Cherokee Nation of Indians*, pp. 55–65.
[41] ASP I, 650–51; Royce, *Cherokee Nation of Indians*, pp. 55–65.
[42] Cherokee Council to Colonel Thomas Butler, March 20, 1801, M-208.

about other Cherokee problems (especially several unpunished murders of Cherokees by whites passing through the nation).[43] This delegation met with Dearborn on June 30, 1801. He parried their request to remove Wafford's settlers by pointing out that the government felt responsible for the settlers' mistake and hoped to work out something in the coming treaty negotiations with the Cherokees. Dearborn then suggested that the Cherokees sell some of their hunting land and also allow the rights of way for the Natchez and Augusta roads to Nashville. The Glass responded that the Cherokees had no interest whatsoever in selling any land because "our country is now small" and needed all that it had left. Glass expressed astonishment and anger that such a request should be made and commissioners appointed when the government had promised in its treaty of October 1798 that it would make no further demands upon them; in its treaty of 1791 the government had solemnly agreed to guarantee their present borders "forever."[44] As for roads through their nation, Glass said these were also out of the question; they "would occasion many difficulties" between the Cherokees and the whites who traveled them.

Dearborn, struck by the vehemence of Glass's reaction, spoke to Jefferson, who agreed to alter his priorities. He wrote to the treaty commissioners telling them to make no "demands" for cessions of land from the Cherokees but merely to "mention" such a sale as a desirable "proposition."[45] The roads, however, were to be pressed as the chief objective. The commissioners were told to do nothing, while among the Cherokees, that would raise "in them unfriendly and inimical dispositions." They still had recourse to Spanish, British, or French assistance if they became upset.

The treaty commissioners finally arrived for negotiations in the Cherokee Nation in September 1801. By then some "frontier citizens" had increased "the pressure for land" and were causing the Cherokees considerable anxiety by saying that the President would insist upon a sale "to extinguish the indian claims to the lands on the right side of the Tennessee" River (the area that remained as their hunting ground).[46] This caused some Cherokees to consult with Benjamin Hawkins about "the propriety of looking out West of the Mississippi for an eventual residence where this nation already have a settlement of nearly one hundred gun-

---

[43] ASP I, 677. Lewis was removed for malfeasance on June 30, 1801; see also Henry Dearborn to Thomas Lewis, March 24, 1801, M-15, reel 1, p. 35.

[44] Conference with a Cherokee delegation in Washington, D.C., June 30, 1801, M-15, reel 1, p. 72.

[45] ASP I, 656.

[46] James Wilkinson et al., "Report of a Treaty Council at Southwest Point, Tennessee," September 4–6, 1801, M-271, reel 1, #0024–0028.

men [about six hundred persons]" on the St. Francis River. These western Cherokees had settled there (in what is now Arkansas) in the 1790s in order to get away from white settlers. The threat of more angry Cherokees across the Mississippi (still in Spanish hands) was bound to worry Jefferson. Hawkins tried to calm the Cherokees by insisting on the "benevolent care manifest towards the Indians" by the American government through "the plan for their civilization."[47]

The commissioners discovered that the Cherokees were unwilling to negotiate about either land or roads. The commissioners pointed out that "your white brethren who live at Natchez, at Nashville, and in South Carolina [and Georgia] are very far removed from each other and have complained to your father, the President, that the roads by which they travel are narrow and obstructed . . . your father is desirous to open wide these roads, but as they pass over the lands of his red children, he first asks their consent." They went on to say that the travelers on these roads would need places "for rest or accommodation" and "your father is desirous that his red children would consent to establish houses of entertainment and ferries on these roads to be kept by persons appointed by himself" (presumably white men). Denying that the government was trying to diminish the possibilities for the Cherokees' future prosperity, the commissioners said that it "intended not to extinguish your rights but to give value to your land values and make it immediately productive to you." Roads would increase land and would give them better access to markets for their livestock and corn. The commissioners admitted that nevertheless, if the Cherokees were disposed to sell any land, such as Wafford's settlement, they were ready to buy it.

Doublehead and Chulio, as Speakers for the council, responded bluntly. Doublehead said that "a number of land speculators" had mistakenly said "we want to sell lands." But the truth was "the Chiefs [i.e., white politicians], the head-men of these frontiers, are themselves interested in these speculations, and they will give you fine talks which are meant to deceive [the President], as they are for their own interest. We think it a shame that the land sellers should impose on the Government and say that we want to dispose of our lands when we do not." This answer adroitly bypassed the fact that the federal government was in fact but the tool of its frontier people in such matters and was as eager to obtain Indian land as any frontier speculator. The Cherokees preferred to avoid embarrassing the commissioner by suggesting instead that the President had probably been misinformed about their intentions.[48]

---

[47] Ibid.
[48] ASP I, 657.

As for "the roads you propose," Doublehead continued, "when you first made these settlements" of frontier people on the Cherokee borders, "there were paths which answered for them," and these paths were still available. "We do not wish to have them [wagon roads] made through our country. Our objections to these roads are these: a great many people of all descriptions would pass [along] them, and that would happen which has recently happened [violence, thefts, and murders of Cherokees], and you would labor under the same difficulties you do now [being unable to find and prosecute the perpetrators]." Roads, in short, would cause as much trouble to their Father, the President, as it would to the Cherokees. The Cherokees "mean to hold fast to the peace" and would cause no trouble, but this would be possible only if unwanted whites were kept out of their country. "We hope you will not make roads through our country, but use those which you have made yourselves . . . within your own limits" and travel around the nation.[49] Realizing that the treaty commissioners and the President would be offended by this refusal, Doublehead added, "I expect you will think [agree] we have a right to say yes or no as answer, and we hope you will say no more on this subject; if you do, it would seem as if we had no right to refuse." The statement was an expression of the Cherokees' belief in their sovereign power over their own land.

In sum, the Cherokees felt that the government was asking them to make further concessions when it had failed to live up to its own obligations. The Cherokees expected, Doublehead said, "to see our rights maintained," especially "that we may not be plagued by those people who want our land" and by those who intruded upon it. Chulio then rose to describe again the government's failure to deal with Wafford's intruders: "We wish to remove those people." Doublehead concluded by reminding the government that it had not brought to justice any of the white men guilty of recent murders of Cherokees though the Cherokees had restrained their relatives from blood revenge. "There are two [lives] which the whites owe us . . . and these debts seem to increase." He hoped "these gentlemen of Tennessee will listen well," for "the State of Tennessee," like the State of Georgia, "had not kept the talks of the Government."[50]

The commissioners left the nation empty-handed and angry. They reported that the Cherokees were stubborn; "their determination was to yield to no accommodation."[51] To get around this, General Wilkinson

[49] Ibid.
[50] Ibid.
[51] James Wilkinson et al., "Report of a Treaty Council at Southwest Point, Tennessee," September 4–6, 1801, M-271, reel 1, #0024-0028.

proposed that the government ignore the Cherokee claim to the area between Nashville and Natchez north of the Tennessee River and deal unilaterally with the Chickasaws: "If the Chickasaw should consent to the
opening of the [Natchez] Road, it is my intention," Wilkinson wrote on
September 10, "notwithstanding the contumacy of the Cherokees, to order the Troops to proceed in that operation [building the road through the
disputed territory] until the Winter stops them, while I leave the Red
people to adjust their respective pretensions to the soil."[52] The Cherokees
were powerless to prevent this. The Chickasaws did negotiate a right of
way with Wilkinson; the Natchez Trace Turnpike was built without
Cherokee consent.[53] Over the next five years, the Cherokees held several
meetings with the Chickasaws and with the Creeks about their joint
claims to the area around the Tennessee River near Muscle Shoals, but
they were unable to reach firm agreements to act in union.

The next step toward acquiring the right of way for the Augusta-Nashville Road (later known as the Federal Turnpike) occurred in April 1802,
when Colonel Meigs, who had replaced Thomas Lewis in June 1801, forwarded a request from the Cherokees that the government provide them
with more technical assistance ("two Blacksmith, two Strikers [ironwork-
ers], two wheel makers and two Card makers and to have them placed in
different parts of their Country for the convenience of their people").[54]
The promise of aid toward Cherokee acculturation, it now turned out, was
contingent on Cherokee cooperation. "The Cherokees have no reason to
expect any more liberality on our part," said Secretary Dearborn, "until
a more friendly disposition shall be discovered on their part." He instructed Meigs: "It may not be improper to inform the Chiefs that from
their conduct at the late treat they must not expect any particular favors
from the United States."[55]

Some Cherokees were ready to see this as a breach of treaty promises.
William Thorp, a former Tory from South Carolina who had married a
Cherokee and, according to Meigs, had "played the Savage" by donning
Cherokee dress and fighting with them in guerrilla wars, sent a letter to
the principal chiefs suggesting that they threaten Jefferson by starting
overtures with the French. "The French have now landed in New Orleans," Thorp said, "and our Father knows they will make offers of Friendship towards [us] and sooner [than] that we should become their friends,
he will give us strong proofs of Friendship, as it is [in] the interests of the

---

[52] James Wilkinson to Henry Dearborn, September 8, 1801, M-271, reel 1, #0113.
[53] W. S. Lovely to Return J. Meigs, February 18, 1802, M-208.
[54] Cherokee Council to Return J. Meigs, April 12, 1802, M-208.
[55] Henry Dearborn to Return J. Meigs, April 7 and April 30, 1802, M-208.

white men to make the Cherokees their friends."[56] But the other chiefs did not care for this kind of intrigue. Some Cherokees did consider moving across the Mississippi where they would be free of this continual pressure from the government,[57] but most Cherokees still believed they would, with patience, persuade the President to see their position and treat them fairly.

Several chiefs, however, who had committed themselves to farming and trade and who wished to remain on good terms with the government in order to advance their private ends, began in 1802 to hint to the agent that they were willing to make a deal. Doublehead, the most powerful chief in the nation, was one of these. He had concluded by 1800 that the days of hunting and fur trading were over for the Cherokees. He was determined to enter wholeheartedly into the life of frontier enterprise and cotton production and had come to believe that rapid acculturation was best for the nation as well as for himself. In July 1802 Doublehead displayed his shrewdness as what Meigs called a "progressive" chief. He wrote to the assistant agent, Lovely, urging the establishment of more gristmills, sawmills, and cotton gins and the need for more white mechanics to manage them. He was hinting that he would like these placed in his area of the nation in exchange for his support of the Georgia Road. He had purchased a number of black slaves and had set the women in his family to spinning and weaving cotton. Lovely sent this letter on to Meigs, who replied that he was "much pleased" with this proposal "from our Friend Double Head. . . . He talks like a man of Sense and reflection on the subject of mechanics and of mills being erected, etc. In the present situation of things I can not say anything more than has been said, that our Government will continue to do them Justice, 'that when they become liberal, they may expect liberality of the Government.' . . ." In short, a subtle promise had been made.[58] Doublehead understood this and decided to push his own advantage a bit farther. In November he wrote to Meigs and made some more immediate personal requests to assist him in his business interests.

My intention is to come and trade with you, But I am so Engaged in Gathering my Beef Cattle that I expect it will be a moone or two before I can come [to the agency]. I . . . have now one Request to ask of you, that is, to have me a boat Built. I want a good Keal Boat some 30 to 35 feet in length and 7 feet wide. I want her for the purpose of Descending the River to Orlians & back by Water. . . . I

[56] Enolee (William Tharp or Thorp) to Cherokee Council, November 20, 1803, M-208.
[57] James Wilkinson et al., "Report of a Treaty Council," September 6, 1801, M-271, reel 1, #0027.
[58] Return J. Meigs to William S. Lovely, July 20, 1802, M-208.

am Determined for to see up the White and Red Rivers in my Route & oppen a trade with the western wild Indians.[59]

Meigs probably obliged Doublehead in this because he could do so out of agency funds. In any case, he told Lovely that he would explain to Dearborn the desire of the Cherokees to have more "mechanics and mills" and that there was now a more "liberal disposition" among the chiefs. "I will make every exertion to obtain what they request" for their improvement, Meigs wrote. Doublehead's town at Muscle Shoals was bound to obtain a major share of this assistance if the negotiations went well.

In his letter to Dearborn, Meigs explained that granting such requests for economic aid would win over some of the influential and "liberal" chiefs, and then they might broach the subject of the Georgia Road or Federal Turnpike again at the council in September so that the initiative might seem to come from within the nation. These chiefs "will expect a Gratuity," he said, but they were aware that the government had planned to make gifts to the nation had the treaty gone through; "they lost, by their imprudence" some advantages which they might have had.[60] Meigs suspected, after this, that chiefs like Doublehead were not really opposed to the road but had only pretended to be. This pretense was motivated partly to sustain their influence among the conservatives who opposed the road and partly to compel the government to recognize their power and to increase the gratuities they expected. Among the "friends of government," Meigs now numbered Doublehead, The Glass, and Dick Justice at the top—all Lower Town chiefs.

Doublehead was fast becoming a wealthy man. Not only did he own many slaves, cultivate large tracts of good soil, and raise cattle for sale in white markets, he had also established a lucrative business by charging whites for pilot fees through the rapids on the Tennessee River at Muscle Shoals. In addition he assumed salvage rights over vessels wrecked on the shoals. His efforts to trade produce, cotton, and livestock in New Orleans for manufactured goods that he could sell to the western "wild" Indians in Arkansas indicated his grasp of the mechanics of the market economy. Meigs described him as one of the most exceptional full bloods he knew, a man "of uncommon powers of mind":

This man, it is true, from the force of his discernment estimates usefull improvements and is exerting himself to live in a stile of some degree of taste; at the same time he is a vindictive, bloody minded Savage and his exertions to raise himself do not appear to arise from any refinement of disposition but to place himself in such a situation as that he may set his foot on the neck of anything that may op-

[59] Doublehead to Return J. Meigs, November 20, 1802, M-208.
[60] Return J. Meigs to Henry Dearborn, July 21, 1802, M-208.

pose itself to his ill founded pride. He is a man of small stature, compact and well formed, very dark skin, small piercing black eyes, the fixture of which when engaged in conversation are as immoveable as diamonds set in metal and seem to indicate clearly that he comprehends the subject and in his reply to an address will omit nothing that has been said. He is occasionally guilty of intemperance and then off his guard, and if he considers himself insulted the explosion of his passion resembles that of gunpowder.[61]

Impressed by Meigs's assessment of the shift in Cherokee attitudes toward the Nashville Road, Dearborn authorized him to negotiate for the right of way at the September council meeting and also to propose to the chiefs the purchase of Wafford's Tract. Meigs planned to do so, but a number of recent assaults, robberies, and murders of Cherokees by frontier whites had so angered both "progressive" and conservative chiefs just prior to the meeting that he felt the moment inopportune for negotiations.

Jefferson and Dearborn became more importunate. In February 1803, Dearborn wrote to Meigs: "The opening of the road through the Cherokee Country to Georgia has become highly necessary, and you will please to take the earliest opportunity of holding a conference with the principal Chiefs of the Cherokees" to obtain it. "You are authorized to make them some presents [another code word for secret bribes] not exceeding 500 dollars for their consent."[62] He also told Meigs to negotiate "for four public houses at proper distances from each other" along the proposed route with good farmland around them to support the landlord and to provide grain for horses and food to travelers and post riders. "Additional presents may be made for the purpose, but at all events, we must have a road." Meigs was to tell the chiefs bluntly that "we shall not consider the Cherokees as good neighbors unless they will allow their best friends, who are taking every means in their power to make them happy, to make a road." Dearborn allowed the question of purchasing Wafford's Tract to be dropped temporarily.

Meigs arranged a treaty conference at Ustanali on April 20, 1803, but four days of angry confrontation only hardened the Cherokees' demand for the right to say no. The conservative majority prevailed again. "We love our land . . . we therefore conclude not to grant our father the President the road through our country." Once again they stressed the failure of the government to bring those who had murdered Cherokees to trial and the demoralizing effect this was having on their people, whom they had to restrain from exercising the clan tradition of retaliation. "Some of

[61] Return J. Meigs to Benjamin Hawkins, February 13, 1805, M-208.
[62] Henry Dearborn to Return J. Meigs, February 19, 1803, M-208.

our people were laid in the ground [murdered and then buried by whites] and the matter was so hidden amongst the white people that no satisfaction was given." The other murders had occurred since the bodies were found but "we cannot find that any satisfaction is given" for them either.[63] Yet when "our people have committed the same thing," they had been quickly apprehended and hanged: "One was hanged agreeable to the white people's laws; the other two were killed by us." Justice was all they asked: "If satisfaction had been given, we should not have hesitated in granting the request" for the road.[64]

Apparently Doublehead and his friends had been quietly at work convincing other chiefs that it was fruitless to oppose the President of the United States. Still the chiefs wanted to obtain some concessions before yielding, especially with regard to apprehending the whites who had murdered Cherokees. Meigs could only answer lamely that these unavenged murders were "much to be regretted" and that the Secretary of War had done "everything in his power to have the murder[er]s brought to justice," including the offer of "large rewards" for their apprehension. He also noted that pursuant to their earlier request, the President had now ordered the army to drive some of the intruders out of their territory in Georgia; these troops had not only expelled the intruding whites but "burned their Houses and their fences, destroyed their corn, carried them before the courts of justice and fined them, etc." However, he had to admit that at the special request of Governor Josiah Tatnall of Georgia, nothing had been done about the intruders on Wafford's Tract.

Dearborn was irate at the continued "obstinacy of the Cherokees." Again he suggested presents and inducements to influential chiefs. Two intermarried white traders, John McDonald and Daniel Ross, volunteered to Meigs the names of some Lower Town chiefs who might be induced to change their votes, "if the road business should be again brought on the carpet"—namely "Katekiska and the Old Cabbin, both of the [Muscle] Shoals, and the Black Fox. . . . These hints to yourself may be of use."[65] Black Fox had only recently been chosen Principal Chief of the nation to replace the deceased Little Turkey. It was not the last time his name was to arise in such a context.

It was at this stage in the bargaining that the Secretary of War finally suggested that if justice could not be obtained against whites who murdered Cherokees, the government would be willing to provide "pecuniary satisfaction." It was embarrassing for the federal government to have to admit that it had no control over justice in its frontier states. Who, the

---

[63] Record of a Council at Eustenalee (Ustanali), April 20–24, 1803, M-208.
[64] Ibid.
[65] John McDonald and Daniel Ross to Return J. Meigs, October 10, 1803, M-208.

Cherokees asked themselves, was running the brave new world they were being asked to enter? The "united states" seemed as divided in their authority as the Cherokees. The Cherokees faced not one harasser but five—the federal government and the four states that surrounded them.

Meigs went about the nation offering his secret inducements to well-disposed chiefs and warning those who objected of dire consequences. He and his assistant discovered that "the white people of property"—"Mr. McDonald, Ross, Rogers, Melton, Woodward and Ratliff, are clear for the road and civilization in its full extent," and only the full bloods seemed opposed.[66] Yet they were the majority. Lovely reported that the conservative chiefs were telling the people "that all the long-haired people are not friends—meaning the halfbreeds—merely because [from Lovely's perspective] they have sense enough" to favor the road. Lovely also suggested that it might give further incentive to allow the road if the Cherokees could "have a toll" on it that would add to their regular income.

In October 1803, the final negotiation over the road from Augusta to Nashville and Knoxville took place. The debate was long and heated, but in the end the so-called progressive chiefs finally had their way. It was significant, however, that only fourteen chiefs dared to sign their names to the agreement out of more than one hundred who were present. Among the signers were Black Fox, Kittagiskee (Katagiska), James Vann, Chulio, Pathkiller, Turtle at Home, Toluntuskee, Tuskeegatehee, and Will Elders. They added a clause to the agreement that tried to quiet rumors of bribery by saying "we are not influenced by pecuniary motives" in signing. The government attempted to make the treaty more palatable by paying the nation $500 for the right to build the road.[67]

Crucial to many who were engaged in trade was whether the road would pass close to their store, farm, or plantation. Critical to others was who would obtain the profits from the public "stands" or taverns along the road. James Vann was eager to have the franchise for the government post riders, supplying horses and providing lodging. Others wanted the income from critical ferries over the rivers along the route. The treaty agreement itself specified that "the ferry at Southwest Point shall be put in the hand of our beloved chief Doublehead and the other two shall be rented by our agent to citizens of the United States to the highest bidders; the preference in Renting these Ferries shall be in favour of persons having connections with the Cherokee Nation"; that is, they were to go to whites who had married Cherokees. Another clause stipulated that after the road was open "the Cherokee Nation with their connections [again,

---

[66] W. S. Lovely to Return J. Meigs, May 17, 1803, M-208.
[67] W. S. Lovely to Return J. Meigs, June 1, 1803, M-208.

intermarried whites] will form a Turnpike Company for keeping the said Road in constant and good repair"—a service presumably to be paid from the tolls. The emphasis on white countrymen indicated that although Meigs wished to have Cherokee citizens profit from the road, he did not trust the full-blood chiefs to manage these important concerns.

To appease those who feared that the road would produce conflict and crime, the chiefs had tried to convince Meigs to establish a twenty-man Cherokee lighthorse patrol to maintain order along the road, half of its pay to be sustained by the Cherokees and half by the War Department. Meigs instead proposed "a small military command" at the Georgia border and the use of the military garrison at the northern border.[68] The Secretary of War vetoed the article on the military command, a decision he was to regret. He agreed, however, to a subsidiary request from the council to supply additional agricultural implements and government-paid mechanics "for us to accelerate civilization." Who was to have the use of these was nowhere specified, but the Lower Towns got most of the benefits.

James Vann, an Upper Town chief heartily in favor of the road, had played a significant but inconspicuous role in the negotiations. When Dearborn later suggested to Meigs that he might "offer an inducement to Vann" to help them settle the controversy over Wafford's Tract, Meigs replied that Vann was too rich for bribes.[69] Nevertheless there were other ways that Vann's interests could be served. "Mr. Vann has done much in bringing the minds of the Indians to the measure of agreement to the opening of the road," Meigs informed Dearborn afterward; "and yet they do not know it and he wishes it to remain so."[70] The road was laid to pass by Vann's trading post; he obtained the ferry rights over the Chattahoochee; he asked that his good friend, John McIntosh (a countryman) be awarded the franchise for another ferry, and he requested the contract for "the Mail business."[71]

Daniel Ross, son-in-law of John McDonald, reminded Meigs afterward that Meigs had made promises to John Lowrey, another countryman, about his reward: "Mr. Lowrey wishes me to remind you of the promise (he says) you made to each other; that is, you requested him to assist you in getting a grant of the road; he has done so; now he wishes the Col. [Meigs] to assist him by directing the Tellico Road [a branch of the Georgia Road] to pass Highwassee at the mouth of the Ammoye where he pro-

[68] The Glass to Return J. Meigs and Henry Dearborn, October 21, 1803, and Return J. Meigs to Henry Dearborn, October 25, 1803, M-208.

[69] Return J. Meigs to Henry Dearborn, June 28, 1804, M-208.

[70] Return J. Meigs to Henry Dearborn, October 25, 1803, M-208.

[71] Ibid. See also W. S. Lovely to Return J. Meigs, November 4, 1803, M-208.

poses to settle" and do business.[72] Doublehead appears to have been given the right to contract out some of the public houses both along the Georgia Road and the Cumberland Road; more important, a spur of the road was later built to his town and trading post in Muscle Shoals.[73] The direct benefit to other chiefs came in the form of trade goods, guns, sheep, and mechanics for their towns.

Not everyone was satisfied. Lovely reported that some of the Upper Town chiefs "take umbrage at the Indulgence of Doublehead."[74] Charles Hicks, son of a white trader and the official interpreter for the agent, reported "that there is some people in the upper towns who are dissatisfied of granting this road as the upper towns [they say] was not present when granted."[75] Whether they resented the dominance of the Lower Town chiefs or felt slighted by Meigs in the division of the spoils is not clear. The conservatives in the Overhill Towns of North Carolina do not appear to have played any part in the whole business; the agent saw no need to consult them because the road did not come near them.

The politicians in the nearby states also had to be given their share of the booty. Governor Tatnall told Meigs that he expected "to have the nomination of the Commissioners for the Road" as his political patronage.[76] When the Cherokees heard about this, they were fearful that surveyors from nearby states would be let loose in the nation. "All the River Town" chiefs (the Lower Towns) held a council at Willstown to protest. This council resolved that "the roads would not have been granted if they had known that the States had the management" of them.[77] The Cherokees would do business only with the federal government. To allay their fears, Meigs said he would appoint some Cherokee leaders to accompany the Georgia surveyors in order to see that they followed the Cherokees', not Georgia's, interests.

The negotiations over this road were eye-opening for those Cherokees who understood all of the machinations involved. They now saw the dangers of their divided regional councils and the real limits on their so-called free consent to such actions. It was clear how dependent they were becoming upon federal aid and how vulnerable they were to threats to withdraw it. In addition, the negotiations made evident that rival claims to land on their borders by the Chickasaws or other neighboring tribes could

[72] Daniel Ross to Return J. Meigs, December 17, 1803, M-208.

[73] Return J. Meigs to Henry Dearborn, November 11, 1803; January 15, 1805; January 31, 1805, M-208.

[74] W. S. Lovely to Return J. Meigs, October 27, 1803, M-208.

[75] Charles Hicks to Return J. Meigs, December 26, 1803, M-208.

[76] W. S. Lovely refers to Tatnall's expectations in his letter to Return J. Meigs, October 27, 1803, M-208.

[77] W. S. Lovely to Return J. Meigs, December 21, 1803, and March 7, 1804, M-208.

easily be used to play one nation off against another. The chiefs could see how the combined and persistent power of the agent, the factor, and the Secretary of War became irresistible and how susceptible some chiefs were to manipulation through greed or ambition.

Still, changes in the Cherokee political structure were not easy to make. In 1804 the council agreed to cede Wafford's Tract to the government for $5,000 in cash and an additional $1,000 annuity *in perpetuum* (it was twenty years before they received this money due to a bureaucratic error that failed to bring the treaty before the Senate for ratification).[78] The government, it appeared, not only refused to survey land promptly when it was ceded but declined to rectify intruder problems resulting from such delays. Under such a system, every cession inevitably led to another cession.

Soon after the negotiations for Wafford's Tract were completed, Doublehead and his Lower Town friends decided to accede to Meigs's insistence that it was time for the Cherokees to sell their old hunting ground north of the Tennessee River. The overwhelming majority of the Cherokees in 1804 were opposed to this, but the council seemed to be falling into the hands of a minority. By cooperating with Meigs, the Lower Town chiefs had become the dominant force in the nation. Nevertheless, their determination to sell the hunting ground eventually destroyed their leadership.

---

[78] Royce, *Cherokee Nation of Indians*, pp. 58–59. Wafford's Tract, ceded in 1804, had expanded by 1812 to an area 34 by 4 square miles; originally it had been only 24 by 4 square miles. See Return J. Meigs to William Eustis, August 26, 1812, M-221, reel 45, #2045.

FOUR

THE SALE OF THE HUNTING
GROUNDS, 1805–1806

The President of the United States presents to Doublehead the sum of one hundred dollars in consideration of his active influence in forwarding the views of Government in the introduction of the arts of civilization among the Cherokee Nation of Indians and for his friendly disposition towards the United States and for the purpose of enabling him to extend his useful example among the Red People. —Thomas Jefferson, January 8, 1806

The decision of the old chiefs in the Lower Towns to sell the last of the Cherokee hunting grounds in a series of treaties in 1805–1806 came as a shock to most Cherokees and precipitated a rebellion against these chiefs that led to their overthrow. The crisis nearly destroyed the nation. It became clear, once these treaties were completed, that a handful of chiefs had made a great profit from them. However, it was not simply the fraud, bribery, and secret treaty clauses that led to the repudiation of the Lower Town chiefs. Popular resentment grew from the manner in which the decision was made and from the fact that the sale of ten million acres of hunting land closed out forever an economic and cultural activity of profound social and psychological significance. The agent and the Secretary of War argued that the fur trade was no longer viable in the old hunting grounds, but whether or not the Cherokee hunters had made a good living from the fur trade in the preceding ten years was not really the point to most Cherokees. Everyone realized that fur trading alone was no longer sufficient for a man to support his family. Yet the option of hunting—the claim that one was a hunter—was there; the tradition remained intact. To lose the hunting ground was to a Cherokee like losing the Latin mass to a conservative Roman Catholic. A sacred, ancient, and apparently timeless tradition—something that God or the Great Spirit had written into the fundamental structure of things—was gone forever. Equally distressing, the decision to end this basic vocation was not made by adequate tribal deliberation and consensus. As in the case of the Augusta-Nashville

Road, the decision was made by a handful of ambitious chiefs working in secret collaboration with the federal agent.

Realizing that most Cherokees were not yet ready to accept such a decision, the agent began in 1804 to hold out rich "inducements" to the old chiefs to take matters into their own hands. These chiefs convinced themselves that the agent was right to suggest the sale of the depleted hunting grounds in return for money that could be used for the purchase of agricultural equipment, sawmills, and gristmills, to improve the life of their people. They told themselves that the majority was too blind to know its own best interest. However, by acting without obtaining a tribal consensus, these chiefs betrayed their trust. It became evident that the Lower Town chiefs, who took the lead in the matter, had become a paternalistic oligarchy rather than spokesmen for the people. Some of the chiefs, like Doublehead, had become frankly contemptuous of those who were upset by the treaties; they were "people without any holes in their head" to let in the light of progress, as he put it.[1] Other chiefs felt that they had simply yielded to the inevitable on the best available terms.

Return J. Meigs felt that the decision was long overdue. He praised the chiefs who had taken matters into their own hands and tried to make a virtue of the large personal rewards they received for cooperating with their Great Father in Washington. For years Meigs told the Cherokees to give up hunting, which "is only a nursery of savage habits."[2] He had noted with pleasure early in 1805 that "raising Cotton, spinning and weaving is carried on the domestic way in almost every part of the nation." Yet, he said, "this is totally done by females who are not held in any degree of reputable estimation by the real Indian and therefore neither them nor their occupation have any charms to tame the savage."[3] As long as Cherokee husbands insisted that hunting was the only acceptable role for "a real Indian," the path of civilization would be blocked. To Meigs, the sale of the hunting grounds was the removal of the greatest stumbling block in the path of Cherokee progress. He had no qualms about bribing the chiefs to do what was right.

Although Henderson's Purchase in 1775 had cut the original Cherokee hunting ground in half by lopping off the northern part of it in Kentucky and subsequent cessions had cut off another quarter of their land in northeastern Tennessee and western North Carolina where hunting had been good, the Cherokees in 1805 still owned over 15,000 square miles of hunting ground in Middle Tennessee and northern Alabama. The most important part of this was the heavily wooded area between the Tennes-

---

[1] W. S. Lovely to Return J. Meigs, June 13, 1803, M-208.
[2] Return J. Meigs to Benjamin Hawkins, February 13, 1805, M-208.
[3] Ibid.

see and Cumberland rivers. Tennessee had been admitted to statehood in 1796; its rapidly expanding population was putting tremendous pressure upon the federal government to free that land from Cherokee ownership. Prior to 1805, despite constant efforts, Meigs and the War Department had failed to convince them to sell any of it. Probably no Cherokee family expected after 1800 to live completely on the proceeds of trapping beaver and selling deerskins; almost all Cherokees kept some horses, cattle, hogs, and poultry and, with the use of axes, hoes, and mattocks, the Cherokees' gardening was more productive even for those who did not have plows. But if a man could not bring back a large catch, at least he could retain his status as a hunter; his wife, the elderly males, and the children in his family could supplement the income he made by selling livestock and garden food. For white easterners like Meigs, hunting was a pastime, but for the Cherokees it had always been a necessity. Without war and hunting a Cherokee man was left only with women's work.

The most persuasive argument Meigs offered for putting an end to the annual winter hunt was that more and more hunting parties, unable to find sufficient furs and hides in the old hunting grounds, were going across the Mississippi to hunt. There they became involved in increasingly bloody battles with the Osages and Quapaws for invading their hunting grounds. After Jefferson purchased the Louisiana Territory in 1803, Meigs suggested several times that Cherokees who were seriously committed to maintaining the fur trade system should consider moving as a body to the west. "They have been expecting," he wrote to Dearborn in May 1804, "propositions for an Exchange of Country for land in Louisiana," but, he added, "there is at present a very great aversion in part of the nation—I believe the greatest part," to such a proposal. Nonetheless, "some ambitious chiefs" might "fall in with such a measure . . . influenced by motives of personal Interest."[4] For the time being, Indian removal to the west seemed unlikely.

In January 1805, Meigs received reports from John (Jack) Thompson, a white man married to a Cherokee, that several Cherokees were killed by the Osages while hunting in the west. Thompson had been in touch with "our Chiefs over the other side of Mississippi on this subject."[5] Many Cherokees combined hunting in Arkansas with visiting old friends and relatives who were now living there permanently. Five months later Meigs heard that a Cherokee war party, led by clan relatives of those slain by the Osages, was leaving for Arkansas to seek retaliation (and to enjoy a little warfare in the hope of taking some scalps, horses, and prisoners).

---

[4] Return J. Meigs to Henry Dearborn, May 31, 1804, M-208.
[5] John Thompson to Return J. Meigs, January 2, 1805, M-208.

He tried in vain to stop them, but he could not.[6] The United States was not happy about Indian wars breaking out across the Mississippi. They produced muddy waters for the British to fish in. This may have been a factor goading Meigs to work with the ambitious chiefs to put an end to hunting entirely by selling the hunting grounds. In addition, Meigs knew that "the Cherokees fall so much in debt" at the government factory and with other traders (white and Cherokee) that they lacked the money to pay them. Those most heavily in debt were the "ambitious," "forward-looking" chiefs eager to become big planters or traders and to own many slaves. (Slave-owning Cherokees did not have to work in their fields.) The sale of land was the quickest way to pay off these debts; there is some evidence that the government factors were told to grant extensive credit to the chiefs for just this reason.[7] Sharing the disapproval of the "forward-looking" chiefs toward the "backward-looking" traditionalists, Meigs pushed hard for the sale of the hunting grounds.

Although most Cherokees thought conservatively about change and wished to proceed slowly with acculturation, Meigs thought in grandiose terms. In 1801 he had proposed the establishment of a giant "manufactory" in the Cherokee nation where all kinds of mechanics would be assembled to train apprentices and provide the tools for their transition to husbandry.[8] He was the original Connecticut Yankee in the primitive Cherokee court. He wanted them to establish a great endowment fund for a nationwide system of public schools; he wanted them to build more roads and plant more cotton and erect more mills and construct more cotton gins and build more river boats and exploit their mineral resources. Meigs was an empire builder; he had visions of making the Cherokee Nation a thriving image of New England. If only they could capture his vision of their future, he would help them inspire red men everywhere to become civilized.

He seems to have instilled some of this entrepreneurial Yankee zeal into the chiefs of the Lower Towns with whom he worked so closely— Doublehead, The Glass, Tolluntuskee, Dick Justice, John Lowrey, and John D. Chisholm. Doublehead, as Speaker for the National Council, saw himself as the chief architect of a revitalized Cherokee Nation and strove to set an example as an entrepreneur. In 1805 he issued a statement of his

[6] Return J. Meigs to Henry Dearborn, May 31, 1805, M-208.

[7] Prucha, *American Indian Policy*, p. 88; see also Henry Dearborn to Silas Dinsmoor, March 20, 1805, M-15, reel 2, p. 47, regarding the Creeks' desire to sell land to pay their debts, and the copy of the Chickasaw Treaty of July 23, 1805 (M-208) in which the Chickasaws say they have sold land to pay their debts. See W. G. McLoughlin, "Thomas Jefferson and the Beginning of Cherokee Nationalism," *William and Mary Quarterly*, 3d ser., 32 (October 1975):562.

[8] Return J. Meigs to Henry Dearborn, November 30, 1802, M-208.

public-spirited enterprise: "I, Doublehead, a principal Cherokee Chief, wishing to accelerate useful improvements in my Nations, and finding that Mills are much wanting in the Cherokee Country for the purpose aforesaid, determine to erect a sawmill and Gristmill on a stream on the South side of the River Tennessee."[9] This statement undoubtedly proceeded from his knowledge that cooperation with Meigs in ceding the hunting grounds would provide him with the rewards that would enable him to undertake this construction.

The primary source of Cherokee credit for capital expansion was the tribal annuity, a sum that varied from $6,000 to $11,000 a year after 1800, depending upon which land cessions were still being paid for in installments. The "perpetual annuity" was slightly over $6,000. In addition, the Cherokee treasury received an income from "stands" along the Cumberland and Georgia turnpikes, from ferry and turnpike tolls, and from the lease of saltpeter caves to entrepreneurs like Samuel Riley, the official interpreter. In addition, private trade generated individual income that was used for developing farms; occasional gifts of $300 to $500 per year in trade goods from the government fund for Indian development assisted them. However, few of the Cherokees were good credit risks and the nation as a whole had a tendency to purchase tools and equipment beyond the scope of the tribal annuity. Meigs saw to it that the nation's credit remained sound by persuading the chiefs each year to pay debts to private traders from the national income; this resulted in enriching the ambitious (heavily indebted) chiefs at public expense. Meigs informed the chiefs that what mattered most was the increase in private enterprise from which, eventually, everyone in the nation would benefit. The prosperous chiefs would set good examples for indolent warriors.

Each year the chiefs decided in council what proportion of their annuity should come to them in cash to pay debts and what proportion should be delivered in trade goods (plows, looms, spinning wheels, hoes, axes) to be distributed among their people. Some chiefs tended to take from the trade goods those items they needed for their own plantations and to leave the rest to be divided among the ordinary Cherokees. Any chief who came to think as Meigs did about the virtues of capital investment for internal improvement was bound to conclude that the primary source of Cherokee income lay in the sale of their unused land. Land they had plenty of and the government always stood ready to buy it. The job of the chiefs was to see that this source of public endowment was used to the best advantage. Under the individualistic ethic of private enterprise and private property

[9] Doublehead's statement: November 16, 1805, M-208. Doublehead could not write English and it is highly probable that Meigs wrote this for him.

that Meigs and the civilization policy held up as the answer to Cherokee development, the sale of the hunting land made some sense. Although the price obtained for the land was tiny in comparison to its market value, in principle the sale of public land to raise funds for private investment was compatible with the best economic theory of the day; it was, in a slightly different form, the policy followed by the federal government in its disposal of the public land. Using the public resources (in land or credit) to subsidize private enterprise was the American way, but it was not, in 1805, the Cherokee way.

Another factor provided a spur to the sale of the hunting grounds in 1805–1806. Some of this land was claimed by the Chickasaws on the west and by the Creeks to the south. The government was aware of these overlapping claims. After investigation, it concluded that no one nation had clear title and the President decided to buy out the claims of all three tribes. However, this created a situation bound to reduce the value of the land—or at least the price the government would pay for it. The jealous regard of each tribe for its own rights enabled the government to play one off against the other. The three Indian nations did not trust each other because each thought the other exaggerated its own claims. The Cherokees met several times after 1803 with the Creeks and Chickasaws on this subject. In June 1805, the Secretary of War wrote to Meigs (as he had written to the federal agents in the other tribes), warning that "a combination of Indian nations" was being formed in the south—"a general confederacy for preventing any particular nation from disposing of their lands without the consent of the whole of the nations combined."[10] Dearborn instructed Meigs to "use every prudent measure in your power to prevent it."

By 1805 all the Indian tribes in the Southeast were aware of the increasing value of their land and of the determination of the federal government to obtain large tracts of it at very low prices. When the War Department approached the Chickasaws in January 1805 about selling their claim to the southwest corner of the Cherokee hunting ground, their chiefs, Chinnubbee King, George Colbert, and Charles's Son, refused, saying: "If we was disposed to sell that land, we will have it surveyed and ask so much an acre for it, the same as the white people does to one another."[11] The thought that the Indians might survey and sell their land by the acre rather than in huge tracts for lump sums sent a chill down the spine of the federal officials. The cost of extinguishing Indian title by this

---

[10] Henry Dearborn to Return J. Meigs, Silas Dinsmoor, et al., M-15, June 20, 1805, reel 2, p. 85.

[11] Chinnubbee, King of the Chickasaws, George Colbert, et al. to General James Robertson, January 25, 1805, M-208.

means would become prohibitive; Indian tribes could not be allowed to act as white land companies and ask the market price for small areas sold piecemeal while holding onto other areas until settlements on what had been previously sold raised the price of what remained. Indians were not entitled to play the great American game of western land speculation.

When Meigs heard of the Chickasaw plan, he told Dearborn that the idea did not originate with them but with Doublehead and the Cherokees. They "have probably suggested to them [the Chickasaws] the Idea of selling lands in small quantities at a high price." Two whites, Loyalists in 1776 and now married into the Cherokee Nation, John Rogers and Jack Thompson, were the persons Meigs held originally responsible for the idea. "I think it is probable that we shall find it necessary to tell them in strong language that the United States is not to be trifled with by Cherokees and Chickasaws."[12] Such a policy would alter the whole structure of established Indian policy. The best way to prevent it was to play upon the jealousies of each tribe and to bribe their influential chiefs.

Meigs was so upset by the thought that the Indians might sabotage the government's benevolent policy that he began to take the same view of the Indians that the frontiersmen had, namely that Indian nations had no real sovereignty over their land and no right to say no to the imperial demands of their conquerors. "If neither [the Cherokee nor the Chickasaw] have the right to sell, the Right lies in the United States who have the most indisputable title, a title acquired in a Just and necessary War." Only "the benevolence of the United States after the war" enabled the Indians to have boundaries protected against intrusion. These boundaries were never meant to give them "absolute right to the soil," he told Dearborn. "It cannot be admitted that they have such tenure in the best tracts of wilderness they pretend to hold—so vastly exceeding their present and future population—that they may refuse at pleasure such reasonable cession as the United States requires."[13] Dearborn and Jefferson heartily agreed. The land in the west belonged to those who would cultivate it.

Declaring that the Indians were being "ungrateful" toward their guardians, Dearborn had determined what he thought a fair price for the unused hunting lands that were so harmful to Indian "progress." In dealing with Indian affairs the Secretary of War thought like a land speculator. There could hardly be "a more equitable mode of calculating the value of Indian title," Dearborn wrote, than on the basis of the "profits they annually derive from hunting" on them. This sum might then be projected to include "what will be the probable profits say for fifty or

---

[12] Return J. Meigs to General Daniel Smith, March 7, 1805, M-208.
[13] Ibid.

more years to come." Assuming that a tribe was making about $3,000 per year from furs and hides taken on this land, Dearborn went on, the government should pay for the land either a sum sufficient to yield "an interest of $3000 a year" or else "an annuity" of $3,000 a year in cash or trade goods. He had used this method in calculating the payment for the Choctaw hunting grounds and now proposed $3,000 in annuities as the sum Congress should offer the Cherokees for their hunting grounds. To demonstrate the generosity of his calculations, Dearborn noted that if he had been strictly practical, it would be "very fair and proper to make very considerable deductions from their hunting profits on account of the decrease of the game" that would occur from year to year. Moreover, when the land was sold and put to productive use by whites, "the labor and trouble of producing peltries and fur hunting will be saved"; the Indians could then more profitably put their energies into developing profits from their own farms or plantations.[14] So went the self-serving theory of white benevolence.

This buyer's mode of calculating the value of Indian land was hardly consistent with prevailing real estate procedures in the United States or in any other Western nation. For the white speculator the value of land was based on what it was worth to the next customer; in this case that would be the frontier farmer, the cotton planter, the cattle herder, the lumberman. But bargaining with Indians was never a normal process. Grown men did not bargain with their children; landlords need not consider the property rights of "tenants at will." On the other hand, Cherokee countrymen like John Rogers, Jack Thompson, and John Chisholm (all of whom were closely allied with Doublehead, The Glass, Tolluntuskee, Toochelar, Black Fox, Pathkiller, and Dick Justice) were thinking primarily of enriching themselves and only indirectly, if at all, of helping the Cherokee Nation. They realized that the government was playing one tribe off against another in bargaining for their overlapping claims. By suggesting that they would survey their land and sell it in small quantities at market value, they were simply improving their bargaining position.

Meigs no doubt explained to Doublehead, as he did to Dearborn, that in making treaties with the government, an Indian nation was making only "such compacts as a minor makes with his Guardian." Ultimately "the United States are their protectors [and] have a just right to determine, and are the best judges of, what lands they can spare."[15] It was nec-

---

[14] Henry Dearborn to Silas Dinsmoor, October 25, 1804, M-15, reel 2, p. 19.
[15] Return J. Meigs to General Daniel Smith, March 7, 1805, M-208.

essary from time to time to show the Cherokees the iron hand inside the velvet glove.

Doublehead and his friends accepted the fact that the federal government had the power to force a sale. Under the rules of the game, they decided to play out the hand and make (at least for themselves) the best profit they could. Their behavior resembled that of immigrant ward bosses later in the century: they took their elective power from the people but sold it to the influential power brokers who ran the United States.

In October 1805, Dearborn told Meigs precisely what could be offered to the Cherokees for their hunting grounds: "The average price paid for Indian lands within the last four years does not amount to one cent per acre" and "the highest price we pay for cession of Indian claims to lands well situated and of good quality is two cents per acre."[16] The outside limit that the government would pay for the first tract of ten million acres of the Cherokee-Chickasaw hunting ground was to be $14,000 cash and a $3,000 annuity in perpetuity (perpetuity meaning until these Indians were civilized and admitted to citizenship).[17]

Meantime suspicion grew among the ordinary Cherokees and Upper Town chiefs that private bargains were being struck without council approval. Rumors became so rife that several of the Lower Town chiefs close to Doublehead wrote to Meigs in March 1805, asking him to clear their names. "We should be glad for you to write us that we sold no land to you." Such a letter from him was needed "to satisfied the young men that we sold no land. . . . the young warriors is tr[y]ing all they can to put us out of place, but we hope to do everything for the good of our Country."[18] Who these "young warriors" or young chiefs were, the writers did not say, but from later events it is fair to guess that they included men like James Vann, Charles Hicks, and The Ridge. The old chiefs who signed this letter were The Glass, Dick Justice, Turtle at Home, Black Fox, and Pathkiller.

The reaction of the young chiefs that began in 1805 against the old chiefs was complex. In its early stage it probably represented a factional dispute over how to manage the sale rather than outright opposition to it. Meigs heard in April 1805 that "there has been a difference between

[16] Henry Dearborn to Return J. Meigs, October 8, 1805, M-15, reel 2, p. 117. For the federal government's method of setting prices for Indian land prior to treaty negotiations see Henry Dearborn to Silas Dinsmoor, October 25, 1804, M-15, reel 2, p. 19, and Henry Dearborn to Silas Dinsmoor, March 20, 1805, M-15, reel 2, p. 47.

[17] Royce, *Cherokee Nation of Indians*, p. 59.

[18] The Glass and other chiefs to Return J. Meigs, March 23, 1805, M-208. These chiefs told Meigs that they were willing to sell Holston Island in the Tennessee River for $2,000 and, although it was not part of the hunting ground, it was included in the treaty for the hunting grounds (The Glass et al. to Return J. Meigs, June 11, 1802, M-208).

Vann and the Glass" but later he wrote that Vann, The Glass, and Tolluntuskee (Doublehead's brother) were working together "to compose the
jealousies between the old and young chiefs."[19] Apart from the dispute
over the sale of land there were quarrels over the excessive numbers of
whites being admitted into the nation and over the reestablishment of the
lighthorse patrol to put down the horse thieves. Land sales alone did not
cause the brewing rebellion.

Meigs first discussed the sale of the hunting lands openly at a council
meeting attended by hundreds of Cherokees in July 1805. He had paved
the way for a cession by offering a new kind of "inducement" to the cooperative chiefs. He told them that certain strategic plots of land in the
hunting grounds along the right or north bank of the Tennessee River
would be reserved as private gifts to them and would not be included in
the cession. These "reserves" would become, under the treaty, fee-simple grants of land to those who cooperated; they could then retain that
land and live on it or they could sell it at market value to whites and
pocket the income. They could also lease it, if they wished. The tribe as a
whole would get the price that Congress had allocated under Dearborn's
calculations, so no one would be the loser. As it turned out, some of these
reserves would be publicly acknowledged as compensation to those Cherokees who now lived on the right bank of the river and who would otherwise have lost their farms; other reserve tracts would be kept secret as
rewards for those who had used their influence to persuade reluctant
chiefs to vote for the sale. Legally there were serious questions about
granting such private reserves to individual chiefs. The opponents of the
sale would claim that tribal land could not be allotted to individuals without full tribal approval; the State of Tennessee would claim that the federal government had no right to make gifts to Indians of Tennessee land,
paid for with public tax money, which could be then offered for sale to
white citizens of that state by the Indians who received it. In addition,
many Cherokees who in previous cessions had been forced to move off
their farms without any compensation questioned why the government
was now so concerned to compensate these particular Cherokees. The answer was that in the past Cherokee houses and farms were so small and
crude they were almost worthless, but in recent years farms had become
larger and more valuable; several of those for whom reserves were
planned in the area north of the Tennessee River were very successful,
well-to-do planters and traders (and several were white countrymen or of
mixed ancestry whose knowledge of federal machinations gave them
great influence). Meigs was also to say later that the granting of fee-sim-

---

[19] Return J. Meigs to General James Robertson, April 26, 1805, M-208.

ple reserves to acculturated Cherokees was the first step in the government's general program for granting citizenship to those Cherokees who were capable of managing their own affairs. Technically these reserves would lie outside the Cherokee Nation and though contiguous to it, the land was taxable by Tennessee; therefore, those who lived on these reserves would be citizens of Tennessee. All of this was not fully clarified to the Cherokees until after the treaty.

Three days before the scheduled negotiations at Hiwassee in July 1805, Doublehead wrote to Meigs, stating that he and his friends were now prepared to give full support to the sale of the hunting grounds provided Meigs carried through "with such Reservations as you have in your proposals offered."[20] From the treaties that finally emerged we know that reserves were offered to Doublehead, Tolluntuskee, Tahlootiskee, John Riley, Charles Hicks, Miles Melton, John D. Chisholm, Autowe, Chechou, and Chetowe.[21] However, even with the strong support of these Lower Town chiefs, the negotiations on July 20 failed. Opposition from the young chiefs and the conservative Cherokees was too strong. Meigs told Dearborn afterward that "those of Mixed blood" supported the cession because they were "in favor of improvement and have very much thrown off the savage manners." But "the real Indians still hug the manners and habits of their ancestors" and refused to give up their hunting grounds.[22]

Despite this initial defeat, Meigs remained confident. Doublehead said that when the regular council meeting was held in October he would have the necessary votes. However, it came as a blow to all the Cherokees to learn that following the fruitless negotiations at Hiwassee, the President's treaty commissioners went west to meet with the Chickasaws on July 23 and persuaded them to sell their claim to a large part of this hunting ground. The Cherokee leaders thought they had worked out an agreement with the Chickasaws and Creeks to support only joint action. Now the Chickasaws had double-crossed them.[23] Meigs told Dearborn that some of the Cherokees were so angry that "it has been with some difficulty that they [the chiefs] could restrain some of their people from committing hostilities on the Chickasaw on account of that cession."[24] He did not say whether these angry Cherokees were traditionalists who wanted to retain the hunting ground or whether they were forward-looking Cherokees who feared that the Chickasaw action would lower the price

[20] Doublehead to Return J. Meigs, July 17, 1805, M-208.
[21] Royce, *Cherokee Nation of Indians*, pp. 62-68.
[22] Return J. Meigs to Henry Dearborn, July 27, 1805, M-208.
[23] Return J. Meigs to Henry Dearborn, August 4, 1805, M-208; Doublehead to Return J. Meigs, August 9, 1805, M-208; Nicholas Byers to Return J. Meigs, August 19, 1805, M-208.
[24] Return J. Meigs to Henry Dearborn, September 22, 1805, M-208.

the Cherokees expected. Because the Chickasaws claimed only the west-ernmost part of the hunting ground, it was still necessary for the govern-ment to bargain with the Cherokees, but the case for retaining the hunt-ing ground was now considerably weaker.

Meigs continued to work on the "influential" Cherokee chiefs between July and October, perhaps at that time increasing the number or size of promised reserves. He also arranged with the government factor, Nich-olas Byers, to give Doublehead $500 worth of credit at the government trading post. Byers reminded Meigs that "D.H. will expect a debt [ar-ranged] in this way [to be] cancel'd by government" when the treaty is concluded. "Doublehead may be bought, but it will be a hard matter to sell him."[25] A month after the Hiwassee negotiations Doublehead and his friends at Muscle Shoals sent a letter to Black Fox and other Lower Town chiefs stating: "We have with much care and attention considered the re-sult of the late Conference [in July] with the Commissioners on the High-wassee, and we think that . . . we shall agree to the request of our Father, at least in part." They had been persuaded because "the Agent had in-formed us that he could not be Justified in continuing the presents of wheels, cards, and implements of husbandry and in giving corn and pro-visions [in times of famine] as he had done before" unless there was co-operation from the Cherokees.[26] Whether Meigs was serious about cur-tailing aid or whether he merely suggested to Doublehead that this would be a good argument to persuade the hesitant is hard to say. The crucial part of this letter, however, was a new plan of Doublehead's to divide the hunting ground into two parts and to sell only the northern part (5.2 mil-lion acres) to the government in October. The southern part, containing the acres claimed by the Chickasaws and Creeks, needed further consid-eration.

Soon after Meigs received a copy of this letter, he wrote to his fellow treaty commissioner, Daniel Smith, saying that he now had assurance from Doublehead, Pathkiller and other chiefs that a treaty would be forthcoming at the October council: "They appear convinced that it will not do to put off the business. They are assured from every quarter that the white people are irritated at their refusal to comply."[27] When the chiefs met the commissioners in late October at Tellico, Meigs stressed to the council the importance of abiding by a majority decision rather than

[25] Nocholas Byers to Return J. Meigs, August 4, 1805, and August 16, 1805, M-208.
[26] Doublehead et al. to Black Fox et al., August 9, 1805, M-208. This letter was signed by Doublehead, Tolluntuskee, Katigiskee, the Seed, Sequeechee, Skiuka, the Redbird, and it was addressed to Black Fox, Dick Justice, Turtle at Home, Chinowe, Slave Body, Eusanalee, Toochelar, Parched Corn Flour, and Taugustuska.
[27] Return J. Meigs to General Daniel Smith, August 19, 1807, M-208.

striving for consensus: "Brothers, in transacting any important publick business where there is [a] number of persons [acting], it cannot be expected that every one will think alike; but where the greatest number agree in their opinion on any point to be determined, such determination is in all well-regulated Society deemed the expression of that Society and [is] conclusive."[28] This renewed effort to persuade the Cherokees to alter their traditional manner of making tribal decisions was in part an effort to force acquiescence from those whom Doublehead and his friends had not yet convinced of the necessity of the sale. Meigs may have feared serious opposition from some of the young chiefs. A system of majority rule was bound to make dealings with the Cherokees easier for the government, but it was a decided departure from the traditional rule of consensual decision making.

As it turned out, the treaty signed by 33 chiefs at Tellico on October 25, 1805, was hardly a majority decision though it may have been a majority of those present and voting at that council. The total number of headmen in the fifty or more towns of the nation was between 100 and 125. The government agreed to pay "three thousand dollars in valuable merchandise and eleven thousand dollars within ninety days after the ratification of this treaty and also an annuity of three thousand dollars [in perpetuity]" for the 5.2 million acres constituting the northern half of the hunting ground. The treaty also granted the right of way for two more roads, one of them to run from Doublehead's town at Muscle Shoals to the Tom Bigbee River leading to the Gulf. By the treaty, three reserves, each one mile square, were set aside "to the use of the Cherokees" without specifying to whom they belonged; a tract three miles square opposite the mouth of the Hiwassee River was also set aside, ostensibly for the use of the United States. (Two of the one-mile-square reserves went to Tolluntuskee and one to Doublehead; the three-mile-square tract was designed in a secret codicil for Doublehead. The large tract opposite the mouth of the Hiwassee was an area that Tennessee was considering as the site of its new capital and as such would net Doublehead a very large sum when sold; he had agreed to give one-third interest in this tract to John D. Chisholm and one-third to John Riley, the son of Meigs's interpreter, Samuel Riley.)[29]

The treaty at Tellico was only the first part of a more complex and far-

[28] Minutes of a Treaty Conference at Tellico, October 22, 1805, M-208.
[29] Royce, *Cherokee Nation of Indians*, pp. 62–68. The treaty mentions "Talootiskie," not "Tolluntuskee," but they are assumed to be the same person. John D. Chisholm, a white man, is reported to have married Doublehead's sister. He also acted as Doublehead's clerk, scribe, and business partner and was heavily involved as a secret negotiator between Doublehead and Meigs from 1801 to 1807.

reaching transaction. A month before the Tellico council, forty-four headmen from twenty-four towns (most of them from the Lower Towns) met at Willstown and requested that Meigs arrange for them to send a delegation to meet with President Jefferson following the Tellico negotiations.[30] They wished to see Jefferson, Meigs told Dearborn, to ask him to settle "the dispute between them and the Chickasaws" over the ownership of the southwestern part of the hunting grounds. While there, outside the eyes of the conservatives who always attended negotiating councils in large numbers, they planned to negotiate for the sale of this area. In December 1805, fourteen Cherokee chiefs, led by Doublehead, went to Washington with Meigs and in January 1806 made a second treaty ceding the other half of the hunting ground for $10,000; in addition, the government agreed to build a gristmill for the Cherokees and to provide them with "a machine for cleaning cotton." The treaty also provided a private annuity of one hundred dollars for the Principal Chief, Black Fox, "during his life." But the most remarkable feature of the Treaty of Washington was the decision to exclude from the cession an area ten miles long and ten miles wide on the northern or right bank of the Tennessee River at Muscle Shoals, where Doublehead lived. The treaty also granted a reserve two miles by three miles to John D. Chisholm, Moses Melton, Charles Hicks, Chetowe, and Cheh Chuh, who had large farms in this area that they did not wish to give up.[31]

Granting a tract of one hundred square miles to Indians in a ceded area was a new idea in American Indian policy, particularly since it seemed to be in the name of one man (it was always known as "Doublehead's Tract"); it was to be his private property to live on, lease, or sell as he chose. The tract became in effect an independent township under the laws of Mississippi Territory; it appears that Jefferson and Dearborn chose to regard it as an experiment in Indian citizenship and self-government. Doublehead was a shrewd and able leader, wholly committed to "the civilization program." The village he was to establish on this tract might become, Meigs hoped, a model of what an enlightened, full-blood chief could do (with a little government aid) to lift his people out of savagery. As it turned out, the tract was nothing but a problem from its conception until it was finally re-ceded to the United States in a treaty in 1817. Doublehead found it more remunerative to lease the land to whites rather than to make it a model Cherokee village. The Cherokee Nation considered the grant a betrayal of tribal right. Most full bloods and young chiefs

[30] Black Fox and other chiefs to Return J. Meigs, September 16, 1805, M-208.
[31] Royce, *Cherokee Nation of Indians*, pp. 62–68.

assumed it was a bribe paid to Doublehead by the government in order to acquire their hunting ground.

Before the Cherokee delegation that negotiated the second phase of the sale of the hunting grounds left Washington in January 1806, President Jefferson made a special gift of $1,000 to Doublehead "in consideration of his active influence in forwarding the views of Government, in the introduction of the arts of civilization among the Cherokee Nation of Indians, and for his friendly disposition towards the United States and for the purpose of enabling him to extend his useful example among the Red People."[32] The final note in this carefully orchestrated cession was an address by President Jefferson to the departing delegation on January 10. In it he outlined his hopes for the Cherokee people and offered them some considerations for their future. First, he praised their progress in "becoming farmers, learning the use of the plough and hoe, enclosing your grounds and employing that labor in their cultivation which you formerly employed in hunting and war." Then he praised the Cherokee women for their "handsome specimens of cotton cloth raised, spun, and wove" by them and presented to him by the delegation. He praised their herdsmen for "raising cattle and hogs for your food and horses to assist your labors." Your "next want," he continued, would be "mills to grind your corn which, by relieving your women from the loss of time in beating it into meal, will enable them to spin and weave" more cloth. Ultimately, Jefferson said, their progress would depend upon changing their laws of inheritance from tribal ownership and a primitive matrilineal system to fee-simple ownership and the patrilineal model of the white man. Now that they lived on single-family farms, their property should descend from the husband to the wife and children, not to the clan relatives—the husband's brothers and the mother's brothers. A man should love his wife and children "more than he does his other relations." Finally, as private property and contractual relationships increased, the Cherokees would need a judicial system to regulate "contests between man and man" over private property and inheritance. This was the path of progress.[33]

However, for those not ready to take this path, Jefferson suggested an alternative: "The Mississippi [Valley] now belongs to us, and it might be that some Cherokees would prefer to move across the Mississippi" to live with the Cherokees on the other side. There they would find more game, fewer white men, less pressure to abandon the hunt and adopt new ways. "That country is ours. We will permit them to live in it." Jefferson did

[32] Henry Dearborn to Return J. Meigs, January 8, 1806, M-15, reel 2, p. 153.
[33] Thomas Jefferson to the Cherokee Delegates, January 10, 1806, M-15, reel 2, p. 169.

TABLE 4

Cherokee Income from Land Cessions, 1791–1835

Year	Location of Cession	Square Miles of Cession		Money Paid by U.S. for Total Cession
		Per State	Total	
1791	Tennessee N.C.	3,435 722	4,157	$1,000 annuity in perpetuity plus trade goods valued at $1,000; in 1792 $500 was added to the annuity; in 1794 the annuity was raised to $2,500 and $2,000 in trade goods was paid to Cherokees.
1798	Tennessee N.C.	952 587	1,539	$1,000 added to the perpetual annuity; and $5,000 in cash.
1804	Georgia "Wafford's Tract"	135	135	$1,000 added to the annuity plus $5,000 in cash (not started till 1824).
1805	Kentucky Tennessee	1,086 7,032	8,118	$3,000 added to the annuity plus $14,000 in cash and trade goods, plus $1,600 for an island in the Tennessee River.
1806 (Oct. 25)	Tennessee	1¼		$10,000 in cash plus another $2,000 in cash in 1807 for "adjusting" the demarcation line.
1806 (Oct. 27)	Tennessee Alabama	5,269 1,602	6,871	
1816 (Nov. 22)	S.C.	148	148	$5,000 in cash from South Carolina.
1816 (Sept. 14)	Alabama Mississippi	3,129 4	3,133	$65,000 from the U.S. in 6 installments.
1817	Georgia Tennessee Georgia	583 435 837	1,855	No payment; land exchanged in Arkansas for western Cherokees.
1819	Alabama Tennessee N.C.	1,154 2,408 1,542	5,104	No payment; land exchanged in Arkansas for western Cherokees.
1835 (final sale of all land in the East)	Alabama Georgia Tennessee N.C.	2,518 7,202 1,484 1,112	12,316	$5,000,000 plus $300,000 for spoliation and $300,000 to cover the costs for removal of the nation to Indian Territory plus a guarantee to 7 million acres in Indian Territory.

SOURCE: Compiled from Charles Royce, *The Cherokee Nation of Indians* (reprint, Chicago: Aldine Publishing Co., 1975).

not press the point, but he was preparing the way for those discontented with the loss of their hunting grounds to emigrate and exchange their homeland in the East for land across the Mississippi. As the Upper Town rebellion led by the young chiefs erupted in 1807, Meigs tried hard to persuade the Cherokees to adopt this alternative.

Perhaps the most controversial aspect of this ill-fated Cherokee delegation to Washington had nothing to do with the treaty but with the decision it made regarding the use of the money obtained by the treaty. Just
prior to leaving the city, the fourteen chiefs voted to dispose of the
$10,000 Congress had paid for the southern half of the hunting ground
by dividing $2,000 of it among themselves (for their own use) and au-
thorizing Meigs to use the remaining $8,000 to pay off debts that they
and other principal chiefs owed to the government factory and to various
private traders, Cherokee and white.[34]

[34] Resolution of the Cherokee Delegates in Washington City, January 4, 1806, M-208. In
the resolution the delegates write that they "wish to receive" $2,000 out of the $10,000 cash
paid for this cession, to pay their hotel bills in Washington "and the ballance of the money
they appropriate to Discharge the debts due to their Traders in the Nation."

FIVE

THE REVOLT OF THE YOUNG
CHIEFS, 1806–1807

The Young chifes, and indede some of them
no chiefes atole [are] trying to Break that Law.
—Chief John Lowrey, October 23, 1806

The Cherokee Rebellion of 1806–1810 occurred in two parts. The first, in 1806–1807, arose over the abuse of the treaty-making power. It led to the official execution of Doublehead in 1807 and the violent repudiation of a treaty that year granting iron-ore rights within the nation to Colonel Elias W. Earle of South Carolina. The second phase of the rebellion took place in 1808–1810, when the Lower Town or "River chiefs" tried to negotiate an exchange of land and the removal of their half of the tribe to Arkansas. In this period a rebellious council representing forty-two towns deposed Black Fox as Principal Chief and installed Pathkiller to replace him. During the first phase, the rebellion was described by Doublehead's friends as a revolt of the young chiefs; it was led by James Vann of the Upper Towns. During the second phase, when Vann himself was killed, the revolt centered around resistance to Meigs's efforts to force the whole tribe to remove to Arkansas. The leaders of the latter phase were Charles Hicks and The Ridge; Meigs called their supporters "the rebel party" or "the insurgents." He believed that the rebels throughout were self-appointed, self-interested men, jealous of the power and influence of the old chiefs, and to some extent he was correct. The great mass of Cherokees, though angry enough to give tacit support to the rebellion, were at first too confused to understand precisely what was at stake. After the secret plan of removal and exchange between Meigs and the Lower Town chiefs was exposed in 1808, however, the rebellion became much more than a factional quarrel between young and old chiefs. It became a struggle to provide clearer definition of Cherokee identity, political structure, and national purpose. In the years 1808–1810, the Cherokees took a major step from being an ethnic nation toward being a nation-state. The traditional definition of being a Cherokee rested upon kinship, clan membership, and adherence to ancient customs, beliefs, and responsibilities.

By 1810, two new tests of Cherokee identity had been added. These defined a Cherokee by residence within specific boundaries (the land where their ancestors had always lived) and by loyalty to the decisions of a representative national council whose policies were arrived at by consensus. Decisions reached by ad hoc councils were not valid; emigration west of the Mississippi was treasonous expatriation. Patriotism required political commitment: lack of political loyalty was grounds, after 1810, for exclusion from the tribe. The United States never acknowledged these important changes, nor did those who emigrated west, but the great body of Cherokees did. Yet the rebellion of 1808–1810 did not resolve the crucial questions of how fast and how far the Cherokees should move toward acculturation and assimilation; these continued to plague them until White Path's Rebellion in 1827.

In addition to the resentment over the loss of the hunting grounds and the secret favors granted to certain chiefs in the treaties of 1805–1806, the young chiefs were concerned about a plan contrived in 1806 by the Lower Town chiefs to survey part of their remaining land on the right bank of the Tennessee River, parceling out that land in pieces for speculative purposes and establishing the principle of granting private reserves (to be owned in fee simple) to the more "advanced" or "acculturated" families. This Lower Town proposal, though in line with Jefferson's message in 1806, was never accepted by the national council and it was strongly opposed by most Cherokees, especially since the Lower Towns assumed that the land to be divided belonged to their region and therefore could be allocated to their people.

The various schemes by the Lower Town chiefs to dispose of tribal land convinced the great mass of Cherokees that tribal security and survival rested upon the maintenance of tribal ownership and control of their land. This, in turn, required an end to the division between the Lower and Upper Towns. As long as certain chiefs assumed the right to control their own area of the nation and to manipulate decisions over the disposal of land in collusion with federal authorities, there could be no national security. The Lower Town chiefs had to be overthrown because they usurped the power to speak for the nation when they had in fact lost touch with the feelings and traditions of the majority. It was too easy for the agent and the War Department to play upon this division to suit their own purposes.

The "young chiefs" who led the rebellion are not easy to identify except to the extent that their names appear on letters or manifestos issued from time to time. In earlier days, a man became a "warrior" at about age twenty-four when he first was allowed to go out with war parties. As he distinguished himself in battle he was given a chance to lead war parties, and at that time he became a "young chief." Young chiefs, though they had a voice in council, were not actually members of the council. They seldom became "old chiefs" until they were past middle age. Cherokee government was essentially a gerontocracy in peacetime; respect and authority came with age, experience, and wisdom. To become an old chief was to become a leading voice in council affairs. This status was usually accorded by a formal vote of the council and could also be withdrawn by its decision to "break" a chief. After 1794 the distinction between young chiefs and old chiefs became increasingly fuzzy because there was no warfare in which young chiefs could distinguish themselves, and other talents became more valuable, such as the power to deal effectively with white officials. Power became factional; in the confusion and disorganization between 1794 and 1810, the clash between young chiefs and old chiefs centered more upon differences in policy than in age or distinction. No doubt the old chiefs remained those who were elected to that rank by the council, but the criteria for such decisions were no longer clearly understood. In this situation, young chiefs became, in essence, "the opposition," or those out of power. The term "young chiefs" did not apply simply to those in the Upper Towns, although that region was a center of opposition to Lower Town hegemony. After 1805 there were opponents of Doublehead and his clique even in the Lower Towns. Nor was a "young chief" necessarily young in years; he was young in that he had not yet earned status as a major chief. It is also not accurate to characterize the rebels or young chiefs as "full bloods" or "traditionalists" in opposition to "mixed bloods" or "progressives" (i.e., those in favor of acculturation). James Vann was not a full blood or an enemy of acculturation; neither were Charles Hicks and The Ridge. Most of those who joined Vann as leaders in the early phase of the rebellion were of mixed ancestry. Mixed bloods dominated the Executive Committee of Thirteen that emerged to lead the reunited nation in 1809. Nor would it be fair to say that intermarried whites (countrymen) had a dominant role on either side. John Lowrey, John Walker, John McIntosh, and John McDonald were white "countrymen" who came to side with the rebels; John D. Chisholm, John Ratliffe, Moses Melton, and Samuel Riley were whites who worked as fervently for the old chiefs. In the years 1805–1810 the leadership was in constant flux; some chiefs changed camps several times. Eventually some who were close to Doublehead, like Black Fox and Pathkiller, joined the rebels, while some, who disliked Doublehead, later joined (after his death) with those Lower Town chiefs who favored removal to the west.

Agent Meigs contributed significantly to the rebellion in several ways, much as he deplored it. He had certainly pushed the old chiefs in 1805–

1806 to act against what he and they knew was the will of the vast majority; that was the principal reason for all the inducements and bribery. He also contributed to the growing gap between the so-called forward- and backward-looking members of the nation, encouraging those chiefs he considered "advanced" or "enlightened" to treat lightly or even scornfully the opinion and values of the "real" or conservative Indians. Ironically, however, his major mistake may have been his continued effort to develop among the Cherokees a sense of national pride. He lost no opportunity to tell them how much they had achieved and how far in advance they were of all other tribes. Upon returning from Washington early in 1806 with the delegation that had sold the last of the hunting ground, he spoke of this nationalistic spirit to a council at Willstown:

Brothers, the visit of your deputation to the seat of Government has done more good to your nation than was ever done to any Indian nation. It has opened the eyes of thousands who were in the dark in regard to your improvements. It has indeed laid the foundation of your future prosperity, and I may say, of your existence to futurity. And it has also been of great advantage to all the red men of America who will now be induced to imitate your people in improvements.[1]

Whether or not a Cherokee agreed with what Doublehead had done, he could take pride, Meigs argued, that his nation as a whole was setting an example of Indian knowledge and ability. Unwittingly Meigs may have suggested to some Cherokees that Doublehead was not indispensable.

Recognizing that many Cherokees disliked the decision to sell the hunting ground, Meigs stressed the success of their rapid acculturation more strongly than he should have at Willstown. He particularly emphasized Jefferson's suggestion that they divide up their remaining land in severalty, making each Cherokee man and his family responsible for their own farm and future by private initiative, hard work, self-reliance, and self-discipline. By putting each Cherokee on his own land, he said, "you will secure your land to your people forever," by which he meant that private property was sacred in America and that Cherokees living on private plots would not have to fear that some faction of chiefs might sell them out: "This proves plainly to you that he [the President] wishes you to live on the land forever." When land is owned in fee simple, the whites "cannot buy your land as has before been done." It will "not be in the power of any council to sell your farms." Meigs had printed and distributed Jefferson's message to their delegates so that "you may be assured that this is the only way to save your Country for yourselves and your children to live in."[2]

---

[1] Return J. Meigs to Cherokee Council at Willstown, April 2, 1806, M-208.
[2] Ibid.

Meigs believed that if he persuaded the Cherokees to divide up their land into farms of about 640 acres per family, perhaps two-thirds of their area would remain empty—that is, it would have no farms on it and would thus become available for cession. When he spoke of saving "your Country" he meant only saving the tracts they farmed as individuals. He spoke in fact for detribalization and denationalization of the Cherokees. The Cherokees had somethng else in mind when they spoke of their country and its future; they meant their national and ethnic identity; they meant holding on to all the lands of their ancestors. The chiefs at Willstown responded to Meigs's statement of March 1806 by saying "you have recommended to this council the division of our lands to individual property," but, they asked, "how much land will we have left to us"—what would happen to the remainder? Some of the chiefs at the council were from the upper parts of the Upper Towns (the North Carolina or Overhill towns) and they said that "these Upper Parts of the upper towns are not well supplied" with the tools necessary to become farmers. Could dividing their land into individual property protect them from whites until such time as they became good farmers? They may have understood Meigs to mean that the total area of the nation would be divided equally among the total number of families, thus securing all of their territory.

Meigs reported to Dearborn after this council that there was "satisfaction with the doings of the deputation" in Washington, but he misread the evidence. The council, for example, had specifically told him not to carry out the final action of the Washington delegation. "You are not to pay any money belonging to the nation to any persons or merchants that has debts in this country because the young chiefs says that they have pass[ed] a law at the Fox's town last fall [which] was [to allow] a twelve months for every man to pay their [own] debts."[3] The council delegates in Washington had usurped authority in designating that money from a land sale, which should be for national use, should instead be used to pay the personal debts of a few individuals. Meigs had tried to explain at Willstown how this happened. The delegates, considering "that numbers of their brethren were in embarrassed circumstances and considering that these people look to the Heads of the nation as their fathers . . . thought it proper while it was in our power for the relief of that description of people, to appropriate the money from the sale . . . to pay their debts."[4] Ap-

[3] Black Fox and other chiefs to Return J. Meigs, August 7, 1806, M-208.

[4] Undated statement by Return J. Meigs in M-208 at the end of records for the year 1806, but probably delivered at Willstown in April, 1806, and at other councils to explain the treaty in Washington.

parently the delegates hoped to disarm criticism by this effort to wipe out all debts, but all they did was arouse suspicion.

Meigs scheduled a second council to hear the results of the Washington Treaty at Ustanali on April 24, 1806. This council expressed opposition to the part of the treaty that allowed "the reservation at Musle Shoals and Spring Creek on the North side of the Tennessee, which lands and reservations shall belong to the whole nation and not to individuals."[5] Meigs explained that the President was pleased by the creation of these fee-simple reserves for individuals "because he saw by these things that you were beginning to encourage your people to have individual property and having a tendency to make your people industrious and to feel like freemen acting entirely for the comfort and benefit of their families."[6] However, the majority of Cherokees were still loyal to their clans and believed in matrilineal inheritance. Meigs, Jefferson, and the delegation had pushed too far ahead in rewarding the highly acculturated (some of them white countrymen) with property that in the opinion of many should have remained part of the tribal land.

One of the leading chiefs of the Upper Towns, Chulio (The Boot) told Meigs that his region wanted "the mill and cotton machine" promised in the treaty to be erected in Ustanali and not in Doublehead's reserve. He also took umbrage at Meigs's reference to Doublehead as a "beloved man" (the Cherokee term for a Principal Chief) when "you know that Doulehead is not a beloved man but only a speaker" of the council. Another prominent Upper Town chief, Katahee (Badger's Son) wrote to Meigs after the council explaining that as their agent Meigs had an obligation to assist all the Cherokees, not just a favored few: "the Chiefs expect that you have regard [to] the welfare of the upper towns as well as [to] the lower towns."[7]

To allay these objections, Meigs attended a third council, at Sawtey (Sautee) in July 1806, to discuss the hunting grounds treaty made in Washington; here he thought he had finally smoothed over all opposition, but further signs of rebellion appeared in August. At that time some Upper Town chiefs made threatening remarks to Doublehead and his friends for betraying the nation. Doublehead bluntly responded that he had no fear of their threats. He was alleged to have claimed that "the United States is to furnish him two or three thousand men to uphold his authority" if any chiefs tried to overthrow him. Other critics accused Meigs of engaging in "land jobbery" because he had approved of Double-

[5] Nepheu, Kalawaskee, and other "Chiefs of the Upper Towns" met in council at Oostenali [Ustanali], April 24, 1806, M-208.

[6] Meigs's statement at Willstown, April 2, 1806, M-208. This was undoubtedly repeated at the Ustanali council and other councils that year to fend off criticism.

[7] Katahee to Return J. Meigs, July 23, 1806, M-208.

head's renting some of the land on his reserve opposite the mouth of Hiwassee to white men.[8] It was common knowledge by then that most of
those who had been awarded reserves under the treaty were making
money by renting all or parts of them to whites.[9]

The controversy over the sale of the hunting ground appeared again at
another council held at Willstown in September 1806. Doublehead was ill
and did not attend, but most of his friends were there. The two chief critics of Doublehead at this council were white countrymen, John Rogers
and John Walker, but there were other young chiefs present who voiced
discontent: John McIntosh (Quotequskey), Will Shorey, John Ross,
George Fields, Dick Fields, John Spears, Charles Hicks, and James Brown.
After bitter recriminations, the council began to break up; Black Fox got
discouraged and drank too much. The Glass and Dick Justice went home
very upset. A group of the dissidents, assuming themselves to represent
the consensus of the council, remained to write an angry letter to the old
chiefs. To give the letter weight, they got Black Fox to sign it (or, according to the old chiefs, they forged his signature). When the old chiefs read
the letter they were convinced that the young chiefs were trying to put
them out of office.

The letter contained a long list of complaints against Meigs, some of
which went back before the hunting ground was sold and grew out of the
effort of the Upper Towns to retain control of the tavern franchises on the
Cumberland and Georgia turnpikes. Once again the young chiefs said
that Meigs should not use any of the purchase price for the hunting
ground to settle the trading debts of individuals because "they owned the
debts and would [should?] pay it themselves." They objected to "any individuals renting land belonging to the nation"—by which they meant
the reserves. They said they no longer trusted the old chiefs and had
therefore appointed a committee to manage all of the nation's funds and
that Meigs should turn the treaty money over to that committee. Most
of the committee members were from the Upper Towns, but it included a
few from the Valley Towns and from the Lower Towns who apparently
agreed with the rebels. The commitee members were Charles Hicks, John
Walker, John Ross, George Glaslin, Kalawaskee, Chatloe, Terrapin, Nettle Carrier, Sequeechee, Tesaiskee, Will Shorey, Young John Watts,
James Davis, and The Big Bear. They were not all young chiefs, but the
younger ones seem to have seized the initiative. The conclusion of their
letter held Meigs responsible for the Treaty of Washington: "Why did
you have these things [reserves] done for individuals when you know it
was not done by the consent of the nation?" They demanded a revision

<hr />

[8] Charles Hicks to Return J. Meigs, August 19, 1806, M-208; Return J. Meigs to Charles
Hicks, September 5, 1806, M-208.

[9] Royce, *Cherokee Nation of Indians*, pp. 62–68.

of the treaty: "What has been done in private manner we desire it might be broke [annulled]."[10]

When Doublehead heard what had happened at this council, he wrote angrily to Meigs, placing the blame upon John Rogers "and his party" of "half breeds," who "thinks he and his party can outdo the United States."[11] As Doublehead interpreted the letter, the young chiefs wished to persuade the nation that he and Meigs were trying "to press on the minds of the people to agree to divide the land" in severalty so that once divided, individual farmers could be cheated out of it by speculators "with whiskey." As for his applying the treaty money to pay personal debts, Doublehead considered this a hollow complaint: "you know and so do the marchants that I can pay my debts myeself," but some who were in debt "are poor people and the best hunting ground now belongs to the United States and I can't see how the poor Indians is to pay their debts" if the nation would not use its tribal resources to do it. "It seems hard to Take away from a family that has but two or three cowes to pay the Trader with it." Doublehead was arguing that many families with small debts to traders (who might seize cows or other effects to pay the debt) would benefit from the decision in Washington. Still, it is obvious that those with the largest debts would be the greatest beneficiaries. Doublehead went on to note that the permanent annuity of $6,000 was insufficient capital for the nation's economic transformation to intensive yeoman farming: "You know very well that this annuity could not support the nation in clothing or houseall furniture; it is the Traders that Brings these things to us and it is the same with the white people; we cannot live without Trade, for the Traders brings his hoes, axes, hatchets, and Brass and Tin Kettles, powder, etc. amongst us and our people has got indebted to them."[12] Doublehead was convinced that he was primarily helping the poor, not the rich, by using the treaty money to pay off private debts. "It seems that my people thinks hard of me, and if you know of anything that I have done that is not Right, Tell it to the people." He had no respect for the complaints of the young chiefs: "Such great and Good men as they pretend to be ought to be ashamed." Their behavior had hardly been unselfish in the past: "when the annuity was give out [in past years] did they not keep some of the Best goods and say they would give in money to the nation, and where is that money?" He was so disgusted with the hypocrisy of these insolent young troublemakers and their supporters that he threatened to "quit my nation['s] Concearns" and "goe hom and mind my own Business."

Doublehead's anger was fully shared by his friend John Lowrey.

---

[10] Council at Willstown to Return J. Meigs, September 19, 1806, M-208.
[11] Doublehead to Return J. Meigs, October 3, 1806, M–208.
[12] Ibid.

Lowrey thought that the nation had confirmed the Washington Treaty at the previous councils that spring. He expressed astonishment that "the yong chifes and indede some of them no chiefes atole [are] trying to Break that law." "If that be the case, what is our cuntry to cum to, if the young, simple, drunken, idel people is to breake laws that all the Chifes and the king makes." The bad faith of these dissidents was proven by their forging of the names of Black Fox ("The King" or Principal Chief), John Thompson, and probably Pathkiller to their resolutions. "My feelings was much Hurte to think these yong people was holding ther Ta[l]ke" in order to demonstrate "that we old chiefs and King shold be made as if they was Nothing." Like Doublehead, he felt that he had done no wrong and charged the rebellion to the ill will of "Mr. Van and Mr. Macdannel [McDonald]" who, though "they were not thare" nonetheless "give their orders to thies men."[13]

The reaction of Doublehead, Lowrey, and other old chiefs to the Willstown resolves indicates their conviction that rapid assimilation was the proper solution to the nation's dilemma. Lowrey spoke of his conversion to the "civilization" program a short while before as though it were a kind of religious awakening: "There is many of them pore simple Createurs [who oppose us] as I was some years ago—co[u]ld see nothing before them; but, dear father, it appearse that few years back that my eise hase Bin opend and I can have nolldge of things that is to come."[14] Naturally those who opposed the "new knowledge" of Cherokee renascence through acculturation were, as Doublehead put it, "Desin[in]g and foolish persons that are Enemies to the improvement and Civeli[s]ation of their People, Enemies to all Improvement, Enemies to all that wish to improve the Blessing that the great and good all-being has Blessed them with; their Eyes and Ears are shut to such things as they ought to know."[15] Black Fox, whom Lowrey described as "the King of the Cherokees," took a similar view. He wrote to Dearborn in December 1806, explaining that the Secretary should pay no attention to the dissident voices in the nation. Meigs, he said, was a good and faithful agent and "we Shall always Look up to him for advise and his assistance; if he had dun Rong, we Don't know it." Although "the upper towns has found fort [fault] with [him] for our grants [reserves], we have not." Black Fox urged Dearborn not to rescind the treaty just because of a few malcontents.[16]

Meigs seems to have considered the opposition to the sale of the hunting ground to be a tempest in a teapot—the work of a few envious minor

[13] John Lowery [Lowrey] to Return J. Meigs, October 23, 1806, M-208.
[14] Ibid.
[15] Doublehead to Return J. Meigs, January 14, 1807, M-208.
[16] Black Fox to Henry Dearborn, December 18, 1806, included in letter from Return J. Meigs to Henry Dearborn, January 11, 1807, M-221, reel 10, #3074.

chiefs, jealous of Doublehead and angry that they had not made any profit for themselves out of the sale. He told Dearborn that the opposition constituted no more than "one in ten" of the 100 to 125 chiefs in the nation. But he underestimated the strength of the opposition among the common people from whom these rebellious chiefs drew their support.

In April 1807, Dearborn discovered that there was a discrepancy between the eastern boundary of the treaty with the Chickasaws of July 23, 1805, ceding their part of the hunting ground and the western boundary of the treaty with the Cherokees, on January 7, 1806, ceding their larger portion to the east.[17] Dearborn did not want another negotiation. He suggested that Meigs quietly persuade those appointed to accompany the surveyors to agree to "an adjustment" of the line: "If the Cherokee Chiefs, when at the place, will consent, for any moderate compensation, to admit the line being drawn in conformity with the Chickasaw Treaty so as to include all the waters of the Elk River," Meigs was authorized to provide such gifts as he thought appropriate. "You will please select 2 or 3 suitabel Chiefs of whom Double Head should be one" who "will consent to it for some handsome present to the Chiefs who may accompany you on the line."[18] The assumption that Meigs, and not the council, could select the chiefs to run the survey indicates how much political power Meigs had assumed over Cherokee affairs.

Meigs talked to Doublehead, who agreed to Dearborn's request; Meigs chose Black Fox, The Glass, Turtle at Home, Richard Brown, and Towalotoh to join him and Doublehead on the surveying party that was to depart in September 1807. He warned Dearborn that the presents these chiefs would demand might be more costly than he expected.[19] Meanwhile, in June 1807, Doublehead and his friends came forward with a new proposition for a land sale. The treaty of 1806 had left the nation with about 1.5 million acres on the right side of the Tennessee River between the Hiwassee River and Chickasaw Old Fields; the tract along the river was 50 to 60 miles wide and 150 miles long, about half of it in Tennessee and half in what became Alabama. Doublehead "consulted a number of Chiefs" in his region and they agreed to "a substitute" proposal for Dearborn's plan to alter the treaty line of 1806. "We have agreed to let our young people take the land that lies on the North Side of Tennessee; they are to do what they please with it, to Lease or sell it to the white people, every one to make his choice, and then to dispose of it as they please."[20]

---

[17] Royce, *Cherokee Nation of Indians*, pp. 67–68.
[18] Henry Dearborn to Return J. Meigs, April 1, 1807, M-208.
[19] Return J. Meigs to Henry Dearborn, May 1, 1807, M-208.
[20] Doublehead to Return J. Meigs, enclosed in letter from Meigs to Henry Dearborn, June 20, 1807, M-221, reel 10, #3132–3134.

What he seems to have meant was that this 1.5-million-acre tract should be surveyed and divided into reserves for the young chiefs of the Lower Towns; each was to have his pick of the plots in the survey and then each either could farm the plot or could lease or sell it to the whites. Before this could be allowed, the whole tract would have to be sold to the United States. Apparently Doublehead considered this a way to buy off the rebellious young chiefs in his region as well as a major step toward acculturation as Jefferson had described it.

Though Meigs was eager to acquire this land, he was not ready to have it all placed in the hands of individual Cherokee chiefs. He promised to consider giving some of that area to some individual chiefs as reserves, but he had already written to Dearborn about a more elaborate scheme to obtain the land still owned by the Cherokees on the right bank of the Tennessee River. "I think the whole might be obtained at the rate of one cent per acre."[21] Although the land on the right bank below the Hiwassee River might (in Meigs's view) belong to the Lower Towns, he wished to give the Upper Towns an incentive to cede land in Tennessee by offering to buy from them a tract of one million acres north of the Hiwassee. The people in the Upper and Valley Towns, he told Dearborn, "are poorer people than the lower Towns" and the money they would make from selling that land "would be of great assistance to them in procuring stocks [cattle]" and farming tools. Some of the money he hoped could be used as an endowment "for the support of schools."

While these plans were in the formative stage, a third issue arose that complicated the matter and finally brought the rebellion to violence. Colonel Elias W. Earle, a wealthy trader from Greenville, South Carolina, who had traveled extensively through the Cherokee Nation, discovered that the nation possessed rich deposits of iron ore on the southern side of the Tennessee River near the mouth of Chickamauga Creek. He wrote to Dearborn early in 1807, proposing that the United States purchase from the Cherokee a region six miles square that would include the iron ore deposits and then commission him to develop an ironworks and erect a government arsenal there. Dearborn thought this an admirable idea, for there was no telling when war in the west would necessitate having cannon and other military hardware at hand in that region. Dearborn convinced himself further that "such an establishment would be of great use to their nation," and instructed Meigs to "endeavour to ascertain the opinion of the Chiefs on the subject."[22]

As usual, Meigs consulted the chiefs of the Lower Towns because they

[21] Return J. Meigs to Henry Dearborn, May 1, 1807, M-208.
[22] Henry Dearborn to Return J. Meigs, February 28, 1807, M-208.

119

were more cooperative; moreover, the iron ore was in their region. By June 1807 he was able to report that "a large majority of Chiefs" were "apparently well pleased with the design." "I have no doubt they will embrace an object that holds forth such great advantages for their people."[23] The advantages presumably were that Earle's foundry would provide cheaper iron goods near at hand and the Indians would benefit from seeing how white men developed nature's mineral resources. They would also profit from the sale. The work at the foundry, however, would be performed by white artisans and black slaves; there was no thought to hire Cherokees.

Meigs's refusal to pay any attention to the various demands of the discontented chiefs and their supporters and his continual effort to play off the Lower and the Upper Towns against each other led the young chiefs to take more drastic action. In July they held a secret gathering and agreed that the chief enemies to the nation were Doublehead and his partner, John Chisholm. One who attended this meeting, George Sanders (Saunders), explained later "that the Indians was much displeased with Double Head and Chisholm and that he [Sanders] Expected they wold be killed as it had been concluded on by a number of the leading characters of the Nation." He also had heard that "Doublehead would be called to account at the Bawl Play" scheduled at Hiwassee Town in August. "A man called the Ridge was appointed to Execute the Business." James Vann was also involved in the plot.[24]

The ball play took place on August 7–8. As usual it was accompanied by great excitement, betting, and drinking among the hundreds in attendance. Shortly after the game, a Cherokee named Bone Polisher saw Doublehead among the spectators and accused him to his face of being an enemy of the people for selling "our hunting grounds." He made some gesture toward Doublehead that Doublehead took to be threatening. Doublehead pulled out his gun, Bone Polisher swung a hatchet, and Bone Polisher was killed on the spot. Doublehead then rode his horse to a nearby tavern at Walker's Ferry kept by Quotaquskee (John McIntosh). While he was drinking inside, someone blew out the candle at his table and a shot wounded him in the jaw. Everyone scattered. Doublehead, though left for dead, was only wounded. His friends carried him to a nearby house but kept his location a secret. The assassins, discovering they had not killed Doublehead, returned. The three persons later accused were The Ridge, John Rogers, and either George or Alexander Sanders (or Saunders). Ridge had formerly fought with Doublehead in

[23] Return J. Meigs to Elias Earle, June 20, 1807, M-208.
[24] Statement of Colonel Joseph Phillips regarding the murder of Doublehead, August 15, 1807, M-208.

the guerrilla war but in the 1790s had moved to Oochegelogy in the Georgia area of the Upper Towns and become a farmer. The three men discovered where Doublehead was hidden, broke into his room, and finished their work with guns, knives, and hatchets.[25] Later, when George Sanders was asked why they had killed Doublehead rather than complaining to Meigs about him, he said "he believed Col. Meigs to be as bad as them, meaning Doublehead and Chisholm." Chisholm was not at the ball play and the assassins took no action against him at this time. There were no witnesses to the murder and despite investigations by Captain A. B. Armistead of the United States Army garrison at Hiwassee, no one was brought to trial for it. More important, though Doublehead had several brothers and many clan kin who should have taken revenge for his death, none ever did so. Apparently his clan accepted the assassination as a semi-official political act taken by responsible chiefs for the good of the tribe and therefore outside the area of clan revenge.[26]

Meigs was terribly upset. He had lost his closest and most powerful ally in the civilization program. He told Dearborn this was "a preconceived plan . . . by a factious party who have always been his enemies, principally from envy of his prosperity and his attachment to the white people."[27] Later that same month action was taken against Chisholm. He had gone to Georgia to meet Colonel James Phillips, who had made an arrangement with Doublehead to lease and develop some land on Doublehead's tract at Muscle Shoals. Chisholm was conducting a party of Phillips's men, including a group of black slaves, to Muscle Shoals along the Georgia Road when a group of Cherokees "stopped the party, took the negroes, and some other property and tyed up a white man [apparently Chisholm] who had charge" of the party; they "kept him tyed up about ten hours."[28] For some reason they did not execute him, probably because he was white. No one ever discovered who had done this, but Meigs was convinced that "Vann is at the head or principal of all these discords."[29] For a time Meigs thought civil war might take place in the nation; he wrote to Governor Sevier of Tennessee to ask him to be prepared to send the state militia to suppress it. Sevier agreed, but the crisis passed.[30]

[25] See Wilkins, *Cherokee Tragedy*, pp. 36–39; Captain A. B. Armistead to Return J. Meigs, August 9, 1807, M-208; Sam C. Hill to Return J. Meigs, August 12, 1807, M-208; Return J. Meigs to Henry Dearborn, August 30, 1807, M-221, reel 10, #3197.

[26] Some reported that Vann was in part motivated against Doublehead because Doublehead had so severely beaten his pregnant wife, who was the sister of Vann's wife, that she had died. See Wilkins, *Cherokee Tragedy*, p. 36.

[27] Return J. Meigs to Henry Dearborn, August 30, 1807, M-221, reel 10, #3197.

[28] Ibid.

[29] Ibid. The slaves belonged to Doublehead and were apparently in payment to him for land that he had leased to a white man on his tract above Muscle Shoals.

[30] Return J. Meigs to Henry Dearborn, September 30, 1808, M-208.

Despite these signs of mounting discontent, Meigs took his hand-picked group of old chiefs (minus Doublehead) to the hunting ground early in September to "adjust" the boundary for the treaty of 1806. Black Fox, The Glass, and the other chiefs involved in this "silent" cession drove a hard bargain, for they now feared that their own lives were in danger. Meigs explained it to Dearborn: "The Cherokees being in debt to the United States $1803 [at the factory], I offered to cancel that debt as compensation to the nation for the attention to the line"; however, "they requested to have it made up to $2000, and $1000 and two Rifles as presents to the Chiefs transacting the business." Meigs agreed; it was "a great acquisition to Tennessee," to whom the government turned over the land, as well as to two hundred families of white squatters who were already settled in the area. The chiefs deserved high pay for this action, he told Dearborn, because "they will have their hands full to satisfy the ignorant and the obstinate and the cunning of their own people, for which they deserve this silent consideration."[31]

Upon his return from this trip, Meigs received a letter from Benjamin Hawkins, federal agent among the Creeks, saying that he had recently talked to a group of Cherokee chiefs who were negotiating with the Creeks, Chickasaws, and Choctaws to try to reestablish the old Muskogee Confederation to prevent further land sales. The Cherokee delegates at this meeting told Hawkins that their problems all stemmed from "the unjust conduct of Doublehead and Chisholm countenanced by the agent [Meigs]." They said "they had executed the first for his crimes against this nation and would have done the same with the second [Chisholm] but for his accidental escape."[32]

Meigs's hope of purchasing the 1.5-million-acre strip along the north bank of the Tennessee River from the Lower Towns and the 1-million-acre tract north of the Hiwassee River from the Upper Towns was postponed because of mounting tensions after Doublehead's death. Nevertheless, Meigs plunged on with the plan to grant Earle thirty-six square miles at Chickamauga for an ironworks in the heart of the Cherokee Nation. On December 2, 1807, Meigs called together twenty-three chiefs, mostly from the Lower Towns, to meet at Hiwassee Town "for an establishment of an Iron works to be carried on under the direction of Government" under "the immediate superintendence" of Colonel Earle. He had selected a tract near the mouth of Chickamauga Creek. The meeting at Hiwassee was not a full or regular council. Meigs had handpicked those who had expressed an interest in it and he was surprised to find consid-

[31] Return J. Meigs to Henry Dearborn, September 28, 1807, M-208; Royce, *Cherokee Nation of Indians*, pp. 68–69.
[32] Benjamin Hawkins to Return J. Meigs, September 16, 1807, M-221, reel 8, #2565.

erable opposition. Earle was present; he told the chiefs that as soon as the treaty was made he intended to move in a large contingent of whites to live there, clear the tract of timber, erect the iron foundry, and start digging and refining the ore. Apart from the purchase price ($5,000 and 1,000 bushels of much-needed corn) no income would come to the tribe. Earle would invest his own funds (or those of the partners in his enterprise) and expected to make his profit from government contracts for war matériel.[33]

The Cherokees had long been aware that they had valuable mineral deposits in their nation. Their silversmiths had found plenty of silver; they had rented out their salines and saltpeter caves to members of their tribe but never given up ownership; rumors circulated of valuable gold deposits. The Cherokees were not eager to have private speculators making money from their resources, nor did they want scores of Earle's white employees and their families living in their midst but outside their control. Meigs assured the chiefs at Hiwassee that this was a government, not a private, project and that the government would assume responsibility for its proper functioning. But the treaty the chiefs were asked to sign allowed the President to cede the land to Earle at some future date; it also stated that if Earle found he had not chosen the best spot for iron ore, he had the right to return this tract and exchange it for another thirty-six square miles at some other place of his choosing in the nation.

Annoyed by resistance to this cession, Meigs began to threaten the chiefs. They would receive no more tools for their farms if they did not sign; they were reminded that there had been a poor harvest that fall and by the following spring they would run short of food and come to the agent to provide corn for their starving people. Meigs boasted to Dearborn afterward that the chiefs reluctantly yielded to these threats. "When the land for Ironworks was ceded, it was foreseen that they must famish without corn, and it was one strong inducement" for them to sign that he added a gift of 1,000 bushels of corn to the sale price.[34] He warned Dearborn, however, that he had promised on "the honor of the Government, that they [the United States] will never let this tract go out of their hands" because if it "should be suffered to go into the hands of private Individuals, there will be no government respectable enough to keep good order between the people employed and the Indians." The reason for this was that "the character of the persons employed in such business is gen-

[33] Return J. Meigs to Henry Dearborn, December 4, 1807, M-221, reel 10, #3246; treaty with Elias Earle, December 2, 1807, M-208; Return J. Meigs to Henry Dearborn, December 3, 1807, M-222, reel 2, #0883; Royce, *Cherokee Nation of Indians*, pp. 71–72.

[34] Return J. Meigs to Henry Dearborn, March 24, 1808, M-208.

erally turbulent and dissipated."[35] The land was "worth $5 per acre" and if the President ceded it to Earle, Earle would certainly sell some of it to speculators. One or two of the twenty-three signers of Earle's treaty were persons who at one point had been among the rebels (like Quotaquskee), but the leading figures were from Doublehead's faction, led by The Glass, John Lowrey, Terrapin, and Big Cabbin.

As soon as the treaty was signed on December 3, Earle left Hiwassee with his copy of it. He returned to South Carolina and began to hire workers and purchase equipment. In addition to ironworkers, carpenters to build housing, and mechanics for the machinery, he needed farmers and slaves to plant and harvest food for the company and its horses.

Meigs was correct that James Vann was behind the opposition to the treaty. "The opposition of Vann" and his party had led them to "threaten the lives of those who are in favor of the Government's view. . . . This threatening the friends of good order is intolerable and requires strong measures of an examplary kind on the part of the United States to deter such hardy villains and their abettors and for the relief of the well affected."[36] Vann, who had a turbulent temper, especially when he drank too much, had had several bloody fights with whites in his home and Meigs was already contemplating ways to have him arrested and taken out of the nation for trial.

When the manner of granting Earle's treaty and its terms became generally known, the rebel faction were furious. Chulio and Sour Mush wrote to John Lowrey in February 1808, holding him to blame and threatening him with retribution for betraying the nation. Lowrey wrote to Meigs asking for protection: "Vann has confused the nation so much that Chulioa sent word to me to get ready for war because I was the head of selling that bit of land. . . . They have threatened to come and rob me and steal all my horses because I sold their land." He had heard that Vann "said some time ago that he intended to turn Bonaparte and now he has turned Bonaparte." But "if that quarter of the Nation is earnest to go to war, I and my quarter is ready to join the white people" to put them down. He obviously expected Meigs and the army garrison to help the Lower Towns in this process. Lowrey closed his complaint by urging Meigs to arrest Vann for his recent assaults on two white men: "This quarter of the nation does give up Vann to you to do what you see cause to do with him. . . . I hope you will have him taken and put to death, for he has reigned long enough."[37]

There were a number of reasons why Vann became a leading figure in

---

[35] Return J. Meigs to Henry Dearborn, December 4, 1807, M-221, reel 10, #3246.

[36] Return J. Meigs to Henry Dearborn, December 3, 1807, M-222, reel 2, #0883.

[37] Jon Lowery [Lowrey] to Return J. Meigs, February 8, 1808, M-222, reel 3, #1311.

the rebellion. Though comparatively young (about thirty-eight), he was very influential and wealthy. He was also shrewd and determined. He felt that Meigs had failed to live up to promises made to him over Wafford's Tract and at the time of negotiations over the Georgia Road. He was among the delegation that went to Washington to sell the hunting ground, but he got into a knife fight with Doublehead in their hotel room during the course of the negotiations. The details were hushed up; Vann received no part of the reserves and probably had argued against them. Vann was most likely envious of Doublehead's influence and power, as Meigs suggested. They were the two most powerful men in the nation. But they were separated by ideology as much as by envy. Vann hated white men and believed that they were taking advantage of his people; Doublehead got along well with whites and thought they were helping the Cherokees. Vann was a mixed blood and Doublehead was a full blood; Doublehead had been a blood-thirsty warrior and had taken many scalps; Vann had been a trader and was never involved in war. Thoroughly acculturated. Vann had no objection to the government's civilization policy, but he realized sooner than most that whites in the frontier would never treat Indians as equals; his own wealth and position did not protect him from insults as a "halfbreed." His patriotism sprang less from any concern to protect tribal traditions or to win approval from the conservative full bloods than it did from his determination to keep the Cherokee Nation strong enough to thwart the efforts of whites to take its land and its sovereignty. He was firmly opposed to a policy that would lead to detribalization.

A month after Earle obtained his iron ore tract, the dissident faction met in council at Ustanali, the capital of the Upper Towns. That council sent letters of protest to President Jefferson, to Dearborn, and to the President of the United States Senate, George Clinton. Meigs dismissed the protest as the work of "a pretended council" that did not speak for the nation (Black Fox, The Glass, and other old chiefs from the Lower Town were not present). However, Pathkiller, the Second Principal Chief, was there and signed the letters. They were signed by forty-six chiefs, a larger number than the Lower Towns had ever mustered. The letter to Clinton simply asked him to persuade the Senate not to ratify Earle's treaty because it "may tend to the Injury of our Nation and yours." Enclosed was a copy of the more detailed letter to Jefferson, which was very specific in its complaints. The young chiefs said they had tried in vain to obtain justice from Meigs and Dearborn but had been ignored. They had then "requested our Friend, Colonel Hawkins of the Creeks" to pass on letters of complaint to Jefferson, but they had received no replies. Ever since the treaty of January 1806, "affairs are still going badly with us." The treaty in Washington was conducted improperly and now "we complain of a Sham Treaty lately held with a few of our people" to sell land to Colonel Earle; such action "ought not to be permitted to an Individual not of our nation for his own benefit." That treaty had been granted under duress: some who signed "were deceived and some of them threatened by the Hand of Power." Others "were induced to sign" because "they were told by your Agent that if . . . they refused it, you would be angry with them and that their annual stipend would in future be withheld." Such high-handed action by the agent was contrary to the harmony he should be promoting among the Cherokees and was "calculated to produce discontent." Meigs, they noted, lived far from the center of the nation at Southwest Point, Tennessee. He was "surrounded by your Merchants and Land Speculators" and he "may be imposed upon" by their arts and bribes. The commander of the army garrison had also threatened some of the dissident chiefs with war.[38]

The heart of the letter was a political manifesto—an effort to assert what the young chiefs considered the right of the Cherokee people to be fully and freely consulted on all treaties. "We, as a free People, have a Right to claim for ourselves and our children" the right of "ratifying or rejecting treaties after they are concluded." Neither the treaty of 1806 nor the treaty with Earle was ever ratified by a full council; they were both the work of only a small minority of chiefs. The Cherokees "can never consider any future Treaty binding upon us until it is reviewed and approved by a Majority of all our beloved Men, Chiefs and Warriors." Meigs, they said, was subverting the idea of Cherokee self-government in his efforts to work with a small number of friendly chiefs and by considering a majority of them to constitute the will of the nation. The Cherokee rebels demanded the right to self-government by their full council in open debate before the whole nation. The letter was signed by those who may be considered the leaders of the rebellious party: Pathkiller, The Ridge, Chulio, Sour Mush, Tuskegetihee, Kelachula, Katihee, Chattloe, Dreadful Water, James David, Nawwayooteaheh, George Sanders, Alexander Sanders, Young Wolf, Currahee Dick, John Doherty, Sharp Arrow, George Parris (or Pearis), and George Fields. Only Vann's name was absent, although he probably wrote the letters.

The young chiefs never received any answers to these letters and they proceeded to take the law into their own hands. If the United States would not repudiate the treaty with Earle, they would see that it was not put into effect. Early in February 1808, Earle sent an advance caravan of wagons

---

[38] Return J. Meigs to Henry Dearborn, January 24, 1808, M-222, reel 3, #1152-1154; Cherokee Chiefs to George Clinton, February 16, 1808, M-222, reel 3, #1154-1156.

containing supplies, workers, and slaves from Tougaloo, South Carolina, to prepare the way for the one hundred families he had signed up for his enterprise. Earle was aware that trouble was brewing; the families he had recruited also knew because Chulio had sent them a letter stating the tribe's opposition. These families refused to start into the Cherokee Nation until they received assurance of their safety. William Brown, Earle's wagoner, was sent ahead to test the situation and prepare the way.

When the Upper Town chiefs learned that several of Earle's wagons would pass through their region on the way to Chickamauga, they held a meeting and planned to stop them. The group chosen to do this included James Vann, Charles Hicks, The Ridge, Dreadful Water, Kelachula, Chulioa, the Halfbreed, George Parris, Tuskegatehee, Necuteou, and Nawwayoutieh, plus "a number of young fellows" like George Sanders, Alex Sanders, and Will Crittenden. They were prepared to use violence if necessary to turn back the wagons. Brandishing guns and tomahawks, this armed party (minus Vann) descended on horseback and surrounded the wagons of Brown and Harrison just as they were about to start on the Georgia Road through the nation. One Cherokee, Calestowee, hit Brown with the side of his tomahawk but did not draw blood. The wagons stopped while Brown visited Vann to appeal for his help—Vann being the headman in the area. But Vann refused it. Vann's sister, Mrs. Peggy Falling, warned Harrison that there would be bloodshed if he persisted. After waiting two days, Brown and Harrison turned their wagons around and went back to Tougaloo.[39]

On February 15, The Ridge, Charles Hicks, Chulio, and the others who had participated in this action wrote to Black Fox, saying that "the late treaty was a cheat put upon the Chiefs" and that they had determined that "the said Earle should not pass through our part of the nation. Accordingly he has been stopped and we desired him to return home, and he has done so."[40] The next day Meigs received a note from Earle describing "how Vann and his party" stopped his wagons saying that this "does not in the least deter me." He now requested a military escort, however, and he warned Meigs to "be carefull of Vann's party who, I am well convinced, is Determined to Kill you if possible."[41] The rebellion of the young chiefs now entered its most critical phase.

[39] See affidavit of William Brown, February 15, 1808, M-208. See also letter of John H. Harrison to Return J. Meigs, February 23, 1808, M-208.

[40] Kattahee [Katahee] and Necuteou to Return J. Meigs, February 15, 1808, M-208.

[41] Elias Earle to Return J. Meigs, February 18, 1808, M-208.

SIX

EFFORTS TO DIVIDE THE NATION,

1808–1809

I understand some years ago that the Government had in contemplation an exchange of land with the Indians South of the Ohio. It is my opinion that if specific propositions were made to the Cherokees . . . that it would in a short time produce a general sentiment amongst them in favor of exchange. —Return J. Meigs, February 1808

After 1808, the critical issue facing the rebellious young chiefs was the effort of the federal agent to persuade the Lower Towns to sell their part of the nation and move to Arkansas. Even before the young chiefs turned against Doublehead, Meigs was convinced that George Washington's original policy of Indian integration was probably unworkable. In part this resulted from his inability to keep white intruders from constantly squatting on land inside the Cherokee borders; it also resulted from the Cherokee's persistent refusal to divide their land among themselves in severalty.

"The Cherokees complain," Meigs wrote to Dearborn on February 9, 1808, "that intrusions on their land on the frontier of Georgia by the white people are still continued and are increasing"; there was as well a "settlement of white people on the N.E. side of Chickasaw Creek" in the Alabama region of the nation, and "the Indians want them moved off."[1] That same day he wrote to Governor Jared Irwin of Georgia to inform him of the intruders and to say that "it is out of all dispute that . . . all of those on the waters of the Chattahoochee are really agressors [intruders] in open violation of the laws, which justifies the complaints of the Indians and disturbs their quiet." Consequently, he told Irwin, he had sent orders to the commanding officers of the United States Army post at Ocmulgee to take his troops and forcibly remove these white Georgians.[2]

However, he had little hope that this would do any good. He had tried these tactics over and over to no avail. "All attempts to remove these people," he told Dearborn, "has hitherto been ineffectual." The troops might

[1] Return J. Meigs to Henry Dearborn, February 9, 1808, M-208.
[2] Return J. Meigs to Jared Irwin, February 9, 1808, M-208.

drive the squatters off, might even burn their log cabins and their crops, but no sooner had the soldiers marched off than the intruders returned, rebuilt their cabins, replanted their crops, and continued as they had before, to live on tax-free Indian land until the government forced the Indians to sell it; then the squatters bought their farms at the preemption price of two dollars per acre regardless of what it was really worth. Meigs believed that only a perpetual military guard marching endlessly round the six-hundred-mile Cherokee border could have kept the squatters out, and the United States could not afford such expenditure. By continually yielding to the intruders' demands and forcing the Cherokees to cede the land squatters were on, the War Department had encouraged further intrusions.

Meigs went on to tell Dearborn in this long, rambling letter, "it is my opinion that there never will be quietness on any of these frontiers until the Indians are removed over the Mississippi." So far as Meigs was concerned, the fault lay as much with the Indians as with the lawless whites. The Indians had too much land. They refused to sell it off and keep only what they needed for their own farms. They declined to become citizens. "I understand some years ago that the Government had in contemplation an exchange of land with the Indians South of the Ohio. It is my opinion that if specific propositions were made to the Cherokees, holding out suitable encouragements and protection, that it would in a short time produce a general sentiment amongst them in favor of exchange."[3] Meigs admitted that "some, who are well situated as farmers, would probably require reservations of competent tracts for their use, but even these would finally sell out and follow the nation [westward]." What reason Meigs had to believe that the poorer Cherokees, like those in the Valley Towns or the Etowah district, would want to emigrate, he did not say. They were to demonstrate precisely the opposite tendency.

Dearborn wrote back immediately to endorse and encourage Meigs's suggestion. "If you think it practicable to induce the Cherokees as a nation generally to consent to exchange of their present country for a suitable tract of country on the other side of the Mississippi, you will please to embrace every favorable occasion for sounding the Chiefs on the subject, and let the subject be generally talked about [among] the natives until you shall be satisfied of the prevailing opinion."[4] For the government, this was the ideal solution to "the Indian question." Jefferson had first suggested the plan in 1803 after the purchase of the Louisiana Territory,

---

[3] Return J. Meigs to Henry Dearborn, February 9, 1808, M-208.
[4] Henry Dearborn to Return J. Meigs, March 25, 1808, M-208.

but when Meigs proposed it to the Cherokees in 1804 he had found no interest in it.[5] Now he thought the climate might be different.

As usual, Meigs began by discussing the matter with the Lower Town chiefs. Suffering from the challenge to their authority from the young chiefs and upset by the accusations of national betrayal, some of them seemed to find the plan attractive, but they first wanted to sell the 1.5 million acres on the north side of the Tennessee River and divide it up as reserves for their young chiefs. Meigs threw cold water on this in a letter to Black Fox in April 1808, noting that it would be difficult to divide that area into reserves because much of it had already been preempted by warrants to Revolutionary veterans. As soon as the Cherokees sold it, these areas would revert to the veterans, their heirs, or assigns. Besides, the Cherokees "have abundance of land on the South side of the River for all your people who wish to live there and become farmers." Meigs was no longer interested in encouraging land speculation that might enrich a few Cherokees. He went on to press for exchange and removal. "It seems as though a great part of your people are not inclined to become farmers; they prefer the hunting life." Even those who had become farmers, he thought, would prefer to be hunters if it were possible. "Numbers, I am informed are already gone over the Mississippi and [I believe] that many others think of going over to that Country where there is good hunting ground." If this were so, then "to divide the land [here] would be of no use." "If they would wish to go over to that Country [Arkansas], your Nation can make an exchange with the U. States, but if you dispose of it [the land you have left in the East] by small parcels, you cannot make an exchange." Meigs had almost totally reversed his position of the previous year when he had praised the Cherokees as a nation of farmers. "Think seriously," he told Black Fox, "and weigh carefully the state of your people."[6]

The Lower Town chiefs did think seriously about it; by May they were ready to enter discussions about the details. They wished to negotiate the matter in Washington, out of sight of the rest of the nation. Meigs wrote to Dearborn on May 17, with plans "relating to a visit of some Cherokee Chiefs to see the Executive and pointing to an exchange of country with the Cherokees."[7] Meigs appears to have kept the Upper Town chiefs in

[5] For early discussion of moving the Cherokees to west of the Mississippi see W. S. Lovely to Return J. Meigs, October 27, 1803, M-208; Return J. Meigs to Henry Dearborn, May 31, 1804, M-208; Return J. Meigs to Henry Dearborn, June 28, 1804, M-208; Return J. Meigs to Henry Dearborn, July 5, 1804, M-208. Most of the Cherokees who moved voluntarily to Arkansas Territory in the years 1800 to 1808 did so because of harassment by white intruders.

[6] Return J. Meigs to Black Fox, April 6, 1808, M-208.

[7] Return J. Meigs to Henry Dearborn, May 17, 1808, M-221, reel 26, #8601.

the dark about his efforts. By a strange coincidence, a group of chiefs in the upper part of the Upper Towns on the Little Tennessee River took a notion at this moment to visit President Jefferson on their own initiative to tell him they wanted to become citizens of the United States. Their trip indicated lack of trust both in Meigs and in their national chiefs. They did not bother to tell Meigs they were going. Led by Stone Carrier, Woman Holder, John of Chilhowee, the Crawling Boy, Chilcohatah, and the Deer Biter, thirty-two Cherokees, including two women, left the nation in March and reached Washington in April. After discussing their problems with Dearborn, this delegation had an audience with Jefferson on May 4, 1808.

Their complaints were simple. They were not part of the rebellious faction led by James Vann. In fact, they told Dearborn they had no use for Vann, whom they called "a turbulent and dangerous man." But they complained strongly about Meigs's favoritism toward the Lower Towns. "For several years," they said, "their part of the nation [the Upper Towns] had received scarcely anything from the United States either as annuities [trade goods for improvement,] or as pay for the land sold." This they attributed to the fact that "the Great chiefs generally live in the lower parts of the nation" and took most of the national income for their own people. Meigs had permitted this to happen; thus they were in great want of plows, spinning wheels, looms, and hoes for their people. They had no gristmill or sawmill in their part of the nation. They said they realized that the hunting days were over; they were ready to become farmers. Their second complaint was of the frequent harassment they suffered from whites who came across their borders to graze livestock and even to live in cabins and plant crops on the Cherokee side of the Little Tennessee River. They reminded Dearborn that Jefferson had told the Cherokee delegation that sold the hunting ground in 1806 that the only way to secure their land to themselves forever was to divide it among them. They therefore wished "to propose a division of the lands of the Nation between the upper and lower Cherokees by a fixed line and to have certain tracts for farms laid off for each family inclined to be farmers [and] to be under the jurisdiction and laws of the United States and become actual citizens."[8] In effect, they wanted the Upper Towns to become a separate Cherokee Nation under the laws of the United States, somewhat like a western territory prior to statehood. Because few of them knew how to read or write English, they could not become individual citizens of Tennessee; they still expected to be under the protection and care of the federal government. Somehow they thought that if they had the status of

---

[8] Henry Dearborn to Return J. Meigs, May 5, 1808, M-208.

131

citizens of the United States they could obtain more respect for themselves and more protection for their land from the whites around them.

Jefferson asked Stone Carrier and his delegation whether they understood what their responsibilities would be as citizens. "Are you prepared for this?" He advised them to return home and consult with the Lower Towns about such a division of the nation. If that could be agreed upon, perhaps Congress would agree to establish some kind of territorial form of government for the Upper Towns under regulations suited to their state of advance and prepare them for full citizenship later. On the other hand, Jefferson thought they might want to consider a different alternative. Those who "still choose to continue the hunter's life" might wish to "settle on our lands beyond the Mississippi."[9] The President hoped to merge the discontented in the Upper Towns with the discontented in the Lower Towns in order to strengthen Meigs's proposal for the total exchange of the Cherokee land and the removal of the whole tribe to Arkansas.

Jefferson was convinced that the grievances of these Cherokees were real; he told Dearborn to have Meigs redress them by seeing that their people received sufficient plows, wheels, hoes, and a gristmill as well as their fair share of the annuity.[10] Meigs had his own interpretation of the various discontents sweeping the Cherokee Nation. "A crisis in their national existence is taking place," he explained to Dearborn in June 1808. Those in the Lower Towns "ostensibly hold up the Idea of becoming farmers," but their real object was to sell their excess land to the white people. Those of the Upper Towns "will try everything before they conquer indolence. . . . They can no more hold their property as citizens than a seive can hold water." Although both the Lower Towns and the upper part of the Upper Towns were talking about dividing their land, Meigs was convinced that neither group really understood what was at stake. Furthermore, he warned Dearborn, "if their land is divided out here to individuals, it will deprive the government of many millions of dollars by the sales of it and the Indians will become more wretched than they now are." In short, he no longer wanted to encourage them to become fee-simple yeoman farmers in the East on their ancestral grounds; he was convinced that they were not ready for it. "There are perhaps two or three hundred families that might hold land as individuals and would make useful citizens," but "the principal mass" of Cherokees would soon be cheated out of what they had by unscrupulous whites. He predicted that at the national council to be held at Broomstown in August, "it is

[9] Thomas Jefferson to Cherokee Delegation, May 4, 1808, M-15, reel 2, p. 374.
[10] Henry Dearborn to Return J. Meigs, May 5, 1808, M-208.

probable that a Division of the Cherokees into upper and lower towns will be agreed on." However, he thought this would be pointless, for "the result of all these alterations will finally eventuate in an exchange of Country." The Cherokees had reached the end of their rope in their present location. "To preserve their national existence" they must emigrate west.[11]

In order to prepare the chiefs for serious discussion of the removal and exchange of the whole nation, Meigs had sent the Lower Towns a message early in June explaining his ideas (and what he took to be Jefferson's) in more detail. Though some Cherokees "have become good farmers," he told them, nevertheless "great numbers who have been bro't up to the hunting life will not, nor can it be expected that they will, change habits too long in use for habits of agriculture and manufacture." Cultural persistence, he recognized, was much stronger than the framers of the original Indian policy in 1789 had realized. It was time to alter that program. "In order to place the Cherokees in a situation where all may have objects of pursuit agreeable to them, it is proposed to place the Cherokees on good hunting grounds" to the west. Although "farming and domestic manufacturers may still be pursued [there] by those who shall chuse those pursuits in preference to hunting," the great benefit of exchange would be that those who preferred a hunting economy could be assured of a good enough catch each year to support their families. "Protection [from other Indians or European nations] and the fostering hand of Government will go along with you"—the factory, the agent, their annuity, technical assistance, and undoubtedly the missionaries and their schools.[12]

This message bore immediate fruit. "The Glass has proposed," Meigs wrote to Dearborn in July, "to have some of their people sent out to explore the country on the West Side of the Mississippi" to find a suitable tract to exchange for their land in the east. Meigs asked that a government military officer be sent with them to see that they found a good location and brought back a favorable report.[13]

Fortunately Meigs was relieved of the problem of Earle's ironworks at this time, when the State of Tennessee claimed that the land granted to Earle in the treaty at Hiwassee Town was located within its state boundary and not, as had been thought, in Mississippi Territory. Tennessee did not want its property to be given to Earle by the United States and the Senate therefore refused to ratify Earle's treaty until the President settled

[11] Return J. Meigs to Henry Dearborn, July 11, 1808, M-208.

[12] Return J. Meigs included that "Talk" to the Cherokee Council in a letter to Henry Dearborn, June 3, 1808, M-208.

[13] Return J. Meigs to Henry Dearborn, June 3, 1808, M-208.

the matter with Tennessee. Earle continued to push his claim for another five or six years, but ultimately the whole scheme fell through. The idea of the arsenal was dropped and in 1814 Earle was reimbursed $985 from the Cherokee annuity for the damage he sustained when the Cherokees stopped him from entering the nation in February 1808.[14] This time luck was on the side of the Cherokees.

Meanwhile, the dissident young chiefs, still led by James Vann, Charles Hicks, The Ridge, and Chulio, seemed unaware of the seriousness of Meigs's efforts to promote removal and exchange in the Lower Towns. In June 1808 they wrote to Jefferson that "for some time past we have reason to believe that your agent has not that good disposition towards us that he ought to have." They suspected that he was negotiating secretly for further cessions and wanted the President to be aware that "in a full Council last April it was determined that no act of any Chief or Chiefs should be considered binding on the nation unless they were first appointed in a council [to act for the nation] and then [their actions] to be ratified by a full council of the Nation before whom their proceedings is to be laid." In short, henceforth treaties should take place in two distinct steps: a negotiating council (presumably with a small number of chiefs appointed for the purpose) would first work out a treaty with commissioners from the federal government, but before that treaty could be considered binding, it would have to be fully discussed and approved by a full national council of all the chiefs and warriors, similar to the United States Senate's ratification of all treaties made by its commissioners. Meigs had never acknowledged such a procedure; for him the action of the negotiating council was final even when he picked those who negotiated or when he knew they represented only a small fraction of the chiefs. Part of the problem was that the Cherokees had never fixed any number or proportion of chiefs to constitute an official council and preferred to live under a decentralized town government. The young chiefs went on to tell Jefferson that they had learned that "Col. Meigs is now about to get The Glass and 2 or 3 other Chiefs to proceed to the Federal City" for some kind of negotiations. What it was for they did not know; "he has kept the object of their journey a profound secret nor can a man amongst us, except two or three favorites [like The Glass], obtain one title of information respecting it." They wished Jefferson to know that The Glass's delegation was "unauthorized" to speak for the whole nation, and that anything they negotiated in Washington would be invalid unless the whole nation ratified it afterward.[15] The letter was signed by Pathkiller, Sour Mush, Job-

[14] Royce, *Cherokee Nation of Indians*, pp. 71–73.

[15] Pathkiller and other Cherokee chiefs to Thomas Jefferson, June 4, 1808, M-222, roll 3, #1342–1345.

bers Son, Chulio, Warrior's Nephew, Nicojack, Lying Fawn, Ootutetah, The Ridge, Kalatahee, Sawanooku, Five Killer, Cautaugatahee, Cawso-coshee, Thomas Pettit, George Parris, Oosaoku, and Ball Catcher.

Jefferson did not know what to make of the letter except that it was from "Vann's party"; Meigs knew nothing about it. Apparently the chiefs who wrote the letter were unaware of Jefferson's earlier meeting with the group led by Stone Carrier and their proposal to divide the nation. As of June, the Cherokee Nation appeared to be divided into at least three distinct political factions, each with its own program and strategy: the Lower Towns were leaning toward removal and exchange; the upper part of the Upper Towns on the Little Tennessee River favored some formal division from the Lower Towns and territorial status; the rebellious young chiefs (most of them living between the Hiwassee River in Tennessee and the Etowah River in Georgia) favored a unified nation, a more highly centralized government, tribal ownership of the land, and a firm stand against removal, division, or any further land cessions.

Meigs favored the first group, whom he still considered the true leaders of the nation, and continued to be sanguine about his removal plan, telling Dearborn in July that "there is a good number who wish to go over the Mississippi."[16] He also explained that although "the general idea of an exchange is that they shall have an equal extent of land [in Arkansas to that] which they now hold here," he did not think parity was necessary. "I think they will think it better to have a less extent of land [in Arkansas], say one half, and that they have the difference in value in cash or goods and payable by installments in ten or perhaps twenty years and without interest." Concerned that Jefferson might continue to hold out the fatal promise of citizenship in the east, Meigs preyed on the government's fear of a war in the west. He reminded Dearborn that the Cherokees, if "well-armed" in Arkansas, would provide "a formidable barrier against the savages or people of any other character" who might threaten the Valley from "the west or northwest."[17] Relations with Great Britain were very tense at this time and Meigs had already broached to Dearborn in March the possibility that James Vann and his rebels "may have been tampered with by the English Emissaries."[18] He also whetted Dearborn's appetite for the total removal of the Cherokees by a speculative estimate of how much land would be gained and how little it would cost.

The land now held by the Cherokees on the South side of the River Tennessee [the Lower Town region] is at least equal to an oblong 100 by 200 miles . . . there is

---

[16] Return J. Meigs Henry Dearborn, July 11, 1808, M-208.
[17] Ibid.
[18] Return J. Meigs to Henry Dearborn, March 24, 1808, M-208.

at least 14,000,000 acres. Suppose the U. States should give them land equal to one half by estimation [in Arkansas] having some natural boundaries, and by the other half at one and one-half cents per acre, say total 105,000 dollars. . . . When this sum is considered separated from the object it appears great, but when compared with the result of the whole exchange, it shrinks to nothing, for in a very few years only a partial sale of the lands acquired will bring millions into the Treasury.[19]

As in all speculation, it took money to make money.

Meigs admitted in the same letter that some of the Cherokees were reluctant to leave the home of their forefathers: "Notwithstanding they are Indians, they have strong local prejudices [sentiments] and to induce them to migrate, they must have strong excitements to leave the place of their nativity and the graves of their fathers." Still, if they could only be made to see that "their existence as a distinct people depends on their migration" and if "solid advantages" were held out, then the plan would work. He hoped to persuade them that a nation with "at least 1600 good, active, gun men," living in Arkansas, could shoot and trap "skins and peltry to the amount of $150,000 annually while the old men, women and Children were raising corn and making cloth." A few months ago he had been praising their progress as farmers. Now he was encouraging them to be hunters and to leave farming to the women.

Meigs was playing a risky game and by late summer he was very apprehensive. It looked as though he might yet face open rebellion from the Upper Towns. He had antagonized some chiefs by firing Charles Hicks, one of the rebels, from his post as interpreter. The incident that led him to demand that the national council turn over Charles Hicks and James Vann for prosecution in white courts was almost a comic opera. On August 31, Charles Hicks, acting in the name of the council, arrested Samuel Riley at knifepoint at Chickamauga Creek. Riley, who was now Meigs's chief interpreter, was carrying an important message from Meigs to the Lower Towns. Hicks told Riley that he was wanted at once for questioning by a council of Upper Town chiefs at Ustanali. Riley said he was on urgent government business and declined to accompany Hicks. Hicks brandished the knife as though to force him, but finally agreed to allow Riley to post $500 bond and promise to appear later at the council to defend himself against unspecific charges. Riley assumed that the rebels would accuse him at Ustanali of betraying the nation and force him to reveal Meigs's secret machinations for removal and exchange. As soon as Hicks had gone, Riley wrote anxiously to Meigs asserting that "the insurgent party" was out to get him and that he feared for his life. Meigs

---

[19] Return J. Meigs to Henry Dearborn, June 3, 1808, M-208.

was outraged that a minor Cherokee chief would arrest "one of the officers of the Cherokee Agency" and insult him while in the execution of his duty. He wrote to Black Fox to say that Hicks must be punished. "The United States," he told the Principal Chief, "are by this conduct insulted by an insurgent party of Cherokees" and "the Government of the United States will not suffer one of their officers to be insulted." "I demand that you punish Charles Hicks or deliver him up to be dealt with as the case may require."[20]

Riley's inordinate fear of Hicks's faction and Meigs's overreaction to this incident resulted from their own bad consciences. Meigs wrote to David Campbell: "Ever since my return from the seat of government [in January] 1806, Charles Hicks has joined the party against Doublehead, of which party Vann is the head." "Hicks had become so insolent" by June 1807, "that I had been obliged to dismiss him as an Interpreter by which the [Lower Town] Cherokee Chiefs were much pleased." This "rebellious party," he said, must be taught a lesson for their arrogance. "If these people are suffered to escape with impunity, they will grow more refractory and oppose every reasonable proposition from the United States and from Tennessee."[21]

Meigs was not placated when he discovered, upon further investigation, that Hicks had arrested Riley over a problem involving the ownership of a slave who had formerly belonged to Doublehead.[22] Since this was entirely a civil matter within the nation, Black Fox did not arrest Hicks nor did Meigs pursue the incident. He decided instead to carry out his old intention to arrest James Vann. In the same letter in which he ordered Black Fox to punish Hicks, he also demanded that the council turn over Vann to him to stand trial for his assaults upon two white men.[23] On January 20, 1808, Vann had shot a Georgian named Leonard Rice during a drunken party at Vann's home; on April 20, he had stabbed a Tennessee wagoner, Samuel Moore, in another brawl at Vann's Ferry on the Chattahoochee.[24] Meigs had received letters from General Buckner Harris of Georgia and Governor Sevier of Tennessee demanding Vann's prosecution for these crimes. Writing to Black Fox and the council about this, Meigs said: "You all know that James Vann is a dangerous man and that he has committed these crimes and others. If you do not check these acts

[20] Return J. Meigs to Black Fox, September 4, 1808, M-208.
[21] Return J. Meigs to David Campbell, September 30, 1808, M-208.
[22] David Campbell to Return J. Meigs, September 23, 1808, M-208.
[23] Return J. Meigs to Black Fox, September 4, 1808, M-208.
[24] Return J. Meigs to Henry Dearborn, February 22, 1808, M-208; Henry Dearborn to Return J. Meigs, May 7, 1808, M-208; General Buckner Harris to Return J. Meigs, June 4, 1808, M-208; Return J. Meigs to Henry Dearborn, July 14, 1808, M-221, reel 26, #8667.

of bad men, they may bring distress on the nation, and in such case the good may suffer for the conduct of their bad men."[25]

Vann, however, had taken care to obtain medical care for both the white men he had assaulted and he paid them well to compensate for their wounds. They had brought no charges. Black Fox and the national council that met at Broomstown in September refused to deliver Vann to Meigs, who then wrote to Dearborn accusing the chiefs of cowardice. "The well disposed Chiefs who are ten to one of the refractory, dare not even make a proposition to have Vann delivered up for fear of assassination when at the same time they would rejoice to see him punished with the utmost severity."[26] Meigs asked Dearborn's permission to have the army arrest Vann and turn him over to Sevier for prosecution in Tennessee. If Vann were convicted, he said, "it would have a good effect and would strengthen the hands of the friends of Government who ought by every reasonable means [to] be supported. Their own Government is nothing, and in the last resort murder and assassination follows as in the case of Doublehead." Meigs displayed his usual contempt for the Cherokee political system: "If a man manifest[s] a decided predilection in favor of complying with the propositions of Government at treaties, his life is threatened and they dare not act." It did not seem to occur to Meigs that the "well disposed chiefs" might be in the minority or had placed their own self-interest before that of the tribe. Meigs once again considered obtaining soldiers from Governor Sevier "to punish the aggressors."[27]

Meigs's resolve to prosecute Vann stiffened when he received a letter from General Harris on October 11 describing how, in June, "James Vann placed himself and the Indian Catahee" at the head of a Cherokee group to accompany the surveyors of Wafford's Tract (which white intruders had tried to expand during the four-year delay between the cession and the survey). Harris's object in the survey was to include as large an area as possible within the grant. Vann believed that Harris's line was designed to exceed the true limits of the cession; his assumption proved correct.[28]

Dearborn gave permission to Meigs to use the troops at the garrison to arrest Vann. Dearborn was hoping to obtain a cession of land for Tennessee at a council in November. Meigs wrote to Sevier: "If Vann is properly brought to Justice, it will have a very good effect, will silence his parti-

---

[25] Return J. Meigs to Black Fox, September 4, 1808, M-208.
[26] Return J. Meigs to Henry Dearborn, September 30, 1808, M-208.
[27] Ibid.
[28] Royce, *Cherokee Nation of Indians*, pp. 58–60; General Buckner Harris to Return J. Meigs, October 11, 1808, M-208.

zans—negociations with the Cherokees will be conducted with ease."[29] Vann was arrested on October 22 and taken to Nashville for arraignment. Much to Meigs's chagrin, Vann was released five days later and he returned home a martyr. "It would appear," Meigs explained sheepishly to Dearborn, "if the opinion of Messrs. Tremble and Dardes [the lawyers hired to prosecute Vann] is correct, that the law as it now stands will not reach the case of Vann."[30] Only those assaulted could bring a complaint, and they refused.

While Meigs's futile efforts to prosecute Hicks and Vann were in process, the national council at Broomstown in September 1808 was taking some of the most important actions in Cherokee revitalization. It was a tense meeting because so many critical matters were before the council: Earle was still hoping to start his ironworks somewhere soon; Meigs had sent the council a long address urging the nation to emigrate west; the Lower Town chiefs were planning their trip to Washington and wanted the council to give them power to act for themselves if not for the nation; Stone Carrier and the upper part of the Upper Towns wanted to divide the nation into two parts; Tennessee was asking for another cession; rumors were circulating about an exchange of land; the number of white intruders pressing onto the Cherokee land all around their borders was in the hundreds; many chiefs feared that too many whites had been given permission to enter the nation as mechanics and sharecroppers; Meigs was requesting the prosecution of Vann and Hicks; and critical new proposals had been offered to establish a national police force that would require further adjustments in the tradition of clan revenge. It took the council almost a month to consider all of these matters. Black Fox served as Principal Chief and Pathkiller as Second Principal chief, but they were on opposite sides in the rebellion; so were Toochelar, the Speaker for the council, and Charles Hicks, Secretary for the council. At one point the Lower Town chiefs withdrew for a secret caucus at which decisions were made about an exchange of land and removal that the council as a whole did not learn about until weeks later.[31]

The Broomstown council refused to take any action on Earle's ironworks or on delivering up Hicks and Vann. Nor could it decide what to do about regulating permits to admit whites to work in the nation. The council members easily agreed, however, to protest strongly to Meigs for not removing the hundreds of intruders on their land. After some difficulty, the chiefs also passed a law establishing a national police force. The resolution of September 11 stated that "regulating parties" were "hereby

[29] Return J. Meigs to John Sevier, October 23, 1808, M-208.
[30] Return J. Meigs to Henry Dearborn, October 28, 1808, M-208.
[31] Return J. Meigs to Black Fox, September 4, 1808, M-208.

authorized . . . to suppress horse stealing and robbery of other property." Groups of lighthorse regulators under local headmen were to be established in different (but unspecified) parts of the nation. They were to "be paid out of the National annuity at the rates of fifty dollars to each Captain, forty to the Lieutenant and thirty dollars to each of the privates." Charges against thieves required "one or two witnesses" and upon conviction, horse thieves "shall be punished with one hundred stripes on the bare back, and the punishment to be in proportion for stealing property of less value." Considering the long-standing opposition of the Cherokees to central law enforcement and corporal punishment, this was a drastic revision in political thought, though not without precedent. Later reports indicate that the law was passed at the urging of the young chiefs and that the Lower Towns had little intention of enforcing it in their area. After the first lighthorse patrols instituted under Major Lewis in 1798 lapsed in 1801, there had been sporadic attempts to revive them in 1802, 1804, and earlier in 1808.[32] Much of the tension dividing the old and young chiefs involved the former's primary concern for individual self-aggrandizement and the profits to be made from land sales and the latter's desire for closer attention to community problems, orderly acculturation, and national survival.

That the clans were still an important element in Cherokee life seems evident from an important clause in the law regarding clan revenge in connection with deaths that might result from resistance to arrest by the lighthorse regulators: ". . . and should the accused person or persons raise up with arms in his or their hands, as guns, axes, spears and knives, in opposition to the regulating company, or should they kill him or them, the blood of him or them shall not be required of any of the persons belonging to the regulators from the clan the persons so killed belonged to."[33] Evidently the similar decision made by the council in 1797 had not been strictly observed.

An equally complex issue over which the clans may have been upset was a clause that ordered the lighthorse regulators "to give their protection to children as heirs to their father's property and to the widow's share whom he may have had children by or cohabited with as his wife at

[32] For discussion of the reinstitution of the Cherokee lighthorse patrol and for some attempts to do this in various parts of the nation after 1801, see The Glass to Henry Dearborn, June 30, 1801, M-15, reel 1, p. 27; Return J. Meigs to Henry Dearborn, December 3, 1802, M-208; W. S. Lovely to Cherokee chiefs, June [no day] 1804, M-208; Return J. Meigs to Henry Dearborn, July 25, 1804, M-208; Quotequsky (James McIntosh) to Return J. Meigs, August 28, 1804, M-208; Tutequskee (probably James McIntosh) to Return J. Meigs, July 8, 1808, M-208.

[33] The Laws of the Cherokee Nation (Tahlequah, Cherokee Nation, 1852), pp. 3–4. Hereafter abbreviated as Cherokee Laws.

the time of his decease." This was, in effect, a repudiation of matrilineal inheritance. The lack of records about the debate in the council leaves it uncertain whether this resulted from a decline in clan ties or the inability of poor clan relatives to take care of a mounting number of fatherless children and husbandless wives or whether this is another example of modernization—the development of middle-class white attitudes (especially among intermarried whites and Cherokees and among mixed bloods). Meigs had reported to Dearborn as early as 1805 that more and more of the wealthy Cherokees were coming to him to have wills made so that upon their deaths their property would go to their widows and children and not to their brothers.[34] He and Jefferson had regularly advised the Cherokees to adopt a patrilineal system, as had the missionaries. The new law read: ". . . in case a father shall leave or will any property to a child at the time of his decease which he may have had by another woman, then his present wife shall be entitled to receive any such property as may be left by him or them when substantiated by two or one disinterested witness."[35]

Traditionally, a man's older brothers or maternal uncles had primary claim on his property, just as a widow's property and children went to her brothers or maternal uncles. Perhaps the women of the nation had complained to the council that wealthy husbands (perhaps white countrymen, perhaps mixed bloods) were abandoning them and leaving their children without support. The Cherokees' marriage and kinship systems were certainly suffering under the strain of their new way of life. Divorce was still easy, but the power of a Cherokee wife to maintain control of her property, her home, and her children was difficult as wealth increased and white manners were adopted. As the conjugal family, living alone on its farm, became the standard pattern of family life, the husband's rights and duties superseded those of the clan. The lighthorse regulators, it appeared, were to be not only a police force, judge, jury, and executioner but a probate court as well. This first major law in the revitalization movement thus instituted a crude instrument for a far-reaching cultural transformation. Though its early enforcement was doubtless weak, it tried to face up to certain basic issues of readjustment and, ultimately, patrilineal inheritance became the norm.

Extant records do not mention any other internal laws passed by this council, but the Reverend Gideon Blackburn, who attended, summarized its activities in a letter to a missionary journal:

---

[34] Return J. Meigs to Henry Dearborn, August 4, 1805, M-208. Meigs explained here the growing preference among some of the mixed-blood Cherokees for patrilineal inheritance as opposed to traditional matrilineal inheritance.

[35] *Cherokee Laws*, pp. 3–4.

A few days ago, in full council, they adopted a constitution which embraces simple principles of government. The legislative and judicial powers are vested in a general council and lesser ones subordinate. All criminal accusations must be established by testimony, and no more executions must be made by the avenger of blood. . . . One law is that no murderer shall be punished until he has been proved guilty before the council. Another, that all Indians who have [live]stock to a certain number specified, shall pay two dollars annually to support their national government; that every white man in the nation . . . shall pay one dollar per annum for the same purpose, and some, whose names are mentioned, are rated as high as five. That all Indians shall be obliged to pay for crossing at ferries in the nation, as the whites do; that all ferries are to be taxed for the same purpose, some as high as fifty dollars, some thirty, some twenty, etc.[36]

If such laws were actually passed, they constituted a major effort to restructure the Cherokee political and legal system. Blackburn's details are so explicit that it seems likely that the matters were at least discussed; he may have seen a draft of proposals brought forward by the young chiefs. However, Meigs makes no mention of such laws, nor are there any records of their implementation. Blackburn was trying to impress the churchgoing public with the success of missionary work. He continued: "I suspect their next step will be the partitioning out of their lands [in severalty] and entering into regular habits of husbandry. Thus far are the Cherokees advanced—further, I believe, than any other nation of Indians in America." Next he expected them to form Christian churches. But Blackburn's optimism tended to run beyond the evidence. Three years earlier he had predicted that "marriage will be soon introduced with some significant ceremony" and written laws would be required "to ascertain the right of property as it increases." Though he mentioned no law on the subject of infanticide, he reported a sharp decline in "procuring abortions," which he attributed to the decline of hunting. Abortions, he said, were undertaken "in order to prepare the females for accompanying their husbands in their hunting expeditions."[37] Blackburn himself took credit for persuading the Cherokees to adopt written laws, but it seems unlikely that he or any missionary was the principal force behind the laws passed at Broomstown.[38] They were the result of the experiential needs of acculturation and adapted white practices to Cherokee needs on Cherokee terms. It is worth noting that Blackburn considered Doublehead's assassination "a serious loss to the nation" for "he entered more fully into the real interest of the nation than any Indian in it, and it was because his

[36] See Gideon Blackburn's letter in the *Panoplist* (Boston), December 1808, pp. 325–26.
[37] *Panoplist*, July 22, 1805, p. 408.
[38] Gideon Blackburn to Return J. Meigs, November 4, 1807, M-208; for a general picture of Blackburn's missionary work see Dorothy C. Bass, "Gideon Blackburn's Mission to the Cherokee Indians," *Journal of Presbyterian History* 52 (1974):203–226.

plans interfered with the selfish designs of Vann and his party that he lost his life."[39]

Meigs was far more interested in the effort of the council to deal with the request of the upper part of the Upper Towns to divide the nation; such a division would make it easier for the Lower Towns to remove and exchange their part of the nation for land in Arkansas. But the council decided not to vote on this matter until after further consultation with Jefferson about its ramifications. This decision allowed Meigs to combine the delegation he had planned to take from the Lower Towns to see Jefferson about removal with a delegation from the Upper Towns to consult about a division line. He hoped to play them off against each other and ultimately to persuade the whole nation to remove to Arkansas.

Meigs did not attend the council, but he sent a message that played upon Cherokee discontents in the east and the rosy future waiting in the west. "You have your choice to stay here and become industrious, like white people, so that the women and children shall not cry any more for bread, or go over the Mississippi, where meat is plenty and where corn may be raised as well as here." "Your Father, the President" wanted what was best for them, but in the East that would be difficult. This was why from time to time "your people Straggle one or two at a time" to the West "or in small parties." If they wanted to go west, they should "go in large parties" and get something in exchange for what they leave. He appealed to their national pride on this score:

Brothers, it is well known everywhere that the Cherokees stand on the highest ground of reputation as a Nation of Red men. The Cherokees have more knowledge as farmers, as manufacturers, and have more knowledge of literature than any nation of Red men in America, I may safely say, than all the Red men in America put together. . . . You have more money, more cattle, more horses, more and better cloathing than any other nation of Red men of equal numbers in America . . . I wish to excite in yourselves a just pride, that is, to have you value yourselves as *Cherokees*; the word "Cherokee" or "Cherokees" should always convey an Idea of Respectability to your people.

But the only way to retain this respectability, he said, was to hold together as a people. The departure of small groups of disgruntled Cherokees was whittling away their strength and unity. "Let them go in large parties" to the West and "let some Respectable Chiefs go with them to keep up good order, that they may be everywhere esteemed as respectable people." Removal was the best way to preserve the nation and to slow

---

[39] Gideon Blackburn to Return J. Meigs, November 7, 1807, M-221, reel 4, #1144.

down the uncomfortable pace of change that living in the East was forcing upon them.[40]

Meigs did not expect the Broomstown council to make a final decision about removal; he wanted the chiefs to authorize a delegation to go to Washington to consult with the President about it. The council did do this, and it chose three chiefs from the Upper Towns (The Ridge, John Walker, and John McIntosh, whose Cherokee name was Quotaquskee) and three from the Lower Towns (Toochelar, Skiuka, and The Seed). Walker and McIntosh (Quotaquskee) were intermarried whites; Ridge was a mixed blood who spoke no English; the rest were full bloods. There was considerable debate over how much authority to give these delegates and how to instruct them. The Lower Towns, following their secret caucus, were determined to pursue the issue of exchange and removal (at least for their part of the nation) and gave their representatives full power to negotiate for them. The Upper Towns seem to have been concerned mostly with exploring the significance of Stone Carrier's proposal about dividing the nation and moving toward citizenship but gave its representatives no power to negotiate. Meigs covered the general confusion by stating that the official purpose of the visit to Washington was to say farewell to Jefferson and to thank him for his help over the preceding eight years. Yet he wrote privately to Dearborn on November 15 that he and the delegates were on their way to Washington "to converse with him on the subject of an exchange of Country."[41] He also said, though on what evidence is not clear, that "more than one half [of the Nation] are in favor of going over the Mississippi." The council had taken no vote on this. Meigs apparently wanted to prejudice Dearborn and Jefferson in favor of his friends in the Lower Towns. He had already appointed an exploration party of Lower Town chiefs to go west; his purpose in coming to Washington was to find out "on what part of the Country [in Arkansas] the U.S. would chuse to place them" if an exchange took place.

At the conclusion of the Broomstown council, The Glass wrote a personal letter to Jefferson expressing the position of the Lower Towns: "Our people expect that Exchange of Land will take place with the United States." He went on, in the style of Doublehead, to say that if a treaty of exchange took place in Washington, he wished to have a reserve set aside for himself and 'likewise one Ileland at the mussel shoals" as a reward for his cooperation; these he would sell after the cession.[42]

Somehow the Upper Town chiefs got wind of what Meigs and Glass were up to; shortly after the delegation had started for Washington on

[40] Return J. Meigs to the Cherokee Council at Broomstown, August 29, 1808, M-208.
[41] Return J. Meigs to Henry Dearborn, November 15, 1808, M-221, reel 27, #8971.
[42] The Glass to Henry Dearborn, November 2, 1808, M-222, reel 3, #1206.

November 15, 1808, they hastily called a council at Hiwassee Town.[43] Chiefs from various parts of the nation were present and accusations were hurled back and forth with considerable passion. The majority then voted to depose (or "break") the Principal Chief, Black Fox, for his part in the secret instructions to the Lower Town delegates; they also deposed three other Lower Town chiefs—Tolluntuskee, The Glass, and John D. Chisholm—from their places as old or principal chiefs. They chose Pathkiller as the new Principal Chief and also chose two additional delegates to represent the nation, John Rogers (a countryman) and Thomas Wilson (a nephew of Charles Hicks who had been educated among the whites). These two were instructed to take fast horses and try to catch up to the delegation before it reached Washington. They carried letters from Pathkiller appointing them as official delegates, thereby giving preponderance in the delegation to the Upper Towns. To satisfy the Lower Towns, the council also sent Cabbin Smith (Big Cabbin) as an additional delegate to speak for his region, though he seems to have been cool toward removal. Vann and the insurgents were certain that Meigs and his Lower Town friends would attempt to make an agreement in Washington for an exchange of land in Arkansas that would leave the Upper Towns little choice but to follow them westward or become United States citizens in the east. If the effort succeeded, there would soon be no Cherokee Nation east of the Mississippi.

[43] W. S. Lovely in a letter to Meigs, November 23, 1808, says this "rump" council met on November 22 (M-222, reel 3, #1314). For a general discussion of this removal effort see McLoughlin, "Thomas Jefferson and the Beginning of Cherokee Nationalism."

SEVEN

THE FIRST STEP TOWARD
NATIONALISM, 1808–1810

*It has now been a long time that we have been much confused and di-
vided in our opinions, but now we have settled our affairs to the satisfaction of both parties and become as one. You will now hear from us
not from the lower towns nor the upper towns but from the whole
Cherokee Nation. —Cherokee council to Return J. Meigs, September
27, 1809*

The three new delegates caught up with Meigs and his party just before they reached Washington, D.C., but Meigs's assistant agent,
Major Lovely, had sent a message by an even faster rider to warn Meigs
of what had happened. Lovely's account was designed to throw doubt on
the validity of the Hiwassee council and thereby allow Meigs to ignore
the new delegates and proceed with his original plan, excluding them
from the negotiations. Lovely heaped sarcasm on the entire proceedings
of November 22, 1808: "I hope this may meet you in time and previous
to the arrival of John Rogers, appointed Ambassador Extraordinary from
the Cherokee Nation to the Government of the United States; it appears
from the information of his friends that he goes by order of the now great
Chief, the Path Killer, Damn his brains, that he could not foresee the consequences that would result by sending one of the greatest Rascalls they
ever cherished amongst them."[1]

Lovely went on to describe Rogers as "a Villain" who was "guilty of
every crime that human nature can be guilty of." Rogers had been a Tory
in 1776, "one of Mr. [Simon] Girts Corps of cut-throats in the State of
Georgia during the revolutionary War." (Lovely had fought on the patriot side with Morgan's Raiders in Virginia.) After the war Rogers fled
to the Creeks and then to the Cherokees where, according to Lovely, he
had engaged in cattle stealing in 1798–1799. As for Thomas Wilson,
"that disafected, owl-looking fellow," Lovely said he was "taken to Philadelphia by Dinsmore and received a tolerable education at a Quaker
school" when he was "a poor, half-starved, ill-looking bouger." Wilson

---

[1] W. S. Lovely to Return J. Meigs, November 23, 1808, M-222, reel 3, #1314.

was "Nephew to Charly [Hicks]" and had "partaken of his mixture of the most poisonous stuff" against Meigs. Lovely concluded by reminding Meigs that Rogers had participated in the assassination of Doublehead and that the new delegates were part of the "deceitful conspiracy" of Vann and Hicks against the United States government and the old chiefs.

Meanwhile the Lower Town chiefs met in a hasty council on November 26 and sent their own messengers after Meigs with a letter to Jefferson giving their view of what had occurred on November 22. Fifteen Lower Town chiefs, led by The Glass, Dick Justice, Turtle at Home, Parched Corn Flour, and John Boggs, signed the account:

It is only 4 days since the upper Division of the Nation met in Council and had very contrary talks and very distant from our wishes; they there [Hiwassee] with a usurped authority, attempted to stop the mouths of four of our old and beloved chiefs and leaders.

The Lower Town chiefs refused to acknowledge the authority of that council and said they still adhered to Black Fox and the other deposed old Chiefs: "They are true friends to you and your Government. These men had done nothing that could be laid to their charge except holding fast to our father the President['s] and Government['s] advice and wishing the true happiness of the Nation and the Interest of the United States." These chiefs claimed to represent "13 Towns composing nearly one half of the Cherokee Nation" in their population, "and taking into view our people that are already crossed the Mississippi, we are a majority." (There are no statistics that support this claim.) Their letter said they were still in favor of "Removing" and wanted to know whether the land they would be given in Arkansas was "the property of the United States" or outside its boundaries, for they wished to remain under the protection of the United States. After expressing their continued confidence in Meigs, they asked the President to pay each of their three delegates $120 for his services and to pay Samuel Riley, who would serve as interpreter in Washington, $1,000 "which the nation owes him" as a trader. The three original Lower Town delegates added their signatures later and presented it to Jefferson after they reached Washington.[2]

Tolluntuskee, angry over his impeachment, sent his own note to the President, explaining, "I have tried to make our people sensible of our own good but they would not listen" (an indication that the Lower Towns represented a minority position). "I and my party are determined to cross

[2] "Headmen of the River Division of the Cherokee Nation" to Thomas Jefferson, no date (probably November 26, 1808), M-222, reel 3, #1157.

the river towards the West. Our bad brothers may dispute, but with me 12 towns go."[3]

Lovely's message caught up with Meigs in Alexandria, Virginia, and on December 13, Meigs sent Riley ahead with a note to warn Dearborn about the newly appointed delegates who would try to participate in the discussions. He told Dearborn that the new delegates were not properly authorized and represented only the dissident faction: "Vann and Hicks having a jealousy that these that were regularly appointed would not transact the business agreeably to their factious views." To permit the "infamous" Rogers to participate would have "a pernicious effect and strengthen the factious party under Vann who are only supported by threats of assassination against those who are friendly to the Government."[4] Meigs wanted no interference in the plan he had worked on for so long.

Dearborn and Jefferson accepted Meigs's negative assessment of the Hiwassee council; the extra delegates took no official part in the deliberations that followed. They did, however, stay at the same hotel as the other delegates and they did participate in informal discussions with them. They signed some of the memoranda to Jefferson from the delegates, but someone, evidently Meigs, crossed off their names. Meigs carefully managed the entire transaction and arranged for the Lower Town delegates to meet separately with Dearborn to present their removal proposals without the knowledge of the Upper Town delegates. When the Upper Town delegates discovered this and realized that if they acquiesced in any division of the nation according to Stone Carrier's plan they would simply facilitate the removal plans that Meigs and the Lower Towns were negotiating, they protested vigorously. Their effort to argue that Black Fox had been deposed and that Pathkiller and the Hiwassee council represented the official view of the nation in opposition to removal was rebutted by Meigs. Meigs believed that if the Lower Towns wished to negotiate a removal in return for an exchange of their part of the nation, they had a perfect right to do so. He argued that the Broomstown council had in effect agreed to a division of the nation when it sent two sets of delegates to discuss their problems with Jefferson. Dearborn was willing to accept Meigs's version; Jefferson was more cautious. The Upper Town delegates told Jefferson: "We did not think that we were bringing the talks of our old chief that we have dismissed. We thought we were bringing the talks of our beloved man, the Path Killer, our present principle Chief and the talk of 42 towns that are also of his mind." The

---

[3] Turtle at Home, Tolluntuskee, and The Glass to Thomas Jefferson, November 25, 1808, M-222, reel 3, #1151.
[4] Return J. Meigs to Henry Dearborn, December 13, 1808, M-222, reel 3, #1306.

decision of the Hiwassee council on November 22, these delegates said, was "to hold fast to our country" and "to hold our country as far as the present boundary lines between us, the Cherokees and the whites." They were now opposed to Stone Carrier's plan to divide the nation in two because this would play into Meigs's hands. They explained to the President that the Hiwassee council was justified in deposing Black Fox and sending new delegates because they had only recently discovered that the Lower Towns "had already made up their minds to move us out of our houses [and off to Arkansas] before we knew anything of it."[5]

The Upper Town delegates admitted that at Broomstown there was a general feeling that separation of the two regions might be useful, but the council favored this only because the Upper Towns considered the Lower Towns to be backward, lazy, and opposed to new laws to improve social order. The old chiefs were against the civilization policy; "very few of the old chiefs has given their children learning" in the mission schools. Most of the old chiefs had opposed the laws institutionalizing the lighthorse regulators. Their children grew up unfit "for any business . . . they want clothing . . . they will steal horses to get them instead of working for them." The Upper Town delegates portrayed the Lower Towns as the most backward part of the nation. As for a dividing line between the Upper and Lower Towns, they were willing to discuss it, but if it were made, it "would be made for no other purpose than to suppress theft and secure our land and keep our chiefs from selling our land."[6] It would not be designed to facilitate removal and exchange of the Lower Town region.

Five days later the Lower Towns, through Toochelar, gave Jefferson their version of why they were there: "My part of the Nation, the Lower towns, is deturm[in]ed to move over the missippa if they like the Cuntry when they exploar it, pervided there father will assist them in their persute." They asked Jefferson to provide them with "Boates to move in" and "Good guns to kill meet to liv on and to Gard our wimmen and Children" from other tribes. They wanted him to put these matters "on paper that we may Carrey it home for our peopel to hear." In short, they wanted a detailed working agreement to emerge from their talk with Jefferson.[7]

The Upper Town delegates said that removal was contrary to all that they had heard for years from the President and their agent. "Your advise has Been to us to lay by our guns and go to farming. Git hoes, plowes and axes. The young peopel [young chiefs] holds your talk fast respecting

[5] The Ridge, John Walker, and John McIntosh to Henry Dearborn, Parker Papers, box 2, Pennsylvania Historical Society, Philadelphia.

[6] Ibid.

[7] Toochalee [Toochelar] to Thomas Jefferson, Parker Papers, box 2.

farming and Industrey"; the old chiefs were fickle, "they throw away the plow and pick up the Gun and also throw away the wimmen's Spining wheles." Jefferson should take no action on removal or division of the nation at this time. These questions "we Leave to be Settled between our present prinsable Cheef [Pathkiller] and our father the President" at some later time.[8]

Jefferson found himself in a quandary. There was no simple way to reconcile the desires of the two sets of delegates nor to negotiate anything resembling a treaty. After two weeks of further discussion he said good-bye to them on January 9, 1809, giving two farewell messages—one to the combined delegation and one to the Upper Town group. He told the former that if the Lower Towns wished to remove across the Mississippi, he would approve of "an exploring party" to find a tract "not claimed by other Indians." When they found a good location, the government "will arrange with them and you the exchange of that for a just portion of the country they leave and to a part of which, proportioned to their numbers, they have a right." To this extent Jefferson was acknowledging in principle the right of exchange and removal by a section of the nation. But to the Upper Towns the essential point in his message was that any such exchange would be arranged later "with them and you" (i.e., those who would emigrate and those who would not)—presumably in a national council. The Lower Towns, however, took the essence of Jefferson's message to be his promise to give "every aid towards their removal" and to provide them with a trading factory and agency once they got settled in the west (i.e., whether the Upper Towns wished to emigrate or not).

The most astonishing thing in what Jefferson said was his claim that every emigrant to the west was entitled to take with him "a just portion of the country they leave." If that were literally true, then the one thousand Cherokees already in the West should be able to negotiate an exchange of their portion of the old nation in the east. It would mean that the land of the Cherokee Nation was in effect already apportioned among its twelve thousand inhabitants and that whenever anyone left, he or she diminished the existing boundaries by his or her "just portion." It left the nation like a barrel with a hole in the bottom constantly leaking people and land. If this were implemented, the national domain would steadily be eroded; it could never hope for any stability or order. Jefferson probably only had in mind a large and concerted migration that would take place at one time by a general agreement with the Cherokee Nation. Meigs, however, had a very different view of the matter and so, it turned

[8] The Ridge et al. to Thomas Jefferson, Parker Papers, box 2.

out, did future Presidents and Secretaries of War. Jefferson's message was to have far-reaching consequences in future years.

In his separate farewell to the Upper Towns, Jefferson was equally vague about the proposed line of division. He said he could not work this out except "on the joint consent of both parties." If a divisional line were worked out, Jefferson suggested that the Upper Towns than hold a kind of constitutional convention in which representatives from each town in the Upper Town region would divide the land in severalty and draw up a set of laws designed to prepare the Cherokees for future citizenship. What would happen to the land not assigned to any particular family he did not say.[9]

The delegates returned to the nation in June 1809, each with his own interpretation of what had happened. Meigs was sure that an agreement tantamount to a treaty had been reached—"an agreement to exchange land here for lands on the Arkansas and White Rivers," as he put it.[10] He was surprised to find that not all of those in the Lower Towns were now certain they wanted to emigrate. Nevertheless he continued to make plans as though most of them would eventually go.

The Upper Towns received a shock when James Vann was mysteriously shot to death on February 9, 1809, at Buffington's Tavern on the Georgia Road. Vann had been out with the lighthorse regulators for a week or more, catching and punishing horse thieves in his district. His punishments had been so severe that some of his men had remonstrated with him. Vann never took criticism well; he insulted and humiliated George Sanders, one of his men, for such a rebuke. It was rumored that Sanders had shot Vann from behind a tree as he stood in the tavern door at night, his back to the light. No one saw the killer and few seemed to care.[11] Despite all he had done to expose the unfair behavior of Meigs, Doublehead, Harris, and others, Vann had never been a popular leader and had many enemies. In 1806 he had killed his sister's husband, John Falling, in a duel over stolen money and the ownership of a slave.[12] He seems to have been reckless, a man grown rich and cynical and tired of living, but neverthe-

---

[9] For Jefferson's messages to the Cherokee delegation in January 1809 see M-15, reel 2, #0414–0416.

[10] Return J. Meigs to William Eustis, August 7, 1809, M-222, reel 4, #1574.

[11] John Gambold to Benzien, February 23, 1809, Moravian Archives, Winston-Salem, North Carolina (hereafter abbreviated as MAS). For a sketch of Vann's life see William G. McLoughlin, *The Cherokee Ghost Dance and Other Essays on the Southeastern Indians* (Macon, Ga: Mercer University Press, 1984), chap. 2.

[12] John Gambold to Benzien, May 30, 1806, MAS. See also Nicholas Byers to Return J. Meigs, May 24, 1806, M-208, and Return J. Meigs to Valentine Geiger, June 6, 1806, M-208.

less a critically important figure at this turning point in the Cherokee renascence.

In March 1809, a month after Vann's death, Meigs received a letter from John Chisholm at Muscle Shoals: "I am preparing to move over the massisipi this summer," he wrote; "all the Indians are preparing in this qarter for the same purpas."[13] Chisholm may have been waiting for some action by a council to ratify removal, for in reply Meigs told him that "the exchange does not depend on the consent of the nation because emigration cannot be restrained. Individuals will go where they please." He also noted that the mass migration being planned required that the Lower Towns "relinquish to the United States land here in quantum proportion to the number they carry over that river, having regard to the whole number of the Cherokee Nation." Carried out literally, this meant that for every Cherokee who emigrated, the land of the eastern part of the nation would be reduced by roughly 1,250 acres; if an average Cherokee family included five persons, then 6,000 acres was to be relinquished or exchanged for every family that went west. Meigs also told Chisholm that "Tollonteskee [Tolluntuskee] says he does not want to explore" in the west "because he has already the necessary information and that he will take over a large number of people" very soon. Evidently the idea of an advance party was given up because the Cherokees who wished to emigrate would simply join those already established four hundred miles up the Arkansas River, near Dardanelles Rock. Meigs hoped that the groups led by Tolluntuskee, Chisholm, and other chiefs from their respective towns would go together in one large body. "The President will, when the migration [date] is determined, give all the facility and aid that may be necessary to carry that establishment into effect."[14]

Tolluntuskee and ten other chiefs came to Meigs on July 20 to say that they had engaged 386 men and 637 women to emigrate with them. Shortly afterward, another 107 names were added to the list.[15] By August 17 Meigs believed it was time for the government to make good on its promises to provide boats, guns, and other necessary aids to those ready to remove to Arkansas. Jefferson had now been succeeded by James Madison and Dearborn by William Eustis; Meigs wrote to Eustis explaining the previous winter's talks with Jefferson and Dearborn. Removal and exchange had been "a subject of negotiation with the President," he said, and "the result was an agreement to exchange lands here for lands on the

[13] John Chisholm to Return J. Meigs, March 18, 1809, M-208.

[14] Return J. Meigs to John Chisholm, March 28, 1809, M-208.

[15] Return J. Meigs to William Eustis, September 16, 1809, M-208. See also Return J. Meigs to Cherokee Council, November 2, 1809, M-208.

Arkansas and White Rivers."[16] Acting on his assurances of government help, he told Eustis, many chiefs had gathered their people together and now "they expect the aid of Government" for their five-hundred-mile journey down the Tennessee, down the Ohio, down the Mississippi, and then up the Arkansas River to Dardanelles Rock. No tract had yet been surveyed for them there because it was not yet known how many would go and how large a tract they would be entitled to. However, Meigs wanted to get the boats, guns, and supplies ready. They were "preparing to move as soon as their crops shall be gathered in." He assured Eustis that "the disposition is so strong for moving that it seems to require the attention of the Government to give it direction and order, or positively to discountenance and repress it." Believing the latter out of the question, he went on to suggest the kind of assistance that the government should now make available: a keel-bottom boat, 200 rifles, 400 lbs. of powder, 800 lbs. of lead, 1,000 flints, 200 beaver traps, 100 axes, 100 corn hoes, 50 grubbing hoes, 200 pairs cotton cards, 50 wool cards, 50 small plows. He estimated the total cost to be $4,100.

To make this expense palatable, Meigs calculated how much land the United States would obtain in the east. There were about twelve thousand Cherokees, and they owned about fifteen million acres; therefore "each man, woman and child are entitled to 1250 acres" in the west. He estimated that there would be "2000 emigrants before next spring" and this "will entitle the United States to 2.5 million acres" from the Cherokee homeland. But this was only the beginning. Once the government had demonstrated its full support of emigration, once thousands had gone ahead and started new settlements between the Arkansas and White rivers, Meigs expected another two thousand emigrants to leave "within two years," and thus another 2.5 million acres would be deducted from the Cherokee homeland for the expanding white populations of Tennessee, Georgia, North Carolina, and what would become Alabama.[17] Ultimately, Meigs was convinced, all the Cherokees would go west.

But while Meigs was doing all he could do stimulate removal, the dissident chiefs were doing all they could to prevent it. This they planned to accomplish by restoring harmony within the nation and reconciling the divisions among themselves. In July 1809, representatives from thirty Upper Towns had met in council at Ustanali and "unanimously" rejected Stone Carrier's plan to divide the nation.[18] The council also wrote to

[16] Return J. Meigs to William Eustis, August 17, 1809, M-222, reel 4, #1574.
[17] Ibid.
[18] Cherokee Council to Return J. Meigs, June 30, 1818, M-221, reel 79, #0060. This retrospective account speaks of a council of "thirty Towns" in July 1809, but a contemporary

Meigs, reminding him that in Washington their delegates had told Jefferson "that the path killer and 42 towns held to their country" and did not want it divided in any way. They also reminded him that "our father told us that our whole nation would be present in the sales of our lands." They expected some kind of deliberation by a national council before any emigration or any exchange of land was formalized. The letter was signed by The Ridge, Oosooke, Kelachulee, and Katahee. Meigs, of course, did not want any such council to take place for fear that the majority would oppose removal; he therefore ignored the letter and continued his plans.

As rumors spread throughout the white frontier that the Cherokees were moving west and that Tennessee and Georgia would soon obtain millions of acres of their land, thousands of whites began to move onto the Cherokee land in Tennessee and Georgia, expecting to squat there and establish preemption rights.[19] Meigs received numerous complaints from chiefs all over the nation during 1809–1810 about these intruders. On two occasions he sent out United States troops to drive them off, but his attitude was ambivalent. At one point in 1809 he described the intruders to the Secretary of War as shiftless desperadoes who were imposing on the government for selfish and dishonest ends:

Should this disposition to make intrusions on Indian land increase, they will perhaps at last put the few troops here at defiance. These intruders are always well armed, some of them shrewd and desperate characters, having nothing to lose and hold barbarous sentiments towards Indians. . . . With these people remonstrance has no effect; nothing but force can prevent their violation of Indian rights.[20]

On another occasion that same year, he painted a different picture for General James Robertson, a Tennessee land speculator and political leader:

I removed 201 families off the Chickasaw lands and 83 off the Cherokee lands—not less than 1700 or 1800 souls. These people bear the appelation of intruders, but they are Americans—our riches and our strength are derived from our Citizens; in our new country every man is an acquisition. We ought not to lose a single man for want of land to work on. A disposition to migrate seems to pervade the whole Eastern part of the U. States. It acts as uniformly as the laws of gravi-

---

letter from The Ridge and other chiefs to Meigs, speaks of a council of fifteen towns; see August 2, 1809, M-208.

[19] Return J. Meigs to William Eustis, October 26, 1809, M-208. There are dozens of letters in Meigs's files regarding intruders on Cherokee lands and the fruitless efforts to drive them off. See, e.g., John Strothers to Return J. Meigs, November 16, 1809; Turtle at Home to Return J. Meigs, October 1, 1809; Return J. Meigs to William Eustis, April 13, 1810. All in M-208.

[20] Return J. Meigs to William Eustis, October 26, 1809, M-208.

tation and can no more be restrained untill the shores of the pacific ocean make it impossible to go farther.[21]

As always, the efforts of the troops against the intruders were useless. Turtle at Home wrote to Meigs on October 1, 1809, thanking him for sending soldiers to remove squatters near his town of Nickajack, Tennessee, yet remarking sadly: "Since the spring that you was down here to drive off the white people who had settled on our lands, they have returned as thick as ever, the same as crows that are startled from their food by a person passing on the road, but as soon as he is passed, they return again. . . . It is very unpleasant to see our lands occupied in this manner."[22]

Meigs was caught between many demands. The state politicians wanted him to go easy on the intruders; he himself knew that the aggravations they caused the Cherokees was a goad to land cessions and emigration. On the other hand, he had to persuade the Cherokees that he was attentive to their rights and to protect the honor of the government so that the Cherokees did not make too many complaints. Generally he erred on the side of lenience toward the squatters because he thought the Cherokees had more land than they needed and acted toward it like dogs in the manger. He would instruct the troops, for example, that they should not force the intruders off their land until they had had time to harvest their crops. General Wade Hampton regarded such orders as counterproductive: "His lenity can but lead to new aggressions."[23]

In 1809 Meigs had good reasons for avoiding trouble with squatters who might in turn complain to their political leaders. He wanted the frontier politicians to help him put pressure on Madison and Eustis for removal. Writing to James Trimble, a prominent Tennessee lawyer, in September 1809, Meigs predicted that "if the United States would be at the expense of thirty, forty or fifty thousand dollars to encourage a migration over the Mississippi" it was probable that "one half at least of the Cherokees would remove to that Country, perhaps nearly all." "What would one hundred thousand dollars be considered [in order] to bring about an exchange of fifteen millions of acres of land and giving us a boundary to near to mobile bay." To effect this end, westerners must lobby the President and Congress. "Now, sir, would it not be strength-

---

[21] Return J. Meigs to James Robertson, Robertson Papers, Tennessee State Archives. In June 1810, Meigs had a map on which he had located over 1,000 intruders on Cherokee land; see Return J. Meigs to William Eustis, June 27, 1810, M-208. For a good general account of the intruder problem see Prucha, *American Indian Policy*, chap. 7.

[22] Turtle at Home to Return J. Meigs, October 1, 1809, M-208.

[23] General Wade Hampton to William Eustis, November 22, 1809, M-221, reel 23, #7673.

ening the hands of the President if your legislature should address him on a subject so interesting to your State and to the United States also?" He would not, Meigs said, urge removal of the Cherokees if he were not convinced that it is in "the interest of the Cherokees" as well; "a gradual but certain extinction" would be theirs if they remained where they were, surrounded "by intelligent and some mischievously cunning people who still keep alive ancient prejudices" and who regularly intruded upon and harassed them. Trimble took the hint and carried the message to Governor Willie Blount, who in turn took it to the legislature. It passed a resolution urging support of removal of the Cherokees and sent it to the President.[24]

Meigs's persistent efforts to promote removal seem to have caused many Cherokees to side with the Upper Towns to save their homeland. At a critical national council at Willstown in September 1809, attended by many chiefs from the Lower and Upper Towns, two important steps were taken toward restoring tribal harmony. First, the council agreed to give no support to the exchange and removal plan, and second, it agreed to restore Black Fox and The Glass to positions as Principal Chiefs. This council wrote Meigs to tell him that the major part of the nation, after many years of division, had finally concluded that their survival depended upon obliterating the old division of Upper and Lower Towns, each with their own regional councils, each with their own self-interests: "It has now been a long time that we have been much confused and divided in our opinions, but now we have settled our affair[s] to the satisfaction of both parties and become as one. You will now hear from us not from the lower towns nor the upper towns but from the whole Cherokee nation."[25]

To show that they were in earnest, this council voted to significantly restructure their governing system. They had suffered much from the cumbersome process of calling ad hoc councils. Councils were now meeting six to eight times a year in various parts of the nation, sometimes even more frequently. Not only did they consume a great deal of time, but attendance fluctuated. Some were regional, some claimed to be national, some were dominated by one faction or another. More important, they were easy for Meigs to manipulate when he wanted something and easy for him to ignore as unrepresentative when he did not like their decisions. The system had no order or direction. To solve this, the Wills-

[24] Return J. Meigs to James Trimble, September 21, 1809, M-221, reel 34, #1751–1752, and Acts of the Tennessee Legislature with respect to Cherokee lands, M-221, reel 34, #1746–1748.
[25] Result of a Council at Willstown, Path Killer and other chiefs to Return J. Meigs, September 27, 1809, M-208; for Meigs's response see Meigs to the Council at Willistown, November 2, 1809, M-208.

town council created "the National Committee," an executive committee composed of thirteen representative and experienced chiefs who had the respect of the nation. Slowly a consensus for patriotic unity and maintenance of the homeland was emerging, contrary to the efforts of the federal government. The role of the newly formed National Committee was to guide the nation between national councils, perform its minor administrative tasks, manage its treasury, deal with the agent on a day-to-day basis, and, when necessary, to call a national council to deal with emergency issues. It went a step beyond the proposal sent by James Vann to the United States Senate in 1806. All the actions of the National Committee were to be subject to ratification at the annual meeting of the National Council in September or October, but the important point was that there was now a permanent, representative authority responsible and available at all times to oversee the general welfare. If this plan worked, it would no longer be possible for the agent to maneuver behind the scenes with a few favored chiefs or to select those whom he considered "well-disposed toward government" when he wanted a treaty line adjusted or needed advance persuasion for a land cession. Hereafter only one group, whose actions were subject to review, was authorized to act for the nation. "We have this day [September 27, 1809] appointed thirteen men to manage our national affairs," the council told Meigs, "for we found it to be very troublesome to bring anything to bear where there were as many as we formally [formerly] had in our council." From this it appears that the National Committee was also to refine and focus issues for debate in the annual Council, to set policies and priorities, and to settle, on its own initiative, certain minor issues (subject to appeal) that took up a great deal of the Council's time (such as personal disputes and business matters).

Those appointed to the first National Committee included prominent leaders among the old chiefs, like John Lowrey, Turtle at Home, and Richard Brown, and important members of the insurgent party, like The Ridge, Charles Hicks, John McIntosh, and John Walker. Other members included George M. Waters (Dreadful Water), Thomas Pettit, George Lowrey (son of John Lowrey), Tuscock, and Sower John (Sour Mush). The reinstatement of Black Fox as Principal Chief returned Pathkiller to Second Principal Chief, so that one leader from each faction held the top posts. Toochelar seems to have agreed to support reunion rather than removal and became Speaker for the nation.

This important council also informed Meigs that it rejected his interpretation of the so-called "agreement" with Jefferson. "Concerning the people that want to move over the Mississippi, we have read and understood the late president's speech, and we understand by it that nothing could be done [toward removal, exchange, or division of the nation in any way] without a national council and by the majority of the nation." At the beginning of this council, a message from Meigs had been read in which he said that Tolluntuskee and other chiefs were about to depart with 1,130 persons for Arkansas. He had enclosed a copy of his letter to Eustis requesting boats, guns, and other supplies for them, no doubt to encourage others to join the group. "We have read the copy of the letter you sent to the Secretary of War," the council said; "you ought not to have wrote so soon on that subject, for it never was brought before a national council." As far as the nation was concerned, Meigs was acting unlawfully.[26] This was signed by Pathkiller, Chulio, The Glass, Dick Justice, Toochelar, Sower (Sour) Mush, Big Half Breed, Keuchesteasky, "and the rest of the Chiefs." The list reveals a remarkable shift in opinion among many of the old chiefs of the Lower Towns and also indicated a conciliatory attitude on the part of the rebels who had so recently had such angry feelings toward the others.

A few weeks later, a group of the chiefs of the reunited nation wrote to Meigs and asked him to put a stop to a new kind of illegal action that stemmed from his interpretation that every emigrant carried with him as his birthright a certain amount of Cherokee land. This letter noted that Richard Fields and others who had enrolled to emigrate had concluded that they had the right to dispose of the farms and plantations they lived on in the Cherokee Nation to white men, as though their farms were their private property. The Ridge, James Foster, Katehee, Kilachulee, Dreadful Water, James Brown, Bushyhead, and Suakee (apparently acting for the National Committee) told Meigs that such acts must be stopped: Tell "your people that sd. Rich'd Fields is not empowered to sell or alienate any Place whatever to any of your people." Emigrants had no right to sell tribal land to whites when they moved west; all the land in the nation belonged to the nation.[27]

In his reply to the resolutions of the Willstown council, Meigs equivocated, not sure what the new political system would mean for his work and plans. He expressed pleasure at the new unity of the nation and said he knew very well all but two of the thirteen chiefs who had been appointed to the National Committee "to transact your national business" and thought well of them. But regarding the views of the council on "the exchange of lands," he demurred. He questioned its right to undermine or stop the removal process he had inaugurated. He tried to argue that a large-scale emigration was superior to the old practice of permitting

[26] Path Killer et al. to Return J. Meigs, September 27, 1809, M-208.
[27] The Ridge and other chiefs to Return J. Meigs, October 23, 1809, M-208.

Cherokee families to straggle west at will without any authorized place to settle. "It is now plainly time that something should be done to regulate these movements or discourage them."[28] Tolluntuskee had heeded Jefferson's wise offer and had gathered a large party to go west under able chiefs. Jefferson had agreed to provide them with a tract of land they could call their own in Arkansas. "National pride," Meigs told the Cherokee chiefs on November 2, required that Cherokee people should not be left to wander around homeless in the West subject to attack by other tribes. "If the exchange is made, it will be in proportion to the number who make the choice and they will be on Cherokee lands" in Arkansas with fixed boundaries guaranteed to them by the federal government, whose care and protection they would be under.

Meigs was trying to make it clear that short of violence, there was no way the new National Council could prevent mass emigration. But if voluntary emigration could not be prevented, the Council believed that it had the right to prevent any land being taken from its eastern territory in order to provide a space for those who emigrated. The Council insisted that under the terms of Jefferson's message in January 1809, any decision regarding exchange of land rested with a council made up jointly of the prospective emigrants and those who remained. Such a council would decide whether and how a division of land should take place for an exchange. Neither Meigs nor the emigrants shared this interpretation, however, and therefore no productive discussion of the problem between the two groups was likely.

Tolluntuskee and his party harvested their crops in October and waited for the boats and supplies Meigs had promised. The Bowl, Saulowee, and other chiefs gradually assembled their parties. But November and December passed without any word from the War Department. People were becoming impatient, and finally Meigs decided that he would have to risk acting on his own initiative. In January 1810 he wrote to Eustis, saying that since he had heard nothing from him, "I furnished this party with provisions" out of agency funds and sent them off lest they conclude that the government wanted "to discourage the migration."[29] The first contingent of emigrants left on January 14, 1810, consisting of sixty-three men, women, and children led by Saulowee and The Bowl. They traveled in twelve canoes and a flatboat; their cattle and horses were sent on ahead with twelve drivers. Meigs noted that this group did not come from the Lower Towns. Saulowee was from Tellico on the Little Tennessee River, an area greatly troubled by intruders.

[28] Return J. Meigs to Council at Willstown, November 2, 1809, M-208.
[29] Return J. Meigs to William Eustis, January 22, 1810, M-221, reel 38, #5071; Return J. Meigs to William Eustis, January 10 and 22, 1810, M-208.

A few days after this, "a large party" of about one hundred left. They came "from two Towns situated about 100 miles below this place" near Muscle Shoals; this contingent was probably led by John Chisholm. About February 26, "Tolluntuskee left this place [Hiwassee] with a considerable party [including] wives and chidren."[30] Meigs had done his best to outfit all three groups, but he had only limited funds and supplies at the agency and factory. He feared that some "improper means would be used" by the opponents of removal to prevent these emigrations, but although the members of the National Committee had come to Hiwassee to watch Tolluntuskee's group leave, Meigs did not see them "use any arguments to dissuade the emigration."[31]

While at Hiwassee, the National Committee told Meigs that they had been given authority to take charge of the nation's annuity and wished to have it provided in specie rather than in trade goods. They probably wanted to make sure that none of it was deducted to pay for the costs of the removal. They also inquired whether the President would continue to supply farm implements and spinning wheels for those who were not migrating. When Meigs wrote Eustis about this, he replied that the President had approved a grant of $450 for farming utensils and also money for the mission schools.[32]

All of this worried Meigs. Not only had the people in the Lower Towns failed to respond as heartily to his removal plan as he predicted but also the new administration seemed reluctant to provide the support he expected. Now Madison said he would continue the gifts of farm tools; the Cherokees could only take that to mean that the new President intended to follow the old policy of helping them to become "civilized" where they were. Meigs wrote to Eustis suggesting that the gifts for economic improvement be "discontinued."[33]

When the reunited National Council met at Ustanali in April 1810, it was determined to act as though the Cherokees and not Meigs had won the battle of removal and exchange. Its first action was to demonstrate its solidarity by adding a number of "beloved old warriors" from the Lower and Upper Towns to the National Committee. These were The Glass, The Seed, John McLemore, The Duck, Sour Mush, Bark, Bark of Chota, Big Half Breed, Katahee, George Parris, The Chip, John Bogg, Parched Corn Flour, Opchata, Nettle Carrier, and Big Cabbin.[34]

[30] Return J. Meigs to Willie Blount, February 16, 1810, M-208, and Return J. Meigs to William Eustis, February 14, 1810, M-208.

[31] Return J. Meigs to Willie Blount, February 16, 1810, M-208.

[32] Return J. Meigs to William Eustis, January 22, 1810, M-208.

[33] Return J. Meigs to William Eustis, March 9, 1910, M-208.

[34] Council at Oostenalee [Ustanali] to Return J. Meigs, April 9, 1810, M-208.

With the express approval of the seven clans, this council again tried to come to grips with the law of clan revenge. Perhaps because of the tensions of the rebellion and the new pressures from white intruders, the Cherokees had seen much anger, bloodshed, and death in recent months. Many incidents were the result of drunkenness or disputes over property. As people moved out of villages to isolated farms, administering the clan system became more difficult. Families tended to become nuclear and patriarchal and the clan system lost much of its relevance. The new law made at Ustanali in 1810 did not abolish clan revenge, but it seriously modified it. The law began by stating that "the various clans or tribes which compose the Cherokee Nation" had agreed to "an act of oblivion for all lives for which they may have been indebted, one to the other." The act was to be "binding upon every clan" and wiped out the duty to avenge murders that may have hung heavily upon some Cherokees. The key portion of the act concerned retaliation for accidental or unpremeditated deaths. The first part of the law reaffirmed the decision made in 1797 about unpremeditated murder: "If, in future, any life should be lost without malice intended, the innocent agressor shall not be counted guilty." The second part was more puzzling. Attempting to deal with the question of deaths within a clan (where all were brothers and sisters) resulting from anger, it made a strange distinction between the angry slaying of a person in a private quarrel (say, a drunken brawl) and the angry slaying of a thief who had stolen a horse:

. . . should it happen that a brother forgetting his natural affection, should raise his hand in anger and kill his brother, he shall be accounted guilty of murder and suffer accordingly, but if a man has a horse stolen and overtakes the thief, and should his anger be so great as to cause him to kill him, let his blood remain on his own conscience, but no satisfaction shall be demanded for his life from his relatives or the clan he may belong to.[35]

At first glance this seems to make a life taken over stolen property more justifiable than a life taken in an angry personal quarrel; the former is excusable, the latter is not. But looked at in another way, it seems to say that although horse thieves have become outlaws and their murder therefore falls on their own heads, killing another man for no reason other than a personal quarrel still merits execution. The law is puzzling because it is open to the interpretation that the lighthorse patrol and not the clan is responsible for justice in both cases, though it does not specifically say this; the lighthorse regulators are not mentioned. The phrase "suffer accordingly" is ambiguous, perhaps purposely so. The law of clan revenge was so basic to the Cherokee sense of order and justice that it had

[35] *Cherokee Laws*, p. 4.

to be dealt with very carefully. Those at the Council probably understood clearly what was at issue here: a basic modification of clan power was being stated; its duties were being altered by the authority of the community as a whole. Blood revenge applied to settling a debt between two clans. A murder within a clan (a brother killing a brother) did not traditionally create such a debt; the acceptance of the concept of personal responsibility for "murder" even within a clan was another mark of acculturation. This is the last reference to clan authority in the published laws of the Cherokee Nation. This does not mean that clan revenge ceased; there were instances of it for many years thereafter. But after 1810 it was not, strictly speaking, legal.

This council also reasserted its opposition to treaties that were not confirmed by national councils, and again it rejected any proposal for exchange of lands to provide a tract for emigrants to Arkansas. Moreover, the Council specifically condemned those Cherokees so lacking in patriotism that they emigrated west at the expense of those who chose to sustain the homeland. This resolution went a long way toward defining what it meant to be a Cherokee after 1810. It was a major manifestation of Cherokee nationalism: "The country left to us by our ancestors has been diminished by repeated sales to a tract barely sufficient for us to stand on and not more than adequate to the purpose of supporting our posterity. . . . Some of our people have gone across the Mississippi without the consent of the nation, although by our father, the President, in his speech, required that they should obtain it previous to their removing." By leaving the nation and endangering the integrity of the ancestral land, these emigrants were not only acting against President Jefferson's speech but were committing treason against the motherland. "We rest assured that the General Government [in Washington] will not attend to or be influenced by any straggling part of the Nation to accede to any arrangement of our country that may be proposed contrary to the will and consent of the main body of the Nation."[36]

Obviously the Council feared that those henceforth to be known as "the Western Cherokees" would call upon the government to survey and guarantee a tract of land for them in Arkansas. They knew that Meigs would support this request by demanding (or seizing) a "quantum portion" of the homeland determined by the number of Cherokees in the west multiplied by 1,250 acres. They also knew that Meigs would not think it necessary to call a treaty council to do this, because in his eyes the "agreement" with Jefferson in January 1809 constituted sufficient basis to require the cession. The "Nation" therefore announced in advance

[36] Council at Oostenally [Ustanali] to Return J. Meigs, April 11, 1810, M-208.

that its "straggling" emigrants had no such claim upon their land. Cherokee citizenship was no longer to be based simply upon kinship, language, or adherence to the traditional ethnic heritage. Henceforth it was defined in terms of living within the boundaries of the homeland and acceding to its laws and treaty obligations as defined by the nation's Council. The Cherokee Nation was not simply a people; it was a place. To leave that place "without the consent of the nation," knowing that the federal government might unilaterally use that action to expropriate land from the nation, was traitorous, a betrayal of one's duties as a citizen and patriot and an act that merited deprivation of citizenship. "Stragglers" were "expatriates."

Like the law redefining clan revenge, this resolution expressed ambiguously an important but as yet barely acknowledged shift in cultural self-definition. Probably most Cherokees did not fully share all that was implied by it. Ties of clan, family, language, and culture were much too strong for such legalistic redefinition of who was or was not a Cherokee. Yet the danger to national survival was so great at this moment that some statement seemed necessary to clarify the commitment to national survival *on the land of their ancestors.* A political and ideological statement was being made. It would take another removal crisis and another decade of experience to make the concept of a Cherokee nation-state explicit.[37]

One other significant act of national self-assertion was taken at the council in April 1810. The Secretary of War had requested that the Cherokees grant a public right of way through their nation for whites "to carry on trade to the Mobile by water down the Coose [Coosa] river and the waters that lead to the mobile."[38] The people of Tennessee wanted a more rapid, direct water outlet to the Gulf of Mexico than the Tennessee and the Mississippi rivers provided. The Council declined to grant it. It did so "because the right of navigating this river does not rest with us alone." It would require the combined consent of the Cherokees, the

---

[37] In 1809 there were perhaps one thousand Cherokees living in Arkansas Territory on the St. Francis and Arkansas rivers; they had moved there in small groups since the 1790s. By 1816, this number had reached almost two thousand. But they had never been given any official recognition. They had no tract of land they could legally call their own and they did not share in any of the annuities that came to the tribe. In March 1816, Secretary of War William Crawford asked a delegation of Cherokees from the eastern part of the nation whether they would not be willing to share their annuities with these westerners and perhaps even exchange a tract of land in the east for land that the government would then set aside for the Cherokees in Arkansas to guarantee their rights. But the eastern Cherokees were totally unsympathetic toward the plight of those expatriates who had deserted the motherland. They told Crawford that these stragglers "should be compelled to return to live with the nation" if they wanted to be considered Cherokees. Crawford to Governor William Clarke, September 17, 1816, M-15, reel 3, p. 423.

[38] Meigs transmitted the letter from William Eustis to the Cherokee Council, March 27, 1810, M-208.

Creeks and perhaps the Choctaws.[39] The United States Constitution said that navigable waters within the United States could not be restricted in use, but the Cherokee Nation seemed to be saying that it must be treated as a foreign nation and waterways within its boundaries were subject to its regulation (and so for the other Indian nations).

With the reunion of the Lower and Upper Towns and the departure of roughly eight hundred Cherokees for Arkansas in the early part of 1810, this removal crisis came to an end.[40] To Meigs's chagrin, the federal government had provided no assistance for his plan beyond what he himself had appropriated. The War Department made no effort to negotiate a western tract for the emigrants. Within six months the emigrants were writing back to Meigs asking for help against the Osages, who resented Cherokee intrusion into Osage hunting ground. Part of the difficulty was that the Lower Towns had not really carried through on their promise to move en masse; at least half of the emigrants had been from the upper part of the Upper Towns. There was no single evacuated block of land available for an exchange. In March 1811, Eustis suggested that perhaps "an exchange so far as to cover the lands of the Cherokees lying with[in] the limits of Tennessee and a small tract lying in the N.W. corner of So. Carolina" might be negotiated.[41] But Meigs thought this was the wrong way to go about it. He wanted to hold out for much more. On May 30, he wrote: "At present it appears to me that an exchange may be effected that will remove the [whole] Cherokee nation to the Arkansa or White river." If the government would simply help him to spur more Cherokees to emigrate by providing him with money for boats, guns, hoes, and supplies, it would demonstrate that the President and War Department took the enterprise seriously. "If the Government can by one convention [treaty] put an end to treaties with these people, I presume it would be desirable."[42] But the government had ceased to be interested; Madison and Eustis were preoccupied with the possibility of war with England.

Frustrated, Meigs decided to suggest a totally different approach to do away with the Cherokee Nation in the east quickly and easily and make its land available to the white poulation. His long letter to Eustis of April 5, 1811, set forth his new proposal. Since 1791, Meigs began, the federal government had spent "not less than one million dollars" to civilize the Cherokees and protect them from white intruders. "The time has now arrived . . . for a change of measures." Reversing his previous claims that

---

[39] Council at Oostenaly [Ustanali] to Return J. Meigs, April 11, 1810, M-208. See also Return J. Meigs to Council at Willstown, November 2, 1809, M-208.

[40] Royce, *Cherokee Nation of Indians*, p. 87.

[41] William Eustis to Return J. Meigs, March 27, 1811, M-208.

[42] Return J. Meigs to William Eustis, May 30, 1811, M-208.

the Cherokees were inherently lazy and preferred to be hunters rather than farmers, Meigs now maintained that the Cherokees were ready for citizenship. "If they can now be placed in a community governed by good laws, they may rise to as high a state of refinement as any other people of agricultural pursuits. . . . It is my opinion that their bodily and mental powers are by no means inferior to those of the white People." Why not "have the civil jurisdiction of the States of Georgia and Tennessee extended over all the [Cherokee] land lying witin their acknowledged limits respectively." Let each Cherokee family head "have a competent farm designated as [his] individual property," grant him federal and state citizenship, and let each family fend for itself. This would "require about two million acres, leaving eleven millions of acres within the limits of those two states," for which the federal government might offer the Cherokee $200,000 to extinguish their title, "payable by small annual installments." Then, "having blended with the citizens under regular Government, their improvement would be accellerated ten fold faster than under the present measures, while they can ramble over 25,000 square miles of land capable of supporting more than 300,000 inhabitants & now lying a dark, unoccupied wilderness." True, "there [were] strong prejudices against them" among the whites because of past antagonisms, but as the Cherokees demonstrated that they were capable of being solid, respectable citizens, this would vanish. They were not dwindling but increasing in numbers: "Since these people have been a little more industrious & live better, they have fast increased in population."[43]

In the same letter Meigs pointed out two dangers ahead for the Cherokees if they were not either moved west or detribalized and made to fend for themselves as citizens. He was right about both. If they did not emigrate, it would be "very difficult for the Government to protect them on the immense tract of land they now claim. If any exigency should require that the military [protection of Cherokee borders by the federal government] be withdrawn, there is danger that intrusion will take such a strong hold of their country as to be without remedy." The whites would overrun, dispossess, scatter, and pauperize them. On the other hand, if the present movement inaugurated by the young chiefs continued to thrive, the Cherokees would create "a Government within a government." Already they were developing "erroneous ideas of their distinct sovereignty & independence; as their numbers increase, those ideas will be fortified" and the United States will be faced with the claim that they are a sovereign nation. "It is of importance that a change [of] measures should take

[43] Return J. Meigs to William Eustis, April 5, 1811, M-208.

place early to put this out of all doubt." They must not be allowed to persist in "their false ideas of their national independence."[44]

Eustis finally conferred with Madison about the floundering exchange and removal venture that Meigs had been pushing so hard for three years. On March 27, 1811, he told Meigs to drop the project. "The removal of the Cherokees and Choctaws to the West Side of the Mississippi as contemplated by Mr. Jefferson has been considered by the present President" and he had concluded against it. Madison found no commitment in Jefferson's message either to support those who unilaterally decided to go west or to negotiate a tract of land for them in exchange for the land they had vacated.[45] As Meigs expressed it in a message to the Cherokee chiefs, "Mr. Madison, the new president, did not think proper to encourage it; i.e., he said that if families chose to remove at their own expense, they might do it," but that the government would not pay for their removal.[46] It was a serious blow to Meigs and even harder on Tolluntuskee, Chisholm, Saulowee, Ooloni, Utsook, Komotawha, Jacket, The Bowl, and the other chiefs who had led their people to the promised land in Arkansas. Meigs had proved to be their Pied Piper. They were now scattered around a vast region, frequently at war, with no government protection and no fixed boundaries.[47] The project had been a fiasco of major proportions, one that would later return to haunt them when Andrew Jackson found reasons to revive it in 1817.

Governor Willie Blount and the people of Tennessee were very displeased. Blount tried to frighten Eustis in 1811 with the specter of an Indian war if the Southeastern tribes were not removed. "My opinion is that a great number of the most wealthy and influential Indians, etc. among the Southern tribes are not friendly to the interest of the United States, and until their ascendancy over the strolling, hunting Indians,

---

[44] Ibid.

[45] William Eustis to Return J. Meigs, March 27, 1811, M-208; see also William Eustis to Silas Dinsmoor, April 20, 1811, M-15, reel 3, #0077.

[46] Return J. Meigs, "Some thoughts on the contemplated exchange of land," addressed to a Cherokee council, undated (inserted at October 18, 1811 letter), M-208. See also William Eustis to Return J. Meigs, March 27, 1811, M-208, and Royce, *Cherokee Nation of Indians*, p. 76. When precisely Madison made up his mind not to follow through on the plan for a removal and exchange of Cherokee lands is not clear, but Eustis implies that it was August 17, 1809. If so, Meigs seemed unaware of this and persisted in trying to promote removal and exchange until April 1811.

[47] Connetue to Return J. Meigs from Arkansas Territory, June 17, 1811, M-208. Connetue said that some Cherokees had been settled at the St. Francis River, Arkansas, since 1790, when land was given to them there by the Spanish. "As they all inclined to farming and raising stock, our stock has become very large. . . . Our women spin and weave almost all the clothing we wear, blankets excepted." Connetue also went by the name John Hill and may have been white or of mixed ancestry. He heartily acceded, he said, to the idea of an exchange of land in Arkansas Territory for the land his people had left behind in the East.

who never may change their habits, is checked," they never would be. "A separation between them [the wealthy Indians] and the hunters" could be effected by urging "the hunters to settle west of the Mississippi in the neighbourhood of certain Garrisons and Factories to be built over there" and encouraging the well-to-do Indians to remain in the East by giving them reserves. The poor hunters would thus "become attached to the United States" because it would protect them in their old way of life in the west, while the rich Indians would become attached because they would be citizens.[48]

But the fear of a war with the British and the western Indians was precisely what had motivated Madison and Eustis not to stir up the southeastern Indians by pressing the policy of removal, exchange, and reserve citizenship upon them. A coercive, large-scale removal would create more, not less, danger; it would certainly arouse the western Indians onto whose lands these thousands of emigrants would be thrust. The result would be more allies for the British and more trouble for white frontier settlers.

Thus the first Cherokee removal crisis ended not with a bang but with a whimper in 1811. The Cherokee patriots had won. Meigs's oversell, the unforeseen expense, the complexity of negotiating the exchange, the antagonism of the western tribes, the new tensions with the British and their Shawnee ally, Tecumseh, and above all the resistance of the Cherokees themselves had brought one of the first victories in the Cherokee fight for survival. Not only did they stop removal, but they refused to cede any more land to Tennessee, Georgia, or the United States. All of the land cessions that had been planned by Doublehead, Meigs, Willie Blount, and Sevier since 1806 were aborted. The initiative for Cherokee revitalization had, for the moment, passed from the federal government and its agent to the Cherokees themselves. After having come to the brink of self-destruction, the Cherokees had managed to pull themselves together. The overwhelming majority was now convinced that security lay in holding on to the homeland and owning it in common, not in severalty. After twenty years of confusion, conflict, and despair, the Cherokees had reached a moment of stability.

[48] Willie Blount to William Eustis, April 24, 1811, M-221, reel 34, #2132.

EIGHT

THE GHOST DANCE MOVEMENT,

1811–1812

You yourselves can see that the white people are entirely different beings from us; we are made from red clay; they, out of white sand. You may keep good neighborly relations with them, just see to it that you get back from them your old Beloved Towns. —Ancestral ghost vision of three Cherokees, January, 1811

As the Cherokees faced the possibility that they might once again exert some control over their destiny, they had to ask themselves what form they wished it to take. If a true Cherokee lived on the land of his forefathers, did he also live in their spiritual world? Or did the Cherokee future require adapting to the white man's world? To control their destiny they needed economic security; to give it shape they needed to instill it with religious meaning. In the years 1811–1812 the Cherokee tried to envision a new way of life that would link their past to their future. Before going forward, they had to look back and ask the spirits of their ancestors for guidance. This was the meaning of their first ghost dance movement in 1811–1812.

In March 1809 Meigs published the results of a tabulation he had hired George Barber Davis to make of the Cherokee Nation.[1] Davis had been working on the survey, which was designed to obtain statistics on a wide range of Cherokee affairs, for over two years. Meigs described it as a "Statistical Table," meant to measure the progress of the nation toward a civilized, agricultural style of life. He found the results so significant that he printed copies and distributed them widely among the Cherokees, missionaries, and state and federal officials. It provided, he said, "a view of their population and of their improvements in the useful arts and of their property acquired under the fostering hand of Government, which has principally been done since the year 1796." Some years later Meigs used

---

[1] Return J. Meigs to William Eustis, December 1, 1809, M-208. Meigs arranged to have the census printed in January 1810 (see Meigs to Eustis, January 30, 1810, M-208). For a general discussion of Cherokee economic development, see William G. McLoughlin and Walter H. Conser, Jr., "The Cherokees in Transition," *Journal of American History* 64 (1977):678–703.

similar statistics to show that the Cherokees had reached a level of civilization and subsistence at which they no longer needed government assistance. In 1811 the government closed its trading post in the Cherokee Nation. The Cherokees could take pride in their economic growth, as they did in the political reorganization, but Meigs's figures also demonstrated that there was a growing gap between the three hundred or so families who were prospering most through acculturation and the two thousand or more families who were still struggling to make ends meet each year. The remarkable revival of traditional religion in the years 1811–1812 resulted in part from these social tensions.

There are no accurate statistics for Cherokee population and economic wealth prior to 1809. In 1794, according to all accounts, the nation was in a state of confusion and devastation after eighteen years of intermittent war and demographic drift. Estimates then placed the population at about ten thousand persons living in sixty to seventy different communities or towns, many of which were palisaded forts enclosing one hundred to three hundred people. By 1809, Davis found that the town system had broken down everywhere. As they adopted the white man's system of family farming, the Cherokees had moved out of their towns, spreading up and down the river valleys wherever they could find good land. However, they continued to define a town in terms of the population that utilized the same town or council house, shared a common set of "headmen" or town chiefs, and celebrated their feast days, religious festivals, dances, and ball plays together in the same town square or stomp ground.

Davis evidently gave names to these scattered centers of population according to his own perspective. Some he called "towns," some "villages," some "-villes," and some "plantations." Vannsville had 3 people in it; Chillhoweeville had 130. The population of "villages" on Davis's table ranged from 12 in Cheowee Village to 326 in Taloney Village. Thirty-six places he designated as "towns," ranging from 10 persons in George Downey's Town to 857 in Etowah Town (the largest town in the nation, scattered over twenty square miles). There were fifteen localities to which he gave the names of rivers or valleys, such as "Etowah River," with 15 persons, and "Hickory Log," with 611. Out of a total of one hundred communities or neighborhoods that Davis visited, he listed thirty-three with 10 persons or fewer. Most of these he called "plantations"; they were probably family farms in which grandparents, aunts, and uncles lived together as extended families. Only forty-one places had a population of over 100. Of these, twenty-two had a population of over 200; ten had more than 250 (about fifty families). The average Cherokee family consisted of five persons.

By 1809 the Cherokee Nation, like the white frontier region around it, consisted of groups who had settled haphazardly wherever soil was fertile and water sufficient. What were called towns had no fixed boundaries, usually extending for miles along a river bank or turnpike. The traditional kind of compact community, centered around a single council house and ceremonial ground, was virtually gone. Davis found the population almost equally divided between 6,116 males and 6,279 females (totaling 12,395). He found 341 whites in the nation, of whom 113 were white men married to Cherokee wives. He did not list the number of white women married to Cherokees. There were 583 black slaves owned by Cherokees, bringing the total population to 13,319. Concerning the whites, Davis noted that many of them were "employed as croppers" (i.e., sharecroppers) on Cherokee plantations—another means by which Cherokee males too poor to own slaves were able to overcome their lack of skill at cultivating fields.

Davis did not take a census of those Cherokees who had already moved to Arkansas, but he estimated that "there are over the Mississippi uperwards of 1000 Cherokees." This did not include the eight hundred whom Meigs had persuaded to emigrate in 1809–1810. Davis made no attempt to distinguish among the descendants of Catawbas, Uchees, Creeks, and other nations who lived in Cherokee territory, some of whom had been captured in war and some of whom had voluntarily moved among them when their own nations dispersed. He also did not mention the existence of offspring of mixed Cherokee and African heritage, nor did he identify the number of those descended from white-Cherokee cohabitation or marriage (the mixed bloods). Whites had been living among the Cherokees for almost a century. The best estimate of mixed bloods as of 1809 would be about 15 percent (by 1830 a judicious estimate by a knowledgeable missionary placed the mixed bloods at no more than 25 percent; a more careful census in 1835 designed to count those of "half blood," "quadroon," and "octoroon," found only 23.4 percent who were not full bloods). Many of mixed ancestry could not speak or write English; it was English-speaking, highly acculturated Cherokees who were identified as a distinct class by the full bloods, the overwhelming majority.

Davis did not organize the census figures by region, so there is no way to distinguish between the Upper and Lower Towns. No map accompanied the survey and today the locations of many of the towns and villages mentioned are difficult to identify. The Cherokees had a habit of carrying a town name with them when they moved (or were forced to move) and maps of the period locate towns of the same name at different spots in different eras. However, Davis did make a special trip to the North Carolina or "Overhill area" to gather data; his letter describing this particular region has survived. Living in the Valley Towns of the

170

Great Smoky Mountains Davis found 1,750 males and 1,898 females for a total of 3,648, or about 30 percent of the national population. There were seventy-two whites in this area but only five black slaves, an indication that the region was poor and not conducive to large-scale farming.[2] Davis also noted that the people there were the most conservative or "backward" he had met anywhere, by his estimate at least a generation behind the rest of the nation. From the best guess that can be made, it appears that there were about 2,000 persons in the Lower Towns, 3,500 in the eastern Tennessee region (north of Chickamauga), and 3,500 in the region within the boundaries of Georgia.

If the eastern Cherokee population increased from ten thousand to thirteen thousand between 1794 and 1809 (in addition to a western Cherokee body of about one thousand) as the data seem to indicate, it is most remarkable that despite all the difficulties they had faced in these years, the predictions of their imminent disappearance were greatly exaggerated. Moreover, the statistics demonstrated a rapid growth in the number and value of their livestock, tools, and mills, including:

6,519 horses at $30 each	$195,570
19,165 black cattle at $8	153,320
1,037 sheep at $2	2,074
19,778 swine at $2	39,356
13 gristmills at $260	3,380
3 sawmills at $500	1,500
30 wagons at $40	1,200
583 Negro slaves at $300	174,900

The net worth of these assets was $571,300, which did not include the cultivated land, houses, barns, and miscellaneous farm buildings. In addition, Davis counted 1,572 spinning wheels, 429 looms, and 567 plows. Finally, he noted that there were three saltpeter works, two powder mills, and five schools in the nation (two conducted by the Presbyterians, one by the Moravians, and two privately supported by well-to-do mixed-blood and white parents). Davis also listed forty-nine Cherokees who still practiced the traditional arts of the silversmith. He did not list other artisans or mechanics, but there were also blacksmiths, wheelwrights, tinsmiths, carpenters, and armorers in the nation. The saltpeter mine and powder mills at Nickajack were run at that time by Colonel James Ore, who leased them from the Cherokees. Within five years Ore mined "upward of 60,000 lbs. of Salt Petre."[3] Another saltpeter mine and powder

[2] George Barber Davis to Return J. Meigs, October 17, 1808, M-208.
[3] Just as the Cherokees objected to whites like Colonel James Ore coming into their country to extract their mineral resources, so they objected to Meigs's leasing saltpeter caves to white entrepreneurs. See John Walker to Return J. Meigs, January 14, 1813, M-208.

mill was run by Samuel Riley, a white man married to a Cherokee. Riley also served as Meigs's official interpreter.

Meigs added to the chart the fact that although in 1796 there was not a single wagon road in the nation, in 1809 there were "hundreds of miles of roads."[4] When Meigs transmitted this "General Statistical Table" to the Secretary of War in December 1809, he noted that when he had first broached the idea for it in 1806, the Cherokees had been vigorously opposed to it, but in 1808 they had acquiesced. Somewhere in those two years a sense of accomplishment had developed. Meigs was particularly interested in the great increase in wagon roads in order to promote a market economy. "Since finding the advantages arising from roads, they have at their own expense open'd upwards of 300 miles of wagon road for communication. . . . One road of 100 miles in length [was] opened by Doublehead, commencing at Franklin County, Tennessee, and runs to the muscle Shoals, and it is contemplated to be continued to the navigable waters of Mobile." The Augusta-Nashville Road had added two hundred miles of federal turnpike that was kept in good enough condition "for Carriages." As Meigs saw it, "thus far . . . have the Cherokees prospered by the pastoral life and by domestic manufactures." However, he added, "the greater number are extremely poor for want of industry; the hunting life here is at an end but a predilection for the hunters state pervades a great part of the Cherokees." He was convinced that "many" would go west with encouragement from the government; "notwithstanding this, they have strong local attachments to the place of their birth and the sepulchres of their fathers" and would need inducements to move.

Meigs might have asked Davis to list the number of boats, ferries, inns, taverns, and trading stores to fill out this picture of prosperity and industry, but he did not. Nor did he make any attempt to estimate the amounts of corn, beans, cotton, potatoes, wheat, melons, peaches, or other crops grown by the Cherokees and sold, along with livestock, to white settlements for extra income. Although Meigs implied that most of the capital investment in tools for domestic manufactures and agriculture had come as gifts from the federal government, in fact the great bulk of this came from purchases made by individual Cherokees from traders or purchased by the tribe as part of their yearly annuity. The annuity in these years varied from $6,000 to $11,000. It was not a government gift but the tribal endowment from the sale of its land. The Cherokees had regularly invested it in farm tools and other equipment. They had also obtained money for their national treasury by leasing to whites their salines and their saltpeter caves. Additional income came from ferry and tavern

---

[4] Return J. Meigs to William Eustis, December 1, 1809, M-208.

leases. White sharecroppers increased the productive wealth of the nation by clearing, cultivating, and fencing land, though there were many complaints that they often cheated the Cherokees who employed them.

One area in which the civilization program had not succeeded was education. Of a potential 3,000 to 3,500 school-age children in the nation, only ninety-four were attending school in 1809. Sixty of these were at Blackburn's two Presbyterian schools in the Tennessee area, according to Davis; eight were at the Moravian school at Springplace, Georgia; two other private schools run by parents educated another twenty-four (see table 5). But there were no schools at all in the Overhill or Valley Town area in North Carolina. Within a year after the census was published both of Blackburn's schools closed, leaving only thirty-four students in the entire nation who were obtaining any formal schooling. Meigs had several times spoken of creating a Cherokee school fund, but only in connection with sales of large tracts of land that the Cherokees did not want to part with. This meant that much of the leadership in the nation's continual struggle with the whites had to come from the three hundred families familiar with English. Davis's census provides only a rough index of this rising middle class—based on what he spoke of as plantations or "-villes," which can be identified as single-family units. The figures in table 6 provide some indication of what a well-to-do, English-speaking mixed-blood family might own. Because Davis was not keeping records by name, this list is purely random. There were many others who fit into this category who are simply not identifiable on the census because it provided only town totals.

Below the 10 percent of the population who were comparatively well-off came the great mass of Cherokees who owned little more than a plow, a horse or two, a spinning wheel, two or three cattle, half a dozen hogs. These families often had to supplement their food supply by hunting, fishing, and gathering. Many did not own even a spinning wheel, a plow, or a loom. Meigs admitted that despite the great progress the nation had made, "the greatest number are extremely poor." These were the people who suffered when their small plots of corn, beans, and melons, tilled by the hoe and mattock, failed in times of drought, pestilence, or frost; for them the hospitality ethic was essential to survival. Davis found only 40 plows among the 3,649 people living in the Overhill or Valley Towns and no wagons, gristmills or sawmills. These Cherokees had 271 spinning wheels and 70 looms for roughly seven hundred families; they had only four blacksmiths and four silversmiths. These were the nation's poorest but most stubborn survivors.

Although, generally speaking, the poorer Cherokees in the more isolated parts of the nation were more traditionalist and continued to prac-

TABLE 5

Schools and Pupils in the Cherokee Nation, 1809

Location	Number of Pupils	Auspices
Near Quotaquskee's, Tenn.	40	Presbyterian (Gideon Blackburn)
Brownsville, Ala.	18	Private tutor
Southwest Point, Tenn.	20	Presbyterian (Gideon Blackburn)
Springplace, Ga.	8	Moravian (John Gambold)
At William Harlin's, Tenn.	8	Private tutor
Total	94	

SOURCE: From statistical table compiled in 1809 by George Barber Davis for his census for Return J. Meigs (Moravian Archives, Salem [Winston-Salem], North Carolina).

TABLE 6

Prosperous Cherokees in 1809 (partial list)

Name	Horses	Black Cattle	Swine	Plows	Whites Employed	Black Slaves
Richard Brown (white)	62	110	215	6	9	14
Robt. Brown	70	70	50	5	19	21
[?] Carter	10	72	9	8	6	22
Dick Fields	127	150	130	3	8	5
[?] Graves	—	—	—	—	6	5
[?] Hammond	10	140	20	3	12	1
Chas. Hicks	20	50	20	3	6	11
[?] Love	14	55	58	3	1	10
John Lowrey (white)	100	200	100	4	4	17
John McDonald (white)	55	110	80	2	1	16
Geo. Pettit	20	104	20	2	7	5
Quotaquskee [John McIntosh] (white)	58	150	50	3	3	7
Daniel Ross (white)	40	90	60	2	1	13
Dick Taylor	—	—	—	—	1	4
Joseph Vann (son of James Vann)	250	1,000	150	10	[3]	115
John Walker (white)	—	—	—	—	—	5
Thos. Wilson	—	—	—	—	—	5
Wm. Woodward (white)	—	—	—	—	—	4

SOURCE: These figures are taken from the statistical table made by George Barber Davis in 1809 for his census for Return J. Meigs (Moravian Archives, Salem [Winston-Salem], North Carolina).

NOTE: This is a partial list. Davis recorded statistics by towns or villages and only in the few cases listed here did he give figures for individual plantations. Other wealthy Cherokees were lumped into town and village totals. Generally speaking, the best indicator of wealth is the number of slaves owned; in 1835, only 7.4 percent of the Cherokee families owned any slaves.

tice most regularly their ancient rituals and festivals, they were not opposed to change. As Stone Carrier's delegation representing thirty-two
chiefs from the Upper Towns had told Jefferson, they wanted to become
farmers but had not been given the tools. They also wanted to make laws
to govern a social order that no longer had the stability of the old town
government with its communal consensus to regulate behavior. Two
chiefs on the upper reaches of the Little Tennessee River wrote to Meigs
in February 1811 that they had met with the other headmen in the valley
at the town of Cowee to try to pass laws to punish stealing. "As we are
Blind as to how to make laws," said Big Bear and The Sharp Fellow, they
wanted Meigs's advice on their first efforts to bring order to the new way
of life in their part of the nation. They had been inspired by the regulator
law of the National Council in 1808 but as yet had organized no lighthorse patrol in their district. A bilingual Cherokee had written out their
laws for Meigs's approval. The first dealt with the theft of livestock:
"Any person stealing a horse shall Receive one hundred lashes on there
Bere [bare] Back; a Cow, fifty, or a hog, twenty-five; A Corn [hoe?] 5;
any small artickel, 10." The poor had not much to steal from each other,
but what little they had was all the more important.[5] The second law
passed by these North Carolina towns dealt with their contractual arrangements with and debts owed to traders, blacksmiths, or neighbors.
"Any person Refusing to pay according to a Contract, his property to be
taken at the validation of two men; the Debtor to be brought before the
head man of his town; a Debt over twenty dollars: stay Acicution [exe-
cution] six months; from twenty to Tenn, three months; under Tenn,
Too months." Its purpose was to see that creditors did not take more from
a poor man than he could afford, to give debtors specific time periods in
which to make good their debts, and to make debtors realize that contractual arrangements must be fulfilled.

Their third law was passed to accommodate the religion of the white
men who lived or worked among them (there were no missionaries in that
region at the time). This was the first Sabbath law in the Cherokee Nation, yet it came from its most traditionalist section. It sought to explain
to the Cherokees that white people did not work on the Sabbath and
ought not to be expected to do so. "Any white man living on our land and
workes on Sunday except the work of Neadsity or gambels on the Day or
huntes for game, shall pay one dollar to every such Afence." The law may
additionally have been intended to keep the whites in order, but the chiefs
explained to Meigs that "this is to let us [k]now when Sunday is comm

[5] Big Bear and Sharp Fellow to Return J. Meigs, February 1, 1811, M-208.

so as we may lern from them." Whether this had any religious significance to the chiefs is not clear.

Meigs kept no copy of his observations on these laws, but it is apparent
from them that old patterns of life and work were changing as rapidly in
the poorest and most remote areas of the nation as in the most acculturated areas. However, there was resistance to the new ways and particularly to the regimentation of life under the market economy. Indians repeatedly told whites that God had not meant the red man to live by the
same rules as the white. God had made specifically different ways for different kinds of men, just as he had given them different colors and placed
them on different continents—the white in Europe, the black in Africa,
the red in America. A chief named The Elk told one of these separatist
myths to the Moravians in 1815: "At the beginning there was only one
man and one woman on earth," but they had two sons. The sons "attempted to take the mother's life," believing "she was a sorceress since
she provided as much food as they wanted without their being able to find
out where she got this." She was Selu, the Earth Mother, goddess of corn.
The mother discovered the plot against her and "she left her sons and flew
up into the heights." When the father, who had been away, came home
and found out what had happened, "he showed the sons his displeasure"
and told them they must "do better." Then he gave them "a book from
which they were to learn how one should act and live." But "one son
seized the book to himself, forcibly and hurried with it away from his father's dwelling." Later, when the father was dying, he "drew a line between the two brothers and their dwellings. This line is the sea [the Atlantic Ocean]." The son who stayed on this side made small canoes able
to go on lakes and rivers, but the son who had the book and who lived on
the far side of the sea "made bigger boats." "Finally," many years later,
King George made such big boats that his people were able "to land on
this side" of the dividing line. "In these large boats, King George sent
presents to his brothers [the red men]. These brothers were quite naked."
Now "the first brother" who stayed here, "was still living, but he was old
and no longer in condition to walk as fast as the young people." As a result, when the people rushed down to get the presents from King George,
the young people "seized all the gifts and kept them for themselves." The
Elk said that he was "really a descendant of the family of the first inhabitants on this side of the sea" and that "the brothers on this side were
originally white like those over the sea, but did not exercise the same care
to protect themselves against the sun" and that is why they became red.[6]

[6] The Moravian missionaries recorded this in the Springplace Diary, October 13, 1815,
MAS. For the myth of Selu, the Earth Mother, and Kanati, the Hunter-Father, see Mooney,
"Myths of the Cherokees," pp. 242–249.

The Elk's account was a combination of other stories, perhaps even including the Adam and Eve, Cain and Abel story, picked up from a missionary. It is similar to the cargo cult stories of twentieth-century people in Melanesia and resembles creation myths told by Africans and other Indians.[7] Its message is simple: there is a fundamental separation between the red and white people that goes back to a primal crime between them that led to the division of the world. The Europeans had broken that division and were perpetuating the crime by imposing European trade goods upon them and causing them to quarrel among themselves, particularly causing friction between the old and the young Indians.

There were other Cherokee myths that stated that the Great Spirit had originally created red, black, and white men. To the red he gave the bow and arrow and set him amidst the game in America; to the white he gave a book in which he could learn many secrets and set him in Europe; to the black he gave a hoe and axe to work in the fields and set him in Africa. All such myths concerned the problems that arose when the separate peoples and their ways of life became mixed up.

The Elk's understanding of cultural pluralism was at odds with that of the young chiefs who dominated the nation after 1811 and directed its acculturation. Young chiefs like The Ridge, Charles Hicks, George Lowrey, and John Ross believed they should accept the gifts that had been brought by the big canoes from Europe and that were now distributed among them by the Great Father in Washington. They thanked President Jefferson in 1808 for establishing schools among them to teach them to read the white man's books and to write his words and for giving them the implements to become farmers because "by means of all these acquisitions the work of civilization advances and will be accellerated." They wished to show the white man that they were his equal, made by the same Great Spirit, and entitled to be called "brothers." "We want to do the best we can for ourselves and our Nation," they told Jefferson in 1808. They regretted that their "old people" did not "understand what is for the benefit of [the] Nation." "If we follow the old customs of our old people, we will never do well." But they insisted that their Father protect them by keeping whites off of their land and leaving them alone to govern themselves. They wished to learn how to be independent and self-reliant—a people able to manage its own affairs. Their elders wished to make only minimal concessing to acculturation and to live as they had always lived, adopting only the changes that made their lives a little easier.[8]

---

[7] See William G. McLoughlin, "A Note on African Sources of American Indian Racial Myths," *Journal of American Folklore* 89 (1976):331–35 and A. W. Loomis, *Scenes in the Indian Country* (Philadelphia: Philadelphia Presbyterian Board, 1859), pp. 52–54.

[8] Cherokee delegation to Thomas Jefferson, December 21, 1808, M-208.

Both programs for the future were patriotic and dedicated to the welfare of their people, but it was difficult to see how they could fit together. Out of this clash of ideas came the Ghost Dance movement of 1811–1812. It was not directed against the missionaries or even against the young chiefs. It was a spiritual struggle to reconcile the old myths and the new ways. The well-to-do were becoming secularists who relied on their own wits and skills; the poor relied upon the supernatural powers of the spirit world. In the calm following the removal crisis, the Cherokees tried to come to terms with the gap that had developed between the intellectual worlds of the young and the old. Having determined that they must remain united on their ancestral homeland, they had to learn how to live together.

The Ghost Dance movement cannot be defined simply as a reactionary effort to return to the past. Only a few looked for a miracle to rid them of the white man and bring back the game. Even the poorest Cherokee shared somewhat in the pride over his nation's survival and growth. The problem was to survive in a way that would retain the essence of the Cherokee identity; they did not want to work and think like white men. The Cherokee felt that they had some special link to the spirit world that the white man did not share, which made them a different and a special people, the favorites of the Great Spirit. One myth said that the Great Spirit had shaped man out of clay and baked him into life over a hot fire: the first clay image baked too long and turned black; the second did not bake long enough and remained pasty white; but the third baked just right and it came out a dusky red. The Cherokees were the color God preferred. The young chiefs had told Jefferson in 1808 that they hoped "the magnanimity of the United States will not suffer 10,000 human beings [to] be lost between whom and the white people the Great Spirit has made no difference except in the tint of their skin."[9] Those who joined the religious revival of 1811–1812 believed deeply that there was, and always must be, something more than "the tint of their skin" that distinguished them from the white man. They were trying to learn from their spirit world what that quintessential difference was.

In addition to this ethnic identity, almost all of the visions, dreams, and prophecies during the revival contained a search for order. They looked forward or backward to a period of peace and harmony; some prophets thought this perfect order would emerge peacefully; others thought it could only come apocalyptically. In an unstable world they sought stability. They knew too little of Christianity to find it any source of help. Their visions were built from their own traditions and were expressed in

[9] Ibid.

terms of their daily experience. As they wavered between hope and fear the visions fluctuated between optimism and pessimism.

No major crisis but a series of small and continual crises provided the general context of anxiety from which the religious revival grew. In 1811 the Secretary of War announced that the war in Europe had destroyed the market for skins and pelts; the government would have to reduce the prices it paid for furs and pelts in its factories.[10] Private traders did the same. Rumors spread that the government would soon close the factory in the Cherokee Nation, which it did later that year; for those who eked out a small living from the fur trade, this was unsettling. In the summer a severe famine spread through large parts of the nation, bringing great hardship to the poor.[11] Black Fox, the old Principal Chief, died; it was unclear who would succeed him. The intruder problem continued to mount and five times in 1811 Meigs sent out troops in fruitless efforts to beat back the white frontiersmen. Rumors of war in the Mississippi Valley increased, given strength by the efforts of Tecumseh and his brother Tenskwatawa (The Prophet) to form a confederacy against further white expansion among all the Indians. Some Cherokees had heard of the inspired visions of The Prophet that set the Shawnees dancing a strange new dance and singing new songs to their spirits. Later in 1811 Tecumseh visited the Creek Nation (his mother was a Creek) to the south; thirty Cherokees went to the Creek town of Tuckabatchee to hear him and see the dances of his prophets. Some said the Creeks would join with Tecumseh and the Shawnees if war broke out. Perhaps the Cherokees should do the same.

The War Department had warned all western federal agents in April 1811 to be alert for foreign spies stirring up the Indians with "hostile dispositions towards the United States"; therefore "be on your guard."[12] In November, General William Harrison led an army that killed many Shawnees at Tippecanoe in Indiana because he suspected that they were about to raid the white settlements in Ohio. The army garrisons near the Cherokee Nation were warned to be ready to move against the British at any time; when they went, everyone knew that there would be no one to hold back the local American intruders.

The first religious incident of the revival preceded most of these problems, but it created a background for the burgeoning of prophetic visions. A Cherokee man and two women were walking at dusk near a hill called Rocky Mountain, apparently in northwest Georgia, in January 1811. Tired after a long day's journey, they entered an abandoned cabin to spend the night. No sooner had they entered it than they heard a loud

---

[10] William Eustis to Return J. Meigs, June 21, 1811, M-221, reel 39, #5528.
[11] Turtle at Home and John Boggs to Return J. Meigs, June 15, 1811, M-208.
[12] William Eustis to all Indian agents, April 15, 1811, M-15, reel 3, p. 75.

noise like thunder in the sky and rushed out to see what it was. To their amazement they saw a band of Indians coming down out of the sky, riding black horses and beating a drum. The apparitions came to earth and rode up to the three Cherokees, saying they had been sent by the Great Spirit with a special message to their people. The Great Spirit was upset with the Cherokees for allowing so many white people into their country "without any distinction" between good and bad whites. The Spirit also did not like their planting the white man's variety of corn instead of the traditional Indian maize. Nor did he want them to have corn ground by the large stone wheels in the white man's mills; their women should grind it by hand in mortars," in the manner of your forefathers." "The Mother of the Nation" had forsaken them and allowed their game to disappear because she did not like these large millstones that "broke her bones." However, she would return to them and bring back the lost game if they would get rid of the bad whites and return to their old ways. The leader of the spirits reminded them that "the white people are entirely different beings from us; we are made from red clay, they, out of white sand." So long as the whites stayed outside the nation's boundaries, the Cherokees might "keep good and neighborly relations with them," but the whites must return the land on which sacred Cherokee towns had stood, like Tougaloo, Chota, and Kituwha, for they had been given to the Cherokees forever. The messenger also told the three travelers that the Cherokees must stop punishing each other so severely, whipping people "till the blood came," under their new laws.

Then the messenger pointed to the sky where there suddenly appeared a beautiful light. Within it were four white houses. The messenger said they were to build houses like these in their beloved or sacred towns for those white men to live in who were good to them and for others "who can be useful to them with writing." The astonished Cherokees who witnessed this vision were then instructed to report all they had heard and seen to their chiefs and also to Colonel Meigs. They were also warned that it would "not be well" for those who refused to believe it; harm would surely come to those who refused to accept this message from the Great Spirit and the Mother of the Nation.[13]

The three Cherokees gave up their journey, returned home, and told their chiefs about the vision. The chiefs asked them to repeat the message at a special council held at Ustanali early in February. Many of the young chiefs were present and one of them, The Ridge, openly scoffed at their story. So angry were the others at this lack of respect to spiritual things,

---

[13] Moravian missionaries, Springplace Diary, February 11, 1811, MAS. This and other accounts by the Moravians are appended to William G. McLoughlin, "New Angles of Vision on the Cherokee Ghost Dance Movement," *American Indian Quarterly* 5 (1979):317–45.

however, that they attacked Ridge and almost killed him before friends intervened.

The Rocky Mountain vision typified much in the Ghost Dance movement. In some ways it looked backward to a better age when much game was present, old ways were followed, and the Cherokees practiced their dances and rituals in the sacred towns. But essentially the vision spoke of a new *modus vivendi* with the whites and a synthetic blending of the old and the new. The vision told them they did not need gristmills, but that they did need to read and write. They did not need renegade or crooked white men among them, but they needed those who were good to them and who would help them. The spirit messenger mentioned one such white man for whom they should build a white house in their sacred city, Captain James Blair of Georgia, a good friend of James Vann, who had assisted them in driving intruders out of their land. Because the only persons teaching them to write at that time were the Moravians, the vision seemed to indicate that these missionaries were good white people. The extreme harshness of the lighthorse regulators was to be rejected but not some kind of law to deal with thieves. Essentially the Great Spirit or "the Mother of the Nation" was asserting the distinctiveness of the Cherokee people who were made from red clay and not white sand. They could be neighborly with the whites who respected them and their way of life, but they must keep a distance between them. This was unlike the angry, vindictive Ghost Dance visions of the Shawnees, which called for the destruction of all whites, for driving them back across the ocean, and for total restoration of the old ways to be brought about with miraculous powers that the Great Spirit would give them to defeat the white man in a final battle.[14] In the later phases of the Cherokee revival some dreams and visions did contain elements of apocalyptic millennialism, but this first vision was, in one sense, reasonable, believable. It won the respect of the great majority of chiefs at the council in February and others who heard it later.

This vision may have played a significant part in a decision taken by the National Council in May 1811 that instructed Meigs to eject every white person from the nation. Meigs protested that this was madness, but he had no choice. He ordered Captain James McDonald and Colonel Alexander Smyth of the army garrison to do as the Council wished; they were to remove not only intruders and renegades but all sharecroppers, mechanics and "those that have indian concubines."[15] If this order had been

[14] For the Shawnee prophesy see "A Talk delivered at Le Maiouitinong" on Lake Michigan by The Trout, May 4, 1807, M-222, reel 2, #0859–0860.

[15] Captain James McDonald and Colonel Alexander Smyth to Return J. Meigs, July 18, 1811, M-208. However, the Cherokee Council at Oostenaleh wrote to Meigs (April 5, 1811,

followed literally, even some of the most dedicated leaders of the rebellion against Doublehead and the old chiefs would have been removed, including John McDonald, Daniel Ross, John McIntosh, and John Walker. But the Council later modified its ruling and allowed intermarried whites to remain, as well as a few useful whites who were teaching schools and building gristmills.

There is no extant record of any other religious vision until late in December 1811. However, in August a blazing comet appeared in the sky that was so large its path could be traced for several weeks. On December 26, the New Madrid earthquake occurred along the Mississippi River between Missouri and Illinois. It shook the entire southeastern part of the United States. Houses in the Cherokee Nation were knocked off their foundations and large sinkholes, thirty yards wide, suddenly appeared and then filled slowly with murky, green water. People were shaken out of bed, and both wild and domestic animals ran about in terror. Subsequent tremors continued in the Cherokee region for another four months. The Moravians recorded at least twelve tremors that shook their houses at Springplace between December 1811 and April 1812.

The earthquake seemed to unleash the fears of many Cherokees about the anger of the Great Spirit and a wave of religious fervor swept through the nation. Some held that the earthquake was caused by a gigantic snake that had crawled under their towns and shaken their buildings as it moved. Some said "the earth is probably very old" and was about to "collapse." Some who had heard missionary sermons talked about a day of judgment or "the end of the world." The Ridge, who had been skeptical of the ghost riders in the sky, now came to the Moravian mission and asked how they explained the earthquakes. Charles Hicks, who had been studying the Bible, said that the quakes foretold "the last day."[16] When the Moravians were asked what they thought, they confessed that God might well send earthquakes to warn his children to repent of their sins and turn to Him, for sooner or later there would be an end to the world. The predictions from Christian and pagan sources seemed so similar that Chief Big Bear concluded that although "the white people know God from the Book," the Cherokees knew him "from other things."

In February 1812 a Cherokee father, caring for two sick children, was sitting in front of his cabin fire late at night. Suddenly a tall man "clothed entirely in the foliage of the trees, with a wreath of the same foliage on

---

M-208) that the chiefs wanted exceptions made for useful whites living in the nation such as blacksmiths, teachers, missionaries, and "other mechanics."

[16] Moravian missionaries, Springplace Diary, March 1, 1812, MAS. Hicks, however, was already a convert to Christianity and in June 1812 presented himself for baptism at the Springplace mission.

his head," appeared in the cabin. He was "carrying a small child and had a larger child by the hand." The visitor said that the child in his arm was the Great Spirit and that the Great Spirit might soon destroy the earth.[17] The Spirit was displeased that the Cherokees had sold so much of their land to the whites and especially that they had sold, in 1777, the sacred town of Tougaloo in South Carolina. Tougaloo was "the first place which God created" and where he had placed "the first fire" for man. Now the whites had desecrated the sacred hill by building a house on it. That house must be destroyed and the hill returned to its natural state. The Great Spirit was angry that the Cherokees were neglecting their religious dances, rituals, and festivals, particularly the festival in which they gave thanks for their harvests. Then the visitor explained to the Cherokee father that his children were sick because the Cherokee had forgotten their Indian herbal remedies; he gave the father "two small pieces of bark from a certain tree" and said if he brewed a drink from the bark and gave it to his children, they would soon be well. He told him about other remedies for sickness and finally said he must take the small child in his arms home, and disappeared.

The white men knew a great many things, but they could not always cure illness. The Cherokees believed that in nature there was a natural remedy for every sickness. These cures were being forgotten. The medicine men knew things that whites did not; the Great Spirit had come to remind this father that he must have more faith in his own Indian understanding of the spirit world and the health-giving remedies of the Cherokee religion.

The religious revival reached its peak that spring and summer, while other pressures mounted. Civil strife broke out among the Creeks, and the Cherokees feared that they might be dragged into it. In June, the United States declared war on the British and the Cherokees had to decide whether to join the war and, if they did, on which side. The young chiefs favored supporting the United States. Most Cherokees preferred neutrality, however, and that was how the Council voted.

Meigs became aware of the Ghost Dance movement in March 1812 when he reported that great efforts were being made in the nation "to appease the Anger of the Great Spirit which they conceive is manifest by the late shocks of the earth." As a result, "they have revived their religious dances of ancient origin," which they practiced with great "solemnity." After these dances they "repair to the Water, go in and wash" in the old ritual of purification. "These ablutions," Meigs said, "are intended to

[17] Moravian missionaries, Springplace Diary, February 17, 1812, MAS. The German-speaking missionaries translated the term "Great Spirit" as "God" but the informant was not Christian and would not have used the term "God."

show that their sins are washed away and that they are cleansed from all defilements." He was not alarmed by the revival. There were "some fanatics" who tried to play upon the fears of the more ignorant, but the acculturated chiefs were opposed to the entire movement. The prophets and visionaries were saying that "the Great Spirit is angry with them for adopting the manners, customs and habits of the white people who they think are very wicked." In Meigs's view, the old people were annoyed at the young mixed bloods who had learned to play fiddles and dance Virginia reels and country dances in the manner of the whites. He did not find any anger expressed toward whites or missionaries. But on some occasions, after dancing for a long time around the fire, some Cherokees "have thrown their clothing into the fire" to show their rejection of "civilization." Even some who were wealthy enough to wear "fine muslin dresses" were burning them.[18]

One prophet had a vision that "on a certain day" hailstones the size of half bushels would fall and destroy all those who did not repair to a certain spot in the hills. The people in his village had fled to that spot on the day he predicted and hidden in caves to escape the destruction. Another prophecy said that there would soon be an eclipse of the moon and when the world was all dark, the nonbelievers would be destroyed. One Cherokee heard that there would be an eclipse of the sun for three days "during which all the white people would be snatched away as well as Indians who had any clothing or household articles of the whiteman's kind, together with all their cattle." One more positive prophecy spoke not of destruction but of the creation of "a new earth" of beauty and harmony.

Had the more immediate problem of war on their borders not forced attention to more mundane matters toward the end of 1812, this religious movement might eventually have produced a single charismatic prophet who, like Tenkswatawa among the Shawnees or Handsome Lake among the Senecas, could have correlated all the feelings and half-articulated hopes and fears of the believers into a single, coherent, and compelling message around which the nation might have rallied. But no such prophet appeared.[19] Many minor prophets rose and fell as their prophecies failed to materialize. Eventually leadership returned to the secular young chiefs who were making Cherokee political nationalism the central aspect of revitalization. These chiefs were able to play upon the emotions aroused in

---

[18] Return J. Meigs to William Eustis, March 19, 1812, M-208.

[19] Thomas L. McKenney, in his account of the movement received from The Ridge in the early 1830s, maintains that it was all centered in a single prophet named "Charles" (or Tsali), but none of the contemporary accounts substantiates this. See Thomas L. McKenney and James Hall, *Biographical Sketches and Anecdotes of Ninety-five of 120 Principal Chiefs from the Indian Tribes of North America* (Washington, D.C.: U.S. Department of Interior, 1967) pp. 191–92.

the revival by directing them toward the old ideal of the warrior who won the approval of his people and of the Great Spirit by victory in battle, thus combining religious fervor and nationalism.

The plan of the young chiefs was to convince the average Cherokee, who was much impressed by the revival, that his enemy was not the white American or his ways but the Creek Indians and the British. Some old chiefs like Chulio believed that "the white people are responsible" for all the troubles the nation faced; he even blamed them for the earthquakes, "because they had already taken possession of so much of the Indians' land and wanted still more." The land was heaving in distress at the white American land hunger and dispossession of the Indians. But young chiefs, like The Ridge, said the earthquake came from the wickedness of the Cherokees themselves, their drunkenness, brawls, and killing of each other in petty quarrels. There were those who saw at the heart of their troubles and emotional malaise a basic moral question regarding personal honesty. One Cherokee woman, for example, who was asked to throw her European clothes into a campfire after a dance, remarked that this "was nothing," that "they ought to become good people and leave off stealing horses and drinking whiskey" if they wished to make the Great Spirit happy. Another Cherokee, told to put off his white man's clothes, said: "It is no matter what cloathes I wear while my heart is straight."[20]

Underlying the Ghost Dance movement was a basic turmoil between the behavior of the inner and the outer man, between the spiritual harmony that should be and the moral confusion that was. At this stage in their renascence the Cherokees were not able to reconcile the old ways and the new. In the end, the spiritual fervor of the revival was turned aside by the excitement of war; moral concern was shunted into national concern. In 1813 the Ghost Dance gave way to war chants.

[20] Return J. Meigs to William Eustis, March 19, 1812, M-208.

NINE

THE CREEK WAR, 1812–1814

Father, your officers treated us as friends embarked in a common cause with them, acting against a common enemy, and we felt honored and felt an emulation not to be outdone in all the offices of friendly communication. . . . —Cherokee chiefs to President Madison after the Creek War

Fearful that the Ghost Dance movement would, as Meigs said, have a "retrograde" effect upon the nation's revitalization, the young chiefs opposed it. They hoped that Cherokee participation in the War of 1812 on the side of the United States would unify their nation and advance its popularity with white Americans. But the Creek War proved to be a tragedy for the Cherokees as well as for the Creeks.

The Creek Nation, like the Cherokee, had fought with the British against the colonists during the Revolution and had joined with the Cherokees in continuing their guerrilla warfare along the southeastern frontier until 1794. When the Creeks finally capitulated in 1794, Benjamin Hawkins was sent to reside among them as their agent. The Creeks, like the Cherokees, were a loose confederation of some sixty towns divided into two regions, the Lower Creek Towns in southern Georgia near Florida and the Upper Creek Towns in central Alabama just to the south of the Cherokee Lower Towns. Hawkins, ignoring their decentralized town system, divided the nation into districts and instructed each district to send from one to five chiefs to represent it at a national council. He allowed the Lower Creeks to elect a chief (or speaker) and the Upper Creeks to elect a chief (or speaker). The council then elected the chief of the whole nation. When the council was not in session, a group of chiefs led by the national chief and the two regional speakers served as an executive committee to consult with Hawkins about all decisions. Thus rather than the long process through which the Cherokees worked out their own centralized system in 1810, the Creeks had centralization imposed upon them by their agent in 1796. Under Hawkins's forceful management, they too began the transformation from a hunting to an agricultural economy.

Those chiefs who worked closely with Hawkins received the lion's share of the annuities and utensils for farming and domestic manufacturing, as was the case with Doublehead's clique among the Cherokees. Hawkins also persuaded the Creeks to adopt a system of centralized police authority many years before the Cherokees, but unlike the Cherokee Lighthorse, the Creek police had power to execute those whom the executive committee of their nation considered to merit it. As among the Cherokees, clan retaliation was declared invalid under this Creek policing system. When the police were reluctant to act, Hawkins threatened to withhold annuities and technical assistance until the chiefs forced the police to punish those whom Hawkins designated. Hawkins also forced the chiefs into major land cessions including most of their hunting ground in southeastern Georgia. By 1810, as in the Cherokee Nation, there was growing resentment against this autocratic system. Under these circumstances, one might have expected the Cherokees to have sided with the Creeks who led the civil war in 1813. They were fighting against an overly rapid and coercive program of acculturation under chiefs, similar to Doublehead, whose views were not representative of their people. Moreover, the Creeks underwent in 1811 much the same kind of religious revival that stirred the Cherokees, although the Creek revival was apparently augmented and shaped from the outside by visits from Tecumseh and the Shawnee prophets. The Cherokees also remembered that a generation earlier the Creeks had befriended those Cherokees who, under Dragging Canoe, refused to yield to the American revolutionists and moved west to found the Lower Towns. The displaced Cherokees had been allowed to found these new towns in 1781 on land in northern Alabama that was in part under Creek control.

In October 1811, Tecumseh and his prophets came to the Creek capital at Tuckabatchee and asked the Creeks to join his confederacy of western tribes. Underneath his request was the distinct possibility that with British help there might soon be a general Indian uprising to throw the white Americans back across the Appalachians. A delegation of Cherokees, led by The Ridge, went to hear Tecumseh talk and was dismayed to hear the message that his prophets had received from the Great Spirit:

Kill the old chiefs, friends to peace; kill the cattle, the hogs and fowls; do not work, destroy the wheels and looms, throw away your ploughs and everything used by the Americans. Sing the song of the Indians of the Northern lakes and dance their dance. Shake your war clubs, shake yourselves, you will frighten the Americans; their arms will drop from their hands, the ground will become a bog and mire them, and you may knock them on the head with your war clubs. I will be with you my Shawanees as soon as our friends the British, are ready for us. Lift up the war club with your right hand; be strong and I will come and shew you how to use it.[1]

[1] ASP I, 845. Whether Ridge and the Cherokees at Tuckabatchee heard exactly this version of the Shawnee prophecy is uncertain, but they heard something similar to it.

Tecumseh's appeal to reject acculturation and prepare for war on the whites made no impression on the Cherokee visitors, but it did receive a warm response from some of the younger Creek chiefs of the Upper Creek Towns who were chafing under the rule of Hawkins and the Lower Creeks. They had never before rebelled against their old chiefs as the Cherokees had, but they had developed strong resentment against them. These young Creek chiefs, led by Opothle Micco, Little Warrior, Peter McQueen, and William Weatherford, secretly accepted the offer to join Tecumseh. They learned the songs and dances of the Shawnee prophets and began to behave more aggressively toward their old chiefs, Big Warrior, William McIntosh, Tustenugee Thlocco, and Tustenugee Hoppoie.[2]

Hawkins refused to take this ghost dance movement seriously. Big Warrior assured him that the Creek people would never accede to the mad ideas of Tecumseh and his prophets. The Cherokees, however, were convinced that there soon would be a British and Indian war against the Americans and that the Creeks (or some of them) would participate in it. Young Cherokee chiefs like The Ridge favored aiding the Americans; some of the ghost dancers probably sided with Tecumseh. The great majority was undecided.

Meigs wrote to the Secretary of War in December 1811 to say he was convinced that the Cherokees "wish to live in peace and be governed by the treaties existing between their nation and the United States."[3] He had warned the Cherokees to ignore Tecumseh. In May 1812, a month before war broke out between Britain and America, Meigs reported to Eustis that "three young chiefs, men of property and considerable information, came into the Council and observed that there would be war between the United States and the English and that they thought it would be for the advantage of the nation to offer their aid to our Government, and that they wished each to raise a number of young warriors and offer their service on the terms of pay and emolument of our military corps."[4] The three chiefs were The Ridge, John Walker, and John Lowrey. Meigs thought the War Department should take up their offer. The volunteers whom the young chiefs could muster would be of "great service in any

---

[2] For the origin and military aspects of the Creek War see Michael D. Green, *The Politics of Indian Removal: Creek Government and Society in Crisis* (Lincoln: University of Nebraska Press, 1982), pp. 37–45; Angie Debo, *The Road to Disappearance* (Norman: University of Oklahoma Press, 1971), chap. 3; Cotterill, *Southern Indians*, chaps. 8–9; Michael P. Rogin, *Fathers and Children: Andrew Jackson and the Subjugation of the American Indians* (New York: Knopf, 1975), chap. 5; and Pound, *Benjamin Hawkins*, chaps. 12–13. For Meigs's version of the origin of the war see his letter to John Armstrong, August 23, 1813, M-221, reel 55, #9217.

[3] Return J. Meigs to William Eustis, December 4, 1811, M-221, reel 47, #1650.

[4] Return J. Meigs to William Eustis, May 8, 1812, reel 47, #1813.

active campaign," he said, especially as cavalry units "because they are real horsemen" and "they love war; it has no terrors for them." Meigs had only one qualm about the plan; he wondered whether the Cherokee warriors "might be restrained from acts of barbarity"—such as scalping British soldiers who fell in combat. "I know that the humanity of our Government would revolt at the idea of Indian Auxilliaries" fighting against white men, but "to employ them against British Indians would not be considered inconsistent with the principles of self defense."[5] He assumed that the Cherokees would be fighting Tecumseh's Shawnees. Meigs and Hawkins did not expect that the Creeks would become allies of the British.[6]

On the other hand, the frontier whites of Alabama and Tennessee not only were fearful of the Shawnees and the Creeks but were even apprehensive about the Cherokees. Governor Willie Blount wrote to the Secretary of War frequently during 1812, telling him the Cherokees were not to be trusted.[7] The general anti-Indian hysteria among Western whites worried Meigs. He believed the frontiersmen were itching for an excuse to start a war with the Cherokees, Chickasaws, and Creeks because "they wish for a pretext to drive them off their lands, and it is with some difficulty that they have hitherto been restrained."[8] The whites would seize upon any incident to accuse the Cherokees of being allied with the British and immediately launch an invasion to wipe them out.

The frontier tension was not wholly unjustified, though it was misdirected. The Shawnees had joined with the British, who had commissioned Tecumseh as a colonel in their army. Meanwhile the young Creeks in the Upper Creek Towns were beginning to flout the authority of their old chiefs. After performing their ghost dances they were destroying their plows, manufactured clothing, cattle, and other property associated with white civilization. The Upper Creek chief, Little Warrior, went north in February 1813 to visit Tecumseh. His purpose was to obtain arms from him and to learn Tecumseh's war plans. On his way home, several members of Little Warrior's party attacked a white settlement near the mouth of the Ohio River and took seven or eight scalps. Upon his return Little Warrior asked the Creek Council to declare war on the Americans. The

[5] Ibid.

[6] Cotterill, *Southern Indians*, pp. 176–78; Pound, *Benjamin Hawkins*, pp. 221–28.

[7] See for example, Willie Blount to William Eustis, July 26, 1812, M-221, reel 42, #8025, and Willie Blount to James Monroe, January 28, 1813, reel 50, #4827. See also John Finley to William Eustis, April 26, 1813, M-221, reel 52, #6637. Blount, like his constituents in Tennessee, was hoping for an excuse to send an army against the Cherokees and thus to acquire by force the land that the Cherokees refused to cede.

[8] Return J. Meigs to William Eustis, January 11, M-221, reel 55, #8838.

council categorically refused.[9] When Hawkins learned of the raid, he ordered Big Warrior and the chiefs to send their lighthorse police to execute Little Warrior and all the others who had participated in it. The chiefs followed Hawkins's orders and their police killed ten of the thirteen in the war party. Before they could kill Little Warrior, however, he and the clan relatives of those executed struck back, taking blood revenge against the members of the police force. This action began the Creek Civil War.

Hawkins and Big Warrior were confident that they could easily put down the rebels, for they were at the outset only a small minority of the Creek Nation. In April 1813, some of the Shawnees and the Creek rebels (called Red Sticks) came to Pathkiller, Principal Chief of the Cherokees since Black Fox's death in 1811. They asked him whether the Cherokees would assist them in their war against the Lower Creeks. Pathkiller declined to get involved, pointing out the danger this would bring upon his nation.[10] In August the Lower Creeks asked the Cherokees to aid them against the Red Sticks; again the Cherokees refused to become embroiled.[11]

On July 30, The Ridge, John Walker and John Lowrey had come to Meigs and renewed the offer they had made in May 1812 to raise a volunteer army to fight against the British and their Indian allies, including the Creeks.[12] Meigs wrote to John Armstrong, who had succeeded Eustis in the War Department: "The civil war amongst the Creeks has placed the Cherokees in a disagreeable situation, and should the insurgent Creeks get the ascendancy, they will, if possible, corrupt the Cherokees."[13] He said he had warned the Cherokees "not to let any of the insurgent party [the Creek Red Sticks] come into their Country because it may subject them to the suspicion of the white people on the frontier." Everyone knew that the British had supplied arms from Pensacola to the Red Sticks in July.[14]

Apparently about seven thousand of the twenty thousand Creeks had joined the Red Sticks of the Upper Creek Towns; those in the Lower Creek Towns realized that it would not be easy to defeat them.[15] Charles

[9] Cotterill, *Southern Indians*, pp. 176–78.

[10] Return J. Meigs to John Armstrong, April 22, 1813, M-221, reel 55, #8891, and Return J. Meigs to John Armstrong, August 6, 1813, M-221, reel 55, #9112.

[11] Return J. Meigs to John Armstrong, August 23, 1813, M-221, reel 55, #9217.

[12] Return J. Meigs to William Eustis, May 12, 1812, M-208; Return J. Meigs to John Armstrong, July 30, 1813, M-208; Charles Hicks to Return J. Meigs, July 31, 1813, M-208; Thurman Wilkins, *Cherokee Tragedy* (Norman: University of Oklahoma Press, 1985), pp. 60, 63, 336–37.

[13] Return J. Meigs to John Armstrong, August 6, 1813, M-208.

[14] Cotterill, *Southern Indians*, pp. 179–81; Rogin, *Fathers and Children*, p. 148.

[15] John Braham to Andrew Jackson, August 29, 1813, M-221, reel 50, #5161. Braham

Hicks and some other Cherokee chiefs expressed sympathy for the rebels, at least to the extent of blaming the old chiefs for being too subservient to Hawkins and too willing to become "land speculators" at the expense of their people.[16] But on the whole, the Cherokees thought the rebels were wrong to accept British arms and foment a rebellion at a time when it would clearly inflame the whole frontier, endangering all the other tribes.

In addition to favoring the offer of Ridge, Walker, and Lowrey to raise an army against the Red Sticks ("the hostile Creeks"), Meigs had advised the Cherokees to declare their support for the Lower Creek Towns ("the friendly Creeks"). This would demonstrate to white Americans that the Cherokees were concerned for the safety of the United States and willing to lay down their lives to protect it.[17] Then, on August 28, 1813, the rebel Creeks attacked a frontier stockade, known as Fort Mims, at the juncture of the Tombigbee and Alabama rivers. They massacred not only the armed garrison but many unarmed farmers and their families who had gone to the fort for protection. Close to five hundred whites were killed and the white frontier was outraged. As the frontiersmen took to arms to retaliate, the Cherokees knew they had no choice but to demonstrate their support for the whites or they too would soon be attacked as potential, if not yet open, enemies.

The War Department, after consulting the governors of Tennessee and Georgia and gaining their legislature's approval, accepted Meigs's suggestion to enroll Cherokee volunteers. They were to be enlisted in the frontier militia and to be given the same rank, equipment, and salary.[18] Although the Cherokee Council never officially voted to join the war, the chiefs who had favored neutrality raised no objections to the volunteers. By the end of October Meigs had enrolled about five hundred.[19]

His plan was to enroll them in companies under their own officers: some were to be lieutenants, captains, and majors; above that rank, command would go to whites. During the course of the next year probably as many as six hundred Cherokees were at one time or another engaged in the war against the Red Stick Creeks. Meigs supplied them with guns, power, lead, flints, and blankets out of the agency funds.[20] At the outset those commissioned as lieutenants included Charles Hicks, John Ross,

---

said he thought the Cherokees would provide one thousand soldiers to fight with Jackson's troops.

[16] Hicks's letter to Meigs is included in Meigs's letter to John Armstrong, August 23, 1813, reel 55, #9217.

[17] Return J. Meigs to John Armstrong, July 30, 1813, M-208.

[18] Wilkins, *Cherokee Tragedy*, pp. 63–65.

[19] Return J. Meigs to John Armstrong, November 17, 1813, M-221, reel 55, #9287.

[20] Ibid. See also Return J. Meigs to John Armstrong June 4, 1814, reel 64, #7130.

The Ridge, Richard Brown, and Big Cabbin; the captains included John Lowrey, Alexander Sanders, Chulio, and David McNair; the majors included Richard Taylor and Gideon Morgan. Pathkiller, as Principal Chief, though too old to fight, was given the honorary rank of Colonel. During the course of the war three Cherokees became colonels: Gideon Morgan, Richard Brown, and John Lowrey (all of whom were whites married to Cherokees); four advanced to major: The Ridge, Sanders, John Walker, and James Brown. Among those who distinguished themselves in battle were George Guess (Sequoyah), White Path, Charles Reece, Chulio, The Whale, Junaluska, and John Thompson.[21] The Cherokees also aided the war effort by providing saltpeter for powder. Richard Riley, son of the interpeter Samuel Riley, was manufacturing 1,000 pounds of powder a day in his powder mill at Creek Path by January 1813.[22]

When Meigs sent the Cherokees off to join the various army units commanded by Generals Andrew Jackson, John Cocke, John Coffee, and James White late in October 1813, he gave them an exhortatory speech about their roles as United States soldiers. "You will find the Army to be a school of instruction that will elevate and raise up your minds to sentiments unknown to barbarous nations, and here it is proper to observe that even in war, we [white Americans] never lose sight of humanity. The United States do not make war on women and children and the aged and helpless, and they always spare the unresisting prisoners."[23] Meigs apparently knew little of the behavior of the frontier militia. They were to perform deeds of barbarity against the Creeks far worse than those of any Cherokee. In any case, neither Cherokees nor white troops had any qualms about shooting unarmed Creek women, children, and aged. The Creek War turned out to be little more than a massacre from beginning to end, a disaster from which the Creek Nation never recovered.

The Cherokees fought in five different engagements in two separate campaigns, one in the fall and early winter of 1813 and the other in March 1814. In most of their engagements they constituted only a small part of the fighting force. The generals permitted them to take their own prisoners, to seize booty, and to take possession of black slaves belonging to Red Stick Creeks. The combination of scalps and booty made the war memorable for those Cherokees who fought. They also enjoyed the honor of fighting side by side with their white brothers; it gave them a

[21] The best account of the Cherokees' part in the Creek War is in Thurman, *Cherokee Tragedy*, pp. 62–78. See also Cotterill, *Southern Indians*, pp. 185–88. For lists of Cherokee war heroes see October 31, 1815, M-208, and May 4, 1816, M-15, reel 3, p. 340.

[22] Return J. Meigs to William Eustis, January 11, 1813, M-221, reel 55, #8838.

[23] Meigs's talk to the Cherokee volunteers is in the Tennessee State Archives, Nashville, Cherokee Collection, VI, C-1, box 3, folder 1. It is undated but probably was given in September 1813.

chance to prove their valor and gain self-respect. Afterwards their white commanders were warm in praise of the Cherokees' courage and daring.[24]

Their first engagement near Turkeytown, late in October, routed the Creeks. Pursuing them, the two groups fought again at Tallashatchee on November 3. The Creeks ran out of ammunition and the Cherokee and militia killed 186 Creek warriors and even more women and children. Only five white soldiers were killed and no Cherokees. John Walker wrote to Meigs after the battle that it was a "dismal" sight "to see Women and Children slaughtered with their father's" by General Coffee's cavalry.[25] On November 9, General Jackson with two thousand militiamen, including some Cherokees, fought at Talladega Town against one thousand Creeks. Three hundred Creeks were killed, again including many women and children. Only fifteen were killed on the American side. On November 19, General White with one thousand militia and four hundred Cheokees attacked a group of sixty Creek warriors at the Hillabee Towns who wanted to surrender.[26] The Creeks offered no resistance and no one on the American side was killed; nonetheless the sixty Creek warriors were wiped out along with many women and children. There were 250 prisoners. In January 1814 a sharp engagement took place at Emukfaw Creek on the Tallapoosa River, in which the Cherokees and "friendly" Creek troops saved Jackson's dwindling army from defeat. Jackson was wounded. Trying to retreat, he was attacked again on January 24 at Enotochopco Creek. The Americans lost one hundred soldiers, but the Creeks lost more and withdrew.[27] Jackson's soldiers, their enlistment time over, refused to reenlist and went home. This campaign ended without victory. Jackson was furious at his troops, calling them "deserters."

Jackson obtained new enlistments in February and left Fort Struther in March for a final battle with the Red Sticks at Tohopeka (Horseshoe Bend). The Creeks, under Chief Menawa, were outnumbered two to one with their backs to a horseshoe loop in the Tallapoosa River. They fought hard but, as so often in this war, ran out of ammunition. When they tried to escape across the river, they discovered that some Cherokees had gone around behind them, swum across the river, and taken all their canoes. Between two and three hundred Creeks were shot in the river as they tried to swim across; only fifty of the one thousand Creeks got out alive.

[24] For Jackson's praise of the Cherokee volunteers see M-222, August 14, 1814, reel 12, #4729.

[25] John Walker to Return J. Meigs, November 5, 1813, M-208.

[26] Gideon Walker to Return J. Meigs, November 23, 1813, M-208.

[27] See Cotterill, *Southern Indans*, pp. 186–87; Mooney, "Myths of the Cherokees," pp. 80–84; Rogin, *Fathers and Children*, pp. 150–54.

The white militia suffered 26 killed, 107 wounded; the Cherokees, 18 dead and 36 wounded; the friendly Creeks, 5 killed and 14 wounded. After the battle the white militia flayed strips of skin from the dead Creeks and braided them into belts and bridles; as they counted the dead Creeks, they cut the nose off each corpse.[28] A few of the Red Sticks continued to fight sporadically until June but most fled to Florida and joined the Seminoles. Jackson chased them there and then had to leave to fight the British at New Orleans. The Cherokees, however, returned home after the Battle of Horseshoe Bend and played no part in the other phases of the war. The total Cherokee losses during the two campaigns were thirty-six killed and fifty-one wounded.

General Jackson praised them and the friendly Creeks: "You have shown yourselves worthy of the friendship of your Father, the President." Madison later gave special awards to about a dozen Cherokees for their bravery.[29] The Cherokee soldiers brought back fifty Creek warriors as prisoners and over three hundred women and children. Most of these eventually were allowed to return to the Creek Nation, though some of the children remained as slaves or were adopted into Cherokee families.[30] No record was kept of the number of black slaves taken from the Creeks by the Cherokees, but it was considerable.

Their service in the war did not bring the respect and fair treatment that the Cherokees expected, though it put an end to the Ghost Dance movement. The federal government was reluctant to live up to its promise to pay Indian soldiers on the same pay scale as white militiamen. The War Department did not want to provide pensions for the Cherokee wounded or to the widows of the Cherokee dead. Even more disheartening, Jackson's militiamen, who had crossed through Cherokee territory to join the troops in the Creek Nation and had then marched through it again to go home, had taken out their hatred of all Indians by committing tremendous depredations upon Cherokee livestock, crops, and dwellings. The most bitter blow of all came when Jackson made his punitive peace treaty with the Creeks at Fort Jackson in July 1814 and included in the cessions demanded 2.2 million acres of land in northern Alabama that be-

[28] Mooney, "Myths of the Cherokees," pp. 83–84; Wilkins, *Cherokee Tragedy*, pp. 75–77; Cotterill, *Southern Indians*, p. 187. For Jackson's description of the Battle of Horsehoe Bend see M-221, April 2, 1814, reel 53, #8414–8418.

[29] For a list of those whom Madison honored see M-208, October 31, 1815. For Jackson's praise of his Indian soldiers see M-222, August 14, 1814, reel 12, #4729.

[30] See Wilkins, *Cherokee Tragedy*, p. 70, on Major Ridge's "adoption" of a Creek child as a slave; Return J. Meigs to Willie Blount, November 4, 1814, M-221, reel 59, #3338; Return J. Meigs to William Crawford, May 2, 1815, M-208. Most of the Red Stick Creek warriors having been killed, their wives and children became subject to slavery by Indian custom and their black slaves became the booty of war.

longed to the Cherokees. He did so in order to open up a broad swath of Indian territory to white settlement stretching all the way from Tennessee to the Gulf.[31]

To his credit, Meigs risked the displeasure of General Jackson and did his best to rectify all of these injuries to the Cherokees. After the Battle of New Orleans, Jackson had become a national hero; it was almost impossible for any politician to stand against him. He was particularly a hero to the frontiersmen of the southeast for ridding them forever of any European threat to the Mississippi Valley and for ending the need to treat the southeastern Indians with kid gloves as Washington, Adams, Jefferson, and Madison had done. The Creek War and the War of 1812 had provided the frontier voters with all the excuses they needed to dispossess the Indians at will and they made no distinction between those who had fought against the United States and those who had fought with them. Meigs and the disheartened Cherokee leaders waged a desperate uphill battle from 1814 to 1816 to try to overcome the intense western prejudice that vented itself upon the Cherokees as well as their neighbors.

In June 1814, Meigs wrote to the Secretary of War that he was truly shocked at the amount of callous devastation of Cherokee property caused by "the Rude part of our armies on their marches to and from the Creek nation."[32] He placed the blame chiefly upon the rank-and-file militia from East Tennessee and attributed it to "prejudice" against all Indians. Jackson's soldiers had shot Cherokee horses, cattle, and hogs for their own amusement and had pillaged and burned Cherokee houses. They had destroyed crops across a wide swath of the Cherokee Nation in northern Alabama. It would take years, Meigs said, for some parts of the nation to recover from these senseless acts. Had the Creeks invaded the Cherokee Nation, they could hardly have caused more damage. The Cherokees demanded reparations and to that end Meigs obtained firsthand accounts from militia officers in Jackson's army, some of whom had tried in vain to prevent their undisciplined troops from such actions. "These depredations may at first seem incredible," Meigs told Secretary of War Armstrong, "but I have no doubt of the justness of the statements; these disorders are well known to thousands. I received a letter from an officer of high rank in the army in which he says, 'The return of the Horse [cavalry] thro' their Country has been marked by plunder and [by] prodigal, unnecessary and wanton destruction of property; their stocks of Cattle and hogs have been shot and suffered to rot untouched, their horses in some instances shared the same fate, their cloathing . . . has been stolen

[31] ASP I, 826.
[32] Return J. Meigs to John Armstrong, June 29, 1814, reel 64, #7672.

195

and in some instances, where they [Cherokees] remonstrated, their lives have been threatened.' "[33] On several occasions Cherokees had appealed to white militia officers to assist them, but they were told "it was of no use, that their men felt themselves unfettered from the laws and that they could not restrain them." Meigs reported that this "fell heavily on some families, having lost all their Cattle and hogs while their young warriors were in the field."[34] Several years later the Governor of Tennessee, Joseph McMinn, admitted the truth of all Meigs said and told the Cherokees: "Jackson's army took your property in the late war. Many very valuable houses were taken possession of by our army and the inhabitants and property thrown out of doors and in some instances the houses ruined."[35]

When Meigs finally tabulated the full amount of the damage, the War Department was shocked. He had verified claims for $22,863.85 that could be proven beyond doubt by testimony of white officers and he said the true damage was at least twice that amount. Seven of the leading Cherokees who had fought with Jackson wrote to President Madison to express their disappointment at the treatment their people received from the militiamen and frankly blamed it on racism. "Father, your officers treated us as friends embarked in a common cause with them, acting against a common enemy, and we felt honored and felt an emulation not to be outdone in all the offices of friendly communication; but we have now to state to our father that a great many white young Warriors, not feeling the ties that should bind them and make them strong by the principles of subordination [to their officers] and feeling liberty in the extreme, it relaxed into licentiousness, and they destroyed our Cattle, sheep, and hogs, and in some instances our horses, for mere sport or prejudice founded only on the differences in shades of complexion."[36]

When the Secretary of War asked Jackson for an explanation of this behavior by his troops, he denied everything. Meigs's verified list of claims he considered fraudulent: "No confidence can be placed in the honesty of an Indian," he said, assuming that the claims Meigs submitted were based upon Cherokee statements.[37] The most Jackson would admit was that some of his soldiers, starving, might have shot a hog or taken a chicken simply to keep alive. The War Department sent this information to

---

[33] Return J. Meigs to John Armstrong, May 5, 1814, M-221, reel 55, #9503.

[34] Ibid. See also Cherokee Council to James Madison, January 10, 1816, M-221, reel 1, #2814.

[35] Joseph McMinn stated this to the Cherokees on November 18, 1818, ASP II, 484–86.

[36] "Outline of an address" by the Cherokee delegation to Washington, D.C., undated but probably in December 1815. It is included on M-208, at the end of reel 6.

[37] Andrew Jackson to William Crawford, July 24, 1816, M-221, reel 70, #2639. See also Jackson to Crawford, December 23, 1816, M-15, reel 3, pp. 449–50.

Meigs, who then conscientiously submitted supporting affidavits from Jackson's officers. He explained to the War Department that the animals shot by the militia could not have been killed for food because "much of the meat was suffered to rot in the woods . . . untouched after being shot." Jackson's immense popularity made it difficult for Armstrong and Madison to refute him by paying the claims. The matter therefore became part of a larger negotiation over other Cherokee complaints at a meeting between the Cherokees and the Secretary of War in Washington in 1816.

The War Department proved as reluctant to admit that it had promised to treat Cherokee volunteers on the same basis as white militia as Jackson was to admit that his soldiers had done anything wrong. It even declined to pay the $5,656 that Meigs had advanced to equip the Cherokee volunteers with ammunition and blankets. Claiming that Meigs had acted without express authority, they demanded that he pay the government back for the equipment out of the Cherokee annuity. Meigs again devoted considerable time and effort to proving that this was standard equipment given to all regular soldiers and that he was told that if the governors of Tennessee and Georgia approved, the Cherokees would be admitted to the militia at equal pay, rank, and pension. He had letters to prove it. Over six hundred Cherokees, he said, had risked their lives, fought bravely, and in the view of some "had saved the lives of 1000 men who must have been lost without their aid." Now the government was denying them equal treatment.[38] Meigs had insisted upon regular enlistment for the Cherokee volunteers because he thought that only in this way could the savage be brought under proper discipline and be subject to court martial if he did not follow orders. Meigs had therefore kept careful records of enlistments, dates of service, killed, and wounded; when he totaled it up, he said that the War Department owed the Cherokees $55,423.84 in soldier's pay. He was particularly angry that widows and wounded were being denied both pay and pensions. For three years the government quibbled about this until finally Andrew Jackson cut the knot in July 1817 with a letter to the Secretary of War. He explained that he had considered the Cherokees under his command to be of equal status with the white militia: "They were to be considered in every respect on the same footing with the militia and entitled to every benefit. . . . I made this promise. . . . I hope it will be complied with."[39] It is significant that at this time Jackson was working desperately to persuade the Cherokees to cede more land or to exchange eastern land for western land. He could have ac-

[38] Return J. Meigs to John Armstrong, June 4, 1816, M-221, reel 64, #7130.
[39] Andrew Jackson to George Graham, July 9, 1817, M-221, reel 74, #5908.

knowledged the government's commitment three years earlier, but he did so only when he wanted a quid pro quo from the Cherokees.

In the end the central issue in this prolonged dispute over claims proved to be land, as always. The Cherokees wanted the President to prevent Jackson from taking 2.2 million acres of their territory in his treaty with the Creeks. To flout Jackson and the frontier voters of Tennessee and Alabama was a decision neither the Secretary of War nor the President wished to make. Yet the Cherokees' claim that the land was theirs, backed by Meigs's testimony and irrefutable historical evidence, was too solid to ignore. Federal and state officials persuaded themselves that if they did go so far as to accept their responsibility and treat the Cherokees honestly, then the least the Cherokees could do in response was to express their gratitude by ceding more land.

The Treaty of Fort Jackson in 1814 between Jackson and the Creeks had been extremely vague in defining the boundary lines of the Creek cession in Alabama that Jackson exacted for their "unprovoked, inhuman and sanguinary war" on the United States.[40] It had, however, defined an eastern and western boundary that Jackson clearly expected to extend north of the Tennessee River to the border of his home state. His view was that the Creeks had always owned the land up to the Tennessee River and that they had merely loaned a strip south of the river to Dragging Canoe and his Chickamauga warriors in 1777. The Cherokees claimed that they had always owned the area extending fifty miles south of the Tennessee River as far west as the Chickasaw boundary at about the present border of the State of Mississippi. Not only had they had settlements there since 1777 without challenge from the Creeks, but in the Treaty of Washington in 1806 the federal government had conceded their ownership of this southern side of the Tennessee River below Muscle Shoals. Both Meigs and Hawkins agreed with their claim. The Creeks, fearing that Jackson would take more land from them elsewhere if they conceded that this area near the Tennessee River belonged to the Cherokees, refused to make any statement.[41]

When Secretary of War William Crawford agreed to discuss this matter as well as their spoliation claims and the military pay and pensions claims with them in January 1816, the Cherokees sent some of their most experienced chiefs to Washington; Meigs accompanied them with the documentation for their positions on all three issues. The Cherokee National Council also asked the delegates to have the Secretary of War remove the intruders who were fast moving into this area on the assump-

[40] ASP I, 826.
[41] Return J. Meigs to Andrew Jackson, August 5, 1815, M-208; September 17, 1815, M-208; September 19, 1815, M-208; Royce, *Cherokee Nation of Indians*, pp. 77–80.

tion that it would soon be surveyed and open for sale. In addition, the Council stated that it wished to make arrangements to develop the iron ore in its territory so that "we may be supplied with iron utensils and the repair of our arms."[42] The nation was preparing for the next step in its economic development—the early stages of industrialization. Knowing that the government would not grant all its requests, no matter how just, without asking for land in return, the Council agreed that the delegates might consider ceding a tract of 94,720 acres on its easternmost border in western South Carolina. The legislature of South Carolina had twice called upon the federal government (in 1801 and 1814) to purchase this land from the Cherokees so that the state could extinguish the last Indian claims within its borders.[43] The Cherokees much preferred yielding this to losing the 2.2 millon acres in the Lower Town area that the Treaty of Fort Jackson would take; much of the area Jackson wanted was rich black-belt soil, suitable for growing cotton. The delegation consisted of The Ridge, John Walker, John Ross, Richard Taylor, and Cheucunnessee (Young Dragging Canoe).

In Washington, the public and press treated them royally as allies who had helped to defeat the Creeks with Jackson. The *National Intelligencer* interviewed them and noted that they were "men of cultivation and understanding," who dressed as white men and whose "appearance and deportment are such as to entitled them to respect and attention."[44] They were wined and dined at several social gatherings and basked in the glow of their acceptance as honored representatives of their people.

The meetings with Madison and Crawford began on February 16, 1816, and it was apparent that the President and Secretary were impressed by their arguments.[45] Madison told them on February 22 that he considered their claims for spoliation just and that he would see that pay and pensions for their soldiers and soldiers' widows were provided. He did not think their plan for an ironworks was adequately worked out, and this issue was put aside. The whole question of how much control Indians had over the mineral deposits on their land was becoming more delicate as the various western states pushed the claim that Indians, as "tenants at will,"

[42] Cherokee Council's instructions to a delegation to Washington, D.C., January 10, 1816, M-221, reel 70, #2820.

[43] Royce, *Cherokee Nation of Indians*, pp. 76–78. See also the resolution of the legislature of South Carolina, M-221, November 30, 1814, reel 60, #4149, and Governor David Williams of South Carolina to William Crawford, December 16, 1815, M-221, reel 72, #4325.

[44] Wilkins, *Cherokee Tragedy*, p. 88.

[45] John Lowery [Lowrey] to James Madison, February 19, 1816, M-221, reel 70, #2814–2820; Cherokee delegation to William Crawford, March 12, 1816, M-271, reel 1, #0935–0939. Many of the documents relating to this treaty negotiation in Washington can be found in ASP II, 88–114.

had no right to exploit any of their natural resources.[46] When they discussed their claim to the land south of the Tennessee River, the Cherokees were blunt in pointing out that Jackson, Coffee, and other Tennesseans had ulterior motives in claiming that land: "The spirit of gain urges them, the laurel of popularity prompts them" to "make crooked talks" and "like the serpent, speak with a split tongue."[47] There was little doubt that Jackson and his friends were heavily engaged in speculation over the ceded land because it was extremely valuable. "The Cherokee nation," said the delegates, "expected nothing but justice" and hoped not "to fall sacrifice to their [the speculators'] rapaciousness." Crawford was already annoyed that this area was filling up with squatters, for it was federal land; he had expected the federal government to sell it for a good price and recoup some of the war costs.[48]

While the delegation was making good headway in Washington, Jackson and Coffee were stealing a march on them back in Alabama. Jackson persuaded Crawford in November 1815 to make Coffee one of the commissioners for the Creek cessions. Coffee took it upon himself (with Jackson's urging) to survey (with some Creek advisors) the northern part of the cession even though he well knew it was being debated in Washington.[49] The line that Coffee ran in January and February 1816 naturally followed the wishes of Jackson, including within the cession the 2.2 million acres claimed by the Cherokees. Richard Riley, who lived near this area at Creek Path, wrote to the delegation on February 10, 1816, informing them that Coffee "insists very strongly that the line should strike the Tennessee at Deposit or Ditto's Landing, taking a part of our nation that the Creeks never laid any colour of claim to whatever. I see Verry clearly that the white people in this part of the country is not disposed to do justice to us." He also reported that "hundreds" of intruders had rushed into this area as soon as they knew Coffee had surveyed it, expecting to pick up land at the preemption price of $2 per acre that on the open market would be worth $20 per acre.[50] Coffee and Jackson had encouraged such an invasion to make it difficult for Madison and Crawford to sustain the Cherokees' claim to it. To do this, the government would now have to remove these intruders at heavy costs in army action and voter reaction. Crawford sent orders to Coffee and the other commissioners to make no final decison on the northern line of the Creek cession until negotiatons

[46] Wilkins, *Cherokee Tragedy*, pp. 90–91.

[47] Ibid., p. 90.

[48] William Crawford to Benjamin Harrison, October 16, 1815, M-15, reel 3, p. 275.

[49] Michael Rogin, *Fathers and Children*, pp. 170–72; Cotterill, *Southern Indians*, p. 195.

[50] Richard Riley to Return J. Meigs, February 10, 1816, M-208; Charles Hicks to Return J. Meigs, April 20, 1816, M-208.

in Washington were completed, but this did not stop the squatters.[51] At one point in the negotiatons Crawford asked whether the Cherokees would be willing to cede the land north of the Tennessee River that Doublehead was trying to sell when he was assassinated, but the delegates said they had no authority to consider this.

Finally, on March 22, to the Cherokees' delight, the Secretary of War agreed to grant all of their demands (including their right to the 2.2 million acres Jackson had expropriated) in exchange for the 94,720 acres in South Carolina (for which he paid them $5,000) and for the rights of way for several roads and navigable streams through their nation.[52] The delegates said this treaty would have to be ratified by the National Council, but they had no doubt of its approval. Crawford then signed the treaty in which the government acknowledged that Jackson had made a mistake; the Cherokee claim to the 2.2 million acres south of the Tennessee River was ceded back to them. This treaty also agreed to pay the Cherokees $25,500 in indemnities for "losses sustained by them in consequences of the march of the [Tennessee] militia" through their nation during the war. Finally, Madison ordered full pay and pensions for their soldiers.[53] The negotiations were in every respect a triumph for Meigs and for the Cherokee delegation. Crawford sent orders to the treaty commissioners to redraw the northern line of the Treaty of Fort Jackson.[54]

The Cherokee triumph was short-lived. The wrath of the whole western region poured in upon the President and Secretary of War once the contents of the treaty became known. General Jackson wrote in exasperation at the "retrocession" of land his troops had won with their blood from the Creeks. The Chickasaws said they were cheated out of some of their claims to the area. The citizens of Tennessee felt that the government had been hoodwinked by savages. The settlers in the Alabama area (then part of Mississippi Territory) were furious that this land would not be open for settlement, and of course the squatters fumed over their imminent ejection. In additon, all the politicians and land speculators in the area resented the loss of an immensely valuable piece of real estate that they had thought was in their grasp. "The Government certainly has been imposed upon," Jackson wrote to Crawford. He warned that it would be impossible to remove the citizens who had already settled in that area. They are "much enraged," Jackson said, and would fight rather than move out. "The militia will not answer for this service" because

[51] William Crawford to John Coffee, March 14, 1816, M-15, reel 3, p. 309.
[52] Royce, *Cherokee Nation of Indians*, pp. 69–70.
[53] ASP II, 88–89, 109–110; Royce, *Cherokee Nation of Indians*, pp. 69–70.
[54] William Crawford to John Coffee, April 16, 1816, M-15, reel 3, p. 328.

"their feelings are the same as the settlers."[55] Jackson also protested the insult to his troops implied in the payment of indemnities to the Cherokees' claims for spoliation and demanded that the whole issue be reopened before the Cherokees were paid anything. Memorials were sent to Madison from citizens of Tennessee and Alabama: "We cannot agree that it is proper to sacrifice the convenience and welfare of so large a portion of the members of the community to gratify the cupidity of any tribe."[56] The "soil [is] fertile beyond description" and the Indians were wasting it. "The Hero who has since immortalized himself" at New Orleans had won this land for American settlement; the land was "propitious to the culture of Cotton" and was not only a matter of great "commercial advantage" but "identified with our National Glory."[57] The westerners were convinced that short-sighted officials in Washington were trying to negate the great victory they had won for the commercial expansion of the United States. They were not to be cheated out of the spoils of victory by a few artful Cherokees who had imposed upon the gullible Madison and Crawford back east.

The President had miscalculated; the political repercussions were too strong. The Cherokees would have to make some concessions. Trying to allay the anger of the westerners, Crawford wrote to Meigs on May 27 that he had authorized new negotiations with the Cherokees. Then on July 5 Crawford wrote to Jackson: "The agent of the Cherokee nation [Meigs] has been directed to renew to that tribe the offer made to their deputation last winter to purchase their claim to the lands lying west of the Chickasaw Old Fields [near Creek Path]. . . . He has also been directed to effect the purchase of all the Cherokee lands lying north of the Tennessee river."[58] This was the land that Madison and Crawford had just declared to be the legitimate property of the Cherokees. The treaty of 1816 was to be a Pyrrhic one. The Cherokees were now told that they must yield all they had regained and more—land north of the Tennessee as well, though this time they would be paid for it. The tract they had given up in South Carolina in May 1816 was a complete loss to them. The government's position was that although it had verified the Cherokee claim to the land Jackson took without recompense, it now wished to take it by paying for it. The Cherokees did not want the money; they wanted their land.

Crawford told Meigs and the senators from Tennessee that the government would offer "$6000 a year in perpetuity" for the tract south of the

[55] ASP II, 110–11, 114.
[56] ASP II, 89–91.
[57] Petition of Leroy Pope et al., July 17, 1816, reel 71,#3678.
[58] ASP II, 100–102, 112.

Tennessee and $20,000 for the 1.2 million Cherokee acres north of the Tennessee. He also provided Meigs with extra funds "to distribute presents among certain chiefs to the amount of $5000 and to John Lowrey the value of his possessions north of the Tennessee [at Battle Creek]."[59] Lowrey indicated that if he could be paid adequately for his holding, he would not oppose a sale. Meigs, whose honor had been vindicated in Washington, now felt free to put whatever pressure was needed on individual chiefs to secure more land for the United States. He had good reason to think that some of the chiefs in this Lower Town area were ready to give it up. Not only was it heavily infested with rough and determined white intruders but this area had been the most heavily devastated by the militia depradations. The people there were discouraged. Clearly there would be no peace for them even if they tried to hang on. The war had unleashed raging hatred of the Indians and irresistible demands for Indian land—particularly land on which cotton could be grown. No Indian treaty could withstand this kind of public pressure.

Still the Cherokees tried. The National Council met on July 20, when Meigs began distributing the first installment of reparation payments for the militia spoliations and the first part of their soldiers' pay for military service. The Council heard the report of the delegation at Washington and happily approved their treaty (with a proviso, later disallowed, that compensation be given to those Cherokees who had to move from good farms in South Carolina). Meigs and Crawford's treaty commissioners from Tennessee then presented the requests of the President that the Council cede the 1.2 million acres the nation still owned north of the Tennessee River as well as the 2.2 million acres that had just been affirmed to it south of the Tennessee. As Meigs later wrote to Crawford: "It was urged on them that their duty to the Government, which had listened to them while at the city by their deputation, and by the constant care of them, required a compliance" with these demands. Further, they were told that "their interest, perhaps their security, required it (having reference to the agitation of the Citizens of West Tennesee)." Nevertheless, the council held firm. "After their slow and tedious deliberations," Meigs reported, "they returned an answer in the negative." Meigs considered this sheer ingratitude. "Their insensibility to the advantage they received from the liberality of the government" in Washington was unforgivable.[60]

Meigs repeated in a letter to Jackson on August 6, 1816, something he had said before the war: the Cherokees had developed "an erroneous Idea

[59] William Crawford to Return J. Meigs, May 27, 1816, M-208.
[60] Return J. Meigs to William Crawford, August 19, 1816, ASP II, 113-14.

of their Sovereignty and independence" but "this fictitious sovereignty was intirely given up [by them] at the treaty of Hopewell" in 1785. It was unfortunate, he added, that in the treaty of 1791 at Holston "the words 'solemn guarantee' are used [for the borders] instead of the word *alotted*." The government had never meant to solemnly guarantee their border to them, Meigs said. It had only meant to allot them that land to live on as tenants at will until the government had need of it. Unfortunately, he said, the Cherokees had developed from this "guarantee" a notion that they could be "an empire within an empire" in which "each [nation, the Cherokees and the United States] having a veto on the other," there might never be any way to obtain their land or to remove them. "They were, at the close of the Revolution, a conquered people," Meigs went on, "their lands were forfeited, and at the treaty of Hopewell they were considered as minors—and there is no way to save them but by considering them as in a state of minority" and compelling them to do what their guardians knew was best. As minors "they are intitled to protection" by the federal government from invasion by frontier whites. As a so-called sovereign nation, they were not entitled to such protection; this "would soon seal their destruction."[61]

From this viewpoint, now pervasive among western whites and close to approval in the War Department, the old Indian policy of "civilization" and integration *in situ* was almost over. It was now possible for the War Department to threaten the Cherokees or any other Indian nation with the withdrawal of federal protection—to leave them to the mercy of the ruthless frontier citizens—in order to compel them to agree to any treaty put before them. Jefferson's statement that the Indian nations had the right to say yes or no to any treaty proposal was now to be described as a temporary expedient, adopted until potential European allies ceased to make the Indians a threat to the westward expansion of the white American population. "The United States have the right to make any arrangements they think proper and just with respect to their lands," Meigs now asserted, and "when the United States propose to them to make cession, they have not the right in fact to put their veto on such propositions."[62]

James Madison and his successor were not quite ready to accept this interpretation of Indian policy, but the various treaty commissioners (usually army generals) from the western states whom the Executive branch invariably chose to negotiate with the Indians fully believed in it and practiced it. John Lowrey, John Walker, and the other chiefs in the

---

[61] Return J. Meigs to Andrew Jackson, August 6, 1816, M-208.
[62] Return J. Meigs to William Crawford, August 19, 1816, ASP II, 113–14.

Lower Towns saw this and were ready to break with the nationalist faction that they had temporarily joined before the Creek War of 1813-1814.

The second victory of the United States over the British had created a tremendous surge of self-confidence and nationalistic expansionism among white Americans. This received added force from the cotton boom in the southern states and the burgeoning northern textile industry. The Cherokees' desire to assert their own sovereignty (though, incongruously, the result of the same shared victory in war) could hardly stand long in the face of the upsurge in American nationalism. This confrontation produced the second Cherokee removal crisis in 1817. There seemed no way the Cherokees could hold their people together; too many were ready to yield to the unrelenting pressure to drive them across the Mississippi.

TEN

NATIONAL UNITY FALTERS,

1816–1817

Those [Cherokees] who choose to remain [in the east and become citizens] where they now reside . . . [will] be considered as entitled to all the rights of a free citizen of color of the United States. —Governor Joseph McMinn of Tennessee, October 25, 1816

The victory over the Creeks and the initial defeat of Jackson's plan to cheat them out of 2.2 million acres of their land in 1816 should have given the Cherokees a renewed sense of self-assurance, but there were too many negative contingencies. The War Department's reluctance to pay their soldiers and return their land, coupled with the obviously increasing animosity of westerners toward all Indians for Tecumseh's "betrayal" and the Creek War, indicated difficult times ahead. The depredations by Jackson's militia and the tremendous number of white squatters on their land further weakened Cherokee confidence. Most devastating of all to their national spirit was the apparent willingness of many Cherokees in the Alabama area of the nation to emigrate west in order to put as much distance as possible between themselves and the aggressive white frontiersmen. The War Department did its best to aggravate this division within the Cherokee people. There was little the more patriotic chiefs could do to allay the fears that, sooner or later, the whites would seize all of their land.

The second Cherokee removal crisis arose from the determination of Jackson and the southeastern states to force further cessions of land from all of the Indians in the region. The expansionist mood of white America promoted the notion that the west should now be fully open for white settlement. The failure of the Indians to keep the peace in the Mississippi Valley ended what little support westerners had ever given to the policy of civilizing them there and then incorporating them as equal citizens. Clearly the Indians were not to be trusted; "once a savage always a savage." Furthermore, it seemed unlikely that the Indians would ever make the most of the rich soil and resources of the trans-Appalachian region. To wait for them to develop it would be to hold back the manifest destiny of the United States to become one of the most powerful nations in the world. Cotton manufacturing was thriving; both New and Old England were eager to buy more raw cotton. The price of cotton had doubled in the years 1814–1816. The first land taken from the Creeks in these years was soon selling for twenty to forty dollars an acre and there were millions of acres of black-belt land still in Indian possession.

Andrew Jackson, himself a large speculator in this land, was determined to use the power and prestige of his victories to free the South of Indians. As a citizen of Tennessee, he was particularly concerned to rid his home state of Cherokees and Chickasaws. If Jackson could obtain the removal of these tribes, other westerners would then be able to remove the Creeks and Choctaws who held even more valuable cotton land to the south and west. White settlers north of the Ohio River felt the same about removing the Indians in the Northwest from land that would soon make that region the corn, wheat, and hog center of the nation.

To overcome the reluctance of some easterners who had accepted the sentimental view that Indians were the equal of whites and could be civilized and Christianized in short order, the westerners, led by men like Jackson and Joseph McMinn, Governor of Tennessee, proposed to reinvigorate Jefferson's alternative program of removal and exchange of lands. This plan was offered as a benevolent solution to a difficult problem. Regrettably, these westerners argued, the simple children of the forest were taking much longer to acculturate than anyone had originally expected. The pressure of western settlements east of the Mississippi, aggravated by certain rough and unruly types of frontiersmen who harassed and cheated the Indians, was making life intolerable for them. Many of the "real Indians" still clung to the ways of their ancestors and preferred to be hunters. Missionaries were as yet too few and had not been able to educate and convert many of them. Would it not be best, then, to give them land west of the Mississippi, rich in game and as yet unsettled by whites, in exchange for the land that they now made too little use of? If the government and missionaries promised to carry their fostering aid west and continue there the original policy of enlightenment under quieter circumstances, would not this be best for the Indians and best for the rapidly expanding population of white Americans eager to settle and exploit the riches of the Mississippi Valley?

Implementation of this new removal and exchange program for the Indians east of the Mississippi would entail a certain amount of sophistry with regard to promises made in previous Indian treaties, particularly if some tribes preferred to remain where they were. It would also require strong efforts to overcome scruples concerning the rights of Indians and the assumption that they should not be moved against their will. Furthermore, generous appropriations would have to be made by Congress from the taxpayers' money in order to "induce" the Indians to cede their land and also to pay for their transportation west. Exactly where the Indians were to be placed when they got to "the west" was to be left to the War Department; the lands on which they would be settled would be federal land and, presumably, unoccupied—except by a few other wild tribes. In some cases, treaties and payments might have to be made to these western tribes to induce them to share their territory with the eastern immigrants. But few white westerners doubted that these obstacles could be overcome or that the plan was absolutely essential to the progress and welfare of the United States. White America seemed convinced that God and natural law had ordained from the beginning that European settlers in the New World, especially those of Anglo-Saxon or Nordic stock, should extend their dominion over the continent from coast to coast.

Jackson and McMinn, ably assisted by Meigs, were in an excellent position to inaugurate this new program and the Cherokees were the logical group with which to begin. Jackson was convinced that the War Department had made a great mistake in returning to the Cherokees the land he had taken in the Treaty of Fort Jackson. Most westerners agreed with him. By invading and building cabins on this land, they were providing Jackson with the argument that only by firing on white veterans of the war could the federal government force them to leave an area for which they felt they had fought the Creeks. At the same time, Jackson was able to argue with the Cherokees in the area that they could no longer hold on to it under any circumstances; thus it would be wiser for them to sell it at a good price and move to a new tract in Arkansas (where their brethren were already living) that the government would survey and cede to them forever. Because the tract in northern Alabama (which became a territory in 1817 and a state in 1819) constituted about half of the area of the Cherokee Lower Town region, where many chiefs had been discontented ever since Doublehead's assassination and the rise of the young chiefs to dominance, Jackson found it easier to make his argument here than elsewhere. He did his best to cajole, bribe, and threaten the Cherokees in Alabama to secede from their nation and go west.

McMinn, an ardent frontier governor, eager to free his state from all Indians, allied himself closely with Jackson and Meigs to find arguments that would persuade Congress to allocate the money needed for the new program. Meigs knew the Cherokees better than anyone and had spent over fifteen years maneuvering with federal officials on Indian affairs. For over a decade he had been convinced that removal and exchange was the best answer to "the Indian problem" and he welcomed the opportunity to have powerful allies in the western Congressional delegations to help him implement it. While Jackson worked on the Lower Town chiefs to split the Cherokees from within, McMinn and Meigs began to unite western policymakers in Congress for another effort at massive removal of the Indians.

One other important ingredient was part of the shift in Indian policy in the postwar years: the unsettled position of those Cherokees who had already gone west. Many of these had gone on the basis of Meigs's promise that Jefferson would grant them a secure tract of land in exchange for the areas they left behind, a promise that had never been kept. Meanwhile the number of Cherokees settled along the upper Arkansas River had grown to 1,500 or more. Jackson, McMinn, and Meigs planned to use these western Cherokees and Jefferson's message of January 1809 as the basis for their argument for removal in three ways: first, they could plead that the government should keep Jefferson's and Meigs's promises, real or implied, which had so far not been kept with those who had removed in 1809–1810; second, they could note that because both the whites in Arkansas and the other Indian tribes there needed to know precisely what land the Cherokees had for their use, some survey and grant of Arkansas land was needed; and third, they explained to the eastern Cherokees that they had some obligation to assist their struggling western brethren by ceding sufficient land to enable the government to grant an equivalent tract in Arkansas.

Thus a successful war, the rise of the Cotton Kingdom, the rapid growth of industrialization, and the sentiments of romantic (and racist) nationalism combined with historical precedents and expediency to inaugurate a major revision of American Indian policy. In this sense, Jackson was the right man in the right place. He took full advantage of the circumstances that provided him with the power and prestige to act.

The first step in the process of dividing the Cherokee Nation in the east took place in September 1816 at the Chickasaw council house in northeastern Mississippi. Jackson had come to negotiate a land cession from the Chickasaws and the Cherokees had sent a delegation to make certain that the Chickasaws did not cede any land claimed by the Cherokees. Most of the Cherokee delegates were from the Lower Towns because they were best acquainted with the area Jackson wanted. Jackson took advantage of the occasion to persuade the fifteen Cherokee delegates that they should cede back to the United States (at a fair price) the area that Madison and Crawford had just returned to them. Jackson had told McMinn in May 1816 that the Cherokees "are inclined, and as I believe will, shortly tender to the United States their whole territory where they now live for lands west of the Mississippi."[1] He seems to have gained this impression from talking to some of the Lower Town chiefs (probably Toochelar, Richard Brown, The Glass, Dick Justice, John Lowrey, John Walker, and George Guess) who were convinced that the intruders in their area would never be removed.[2] Jackson also seemed to think that Pathkiller and The Ridge (now Major Ridge) might be persuaded to support removal. However, he had little respect for most of these chiefs whom he characterized as "half-breeds." Jackson considered himself the friend of "the real Indians"—the common people. He had told his friend Coffee to sound out Lowrey, Brown, Pathkiller, and Ridge during the summer of 1816 regarding the retrocession of the 2.2 million acres in northern Alabama: "They knew they never had any rights [to that area] and they will be glad, as I believe, to swindle the U. States out of a few thousand dollars to bury their claim, which they know, if persisted in might bury them and their nation.[3]

By a combination of threats and bribes, Jackson persuaded the fifteen delegates to the Chickasaw council to overstep their assignment and sign an agreement (Jackson called it a treaty) to cede back the 2.2 million acres. Because the Cherokee Council had expressly forbidden these delegates to sign any treaty, the signers told Jackson that their signatures on the "treaty" meant nothing unless the full council later ratified it. "In concluding the treaty with the Cherokees" (at the Chickasaw council), Jackson told the War Department on September 20, "it was found both wise and politic to make a few presents to the chiefs and interpreters." Of course, he added, "secrecy was enjoined as to the names [of those bribed]. Secrecy is necessary or the influence of the chiefs would be destroyed, which has been, and may be useful on a future occasion."[4] In this treaty the government agreed to pay the Cherokees $60,000 (or less than 3 cents per acre) for the land.[5] The delegates who signed were Toochelar, Oohulooke, Wasosey, Ganoa (The Gourd), Spring Frog, Oowatata, John Benge, John Baldrige, The Bark, George Guess (Sequoyah), Arch Campbell, The Spirit, Young Wolf, and Ooliteskee. They later excused their actions to the Cherokee National Council at Turkeytown on September 28 by saying that Jackson had told them that the Cherokees would lose all

[1] ASP II, 115.

[2] ASP II, 110, 114.

[3] Wilkins, *Cherokee Tragedy*, p. 94.

[4] ASP II, 92, 104–105; Cotterill, *Southern Indians*, pp. 199–202; Wilkins, *Cherokee Tragedy*, pp. 94–95.

[5] Royce, *Cherokee Nation of Indians*, pp. 81-83; ASP II, 92. The Cherokee Nation noted that previously, in the spring of 1816, Crawford had offered them an annuity of $6,000 "in perpetuity" for this tract; now Jackson had cut the offer to $60,000 in ten installments. See Going Snake and Cherokee delegation to John Calhoun, November 22, 1817, M-271, reel 2, #0014.

their land north and south of the Tennessee River if they did not cede this region to the south of it. They also pleaded that they had held out against Jackson's effort to obtain other large tracts in Tennessee, North Carolina, and Georgia. If the National Council did not agree to ratify what they had signed, they said, it had only to take no action during the negotiations that Jackson was to hold with the Cherokees at Turkeytown in October.

The Council expressed intense anger toward its delegates for allowing themselves to be browbeaten into this agreement, which it took no official action to ratify. However, Jackson was not to be denied when he got to Turkeytown. Late in the evening of October 4, after Jackson had made no headway with the Cherokee Council and it had adjourned for the day, he met with eight of the old chiefs and persuaded them to sign a statement saying that they, acting for the Council, had ratified what its delegates had agreed to earlier on September 28 at the Chickasaw council house. Under their signatures (which were added below those of the fifteen delegates to the Chickasaw conference) Jackson wrote in his own hand, "and ratified at Turkey Town by the whole nation."[6] The eight who signed away these 2.2 million acres on October 4 were The Glass, Sour Mush, Chulio, Dick Justice, Richard Brown, The Bark, The Boot, and Pathkiller.[7]

When the rest of the chiefs learned what had happened, they immediately wrote to the Secretary of War protesting that this treaty was not the work of the whole nation but only "the minority of our nation."[8] The War Department was in no mood to repudiate Jackson a second time. The Senate ratified the treaty and the westerners expressed great satisfaction that Jackson had preserved for them this valuable tract of land that they had won by their guns and that Crawford and Madison had almost let go. Governor McMinn wrote: "The possession of that country will enable not only the citizens of Tennessee but also those of the western counties of Virginia to find a market for their surplus produce and domestic manufactures infinitely nearer home than any other which has been or ever will be discovered."[9] But McMinn was unhappy that Jackson had not obtained in this treaty a single acre of Cherokee land in Tennessee. The treaty only concerned land south of the Tennessee River, in Alabama. Jackson, however, had now talked with enough chiefs from the Lower Towns to realize that some of them were ready to move west and that they would sell the land north of the Tennessee River (claimed to belong to the Lower Towns) if they could arrange it. Jackson reported to Craw-

[6] See the copy of the treaty, September 14, 1816, M-668, reel 4, #0201.
[7] Royce, *Cherokee Nation of Indians*, p. 82.
[8] The original protest is missing but it is restated in a letter from Return J. Meigs to John Calhoun, December 16, 1818, M-208.
[9] ASP II, 115–16.

ford on October 18 that "a [Cherokee] council is to be held shortly at Willstown, probably to select persons to explore" the area of Arkansas; "as soon as that is done, a delegation will be sent to the President to effect the exchange" of eastern Cherokee land for a western tract.[10] The implication was that the Lower Town chiefs would carry out this plan regardless of the will of the rest of the Cherokee Nation. Jackson, McMinn, and Meigs seem to have convinced themselves that most of the "real" Cherokees (the full-blood majority) could be persuaded to move once the hold of "the halfbreds" over them was broken. Nevertheless, all the evidence indicates that only a very small part of the nation, located only in the Lower Town region, was ever in favor of this action.

Within three weeks after Jackson had regained the tract in northern Alabama, McMinn and Meigs began their efforts to persuade Crawford to ask Congress for an appropriation to promote removal and exchange by the Cherokees. McMinn wrote to Crawford on October 25, taking the liberty of "suggesting to your honor the propriety of renewing to the Cherokees a proposition made to them during the administration of Mr. Jefferson."[11] That proposition, as McMinn chose to interpret it, was to tell the Cherokees that they had two alternatives: removal or detribalization and state citizenship. He explained how he thought this proposition should be made:

Each able-bodied Cherokee embracing the plan [of removal] shall be furnished at some suitable point west of the Mississippi with a good new rifle gun, some powder, lead, &c., and allot to those who choose to remain where they now reside, say 640 or 1000 acres of land to each family, to them, their heirs, &c. during their continuance thereon, and each Cherokee Indian thus settled to be considered as entitled to all the rights of a free citizen of color of the United States, to be subject to the payment of taxes for their lands, polls, &c.[12]

That is to say, a Cherokee who agreed to remove would simply be given a gun and sent to Arkansas; a Cherokee who did not would obtain the tract on which he had his farm and become a second-class citizen of whichever state his farm happened to be located in. Thereafter, there would be no Cherokee Nation in the east. The only nation that would remain would be those who had moved to Arkansas on a tract more or less proportionate in size to the percentage of Cherokees who emigrated.

In most southern states, "free people of color" had almost no rights beyond holding the land they paid taxes on. They could not vote, hold office, serve in the militia, or testify in court against a white man; they

[10] ASP II, 107–108.
[11] ASP II, 115.
[12] Ibid.

could not marry whites or send their children to public schools. They were a separate and distinct caste. This was hardly the kind of citizenship for acculturated Indians that Washington and Knox had envisioned under the original Indian policy. Furthermore, to say that they could hold their homesteads only as long as they continued to live on it implied that they did not really have the right to sell it and buy other land. McMinn seemed to say that each Cherokee family that declined to go west would be forever rooted in that spot; its only other option would be to give up the land to the state and move to Cherokee land in Arkansas.

Meigs does not seem to have ever adopted McMinn's position that Indian citizens should be treated as "free persons of color." In fact, in April Meigs had congratulated Crawford on his report to Congress in which he seemed to argue that Indians would make better citizens in the long run than most of the new immigrants from Europe. Crawford had told Congress in March 1816 that he intended to carry on the original Indian acculturation policy, to provide "a judicious supply" of articles to make the Indians into farmers, to "let intermarriages between them and the whites be encouraged," and to look forward to their full "enjoyment of civil liberty and social happiness" once they were incorporated into the republic as civilized men. "It will redound more to the national honor," Crawford told Congress, "to incorporate by a humane and benevolent policy, the natives of our forests in the great American family of freemen than to receive with open arms the fugitives of the old world whether their flight has been the effect of their crimes or their virtues."[13]

When Meigs read this he responded enthusiastically. He deplored the fact that "the great number of people who compose our population have, I think, illiberal, and many of them, very contemptible and barbarous ideas in relations to all Indians." Such people believe that "they should never be men" and that "they may be subjects but not citizens." Meigs disagreed. He applauded the policy of "intermarriage with our citizens" and believed that "in time, by such a measure, the shades of complexion will be obliterated and not a drop of human blood be lost." Like Jefferson, he admired the Indians, "whose physical and intellectual power are equal to those of any other people in the same latitude." He had no doubt that "within a short time we may incorporate them and identify them as American citizens." "Nature has been liberal towards them in their physical and intellectual forms and capacities, and we have no right to conclude that she has been niggardly toward them in anything that can prevent their arriving at the same elevation" as "other human beings."[14]

[13] ASP II, 26–28.
[14] Return J. Meigs to William Crawford, April 14, 1816, M-221, reel 70, #3110.

But at the same time Meigs could not help agreeing with McMinn and Jackson that the task of "elevating" the Indians was taking longer than originally expected—a situation he blamed on the "backward" full bloods. Consequently, late in 1816, Meigs willingly threw his weight behind McMinn's plan for removal and exchange. He wrote a long letter to Crawford on November 8 pointing out the importance of careful planning and adequate funding to transport thirteen thousand Cherokees six hundred miles to a new home in Arkansas. "They will require a considerable number of boats to move their families of old men and young children and such articles for housekeeping as are necessary for them. The [able-bodied] men will principally go with their livestock by land. . . . The whole expense of moving" would require a large appropriation by Congress. However, that sum "is only a feather contrasted with the great advantages to be derived to the United States by the exchange. . . . We shall gain eleven or twelve million acres of land. . . . Georgia will be made immensely rich. . . . Tennessee will acquire a very great addition to her wealth, and the United States will have a valuable tract for sale" in the Alabama region.[15]

In this same letter he offered a model of the kind of treaty he hoped to see emerge from negotiations. It included the granting of special "reserves" and citizenship to those who did not want to move, but only if they seemed capable of managing their own affairs as citizens. He expected those on such reserves to be treated as full citizens and not as free people of color. Those who did choose to emigrate would want far more than the gun and ammunition that McMinn offered. For example, they might want reimbursement for improvements left behind as well as government assistance after they arrived in Arkansas "for the encouragement of agriculture, domestic manufactures" and so forth. Meigs suggested that Congress appropriate at least $20,000 for such economic aid and also funds to supply them with blacksmiths, an armorer, an agent, a factor, an army garrison, a trading post, and assistance for mission schools. He told Crawford he had talked with McMinn about all this and had agreed that negotiations for a removal treaty could go more smoothly if the Council could be persuaded to send a delegation to Washington with power to work out the details. He was convinced that there would be strong opposition from the "unenlightened" members of the tribe.

As rumors began to circulate in the Cherokee Nation that some chiefs were contemplating removal and exchange, protests were sent to Meigs. A council held at Tuskquittee Town by the Valley Town chiefs of North Carolina early in December sent Meigs a message saying that the people

[15] Return J. Meigs to William Crawford, November 8, 1816, M-208.

in that area "wish still to live where they are [for] many ages or generations. The Great Spirit is above us all. . . . We want the ancient lines yet
to stand. . . . We do not want to go towards the setting sun. We want to
remain toward the rising sun."[16] On December 18 he received a petition
signed by "the heads of all the up[p]er towns" stating "we are jealous
[suspicious] that the lower towns wishes to sell all our land Away and we
might know nothing about it." They said they supported the position of
the Valley Town chiefs and wished to be notified of any discussion taking
place with the Lower Towns concerning removal.[17] Other chiefs of both
regions asked Meigs to inform the President that they were determined
to remain on their ancestral land.

Signs of opposition, however, did not bother McMinn and Meigs any
more than they did Jackson. On December 25, the western Senators, instigated by politicians in Tennessee, introduced in the Senate a resolution
requesting the Secretary of War "to inquire into the expediency of authorizing, by law, an exchange of territory with any of the Indian
tribes."[18] This was referred to the Committee on Public Lands for consideration. That committee reported on January 9, 1817, that the treaty-
making power itself was not sufficient authority for a President to exchange public land in one area for federal land in another area. However,
the committee discovered that in 1804 "a former Congress did by law authorize the President to stipulate with the Indian tribes residing east of
the Mississippi for an exchange of lands the property of the United States
on the west side of that river." This had been done at Jefferson's request
after the Louisiana Purchase, but nothing had come of it. Even so, "that
law remains in force"; hence there was no need to provide further legal
authorization. All that was needed was a law to create "an appropriation
of such sum of money as will enable the President to carry into effect the
provisions of the former law and form treaties with the other tribes for
that purpose." The committee then recommended such an appropriation
and the pursuance of such treaties.[19]

The westerners were delighted. Two weeks later McMinn wrote to tell
Meigs that the western Congressmen had introduced a bill to "give the
President power and money to open and hold Treaties for an exchange of
land with any of the Southern tribes."[20] McMinn thanked Meigs for his
suggestions on how best to draft such treaties and for his suggestions on
promoting emigration. He did not discuss the status of those Cherokees

[16] Valley Towns chiefs to Return J. Meigs, December 18, 1816, M-208.
[17] Upper Town chiefs to Return J. Meigs, December 18, 1816, M-208.
[18] ASP II, 123–24.
[19] Ibid.
[20] Joseph McMinn to Return J. Meigs, January 29, 1817, M-208.

who might choose citizenship; in any case, that was a matter not for the federal government but for each state to decide.

Early in January 1817 Meigs met secretly at the agency at Hiwassee with some of the Lower Town chiefs. Toochelar was there. He was Second Principal Chief of the nation now, under Pathkiller. He told Meigs that the Upper Town chiefs were well aware of his determination "to go to Arkansas." They had told him also that if he persisted in this effort, they would remove him from his office.[21] Soon after this, a group of Cherokee women in the Georgia area of the nation began circulating a petition to present to the Council, protesting that as mothers of the warriors and the chiefs they were "against an exchange of country" because of "the hardships and sufferings to which it is apprehended the women and children will be exposed by a removal."[22]

While the appropriation bill was working its way through Congress in January and February, Pathkiller called a National Council at Big Spring, Georgia, on February 18, to discuss a request from Madison that the Cherokees consider ceding all of their remaining land in North Carolina. The Council wrote a memorial stating that only four months ago they had given up all their land south of the Tennessee River "and now the state of North Carolina wants to take all the land in her charter limits and the states of Georgia and Tennessee will want to take their limits too, and if they all get [their desires] we shall then have no lands for our people to live and raise their stocks on" or "to Raise our Children" on. The Cherokees wished to make their position very clear: "[We] do not wish to part with any more lands." Someone, they said, must have been misinforming the President about this. Probably "designing men," land speculators, and some "of our white brothers on the frontiers." Perhaps there were some of "our Idle people wishing to go over the Mississippi, but the body of the Cherokee nation wishes to remain on the land on which they were raised." The Council then expressed its strong objection to Meigs's effort in January to meet with a few handpicked chiefs at the agency to suggest to them "the terms on which the United States would exchange with us the lands here for that over the mississippi." Such a plan had "been given our people nine years [ago] in Double Head's time"; it was rejected then and it was not wanted now.[23]

At this point the Arkansas Cherokees were brought into the picture by instructions from Meigs that they should send a delegation of those who owned land on Doublehead's reserve at Muscle Shoals so that General

---

[21] Toochelar to Return J. Meigs, January 9, 1817, M-208.

[22] Brainerd Journal, February 13, 1817, ABCFM.

[23] Charles Hicks to Return J. Meigs conveying the message of Pathkiller and the council at Big Spring, February 18, 1817, M-208.

Jackson could offer them "a reasonable price" for it, because the government wished to extinguish all such reserves.[24] When this delegation arrived at Hiwassee in April it was used to apply pressure on the eastern Cherokees. As Meigs knew they would, the western Cherokees told the eastern members of the tribe of their desperate need for a tract of land in Arkansas that would protect them from white intruders as well as from the warriors of the Osages and Quapaws, who considered them wandering intruders.

Thomas Nuttall, an American naturalist who visited the Cherokee settlement on the Arkansas River in 1819, provided a glowing account:

Both banks of the river, as we proceeded, were lined with the houses and farms of the Cherokee, and though their dress was a mixture of indigenous and European taste, yet in their houses, which are decently furnished, and in their farms, which are well fenced and stocked with cattle, we perceive a happy approach toward civilization. Their numerous families, also, well-fed and clothed, argue a propitious progress in their population. Their superior industry either as hunters or farmers proves the value of property among them, and they are no longer strangers to avarice and the distinctions created by wealth. Some of them are possessed of property to the amount of many thousands of dollars, have houses handsomely and conveniently furnished, and their tables spread with our dainties and luxuries.[25]

Tolluntuskee and other chiefs who had arrived in Arkansas in 1810 considered themselves far superior in manners and life style to the "savage" and "barbarous" Osages and Quapaws who were indigenous to that region. They spoke of them as "rude, uncultivated" and "childish," "wild Indians."[26] In part the difference was the progress the Cherokees had made in acculturation; in part it was the intermarried whites (like John D. Chisholm) or those of mixed ancestry (like Walter Webber), who set the style for the Arkansas settlement. For the full bloods, however, the western settlements were a haven where they could bring up their children in a more stable, conservative tradition, teaching their sons the arts of hunting and of war.

Yet the life of the western Cherokees was far from idyllic, which was why more did not join them and many returned east. War with the Osages and Quapaws was a constant problem and often the western Cherokees called upon their eastern brothers to come and help them fight, for

[24] Return J. Meigs to William S. Lovely, March 6, 1817, M-208. Lovely, who had been assistant to Meigs, was sent to Arkansas in 1813 to act as agent for the Cherokees who had emigrated to Arkansas Territory.

[25] Mooney, *Historical Sketch*, p. 133.

[26] Tolluntuskee to Return J. Meigs, June 28, 1812, M-211, reel 47, #2012. Tolluntuskee was one of the chiefs of the Western Cherokees.

they were outnumbered. Cherokee hunting parties were constantly under threat of attack and large-scale warfare occurred in 1805–1807, 1812–1813, and 1816–1818, in which no quarter was given on either side. There were no army garrisons to intervene and the Cherokees had no legitimate treaty boundaries to call their own. They were there only as long as they could defend themselves.

They also had no government factories to which they could sell their furs and skins or from which they could obtain reliable guns, hoes, knives, ammunition, spinning wheels, or looms at fair prices. They were at the mercy of unscrupulous traders who paid them far too little for their catch and overcharged them for the manufactured goods they needed. Meigs always felt guilty over his failure to carry out the promises he had made to them when they left after 1809. He tried in 1811 and 1812 to send them part of the Cherokee annuity so that they would have some capital to make a beginning as farmers. But after 1812 the eastern Cherokees prevented this. They wanted no assistance given to those who had deserted the motherland and nothing done to encourage others to make similar arrangements. When the War of 1812 began, Meigs persuaded the federal government to send his assistant agent, Major Lovely, to live among the Arkansas Cherokees, but apart from his good advice, Lovely brought them no other benefits. His job was to keep the War Department informed of their friendly or unfriendly disposition and happily for the Cherokees he reported that they had no desire to join with Tecumseh and the British.

Lovely's reports, however, were a major source for the effort to revive Meigs's plan for removal and exchange. Like Meigs, Lovely believed the emigrants had been treated unfairly by their brethren and by the government. When the war was over, his pleas for assistance to these deserving Cherokees struck a responsive chord in the minds of Jackson and his western friends. "The worst banditti" from among the whites, Lovely wrote in 1813, "have made their escape to this Country, guilty of the most horrid crimes, and now depredating on the Osages and other tribes, taking often 30 horses at a time."[27] The land was good, "the most valuable as to soil and valuable minerals" in the whole Louisiana Purchase, he thought, and "I never saw such quantitys of the very best kind of furs, dressed deer skins, bear skins etc." as the Cherokee hunters were able to obtain; "but these poor fellows get little or nothing for them" from dishonest white itinerant traders.[28] Three years later Lovely wrote: "Their women spin and weave cotton cloth while the men are hunting and yet they cannot

[27] W. S. Lovely to Return J. Meigs, August 6, 1813, M-208.
[28] W. S. Lovely to Return J. Meigs, July 10, 1813, M-208.

dispose of their furs and skins to any advantage—the travelling traders impose on them unfairly—in the sale of goods and ammunition and blankets [the traders] charge at two or three prices, that is, of the value."[29] The western Cherokee chiefs, Takatoka and Tolluntuskee, complained throughout 1816 that "the Osages do frequently throw some of my people to the ground [shoot them], and I feel that I am under the painful necessity of resisting the wrong they do me . . . my young men are now so exasperated from the Injuries and Insults offered them that it is now no longer in my power to restrain their fury." Recently the Osages had enticed a young man from his hunting camp and then "they most inhumanly butchered the Inocent victim. Such insults we cannot bear as a nation."[30] Claremont, the chief of the Osages, reported that similar murders of his warriors had been commmitted by the Cherokees.[31]

The chief problem for the Cherokees and for the other Indians in Arkansas was the rapid advance of the white frontier. Arkansas was then part of the Missouri Territory. The majority of white settlements in the territory were along the Mississippi River, especially near St. Louis. Following Jefferson's advice, the Cherokees had gone four hundred miles up the Arkansas River to avoid the white settlements. After the war, however, the same mad scramble for land occurred west of the Mississippi as east of it. The legislators of the Missouri territorial legislature and the land speculators (often one and the same) decided in 1813 to set off the region in the southern part of the territory as the county of Arkansas, which included at first the whole of what is now the State of Arkansas. As a county, the land came under the jurisdiction of the whites, living in it and under the jurisdiction of the legislature of Missouri Territory. Suddenly the Indians (Osages, Quapaws, and Cherokees) found that they had no legal rights there.[32] What was more, land speculators immediately incorporated the Missouri Company in St. Louis and purchased large tracts of the best land in the new county. They sent out surveyors to survey it and sheriffs to put off any persons, white or Indian, who were illegally "squatting" on it.

Lovely was horrified, as were the Indians. He wrote to President Madison in September 1815 that the Cherokees "have been most extraordinarily dealt with. The legislative authority of this Territory, having in-

---

[29] Return J. Meigs to William Crawford, February 17, 1816, M-208. See also Return J. Meigs to William Eustis, August 12, 1812, M-221, reel 47, #2010.

[30] Tolluntuskee to Return J. Meigs, January 25, 1817, M-208.

[31] Clermont, Chief of the Osages to W. S. Lovely to Meigs, June [30], 1814, M-208. There are many other letters from the Osages and Quapaws complaining that the Cherokees who had emigrated to Arkansas Territory were interfering with their hunting, settling on their land, and harassing their people.

[32] W. S. Lovely to James Madison, September [no day], 1815, M-221, reel 64, #7047.

cluded all that tract of country so settled by the Cherokees into the county of Arkansas and so far West and South of them that they cannot get out of it without excluding themselves from the protection of the United States" (i.e., they would have had to leave the United States and enter Spanish territory). "Indians are daily moving [here] from the old nation . . . thinking they are placing themselves on land for which they have paid" by relinquishing their rights in the old country. But when they arrive, they find "their [new] country is daily infested with constables, sheriffs, etc." telling them to move on because they had no right to live there.[33] Meigs had already written to the Secretary of War in June 1814: "By an act of the legislature of Missouri in December last, it is supposed that the Cherokee villages and all their hunting grounds are included in the County of Arkansas. This has alarmed the Cherokees. They are afraid of losing their fine improvements on the land." He explained that there were now about 3,600 people in the Cherokee community (probably exaggerated by at least half) and "they have fine plantations enclosed with good fences," all of which they would lose to the land speculators.[34] The Arkansas Cherokees appointed John D. Chisholm to hurry east and discuss the matter with Meigs, who sent Chisholm on to Washington, but the Secretary of War was not willing to help. He referred the westerners to their eastern brethren, who were, he said, supposed to have exchanged land for them in 1810–1811 but did not. The eastern Cherokees told the westerners to return east and strengthen their homeland. The National Council had no intention of ceding any of their land to help expatriates.

Governor William Clark of Missouri realized that something must be done about Indian claims in Arkansas County. He received permission from the Secretary of War to survey some land to be set aside for the Quapaws and the Osages. When the survey was being conducted in the summer of 1816, Clark wrote to Crawford to ask whether he should also set aside some land for the western Cherokees. Crawford replied: "Should the line of the Osage treaty prove that they [the Cherokees] are settled upon the Osage lands, nothing can be done for them." Emigration of the Cherokees to Arkansas, he said, had been permitted by Jefferson on the condition of a proportional exchange of land, but "this condition has never been complied with on the part of the nation and of course all obligation on the part of the United States to secure the emigrants in their new possessions has ceased."[35] The War Department intended to make

---

[33] Ibid.

[34] Return J. Meigs to John Armstrong, June 24, 1814, M-208.

[35] Royce, *Cherokee Nation of Indians*, p. 88, n. 1; William Crawford to Return J. Meigs, September 18, 1816, M-208; ASP II, 97–98.

the eastern Cherokees bear the responsibility for the plight of their brethren.

Meigs, of course, felt that Crawford had missed the point. It was not, in Meigs's opinion, a matter of free choice for the Cherokees in the east to accept or reject the conditions Jefferson had set for exchange in 1809. The government had made an agreement or pledge to the Cherokee emigrants that could not be abridged by the obstinacy of the eastern Cherokees; the Cherokee Council could and should now be forced to yield a proportional amount of land so that a tract could be set aside in Arkansas County for their countrymen. It was upon this point that McMinn and Jackson seized so avidly after 1816 in their efforts to effect a massive Cherokee removal. Crawford, though not averse to this, thought he had done all that was necessary or proper for the western Cherokees when, in March 1816, he had urged the eastern Cherokee delegation in Washington to take pity on their brethren. He had asked them to cede some of their land in Georgia or Tennessee so that the government could provide an equivalent tract in Arkansas. As Crawford later reminded Meigs, the Cherokee delegation flatly refused: "When this subject was mentioned to the Cherokee deputation last winter, so far were they from acknowledging its force that they declared the emigrants should be compelled to return and live with the nation."[36] Jackson too had urged the eastern Cherokees to cede land to help their brethren, but the delegation at the Chickasaw council house in September 1816 refused to acknowledge any such obligation.

Nevertheless, the people of Tennessee persisted. As the time approached for negotiations in the summer of 1817, McMinn, Meigs, and Jackson were determined to use Jefferson's message of 1809 as the wedge to force the Cherokees to relinquish all or most of their eastern land. James Monroe succeeded Madison in March 1817 and appointed George Graham as Secretary of War. Anxious to please the Western Congressmen, Graham and Monroe designated McMinn, Jackson, and David Meriwether of Georgia as commissioners to negotiate with the Cherokees. They did this even before Congress had appropiated any money for removal. To make sure that the western Cherokees were included in these negotiations, the President placed on the agenda the problem of settling the controversy over Doublehead's reserve.[37] When Graham discovered that Congress had adjourned without passing an appropriation for these negotiations and when he read the strongly worded letter from Pathkiller

[36] William Crawford to William Clark, September 17, 1816, M-15, reel 3, p. 423.

[37] Return J. Meigs to W. S. Lovely, March 6, 1817, M-208; George Graham to Andrew Jackson, January 13, 1817, M-15, reel 2, p. 2; George Graham to Andrew Jackson, March 22, 1817, M-15, reel 4, p. 19.

and the Council at Big Spring saying that the Cherokees were firmly opposed to removal, he wrote to Jackson saying it might be "inexpedient to enter into negotiations with the Cherokee for an exchange of territory at so early a period"; the President was of "the belief that the mind of the natives is not sufficiently made up to meet that question."[38] Jackson said he saw no reason to postpone the negotiations. Monroe and Graham backed down and the date was set for June 20, 1817.[39] The western politicians had the bit in their teeth and were not to be stopped. They felt certain the Cherokees—especially those living in Alabama—could be started west by the end of the summer.

The Cherokees were now fully aware of what was going on. The pressure for removal was mounting on all sides, yet their own ranks were badly split. Moreover, they were faced at that moment with one of the worst famines they had had in years. In part this was the result of a bad drought throughout the southeast in 1816 that had ruined the crops of both Indians and whites. But it was also the result of the general discouragement of those in the Lower Towns, so beset by intruders that many had not planted enough corn in 1817 to see themselves through the winter and summer. They were not sure whether they would be able to remain where they were or to harvest what they planted. The impact of these intruders upon the Cherokees in Tennessee and Alabama was described in a letter to Meigs in March 1817 from the chiefs of Fort Deposit, near Huntsville, Alabama: "Friend, there is at this place 93 [Cherokee] Familys in all [that] is like to suffer this summer unless there is some provision could be made through yourself" to provide corn. Eighteen of these families had recently come into the town because they were forced out of the Muscle Shoals area: "The corn they had down there was taken or stole by white people." These families had been told "they was to be paid for their places [farms]" but had received no payment. "We all have divided [our supplies] with them as long as we had [any food] in this place, and [now] we have all become alike [poor] for our crop of corn was but lite last year in these parts and the Intruders, by driving their stocks on the land, has destroyed all the cane Range" so that the Cherokees' hogs and cattle died or were only skin and bones.[40] Between February and April 1817, as the meager harvest of the previous fall was exhausted, Meigs received desperate requests from ten different towns in the Lower Town region to send corn to feed their starving people. Meigs wrote to

---

[38] Graham's letter to Jackson on March 25, 1817, is missing but Jackson quotes it in Andrew Jackson to George Graham, April 22, 1817, M-221, reel 74, #5883.

[39] Andrew Jackson to George Graham, April 22, 1817, M-221, reel 74, #5883; George Graham to Andrew Jackson, May 14, 1817, M-15, reel 4, p. 36.

[40] Chiefs Cunchestenaske, Spring Frog, et al. to Return J. Meigs, March 20, 1817, M-208.

the Secretary of War that "the shortness of crops which pervaded the greatest part of our country, greatly affected the Cherokee country. I have been obliged to draw orders . . . to prevent actual suffering." The Cherokees had told him that "a father will not let his children perish with hunger" and he had "bought six hundred bushels of corn for them."[41] It was customary in these situations for Meigs to draw an order against the Cherokee annuity and authorize some trader (Joseph Vann, Samuel Riley, or John or Lewis Ross) to provide the corn with the understanding that they could collect on the draft from the Council at annuity time. Corn being scarce everywhere, it sold for $1.00 to $1.50 per bushel. Over the course of several months this drained thousands of dollars from the annuity as one town after another requested two or three hundred bushels.

Theoretically, the National Committee was supposed to have control of the annuity and any drafts upon the National Treasury. But the requests were so frequent and so urgent that it was not feasible for the Committee to meet every week, and it permitted Meigs to manage these matters on his own. By May, Meigs had given out so much corn that he no longer dared charge it against the annuity for fear of angering the National Committee. He told the Secretary of War that he wished to take this expense out of the agency funds and noted that such generosity would pay off in good will at the time of the negotiations. After all, he said, "one or two thousand bushels of corn would not be thrown away upon these people even in an Interesting [self-interested] point of consideration, especially when important negotiations are pending."[42] He did not note that the inability of the government to keep out intruders was in part to blame; he preferred to blame the shortage upon the laziness of the Cherokees: "They do not love labor." The demoralization that had struck the Lower Towns since 1814 was taking its toll. Fortunately for those who opposed removal, the war between the Osages and the western Cherokees had burst out with such fury in 1816–1817 that the Arkansas Territory did not look much more inviting than their own desolate region.

The crisis over the food shortage revealed another problem to some Cherokees. Meigs was now in his seventies. The strain of his many activities and the absence of his assistant led him to turn over some of his duties to his son, Timothy. Timothy Meigs was not a competent administrator and in addition he was either dishonest or easily manipulated by others. Gideon Morgan complained in 1816 that Meigs and his son were mismanaging the Cherokee annuity and illegally using it to pay off the

[41] Return J. Meigs to George Graham, May 6, 1817, M-221, reel 75, #6401.
[42] Ibid.

private debts owed to traders by individual Cherokees. Morgan said that Meigs had charged the annuity $10,000 for corn the previous year and that some Cherokee and white traders were making inordinate profits from this. He also said that Timothy Meigs purchased debts at a discount from traders and then would persuade his father to use the annuity to pay him for them in full.[43] In the fall of 1816 Pathkiller as Principal Chief had ordered Meigs to make no more deductions from the annuity for corn, but Meigs nonetheless continued to do so.[44]

Clearly the Cherokee needed to tighten up their system of administration. The establishment of the National Committee in 1811 had been a start, but since then too many new problems had come up for which provision had not been made. Inefficiency in administering the National Treasury and the danger of tribal division over the new removal and exchange threat caused the Council to pass important new legislation in the Council at Amohee in early May 1817. The new laws constituted a major reform in the Cherokee political structure. Meigs was so busy over pending negotiations that he seems to have been largely unaware of the changes and made no comments about them in his reports. Perhaps he thought that after negotiations in June such efforts by the Cherokees to strengthen their "fictitious sovereignty" would be rendered obsolete.

The political reform law of 1817 made it clear in its preamble that the fundamental purpose of the legislation was to prevent any fraction of the nation from effecting an exchange of land: "Whereas fifty-four towns and villages have convened to deliberate and consider on the situation of the Nation, in the [matter of] disposition of our common property of land without the consent of the members of the Council, in order to obviate the evil consequences resulting in such a course, we have unanimously adopted the following form of the future government of our nation." The law then spelled out six major revisions in the governmental system. The first redefined the role of the National Committee. It was now specifically limited to "thirteen members elected as a Standing Committee for the term of two years"; before it had apparently had no set tenure and may not even have been limited to the number thirteen with which it had begun in 1810. If vacancies occurred in this committee during the two-year period, the "head chiefs" were to fill them.[45]

The second article defined the specific duties of the National Committee: to take "care of . . . the affairs of the Cherokee Nation" when the National Council was not in session by making decisions for the nation. Such acts were not "binding on the Nation in our common property

[43] Gideon Morgan to William Crawford, May 14, 1816, M-221, reel 70, #3041.
[44] Return J. Meigs to Ecacalan (Young Glass), July 17, 1817, M-208.
[45] *Cherokee Laws*, pp. 4–5.

without the unanimous consent of the members and Chiefs of the Council." All acts of the Committee had to be presented to the Council annually "for their acceptance or dissent." Treaties were not to be made by the National Committee because they concerned land—"our common property"; only the Council could make a treaty. This article also stated that the National Committee was to elect a President and to have a clerk to keep written records, in English, of all its resolutions or acts. The Council was to appoint its own Speaker, who could not be the same person as the President of the Committee. Although the law did not say so, it was assumed that most of the National Committee would be made up of those of mixed ancestry who could speak and write English; the Council would be dominated by representatives of the three-quarters of the nation who were full bloods. In effect this law created a bicameral legislative system in which the National Committee of thirteen initiated the laws and the National Council of headmen from the towns concurred in or rejected them. Subsequent laws of the nation were usually prefaced: "Resolved by the National Committee and concurred in by the National Council."

The third article dealt with the anticipated emigration of some of their people to Arkansas and the alleged claim that such emigrants carried with them a proportional tract of the nation's total land: "The authority and claim of our common property shall cease with the person or persons who shall think proper to remove themselves without the limits of the Cherokee Nation." In a sense this was a reaffirmation of the decision announced in 1810 that "stragglers" to the west were not to be considered part of the nation. Should any group of chiefs make a treaty of removal and exchange, this law was designed to neutralize it. A western emigrant had no standing and neither the tribal land nor the tribal annuity funds were to be divided between those in the homeland and those who deserted it. The sovereignty of the nation was indivisible and rested with the resident citizens of the motherland.

Article four reasserted the traditional system of matrilineal property rights, at least to the extent that husbands could not dispose of their wives' property. This would become critical if the government of the United States were to reimburse emigrants for their improvements and if husbands and wives separated over emigration. Whites defined "heads of family" in terms of males only; "the improvements and labors of our people by the mother's side shall be inviolate during the time of their occupancy." Women who emigrated were subject to the same loss of claim upon the common land of the nation as men; conversely, if a husband left for Arkansas and his wife remained, the United States could not dispossess her or claim the husband's proportionate share of the nation's land.

Article five reasserted the control of the National Committee over the

National Treasury, annuity, and all disbursement of funds. "This Committee shall settle with the Agency for our annual stipend and report their proceedings to the members of the Council." It was to keep strict accounts and to be held responsible for those funds. To make it clear that Meigs was not to have any part in expenditures from the Treasury, an explanation of this clause was passed two months later by the National Committee and sent to Meigs: "Agreeable to a Resolution passed by the National Committee and Principal Chiefs of the nation, it is resolved that there shall not be an order for any amount for individual accounts against the Nation given on our agent for the term of two years from the 6th May, 1817."[46] Traders must now come to the Committee to settle their debts.

The final article of this law set out the method of amending this new structure and a pledge to uphold the act, which seems to substantiate a later claim that the six articles together constitued a constitutional framework or fundamental law that bound even the Council: "The above articles for our government may be amended at our electional term, and the Committee is hereby required to be governed by the above articles and the Chiefs and Warriors in Council unanimously pledge themselves to observe strictly to the above articles." Whether "electional term" meant the annual council to which each town sent its headmen or whether it meant only those councils at which the two-year terms of the National Committee expired, is not clear.[47]

The political reform act of 1817 (or "the first Cherokee constitution," as some historians have called it) revealed that the Cherokees had come a long way from their traditional reliance on unwritten custom, oral law, ad hoc councils, and decentralized town autonomy. They were ready now to institutionalize their sense of nationhood. The complex structure of their market economy, the danger of encroaching white settlements, and combined state and federal efforts to manipulate them made written records, administrative accountability, and stronger centralization of authority essential. Also required were clearly defined statements of national identity, citizenship, common ownership of property, and the rights of women. Cherokee revitalization continued to be a secular movement led by creative, collective statesmanship. The old religion was not dead nor were the roles of medicine men and priests by any means defunct, but the adonisgi were not the persons responsible for coping with the political and economic problems the nation now faced. In a profound way, the Cherokee renascence was based upon a separation of church and

---

[46] Cherokee National Committee to Return J. Meigs, July 14, 1817, M-208.
[47] *Cherokee Laws*, p. 4; see also Strickland, *Fire and the Spirits*, pp. 61–62.

state as important as that which the United States had effected in its birth as a nation. No longer did all Cherokees share the same view of nature, the supernatural, or human nature, and certainly they did not agree on specific ethical or ritual behavior. The varieties of belief indicated a new religious pluralism. Separation of church and state was not complete (any more than it was in the United States) but neither could it be said that there was a formal establishment of religion. Political centralization forced secularism and acknowledged religious pluralism. Many Cherokees did not fully realize this subtle shift in their definition of the Cherokee Nation. When they did become aware a decade later, this spurred a major social rebellion.

The law of 1817, agreed to by fifty-four towns, was clearly the will of the great majority as they faced their new confrontation with white negotiators. But it was not unanimous. The absence of Toochelar's name as a signer of the law indicates that he may already have been deposed as Second Principal Chief because of his determination to support removal and exchange. His formal impeachment was not long in coming. On the other hand, it was significant that the first president elected by the National Committee was Richard Brown, a man who had told Meigs he was fully in support of removal (though the nation may not have known this). The Cherokees felt that they were now prepared to meet with Jackson, McMinn, and Meriwether, but they had underestimated their foes and overestimated their unity.

ELEVEN

THE STRUGGLE FOR SOVEREIGNTY,
1817–1819

We consider ourselves as a free and distinct nation and the Government of the United States have no police over us further than a friendly intercourse in trade. —Cherokee memorial, June 1818

There was no way the Cherokee leaders could prevent a sizable number of their people from moving to Arkansas in 1817–1819 if they chose to go. Voluntary emigration had started again in 1814, and it continued after 1819. The western Cherokees desperately wanted a tract of their own to live on. The question was whether the National Council could prevent the whole nation from being forced to remove (or forced to accept second-class citizenship in the east). Or, to put it another way, the Council had to insist that emigrants never carried with them a right to part of the soil of their homeland that could be exchanged, pro rata, for western land. For two years the eastern Cherokees engaged in a desperate struggle to preserve their right, guaranteed by their treaties, to the land of their ancestors. At one point in this struggle, Joseph McMinn claimed that threats were made on his life and called in the United States Army to protect him. Several chiefs claimed intimidation by the patriots; others were "broken" for their support of removal. Saving their country in these years proved a hard, dirty business that bore most heavily upon the poorest Cherokees and particularly those in the Lower Towns. In the end, the whole nation had to make bitter sacrifices of land and kinship loyalties in order to sustain their claim to sovereignty in the east. Some Cherokees felt that only the timely help in 1817 of the newly arrived Congregationalist missionaries from New England had turned the tide that was running so strongly against them as the sectional schisms began in the United States that culminated in Civil War. But this was not wholly true; there were also weaknesses in the strategy of the westerners as well as in McMinn's management of the whole business that undermined this removal plan. But ultimately the Cherokees could take pride in their victory over McMinn, Jackson, and Meriwether and in the resourcefulness of their leaders—some of them old hands at dealing with the government (like Charles Hicks and Major Ridge), others (like John Ross and George Lowrey) gaining new prominence.

Jackson, McMinn, and Meriwether, with two of the fifteen delegates from the Arkansas Cherokees (John D. Chisholm and John Rogers), arrived at the federal agency at Hiwassee on June 20, 1817, to negotiate the plan for Cherokee removal. In this plan they were fully supported by agent Meigs.[1] The instructions from George Graham, the Secretary of War, stated that a rifle, a blanket, and transportation to a specific area in Arkansas (the first of a new kind of Indian reservation) were available for those Cherokees who wished to emigrate and that 640 acres of land and citizenship (according to "the laws of the particular state or territory in which they may respectively reside") were available to those who did not emigrate. These were the two choices that the negotiators were to put before the Cherokees.[2] When the Cherokee National Council had assembled, Jackson began by reading Jefferson's message of January 9, 1809, arguing that it constituted a binding agreement for removal and exchange that the Cherokees had for too long neglected to fulfill. The Council responded that Jefferson's talk was not a treaty; no council had ratified it and the delegation to which he spoke had not signed it; they had had no authority to make such a treaty. Furthermore, Jefferson had said in his talk that any such exchange had to be agreed to by both the Lower and Upper Towns meeting in council; no such council had ever met to discuss the removal of 1809–1810.[3] In fact, they said, on April 10, 1809, a council had specifically declined to authorize any division of the nation. Those who went west in 1810 therefore went as individuals and had been officially designated by the Council at that time as "stragglers" and expatriates. If the Cherokees in Arkansas had encountered difficulties there, they had no one to blame but themselves.

A fruitless debate over the meaning of Jefferson's message continued for eight days until finally, on June 28, the Cherokees withdrew for four days and drew up a long and detailed statement of their arguments, signed by the sixty-seven most important chiefs in the nation, including most of those from the Lower Towns. This memorial was presented to Jackson and the other commissioners on July 2. After flatly denying any commitment to exchange of lands in 1809, the memorial concluded: "We feel assured that our father, the President, will not compel us into meas-

---

[1] The other thirteen delegates from Arkansas had returned home. Most of the documents for these negotiations can be found in ASP II, 140–47, 478–90; M-221, reel 79, #0053–0080; and M-15, reel 4, pp. 2–70. The treaty of July 8, 1817 is in ASP II, 129–31; see also Royce, *Cherokee Nation of Indians*, pp. 84–91.

[2] George Graham to Andrew Jackson, May 16, 1817, M-15, reel 4, p. 37.

[3] ASP II, 142–43.

ures so diametrically against the will and interest of a large majority of our nation." There might be some chiefs and families who were ready to emigrate, but as a nation, "we wish to remain on our land and hold it fast. We appeal to our father, the President to do us justice."[4] The statement also reproached the treaty commissioners for confronting them with an illegal choice: "We are now distressed with the alternative proposal to remove from this country to the Arkansas or stay and become citizens of the United States." They opposed both. "We are not yet civilized enough to become citizens of the United States nor do we wish to be compelled to move to a country so much against our inclination and will." To go west would mean to "return to the same savage state of life that we were in before" and start all over again. "You tell us to speak freely and make our choice." There was a third choice and that was the one they wanted and believed they were entitled to: "Our choice is to remain on our lands and follow the pursuits of agriculture and civilization."

Jackson and his fellow commissioners were not willing to allow the third option.[5] They demanded a decision on the two options outlined and threatened that if the Cherokees did not choose one of these, they would be deemed unfriendly: the government would cease to use its power to protect them from frontier intruders and their annuities and all technical asisstance would be cut off. After considerable haggling, the commissioners found thirty-one chiefs willing to sign a treaty on July 8 that the commissioners considered compliant with their either-or terms (i.e., citizenship or removal) but that many of the signers evidently considered a compromise allowing the third option of remaining as a nation in the east. Although only thirty-one of the sixty-seven chiefs at the Council signed this treaty, by adding the two delegates from Arkansas (who also signed, by proxy, the names of the thirteen other western delegates who had gone home), the total signatories came to forty-six. Because the treaty commissioners considered the Cherokees (east and west) to be one people, they felt justified in counting the fifteen signatures of the Arkansas delegation. Meigs believed the treaty was valid because all thirteen members of the National Committee had signed; he felt that they were the official representatives of the nation by its own definition.[6]

It is not hard to explain why chiefs like Toochelar, The Glass, Richard Brown, Cabbin Smith, and John Walker signed this treaty. It is difficult to explain why Charles Hicks, John McIntosh, Kelachulee, Katahee, and Going Snake signed it. The former were all from the Lower Towns and many of the signers were persons who had been supporters of Double-

---

[4] Ibid.

[5] See Graham's instructions to the commissioners, May 16, 1817, M-15, reel 4, p. 37.

[6] For the signatures to the treaty, see M-668, reel 4, #0336.

head. But the latter group were all opponents of Doublehead and since 1810 had been staunch nationalists. The non-signers, led by Major Ridge, John Ross, George Lowrey, and Pathkiller, were considerably taken aback by this division in their ranks. The non-signers clearly represented the majority of those in the east; with the staunch backing of the Valley Town chiefs and most of the Upper Town chiefs, they constituted thirty-six of the sixty-seven signers of the memorial of July 2, opposing the negotiations.

The treaty can best be explained in terms of its vague wording and the willingness of each side to believe what they wished to believe it said. Persons like Hicks, McIntosh, and Kelachulee apparently thought that they had signed a compromise treaty that included the third alternative within it. They based this on the fact that the treaty did not specifically say they had only two choices, to remove or to become citizens. By this treaty the Cherokees agreed to give up two large tracts of land (one of 373,000 acres in Georgia and one of 278,000 acres in Tennessee), on the basis of which the government was to provide a tract of similar size for Cherokees who wished to live in Arkansas. The treaty also said that the annuity of the nation would be "divided between the two parts of the nation" in proportion to a census to be taken after all those who were considering emigration had enrolled to do so. The census was to be taken on June 30, 1818, after which, presumably, the government would withdraw its offer to provide guns, blankets, transport, and supplies to emigrants. The treaty also said that those Cherokee heads of family "who may wish to become citizens" would be given a reserve of 640 acres, "to include their improvements" (i.e., the reserve would be centered on their present farms). The signers of the treaty who opposed both removal and detribalization assumed that the treaty left open a third alternative, though it was unspoken; they believed those who did not enroll to emigrate or request a reserve would remain as they were—they would constitute the Cherokee Nation in the east minus the emigrants and minus those who chose to become citizens. Signers like Charles Hicks assumed that this would constitute the vast majority. The non-signers felt that the treaty was a trap. It gave the government a year to put all the pressure it could on every Cherokee to emigrate and, at the end of that time, it could simply grant reserves to the rest and detribalize the nation. How else could reserves with citizenship be granted to individuals on their own farms scattered throughout the nation? Those like Hicks, who signed but opposed the government's two options, assumed that the persons who requested reserves would be located on the land that was specifically ceded in the treaty. The unceded land would remain for the rest. They signed a treaty including these specific land cessions because they felt it was the only way to solve the problem of the western Cherokees and still save something of the old nation.

The treaty commissioners and Meigs, however, felt that the treaty had accomplished exactly what they wanted. They believed that almost total removal—except for three hundred or so reservees—would result and that so few would want reserves that in effect nothing would be left of the nation in the east. Their only difficulty was that they had allowed themselves only one year to accomplish total enrollment, because in June 1818 they were committed to taking a census and dividing the annuity between those who had enrolled and those who had not.

The opponents of removal, however, were convinced they could succeed in saving the nation if they could prevent a sizable body of Cherokees from making one of the two choices offered in the treaty. Hicks, McIntosh, Kelachulee, and the other signers who were ardent nationalists realized this soon after signing the treaty and joined forces with Ross, Ridge, and the other non-signers to achieve that goal. Their first step was to create obstacles to enrollment and to enforce the law of 1817 that disenfranchised or deprived of citizenship any Cherokee who emigrated (or, in this case, enrolled to emigrate) from the nation. Enrollment thus became tantamount to treason. Toochelar and The Glass were the first to suffer under this ruling. On August 6 the National Council informed Meigs that these chiefs were no longer part of the nation; as Pathkiller put it, they "have let go of my people and country and joined themselves to the Arkansaw Cherokees, and they have no business to speak for the people and country here, as you and the commissioners have divided my warriors and made us two Nations."[7] McMinn, writing to the Secretary of War, noted that Toochelar and The Glass "have enrolled themselves as emigrants . . . for which cause alone, as I am informed, they have both been discarded and struck from the list of chiefs notwithstanding they have become Gray in the service of their Country."[8] McMinn, of course, wished them to remain part of the Council during the next year in order to promote the goal of total removal.

Charles Hicks, having repented of signing the treaty and made clear his determination to oppose removal, was named Second Principal Chief to replace Toochelar; John Ross became President of the National Committee to replace Richard Brown; Going Snake (Ehnautaunnueah) became Speaker of the National Council.[9] Thus reconstituted, the Council and Committee were firmly in the hands of staunch nationalists who now prepared for a long, hard fight to retain as much as possible of their home-

[7] Pathkiller et al. to Meigs, August 6, 1817, M-208.

[8] Joseph McMinn to George Graham, M-221, reel 15, November 13, 1817, #6626.

[9] Payne Papers, VII, part 1, 26–27; ASP II, 145.

land and sovereignty. The fight created lasting divisions among the Cherokees. Those who went west felt they had been unjustly branded as traitors and did not easily forget the hatred vented against them. Those who remained in the east believed that they were the true patriots. In the memorial of July 2 to the treaty commissioner, the sixty-seven chiefs had referred to the eastern area as "their native country" and "our beloved country." After the treaty was signed, Pathkiller said they were now "two Nations."

Return J. Meigs, the eternal pragmatist and "honest broker," preferred to avoid the issue of Cherokee nationalism except in the abstract sense of ethnic pride. "Brother, your nation is not divided," he replied to Pathkiller on August 9: "The Cherokees here and on the arkansas are one people . . . you are both here and there only one family." For Meigs it was not in the government's interest to recognize any sense of homeland, fatherland, or motherland where the Cherokees were concerned. He had always discouraged their sense of nationalism and sovereignty. Although Pathkiller did not sign the treaty of July 8, 1817, Meigs acted as though he would and should support it as the will of the majority. "Your best friends think that you have taken the only method in your power to preserve and perpetuate your national existence" (i.e., removal). "Your existence could not be effected here to remote time." To remain in the East would mean certain extinction as a people. "Therefore to save your people, you have done right to place them on ground [in the West] which you can call your own; this will keep your national pride because they are not beggars [on the land of the Osages]; they stand up and lye down on their own soil." He wished Pathkiller to be optimistic about his nation's future in Arkansas: "Schools will be continued and extended, agriculture and manufactures will still be encouraged here and in Arkansas. You must not suffer yourselves to believe that the United States wish to aggrandize themselves on the ruin of your nation."[10]

---

[10] Return J. Meigs to Pathkiller et al., August 9, 1817, M-208. Meigs's true sentiments toward Cherokee nationalism appeared in a letter to George Graham a few months later: "They still silently adhere to the wish to remain on their old ground as one people, subject only to their ancient laws and customs; this is perhaps a National sentiment in man, but in the present case it is, I conceive, utterly inadmissible and impracticable; inadmissible because an independent Government placed within the center of another independent Government would be a phenomenon, if not a monster in politics. The Indian tribes have had, and many of them still have, erroneous ideas of their sovereignty and independence. We must keep them dependent. It will not be understood that I would deprive them of their natural right—my mind would revolve at such a sentiment. Their political state in relation to the United States is that of minors. . . . By their local and moral condition [they] are appendages only to the United States . . . [they] refuse to saved by us . . . it is of the first importance to the peace, even to the safety of the U. States, that we occupy and fill with good citizens all the Country from the interior to the seashore, from New Orleans to the

Meigs lost no time in getting enrollment for removal under way. For obvious reasons those who planned to go west were eager to leave as soon as possible. They began applying to Meigs immediately for the rifle, ammunition, traps, blankets, and kettles that had been promised. "The commissioners were of opinion," Meigs wrote to Graham July 24, "that the tide of emigration should not be retarded by waiting for the ratification of the treaty" by the United States Senate.[11] He had already placed orders for boats and supplies to transport the first emigrants even though Congress had not yet appropriated the money for it. "Upwards of 700 Cherokees" had enrolled by July 24; he asked for an assistant to help him with the complex arrangements.[12] The first names on the first enrollment list, dated July 8 (the day the treaty was signed), were Toochelar, James Rogers, The Gourd, Spring Frog, John Jolly, Blackbird, No Fire, Charles Rogers, John W. Flowers, and Kulsatahee.[13] Some signed as individuals, but most signed as headmen of their towns and indicated how many men, women, and children they expected to take with them. It was not to be an exodus by families but by whole communities. The first thirteen to enroll spoke for a total of 552 emigrants.

The logistics of removal and exchange were more complex than anyone had imagined they would be. The treaty required that government appraisers should visit the farm of each enrollee and evaluate his "improvements" (houses, orchards, barns, fences, cultivated land) and provide a figure for his reimbursement. Most farms, it was expected, would be valued at under $50 and therefore the guns, blankets, kettles, and other items would cover reimbursement. But some of the enrollees were wealthy men with large establishments and they expected full compensation. Surveyors also had to survey the tracts for those who chose citizenship and a 640-acre reserve around their farms or plantations.

Graham authorized Meigs to proceed at once with transporting those who were ready to go and said: "You will make use of all the means at your disposal to induce the Indians generally to remove, and impress on the minds of those who are desirous of remaining, the advantages of selecting a section of 640 acres and of becoming citizens of the United States."[14] The War Department would underwrite removal costs until Congress passed the appropriation. Typical of the confusion that was to mark the whole proceeding was Graham's decision to order flatboats built

---

State of Georgia." Meigs wrote this to Graham on October 30, 1817 (M-208). It was designed to help him persuade the Senate to ratify the treaty of 1817.

[11] Return J. Meigs to George Graham, July 24, 1817, M-221, reel 75, #6512.

[12] Return J. Meigs to George Graham, July 24, 1817, M-208.

[13] "Register of Cherokees who wish to Emigrate to Arkansas River," July 8, 1817, M-208.

[14] George Graham to Return J. Meigs, August 9, 1817, M-208.

for transport when Meigs, knowing the difficulty of beating upstream on the Arkansas River, had already placed orders for keelboats.[15]

To the western Congressmen's surprise, their removal bill met with considerable resistance in Congress. Many easterners were not yet ready to abandon the old Indian policy or to abandon the treaty commitments that supported it. The bill requested $50,000 to accomplish removal of the Cherokees (as it turned out, a ridiculously low figure). The Senate had passed it in March 1817 but the House had turned it down. Even in the Senate the bill received severe criticism, particularly from northeastern Senators. Some of the negative votes, Graham said, came from "opposition to the general policy of removing the Indians west of the Mississippi" rather than adhering to the promise to civilize and incorporate them where they were. "It is also probable," he told Meigs, that when the bill was reintroduced in January 1818, "there will be opposition founded on the assumption that the Treaty has not received the unbiassed sanction of the portion of the nation residing east of the Mississippi, as evinced by the small number of chiefs who signed it." Others would object "that no right to any portion of the Cherokee land had accrued to the United States in consequence of the transaction which took place in 1809." Furthermore, the debate on the treaty might reveal that "such a right had been assumed and too strongly enforced by the Commissioners."[16] These were precisely the grounds on which the Cherokees hoped they could defeat ratification of the treaty in the Senate.

Meigs tried to provide Graham with arguments to counter these objections. "I beg leave to observe that there never was any definite number of Chiefs required to authenticate a treaty, the number depending on contingent circumstances."[17] It was true, he said, that Pathkiller, the Principal Chief, and many other chiefs did not sign, but "all of their National Committee" had signed and "their Clerk" and "Sower Mush, one of the oldest and most respectable chiefs." Ignoring the nation's law that ratification of a treaty must be made by a full National Council, he argued that "the National Committee in the act of signing were in fact the nation." He then went on to reveal his own contempt for Indian councils and to defend the necessity for threats, browbeating, bribes, and intimidation. The Cherokee government, he said, was "in fact a Democracy" but a democracy that "has no tone." The petition of sixty-seven chiefs opposing removal was of little consequence because the signers had been intimidated by the opponents of removal. "Some daring individual will keep

---

[15] George Graham to Return J. Meigs, August 13, 1817, M-15, reel 4, p. 74.
[16] George Graham to Return J. Meigs, August 1, 1817, M-208.
[17] Return J. Meigs to George Graham, October 30, 1817, M-208.

even the best Chiefs in awe by the threatening with death any man who would consent to sell land."

The Cherokees' desire for harmony and consensus simply did not measure up to Meigs's concept of getting thing done in a democracy. Their democracy had "no tone" because the chiefs, though "ostensibly a mild Aristocracy" were not the kind of "natural *aristoi*" to whom Jefferson (and the Federalists of New England) thought democracy ought to be entrusted. The chiefs were too much in awe of the masses. "Their power and authority is only nominal." They would not act until they felt their people were solidly behind them. Hence it was almost impossible to get decisions from them without countering the pressure of the Cherokee masses with the belligerence of the treaty commissioners. There was no other way to do business with Indians. In fact, some chiefs who were favorably "disposed to comply with the advice and wishes of Government" welcomed the pressure the treaty commissioners put on the Council; "they are well pleased to be strongly urged to do that which they are perfectly willing to do. This being done, they are safe from the Censure of their own people." They could say they had no choice but to yield; then the people would acquiesce. But if Meigs was right, why was Doublehead executed in 1807? Why was Black Fox deposed as Principal Chief in 1809? Why was Toochelar deposed as Second Principal Chief in 1817? Meigs blamed the continued opposition to the treaty upon a small but wealthy group of chiefs who were fully capable of "becoming citizens" but who would not like to be "under the restraint of [the white man's] laws" and who, after detribalization, would "lose that decided and marked ascendancy they now enjoy" over their backward people. "The real Indians" would prefer to go west and retain their old ways, but the "halfbreeds" favored "retaining all their lands" in order to enrich themselves at the expense of the poor.[18] He made only one concession to the legitimacy of opposition to Jackson's treaty; he acknowledged the sentimentalism of the full bloods who "wish to remain on their old ground as one people subject only to their ancient laws and customs."

Some of the Cherokees may be destitute of local attachment, but these are few. The greater number have strong local attachments—the rivers, the springs, and the mountains, their old hunting grounds, and more than all, the bones of several generations of their ancestors, lie buried in their plantations and on the battlegrounds in their wars with the northern tribes. . . . Although told that they are going to a country with the same mild climate and temperature as this, their philosophy [state of knowledge] is not sufficient to silence local recollection.[19]

[18] Ibid.
[19] Return J. Meigs to [John Calhoun], "Outline of Subject of Emigration," December 16, 1818, M-208. This is unsigned and may simply be a rough draft.

The government gathered its arguments and the Cherokees gathered theirs for the Senate debate on ratification and general removal. Because Pathkiller spoke no English, Charles Hicks played the major role in coordinating the Cherokee opposition. McMinn paid tribute to Hicks's authority and leadership a year later: "Hicks may be justly ranked as the standard of opposition to the execution of the treaty; in fact, he is their principal legislator and sole judge, and in every measure commands the esteem and confidence of all that part of the nation."[20] He was also uncorruptible.

Hicks had come a long way since he began at the turn of the century as an official government interpreter. He had grown wealthy as a trader and planter. He owned at least a dozen black slaves. He had many times participated in treaties and trips to Washington to see the President and confront Secretaries of War. After sending his sons to the Moravian mission school he became interested in Christianity and was one of the first to be converted (in 1813) by the Moravians. Although they were pacifists, the Moravians had not objected when he volunteered to fight in the Creek War. An ardent patriot and nationalist since he had first joined the effort to overthrow Doublehead, Hicks had devoted himself to the civilization program and opposed what he considered the pagan fanaticism of the Ghost Dance movement. His influence stemmed from his quiet, firm, patient determination to put his country first.

In order to protest against the ratification of the treaty, the Cherokee National Council decided to send a delegation to Washington. Hicks did not go with them, but he probably drafted the very explicit instructions they were given. They were to tell the President that "we have of late years been subject to the control of the minority of our nation"—a reference to Lower Town chiefs like Toochelar, The Glass, and Richard Brown who had made the treaty with Jackson in 1816 and promoted the removal treaty of 1817. The delegates were to present a memorial to the Senate explaining why the treaty should not be ratified. They were also to say that henceforth they wanted the agent to turn over their annuity to them in cash each year and to point out that the nation had never received the money promised for Wafford's Tract in 1804. As always, they were to ask for the removal of intruders and point out that the intruders were extremely lawless, committing "unwarrantable murders," stealing property, and "destroying" the range by driving large herds of cattle onto their land. The delegation was to request more schools for their children and to say that they were making progress as a people toward Christian-

[20] ASP II, 482.

ity.[21] Their reference to additional schools and Christianity may have been prompted by the recent advent of New England missionaries into the nation in the spring of 1817. The Cherokees knew that the New Englanders were opposed to removal and no friends of General Jackson. Their Senators could be counted upon to oppose the treaty.

The delegates were Going Snake, George Harlin, James Brown, Roman Nose, Richard Taylor, and Richard Riley. They met with Graham in November and then, in December, with his successor, John C. Calhoun. They said the nation was ready to make a treaty that would provide sufficient land and a fair proportion of their annuity to help the Cherokees in Arkansas if the government would retract the treaty of July 8 and cease all efforts to promote removal.[22] Graham declined this offer and told them that the treaty "must be strictly adhered to."[23]

On December 26 the delegates attended Congress and were at the Capitol when the Senate ratified the treaty despite their memorial against it. But they had the satisfaction of finding that some Senators strongly opposed the measure. They returned to find their nation in turmoil. McMinn, having left the governorship of Tennessee, had been appointed by the President as agent for the treaty commissioners.[24] He came to live in the nation at the garrison and to work with Meigs. His duties were to manage the enrollment and transportation of emigrants, to supervise the surveying of tracts for citizenship and the evaluation of improvements, and to take the census. He proved to be both energetic and ruthless in his efforts to destabilize the nation in order to increase enrollment.

One of McMinn's first acts was to withhold the Cherokee annuity of 1817 on the ground that by the recent treaty it was to be divided with the western Cherokees and thus the proper division could not be ascertained until the census was taken in June 1818. His real purpose was to increase the difficulty of the Council to pay its debts, to support deputations to Washington, and to find corn for those still suffering from the famine. Faced with a shortage of cash, the Council struck back by passing a law ordering the lighthorse regulators to collect any debts owed to the nation by those who were departing for Arkansas. The Lighthorse were told that if emigrants refused to pay, they were to dispossess them of any goods they had (including the new rifles, blankets, traps, and kettles that the government was providing to enrollees) and sell these to pay the debts. McMinn denounced this as an effort to harass those who wanted to emi-

---

[21] ASP II, 145.

[22] ASP II, 146.

[23] George Graham to Joseph McMinn, November 29, 1817, M-15, reel 4, p. 101; ASP II, 464.

[24] ASP II, 478.

grate.[25] "I issued an order forbidding all such attempts," he told Graham on December 29, "and declaring that I would view it in the light of hostility against the United States and would punish its perpetrators accordingly." This was only the first in a series of confrontations between tribal authorities and McMinn over the next year. For example, when appraisers were on their way to evaluate the property of an emigrant, nationalist Cherokees would burn down the emigrant's houses and barns to prevent the "traitors" from receiving any remuneration.[26] To stop such actions McMinn had to place armed guards around emigrants' farms and plantations until the appraisers arrived.

The angry confrontations only contributed to the determination of the emigrants. On February 15, 1818, Chief John Jolly, brother of Tolluntuskee, departed in a flotilla of fifteen boats carrying 331 persons from his town at the mouth of the Hiwassee River.[27] Soon after this, another group left with Chiefs Thunder, Te-esliskee, and No Fire.[28] Fortunately for McMinn, Congress finally passed the appropriation bill for this removal on April 20, 1818, allotting $80,000 to cover all expenses under Jackson's treaty. By that time McMinn had already spent $21,255 and the rest was going fast.[29]

After March 1818 the number of emigrants began to decline for various reasons: rumors of renewed warfare with the Osages were rampant; in the summer the Arkansas River became too shallow for heavy transport in its upper reaches; those who were most eager to leave were already gone; and McMinn was having trouble with emigrants who accused him of failing to reimburse them properly. He, in turn, claimed that many emigrants, particularly those with large plantations, were trying to obtain more from the government than they were entitled to. Some of these, like Major James Brown, used their slaves to clear new land after the treaty and then expected McMinn to pay for this "improvement."[30] The Council accused McMinn of using devious methods to increase enrollments: "We have understood that there is numbers of our people that have drawn guns and other articles [as emigrants] that were made drunk to induce them to take these things to go over to the Arkansas. This ought not to be allowed when drunk."[31]

[25] ASP II, 481.

[26] Joseph McMinn to John Calhoun, March 1, 1818, M-221, reel 78, #9024.

[27] John Jolly to John Calhoun, January 28, 1818, M-208; Return J. Meigs to John Calhoun, February 19, 1818, M-221, reel 78, #9043.

[28] Te-esliskee et al. to John Calhoun, February 21, 1818, M-221, reel 77, #8078.

[29] John Calhoun to Joseph McMinn, May 11, 1818, M-15, reel 4, p. 161.

[30] Joseph McMinn to John Calhoun, March 1, 1818, M-221, reel 78, #9024.

[31] Letter of twenty-two chiefs from Broomstown council to Return J. Meigs, May 10,

When John Walker, a Cherokee who favored removal, suggested to Calhoun that if enrollment was going too slowly, the wise course would be to postpone the census for another six months, Calhoun agreed: "The longer it can be fairly postponed, the better for us," he wrote to Mc-Minn.[32] McMinn announced that the census was being delayed because measures adopted by the Cherokees had intimidated many who wanted to enroll. The Council claimed that postponement was a breach of the treaty. McMinn instructed Meigs to call a council in May so that he could upbraid the chiefs for their opposition, but they refused to come. In June, McMinn told Calhoun that the intransigent chiefs had sent "runners with orders to threaten the lives of those who would attend."[33] Nonetheless he claimed to have enrolled 223 families for emigration and 56 for reserves in the month of May. To assist him in this process, Calhoun appointed John Walker, who had already been to Arkansas and was considered valuable to the government because he could overcome the fears of those hesitant to go to a place they had never seen.[34]

When the chiefs became aware that McMinn had postponed the census indefinitely, thereby leaving the nation open to continuing chaos as long as the government thought it had hope of enrolling more Cherokees, they called a council at Ustanali to protest this and other "improper" actions taken by McMinn. It also seemed likely that McMinn would once again withhold their annuity. The council was held from June 20 to July 3. Here the women of the nation presented their petition to "the headmen and warriors." They pointed out that "the land was given to us by the Great Spirit" and urged the Council members, "our beloved children, . . . to hold out to the last in support of our common rights." Because the Moravian and the new missionaries from New England were present, the women also noted that "some of our children have become Christians; we have missionary schools among us; we have heard the gospel preached in our nation."[35] They pointed out that removal would be particularly hard upon the women and children and said that they did not want to leave their homeland.

McMinn was not invited to this council. He told Calhoun: "Many attempts were made to prevent [my] attendance; some by threatening my

---

1818, M-221, reel 79, #0070; see also enclosure from Ard Hoyt to S. A. Worcester, July 25, 1818, ABCFM.

[32] ASP II, 480; Calhoun had succeeded George Graham as Secretary of War early in 1818. See also John Calhoun to Joseph McMinn, April 11, 1818, M-15, reel 4, p. 135.

[33] ASP II, 481.

[34] John Calhoun to Joseph McMinn, April 11, 1818, M-15, reel 4, p. 135.

[35] See enclosures of Ard Hoyt to S. A. Worcester, July 25, 1818, ABCFM. Details of this negotiating council at Ustanali are in M-221, reel 79, #0053–0080 and M-234, reel 71, #0284–0295.

life." Nevertheless, he came and found "upward of 2000 warriors" present. He seemed surprised to find their "hostility" toward the removal policy "much stronger than I anticipated." But what shocked him most was the assertion in the memorial the Council presented to him, which said: "We consider ourselves as a free and distinct nation and that the Government of the United States have no police over us further than a friendly intercourse in trade." The statement went on to say that the census should be taken no later than September of that year and that Elijah Hicks, the son of Charles Hicks, had been appointed to be their representative for the census. It concluded by expressing strong disapproval of "the practice of registering the names of people for reservations who do not live within the tracts of land ceded in the first and second articles of the treaty."[36] McMinn was granting reserves throughout the nation, assuming that no land would remain for the Cherokees in the east.

In response to the charges, McMinn told the Cherokees that the treaty would be executed as written. Those who wished to be citizens would get reserves wherever they now lived; "it must be understood the remaining part of the nation must remove west of the Mississippi." For them to continue to suppose otherwise was self-deceptive and a misreading of the treaty. They had no other option but to remove or become citizens. Resistance was futile. Apparently without prior consultation with the War Department, McMinn also said he wanted to meet with the Council again in September, when he hoped to propose to them that the government pay "upward of $100,000" for "an entire extinguishment" of all their eastern land claims.[37] Where he expected to obtain this money he did not explain nor did he say why such a sum should suddenly be offered when there was nothing in the treaty about it. Apparently, as it turned out, the idea had simply occurred to McMinn on the spur of the moment as a further means to confuse the nation and perhaps win over some of the reluctant chiefs. He assumed he could get the money from the government if he needed it.

The Council suspected that McMinn had received new instructions and was planning to negotiate a new treaty with friendly chiefs. It therefore passed a law on July 7 affirming that any Cherokee who agreed to sell any land of the nation without the approval of a full council would be subject to death.[38]

McMinn wrote a stark account of this Ustanali Council to Calhoun, describing the Cherokees' increasing "enmity to Government," stressing

[36] Cherokee memorial to Joseph McMinn, June 30, 1818, M-221, reel 79, #0060–0069.
[37] Talk by Joseph McMinn to Cherokee Council, M-221, July 1, 1818, reel 79, #0067; ASP II, 480–81.
[38] Joseph McMinn to John Calhoun, July 7, 1818, M-234, reel 71, #0284.

the threats made against his life and those of would-be emigrants, and characterizing the Council's statement about the Cherokees' being "a free and distinct nation" as an arrogant "declaration of Independence on the part of the Cherokees" that must be corrected before the wild idea spread to other tribes. "This principle, once established, could be subversive of all order, peace and happiness, as well as to over throw the present Treaty."[39] The Council's law threatening death to those who sold land without authority had, McMinn claimed, frightened many well-disposed Cherokees: "Were it not for these declarations, I should be able to enrol for Emigration nearly their whole Nation." He laid the chief blame for Cherokee opposition at the door of Charles Hicks. "So completely are they under the control of Hicks and others that those who have given me assurance of their going to the West dare not even look at me nor speak to me." The position of Hicks and "of the opposing part is now pretty clearly developed. . . . Their avowed object is to take the Enumeration [census] as soon as possible with the expectation that the greater part of the people will be found here, where, by the terms of the treaty, a tract will be laid off for them upon which they and their heirs will live in the full enjoyment of all their savage customs."[40] McMinn was determined that such an interpretation of the treaty should not prevail.

To prevent this, he told Calhoun, "I have assumed a much higher ground" in dealing with them than previously. He had made it clear that there was no alternative to removal or citizenship. In order to make total removal more palatable, he had suggested that the government would be willing to pay them an additional $100,000. He requested that Calhoun now draft instructions to him authorizing him to offer such a sum for an outright cession of all Cherokee land in the east.

Five days after the Ustanali Council, Hicks protested to Meigs that "as to total exchange of lands, I never understood that was the meaning of the treaty." He believed that McMinn must have erred "to [tell us to] become citizens or [we] must go over the Mississippi." That "would be a [use of] force which you said we were free [from]." Hicks had not seen Meigs's correspondence over the last eight years in which he had said that the Cherokees did not have the right to be free from compulsion when the government acted in their best interest. Hicks now implored Meigs to assert that the Cherokees retained the right to say no to treaty requests and particularly to this cruel choice.[41]

Pathkiller also wrote to McMinn: "It appears to me that you want to dispossess us of our habitation . . . but I will hold my country fast. . . .

[39] ASP II, 479–80, and Joseph McMinn to John Calhoun, M-234, July 7, 1818, reel 71, #0284.

[40] Joseph McMinn to John Calhoun, August 7, 1818, M-221, reel 79, #0053–0054.

[41] Charles Hicks to Return J. Meigs, July 5, 1818, M-208.

I love my country where I was raised. I never will find such another Country if you was to dispossess [us] of our boundary.''[42] The genuine surprise in these statements by Hicks and Pathkiller at the ''high ground'' taken by McMinn in July may reflect a sense of despair at the thought that there might be no way to save their homeland. It is hard to believe that they had not recognized earlier that total removal was the intention of the treaty commissioners.

When Calhoun read McMinn's inflammatory report of Cherokee obstinacy, he decided to back McMinn's new plan. He wrote on July 29: ''The conduct on the part of the Cherokee nation merits the severest censure. After ratification of the treaty, resistance to its fair execution can be considered little short of hostility. The menaces offered to those who choose to emigrate or to take reservations cannot be tolerated.''[43] He considered that the Cherokee actions were in ''open violation of the treaty'' and said ''the United States will not permit the treaty to be defeated by any such means.'' Calhoun also agreed to send new instructions to allow McMinn to offer the Cherokees $100,000 to confirm the plan for total extinction of the eastern land claims. ''I have examined with care the project of an arrangement which you purpose to carry the treaty into effect. Such an arrangement accords entirely with the views of the Government.'' As for the sum proposed, ''even that sum might be considerably enlarged'' if necessary to effect the purpose. He cautioned McMinn that ''so bold a scheme'' might alarm the Cherokees and ''augment the violence of the opposition.'' However, he left this to McMinn's judgment.[44]

Shortly after Calhoun wrote, Meigs sent him a letter saying that the Cherokees were now so heavily in debt that if they were offered $120,000 to move west they would undoubtedly agree.[45]

McMinn postponed the Council meeting at which he was to present this new inducement until November 13. When the Cherokees arrived at the agency, they found that McMinn had stationed a group of soldiers around it. The soldiers were ostensibly present to protect emigrants from intimidation, but their real purpose was to intimidate the Council. From the outset McMinn took a severe tone, reasserting the correctness of his interpretation of the treaty and reading the letter from Calhoun saying

[42] Pathkiller to Joseph McMinn, July 12, 1818, M-208.

[43] ASP II, 479–80.

[44] Calhoun's reasoning on Indian removal at this time can be seen in a letter he wrote to McMinn on July 29, 1818: ''Surrounded as the Cherokees are by the white population, they are in danger of perpetual collisions with them, or, even if disputes can be avoided, to fall under the train of vice and misery to which a savage people are doomed when they come into contact with enlightened and civilized nations. It is vain for the Cherokees to hold the high tone which they do as to their independence as a nation; for daily proof is exhibited that, were it not for the protecting arm of the United States [against white frontier ruffians], they would become victims of fraud and violence'' (ASP II, 479).

[45] Return J. Meigs to John Calhoun, August 7, 1818, M-208.

that he agreed with that interpretation. He also read Calhoun's statement that the Cherokees deserved severe censure for opposing the treaty by actions hostile to the United States.[46] He said that by his calculation over half their nation had already relinquished their title to land in the east through enrolling or reserves (a wild exaggeration). He urged the Council to end the whole matter quickly and easily by accepting the $100,000 that the government was now willing to add as a codicil to the treaty.

The Council deliberated and then replied: "If we were to accede to your propositions to compel a whole nation of people, contrary to their free will and choice, to leave the land of their nativity . . . which all the solemnity of a treaty" had guaranteed them (in 1791), and to do this by accepting a pittance not more than one-tenth its true worth, they would be both dishonest and inhumane toward their people.[47] Therefore, "we have decisively rejected your propositions for an entire extinguishment of all our claims to land east of the Mississippi river." They again insisted that the census be taken at once. The response was signed by seventy-two chiefs.

McMinn answered that in all his public life he had never received a reply "more unexpected or better calculated to wound my feelings." The Cherokees' ingratitude toward the government was unbelievable. However, he was willing to raise the offer for their land to $200,000 and give them until 1822 to complete their removal. When the Council also rejected this offer, McMinn lost his temper. He threatened to withdraw all protection of their borders and leave them at the mercy of white intruders. Let them see then how much their vaunted "independence" would do them. He demanded a censure of those members of the Council and National Committee who had personally intimidated emigrants and threatened the life of his interpreter, Captain James Starr. He also demanded that the Council pass a resolution to punish anyone else who tried to prevent fulfillment of the treaty. Only by such actions could the Cherokees purge themselves of the contempt they had shown to the authority of the United States.[48] The Council declined to take any of these actions. McMinn then announced that he would forwith send all the government troops "on furlough"—tantamount to inviting the frontiersmen to enter the nation and plunder it at will.

When the Council was just about to break up in this confrontation with McMinn, he narrowed his demands and made a concession. He said that he would have the census taken as soon as the Arkansas chiefs sent their commissioner for this purpose (as the treaty designated) and that he

[46] ASP II, 481–88.
[47] ASP II, 487.
[48] ASP II, 482, 489.

would be satisfied of the Council's friendliness if it would remove from office Thomas Foreman, a member of the National Committee and the man who allegedly threatened Starr's life. The Council decided to sacrifice Foreman for the sake of ending the crisis.[49] When the census was taken, enrollment would end and the Cherokees would be allowed to keep what was left of their land.

Once they voted to expel Foreman from the National Committee, McMinn accepted this as proof that he had broken the hostility of the Council and had won the contest of wills with Hicks. He wrote to Calhoun that he was now "most sanguine" that the aims of the treaty would be completed "in a much shorter period."[50] Evidently he assumed that emigrant enrollment would suddenly flourish. He also informed Calhoun that he had persuaded Pathkiller to send a delegation to Washington "to settle everything according to his father's wishes." Calhoun, presumably, would be able to persuade them to accept the $200,000 for their land. "Now is the auspicious moment; the most violent opposition is silenced and the friends of an exchange have at last assumed an air of independence." The Cherokees were now prepared, he said, to demonstrate a "spirit of conformity" to the benevolent aims of the government.

The Cherokees were indeed worried, but they were by no means as totally cowed as McMinn assumed. His claim that he had "one-half the Cherokee population on our side" because he had a list of 864 families who had "relinquished their claim to land east of the Mississippi" was based on false statistics. He estimated that there were 2,900 Cherokees in Arkansas prior to the treaty and insisted that there were only 10,000 Cherokees in the east. Assuming that each of the 864 families had "three or four members" (though probably many of the 864 had enrolled as individuals), he claimed a total of 3,456 Cherokees in the east and 2,900 in the west who were "on our side" (i.e., in favor of removal and exchange), which was more than half of 10,000. But if Meigs's census in 1809 was correct, there were over 13,000 Cherokees in the east in 1809 and there were probably more by 1818. In 1818 there were perhaps 2,500 Cherokees in the west. The Cherokees then totaled close to 16,000 or 17,000 people. Moreover, many in the east who put their names on the rolls to go west in 1817–1819 never did go.[51] Of the 864 on McMinn's list, 146 took reserves and planned to stay in the east.

[49] ASP II, 482; Cherokee Council to Joseph McMinn, November 28, 1818, M-208.
[50] ASP II, 482.
[51] Royce, *Cherokee Nation of Indians*, p. 100; Royce here states that 817 Cherokees who enrolled for Arkansas between 1817 and 1819 never left their homeland. See also ASP II, 480–83. A census taken of the Cherokees in 1825 reported a total of 14,972 Cherokees living in the east and an estimate of 3,500–4,000 in the west. See McLoughlin and Conser, "The Cherokees in Transition," p. 681.

But statistics were not the issue. The question at this stage was whether the Cherokees now had the initiative or whether Calhoun had it. The Council met in December and picked new delegates to go to Washington. Some of the missionaries from New England heard a rumor that these delegates had been given the authority to take the best offer they could get for their land and sign a treaty of total removal. But others heard that the Cherokees expected to persuade Calhoun to let them remain in the east. Cherokee revitalization hung in the balance.

TWELVE

"FRIENDS AT THE NORTH,"

1819

They have a strong desire to perpetuate their national existence and name, but this can only be done if they remove to the West. —Return J. Meigs to John C. Calhoun, February 10, 1819

For several weeks after the Cherokee delegation left for Washington to make a final effort to save their homeland, Meigs and McMinn continued to believe that their original plan had finally succeeded—that all of the Cherokees in the East would either emigrate or become citizens. McMinn did not go to Washington because he wished to continue to enroll Cherokees to go west. He was confident that Calhoun would push the treaty through to this intended effect. On January 26, he wrote to Calhoun: "Should a failure ensue in the anticipated negotiations at the city (which we trust is not probable), I think I can venture to state that $300,000, including all former expenditures will cover every necessary expense attending their removal . . . which would be a little more than two cents per acre" for 14 million acres, "a great proportion of which is rich land and well-watered and particularly in the Alabama Territory." Most of this was suitable for cotton growing and therefore "certainly contains the most valuable part of the Cherokee country."[1]

But Calhoun had already decided not to push for total removal and detribalization. Cherokee resistance had succeeded better than they knew. The mounting cost of the effort put an end to it. The Cherokees were saved by the growing economic crisis in the United States known as the Panic of 1819—caused in large part by overextended credit for speculation in western land. McMinn had, by December 1818, spent the full $80,000 appropriated by Congress for removal. It was not likely that Congress would now appropriate two or three hundred thousand dollars more, especially when the Cherokees had made it clear how strenuously they opposed removal. On December 29, Calhoun told McMinn that "the state of the Indian fund and particularly that for carrying the Cherokee

---

[1] ASP II, 483.

treaty into effect will not permit arrangements so extensive" as McMinn had outlined for total removal. "It is to be hoped that the effects of the measures which have been pursued will, in a few years, accomplish the object of Government," but for now, the President was willing to let the matter rest.[2]

Because the Cherokees were unaware of this when they arrived in Washington, they were prepared to make further concessions; Calhoun was prepared to squeeze all the land out of them he could. Among other things, he hoped to persuade them to yield all of their remaining land in Georgia in order to fulfill Jefferson's Compact of 1802. The Cherokees had only one card left to play in their negotiations: to enlist the political aid of the distinguished and well-connected mission board of the newly arrived missionaries from New England. Known as the American Board of Commissioners for Foreign Missions, this missionary society in Boston included among its members and former members some of the wealthiest businessmen and most influential political leaders in New England and the Middle Atlantic states. Though dominated by New England Congregationalists, it was also allied with the Dutch Reformed Churches of New York and New Jersey and the Presbyterians, who were powerful in New York and New Jersey. The politicians for these states had been among the most strenuous opponents of the bill for appropriations to remove the southeastern tribes both in the Senate and in the House. Their opposition was in part political (they were no friends of Jackson and the westerners) and in part philanthropic. They strongly preferred the original Indian policy of civilizing and incorporating the Indians and they firmly believed that the United States must live up to its treaty pledges.

The American Board of Commissioners for Foreign Missions had decided in 1816 to send missionaries to establish schools and churches among the Cherokees and other Southeastern tribes. The American Board had been founded in 1810 to undertake overseas missions in the Far East, but after the War of 1812 many churchgoers wanted to help the Indians to become good Christian citizens and to share in the nation's manifest destiny. The Presbyterians on the Board, having lost Gideon Blackburn's schools among the Cherokees in 1810, may have suggested the appropriateness of concentrating their efforts on the Southeastern Indians. The Board sent the Reverend Cyrus Kingsbury as its agent to travel through the south in 1816 and determine the feasibility of starting Indian missions. When Kingsbury reported that the southeastern Indians were potentially ripe for mission activity because of their rapid acculturation,

[2] ASP II, 480.

the Board corresponded with President Madison and received his full approval. They also asked the government to grant their agency a monopoly of missionary work among the Cherokees, Creeks, Choctaws, and Chickasaws and to commit itself to providing funds and equipment to assist their schools as it had assisted those of Blackburn and, after 1808, the Moravians.[3] The President agreed to provide some financial aid, but he could not grant the Board exclusive Christianizing rights among the southeastern Indians.

In the course of his travel, Kingsbury discovered that Andrew Jackson was doing his best to promote total removal and exchange of land among the Cherokees and other tribes. "I ought to observe," Kingsbury wrote in November 1816 to the Prudential Committee that managed the American Board's affairs, "that I expect an attempt will be made at the coming session of Congress to induce the Cherokees to remove over the Mississippi."[4] Jackson's failure to obtain Cherokee acquiescence to removal in October 1816 evidently convinced the Board to go ahead. Jackson, in fact, introduced Kingsbury to the Cherokee chiefs at the Council in Turkeytown that October. Kingsbury reported that he "told them we would take their children, teach them freely without money. That we would feed as many as we could and furnish some clothes to those that are poor." In addition, Kingsbury said, his Board wanted a tract of land on which they could start a farm to provide vocational training for young Cherokee boys, teaching them husbandry and the girls domestic manufactures.[5]

The Council agreed; with their approval Kingsbury chose a tract near Chickamauga (later named Brainerd Mission) and purchased the improvements there of old "Tory" John McDonald, now too old to manage a farm and about to move near his grandson, John Ross, a few miles away. Kingsbury told the Board he hoped to have the school started by February 1817 but he warned them that Jackson and the westerners had by no means ended their efforts to remove the Indians to Arkansas. He considered this policy contrary to all treaty guarantees and cruel to the Cherokees: "If the attempt should succeed, I should blush for my country."[6] However, he admitted that he had found intense hatred of the Indians among the whites everywhere on the frontier. "I hope to remove some of the prejudices against them," Kingsbury wrote, by showing that the Indians were capable of education and conversion to Christianity. "But you

---

[3] For a detailed study of the missionaries to the Cherokees, see McLoughlin, *Cherokees and Missionaries*. On the effort of the ABCFM to attain a monopoly of missionary activity among the five southeastern Indian nations see ibid., p. 105.

[4] Cyrus Kingsbury to S. A. Worcester, November 28, 1816, ABCFM.

[5] Cyrus Kingsbury to S. A. Worcester, October 15, 1816, ABCFM.

[6] Cyrus Kingsbury to S. A. Worcester, November 28, 1816, ABCFM.

cannot conceive the state [of] feeling [against them] even among professors [of religion]."[7]

The Congregationalists of New England (descendants of the Puritans), who constituted the major part of the American Board, had never been shy about uniting the aims of church and state for the maintenance of moral, orderly, Christian society. Unlike the Moravians, whose persecution in Europe led them to keep as far from secular governments as possible, the Congregationalists were prepared to establish close cooperation with the federal government. Their school at Chickamauga got under way in February 1817 and the missionaries who were sent there soon found themselves caught up in the problem of removal and exchange. Agent Meigs, eager to have the missionaries on his side, informed them that "about one-third of the Cherokees" were living in Arkansas. "Col. Meigs has more than once suggested," Kingsbury reported in June, "the importance of establishing a school in that country and has said that Government will furnish almost any aid we might wish," if the Board would do this.[8] Kingsbury realized that the government was trying to use the Board for its own purposes: "The object of the Government would be to get as many of these people over there [in Arkansas] as possible." If the government could assure the Cherokees that there would be schools available in Arkansas, this might be another inducement to emigrate. Not wishing to offend the government, which had agreed to pay for the cost of their school buildings and provide them with tools for vocational training on their farm, the Board agreed to establish such a school at once. This pleased Meigs and McMinn, but the Cherokees could not help viewing it as inimical to their efforts to prevent removal. Missionaries who supped with the Devil needed a long spoon. The American Board was soon engaged in a complicated game of trying to appear neutral and yet remain friendly with both sides in the struggle. "We wait with some solicitude to learn the probable effect of the new arrangement made by the Government with the Cherokees," wrote Dr. Samuel A. Worcester, one of the Board's leading members, to Kingsbury in August. "We hope it will not be inauspicious to our great design."[9]

The Board's missionaries in the field were personally sympathetic to the Cherokee desire to remain in their homeland. The Reverend Elias Cornelius, the Secretary of the American Board, who traveled to Chickamauga in October to meet the chiefs and report on the progress of the school, made little effort to hide his distaste for the policy of Jackson and the westerners. Like the eastern Congressmen who opposed the removal

---

[7] Ibid.
[8] Cyrus Kingsbury to S. A. Worcester, June 30, 1817, ABCFM.
[9] S. A. Worcester to Cyrus Kingsbury, August 22, 1817, ABCFM.

bill, Cornelius thought Jackson and the other treaty commissioners of 1817 had distorted Jefferson's message of 1809 and had bullied the Cherokees into signing the treaty of July 8. "The Commissioners who held the treaty in July last acted entirely without authority from the President of the United States," Cornelius was alleged to have told the chiefs. He assured the Cherokees that Congress would never approve of removing them against their will.[10]

When the pro-removal chiefs heard of this, they told Sam Houston of Tennessee, who had been appointed to assist McMinn with the enrollment of emigrants. Houston wrote to the Secretary of War, accusing Cornelius and Kingsbury of using their "influence to prevent the Cherokees from removing."[11] Upon discovering this accusation of political meddling, Kingsbury rushed to McMinn to disavow any such intention. He said that Cornelius had merely shown to a few Cherokees a letter from the Secretary of War in which Graham himself had said "that it was doubted whether the treaty would be ratified" because of the strong arguments made in the Senate by opponents of the removal bill. Kingsbury then wrote to the Board in Boston stating that neither he, Cornelius, nor any missionary was engaged in political activity. He also remarked that Houston was an officious man "much engaged to get the Indians away from their country."[12]

Calhoun, replacing Graham in December, took the word of Dr. Worcester in Boston that the missionaries were not opposing removal and the matter dropped.[13] Still, the Cherokees, both pro- and anti-removal, could not help realizing that these northern missionaries disliked the efforts being made to move them. "Some of the emigrating party" said Kingsbury, "circulated a report that it was our object to form a large settlement of white people to get possession of their land."[14] They spread this report in order to turn the Cherokees against the mission. "The white people" of Tennessee, who lived near the mission, also sensed the dislike of these northerners for the new removal policy. They "think it of great importance that all the natives should be removed," Ard Hoyt wrote; the New Englanders had to be very careful "lest our good intentions should be misconstrued."[15]

The anti-removal chiefs, however, were eager to make the most of

[10] Cyrus Kingsbury to S. A. Worcester, December 11, 1817, ABCFM.
[11] See ibid. and Joseph McMinn to John Calhoun, November 25, 1817, M-221, reel 75, #6641.
[12] Cyrus Kingsbury to S. A. Worcester in his "Post scriptum" dated December 15 in his letter of December 11, 1817, ABCFM.
[13] John Calhoun to Thomas McKenney, February 16, 1819, M-15, reel 4, p. 119.
[14] Cyrus Kingsbury to S. A. Worcester, March 6, 1818, ABCFM.
[15] Ard Hoyt to S. A. Worcester, July 25, 1818, ABCFM.

these new allies. They embarrassed the American Board missionaries in their memorial to the treaty commissioners of July 1817 when they implied that the start of its mission school at Brainerd (Chickamauga) was proof that the old Indian policy would prevail. Why else would President Madison lend his support to the Board? "We hope by the [aid of the] benevolent societies of our white brothers from the north, that in course of time, if we shall be allowed to keep our country, our white brothers will not blush to own us as brothers."[16]

However neutral they tried to be in their public statements after that, the Board's missionaries minced no words in their private letters. "We think," wrote Ard Hoyt, who took over Brainerd Mission when Kingsbury moved on to set up a school among the Choctaws, "with the Chiefs of this people, that a general removal would greatly distress this people and in a great degree retard, if not ultimately defeat, the benevolent design of bringing them out of their state of darkness to the light of divine truth and the privileges of civilization."[17] The missionaries greatly admired Charles Hicks, whom they called "Brother Hicks" because he was a Christian and a supporter of missions. He is "an observing brother who is ever attentive to the best interest of his people," Hoyt wrote to the Board in July 1818.[18] Hoyt quickly understood why the Cherokees did not support the alternative of citizenship offered in the treaty: "This people consider the offer of taking reserves and becoming citizens of the United States as of no service to them. They know they are not to be admitted to the rights of freemen or the privileges of their oath, and say no Cherokee or whiteman with a Cherokee family, can possibly live among such white people as will first settle their country" and surround the reserves.[19]

By December 1818 the missionaries feared that the pressure on the Cherokees had become too strong to resist. "The great part of the Cherokee nation will cross the Mississippi," wrote Hoyt, as the Cherokee delegation prepared to depart for Washington. "The delegates have full power to negotiate an entire exchange of country if they think best after a conference with the President."[20] A combination of sympathy and self-interest led the Board to decide to intervene in January 1819 and to offer its good offices to aid negotiations between the Cherokees and the federal government. One incident in particular helped to turn the Board against

[16] ASP II, 143.

[17] Ard Hoyt to S. A. Worcester, July 25, 1818, ABCFM.

[18] Ibid. For other statements in praise of Charles Hicks see Brainerd Journal, April 12, 1819, and July 15, 1818, and Ard Hoyt to S. A. Worcester, March 18, 1818, ABCFM.

[19] Brainerd Journal, November 25, 1818, ABCFM.

[20] Ard Hoyt to S. A. Worcester, January 11, 1819, ABCFM.

McMinn and his high-handed efforts to dispossess the Cherokees: "He opened an office," one of the missionaries wrote to Boston in January, "at the Cherokee Agency, for the sale of all improvements made by Arkansas emigrants to the highest bidders, thus to fill the country with whites, and, as he might expect, with whites of the most abandoned character."[21] The treaty gave McMinn no authority to lease or sell land in the Cherokee Nation to whites just because a Cherokee had enrolled to emigrate or even if he had departed for Arkansas. His purpose, he said, was to provide emigrants with cash and to avoid the delay and trouble of having the government appraise the land and remunerate the emigrant. McMinn encouraged the emigrants to arrange sales or leases on their own terms and he ignored protests by Pathkiller and the Council. However, he overreached himself when he put up the American Board mission at Brainerd for sale and accepted an offer for it from a citizen of Tennessee. "Some say he was intoxicated when he did this," the head of the mission wrote to the Board in Boston, "and think he will in some way disannul this sale in his sober moments—others think it quite possible that this may in a future day occasion some dispute."[22] "All these sales are contrary to the express language of the treaty," Hoyt said, urging the Baord to take some action before the missionaries were dispossessed by the purchaser.

Whether McMinn adopted this tactic out of a genuine belief that it was good policy or as a last desperate effort to disrupt and demoralize the Cherokees by filling their land with white speculators cannot be said. However, the muddle over ownership that this was bound to produce may well have been one of the reasons Calhoun decided to end the whole business and send McMinn packing.[23]

John Ross, who was chosen a member of the delegation to visit Washington in January 1819, realizing that the missionaries disliked McMinn and were sympathetic toward the effort to avoid removal, paid a visit to Brainerd Mission before he left. He wished to explain the strategy of the delegation and to enlist the missionaries' help. Ross began by telling them confidentially that the Cherokees might have to give up all their land and go west. If this were forced upon them, he said the delegation would do its best to make some arrangement with Calhoun to preserve the mission property from white land speculators and reimburse the Board for its heavy investment there: "He thought the mission families must have a reserve, at least equal to the Cherokees who choose to re-

<hr/>

[21] Daniel Butrick to S. A. Worcester, January 1, 1819, ABCFM.

[22] Ard Hoyt to S. A. Worcester, March 17, 1819, ABCFM.

[23] Calhoun wrote to McMinn on September 7, 1819, that "with respect to the validity of the leases," he had talked to the President, "and after due consideration, the President, as well as myself, was of the opinion that they were not good" (M-15, reel 4, p. 321).

main, i.e., 640 acres to each family—that the grant for Chickamaugah [Brainerd] must be sufficient to include all our buildings and improvement." From the sale of such a reserve, the Board could recoup the money it had put into the school or farm. On the other hand, Ross said, if the delegation was able to avoid removal, the nation planned to establish an endowment to support schools by selling a tract of its land that would fetch a good price. He asked Hoyt's advice on how such a fund might be administered, suggesting that the American Board might participate in that process to support its own schools. "The great object of his inquiry," Hoyt wrote to Boston, "was how a large tract of good land at some place where it would sell high, could be secured in the hands of some white people (as they had no law by which it could be secured among themselves) so that the nation should hereafter have the benefit of it for the support of schools."[24] Hoyt thought both suggestions were important. He told the Board: "Perhaps this may be the best time to secure the property of the Board here," and urged it to send representatives to "visit the delegation at Washington and grant them friendly aid in their time of trouble." The Board agreed and appointed Dr. Worcester to go to Washington at once to confer with the Secretary of War regarding the future of the Cherokee Nation.

The Cherokee delegation arrived on February 1. Its members were Charles Hicks, John Ross, Lewis Ross, John Martin, James Brown, George Lowrey, Gideon Morgan, Jr., Cabbin Smith, Sleeping Rabbit, Small Wood, John Walker, and Currahee Dick. In their first meeting with Calhoun, apparently unaware that he was prepared to give up total removal, they asked him to take pity on them. Despite many difficulties, "our manners and customs are rapidly assimilating to those of our white Brothers and Sisters who surround us, and we fondly look forward to the time when we shall see those dark clouds of superstition and ignorance vanish from among us." They took note of the argument that their slow progress was considered by some a sign of their innate inferiority: "It is to the want of education and not to a defect in nature to which we must ascribe nearly all of our evils. Natural man is in every country and in every age nearly the same. It is to the Lights of education to which every nation owes their distinction, excepting in Colour. It is a degradation to the American character to say that her natural Sons are incapable of improvement."[25] (Perhaps some of them had read Jefferson's *Notes on Virginia*.)

To demonstrate their advances in civilization the delegates informed

[24] Ard Hoyt to S. A. Worcester, January 11, 1819, ABCFM.
[25] Cherokee delegation to John Calhoun, February 5, 1818 [misdated, should be 1819], M-271, reel 2, #0576.

Calhoun that "the Laws of the Cherokee Nation are now recorded in a book and Communicated verbally to the people. . . . we propose establishing within the nation a printing office and publishing a periodical magazine or newspaper [and] to give to each head of family a copy gratis who has a member in it who could read the english language." Furthermore, "to secure a proper management of this establishment," they proposed "to place it under the direction of the Society of Friends or the foreign missionary society [the American Board] and solicit the citizens of the united states to become subscribers to it." Any profits from the paper would go "exclusively to the education of Indian youths." They said they wished to sell some of their land to establish a school fund to supplement the benevolence of the government and missionary societies.

Then they complained about McMinn's "late conduct in leasing out our lands [to whites] contrary to the spirit and meaning of the treaty." They were willing to deal liberally with their brothers in Arkansas if they could find some way to do so without giving up all their land.[26]

Calhoun took a hard line with the delegation. "You see that the Great Spirit has made our form of society stronger than yours and you must submit to adopt ours if you wish to be happy by pleasing him."[27] If the Cherokees wished to avoid total removal, they must be prepared to give up additional tracts of land: "It is indispensable that the cession which they should make should be ample and the part reserved to themselves should not be larger than is necessary for their wants and conveniences." This was the first hint they had that perhaps some compromise could be worked out. The question then became how great a sacrifice would be required.

From February 5 to 27, Calhoun and the delegates huddled over a map of the Cherokees' lands, trying to decide just how much they should cede and where it should be sliced from their country. Calhoun kept urging that it should all be taken from the part of their country lying within the

[26] Meigs, who had accompanied the Cherokee delegation to Washington, wrote to Calhoun on February 10: "If they wish to remain here, I mean on the present ground, it appears to me indispensable that they should receive laws from Georgia and Tennessee, mild laws, adapted to their state of information. . . . It is time that their present customs . . . should be abolished. If this is done and complete enfranchisement accorded to all those whose merit and information will justify it, it will be making a benevolent experiment. . . . But it will, in my opinion, be only a temporary expedient on their part to gain time; it will not stop the current emigration to the west of the Mississippi river. Their country on the east of that river will not support them without industrious habits of labour, and this they will not submit to. If it is desirable to perpetuate their national existence and name, and I think they strongly desire it, they must take new ground where the pressure of white population will not be great for many years to come. . . . They have had erroneous ideas on subject of their relations with the Government. Their safety depends on their dependence, but it is difficult to make them comprehend this" (M-271, reel 2, #1351).

[27] ASP II, 190.

bounds of Georgia, but this was the seat of their government, Ustanali, and the site of much of their best and most highly developed land. It was also the location of the Moravian mission and of the major full-blood towns along the Etowah River. "It was found impossible," Calhoun explained later to the angry Georgia politicians, to induce the delegation to yield to this demand; "they were fixed in their determination particularly not to be separated from the Creek nation by any intervening white population and to cover their northern boundary to the Tennessee River, which necessarily threw the cession made by the treaty into Alabama, Tennessee and North Carolina" with only a small tract in Georgia.[28] In the end the Cherokees ceded in 1817 and 1819 a total of four million of their remaining fourteen million acres: 1,540,000 in Tennessee (north of the Hiwassee River); 986,880 in North Carolina; 739,000 in Alabama Territory (north of the Tennessee River on its right bank); and 536,000 in Georgia (making the Chattahootchee River the new boundary).[29] These cessions would require almost two hundred Cherokee families or, more precisely, 870 persons to move from their homes and crowd into what was left of the nation.[30] The government agreed to grant an equivalent area in Arkansas to the western Cherokees.

The delegates then faced the problem of dividing their annuity with the western Cherokees. For that purpose the census was supposed to be taken, but neither side wished to undergo the trouble and expense. Instead the delegates and Calhoun tried to estimate how many Cherokees were in Arkansas or enrolled to go there and how many would remain in the east. The delegates claimed that three-fourths of the Cherokees (12,544 according to a census ordered by Pathkiller in 1818–1819) would remain in the east and only 3,500 would be in Arkansas. Calhoun estimated that there would be 5,000 Cherokees in Arkansas and that 10,000 would remain in the east. Reluctantly, the delegation accepted Calhoun's figures and agreed to give one-third of their annuity to the Arkansas Cherokees.[31] No official census was taken.

As stipulated in the treaty of July 8, 1817, and the treaty of February 27, 1819, those who wished reserves and citizenship would obtain them if they lived on ceded land; in the 1819 treaty, anyone who lived on land ceded in 1817 and who did not wish to emigrate could also obtain 640 acres around his farm and become a citizen. Over three hundred Chero-

---

[28] ASP II, 462, 500.

[29] Royce, *Cherokee Nation of Indians*, pp. 91–100; ASP II, 461–62.

[30] ASP II, 495, 498; list of Cherokees forced to remove from land ceded 1817–1819 (undated), M-221, reel 98, #2425.

[31] Royce, *Cherokee Nation of Indians*, pp. 90, 98; Cherokee delegation to Calhoun, February 17, 1819, M-271, reel 2, #1111.

kees "took reserves" under these treaties, but they were to have great difficulty sustaining their claims on these tracts in the ensuing years.[32] The delegates also received a pledge from Calhoun to remove any intruders from what was left of the nation, including those to whom McMinn had illegally leased or sold emigrants' land.

Finally the Cherokees raised the question of selling some of their land to establish a permanent Cherokee school fund. Dr. Worcester did not reach Washington until February 18 to speak for the American Board. By then the negotiations were far along. Whether he exerted a major influence on the final version or not is hard to tell, but the delegates gave him credit for helping. A tract of twelve square miles of good Cherokee land along the Tennessee River (not included in any cession) was set aside in this treaty to be surveyed and sold as soon as possible by the government. The money from the sale was to be invested by the President in trust for the education of the Cherokees' children. Worcester assumed that the bulk of this fund would go annually to support the schools of the American Board.[33]

The Cherokees expected that the treaty they signed with Calhoun on February 27 would at last secure for them a permanent agreement with the United States and that there would be no further attempt to remove them and no further effort to ask them to cede more land. Although Calhoun refused to write any such guarantee into the treaty, the Cherokees and Dr. Worcester chose to believe that this treaty would be their last. When they bid farewell to President Monroe, the delegation said they firmly hoped that "you will not solicit us for more land" in the future.[34] They were determined never to yield any more. Monroe made no promises and within four years the government, urged on by the politicians of Georgia and the other states, was at them again. Calhoun, of course, had no doubt that ultimately the southeastern Indians would all be removed.

Two weeks after the delegates signed the treaty, the Senate ratified it and the Cherokees' second removal crisis was over. When the news reached the nation that they would not have to sell all of their country and go west, there was a tremendous sense of relief and elation. Somehow the nation had managed to survive another threat to its existence; perhaps they too had a peculiar manifest destiny. Perhaps the Great Spirit had singled them out as a specially chosen people.

[32] See William G. McLoughlin, "Experiment in Cherokee Citizenship," *American Quarterly* 33 (1981):3-25, for a discussion of what happened to the Cherokees who were given reserves as a result of the treaties of 1817 and 1819.

[33] The Cherokee delegation first mentioned to Calhoun their desire to establish an endowment for a school fund on February 12, 1819 (M-271, reel 2, #1106); see also ASP II 190, 232-33.

[34] Cherokee delegation to James Madison, March 5, 1819, M-271, reel 2, #1123.

The American Board's missionaries at Brainerd were as pleased by the outcome as the Cherokees. Hoyt wrote to thank Dr. Worcester for "the joyful information that God has heard the prayers of his people in behalf of the poor, despised and afflicted Cherokees. . . . This deliverance, beyond expectation, has spread joy and gladness through the nation, and we are happy to learn that some ascribe it to the true cause [viz., God's will]."[35]

John Ross had written to Hoyt from Washington to thank him for the Board's help: "I have the pleasure and satisfaction of becoming acquainted with the Rev. Dr. Worcester who has been here several days and been very active in promoting much good towards our welfare and future happinees. I cannot express my feelings of gratitude in behalf of the Cherokee Nation to those religious societies who has so much softened the hearts and influenced the minds of the gentlemen of Congress, as well as the heads of department towards the interests of the poor red children of nature."[36] Hoyt relayed this message to Boston and Dr. Worcester wrote to Charles Hicks in March 1819 to congratulate him on the outcome:

I rejoice with you and thank the Great and Good Spirit for his kindness to you and your nation. It was a day of darkness. . . . You feared that you would be compelled to give up your houses, your cornfields, your rivers, plains and mountains. . . . The dark Cloud has passed away. . . . A good portion of your land is secured to you; the wicked men who seek your hurt are to be kept from troubling you. You are allowed to sit quickly around your own fires and under your own trees and all things are to be set before you and your children.[37]

Worcester also told Hicks that the Cherokees were now becoming a well-known people and an important benevolent cause among white Americans in the northeast. "Hundreds of thousands of good men and women in all parts of this country" were coming forward to aid them. The Cherokees at last had found a source of political power within the United States in the churchgoing, philanthropic voters. The Quakers of Philadelphia, for example, had sent petitions to the Secretary of War on their behalf in 1818–1819,[38] and the united forces of the Congregationalist, Presbyterian, and Dutch Reformed denominations were with them through the American Board. Indian reform had now joined the temperance movement, African colonization, religious education, prison reform, world peace, and the moral improvement of the urban poor in the great

---

[35] Ard Hoyt to S. A. Worcester, April 10, 1819, ABCFM.
[36] Quoted in Ard Hoyt to S. A. Worcester, April 10, 1819, ABCFM.
[37] S. A. Worcester to Charles Hicks, March 4, 1819, ABCFM.
[38] For a typical Quaker petition on behalf of the Cherokees see M-221, reel 78, #9207.

religious revival sweeping across America to elevate and Christianize the republic. The heroic determination of the loyal Cherokees to preserve their homeland had given the philanthropic public a romantic new cause to champion.

Charles Hicks, who had borne the great burden of the two-and-a-half-year struggle, returned to the nation with renewed vigor, said Hoyt. He "is much engaged for the instruction of his people" in Christianity. "While an entire exchange of country was thought of as a measure they might be pressed to adopt, his spirit was often greatly borne down with discouragement; but since they have succeeded in getting a part of their country guaranteed to them anew and so many christian people are engaged for their instruction," his spirit had been raised up.[39] The power of the Great Spirit was for him to be found most clearly now in the teaching of the Christian faith. Over the next decade, many Cherokees were to find a new hope in the spiritual power of the white man's religion as they understood it. Serious divisions arose, however, over whether Christianity would strengthen or weaken Cherokee nationalism.

[39] Brainerd Journal, April 12, 1819, ABCFM.

THIRTEEN

THE CREEK PATH CONSPIRACY, 1819–1822, AND THE EXPERIMENT IN CITIZENSHIP, 1818–1832

This is a precedent much wanted, that the absurdity in politics may cease of an independent sovereign nation holding treaties with people living within its territorial limits, acknowledging its sovereignty and laws who, although not citizens, cannot be viewed as aliens but as the real subjects of the United States. —Andrew Jackson, January 1821

Although the mood of the Cherokee nationalist leaders in 1819 was again hopeful, certain elements within the nation were profoundly dissatisfied. Discontent was also rife among the frontier whites in the region, who had hoped for the total removal of the Cherokees. Although these feelings did not prevent rapid improvement in Cherokee life over the next decade, they did provide continual problems for the Council. Andrew Jackson and his friends did their best to use the Cherokees' internal disagreements as wedges to divide the nation, the most extreme example being Jackson's aggressive encouragement of dissension among the chiefs in what was left of the Lower Towns, especially in the Creek Path area of northeastern Alabama. They had borne the brunt of spoliations in 1813–1814, of land cessions from 1816 to 1819, and of intruders ever since. Almost three-fifths of the Lower Town region was taken from the Cherokees between 1816 and 1819. Jackson maintained a regular correspondence with his Cherokee friends there, hoping to negotiate a cession of the whole area. In the end, he succeeded in generating a conspiracy by the chiefs in and around the town of Creek Path to sell their part of the nation without asking the permission of the National Council. When the plotting was discovered in 1821, the Council impeached the conspirators for treason.

Discontent after 1819 was also acute among three other groups of Cherokees: the 3,000 to 3,500 already in Arkansas; a group of over 800 in the Lower Towns who had lost their citizenship by enrolling to go west but then had changed their minds; and the 311 Cherokee heads of families (totalling 1,173 persons) who had taken out reserves as United States citizens under the treaties of 1817 and 1819 only to find it impossible to sustain possession of them.

The strong antipathy among whites surrounding the Cherokee Nation was manifested in many quarters. The State of Georgia printed a resolution that it circulated far and wide, protesting that the treaty of 1819 implicitly, if not explicitly, broke the compact that Jefferson had made with the state in 1802; Georgia demanded immediate and total extinction of all Cherokee title to land within its borders.[1] The legislatures of Tennessee, North Carolina, and Georgia also protested that the federal government had no right to grant reserves and citizenship to Cherokees within their states' borders. A group of whites to whom McMinn, during his last desperate effort to promote total removal, had leased the improvements of Cherokee emigrants or Cherokees enrolled to emigrate was angry that these leases were now challenged by the Cherokees; the Cherokee Council claimed that any money paid for such leases, if they were legal at all, should come to the national treasury and not to the United States, because it was Cherokee land that had been leased.[2]

Finally, the Cherokee Council felt itself badly abused when the surveys of the land ceded in 1817 and 1819 were completed. The Council asserted that the surveyors had purposely or erroneously included areas that the Cherokees had not intended to cede. The most egregious example of fraudulent survey was "Lumpkin's Line," run by Wilson Lumpkin of Georgia. The Cherokees said this line improperly took thousands of acres from them because Lumpkin had misidentified the upper source of the Chestatee River; if allowed to stand, this line would force a whole town of Cherokees to move that the Council had never intended to displace.[3] The vague wording of the treaties and the inaccurate maps upon which they were based always produced such geographical misinterpretations, but the Cherokees claimed that the surveyors of these treaty bounds had been deliberately encouraged by state politicians and land speculators to choose landmarks that maliciously included the largest possible areas for the state and federal governments at the expense of the Cherokees.

The western Cherokees had almost as many complaints against the

[1] Memorial of the State of Georgia, December 11, 1819, M-221, reel 92, #8105. See also Royce, *Cherokee Nation of Indians*, pp. 105–106.

[2] Royce, *Cherokee Nation of Indians*, p. 99. Ultimately all the leases made by McMinn were cancelled; see Joseph McMinn to John Calhoun, March 17, 1821, M-221, reel 90, #6858.

[3] Royce, *Cherokee Nation of Indians*, pp. 99–100; Hugh Montgomery to Cherokee Council, September 26, 1826, M-208; Charles Hicks and Return J. Meigs to John Calhoun, June 25, 1820, M-271, reel 3, #0408; Cherokee Council to John Calhoun, January 26, 1820, M-15, reel 4, p. 358.

eastern Cherokees and the government after 1819 as they had before 1817. In fact, in January 1818 they had become so upset at the behavior of their eastern brethren that they officially (but unsuccessfully) requested the Secretary of War to constitute them as a separate and distinct Cherokee Nation.[4] They were angry because they had not been asked to participate in the negotiations with Calhoun in Washington in 1819 that so intimately concerned them. As a result, they said, they had been cheated of their fair share of the annuity. Like McMinn, they believed that at least half of the nation had gone west or was enrolled to go west. Furthermore, they said that since the first removal in 1810 or really since Doublehead's cessions of 1805 and 1806, they had given up almost half of the original land of their nation (i.e., half of "all the lands watered by the Tennessee River," as John Jolly put it).[5] Yet when the government finally estimated the land they were to receive in Arkansas (between the Arkansas and White rivers), it came to only 3,285,710 acres.[6] This the western Cherokees considered to be far short of what they deserved. Furthermore, the Arkansas River was designated as the southern boundary of their tract in Arkansas, which meant that hundreds of Cherokees who had established farms on the south side (or right bank) of the river had to give up their farms and move to the north side without any compensation. Several hundred of these Cherokees simply moved west and settled on the banks of the Red River, which bordered Mexico at the outer territorial limits of the United States. Others later moved south of the Red River into the part of Mexico that became Texas.[7] If the government defined the Cherokee Nation ethnically, or if it considered the "Western Cherokees" to include all those west of the Mississippi, these Red River emigrants wanted to know what help they would be provided. The government disavowed any interest in or responsibility for any Cherokees who refused to live within either the new tract in Arkansas or the old nation in the east.

Even the Cherokees in Arkansas who were now guaranteed by treaty the protection and assistance of the United States found much to complain about in their treatment. They did not feel that they had been adequately reimbursed for the improvements they had left behind; they were not protected from the Osages; the white intruders on their new tract were not ejected; the government failed to provide them with a

[4] Tolluntuskee to John Calhoun, January 14, 1818, M-271, reel 2, #0567.

[5] Joseph McMinn to John Calhoun, February 9, 1824, M-221, reel 98, #2244.

[6] Royce, *Cherokee Nation of Indians*, pp. 115–21; John Calhoun to the western Cherokee chief, February 12, 1823, reel 6, p. 384; Joseph McMinn to John Calhoun, February 9, 1824, M-221, reel 98, #2244.

[7] Mooney, "Myths of the Cherokees," pp. 99–103.

promised "western outlet" to their tract (a belt of land to the west through which they could travel to obtain furs and pelts further west or to leave the United States entirely without crossing through any land owned by whites); and finally, they complained that a number of other Indian tribes had been moved by the government into western Arkansas and their settlements were impinging upon land that the Cherokees felt was theirs (these included Shawnees, Delawares, Oneidas, and some of their old enemies, the Upper Osages and the Quapaws).[8]

The papers of the Cherokee Agency and the Secretary of War's office for the years 1819 to 1829 are crammed with documents regarding questions of reimbursement for the improvements of emigrants and of persons who were forced off ceded land. Neither the government nor the eastern or western part of the nation was ever able to resolve all of these claims. In 1824, for example, the eastern part of the Cherokee Nation presented a bill to the Secretary of War for $581,000 worth of valuations and improvements in territory ceded between 1817 and 1819 for which the government had agreed to reimburse them. Similarly, the western Cherokees continued to claim that they were owed several hundred thousand dollars for improvements they had given up when they moved west. Fraud and confusion abounded on both sides; collecting claims from the government became a major occupation of the Cherokees and of all other tribes from this time forward. It turned them all into lawyers (or the clients of lawyers), creating a vast bureaucracy for record keeping that overwhelms the archives on Indian affairs to this day. It became common to sell such claims to white (or Indian) speculators who then brought their own suits against the government. Certain Cherokees, like Major John Walker, went bankrupt after buying up many such claims and finding themselves unable to persuade the courts to substantiate them.[9] The worst sufferers, as always, were the poorest Cherokees, who sold their claims cheaply and never received adequate recompense for the years of effort they had put into improving their farms. This meant they had little, if any, capital to start over again if they went west or if they had to move from some ceded area into what was left of the old nation.

To stop the war with the Lower Osages that made life difficult in Arkansas the federal government had arranged a truce between the two nations in October 1818, but once the Osages saw the vast numbers of additional Cherokees and other tribes moving into their area, they would no longer honor the agreement. War broke out in 1819 and continued sporadically until 1824. It brought death, loss of property, and a number of

---

[8] Royce, *Cherokee Nation of Indians*, pp. 93–94; John Jolly to John Calhoun, March 17, 1821, M-271, reel 3, #0796.

[9] Return J. Meigs to John Calhoun, February 25, 1823, M-221, reel 96, #0856.

outright massacres on both sides during that period. In March 1821, the Arkansas Cherokees sent a delegation to Washington to protest that "our people have been most inhumanly murdered, butchered and plundered" by the Osages.[10]

In 1819–1820, the major complaint of the Arkansas Cherokees was that the government had not kept its promise to supply the new emigrants with corn and other food for a year after their arrival in Arkansas—until their first crops could be harvested.[11] They were also promised "that we should have good millseats and plenty of game and not be surrounded by white people." But these promises were not kept. Whites were intruding everywhere.[12] Furthermore, "the greater part of the Country we possess between Arkansas and White river is so encumbered with barren mountains that scarce a deer inhabits it."[13]

President Monroe had ordered a survey in 1818 to draw an eastern boundary for the Cherokee tract in Arkansas between the White and Arkansas rivers within Arkansas County, beyond which no whites were to emigrate. The land speculators and frontier whites in Arkansas were furious when told that a large tract of their best land was to be reserved for Indians. This survey was not completed until April 1819 and by then many hundreds of whites had already moved into the area. Drawing the western boundary of the Arkansas tract took even longer because the land ceded by the Cherokees in the east had first to be surveyed and its total ascertained. When this western boundary in Arkansas was completed in 1824, the western Cherokees claimed that it gave them much too small a tract, not a fair exchange at all for what they had given up in the east.

By 1824 some white settlers were already living to the west of the western border of the Arkansas tract (about where the present state of Oklahoma borders on Arkansas). The Cherokees had long feared that even in the west they would soon find themselves surrounded by whites, which was why they had asked for a "western outlet" from their area as early as 1817. At that time President Monroe had agreed to it in principle. In order to effect it in 1824, however, so many whites would have had to be removed that the government preferred to ask the Arkansas Cherokees to move further west. Arkansas was now a territory (set off from Missouri in 1819) and fast filling with white settlers. The western Cherokees and other tribes placed in that area were offered another exchange of land in what became known as "Indian Territory," west of Arkansas and Missouri in the western part of Arkansas Territory (now Oklahoma). Once

[10] John Jolly to John Calhoun, March 17, 1821, M-271, reel 3, #0796.
[11] Robert Lewis to John Calhoun, M-221, reel 82, #1438.
[12] Western Cherokee chiefs to John Calhoun, March 17, 1821, M-221, reel 73, #8894.
[13] Ibid.

again all of their farms and improvements would go to whites; for a second time they would have to start over again on new land, with a new round of "claims for reimbursement" that the government would have to settle.

When this occurred in 1828, the Cherokees in the east felt that their western brethren got just what they deserved for trusting the government's empty promises, but those in the old nation had their own share of problems. The most serious of these after 1819 developed among Cherokees in northeastern Alabama, in what remained of the Lower Towns. A considerable number, more than eight hundred, had enrolled for emigration because they felt there was no chance of avoiding total removal.[14] A few had enrolled simply to obtain new guns, blankets, and kettles and had never intended to remove. By placing their names on the roll of emigrants, however, they all became expatriates under the Council's law of May 6, 1817. When they decided in 1819 that they would not go west after all, they were considered aliens in their own land; they had no rights as Cherokee citizens and their headmen could not represent them in the National Council. The status of these alien Cherokees was further degraded by a new law passed by the Council on November 1, 1819, which stated that "any citizens of the nation, not enrolled for the Arkansas country, who has or may take possession of . . . any improvement . . . where Arkansas emigrants had left . . . shall be entitled to an exclusive right to the same."[15] This meant that if a Cherokee had left his farm thinking he was going to Arkansas or had actually departed and then returned, he might find that some other Cherokee now occupied his house and farm and that he had no right to reclaim it; he must find some other unoccupied area and start over. These people were, as Return J. Meigs put it, "a kind of Aliens" in their own country, and he put their number at "upwards of eight hundred . . . who had imprudently declined going [west] after all."[16] The Cherokee Council had "permitted [them] to remain in this part of the nation [the Lower Towns] but under sundry mortifying disabilities" with regard to their role in tribal affairs. Meigs, who had no use for the "barbarous Aristocracy" who ruled the nation, sympathized with these people. He wrote of their "degradation" by the Council and defended their "efforts to place themselves independent of a

[14] Royce, *Cherokee Nation of Indians*, p. 100, sets the number of who signed up to emigrate and did not go or returned at 817, Return J. Meigs sets it at 837; see Return J. Meigs to John Calhoun, M-271, February 9, 1820, reel 3, #0472.

[15] *Cherokee Laws*, pp. 9–10.

[16] Return J. Meigs to John Calhoun, March 27, 1821, M-221, reel 90, #6836; Calhoun told Meigs in June 1820 that the government would no longer pay transportation or provide provisions and remuneration for improvements to any Cherokee who had enrolled to emigrate but had not yet done so (Calhoun to Meigs, June 15, 1820, M-208).

very barbarous Aristocracy who, very impolitically, affect to look down upon them." To Meigs, these former enrollees "are as respectable as any part of the Cherokees. Many of them having acted well under General Jackson in the Creek War." Eventually many of them became involved in the Creek Path conspiracy.

The leaders of this conspiracy lived in or near the towns of Creek Path and Brownsville in northeastern Alabama. When General Coffee had drawn the line for the eastern boundary of the Creek cession in 1814, he had generously excluded these towns because of Jackson's affection for Colonel Richard Brown, the Cherokee mixed blood who was the headman or town chief in Brownsville.[17] But Jackson and Coffee could not prevent this area from being overrun by white intruders. John Brown, the brother of Richard Brown, explained to a Congregational missionary in 1818 why he had decided to move to Arkansas even though he did not want to do so: "Living near the United States line he has great trouble from some of his white neighbors who steal his horses, hogs, etc. and on this account he does not know but he shall be compelled to move over the Mississippi.[18] The chiefs in this area who conspired to act as if "independent" of the Council and sell the land were George Fields, Turtle Fields, The Speaker, Wasosey, Bear Meat, John Brown, The Mink, Parched Corn Flour, George Guess (Sequoyah), Young Wolf, Arch Campbell, Night Killer, James Spencer, and Captain John Thompson, who was also interpreter and scribe for the group. They were assisted in the plot by several western Cherokees, notably John Rogers and Walter Webber.[19] But Andrew Jackson was the prime instigator.

Jackson was deeply annoyed by the failure of his effort in 1817–1819 to remove the Cherokees or even to extinguish all their claims to land in Tennessee. He kept in close touch with his Cherokee friends in the Lower Towns, John Brown, George Fields, The Speaker, and John Thompson. They in turn relied upon him to help them out of their awkward position. Having enrolled but failing to take advantage of emigration before June 15, 1820, they were no longer eligible for government aid if they wished to go to Arkansas. They could get no remuneration for their improvements (some of which were substantial), no support in transporting themselves and their families, or any assistance after they got there.[20]

[17] Rogin, *Fathers and Children*, pp. 170–71, and Royce, *Cherokee Nation of Indians*, pp. 78–79.

[18] Brainerd Journal, January 24, 1818, ABCFM. Richard Brown died in 1819.

[19] Wasasy et al. at Creek Path to John Calhoun, November 2, 1822, M-221, reel 95, #0196; John Calhoun to Return J. Meigs, March 21, 1821, reel 93, #9070; John Calhoun to Return Meigs, June 15, 1820, M-208. Chiefs such as Two Killer and Clubfoot may also have been involved in this plot.

[20] John Calhoun to Return J. Meigs, June 15, 1820, M-208.

Colonel Return J. Meigs (1740–1823). A Connecticut Revolutionary veteran and staunch Jeffersonian, Meigs played a double-edged role as federal agent to the Cherokees from 1801 to 1823.

Cherokees of the early to mid-1800s adopted a wide range of dress. Some retained traditional clothes, turbans, and ornaments, some wore garb similar to white frontiersmen of the time, and some wore the latest in European fashion. Sequoyah (George Guess), shown above in 1828, was a mixed blood who opposed acculturation. Famous for his invention of the Cherokee syllabary in 1821, he moved to Arkansas around that time and became a chief among the western Cherokees. Here he is wearing the ornament struck in his honor by the Cherokee National Council in 1824. At the right, above, is Major George Lowrey (c. 1844), Assistant Principal Chief of the Cherokee from 1828 to 1838. A mixed blood who favored acculturation and Cherokee nationalism, he is wearing traditional silver ornaments in his ears and a U.S. presidential medal around his neck.

Sketch: The New-York Historical Society, New York; Sequoyah: National Anthropological Archives, Smithsonian; Lowrey: Thomas Gilcrease Institute of American History and Art, Tulsa

Major Ridge (The Ridge), shown c. 1835 (top left), was a mixed-blood Upper Town chief and longtime member of the National Council. He participated in the plot against Doublehead, fought under Andrew Jackson in the Creek War, and though a major figure in the Cherokee renascence, was persuaded to sign the fraudulent Treaty of New Echota by his son John, who led the pro-removal wing of the nation after 1832. John Ridge (below left, in 1828) was educated with his cousin Elias Boudinot (Buck Watie) at Cornwall Seminary in Connecticut, where both married whites. Boudinot (below right, c. 1835), was editor from 1828 to 1832 of the *Cherokee Phoenix*, the nation's official weekly newspaper and the first wholly Indian-published paper in the United States. He was devoted to the process of acculturation and Christianization and favored removal to the west. All three men were assassinated on the same day in 1839. The newspaper (above right), which first appeared in 1828, was forced to suspend publication in 1834 but was later revived after removal. It contained articles both in English and in the syllabary invented by Sequoyah.

The Ridges: National Anthropological Archives, Smithsonian; Boudinot: Western History Collections, Univ. of Oklahoma; newspaper: American Antiquarian Society, Worcester, Mass.

ᏣᎳᎩ ᏧᎴᎯᏍᏆᏁᎯ

CHEROKEE PHŒNIX.

VOL. I.   NEW ECHOTA, THURSDAY MARCH 13, 1828.   **NO. 4.**

...D BY ELIAS BOUDINOTT,
...ACH. HARRIS,
... THE CHEROKEE NATION.
...50 if paid in advance, $3 in six
...or $3 50 if paid at the end of the

...scribers who can read only the
... language the price will be $2.00
...e, or $2,50 to be paid within the

...subscription will be considered as
...d unless subscribers give notice to
...ry before the commencement of a

...œnix will be printed on a Super-
...et, with type entirely new procur-
...purpose. Any person procuring
...ibers, and becoming responsible
...ayment, shall receive a seventh

...sements will be inserted at seven-
...ts per square for the first inser-
...thirty-seven and a half cents in pro-
...uance; longer ones in propor-

...letters addressed to the Editor,
...will receive due attention.

...ROKEE LAWS.

...wing laws of the Cherokee Na-
...blish as we find them in print,
...y corrections, except what was
...y be typographical errors. They
...ly been circulated in this Nation
...ter form.—Our readers at a dis-
...perhaps be gratified to see the
...acement of written laws among
...ll. We publish some that are
...orce. The repealing laws will
...e order of time they were pa...

Be it known, That this day, the various clans or tribes which compose
the Cherokee Nation, have unanimously passed an act of oblivion for all lives
for which they may have been indebted, one to the other, and have mutually agreed that after this evening the
aforesaid act shall become binding upon every clan, or tribe; and the aforesaid 'clans or tribes' have also a-
greed that if in future, any life should
be lost without malice intended, the
innocent aggressor shall not be accounted guilty.

Be it known also, That should it so
happen that a brother, forgetting his
natural affection, should raise his hand
in anger and kill his brother, he shall
be accounted guilty of murder and suffer accordingly. And if a man has a
horse stolen, and overtakes the thief,
and should his anger be so great as to
cause him to kill him, let his blood remain on his own conscience, but no
satisfaction shall be demanded for his
life from his relatives or the clan he
may belong to.

By order of the seven clans.
TURTLE AT HOME,
Speaker of Council.
Approved.
  BLACK FOX, Principal Chief.
  PATH KILLER, Seed.
  TOOCHALAR.
CHARLES HICKS, S—'y to the Council.
Oostnallah, April 10, 1810.

WHEREAS, fifty-four towns and villages having convened in order to deliberate and consider on the situation of our nation, in the disposition
of our common property of lands,
without the unanimous consent of
the members of the Council, and in
order to obviate the evil consequences resulting in such course, we
have unanimously adopted the following form for the future government of our nation.
ARTICLE 1st. It is unanimously a-
greed, that there shall be thirteen
members elected as a Standing Committee for the term of two years, at
the end of which term they shall be...

There are people,' continued the
corporal, 'who can't even breathe,
without slandering a neighbor.'

'You judge too severely,' replied my
aunt Prudy, 'no one is slandered who
does not deserve it.'

'That may be,' retorted the corporal, 'but I have heard very slight
things said of you.'

The face of my aunt kindled with
anger. 'Me!' she exclaimed, 'Me!—
slight things of me! what can any body
say of me?'

'They say,' answered the corporal
gravely, and drawing his words to
keep her in suspense, 'that—that you
are no better than you ought to be.'

Fury flashed from the eyes of...

SCANDAL.

This rough-hewn log cabin on the Qualla Reservation, North Carolina, although photographed in 1888, is also typical of the homes of ordinary Cherokees in the years 1810–1838. A woman is pounding corn in a tree-trunk mortar. Ears of corn, a stick for ball play, a splint basket, and other objects can be seen between the chinks of the house, on the roof, and suspended from the eaves. Walini', a Cherokee woman also from 1888, probably did not differ greatly in dress from some women of an earlier period.

National Anthropological Archives, Smithsonian

James Vann's tavern (above) and home at Diamond Hill, Cherokee Nation, near Springplace, Georgia, were built in 1803–1804. Vann, one of the nation's most prosperous and controversial chiefs, was murdered in 1809. These buildings were near his trading post on the Connasauga River, along the federal turnpike from Augusta to Nashville. Both still stand; the tavern has been moved to New Echota, Georgia.

John Ross (left, c. 1835) was President of the National Committee, 1817–1827, and Principal Chief of the Cherokee Nation, 1828–1866. One-eighth Cherokee, he was strongly in favor of acculturation and Cherokee nationalism. His second home (above) in Rossville or "Head of Coosa," Cherokee Nation, was at the headwaters of the Coosa River. He moved here in 1827 from his first home at Ross's Landing, near present-day Chattanooga.

State of Tennessee Tourism Development Office

The western Cherokees would have been happy to have them, but when they arrived they would have had no capital with which to reestablish themselves. Clinging to the attitudes prevalent in Doublehead's day about Lower Town independence and estranged from their brethren to the east, the chiefs decided that the land of the Lower Town area belonged to the people who lived there and not to the tribe as a whole. They felt no allegiance to a people who had ostracized them. What they needed was some way to obtain a good price for their region. Andrew Jackson was more than willing to help, but it all had to be done with great secrecy. If the Council found out what they were up to, some might pay with their lives.

As always in such machinations, there were many irons in the fire. Jackson was determined that what he called "the farce" of holding treaties with Indians should cease.[21] He saw the Creek Path conspiracy as a way to force Congress to act without a treaty and thereby set a precedent for unilateral removal actions. Certain whites who had moved into the Lower Town area, like Captain James Reed, had made a contract with the Creek Path chiefs to develop their lucrative saltpeter caves and wished to get rid of Cherokee sovereignty in order to assume private ownership of these resources. Some of the chiefs were out to make a good profit for themselves in order to spite nationalist leaders like Charles Hicks and John Ross, whom they accused of having enriched themselves by reserves they took in the treaties of 1817 and 1819.[22] Other Lower Town chiefs, like John Rogers, were friendly to Jackson and eager to enlist in his cause and share in his power.[23] Some, like George Guess, probably believed that sooner or later the white man would get all the Cherokee land in the east and considered the nationalists' policy unrealistic. Guess also opposed the extreme assimilationist outlook of some of the nationalists (like Hicks and Ross) and their support for Christian missions. He was at this time close to completing his system for writing the Cherokee language; once that was accomplished a major force for the preservation of Cherokee traditionalism would be available. He did not want to see the disappearance of the Cherokees' ethnic identity and thought the best place to nurture that heritage would be in the west, as far away as possible from the whites.

The Creek Path conspiracy may have begun as early as October 18,

[21] Andrew Jackson to John Calhoun, September 2, 1820, M-271, reel 3, #0360; see also Jackson to Calhoun, January 18, 1821, M-221, reel 89, #6234.
[22] Some of the nationalists, such as John Ross and his brother, Lewis, did request and receive reserves because they thought they could make money from them. See Gary Moulton, *John Ross, Cherokee Chief* (Athens: University of Georgia Press, 1978), p. 78.
[23] John Rogers to Andrew Jackson, August 17, 1820, M-271, reel 3, #0363.

1819, when, as Jackson later told Calhoun, a delegation of chiefs from Creek Path came to visit him while he was making a treaty with the Choctaws. This delegation told him that for three years they had been excluded from participation in Council affairs and that they had no confidence in Charles Hicks.[24] Hicks, they said, would "cheat them out of their land"—probably by ceding it in order to preserve the rest of the homeland. (In 1819 the nationalist leaders did in fact cede some land that the Lower Towns considered part of their domain.) Therefore, they told Jackson, they wished to have their farms set aside as reserves (so that the Cherokee Council could not sell them out) and in turn they would cede all the rest of the Lower Town area to the government. (Then, no doubt, they would sell their reserves to whites at the market price and use the proceeds to move to Arkansas.) Jackson was convinced that this was a good opportunity for the United States to obtain the area.[25]

In August 1820, Jackson was told by John Rogers that various chiefs in the Creek Path area had asked him to obtain boats and provisions for them to go west.[26] From 1819 to 1821 Jackson tried in vain to persuade Calhoun to reopen emigration: "I have now but little doubt that a large portion of the real Indians wish to pass to Arkansas if they had means."[27] The Panic of 1819 however, had left the government, like everyone else, severely strapped for cash; Calhoun declined to support the expenditure that Jackson's requests would have required.

Unable to obtain reserves or to persuade Calhoun to reopen emigration and provide transport for it, the Creek Path chiefs next tried to persuade the political leaders of Tennessee to help them negotiate an outright sale of their land. Explaining their inconsistent behavior over removal in 1817–1819 to Governor William Carroll of Tennessee (in 1822), the Creek Path chiefs said: "True it is some of us did enrole our name as Arkansaw Emmigrants, not knowing but our Lands were sold at the same time [i.e., expecting them to be ceded by the council], and finding shortly after they were not, we set still on our farms that we had made thinking no one else has a better right [to them] than we who made them. Nevertheless, we plainly see [now, that] there is no peace for us on this side of the Mississippi—therefore we have sent our long tryed friend, Captain James Reed, to you for the purpose of giting you to use your influence with General government and your state members in Congress for us, the

[24] ASP II, 502–506; Andrew Jackson to John Calhoun, January 18, 1821, M-221, reel 89, #6234. This group had been excluded from participation in tribal affairs because once they had enrolled to emigrate they were, by Cherokee law, no longer citizens of the nation.
[25] Andrew Jackson to John Calhoun, January 18, 1821, M-221, reel 89, #6234; Andrew Jackson to John Calhoun, September 2, 1820, M-271, reel 3, #0360.
[26] John Rogers to Andrew Jackson, August 17, 1820, M-271, reel 3, #0363.
[27] Andrew Jackson to John Calhoun, September 20, 1820, M-271, reel 3, #0360.

Creek Path people, to have [the] privalege to sell our own part of the Country at a Reasonable price to the United States and for us to reap the benefits of the proceeds of the sales to enable us to move away in peace. . . . We are not able to move without we can have that privilege."[28] The land they felt entitled to sell as their own included 1.25 million acres in Tennessee and northeastern Alabama. The western Cherokees, whose total land area had not yet been surveyed in Arkansas, would of course be able to claim this as an additional allotment to their area and thus enlarge their tract in Arkansas. The Creek Path chiefs said they had over eight hundred persons ready to go west and that they had the right to carry with them to Arkansas one-eighth of the Cherokee annuity.[29]

Jackson had no compunction about secret negotiations with a faction of the Cherokee chiefs. "It is high time to do away with the farce of treating with Indian tribes' as sovereign nations," he wrote in September 1820. There was no need for the travesty of prolonged treaty negotiations when the Indians had no right to refuse government requests. "There can be no question but congress has the right to legislate on this subject." It "has always appeared very absurd to me" to pretend that Indians were sovereign nations. "More justice can be done the Indians by legislation than by treaty," for in treaty making the scheming halfbreeds always ended up enriching themselves at the expense of "the real Indians."[30] Jackson, the enemy of aristocratic privilege among the monopolists and bankers of white America, saw himself as equally the protector of the simple, "real Indians," who wanted only to be hunters and live by their old honest skills, against the half-breed aristocrats.

He was not above using a few wiles to do what was right. When first approached by the Creek Path chiefs in 1819, he had told them they must put their plan in writing. He evidently implied that they should obtain some support from Pathkiller, the Principal Chief.[31] By some means they were able to get Pathkiller to sign his "mark" to a document supporting their request (though the letter was in English and Pathkiller could not read English). Later, when the plot was uncovered, the National Council insisted that Pathkiller's signature had been forged, which implies at least that he repudiated it. When Jackson received this Creek Path plan in January, 1821, he wrote again to Calhoun. Again he insisted that "Congress take up the subject and exercise its power under the Hopewell treaty [of

[28] Wasasy and the Creek Path chiefs to William Carroll, November 2, 1822, M-221, reel 95, #0196.

[29] Andrew Jackson to John Calhoun, January 18, 1821, M-221, reel 89, #6234; see also Jackson to Calhoun, September 2, 1820, M-271, reel 3, #0360.

[30] Andrew Jackson to John Calhoun, September 2, 1820, M-271, reel 3, #0360.

[31] Andrew Jackson to John Calhoun, January 18, 1821, M-221, reel 89, #6234.

1785] regulating all Indian concerns as it please. This is a precedent much wanted, that the absurdity in politics may cease of an independent sovereign nation holding treaties with people living within its territorial limits, acknowledging its sovereignty and laws who, although not citizens, cannot be viewed as aliens but as the real subjects of the United States."[32] To call the Cherokees "subjects" was to admit that the United States had always been an empire, not a republic. It was strangely inconsistent with the image of Jackson as the great American democrat, but wholly consistent with his image as a westerner with little respect for Indians.

Soon after this letter, Charles Hicks and the National Council became aware of how far the Creek Path conspiracy had progressed. Hicks attributed it primarily to the speculating schemes of Jackson's friend and other Tennessee speculators. He also was convinced that "they have unfairly obtained Path Killer's signature" to further their object of "attempting to establish a distinct claim to lands here" in the Lower Towns.[33] Suspecting that Meigs had known of the plot and done nothing to warn them of it or to discourage it, the Council decided to take matters into its own hands. It convened at Fortville, Hicks's town, on March 21, 1821, and proceeded to indict the leaders of the plot for treason. This Council voted to condemn "the Illegal proceedings of the emigrant Cherokees at the Creek Path." It charged the plotters with "attempting to take off a piece of land lying in the neighbourhood of said town as their separate property" although it was "reserved to the said Nation in a treaty of the 27th Feburary, 1819." Named in the indictment were "Wasasey, Speaker, Turtle Fields, Young Wolf, James Spencer, Archibald Campbell, George Fields, and the Night Killer." There may have been other charges as well. It ordered the conspirators to "be brought to trial before the National Committee and Council to be held at Newton [New Echota]" and to suffer "such punishment and fine as shall be decreed by the committee and council for acting in defiance and direct violation of the rights of the Cherokee Nation . . . and for stealing the signature of our beloved head Chief in a fraudulent manner to aid them."[34]

If this trial of the Creek Path conspirators ever took place, no records of it exist. However, the oral tradition among the Cherokees recalls that it did occur and that the accused were severely punished, including George Guess (although he was not named in the indictment).[35] More

---

[32] Ibid.

[33] Return J. Meigs to John Calhoun, January 31, 1821, M-221, reel 90, #6769; Return J. Meigs to John Calhoun, March 27, 1821, M-221, reel 90, #6836.

[34] Return J. Meigs to John Calhoun, March 21, 1821, M-221, reel 93, #9070.

[35] See Traveller Bird, *Tell Them They Lie: The Sequoyah Myth* (Los Angeles: Westernlore Publishers, 1971), pp. 105–107.

likely they were all condemned in absentia; had they been punished, Andrew Jackson would surely have come to their defense. The plotters' actions in subsequent years are well documented by extant papers, but nowhere in their writings do they mention that they had been punished in 1821. In all likelihood Hicks and the nationalists wanted only to make their treachery public and thus make it harder for Jackson, Carroll, and Reed to continue to support them. Whatever happened, it did not end the conspiracy.

In 1824, when President Monroe sent commissioners to negotiate with the National Council for a cession of land, Calhoun provided them with copies of the correspondence between Jackson and the Creek Path chiefs in which they stated their desire to sell the land and remove west. Calhoun's purpose was to undermine the claim of the Council that "their people" were "unanimously" opposed to any sale or emigration.[36] But since the Cherokee Nation did not recognize these enrollees as "their people," the Council simply reaffirmed that no true Cherokee favored removal. It told the treaty commissioners that nothing prevented the people at Creek Path from moving west at any time. In fact, the Council urged Calhoun to provide them with boats and provisions to make the trip. But having already once enrolled and having by that act taken their toll of the nation's land and annuity, those people could hardly expect the Council to repeat the process. In the end, some, like George Guess, did go west on their own initiative, but the bulk of them remained on their farms in the east. Meigs was probably right that the Council was not politic to deny them a pardon and reinstate them to equal status upon taking some oath of fidelity, but feelings ran high at that time and the Cherokees wished to make an example of those who infringed the nation's highest law.

The chiefs of Creek Path were by no means intimidated by the exposure of their conspiracy. They continued to correspond with Jackson, Governor Carroll, and others for another two years.[37] But when they found that the federal government would act only through the National Council, they finally gave up. Jackson's day had not yet come.

Next to the Creek Path plot the most awkward issue facing the nation after 1819 was the experiment in citizenship that grew out of the treaties of 1817 and 1819. In order to induce some of the wealthier Cherokees to

[36] ASP II, 507–506.

[37] See Wasasy to John Calhoun, November 2, 1822, M-221, reel 95, #0196; John Calhoun to Return J. Meigs, December 30, 1822, M-208. Calhoun's letter names as among those Creek Path Chiefs interested in selling their part of the nation to the federal government: Wasausa, George Fields, Turtle Fields, George Guess (Sequoyah), James Spencer, Young Wolf, and John Thompson.

support emigration, Jackson, McMinn, and Meriwether wrote into the treaty of 1817 the system of granting reserves to those who said they would accept citizenship. They did not think many Cherokees would be able to sustain this status of citizenship and assumed that those who took the reserves would ultimately sell them and move to rejoin the nation (east or west); those tracts would then revert to the United States. Yet the United States did not want the experiment to be a complete failure lest it not be able to induce wealthy Indians in other tribes to try the same tactic. Agent Meigs had estimated that there were perhaps three hundred Cherokees capable of sustaining the status of citizenship, most of them intermarried whites or mixed bloods. Their interest in maintaining their rich farms or plantations could have made them formidable opponents to any removal project had they not been offered this alternative.

To the federal government, the grant of 346 tracts of 640 acres each was a small concession to make if it would bring millions of acres to the states and their white citizens. But to the states, land speculators, and individual frontiersmen, every 640-acre plot reserved to an Indian was that much fertile land taken from a deserving white farmer and from land-sale revenues. Moreover, the states resented the fact that the federal government was granting citizenship to an alien or "subject" people of color within their sovereign boundaries. None of the southeastern states was prepared to grant equal citizenship to Indians. Furthermore, much of the land in Tennessee and western North Carolina that had been ceded in 1817 and 1819 had Revolutionary bounty warrants included on it that Calhoun had failed to take into consideration when he permitted the granting of reserves. Georgia cited its compact with Jefferson to oppose the reserves and insisted that all land extinguished from Indian claims must revert to the state.

No sooner was the treaty of 1819 signed than the government had to defend itself against claims by the states, while many of the Cherokees found themselves battling desperately against white frontiersmen trying to oust them from their reserves by fair means or foul.[38] Although the Cherokee Council insisted that the government honor the treaties of 1817 and 1819 and protect those who had been given reserves, it said at the same time that those Cherokees who had taken out reserves in the ceded areas were no longer Cherokees. They were now United States citizens and must not look to the Cherokee Nation for help. For those philanthropists who hoped that this experiment would substantiate the original Indian integration policy of George Washington, the weak support given to the reserves proved a deep disappointment. For those Cherokees who

---

[38] McLoughlin, "Experiment in Cherokee Citizenship."

suspected that the white man would never treat the Indians as equals, this first experiment in Indian citizenship hardened their separatist and nationalist ideology. It took almost a decade for the reserve problem to play itself out, but ultimately it appeared that not a single Cherokee reservee was able to sustain his hold upon citizenship. Their fate was not unlike that of those who had been given the chance to form a model community under Doublehead at Muscle Shoals in 1806. Their land returned to the white man's government.

The reserves in Georgia were the first to go. The Governor of Georgia, George M. Troup, shared the view of McMinn of Tennessee on the racial inferiority of Indians. When Calhoun wrote to him in 1824 asking whether Georgia would consider integrating civilized Indians into its citizenry, Troup replied: "If such a scheme were practicable at all, the utmost of the rights and privileges which public opinion would concede to Indians would be to fix them in a middle station between the negro and the white man; and that, as long as they survived this degradation, without the possibility of attaining the elevation of the latter, they would gradually sink to the condition of the former."[39] Two years before this, Congressman George Gilmer of Georgia persuaded Congress to appoint a special committee to investigate the status of Georgia's Indian land. As chairman of this committee, Gilmer reported to Congress that the treaties with the Cherokees in 1817 and 1819 had done little to fulfill the compact that Jefferson had made to rid that state of Indians. In fact, the efforts to civilize the Cherokees and to give them reserves was having a contrary effect: "It appears from the last treaty that the United States are endeavoring to fix Cherokee Indians upon the soil of Georgia" forever. "It will be necessary for the United States to relinquish the policy which they seem to have adopted with regard to civilizing the Indians and rendering them permanent upon their [Georgians'] lands."[40] Gilmer's committee recommended further treaty negotiations to remove the Cherokees and an appropriation by Congress to buy out all of the reserves. President Monroe appointed two commissioners from Georgia, Duncan Campbell and James Meriwether, to travel through the state and purchase, for no more than two dollars an acre, all the Cherokee reserves granted in 1817 and 1819. By December 1823 the commissioners reported that they had completed their task. They had to pay an average of $1,627 for each 640-acre reserve because some whites who had purchased them from Cherokees refused to sell for less. Some cost as much as $4,000. The reserves

[39] ASP II, 735.
[40] ASP II, 259–60.

thus purchased were immediately turned over to the State of Georgia for distribution to its citizens.[41]

The State of Tennessee adopted a variety of measures to rid itself of Cherokee reserves. First it claimed that many of them overlapped Revolutionary veterans' warrants and simply appropriated those that did. Next it claimed that Calhoun had no right to extend the date for taking out a reserve past July 1, 1818, under the terms of the treaty of 1817, and by an act of its legislature this was used to invalidate 184 reserves, which were immediately surveyed and sold. William Wirt, the Attorney General of the United States, stated that this was illegal because treaties were the supreme law of the land under the Constitution, but he had no effect. When Tennessee placed on sale the areas ceded in 1817 and 1819, it took no cognizance of the reserves. Those who purchased land on which Cherokees were living on reserves considered their rights superior. The Cherokee agent at the time, Hugh Montgomery, reported in 1826 that "the purchasers in some instance have by force and arms dispossessed the Cherokees."[42]

The War Department hired lawyers to defend some of the reservees in Tennessee against the various efforts by the state to dispossess them, but the cases were tedious and expensive. Finally Montgomery recommended in 1827 that the department evaluate the improvements of those few Cherokees still on reserves in Tennessee, pay them the appraised value, and persuade them to move back into the Cherokee Nation. The department agreed that this was the best solution and carried it out.[43]

North Carolina was equally determined to rid itself of Cherokee reserves and used the decision of one of its judges in a case in which a Cherokee named Euchellah sued a white man named Welsh for ejecting him from his farm as the basis for doing so. Euchellah had offered as proof of his claim to the reserve the certificate of a survey given to him by the federal agent. The judge ruled that the certificate was invalid because it had not been signed by the President of the United States or by a surveyor commissioned by him.[44] Again the War Department hired attorneys at great expense to try to defend the Cherokee reservees. Although the attorneys won several cases, the War Department finally gave up the effort to help the Indian reservees in 1829 when Congress appropriated $20,000 and appointed two commissioners to buy out all of the reserves in North Carolina.[45]

---

[41] Duncan Campbell to John Calhoun, December 24, 1823, M-221, reel 97, #1680.

[42] Hugh Montgomery to James Barbour, May 10, 1826, M-208.

[43] Ibid.

[44] William Roane to James Barbour, July 8, 1827, M-234, reel 72, #0425.

[45] Thomas L. McKenney to Humphrey Posey and R. M. Saunders, June 5, 1829, M-21, reel 5, p. 466.

Alabama had been admitted as a state in 1819; like Georgia it appealed to Congress in 1823 to appropriate money to buy out the reserves within its borders. When Congress postponed a decision, Alabama used North Carolina's technicality of claiming that all surveys of reserves must be signed by the President or his authorized surveyor. In those cases where a reserve could meet this criterion, the state tried other tactics, such as declaring that the Cherokee who owned the land had failed to occupy it or had left it vacant for some time. In 1828 Alabama again asked Congress to buy out the reserves, but by then there were almost none left. Many Cherokees had themselves invalidated their claims because they had not taken them out on land they resided on as the treaty required. Montgomery reported in 1826 that "they have all, or with few exceptions, been driven off their land. . . . I have been able to give them no incouragement . . . a great number of them are giving to a set of speculators use of the land . . . many other are selling out for a Song."[46]

The Cherokee agents and War Department lawyers reported numerous cases of fraud against reservees or violent and illegal dispossession by whites. Peggy Shorey had a life estate in Marion County, Tennessee. Fearing that she would be dispossessed, she signed a paper deeding it to a white man who promised to defend her rights to it. Once he had the deed, he put her off and took the land for himself.[47] Eight Killer, who had a reserve in the same county, was driven out of his house by whites and appealed to the captain of the garrison nearby. The captain talked to the intruders, who promised to leave in a few days and gave their bond and security to him. When the time had elapsed, Eight Killer went back, but the intruders refused to honor their agreement; instead "they beat and abused him very much and drove him off" and the agent reported "he has been afraid ever since to go back."[48]

Eight Killer and Peggy Shorey were poor Cherokees who had no education or influence. But although Templin Ross was well off and well educated, he too was unable to defend his claim. He reported that he left his reserve on a short trip in June 1819 to take his pregnant Cherokee wife to stay with her family until their baby was born. When he returned to his farmhouse, he found "my doors were broken open and possession taken of the premises" by several white men. They refused to let him in the house, he reported in 1827, "and out of which I am kept to this day."[49]

Records show that a few Cherokees in Tennessee and Alabama continued to sue for their land until the 1830s, but the wisest reservees were

[46] Hugh Montgomery to James Barbour, May 10, 1826, M-208.
[47] Peggy Shorey to Hugh Montgomery, October 24, 1825, M-208; Hugh Montgomery to James Barbour, December 31, 1826, M-234, reel 72, #0201.
[48] John Ross to Hugh Montgomery, July 2, 1825, M-234, reel 71, #0611.
[49] Templin Ross to Thomas McKenney, February 16, 1827, M-234, reel 72, #0417.

those who sold out to whites while they still had possession. Some of these managed to make as much as $4,000 for their reserves; George Harlin received $5,120 for his reserve in Alabama. Even so, Harlin's land was alleged to be worth five times what he received for it.[50] This was the era of the great boom in "black belt" cotton land. Speculators were getting thirty dollars or more an acre in some of the areas the Cherokees had ceded in 1819. The Cherokees who hoped to become citizens and live as equals on this land were doomed to disappointment. They could not overcome the prejudice against them, even when the Federal government belatedly tried to help. It was an important lesson for those who had believed that someday the Cherokees should divide their land in severalty and become citizens as Washington and every succeeding President had told them to do. The reserve problem taught them that as long as the hostile attitude of southeastern whites remained unchanged, it was essential to hold their land in common. Without national ownershp they would be completely at the mercy of the whites, as the 356 reserves of 1817 and 1819 discovered.

Nevertheless the hopes of the remaining Cherokees in the East continued high. The reservees had taken a chance, against the advice of their leaders, and had paid the price. But the Cherokees who persisted in the defense of their homeland had survived. In the decade following the treaty of 1819, Cherokee renascence was to reach its peak. For all the Cherokees' problems, this was a halcyon era full of national accomplishment, confidence, and pride. At last they seemed to have attained control of their own destiny.

[50] Gideon Morgan to Thomas McKenney, August 1, 1828, M-234, reel 72, #0589.

FOURTEEN

CHEROKEE RENASCENCE, 1819–1829:
POLITICS AND ECONOMICS

I can view my native country, rising from the ashes of her degradation, wearing her purified and beautiful garments, and taking her seat with the nations of the earth. . . . on her destiny hangs that of many [Indian] nations. —Elias Boudinot, Address to the Whites, 1826

The essence of Cherokee renascence was to establish a distinct national identity, firmly grounded in economic self-sufficiency and political self-determination. Prior to 1819 this was frequently asserted but not realized. The Cherokee annuity was too small to support the nation's revitalization. Economic development depended upon financial assistance from the federal government in many forms. Political development was directed assiduously by the federal agent. Much of the Cherokees' early progress was made by learning from their mistakes and discovering that the agents and the federal government were not always looking after the Indians' best interests. They learned that if they did not look out for their own economic advantage, there were plenty of whites who would enter their nation to enrich themselves. They found that political leaders who were not accountable to the National Council were easily manipulated by the agent and by treaty commissioners. To be truly self-governing, they had to learn the lessons behind what they were officially taught. They had to become less trusting, more careful, more hard-headed and more skeptical of those whites who claimed to be leading them to become more civilized and democratic. They also had to devise means to guard against mismanagement, dishonesty, and betrayal from within their own ranks. They had to keep written records. They had to study the white man's laws—how they were made and how they were interpreted, how they were enforced or not enforced. Then they had to appropriate these lessons to their own needs. In the most critical areas of revitalization the Cherokees were self-taught. The white man's government and practices provided the tools for the Cherokee renascence, but the Cherokees had to learn how to use them for themselves.

In 1819 the Cherokee Nation numbered about twelve thousand men and women in the midst of over one million whites south of the Ohio River and west of the Appalachians. The primary and persistent goal of the white people was to dispossess the Cherokees of a generation of hard-won farms, plantations, roads, ferries, orchards, pastures, trading stores, mills, cotton gins—all the features of a thriving frontier community, not to mention their still untapped timber and mineral resources in the woods, hills, and mountains surrounding their settled towns and villages. Frontier politicians like Andrew Jackson, Joseph McMinn, George Gilmer, Wilson Lumpkin, John Eaton, and John Coffee who persisted in describing the Cherokees as "hunters" and "savages" did so in order to sustain a stereotype in the public mind that would excuse their seizure of the Cherokees' farms and towns. The frontier whites complained that these "savages" were not making the most of the tremendous resources of their region, yet the more rapidly the Cherokees succeeded in doing so, the more eager the whites became to take it from them. It was the achievements, not the failures, of the Cherokees that had continued to haunt white Americans all these years.

The essence of equality is the ability to act and speak as equals, as one person to another and not as pupils to teachers, wards to guardians, or children to fathers. By 1819 the Cherokees had learned this difficult lesson; if they wished to be treated as equals, they must be as determined, united, and aggressive as whites. They were at last ready to take charge of their own affairs and assert their own forms of pressure upon the federal and state governments. Self-assertion had replaced self-doubt; they would no longer be deferential or easily intimidated. This resulted not simply from drastic changes in the structure of their governance and way of life, but from hard experience and profound inner transformations in their patterns of thought, behavior, and belief. This was a crucial aspect of their acculturation. They had learned that their old ethic of harmony, cooperation, and slow popular consideration of issues to reach consensus was not effective in dealing with white officials and frontier politicians. They had to learn to deal with whites as adversaries, to confront white self-interest with their own self-interest, to combat power with power. The Cherokees' sources of political power were woefully limited, but as long as the United States claimed to be a government of law and of adherence to contractual agreements, as long as the states of the Union agreed that under the Constitution treaties were the supreme law of the land, and as long as the American public felt some moral obligation to help the Indian lift himself by his own bootstraps, the Cherokees were able to use these aspects of legitimizing power underlying the white man's system to their advantage. In the years 1817–1819 they discovered another source of power: they learned how to mobilize and use public opinion (through the missionaries, through white churchgoers, through philanthropists) to support their demands for Christian philanthropy, American justice, and fair play.

Increasing Cherokee self-assurance and self-sufficiency can be measured in many ways besides the increasing complexity and sophistication of their legal and political system. Statistical measurements of economic growth are available by comparing the censuses of 1809, 1826, and 1835. The censuses reveal an astonishing though incomplete picture of advances in numerous aspects of Cherokee life—in population, productivity, resources, educational skills, and enterprise. In addition, the codified laws of the nation from 1808 to 1827 reveal the rapid elaboration of their executive, legislative, judicial, and administrative structure, especially after 1819, culminating in their constitution of 1827. The number of schools and churches in the nation grew rapidly after 1819 and so did enrollments; literacy increased. In addition, less precise but more dramatic indices are available from the development of important new institutions, such as the capital town of New Echota, the first printed Cherokee book of laws, and their bilingual newspaper. Visitors to the nation in the 1820s wrote admiringly of their prosperity and good order, making the Cherokees the prime example in the public mind of Indian progress—"the most civilized tribe in America."

There were also less obvious measures of change. As the self-sufficiency of the Cherokee people increased, the assistance of the federal government gradually decreased (or was transformed at the Cherokees' request from goods and services to cash). The federal government had closed its factory in 1811 because it was losing money. Located at first in the northwest corner of the nation at Southwest Point, Tennessee, and after 1807 at Hiwassee Town, it had not provided a very good yardstick to determine fair trade. The great distance it had to transport goods to stock the factory forced the government to charge high prices. Some Cherokees complained that government trade goods were not the best quality, apparently because the government did not think Indians could afford superior products. By 1811 the Cherokees had enough private traders among their own people to provide effective competition with white traders and sufficient skill to make their own bargains. The Cherokees did not miss the factory when it was gone; Cherokee traders like Joseph Vann, Samuel Riley, John and Lewis Ross, John Martin, and David McNair were easily available to take over its business. In fact, some were pleased to see it go because they had always suspected that it was used by the agent to grant favors (through extending credit) to well-disposed chiefs. Moreover, excessive amounts of the Cherokee annuity were taken each year by the agent to pay off debts at the factory—especially tribal debts such as emergency grants of wheat and corn in times of famine or repairs for gristmills.

The government had removed its army garrison from Hiwassee Town in 1812 because the troops were needed elsewhere during the war. After 1815 regular army soldiers were only intermittently located in the vicinity of the Cherokees. As the white frontier moved farther west, new forts were opened across the Mississippi, where Indian wars were still a daily occurrence. The absence of troops near the Cherokee Nation made it very difficult for the agent to remove intruders. In 1819 the regular troops closest to the Cherokees were sent to Florida to fight against the Seminoles and the garrison was never reopened. This was harder on the Cherokees than on the government, except when the government was about to negotiate a treaty and wanted to impress them with its concern, efficiency, and protection of their rights. In the 1820s the agent several times authorized the Cherokee Lighthorse to remove white intruders; in one respect this was a striking sign of their maturity, in another a very risky assignment that could easily lead to a bloody skirmish.

In 1819 Meigs suggested to Calhoun, Secretary of War, that it was time for the government to end its civilization program and phase out its gifts of technical and economic assistance to the Cherokees. Calhoun, facing government austerity due to the financial panic, agreed. "My own opinion," he wrote in April 1820, "is that so long as the United States continue[s] to furnish them" with "articles for manufacturing and agricultural purposes, the Indians will make no effort to procure them themselves. . . . they will do nothing for their own accommodation and support."[1] Meigs replied: "The Cherokees are now better provided with utensils for agricultural and manufacturing purposes than ever they were before and . . . there cannot perhaps be a better time to commence a retrenchment of these expenses and to let them know that it was not to be expected that these gratuities should alway[s] be continued." He shared Calhoun's view that continued gifts from the government would only undermine the development of individual self-reliance: "Twenty-four years have elapsed since the commencement of these bounties and the measures have had a good effect, but to continue them longer would really hurt them and only be throwing cold water on their personal exertions and nursing indolence. They actually want some stronger excitements to industry than they have now. If they were my own Children I would say the same." Although these arguments were obviously self-serving, they were also a left-handed compliment to Cherokee self-sufficiency. Having rationalized with typical inconsistency the notion that

[1] John Calhoun to Return J. Meigs, April 30, 1820, M-208.

the way to reward Indian effort was to punish Indian indolence, the government had no compunction about taking unilateral action to abridge this treaty promise. Nor did Meigs try to ascertain how many Cherokees in the remote districts still needed hoes, plows, spinning wheels, or looms. The impression left by this bit of correspondence is that the government sulkily resented the success of its own program because it undercut Cherokee dependence. "It is time," Meigs said, "that they should, like white people, depend on their own exertions. They have good land, a mild climate; they have now attained a competent knowledge of agriculture, of household manufactures by the aid of Government; as herdsmen, they raise large stocks of all the valuable kinds of domestic animals and without labor." This was a grudging recognition of Cherokee economic maturity: "They now ought no longer to be kept in leading strings, but to stand up like men on their own feet." When they did begin to stand up against their "Great Father" however, they were told that they were insolent, ungrateful minors who did not know what was best for them.[2]

On May 3, 1820, Meigs proposed "to issue no more orders for utensils for agricultural [purposes] and for the purposes of domestic manufactures" to be distributed gratis among the Cherokees "except in extraordinary cases." So ended the long federal effort to help the Cherokees through their transition from the hunting to the agricultural stage of their "civilization." The Cherokees made no official complaint, though from time to time some of the poorer Cherokees continued to send requests for help. It is doubtful that the National Council was even informed of this decision.[3]

In 1819 the Cherokees had initiated a significant change in governmental practice when it negotiated with Meigs for a flat cash grant of $1,280 in exchange for the expense incurred by the government each year to provide a council at the agency at the time the annuities and economic aid were awarded. For various reasons the agent had found it useful to call a large gathering of the chiefs and their people every year in the late summer or early fall. He liked to pose as a benevolent dispenser of gifts from the government; he wanted to show that he was doing this openly and honestly; he wanted to see that the chiefs distributed the trade goods fairly; and frequently he wished to create a friendly atmosphere to conduct negotiations for land or a right of way. These were usually festive

[2] Return J. Meigs to John Calhoun, May 3, 1820, M-208.

[3] Ibid. For an example of a request for help from the Cherokee town of Etowah, one of the poorest parts of the nation, and Calhoun's refusal to honor it, see Return J. Meigs to John Calhoun, May 25, 1822, M-208, and John Calhoun to Return J. Meigs, August 12, 1822, M-208. To Meigs's credit, he supported the request for more technical assistance to Etowah on the grounds that its people had not received their fair share of economic aid over the years.

social occasions, sometimes coordinated with the Green Corn Dance or a ball play. As many as 2,500 to 3,500 Cherokees would attend from all over the nation. The government provided the food for such gatherings; rations for three to five days could be very expensive. After 1810 the National Committee began to ask that the annuity be turned over to it in cash, but nonetheless the agent continued to call annual gatherings because the chiefs had to agree to deductions from the annuity to pay tribal debts. By 1819 fewer people attended the distribution of annuities because they trusted the National Committee to handle the nation's funds. There were enough other occasions for festivals. That year the National Committee, through Charles Hicks, asked Meigs precisely how much money, on the average, the government spent each year to provide rations for this annuity meeting. Hicks suggested that this amount instead be paid to the tribe in cash as part of the annuity. Meigs and Hicks settled on the sum of $1,280 and Thomas L. McKenney, the Director of Indian Affairs under Calhoun, agreed to grant it "in perpetuity" from the agency funds in lieu of the older arrangement. This prevailed for the next three years until Calhoun questioned the grant. Meigs said that it in fact saved the department at least 50 percent over the previous system and that he had pledged his word to the nation to sustain the agreement.[4] The War Department allowed the arrangement to continue until 1827 and then arbitrarily refused to pay it any longer. Meigs had died four years earlier and the agent at that time, Hugh Montgomery of Georgia, was not inclined to defend the agreement.[5]

Another form of government assistance cut off after 1819 was the practice of paying sums of money to Cherokee relatives for an unpunished murder by a white. In 1819 Meigs wrote to Calhoun to tell him how an insane soldier at the garrison, who had killed a Cherokee with a knife several years before, had been brought to trial but escaped and had since eluded capture. "A considerable number of Indians have been killed (generally speaking, murdered) since I have been in this Agency." He reminded Calhoun of the long-established policy of "making presents to the relatives of those killed on their solemnly promising to cease all thoughts of taking satisfaction, as they call it."[6] In some cases he gave as little as $100 or $130, he said, but in this case he thought $160 would be more appropriate. To his surprise, Calhoun refused to authorize it: "You will inform the chiefs that the practice will not be continued in future as it is repugnant to those principles by which we govern ourselves."[7] Cal-

---

[4] Return J. Meigs to John Calhoun, October 8, 1822, M-221, reel 96, #0797.
[5] Thomas L. McKenney to Hugh Montgomery, March 24, 1827, M-21, reel 3, p. 467.
[6] Return J. Meigs to John Calhoun, November 14, 1819, M-271, reel 2, #1391.
[7] John Calhoun to Return J. Meigs, January 6, 1820, M-15, p. 354.

houn had evidently forgotten that the frontier governed itself by refusing to accept Indian testimony in state courts and that frontier whites never convicted one of their own people for murdering an Indian. It is also worth noting that the value of a Cherokee life had declined considerably over the years. Earlier in the century Meigs had regularly given $200 to $300 in such cases. It is also ironic that when a Cherokee killed a black slave and was acquitted, Meigs nevertheless accepted a claim by the slave's master of $500 for the loss of his "property." In that case, the money was taken from the Cherokee annuity.[8]

When Joseph McMinn succeeded Meigs as the Cherokee agent in 1823, he phased out another important aspect of government aid relating to the complications of white jurisprudence on the frontier. To protect Cherokee civil rights in cases where they became embroiled in a civil quarrel with a white man, the agent had always hired white lawyers to argue the Cherokee case. In 1823 a Cherokee asked McMinn to "institute suit in the Federal Court against a white man charged with having robbed or stolen two slaves from a native." McMinn said he would first have to ask the Secretary of War. The Cherokees "remonstrated by saying Colonel Meigs never waited for your instructions on such occasions; I replyed to them that they were in quite solvent circumstances and able to support the suit."[9] He also told them that "during their minority they had a just claim upon the resources of the Government of the United States, but that this claim would diminish in the precise ratio that their Nation would approximate towards a state of civilized life." Besides, he said, the government was trying to curtail expenses in Indian affairs and could no longer bear this burden. In his letter to the War Department McMinn also mentioned that the Cherokees had been very truculent toward government treaty commissioners that year, refusing to cede any more land. It seems likely that as former Governor of Tennessee he did not want to be put in the position of using his authority as a federal agent to prosecute citizens of his state who had voted, or might yet vote, for him. "If the Cherokees are highly indulged in having their suits brought for them," he warned Calhoun, the suits "will become very numerous" because of the increasing friction between whites and Indians on their borders and the willingness of the Cherokees to take the disputes to court. He seems to have feared that because the Cherokees were "advancing with great rapidity" toward the status of civilized people, they might soon be given the right to testify in court, particularly those whom the missionaries were converting to Christianity. In that case, the states might find the "courts

---

[8] See Jenkins Whiteside to Return J. Meigs, March 24, 1810, M-208, and Return J. Meigs to Jenkins Whiteside, April 20, 1810, M-208.

[9] Joseph McMinn to John Calhoun, June 24, 1823, M-221, reel 98, #2126–2127.

of justice open to every class of people." This boggled the mind of a man who thought Indians should have no more rights than "free people of color."

In short, it became increasingly difficult after 1819 for government officials to assert on the one hand that the Cherokees were "minors" and on the other that they were old enough to manage their own affairs. What the nation saw as the reluctance of the government to provide them with customary protection and assistance also constituted an increasing governmental awareness that the Cherokees were approaching the point at which they would have to be treated as equals. This was why Calhoun asked Governor Troup in 1824 whether he would accept the Cherokees as citizens. The refusal of Georgia and the other states to consider this made it awkward for the government to continue aid to the Indians. Every act to assist in civilizing the Indians and granting them equal protection before the law was an offense to the states, which wanted them removed to the west as feckless, irresponsible savages. Every step toward the Indians' integration or incorporation was an affront to those who believed them to be racially inferior.

Another striking aspect of the Cherokee renascence to men like Meigs, McMinn, and Calhoun was a series of eleven laws passed between 1820 and 1823 that together constituted a political revolution in the structure of Cherokee government. Under these laws the National Council created a bicameral legislature, a district and superior court system, an elective system of representation by geographical district rather than by town, and a salaried government bureaucracy. These laws completely replaced the traditional decentralized town government system under locally chosen "headmen" and town councils. They represented a definite move by the nationalist leaders toward a replication of the American political system, including overlaying many aspects of Anglo-Saxon jurisprudence on Cherokee customs. Although there was no outright attack upon Cherokee traditionalism by the Council (and could not be, because the majority of the Council were traditionalists), there was a clear effort by strong, mixed-blood leaders to adjust tradition to current circumstances. It was no easy matter to convince a Council that had a majority of full bloods who spoke no English to graft all of these innovations onto traditional practices. The leaders in these innovations—Charles Hicks, John Ross, Major Ridge, William S. Coody, and John Martin—risked alienating their conservative people in order to prove to the white man that the Cherokees could understand and manage a republican form of government. Not all of the Cherokees approved of these laws or followed them in detail, but most acquiesced. They did so in the hope of improving their standing with the whites who kept calling them savages. The new laws had considerable appeal to the missionaries whom the Cherokees were eager to have on their side; they were widely publicized in missionary and other philanthropic journals as proofs of Cherokee civilization.

The first basic step in this new political structure was the judiciary act passed on October 20, 1820. The National Council concurred in dividing the nation into eight irregularly shaped but equally populated "districts" and established a district court in each.[10] A month later a second law defined the boundaries of these districts and decreed fixed salaries for all state officers. This law also specified that henceforth the Council would no longer consist of seventy to one hundred headmen representing each of the so-called towns or villages in the nation (the boundaries of these towns no longer having much meaning or definition except the adherence to a particular town council house), but would consist of thirty-two "representatives," four elected annually from each of the new judicial districts.[11] In addition, local administration was no longer to center in the fifty to sixty town council houses but in a district "council house," really a county courthouse, to be built "for the purpose of holding councils to administer justice in all causes and complaints." The term "council" was used to mollify opposition; although Cherokee town councils had sometimes functioned as courts to adjudicate local problems, they originally functioned as town governments, deciding everything from whether to go to war or make peace to when to hold religious festivals or ball plays. Many of the functions of the town councils had withered away since 1794. The most common aspects of conflict among Cherokee citizens now involved issues of private credit and debt, contracts, inheritance, and property ownership that were difficult to adjudicate in town councils where everyone could speak. Prior to 1822 private controversies frequently came to the National Council for resolution. By 1820 the National Council felt overburdened with these private quarrels and established district courts to be staffed by those competent to handle them. One "judge" was appointed for each of the eight district courts and in addition four circuit judges were appointed, each "to have jurisdiction over two districts"; the circuit judges were to "associate with the district judges in determining all causes agreeable to the National laws." This left only a few local matters to the old town councils, particularly ceremonial issues, marriages, and clan matters. But the complexity of the new national laws, most of them concerned with the economics of a free enter-

---

[10] These laws and those cited below are all quoted in *Cherokee Laws* (Tahlequah, C.N., 1852) in order of their date of passage by the National Council. See also Rennard Strickland's discussion of Cherokee law and government in *Fire and the Spirits*.

[11] *Cherokee Laws*, pp. 11–12, 15–18. See also Elias Boudinot, *An Address Delivered to the Whites* (Philadelphia, 1826), p. 11.

prise system, required a different kind of law and justice. Traditional town councils ceased to function well when the population became widely dispersed on individual farms.

The new laws instituted officials called "marshals" (in effect lighthorse regulators) to execute the decisions of the district courts. The first judges were chosen by the National Committee, but in 1828 this law was amended to have them chosen by joint vote of the National Committee and National Council (when acting together they were known as "the General Council" of the nation). The law did not specify how judges were to conduct their cases; the wording of the original judiciary law indicates that the district judges may have met in conjunction with local headmen and acted as moderators. In 1824, a new law specified that legal matters were to be heard before juries; jurors were to be "disinterested men of good character and judgment," impaneled by the marshal in each district. The marshal was also given the power to subpoena witnesses at the court's request and "to collect all debts" of the nation (deducting 8 percent for his pay as collector). Eventually the marshals ceased to be leaders of the Lighthorse, and in 1825 the lighthorse units were disbanded. The laws in each district were thereafter enforced by the marshal, a sheriff, a deputy sheriff, and two constables. The Cherokee Nation did not erect any jails. Punishments set by the courts for criminal cases (whipping or execution) were administered by the marshal, sheriffs, or deputies upon conviction. Fines and other penalties or court orders were executed by the marshals, who had the power to distrain or confiscate the property of those convicted and auction it off to pay the fines if the person convicted did not have the cash.

At first, appeals from the district or circuit courts could be made to the National Council, but in 1821 a new law established a Superior or Supreme Court for the nation. It consisted of the district judges and circuit judges meeting together at the national capital once a year for this purpose. Eventually a handsome two-story clapboard building was erected in New Echota to house the Supreme Court. By 1822 the nation had a three-tiered judicial system: the district courts heard criminal cases, except for murder, and civil cases involving less than $100; the circuit courts heard murder cases and civil cases involving more than $100; the Supreme Court heard appeals from the lower courts. Each court had its own salaried clerk, who was required to keep written records of all cases and to issue subpoenas for witnesses. In 1825 the judiciary was declared "independent" of the Council.

The same law that in 1820 provided for elected representatives from each of the eight districts also provided for the payment of salaries to all national officers. Pathkiller, now seventy-five years old, received $150 as

Principal Chief; Charles Hicks, the Second Principal Chief, who handled most of the official correspondence of the nation, received $200; and the clerk and the Speaker of the Council each received $2.50 per day during Council sessions. The President of the National Committee (which was henceforth the upper house of the bicameral legislature) received $3.50 per day. From 1817 to 1827 John Ross served as President. The clerk of the National Committee (at first Thomas Wilson, later Elijah Hicks) received $2.50 per day when the National Council was in session. The Council's interpreter received $.50 per day. Council sessions were conducted in Cherokee and English depending upon the preference of the speakers, but all official documents had to be written in English. Council members received $1.00 per day; members of the National Committee, $2.00 per day. It appears that legislation might originate in either the Council or the Committee, but the Council generally asked the Committee to draft any legislation it wanted. Both houses had to concur for a law to pass. The Principal and Second Principal Chiefs had to sign all laws and usually the Speaker of the Council signed as well. There was probably no veto power because tradition still assumed that consensus preceded passage.

The purpose of this republican system of government, clearly modeled on that of the surrounding states (though not specifically copied from any one of them) was to increase the efficiency and centralize the authority of the Council. The laws were Cherokee versions of white political structures. They created a professional bureaucracy for administration and record keeping. The General Council tried hard to reconcile old communal patterns and nomenclature (chiefs, council, speaker) with new structures. Behind the restructured system lay a new individualistic, competitive, acquisitive system of values that was almost impossible to reconcile with the tradition of harmony and cooperation. The Cherokees wished to demonstrate that they could govern themselves in an orderly, democratic, efficient manner while providing civil liberty for the individual. In the new market economy that generated the nation's prosperity, the political structure was designed to protect property and contractual rights with which the older generation and town councils were not familiar and could not deal adequately. A centralized, tripartite republican government constituted a major transformation from the older decentralized town council system. The Cherokees had clearly moved, in Ferdinand Tönnies's terms, from *gemeinschaft* to *gesellschaft*, and from an oral to a written system of order. This new respect for written law was evident in the Cherokees' request that their agent should have all new laws printed annually and distributed throughout the nation. Laws were changing and being created too quickly for an oral tradition to have coped with them. In addition, the Cherokees wanted the whites to be aware of their progress.

In 1826, John Ridge, the son of Major Ridge and one of the new generation born into a different political world, educated by missionaries, and readily adapting to the new ways, wrote a letter to Albert Gallatin (Jefferson's former Secretary of the Treasury, now retired and dabbling in anthropology), explaining to him the significance of the political restructuring that had taken place in the early 1820s. Formerly, Ridge said (describing his people in the third person),

their chiefs were numerous and their responsibility was a trifling [one]. Lands then could be obtained of them at a price most convenient to the United States as their commissioners, with the assistance of their agent, could always procure a majority for a cession, and when this was done, all yielded to secure their share for the trifling equivalent. At length the eyes of our Nation were opened to see their folly. Their existence was in danger and the Remedy was within themselves, and this could only be effected by the amendment of their Government. Useless members were stricken off—a Treasurer was appointed and a National seat for their future Government was selected. In short, these Chiefs organized themselves into a Standing body of Legislators.[12]

Charles Hicks took the same view of this political transformation. Writing to Meigs a few days after the first laws that replaced town government by district government were enacted, he said this new measure had been passed "for the interest of perpetuating the nation."[13]

Elias Boudinot, the nephew of Major Ridge, educated at mission schools and shortly to become editor of the nation's bilingual newspaper, described the economic and governmental changes to a white audience in Philadelphia in 1826 and concluded with these fulsome remarks:

The Cherokee authorities had adopted the measures already stated with a sincere desire to make their nation an intelligent and virtuous people, and with a full hope that those who have already pointed out to them the road to happiness will now assist them to pursue it. . . . I can view my native country, rising from the ashes of her degradation, wearing her purified and beautiful garments, and taking her seat with the nations of the earth. . . . on her destiny hangs that of many [Indian] nations. If the General Government continues its protection and the American people assist them in their humble efforts, they will, they must, rise.[14]

The dynamic nature of Cherokee society, its fluid and rapidly evolving political order, reflected an equally dynamic economic and social order. The claims of John Ridge and Charles Hicks that the purpose of the polit-

[12] John Ridge to Albert Gallatin, Payne Papers, VIII:106.
[13] Charles Hicks to Return J. Meigs, November 27, 1820, M-208.
[14] Boudinot, *Address*, p. 14.

ical revolution of 1820–1823 was to save and perpetuate the nation in its struggle with the United States was only half of the story. Centralization and efficiency also made it easier to expand the economic development and prosperity of the nation—raising the standard of living for all. Of the 115 recorded laws passed between 1817 and 1828, forty-eight or 42 percent were concerned very specifically with economic issues such as trade, transport, labor, land use, credit, loans, development of resources, regulation of livestock, fencing of property, regulation of turnpike and ferry tolls, business franchises, and similar aspects of a market economy. Another 20 percent of the laws were concerned with social and cultural change, such as the role of women, marriage, inheritance, education, the sale of liquor, gambling, schooling, Sabbath observance, and the status and rights (or limits on rights) of slaves and of intermarried whites. The Cherokee people were told that all of the restructuring—political, economic, and social—was necessary "to preserve the country," but some began to ask how the country was being preserved when it was daily changed to conform to white patterns. This was the Cherokee dilemma, the dilemma of all Native Americans: in order to survive as red men, they were told they must become more and more like white men.

The forty-eight laws dealing with economic questions indicate the high state of acculturation that some parts of the Cherokee nation—or at least the three hundred Cherokee families at the center of the nation's development—had reached. Although the nation still retained common ownership of its land, the use it made of its land and its resources differed little from that of surrounding white settlements. Those with high ambitions and entreprenuerial skills worked primarily for their own aggrandizement. At best the nation made a nominal income from leasing a franchise for a turnpike, ferry, tavern, or a saline or saltpeter cave. Private initiative and private profit were the chief spurs to the expansion of the economy. Dividing these forty-eight laws into rough categories indicates that eleven dealt with transportation, ten with the labor force (including black slaves), seven concerned stray livestock, six regulated land use, three were concerned with forest and mineral resources, eight dealt with public monies and credit, one each dealt with debtors, vagabonds, and wills.

Most of the transportation statutes were concerned with turnpikes or roads, the basic arteries for the market economy. Cotton, corn, wheat, barley, melons, beans, and salted pork or beef traveled by wagon out of the nation and manufactured goods returned the same way. Livestock and poultry were walked to market in the neighboring communities. Traders or middlemen usually bought up most of the produce of the individual farmers and herders and disposed of it in bulk, although some Cherokees took their own livestock and produce to market. A smaller amount of agricultural produce and livestock was carried by flatboats or keelboats (and eventually by steamboats) on the local rivers, which provided good arteries as far south as Natchez, Mobile, and New Orleans and as far west as the Arkansas Cherokees. The chief eastern markets were Savannah, Augusta, and Charleston. The bulk of Cherokee trade went to Knoxville, Nashville, Athens, or Huntsville on the periphery of the nation. By 1824 the federal government was sending negotiators on behalf of the states to ask the Council for rights of way through the nation to dig canals and build railways (for horsedrawn cars). The Council refused such requests in 1826, 1827, and 1828, much to the annoyance of whites seeking easier access to markets.[15] Had the Cherokees remained long enough in the east they would undoubtedly have had to grant such rights; some of their own traders favored them in the 1820s.

Most of the turnpike laws were concerned with proper upkeep by the various turnpike companies that had built spurs or connecting links to the federal turnpikes. The nation incorporated some of its own traders in order to build turnpikes.[16] Some of the laws concerned regulating the toll rates at the gates of the various turnpikes. One law forbade any person to cut a road without approval of the Council, which indicates that Cherokee farmers were apt to do just what white farmers did and cut the shortest path from their farms or plantations to the nearest highway or market. The Council also had to settle the disputes between competing turnpike companies that complained of new roads being built "in opposition to the interest of" the existing "proprietors of a privileged turnpike."[17] The Council set standards for the construction of roads, which were "to be cut and opened twenty-four feet wide, clear of trees, and the causewaying to be covered with dirt . . . and the banks of all water courses to be put in complete order."[18] Turnpike companies either paid an annual rental fee or deposited a fixed portion of their revenue into the Cherokee National Treasury. In short, every aspect of highway construction, upkeep, and regulation was controlled by the Council. It similarly regulated ferries, inns, taverns, and trading posts located along the highways.

As in every frontier community, there was always a shortage of skilled labor. The Cherokee Council licensed all white craftsmen, mechanics, artisans, traders, teachers, clerks, and sharecroppers who entered the nation to take up residence. This had originally been done by the federal agent, but the Council took this task under its own control after 1811. The prob-

---

[15] The documents regarding these treaties may be found in M-208, M-15, M-221, and M-271.

[16] *Cherokee Laws*, pp. 20–21.

[17] Ibid., p. 7

[18] Ibid., p. 35.

lem was complex because of the touchy nature of Indian-white relations. The Cherokees needed honest, competent white labor. Sharecroppers, for example, sought the advantage of a tax-free farm on rich virgin land and agreed to work a tract for Cherokee landholders; often they failed to pay their share of the crop to the Cherokee they worked for and after several good crops simply absconded with their profits to buy their own farms outside the nation. In 1819 the National Council unanimously agreed "that schoolmasters, blacksmiths, millers, salt petre and gun powder manufactures, forgemen, turnpike keepers, and mechanics" who were "privileged to reside in the Cherokee Nation" must acquire permits from the Council through their Cherokee employers, who must stand "responsible for their good conduct and behavior."[19] A similar law applied to "single white men . . . admitted to be employed as clerks" and all white traders and storekeepers were required to obtain permits from the Council.[20] Nor were free blacks or slaves allowed to labor in the nation without a permit.[21] However, the Council tried hard to encourage mechanics "of good character and sobriety and well-skilled in their respective professions" to come to the nation, provided they would agree to stay for four or five years and "take under their care for instruction as many apprentices as practicable."[22] By 1827 the Council was regulating mission schools and preparing to start public schools.

The Cherokees were eager to train their own mechanics. Charles Hicks reported in 1820 that "the art of making the spinning wheel and loom has been acquired by five or six Cherokees" and some had learned enough coopering so that they were "making water vessles out of wood." "Besides, there are six or seven others who work at the blacksmith's trade . . . repairing the plough, the axe, the gun, and shoeing of horses." There were some even who "make the plough."[23] The number of Cherokee mechanics grew steadily in the 1820s.

Laws governing the control of livestock were common on every frontier. Their purpose was to hold owners responsible if their hogs, goats, sheep, cattle, or horses entered the land of another person and destroyed his crops. These laws also concerned the retrieval of stray animals. Part of the responsibility lay in proper fencing; Cherokee laws prescribed the height and quality of "legal fences" to establish the blame for destruction of crops. One law created "rangers," whose job was to impound stray

[19] Ibid., p. 6.
[20] Ibid., p. 11.
[21] Ibid., pp. 34, 37.
[22] Ibid., pp. 61, 6, 11.
[23] See appendix to Jedidiah Morse, *A Report to the Secretary of War* (New Haven, Conn., 1822), p. 169.

livestock, to advertise them, and to care for them until their owners claimed them and reimbursed the ranger according to fixed fees.[24] The most difficult aspect of this problem was on the edge of the nation, where whites failed to observe the boundary line. "Much injury is sustained," the Council said, "by the inhabitants living on the boundary lines, from citizens of the United States feeding and keeping their stock of property on Cherokee lands whereby horses, cattle, hogs, etc. belonging to the citizens of this nation are exposed to be taken off by such person or persons trespassing." To prevent this, a law required the judges of each district to "appoint an assistant ranger . . . whose duty it shall be solely to pay strict attention to such trespassers . . . and to forwarn the frontier inhabitants of the United States" to keep off Cherokee land. The strays of whites that were caught in the nation were to be impounded.[25]

The Cherokee laws regarding land usage were unlike those of white settlements because of the tribal ownership of all land. The law forbade the sale of any Cherokee land or improvements on it (such as houses, barns, or stables) to whites, although Cherokees could sell any improvements to each other.[26] The law said that no Cherokee could take up or settle upon land formerly used by another Cherokee unless it had been abandoned for three years.[27] Another law stated that no Cherokee could take up land for a farm or plantation closer than a quarter-mile to another Cherokee without his permission.[28] Most of the land tenure problems arose from the emigration or enrollment for emigration of Cherokees during the removal crisis of 1817–1819. If an emigrant moved west, he immediately lost all right to his land and improvements. If he later changed his mind, he had to come back and start over somewhere else (unless no one had moved onto his farm).[29] Anyone who wanted to move west after 1821 was not allowed to sell his improvements to another Cherokee to subsidize his removal; the nation did all it could do to discourage emigration. The land of an Arkansas emigrant was declared abandoned after one year.[30]

A major unresolved problem for the Cherokees and for all Indians was whether they had the right to develop their own mineral resources.[31] They were damned if they did (because they were considered only tenants on the white man's land) and damned if they didn't (because white Amer-

---

[24] *Cherokee Laws*, pp. 34–35.

[25] Ibid., p. 54.

[26] Ibid., p. 45.

[27] Ibid., p. 59.

[28] Ibid., pp. 40–41.

[29] Ibid., pp. 9–10.

[30] Ibid., p. 80.

[31] The governor of Georgia said in 1830 they lacked this right (M-221, reel 110, #8773).

icans believed that God required man to exploit His natural bounties).
The federal agents always encouraged the Cherokees to lease their resources to whites but did not object to leases to competent Cherokees (intermarried whites or mixed bloods). Salines and saltpeter caves were the
first resources to be developed in this way. The Cherokees never doubted
their right to use all their resources. They had made turpentine, pitch,
tar, potash, and maple sugar from their trees long before 1794. They had
also become excellent silversmiths and they knew places where gold was
to be found, though they kept these secret. Cherokee laws protected the
rights of those who were given concessions to mine salt, thereby taking
what had previously been a public resource and making it a private,
money-making enterprise. Those given a franchise to mine salt or saltpeter paid a fee to the state. Although they had opposed the effort to allow
Colonel Earle to develop their iron ore resources for his own profit, the
Cherokees were eager to find some way to develop it themselves; they
were disappointed when President Madison declined to assist them in this
project in 1816.

Formerly, the Cherokees, like most woodland Indians, had periodically
burned off the underbrush in their woods to improve the growth of new
forage for deer and to increase the yield of berries for human and animal
(particularly bears) use. But with the advent of elaborate private farms
throughout the nation, this had to be abandoned.[32] In 1825 the Council
forbade anyone to set fires even in the most remote regions "before the
month of March" in order to protect timber that was now more important
than deer or bears.[33] The Council asserted the nation's right to its ferrous
minerals in 1825 stating that "all gold, silver, lead, copper or brass mines
which may be found within the limits of the Cherokee Nation shall be the
property of the Cherokee Nation."[34] The law allowed one-fourth of the
proceeds from any mine to accrue to the person who discovered it.[35] Development of the nation's rich mineral resources was slow because the
Cherokees still lacked the skills and the capital for large-scale manufacturing.

Most of the laws regulating monies were designed to increase the efficient management of the National Treasury, which provided the principal
source of capital for those who lacked the credit to borrow from traders.
Despite their claims to sovereignty, the Cherokees never tried to exercise
the right to coin money. The Treasury did accept promissory notes at 6
percent for debts owed to the nation and allowed these to circulate as cur-

[32] See Goodwin, *Cherokees in Transition*, pp. 63–64.
[33] *Cherokee Laws*, p. 41.
[34] Ibid., p. 50.
[35] Ibid., p. 50.

rency. In 1825 the Council encouraged local enterprise by permitting the Treasurer "to loan out at interest, at six percent per annum, such surplus public monies as may be in the treasury." Surety and bonds were required from those taking such loans and no loan was to exceed $500. The Treasurer evidently made some bad investments in this and after some defaults the Council ordered the process stopped in 1827.

Perhaps the most obvious signs that the Cherokees were developing an entrepreneurial bourgeoisie were the laws passed regarding those who died intestate. The law did not broach the delicate question of whether maternal clan relatives of a widow or divorced woman or the elder brothers of a deceased man had the first claim upon the property of the deceased who died without a will. It simply said that "the nearest relatives of the deceased" had a right to apply to the district court to have an administrator of the estate chosen. How the administrator was to decide between the claims of wives (or ex-wives) and children (of various wives) and the claims of clan relations, the law did not say, though presumably under the inheritance law of 1808 both categories of claimants were to be given a share. In the old days when a Cherokee man died, he might at the most own a gun, a horse or two, and perhaps a slave, which went to his older brothers as his clan protectors; an unmarried or widowed Cherokee woman might own a cabin, several knives, blankets, and kettles, a horse, and perhaps also a slave (and if she had formerly had children by a husband or two, these children were in her care), which at her death went to her older brothers as the protectors of her and her children. But now that some families owned many horses, cattle, and hogs, valuable black slaves, and perhaps an extensive farm or plantation with all the requisite outbuildings and a well-constructed house, "the legal heirs" (as the law termed them) might come from all directions to claim a share of it. In most cases, the well-to-do took pains to make wills and the Council honored these even though most of them followed patrilineal rather than matrilineal practice. As early as 1805, Meigs had noted that the more well-to-do Cherokees like James Vann and Doublehead were concerned that their estates should pass to their children and not to their brothers:

Several have spoken to me on the descent of property. At present the property left by the decease of the head of a family descends to the male who is nearest a kin, which by their custom is the oldest brother of the deceased. He takes all the property and the widow and her Children are left destitute unless she had some property which she brought to the family or acquired by her industry afterwards. Two persons of the half Breeds have requested me to write their wills hoping that might be a means of breaking thro the old custom. . . . They now see the great impropriety of estates going out of the family in this side way manner as it is a

TABLE 7
Cherokee Economic Growth, 1809–1835

	1809	1826	1828	1835
Cherokees	12,395	13,963[a]	14,972	16,542
males	6,116	—	—	—
females	6,279	—	—	—
Whites intermarried	341	211	205	201
males	—	147	144	—
females	—	73	61	—
Black slaves	583	1,277	1,038	1,592
Black cattle	19,165	22,000	22,405	—
Horses	6,519	7,600	7,628	—
Swine	19,778	46,000	38,517	—
Sheep	1,037	2,500	2,912	—
Looms	429	762	769	—
Spinning wheels	1,572	2,488	2,428	—
Wagons	30	172	130	—
Plows	567	2,943	2,792	—
Grist Mills	13	31	20	—
Sawmills	3	10	14	—
Powder Mills	1	—	6	—
Ferries	—	18	10	—
Silversmiths	49	—	55	—
Blacksmiths	—	62	—	—
Cotton Gins	—	8	—	—
Salt Petre works	2	—	9	—
Schools	5	18	19	—
Pupils	94	—	292	—

SOURCES: Return J. Meigs, Census, Moravian Archives (Winston-Salem, N.C.); Elias Boudinot, *An Address Delivered to the Whites* (Philadelphia, 1826); *The Cherokee Phoenix*, June 18, 1828.

[a] Plus 3,500–4,000 living in the west.

great discouragement to industry as well as cruel to the Children of the deceased.[36]

This practice grew steadily among the more well-to-do. The growth of private property (see table 7) on private farms and the concomitant development of the nuclear family as the basic kinship loyalty clearly placed a strain on traditional patterns. Tensions within the developing legal system slowly generated fears and resentments among conservative Cherokee.

The most basic right and necessity of a nation-state is its right to levy taxes for the support of its institutions. The Cherokees had been given the

[36] Return J. Meigs to Henry Dearborn, August 4, 1805, M-208.

right to local self-government by their treaties and they assumed the right to tax their inhabitants. The administration of their system was growing more expensive and their annuities were not always sufficient to meet their annual expenses. In 1819 the Council laid a tax of $25 per year upon "all citizens of the Cherokee Nation establishing a store or stores for the purpose of vending merchandize" and a tax of $80 per year on all noncitizens "permitted to vend merchandise in the Nation" either as itinerant or fixed traders.[37] This law had three purposes: to raise revenue, to equalize the position of Cherokee traders in competition with whites, and to regulate the number of white traders in the nation. Enforcement of this law created considerable trouble with the federal government. Some of the white traders protested against it, declined to pay their tax, and had their goods seized and sold by Cherokee sheriffs to force payment. In addition, a year later, the Council required "each head of family" to pay "a poll tax of fifty cents and each single man under the age of sixty years also shall pay fifty cents" per year to the government. Most Cherokees, especially in the outlying districts, refused or failed to pay, and this tax was suspended in 1825.[38]

With the power to tax came the power to regulate internal trade, a bone of considerable contention among the thirteen British colonies of North America after 1763. The same law that laid a tax upon Cherokee and white traders in the Cherokee Nation also prohibited the import or sale of alcoholic beverages by non-Cherokee citizens, and those who did import or sell it risked a $100 fine; "neverthless," the law continued, "nothing shall be so construed in this decree to tax any person or persons bringing sugar, coffee, salt, iron and steel into the Cherokee Nation for sale; but no permanent establishment for the disposal of such articles can be admitted to any persons not citizens of the Nation." The federal agent granted licenses to alien white traders (another bone of contention); the Cherokee Council (through its clerk) issued licenses to traders who were Cherokee citizens. These tax laws of 1819–1820 were approved by Meigs and Calhoun before they were printed and published, but many frontier whites did not like to see the Cherokee Nation exercise the sovereign power to tax. Meigs said of the new laws, "I think you have made some good regulations."[39] Calhoun wrote in April 1820: "The Cherokee Nation has a right to adopt any rules and regulations it pleases for its own policy not inconsistent with existing treaties and the laws regulating intercourse with the Indian tribes." Few saw at the time where all this was leading with respect to Cherokee claims of national sovereignty.

[37] *Cherokee Laws*, p. 6.
[38] Ibid., p. 48.
[39] Return J. Meigs to Charles Hicks, January 20, 1823, M-208.

Taxation and income from public loans and franchises granted by the nation were never a major source of income for the Cherokee National Treasury. The principal source of income (outside land sales) always remained the annuity. Of course, had the Cherokees ever succeeded in persuading the government to pay the claims of $581,000 sustained by damages from the inadequate evaluation of Cherokee improvements on land ceded in 1817 and 1819 (as well as from the misdeeds of McMinn in leasing Cherokee property in 1818–1819 and from the failure of the reserve system), it would have had much less difficulty in paying expenses and stimulating economic growth. The federal government denied the validity of the figure and the negotiations over the claims dragged on year after year with no resolution. The major part of the Cherokee revenue came from $4,000 granted "in perpetuity" by the federal government for land ceded between 1791 and 1806 and various lump sums for land ceded in 1816–1819 that were divided into annual increments ranging in total from $10,000 to $11,000. The federal government's payments were frequently slipshod. This was revealed in the long delay over the payment of $4,000 for Wafford's Tract agreed upon in 1804. Somehow the government failed to have this treaty ratified by the Senate, though white settlers immediately took over all the land. In 1811 when, at the request of the Council, Meigs asked when this money would be forthcoming, he received no reply. The Cherokees brought the matter up again in 1824, but after a diligent search through its files the War Department said it had no record of such a treaty.[40] The Cherokee Council then went into its files and produced a certified copy. After hemming and hawing over the validity of the copy, the government finally conceded that it was genuine and proceeded to present the treaty for ratification. When the Cherokees requested that they receive interest that had accrued on the sum for the intervening years, the government refused. The Cherokees received their $4,000 in a lump sum in 1825. The annual income from annuities in the 1820s, including the $1,280 that Meigs had negotiated in place of the government's annuity festival, came to between $14,000 and $16,000 per year. Because the Cherokees used it wisely and honestly, it provided the basis for their new system of government and their remarkable economic development from 1819 to 1829.

Although there had been a National Treasury ever since annuities began in 1791, the income had at first been distributed by the agent to the town chiefs in the form of trade goods. Meigs usually tried to keep several thousand dollars of it at the agency during the year to cover contingencies (usually claims by whites for theft or destruction of property). Every year

[40] Royce, *Cherokee Nation of Indians*, pp. 58-60.

before the annuity was paid, he tallied up all claims against it by whites, by the factory, and by the government (for special gifts) and deducted that from the total before he distributed what was left. Not until 1817 did the National Committee successfully take control of the annuity away from the agent, though on several occasions it had requested that the annuity be paid in cash rather than in trade goods. The Committee's clerk did not keep records of these funds prior to 1817. Charles Hicks seems to have done so, however, as unofficial treasurer,[41] and his home in Fortville, Tennessee, became the site of the National Treasury after 1817. He reminded Meigs's successor, Joseph McMinn, in 1823 that "a National Treasury was established at this place" by the Council.[42] After 1823, Hicks sometimes referred to himself as "treasurer of the Nation" as well as Second Principal Chief. Though Hicks was careful and honest, he does not seem to have been able to balance the nation's budget. No records of the national income and expenditures have survived.

Nor is there any adequate way to measure the gross national income of the nation in these years. The closest we can come to measuring economic growth is through statistical tables compiled in 1809 by Meigs, in 1825 by act of the Council, and in 1835 by commissioners of the United States. Only in the last census were figures taken concerning the estimated values of farm produce, and there were important omissions from these (particularly with regard to such important products as cotton production, truck gardening, poultry, orchards, manufactured goods, and silversmithing). Nevertheless these statistical tables deserve to be cited as at least a minimal statement of Cherokee develoment until a means is found to extrapolate more complete estimates of family or farm income and the wealth generated from trade, timber, minerals, water power, and other resources (see table 8).[43]

Beyond these bare statistics there are many eyewitness accounts by persons who lived in or traveled through the Cherokee Nation in the 1820s, when it became a showpiece for foreign and domestic visitors who wanted to discover how the Indians were faring under the benevolent policies of the new republic and the missionary societies. One of the more interesting of these comments was written by a Moravian missionary, Abraham Steiner, who had visited the nation in 1801 and then returned in 1820: "I cannot express the astonishment and delight I felt," he wrote to the Secretary of War after his return visit, "in observing the progress of civilization in that country. . . . The well-cultivated plantations here

[41] Meigs addressed a letter to Hicks on June 20, 1820, to "the Treasurer of the Nation," June 20, 1820, M-208.

[42] Charles Hicks to Joseph McMinn, May 17, 1823, M-208.

[43] McLoughlin and Conser, "Cherokees in Transition."

TABLE 8
Cherokee Agricultural Production, 1835

A. Acreage and Farms by State

State	Total Tillable Acreage	Acres in Cultivation	Number of Farms	Average Number of Acres in Cultivation per Farm
Tennessee	251,005	10,692	412	25.92
Alabama	292,480	7,256	259	28.01
North Carolina	35,000	6,906	714	9.67
Georgia	614,400	19,216	1,735	11.07
Total	1,192,480	44,070	3,120	14.12
[True total: 1,192,885]				

B. Grain Production and Land Value by State

State	Total Bushels of Wheat Grown	Average Bushels per Farm	Total Bushels of Corn Grown	Average Bushels per Farm	Estimated Worth of Tillable Land
Tennessee	976	2.37	129,179	313.54	(at $2 per acre) $443,290
Alabama	240	.92	88,776	342.76	(at $2 per acre) $594,640
North Carolina	65	.09	78.392	109.79	(at $5 per acre) $175,000
Georgia	1,221	.70	267,664	154.26	(at $2 per acre) $1,228,800
Total	2,502	.80	563,991	180.76	$2,441,730

SOURCE: Federal Census of 1835, Bureau of Indian Affairs.

and there do credit to their industry, judgment and arrangements. . . . All seem intent to have among them more and more of the benefits of civilization. . . . The English language is also beginning to prevail and will soon predominate. . . . The Cherokees are the most advanced in civilization of any of the Indian tribes without exception. . . . The United States are now in a fair way of successful experiment that Indians can be civilized.[44] By 1822 Steiner had no doubt that the Cherokees were now ready to "become worthy citizens . . . and useful members of the Union,"[45] and he was surprised and dismayed that there was still talk of forcing them to remove to Arkansas.

John Ridge, writing in 1826, explained to Gallatin that there were no longer any Cherokees who tried to make a living by hunting; those Cher-

[44] Abraham Steiner to John Calhoun, April 26, 1820, M-221, reel 87, #4606.
[45] Abraham Steiner to John Calhoun, January 25, 1822, M-221, reel 94, #9527.

okees had gone west. In the east the Cherokees "prefer to clear the forest and govern their own individual plantations . . . they are farmers and herdsmen." He admitted that there were great variations "in value of property possessed by individuals" and "increasingly so," but "this only answers a good purpose, as a stimulus to those in the rear to equal their neighbors." For all Cherokees, "their principal dependence for subsistence is on the Production of their own farms. Indian corn is a staple production. . . . Wheat, rye and oats grow very well. . . . Cotton is generally raised for domestic consumption and we have grown it for market and have realized very good profits." Men work behind the plow and women "sew, . . . weave, . . . spin, . . . cook."

The African slaves are generally mostly held by Half breeds and full Indians of distinguished talents. In this class the principal value of property is retained and their farms are conducted in the same style as the southern white farms of equal ability in point of property. Their houses are usually of hewed logs, with brick chimnies, and shingled roofs; there are also a few excellent brick and frame houses. Their furniture is better than the exterior appearance of their houses would incline a stranger to suppose; they have their regular meals as the whites [with] servants to attend them in their repasts, and the tables are usually covered with a clean cloth and furnished with the usual plates, knives and forks, etc. Every family more or less possess hogs, cattle and horses, and a number pay attention to the introduction of sheep. . . . Domestic manufactures are still confined to women. . . . These consist of white or striped homespun, coarse woolen blankets and in many instances very valuable and comfortable twilled and figured coverlets. Woolen and cotton stockings are mostly manufactured for domestic use within the Nation. . . . calicoes, silks, cambrics, etc. . . . are introduced by Native merchants who generally trade in Augusta. . . . Cherokees on the Tennessee river have already commenced to trade in cotton and grow the article in large plantations and they have realized a very handsome profit. All those who have it in their power are making preparations to grow it for market and it will soon be the staple commodity for the Nation.[46]

He noted that schools were flourishing and "A National Academy of a high order is to be soon established. . . . The edifice will be of Brick and will be supported by the Nation. It is also in contemplation to establish . . . a printing press and a paper. . . . at our last session $1500 was appropriated to purchase the press. . . . We also have a Society organized called 'The Moral and Literary Society of the Cherokee Nation.' A library is attached to this Institution." That same year, David Brown, another young Cherokee educated by missionaries wrote a similar description of the nation's progress that was included by the Secretary of War in his report to Congress:

[46] John Ridge to Albert Gallatin, February 27, 1826, Payne Papers, VIII:103–115.

In the plains and valleys the soil is generally rich, producing Indian corn, cotton, tobacco, wheat, oats, indigo, and sweet and Irish potatoes. The natives carry on considerable trade with the adjoining States and some of them export cotton in boats down the Tennessee to the Mississippi and down that river to New Orleans. Apple and peach orchards are quite common, and gardens are cultivated . . . butter and cheese are on Cherokee tables. There are many public roads in the nation and houses of entertainment kept by natives. Numerous and flourishing villages are seen in every section of the country. Cotton and woolen cloths manufactured here [by hand]; blankets of various dimensions, manufactured by Cherokee hands, are very common; almost every family in the nation grows cotton for its own consumption. Industry and commercial enterprise are extending themselves in every part.[47]

Such statements by the rising generation of Cherokees were of course designed to impress sympathetic whites and tended to overemphasize the situation in the middle region of the nation (from Augusta to Knoxville) and to neglect the poor areas along the Creek border and in the North Carolina mountains. Nevertheless, their importance as descriptions lies essentially in their tone of optimism, self-confidence, and hope. The nation had passed through its time of trial, its wandering in the wilderness, and had now entered into the Canaan of contentment.

On the other hand, many Cherokees were not ambitious for wealth and did not seek out the best land. Although most full bloods mastered the art of plowing, they did not really understand how to get the best yield from the land. The New England missionaries believed that the government had failed to provide the Cherokees with adequate knowledge of the scientific aspects of farming. The gap between the few rich and the many poor that Ridge noted marked not only a difference in knowledge or industry but also a fundamental clash in social ethic. Something like a landed, entrepreneurial class and a poor, peasant class had evolved by 1825, and they did not always get along. It was not unlike the friction between the rising cotton capitalists and the poor white dirt farmers in the surrounding southern states.

[47] ASP II, 651–52.

FIFTEEN

TESTING THE LIMITS OF SOVEREIGNTY,
1819–1826

*Their declaration not to meet with the [treaty] Commissioners is little
short of a declaration of independence, which they never lose sight
of.* —Return J. Meigs to the Secretary of War. 1822

If the Cherokees thought that the treaty of 1819 had guaranteed that
they could remain permanently on what was left of their original soil,
they were soon disappointed. Neither acculturation, prosperity, political
unity, nor their obvious determination to sell no more of their land was
sufficient to keep the federal and state governments from trying to obtain
further cessions. At the request of the people of Georgia, Congress appropriated $30,000 in June 1822 to negotiate for the extinction of the
Cherokee title to 7,200 square miles of land within the boundaries of that
state. As soon as the Cherokee National Council learned of this, it "requested the [district] Judges to ascertain the sentiments and disposition of
the citizens [of the Cherokee nation] of their respective Districts on the
subject." The judges reported to the Council in October that "unanimously, with one voice and determination" their districts had decided "to
hold no treaties with any Commissioners of the United States to make
any cessions of land, being resolved not to dispose of even one foot of
ground."[1] No tabulation of votes or other evidence was recorded of this
sentiment and, given the feelings of many Cherokees in Creek Path and
other Lower Towns, the claim of unanimity was somewhat exaggerated.

Nevertheless, the Council sent word to the Secretary of War that it was
not willing to meet with any treaty commissioners on this subject. Their
letter was signed by the members of the National Committee: John Ross,
George Lowrey, Richard Taylor, Thomas Foreman, John Beamer,
Thomas Pettit, John Downing, John Baldrige, Cabbin Smith, Sleeping
Rabbit, Kelachulee, Currahee Dick, Roman Nose, and Comanahee. It was
also signed by the following members of the Council: Pathkiller, Charles
Hicks, Ollayeh, Big Rattling Gourd, Ahneyaly, Samuel Gunter, Terrapin

[1] *Cherokee Laws*, pp. 23–24.

Head, Rising Fawn, William Hicks, Tunnittehee, Walking Stick, Old Turkey, The Feather, Going Snake, Tusquieh, Oowanekee, Chunayahee, Slim Fellow, Gone Up To, Major Ridge, and Alex McCoy. These were now the leaders of the nation and they spoke with a new sense of nationalistic self-confidence. The skill with which they handled treaty negotiations with the federal government from 1822 to 1828 provides the best evidence of the nation's political maturity.

Meigs was shocked. He told Calhoun: "Their declaration not to meet with the Commissioners is little short of a declaration of independence which they never lose sight of." In his opinion "such a declaration" was "disrespectful to the United States Commissioners and to the Government." He blamed a few artful Cherokees for the impasse. "Their government is an aristocracy consisting of about 100 men called Chiefs and those Chiefs are controlled by perhaps twenty speculating individuals." Forgetting how often in the past he had praised such chiefs for promoting civilization and the good order of their people, he now concluded that "the conduct of these individuals is to perpetuate barbarism by encouraging indolence." If they persisted in their intransigence, "the citizens of Tennessee, Georgia and Alabama would probably hardly be restrained long from taking possession of their respective claims" to Cherokee soil. And Meigs implied that he thought these citizens would be fully justified in doing so.[2]

Thus began six more years of wrangling between the Cherokees and the government. Throughout this period, however, the Cherokees held firm; one set of commissioners after another went away empty-handed, frustrated, and angry. Several aspects of the negotiations in 1823–1824 revealed how adept the Cherokees had become in dealing with white officials. When the treaty commissioners, Duncan Campbell and James Meriwether, arrived in the nation on January 15, 1823, despite the Council's assertion that it did not want to negotiate, they found no chiefs or warriors at the agency, the place they had appointed for the meeting. After waiting a week, the commissioners had to return without even presenting their arguments, much less using the bribes they had brought or the rations for the subsistence of the hundreds of chiefs and warriors whom they had expected to attend. The Council said it was sorry for the inconvenience, but it had tried to save the commissioners the trouble of making the trip. The Council also "protested against being told when and where they should meet" the commissioners: "We know of no instance of Ministers or commissioners to a foreign court persisting in selecting a

[2] Return J. Meigs to John Calhoun, November 22, 1822, M-208. For a general discussion of these treaty negotiations see Annie H. Abel, "The Cherokee Negotiations of 1822-1823," *Smith College Studies in History* 1 (July 1916).

spot remote from the Seat of Government to which their embassy were directed for negotiation and of taking it entirely upon themselves to fix the time for a convention." When the Secretary of War complained of the grossly impolite behavior of the Cherokees, the Council said that in its opinion "the 'failure, exposure, expense, and trouble' which you complain of . . . may be attributed . . . to the very little confidence and respect you had for the proceedings of our Council."[3] Thereafter, to show that they must be taken seriously and with respect, the Council said treaty commissioners would be welcome only at the national capital of the nation, New Echota, at a time mutually agreed upon in advance.

Nevertheless, the commissioners tried to schedule a meeting for negotiations in the Cherokee town of Taloney, in the Georgia part of the nation, on August 9, 1823.[4] When the Council reiterated its stand that it would meet nowhere but New Echota, Campbell and Meriwether were forced to yield. They appeared at the Cherokee capital on October 4 and brought with them Johnson Wellborn and James Blair, commissioned by the State of Georgia to negotiate its claims against the Cherokee Nation. Wellborn and Blair informed the Council that the Cherokees owed Georgia over $100,000 for spoliations that had occurred between 1775 and 1794. Georgia, having recently browbeaten the Creek Nation (with the help of the duplicitous Creek chief, William McIntosh) into ceding five million acres to pay for $200,000 worth of similar Revolutionary claims, thought it could do the same with the Cherokees.[5] Among other things the Georgians demanded "the immediate restoration of all negroes and their increase which had run away or been taken from the citizens of Georgia at any time previous to the 20th day of June, 1794" and, "in money, a reasonable hire for all such Negroes" for the years since 1794.[6] The Cherokee leaders considered this ridiculous and illegal. They pointed out that under Article 9 of the Treaty of Tellico in 1798, the United States had agreed that "all animosities, thefts, plundering, prior to that day, shall cease and be no longer remembered or demanded on either side." Georgia's claims were therefore no longer valid and the Council refused to consider them. Wellborn and Blair left empty-handed.

When the Secretary of War had first mentioned these negotiations in October 1822, Meigs had written to suggest that the commissioners

[3] The Chiefs in Council to Duncan Campbell and James Meriwether, April 25, 1823, M-208.

[4] For the commissioner's account of the failure of the negotiations of January 1822, see Duncan Campbell and James Meriwether, reports to John Calhoun, January 18, 1823, M-208 and January 22, 1823, M-221, reel 95, #0219; and the commissioners' journal, February 21, 1823, M-221, reel 95, #0237 and #0427.

[5] See Angie Debo, *The Road to Disappearance*, p. 86.

[6] The Georgia Commissioners to the Cherokee Cuncil, October 27, 1823, M-208.

should be prepared by bringing "tangible" funds with them, up to $20,000 with which to bribe susceptible chiefs.[7] Campbell and Meriwether did this, but instead of passing this money out themselves, they arranged for Chief William McIntosh of the Creeks to come to the negotiations and do so. McIntosh had a Cherokee wife and as a Cherokee countryman of some status, he was welcome to attend. Secretly he offered thousands of dollars each to Charles Hicks, John Ross, and Alex McCoy on October 24, 1823. They in turn asked him to put his offer in writing. When he did so, they took his letter to the Council and read it out loud in his presence. Thoroughly embarrassed by this exposure, McIntosh beat a hasty retreat to his own nation.[8] (Two years later McIntosh was executed by his people for betraying them.) Campbell and Meriwether claimed to have no knowledge of McIntosh's actions, but his exposure severely undermined their position.

The negotiations proceeded nonetheless. The commissioners offered the Cherokees the perennial choice of an exchange of lands in the west or fee-simple reserves and citizenship in the east. The Council reminded them that it had already twice declined the first alternative (in 1809 and 1819) and that it considered the second one specious: "What has been the course pursued by the States of Tennessee and Georgia and some of their citizens" toward the 311 Cherokee families who were granted reserves in 1817 and 1819, they asked. "We find opposition, fraud, and every species of injustice were raised against the interests" of those who had honestly accepted the offer of citizenship in those states. Most of them, the Council noted, had suffered "an entire ruin and loss of properties" before the federal government provided lawyers for a few of them and then decided to buy them all out.

When the commissioners, angry and frustrated, said that the land the Cherokees occupied belonged to the United States by "discovery" and "by conquest," the Council answered calmly: "Our title has emanated from a Supreme source which cannot be impaired by conquest or by treaty" and if the United States had title to it, "why should [it] purchase, time after time, by treaties, lands to which you would wish to convince us we have no title?" Did the treaty commissoners' threat of withdrawing protection for Cherokee boundaries mean that the government "will trample justice under foot?"[9]

[7] Return J. Meigs to General John Floyd, October 24, 1822, M-208; Return J. Meigs to John Calhoun, November 22, 28, 1822, M-208.

[8] For William McIntosh's effort to bribe the Cherokee chiefs on behalf of the commissioners see Duncan Campbell to John Calhoun, October 27, 1823, M-208, and Brainerd Journal, November 11, 1823, ABCFM.

[9] ASP II, 464, 472–73 and Abel, "Cherokee Negotiations."

The commissioners had no answer and the negotiations ended with no concessions by the Council. Campbell and Meriwether admitted to the Secretary of War that they had been bested: "The Cherokees are far in advance of any other tribe in civilization," they told Calhoun, and their hostility to any further cession of their land "may be ascribed in a great degree to the fondness with which they cherish the feeling of National pride and to a determination to perpetuate their National Character." People with such pride could not be easily browbeaten. Furthermore, the commissoners correctly observed, "they have a great abhorrence to the idea of being merged [incorporated as citizens] in the general government [or state governmnts] and having foreign laws extended over them." What the commissioners did not note was that the Cherokees had indicated that the policy of integration was doomed by the inveterate racist hatred and contempt that the frontier whites felt toward Indians no matter how civilized or Christianized they might become. The commissioners also noted that the Cherokees were determined to preserve their autonomy: "They plume themselves upon the fact of having organized a government of their own and consider a further sale of land as endangering its perpetuity." The commissioners had to admit: "There is too much truth in their arguments to be easily combatted, and so long as they are recognized as having equal share in the contractual arrangements [i.e., the right to say no], negotiations will be difficult."[10]

Having stood off the federal negotiators seeking their land and their removal, the Cherokees countered by sending their own negotiators to Washington in 1824 to demand attention to some of their claims against the government. They did not ask permission of the agent to go, as they had in years past when the War Department had paid their expenses. Now they paid their own way and made their own appointment with the Secretary of War. Agent McMinn, who had succeeded Meigs in March 1823, told Calhoun: "They are entitled at least to the merit of consistency," but he thought they needed to be taught "better manners."[11]

The members of the deputation that went to Washington in January 1824 were John Ross, Major Ridge, Elijah Hicks (son of Charles Hicks), and George Lowrey. They had a number of issues they wanted settled. They wanted to know why the government had not yet paid them for Wafford's Tract, which they had ceded in 1804; why it had not remunerated those Cherokees forced to move from the land ceded in 1817 and 1819; why it had not removed the hundreds of intruders on their land; and why it had refused to accept the fact that "the Cherokee Nation have

[10] Duncan Campbell to John Calhoun, February 28, 1823, M-221, reel 95, #0237.
[11] ASP II, 473–74.

306

now come to a decisive and unalterable conclusion not to cede away any more land."[12] The Cherokees also had an interesting proposal to make in order to solve the thorny problem arising from Jefferson's compact with Georgia in 1802. The Cherokees had always considered this pact an injustice to them. Jefferson, they believed, had no right to promise to extinguish their title to all land in Georgia when Congress had already solemnly guaranteed their land to them in the treaties of 1791 and 1798. They told the Secretary that this matter should be reopened by Congress and proposed a solution: "Why not extend the limits of Georgia" into the "extensive territory in the Floridas" that bordered on Georgia and now belonged to the United States. Florida was still a territory under Congressional jurisdiction and it had little white population. The Seminoles had been defeated there and were in the process of being removed to the west. Florida's land was more suitable for cultivation than the red clay areas and rocky mountains of northern Georgia where the Cherokees lived. This proposal struck the Cherokees as a logical and constitutionally sound way around a dilemma difficult for them and for the federal government. Calhoun, however, refused even to consider it. Who were the Cherokees to tell the United States how to solve its problems? "You must be sensible," he said coolly, "that it will be impossible for you to remain for any length of time in your present situation as a distinct society or nation within the limits of Georgia or any other States. Such a community is incompatible with our system."[13] The Cherokees replied that they were located on their land before the Constitution was written or any Englishmen had settled in Georgia. "The Cherokees are not foreigners but original inhabitants of America." The American states were the intruders; the Cherokees "cannot recognize the sovereignty of any State within the limits of their territory." Meriwether and Campbell had told them in October 1823 that when the President "qualifies you as citizens you must become so," but they believed they had the right to apply for citizenship when they were ready and meanwhile to "remain as a separate community" as long as they chose. The Cherokees, seeing the Creeks, Choctaws, Chickasaws, and Seminoles being deprived of their rights and sent west (along with many other tribes from north of the Ohio River), were determined not to follow that path. The Cherokee applied the myth of the Garden of

[12] John Ross and Cherokee delegation to James Monroe, January 19, 1824, M-221, reel 98, #2432; also see John Ross to John Calhoun, February 11, 1824, M-234, reel 71, #005–0013; and ASP II, 473–74. See also Moulton, *John Ross*, pp. 26–28.

[13] ASP II, 473. Calhoun cites the clause in the Constitution forbidding Congress to create any new states from the boundaries or within the boundaries of already existing states without the permission of that state.

Eden to the Cherokee situation in their address to Calhoun on February 11, 1824, to explain why they were no longer interested in integration:

The happiness which the Indians once enjoyed . . . in their primitive situation . . . was now poisoned by bad fruits of the civilized tree which was planted around them . . . overshadowed by the expanded branches of this tree [many tribes] dropped, withered and are no more. . . . [Victims of the] ambition, pride and avariciousness of the civilized man . . . the untutored sons of nature became a prey. Defrauded of their lands; treated as inferior beings. . . . They became associated with the lowest grade of society . . . [and] considering themselves degraded [lost incentive, and became drunkards and criminals], and such must be the fate of those tribes now in existence should they be merged into the white population before they became civilized.[14]

As for the plan of ultimate incorporation into the United States, the delegation, playing the white man's tune of "someday," answered: "Whenever the whole nation shall have been completely and fully civilized," they would give serious consideration to the notion of incorporation or integration as citizens. Meanwhile their only hope for survival was through a separate national existence under their own laws and leaders.

The conduct of these Cherokee nationalists in the treaty negotiations from 1822 to 1828 struck white officials as arrogant and improper. But this was only one aspect of their search for self-respect and their efforts to define the outermost limits of their sovereignty under the treaty rights. Cherokee sovereignty was tested to the limit in four other areas in the early 1820s. In each of these confrontations the Cherokees demonstrated remarkable skill. They defined their positions carefully; they provided specific historic precedents and legal documentation for them; they persisted in their efforts to obtain clear and definitive answers; and they offered patient and astute responses to the indignant reactions by white officials. One of these issues was their right to police their own borders when the government army garrisons were not willing or able to do so. Another was their disclosure of the government's failures to carry out its obligation to establish a Cherokee school fund under the treaty of 1819. A third was their protest against the government's effort to cheat them of part of their annuity by paying it in depreciated paper money. And, finally, they displayed remarkable tenacity in carrying to the Attorney General and then to Congress their claim that they had the right to lay internal taxes on white traders (or anyone else) within their borders.

Of all the daily problems in Indian affairs, the most difficult was always that of preventing white intrusions across treaty lines. By the Treaty of Philadelphia in 1791, the government had agreed that "if any citizens of

14 ASP II, 474.

the United States, or other person not being an Indian, shall settle on any of the Cherokees' lands, such person shall forfeit the protection of the United States and the Cherokees may punish him or not as they please."[15] However, the danger faced by an Indian force that tried to remove a frontier family from its land was so great that in practice this was always done by soldiers of the United States Army. In later treaties the United States accepted this responsibility. The treaty of 1819, for example, said that "all white people who have intruded or may hereafter intrude on the lands reserved for the Cherokees shall be removed by the United States."[16] The departure of the regular army garrison at Hiwassee after 1819 made it difficult to police the Cherokee borders on a regular basis. The question arose whether the Cherokee Lighthorse might take on the task. If they did, the Cherokees expected them to be paid at the same rate as the United States Army's soldiers whose work they were taking over.

Meigs had told the War Department in 1819 that he could not possibly eject each intruder at the moment he settled. He waited until large numbers of them had moved into an area before he went to the trouble of getting out the troops who sometimes had to travel 150 miles each way to eject them. In September 1819, Meigs reported that there were 1,500 intruders in the nation, doing a tremendous "amount of damage" and constantly harassing the Cherokees.[17] The Cherokees were not entirely innocent and sometimes stole horses from the intruders or otherwise tried to make life unpleasant for them. Nevertheless, as Meigs wrote in this letter, the intruders "always outdo the indians in the amount of damage" inflicted. At this time all the troops in the southeastern part of the United States had been sent to Florida to fight the Seminoles and General Jackson would not allow any of them to be relieved for this police work.[18] Calhoun wrote to Jackson about this, and he suggested that perhaps it was time to let the Cherokee Lighthorse take over this task. Calhoun told Meigs in April 1820 that he approved of Jackson's proposal for "the employment of the Indian Light Horse company, as he suggested, instead of a detachment of the United States troops for the purpose of removing refractory intruders." Calhoun thought this would "operate advantageously by preventing the return of the intruders (as they will know that this [Cherokee] force is always at hand to execute your order . . .)." He also favored the plan because it would be "saving the government the inconvenience

[15] The texts of Cherokee treaties can be found in Richard Peters, *The Case of the Cherokee Nation against the State of Georgia* (Philadelphia, 1831), p. 252.

[16] Ibid., p. 271.

[17] Return J. Meigs to John Calhoun, September 19, 1819, M-271, reel 2, #1373.

[18] Return J. Meigs to John Calhoun, May 17, 1822, M-208.

and expense of marching troops.''[19] President Monroe approved the plan wth the provision that the Cherokees must consult the agent before sending the Lighthorse on such missions, and they were to be accompanied by some "whiteman for their protection.''[20] This last provision was not carried out.

Accepting the task, the Cherokee Council in June 1820 commissioned John Ross, Elijah HIcks, and Daniel Griffin to lead picked members of the Lighthorse on a tour of the six-hundred-mile Cherokee frontier.[21] They were first to warn the intruders in each state to leave and then, if they refused, to put them off with their livestock and their slaves at gunpoint. It was not an easy task. Meigs reported that the intruders were armed and dangerous and not apt to take orders from Indians. McKenney later described the activity:

Col. Meigs ordered the [light]horsemen to simply warn the settlers to leave. Ross protested against a powerless attempt of the kind, and they were reluctantly granted authority to remove those who refused to go. The first settlement to be purged of intruders was near the agency [in Eastern Tennessee] and these, at the approach of Ross with his troopers, fled. . . . At Crow Island, they found a hundred armed men who, upon being approached by messengers with peaceful propositions, yielded to the claims of Government and disbanded.[22]

By acting judiciously, Ross cleared all the intruders from the Tennessee and Alabama borders of the nation, but expecting more violent resistance in Georgia, he wrote to Meigs that he thought it unwise to take the Cherokee Lighthorse into that area. Meigs finally persuaded Jackson to send white troops to clear out the Georgia intruders.[23] Hicks later told Meigs that Ross had "encountered some risk from the uncivilized intruders on our borders," but that he did his job well. The United States Army temporarily cleared the Georgia frontier, but no one removed the numerous intruders in North Carolina at Standing Peach Tree and Valley Towns.[24] The mountainous areas of North Carolina were always the most neglected area of the nation both by the agents and by the Cherokee leaders.

Afterwards Meigs asked Calhoun that the Lighthorse be paid for their services at the same rate as regular militia. They deserved this, he said, not only because of the risk they took but because they had to leave their own farms and other work to attend to this duty.[25] Calhoun, who had expected to save money on the plan, expressed considerable surprise that

[19] John Calhoun to Return J. Meigs, April 20, 1820, M-15, reel 4, p. 403.
[20] John Calhoun to Return J. Meigs, October 14, 1820, M-208.
[21] Charles Hicks to Return J. Meigs, June 10, 1820, M-208.
[22] McKenny and Hall, *Biographical Sketches* (1967), p. 443.
[23] Captain R. C. Call to Return J. Meigs, June 28, 1820, M-208.
[24] Charles Hicks to Return J. Meigs, September 12, 1820, M-208.
[25] Return J. Meigs to John Calhoun, October 20, 1820, M-208.

the Cherokees wanted to be paid. "When the Department authorized the employment of the Indian Lighthorse for the removal of intruders, it was done under an impression that the service, being exclusively for their own benefit, no pay would be expected for it from the Government." Far from conceding that the Cherokees had in fact taken over the work that the government should have done, Calhoun argued that "the Department considered in directing the employment of the Cherokee Light horse that it was conferring upon the nation an essential favor" because it implied that they were no longer "dependent on the Troops of the United States" to protect them. He reluctantly agreed that "under the circumstances . . . of the present case as you have stated them (although it is one in which there is no obligation on the Government to make compensation) it would perhaps be proper to make the individuals composing the detachment a gratuity proportioned to the damage which each may be considered to have sustained by being engaged with it." Meigs would have to provide Calhoun with estimated damages to the crops of each Lighthorse soldier and officer in order to obtain the compensation; that way the government could avoid admitting that it had actually paid the Indians a salary for this service. It had only compensated them for specific damages. "It is to be understood," Calhoun concluded, "that this case is not to form a precedent."[26]

Meigs tried to persuade the Cherokees to pay the Lighthorse out of their own Treasury. The Council refused. It declined "to undertake solely on ourselves the protection of our land from its aggression by lawless white men." Not being "a national act" but a service to the United States, this could not be paid out of the nation's funds.[27] Embarrassed, because he had in fact kept muster roles of the Lighthorse and the Cherokees knew it, Meigs wrote to Calhoun that he thought the "gratuity" ought to amount to the same rate as regular militia pay. Calhoun in annoyance offered half pay.[28] Meigs paid it, but the Cherokees refused to accept this as full payment and continued to press for the other half. To strengthen their case, they obtained a letter from Jackson saying they deserved full pay and presented this to Calhoun when they were in Washington in 1824. In his letter Jackson had said that it was his distinct impression "that the Light Horse pay would be regulated by the pay allowed to the United States militia as mounted gunmen for similar services."[29]

While this dispute over paying the lighthorse regulators was still drag-

[26] John Calhoun to Return J. Meigs, November 14, 1820, M-15, reel 5, p. 30.

[27] Charles HIcks to Return J. Meigs, November 27, 1820, M-208.

[28] John Calhoun to Return J. Meigs, August 4, 1821, M-15, reel 6, p. 140.

[29] Cherokee delegation to John Calhoun, May 3, 1824, M-234, reel 71, #0085 (Jackson's letter is included with this).

ging on, the intruders were returning. On March 6, 1822, Meigs again requested troops to remove them.[30] Hicks wrote him that horses and cattle were being stolen from the Cherokees and those robbed had no recourse because in a white court of law the Cherokee owner was "not allowed to prove his property by his oath."[31] "The Chief says," Meigs told Calhoun in May, "that the intruders had added to intrusion the killing [of] their domestic live stocks and in one instance they had turned one of their best men off his plantation and now occupy it themselves."[32] Calhoun still seemed unaware of the fact that state courts would not allow an Indian to testify on his own behalf. He had said earlier: "The Indian upon whom the fraud was committed has his remedy against the citizens who committed it by suit in any of the courts of the state or territory in which he may be found."[33]

Angry over the lawless behavior of the intruders and the reluctance of Meigs to do anything about it, the Council met in May 1822 and said that it was willing to use its Lighthorse once again even though it had not yet fully been paid for its work in 1819. Meigs advised against it "because I think there would be bloodshed." He admitted that under the treaties "you have a right" to take such action, but "it must be at your own expense."[34] Explaining to Calhoun why he had advised against the use of the Lighthorse, he said that the anti-Indian feelings of the intruders, particularly in Georgia, were so intense that they would simply engage in a shoot-out. He also advised that the use of state militia was "not desirable" because its members were likely to be the friends and neighbors of the intruders and share their views. The only answer was the United States Army. "Twenty regular troops having orders and commanded by a Good subaltern officer would be respected by the intruders when two hundred indians would be driven home with loss. Blood would probably be shed on both sides and the attempt would be abortive."[35] Calhoun replied in June that it was too late in the year to take any action against intruders and that it would be better to let them harvest the crops they had planted before trying to remove them.[36]

In April 1823, the Council appealed to Meigs's successor, Joseph McMinn, for help with this problem. "It is a grievous truth that the interest of this Nation has been for a long time trampled upon by the frontier White people with impunity in defiance of existing Treaties and thro'

[30] Return J. Meigs to Charles Hicks, March 6, 1822, M-208.
[31] Charles Hicks to Return J. Meigs, March 1, 1822, M-208.
[32] Return J. Meigs to John Calhoun, May 17, 1822, M-221, reel 96, #0755; see also Charles HIcks to Return J. Meigs, March 1, 1822, M-208.
[33] John Calhoun to Return J. Meigs, April 20, 1820, M-15, reel 4, p. 405.
[34] Return J. Meigs to Charles Hicks, May 13, 1822, M-208.
[35] Return J. Meigs to John Calhoun, May 17, 1822, M-208.
[36] John Calhoun to Return J. Meigs, June 26, 1822, M-208.

disrespect for [due to] the drowsy relaxation and want of energy from sources best known to the Department you occupy." The Council described the intruders as "whites of the lowest cast[e]."[37] Knowing that treaty commissioners were on the way, McMinn decided to call upon the state militia and sent orders to Captains Archibald R. Turk of Tennessee to prepare his troops. He warned Calhoun, however, that this would certainly irritate the politicians of Georgia. "The present appears to be a precarious crisis in the state of affairs between the People of Georgia and the Cherokees in relation to the Pending treaty as well as to other claims against the Cherokees by the State." McMinn's sympathies were with the Georgians: "I labour under the impression that a suspension [of intruder removal] until the latter part of the next fall season would be preferable."[38]

Calhoun thought treaty negotiations would go better if the intruders were removed and ordered Turk to proceed to this task with sixty of the Tennessee militia. He suggested that the Cherokee Lighthorse might accompany Turk, but if so "not to be paid by the United States but volunteers for the benefit of their own nation, in order that they may become accustomed to prevent such intrusions by their own force with little or no aid from the government in the future." In this case he was willing to encourage Cherokee independence; "they *assume* to be an *independent* people, they ought to act up to its Spirit."[39] The Cherokees declined to participate, reminding the government that this was a treaty obligation of the United States.[40]

Captain Turk found his job extremely difficult. With sixty militiamen he started his six-hundred-mile journey in October 1823 and did not complete it until July 1824.[41] The intruders proved stubborn and truculent. Some were prepared to fire on the troops. One of these was James Dickson of Georgia, by all accounts a rough and unruly character. When Dickson aimed his gun, threatening to shoot Lieutenant Benjamin Hambright, one of Turk's officers, Hambright shot first in self-defense. Dickson died three days later. The State of Georgia arrested Hambright for murder and put him on trial before a frontier jury in September 1824. The jury heard the evidence and pronounced Hambright guilty as charged.[42]

Turk was incensed. "The prejudice the state of Georgia has, both

[37] Cherokee Council to Joseph McMinn, April 26, 1823, M-208.
[38] Joseph McMinn to Cherokee Council, April 28, 1823, M-208.
[39] John Calhoun to Joseph McMinn, April 22, 1823, M-15, reel 6, p. 491. Emphasis in original.
[40] Cherokee Council to Joseph McMinn (quoting Calhoun), October 11, 1823, M-208.
[41] Joseph McMinn to John Calhoun, September 24, 1823, M-208; Joseph McMinn to Thomas McKenney, July 23, 1824, M-234, reel 71, #0302.
[42] Captain Archibald Turk to John Calhoun, September 29, 1824, M-234, reel 71, #0425.

against the Cherokees and the United States, about the Cherokee lands," he wrote to Calhoun, "induces me to believe that we cannot by any means have justice done us" in such cases.[43] Later it was discovered that friends of Dickson had threatened government witnesses who were to appear to support Hambright's testimony of self-defense. These friendly witnesses never appeared. Dickson's friends then took the stand and lied about the incident, making Hambright the aggressor. Only when the federal government obtained a new trial in a federal court was he exonerated. The lawyers' fees cost the government $1,500.[44]

The Cherokees' success in forcing the government to acknowledge that policing Indian borders was difficult work that even the army could scarcely manage was not matched in their long effort to discover what had happened to their plan to sell twelve square miles of their best land south of the Tennessee River in order to create a permanent endowment for schools. According to the treaty of 1819, the government agreed to survey the designated land and sell it at the same time it sold the other land in Alabama ceded in that treaty. The proceeds from this school tract were to be placed in a trust fund; successive Presidents were to be its trustees. The income from the fund was to go annually to the Cherokee Nation. When originally considered, the Cherokees planned to use this money for grammar schools, perhaps supplementing the missionary school funds and perhaps locating public schools in areas that the missionaries did not serve. However, as time went by and missionary schools increased, the Council debated whether to use the fund instead for a national academy or secondary school. In October 1825, the Council decided on an academy that would prepare the better mission school students for college.[45]

Six years after the treaty of 1819, the government still had not sent the nation any information about the school fund. The Council asked one of its deputations to Washington to look into the matter and to inform the President that "there are many settlers on those reserved lands who are destroying the timber and tilling the soil free of rent and the number of Cherokee children under tuition [instruction] is curtailed for want of the means anticipated from the sale of the lands."[46] The delegates were to urge the President to "take measure to have the [designated] lands sold as soon as practicable and the proceeds applied as stipulated in the Treaty."

[43] Ibid.

[44] Archibald Turk to John Calhoun, September 29, 1824, M-234, reel 71, #0425. For the trial of Turk's men see Archibald Turk to John Calhoun, January 6, 1825, M-234, reel 71, #0683; Archibald Turk to James G. Williams, January 7, 1825, M-234, reel 71, #0703; James G. Williams to John Calhoun, October 14, 1824, M-234, reel 4, #0452.

[45] *Cherokee Laws*, p. 47.

[46] Instructions of Cherokee Council to its delegation, February 17, 1825, M-234, reel 71, #0488.

John Ross, Charles Hicks, and George Lowrey arrived in Washington on February 17, 1825, and went to see Thomas L. McKenney, the Director of the new Office of Indian Affairs that Calhoun had created within the War Department. McKenney was unable to explain the delay and the Cherokees were fearful that the government had not yet surveyed the tract. McKenney reassured them: "The lands have all been surveyed, etc. leaving therefore nothing to be done but to dispose of them" and transfer the money into the trust fund. Several days later, Ross went to the General Land Office to look up the records. He discovered that McKenney was wrong; the land set aside had not been surveyed. When the delegation informed McKenney of this, he expressed great surprise and said that he would attend to the matter at once.[47] It turned out that the land had inadvertently been sold to white citizens and the money deposited in the United States Treasury. The embarrassed McKenney agreed to find another tract of land of equal quality to make up for the mistake.

Another year went by. In December 1826 the Council again inquired into this matter, expessing its hope "that an arrangement will be made as soon as practicable to bring those lands into the market so that the youths of this nation may enjoy the priviledge and benefit of education from the funds which will arise therefrom."[48] Nothing happened. In October 1828 the Council delegated John Ross and William Hicks to go to Washington to ask why the government had for so long failed to live up to the treaty.[49] Before leaving, they culled over their treaty records and discovered that back in the Treaty of Tellico, in 1805, a similar reservation of land in Tennessee had been "set apart for school purposes" and had never been acted upon by the government.[50] By this time the Cherokees had become very good at checking up on government negligence. The War Department conceded the obligation and asked the agent to look into the matter of the 1805 reserve and to "rent said reservation for the most you can obtain and collect the same and pay over the amount of the Cherokees."[51] But nothing was done about the land set aside in Alabama in 1819 and it became evident to the Cherokees that nothing would ever be done about it. Nor, in fact, did the agent ever find and sell (or rent) the educational reserve in Tennessee designated by the Treaty of Tellico.

Probably the War Department decided to neglect this matter because of the report of the select committee established by Congress in 1822 under

[47] Thomas McKenney to John Ross and Cherokee delegates, March 1, 1825, M-21, reel 1, p. 380.
[48] Charles Hicks and John Ross to Hugh Montgomery, December 11, 1826, M-234, reel 72, #0042.
[49] *Cherokee Phoenix*, October 22, 1828.
[50] Thomas McKenney to Cherokee delegation, April 25, 1829, M-21, reel 5, p. 422.
[51] Ibid.

George Gilmer of Georgia. That committee specifically objected to the clause in the treaty of 1819 establishing a permanent school fund for the Cherokees. The matter was "too objectionable to pass over in silence," the committee said. Such an action "does not accord with the general policy of this Government," which was bound by the Jefferson Compact of 1802 to remove the Indians and not to secure a permanent fund for them. Furthermore, this clause in the treaty infringed "the power of Congress over the public property of the United States"; the treaty-making power of the Executive could not take public land for any other purpose than to sell it to the public.[52] Apparently the War Department decided not to risk a confrontation with Georgia and Alabama over this issue and proceeded to ignore this requirement of the treaty, despite the fact that neither John C. Calhoun nor the United States Senate had seen anything unconstitutional in that clause when the treaty was ratified in 1819.

The effort of the War Department to pay the Cherokee annuities in depreciated paper money from state banks began during the Panic of 1819, which in other ways had worked to the Cherokees' advantage by curtailing funds for their removal. The annuity came to the agent each year in the form of drafts drawn against the United States Treasury by the Secretary of War. It was the agent's job to convert these to specie or bank notes through the receivers of public monies and the banks in the immediate vicinity. In earlier days he could convert the drafts into trade goods, but after 1813 the Cherokees preferred to be paid in cash. When the Cherokees officially created the post of National Treasurer in 1825, it provided him with a salary of $300 a year, made him post a bond for $50,000, and demanded strict accounting for all the money he received and spent.[53] The law also stated that "the annuities arising from treaties with the United States and the revenue arising out of the tax law shall be funded in the National Treasury and be the public property of the Nation." But even before this, Charles Hicks had long been carefully watching over the money due the Cherokee Nation.

In 1819 there was no branch of the Bank of the United States in Tennessee upon which Meigs could draw to convert his drafts into specie. The nearest branch was in New Orleans. Consequently he began that year to accept paper money from the state banks of Tennessee, Alabama, and Georgia. State bank notes varied widely in value, depreciated rapidly, and often were not acceptable outside the state in which the bank was chartered. When Charles Hicks first received this depreciated currency in 1819, he found that he was short in his accounts to the nation because he

[52] ASP II, 260.
[53] *Cherokee Laws*, pp. 45, 58, 59.

could not convert it at face value. He complained to the agent, stating that the banks in Georgia would not accept paper money from banks in Tennessee, and therefore requested in 1820 that the annuity be paid either in gold, silver, or notes of the Bank of the United States.[54] Meigs did not do so. In 1821 Meigs, who was now eighty-one years old, suffered "a stroke of palsy" and temporarily lost his power of speech. The nation had already begun to complain that in recent years Meigs had become very slipshod in financial affairs.[55] To make matters worse, his subagent, James G. Williams, was an alcoholic.[56] Hicks wrote to Meigs in June 1821 saying, "I will again complain to yourself" about "the kind of money you have paid the Nation these two years annuity, which I am confident the Government do not wish the Nation should be paid in bad money." He himself would not have accepted the money in 1820, but John Ross, as President of the National Council, had accepted it for the nation and foolishly signed for payment in full. "I am confident," Hicks continued, that the "government could as easily convey the United States bank bills as the checks [drafts] which I understand is exchanged for Tennessee bills which bills are no more account in Georgia or [other] southern states than blank bills for our annual stipen[d] and the Nation can act as they think proper."[57]

Meigs assigned the duty of converting the drafts into cash in 1821 to Thomas C. Hindman, who had been appointed to assist him during his illness. Hindman, a partner of Lewis Ross and brother-in-law of John Ross, took drafts totaling $18,926 to Huntsville, Alabama, and to New Orleans to have them converted. But according to Meigs he converted these "public funds into depreciated currency" and pocketed a "premium" (or discount) of over $2,800. "The damage sustained by the Government by Mr. Hindman's conversion" of "sound currency into uncurrent bank notes" also meant damage to the Cherokee treasury.[58] When Meigs recovered his speech and health in the fall of 1821, he confronted Hindman with this embezzlement. Hindman "did not consider himself any further accountable" and Meigs was not sure whether to prosecute him or not. "I never knew," he said, "in what point of light the government views these transactions [discounts], wheher they are admissible or honorable."[59] Calhoun replied that in his opinion such actions were

[54] Charles Hicks to Return J. Meigs, November 27, 1820, M-208.

[55] Charles Hicks to Return J. Meigs, June 28, 1821, M-208.

[56] John Calhoun to Return J. Meigs, November 3, 1821, M-15, reel 6, p. 180.

[57] Charles Hicks to Return J. Meigs, June 28, 1821, M-208.

[58] Return J. Meigs to John Calhoun, November 27, 1821, reel 93, #9067; Return J. Meigs to John Calhoun, December 2, 1821, M-221, reel 93, #9069. Apparently this sum included both the agency funds and the Cherokee annuity.

[59] Return J. Meigs to John Calhoun, November 27, 1821, reel 93, #9067.

"highly improper" and told Meigs to hire a lawyer and bring suit against Hindman for the return of the $2,800.[60]

Meigs then wrote to Hicks in March 1822 and apologized for the transaction, noting that he had himself been very ill and had "been deceived by men I confided in." He promised not to pay the annuity in depreciated Tennessee bank notes again and was as good as his word.[61] The annuity in 1822 was paid "in silver."[62] After Meigs's death McMinn proved unable to continue paying the annuity in specie. He told Obadiah Jones, the Receiver of Public Monies in Huntsville, that John Ross, as President of the National Committee, had been instructed by Hicks "to receive nothing but specie or notes of the Bank of the United States of some of its branches" for the annuity. As "there is a treaty pending," he told Jones, "he hoped this could be possible."[63] Yet despite their best efforts, Jones and McMinn were unable to obtain more than one-third of the annuity (about $3,000) in specie. The remaining two-thirds came "in Southern Paper" on Georgia banks.[64] McMinn used the specie to pay off the nation's debts to white citizens; by the time he had deducted this sum, there were only paper bills left for the nation's Treasury. Hicks protested again. "I deem it necessary as Treasurer of the nation, to apprize you on this subject that only silver or gold or the United States bank bills will be received for the current year's annuity and succeeding annuities thereafter." This was necessary, he said, because "I find the Southern bank bills are already begun to depreciate their nominal standured from 4, 5, 6, & 7 per cent below par, and I make no doubt you will do every thing to accommodate the nation on this subject."[65] In support of Hicks, the Council resolved "that the Treasurer" was "not to receive into the Treasury . . . on account of the annual stipends . . . any other description of money than Specie, Treasury [notes] or Notes of the United States Bank."[66]

McMinn died in 1825. When the new agent, Hugh Montgomery, again offered paper money from state banks in 1826, Hicks returned it. The money was from the banks of Newbourn and Cape Fear, North Carolina, and Hicks said the Council had refused to accept it. These paper bills were, he said, "five percent under par both in Georgia and South Carolina."[67] Montgomery told James Barbour, John Quincy Adams's

---

[60] John Calhoun to Return J. Meigs, January 4, 1822, M-15, reel 6, p. 210.
[61] Return J. Meigs to Charles Hicks, March 6, 1822, M-208.
[62] Charles Hicks to Joseph McMinn, May 4, 1823, M-208.
[63] Joseph McMinn to Obadiah Jones, May 2, 1823, M-208.
[64] Joseph McMinn to Charles Hicks, May 16, 1823, M-208.
[65] Charles Hicks to Joseph McMinn, May 4, 1823, M-208.
[66] *Cherokee Laws*, p. 83.
[67] Charles Hicks to Hugh Montgomery, December 13, 1826, M-208.

Secretary of War, that the nearest bank from which he could get the kind of money the Cherokees would accept was in Savannah, Georgia, over two hundred miles from his agency in Tennessee. Nowhere in Tennessee could he obtain specie or United States bank notes. However, he said he hoped to be able to persuade the Cherokees to accept Carolina and Georgia paper that he could obtain from certain Tennessee merchants. He explained that he had been forced to take bills from the Cape Fear and Newbourn banks because nothing else was available when the annuity came due. He knew they were "not as current in Georgia as their own or South Carolina paper," but he thought the Cherokees were being too demanding. "I suppose they have been asked a small percent [discount] on them in August" but he did not think that a cause for complaint. "Until the United States Bank establish[es] a branch in Tennessee, we shall never be able to exchange large drafts with any degree of facility as there are not [in Tennessee] monied Capit[al]ist[s] and their Banks deal chiefly in Trash which will not pass current out of sight of their Banking houses."[68] Montgomery got to the crux of the matter when he spoke of "the degree of facility" involved. It was not worth his while to travel to Savannah or worth the government's effort to find some way to pay the Cherokees what was due them. This issue was never fairly solved. As in similar Indian affairs, the problem was allowed to linger while the government waited for some way to remove the Indians to the west.

The Cherokee problem over the right of internal taxation did not arise until white traders challenged it. In the tax law passed in 1819 it was specified that a tax of $80 on "pedlars not citizens of the Nation" must be paid when they obtained a license from the Council; a $200 fine was prescribed for all violations. When several traders declined to pay it, the Cherokee courts fined them accordingly. When they refused to pay the fine, the Cherokee marshals seized and sold enough of their goods to pay the fines. These merchants complained to the agent and to the Secretary of War. The nation was soon embroiled in the thorny question of whether the law conflicted with the Treaty of Hopewell or with the Trade and Intercourse Acts or not. Technically the issue was whether the Cherokee courts had the right to try and fine white traders under the law of their Council.

The white traders argued that under the Treaty of Hopewell and the Trade and Intercourse Acts they were subject only to the laws of the United States, because only the United States controlled trade with the Indians. They said they willingly complied with the law requiring them to obtain a license from the federal agent but that the Cherokees had no right to establish other regulations for them. The power to tax was the

---

[68] Hugh Montgomery to John Calhoun, January 6, 1826, M-234, reel 72, #0322.

power to destroy, or at least to discriminate and in this case the Cherokees had discriminated by charging native traders only $25 for a license.

The Cherokees said that when they said that the United States could regulate their trade in the Treaty of Hopewell, they had merely yielded their right to conduct trade with other foreign nations. As for the Trade and Intercourse Acts, they had been passed to protect them from unscrupulous and dishonest white traders and to limit the number of such traders who might enter their nation. These laws did not prohibit them from taxing persons who lived in the nation, did business there, and made profits under the protection of their laws.

In 1820 there were fourteen American citizens engaged in trade in the Cherokee Nation, some of them in partnerships.[69] Nine of these willingly paid the tax; five refused and took their cases to the government. The five were Jacob Scudder, the partnership of Gideon Morgan and Michael Huffacre (or Huffaker), and the partnership of John S. McCarty and John McGhee. (Apparently some of the Cherokee traders also refused to pay their tax and their property was also distrained, but they did not appeal to the government for help.)[70] The Cherokees, expecting trouble over this action, had obtained a legal opinion from a prominent American jurist, the Honorable Hugh L. White, before they enforced the law against the noncompliant white traders. White, a Tennessee judge, was a brother-in-law of Governor Willie Blount and, at that time, a close friend of Andrew Jackson (though he later quarreled with and opposed him). White was probably paid a fee for his services. "In my opinion," he wrote, "the Nation have the right to impose this tax. By treaty the United States have the power to regulate trade and intercourse with the Cherokee Indians," and to license white traders, but such a license merely certified that "the individual may be trusted in the Nation"; it was "not intended to take from this Nation the right of judging whether their people should trade with him or not nor the right of fixing the terms and conditions upon which such trade should be conducted."[71]

Armed with this support, the Cherokees had proceeded to fine and distrain the five delinquent traders. By the time they took this action, in 1824, several years of back taxes were outstanding and thus a sizable amount of the traders' goods had to be seized and sold at auction. An-

---

[69] For the list of Cherokee traders in 1823–1824, see Joseph McMinn to John Calhoun, August 31, 1825, M-234, reel 71, #0363; see also letter of Joseph McMinn sent to Thomas McKenney by J. G. Williams, December 16, 1824, M-234, reel 71, #0467.

[70] Cherokee delegation to John Calhoun, February 25, 1824, reel 71, #0073.

[71] Hugh White's letter, dated May 27, 1823, is contained in the letter of the Cherokee delegates to John Calhoun, February 25, 1824, M-234, reel 71, #0073.

thony Foreman was the marshal who carried out the penalty.[72] The five traders later claimed their losses totaled over $1500 worth of goods.[73] They had appealed to the agent even before some of them were distrained. McCarty told McMinn that "the Principle of Equality" was at stake, because white traders had to pay higher taxes than Cherokee traders. McMinn advised the Cherokees to be cautious. "I beg leave to propose to you as a friend to both parties that you suspend the collection of this debt untill you can forward a memorial to [the] next Congress . . . and let the memorial exhibit your true situation (namely) that you have a government to support which cannot be carried on without actual resources, that many of your people are unable to contribute any considerable amount without great embarrassment and hence the necessity of resorting to a tax on merchants, etc. and ask Congress to pass a law vesting the Cherokee Nation with Power to levy taxes and raise revenue under such limitations as they may prescribe." In his opinion, however, they were probably "infringing either upon the Constitution or the Laws of the United States."[74]

Hicks replied that white citizens were asked to pay more than Cherokee traders because the white trader had more money and more credit and therefore had a decided advantage over his Cherokee competitors. The Council had worded the law to take account of "the different advantage enjoyed by the partys in their capitals and opportunityes of laying in their goods in the United States, as one has ample resources to lay in fresh goods should his old stock remain on hand at the end of the year and the others are obliged to sell out his old stock before he is enabled to make remittance to his creditors in order to obtain fresh supplies of goods to enable him to continue in his mercantile pursuit."[75] The Cherokees saw the power to tax as the power to equalize.

In August 1823 Hicks went on to assert the nation's right to govern its own internal affairs and to lay internal taxes. He said the nation had enjoyed the right of managing its own affairs by law for "upwards of thirty years to my knowledge." The Cherokees believed the tax law was entirely within their powers of self-government; "the treaties and intercourse law does not forbid of the internal regulation of our Government" and the Trade and Intercourse Act "never was intended to take from the nation the right of judging whether their people should trade" with certain per-

[72] Joseph McMinn to Charles Hicks, July 19, 1823, M-208; Return J. Meigs to John Calhoun, February 12, 1824, M-221, reel 3, #9083; Gideon Morgan to John Calhoun, February 12, 1824, M-234, reel 71, #0075.
[73] Gideon Morgan to John Calhoun, February 12, 1824, M-234, reel 71, #0075.
[74] Joseph McMinn to Charles Hicks, July 19, 1823, M-208.
[75] Charles Hicks to Joseph McMinn, August 8, 1823, M-208.

sons "nor the right of fixing the terms and conditions upon which such trade should be conducted." Hicks said that McMinn was the lawbreaker, for he had broken a long-standing agreement between Meigs and the Council. Meigs had said that he would never license a trader without first obtaining the consent of the Council. McMinn, however, had "failed to do this in the cases of Jacob Scudder and Simon White," whom he permitted to keep houses of entertainment as though this were a licensed trade. Meigs had said that tavern keepers were not licensed traders; McMinn had violated that agreement. "I solemnly protest against such libertys being taken," Hicks said. All franchises for inns, taverns, or stands were to be granted by the nation and the nation was entitled to charge rent or obtain a share of the profit from them. McMinn was infringing on the nation's rights to regulate its internal affairs and might well be guilty of doing favors for his friends.

Huffacre and Morgan entered a claim against the nation for "spoilation [sic] on our Merchandize by the Cherokees" and for infringing the Trade and Intercourse Act.[76] They argued that because they had a license to trade from McMinn they should be subject to no other regulation from the nation. Because Gideon Morgan was a Cherokee countryman, the other merchants gave him their power of attorney to plead their case and collect their claims. McCarty and McGhee claimed $557 damages; Morgan and Huffacre, $474; Jacob M. Scudder, $507. William Throp, another intermarried white who had paid a tax as a Cherokee trader, now decided to oppose the law and gave Morgan the power to act for him.[77] Morgan had already brought his case before the Council and been turned down; the Council had ruled that the nation had "the right to tax traders in their nation whether licensed or not."

McMinn sent the problem to the War Department and Calhoun discussed the matter with the Cherokee delegation in February 1824. They told him: "We cannot see that the Cherokees conceded [in any treaty] their own right of making municipal regulations for themselves," and they declined his request to repeal the law.[78] To do so would undermine the whole principle of their right to self-government. Calhoun submitted the case to the Attorney General, William Wirt. Wirt, in a long and labored response on April 2, 1824, stated that in his opinion the Cherokees had acted unconstitutionally. He added in an important obiter dictum, however, that this was not their fault so much as it was the fault of Congress for failing to take into consideration the changing nature of the

[76] Gideon Morgan to John Calhoun, February 12, 1824, M-234, reel 71, #0175–0176; see also J. G. Williams's copy of a letter from Joseph McMinn to John Calhoun, December 16, 1824, M-234, reel 71, #0467.

[77] Ibid.

[78] Cherokee delegation to Joseph McMinn, February 25, 1824, M-234, reel 71, #0073.

Cherokee Nation as it had advanced in wealth, economic stability, political order, and civilization. He based his opinion on the argument that when the Treaty of Hopewell was "entered into, there was no such things as municipal regulations in the Cherokee Nation" and hence the Cherokees had in fact handed over "the whole system of regulation *on both sides* [internal and external] under which trade should be carried on." He also cited John Marshall's decision in *McCullough* v. *Maryland* that the power to tax was the power to destroy. In his obiter dictum, however, Wirt suggested that Congress should consider changing its paternalistic relationship with the Cherokees. Could not Congress "have respect to the altered condition of the Cherokees, to the stage of civilization to which have been now carried by the measures adopted by the United States to produce this very effect," and "adopt their further regulations to their altered condition so as to enable that nation to raise a revenue for the support of their government by an equal tax upon our traders as well as their own"? In his opinion "the time has passed away in which it could be tolerated to treat these people as we please because we are christians and they are heathen."[79] It was the nicest possible way to let the Cherokees down.

Calhoun forwarded Wirt's opinion to McMinn on June 18, 1824, with instructions to tell the Cherokee Council to repeal its tax law on traders and to refund the money taken from them. McMinn did so, and that October Huffacre and McCarty appeared at the Council expecting to receive their refund.[80] The Council, rejecting Calhoun's order, refused to pay them. It told McMinn that it had already "appealed from the opinion of the attorney General" to the Congress of the United States.[81] It had done this by sending a memorial to Congress, "and as the subject has not been acted upon and is now pending in Congress, the law imposing the taxes still remains in force." They had sent their message in April, three days after Wirt released his opinion. The memorial had the full support of McKenney of the War Department.[82] Nevertheless, McMinn deducted from their annuity in November 1824 the amount claimed by Huffacre and McCarty and paid it to them (in specie).[83] When the other traders

[79] William Wirt's opinion for John Calhoun, April 2, 1824, M-234, reel 71, #0441–1450. Emphasis in original.

[80] Joseph McMinn to Cherokee Council, October 20, 1824, M-234, reel 71, #0471, and J. G. Williams to John Calhoun (enclosing letter of McMinn), December 16, 1824, reel 71, #0471.

[81] Cherokee Council to Joseph McMinn, November 5, 1824, reel 71, #0474.

[82] Thomas McKenney to Cherokee delegation, April 7, 1824, M-21, reel 1, p. 27, and Thomas McKenney to Cherokee delegation, April 15, 1824, M-21, reel 1, p. 52.

[83] John Calhoun to Hugh Montgomery, June 10, 1825, M-208; for John Ross's protest against this see John Ross to John Calhoun, February 28, 1825, M-234, reel 71, #0497.

learned of this, they also asked McMinn for reimbursement; he then deducted their claims as well from the annuity.[84]

In 1825, agent Montgomery continued to press the Cherokees to repeal the law. Instead, they merely voted on November 10, 1825, to suspend that part of it applying to Cherokee traders (the whites were no longer paying) for two years. When Congress declined to act on their memorial, Charles Hicks and John Ross wrote a detailed rebuttal to Wirt's opinion, based upon the position of the American colonists against Parliament in 1775 (with McMinn in the role of a royal governor). Since the American Constitution forbade their representation in Congress, they had the right to lay taxes for their own support and Congress had no right to interfere with this. They claimed that the wording of the Constitution virtually acknowledged their sovereignty because Section 8 of Article One said Congress had the power to regulate commerce "with foreign nations and among the several states and with the Indian tribes." As Hicks and Ross read this, "we are placed precisely on the same footing with Foreign Nations and the several states . . . and have not the several states ever exercised the right of taxing merchants, pedlars, etc?" Could Congress regulate Great Britain's or France's internal trade? "In the name of common sense and equal justice, why is the right of the Cherokee Nation in this respect disputed?"[85] Moreover, "the American government, we believe, never has advocated the doctrine that taxes can be imposed where the people taxed are unrepresented." How could Congress regulate the Cherokees' trade when they were "unrepresented in Congress"?

The thrust of the argument was clear. The time had come for the United States to recognize the Cherokee Nation as either an independent, sovereign state (with the same state's rights as other states in the Union) or an Indian territory. Having never ratified the American Constitution, the Cherokees believed they were like the thirteen original states prior to 1789 or like Rhode Island from 1789 to 1791. Considering the dilemma they were in, it is hardly surprising that a number of Cherokees were beginning to think in such terms. In 1823, one young Cherokee who had recently been graduated from the missionary schools and was considered a rising star of the younger generation suggested in a letter to the public published in a Virginia newspaper: "In a few years . . . you shall see an aborigine in congress who will act in the capacity of a representative from

[84] Thomas McKenney to Cherokee delegation, February 22, 1825, M-21, reel 1, p. 364; John Calhoun to Robert Houston, January 24, 1825, M-21, reel 1, p. 321; John Calhoun to Hugh Montgomery, June 10, 1825, M-208.

[85] John Ross and Charles Hicks to Hugh Montgomery, December 11, 1826, M-234, reel 72, #0042–0046. On October 18, 1827, the Council made the tax on white and Cherokee traders equal (*Cherokee Laws*, pp. 88–89).

the Cherokee Nation."[86] Such young nationalists fully believed that their nation was moving through the normal phases of any western area of the United States—it would soon have territorial status and then statehood. On those terms, within those limits of sovereignty, the Cherokees were still willing to consider the possibility of fulfilling George Washington's original policy of incorporating with the people and destiny of the United States. They would come in as equals or not at all.

Yet the Cherokee nationalists had not really thought through their position. They had rejected territorial status in 1824, yet in 1827 they adopted a constitution. They preferred in fact to negotiate with the United States by treaties and remain a foreign nation for as long as possible. To be a territory would mean opening their land to all white citizens who wished to enter it. It would probably also mean that they must give up communal ownership of their land. Congress would hardly approve a territorial constitution advocating communism. In the years 1825 to 1833 the Cherokees and the United States debated what kind of sovereignty or self-government was viable for Indian peoples.

[86] David Brown to Thomas McKenney, February 28, 1823, M-221, reel 95, #0003.

SIXTEEN

CLASS, GENDER, AND RACE IN THE
NEW CHEROKEE STATE, 1819–1827

*Resolved by the National Committee and Council, That intermarriages
between negro slaves and indians or whites shall not be lawful . . . Resolved . . . That all free negroes coming into the Cherokee Nation . . .
shall not be allowed to reside in the Cherokee Nation without a permit.*
—Laws passed November 11, 1824

The political acumen and economic enterprise that enabled the Cherokees to achieve a sense of self-determination and national destiny in
the 1820s came at a heavy cost to those Cherokees who adhered to the old
ways. By 1825, Cherokee society was politically centralized but socially
diverse. It had always been divided regionally; now it was also divided by
class and race. There was also a new kind of generational division and educational division. In the past there had been an unbroken harmony
among grandparents, parents, and the rising generation. Through the
clan system of matrilineal kinship responsibilities and inheritance, the
Cherokees had reenforced each others' identities, values, and sense of
timeless continuity within a single community. Now the three living
generations seemed unable to comprehend each other; they lived in different worlds. The members of the youngest generation, born after 1789,
especially those who had attended school and had come of age by 1820,
thrived on the changes that had revitalized a fallen people and were willing to accept more acculturation. Their parents, born in the Revolutionary Era and having waged the hard struggle for survival after 1789, were
convinced that they must protect what they had attained at all costs but
were not eager for more change. The generation of the grandparents (and
beyond them) understood in a general way the necessity for some of the
changes that had come about, but emotionally—in their hearts and
minds—many of them found the new ways unsettling and strange as well
as destructive to tribal coherence; in their confusion, these older people
clung to whatever they could of their traditional way of life and resisted
change.

The greatest source of division among the Cherokees, one that cut across generational lines, was between those who held to the ideal of a communal ethic and matrilineal kinship and those who were adopting an individualistic ethic and the patrilineal family. The adoption of horse-and-plow agriculture and the placing of women in the house were not the great difference between generations. The basic difference concerned the values of a commercial, market economy and a subsistence economy of sharing. Leadership at the top of the new commercial order was provided by a small group of well-to-do, influential merchant-traders, large planters, slave-owning farmers, and entrepreneurs, who understood and found satisfaction in the capitalistic system of trade, profit, and manufacture. They had accepted the individualistic values of the acquisitive society, though most retained some feeling for the older ethic. Below this financially successful elite was a somewhat larger group of farmers and herdsmen who mixed small-scale farming with another enterprise—running a tavern or ferry, owning a gristmill or sawmill, acting as middleman for large traders and plantation owners. Next, and by far the largest class, were the small farmers who barely made enough to live on, who engaged perhaps in a little barter, sold a few cattle or hogs, and clothed themselves from the homespun made by the women of the family from small patches of cotton. Some of these might have a couple of horses, a plow, and a milk cow from which their wives could make butter and cheese, but many had to supplement heir farming by hunting and their wives still planted a truck garden using a hoe. Although most Cherokees lived in some kind of log cabin, these ranged from the barest one-room, dirt-floored, and stick-chimneyed style to elaborate double-houses with brick chimneys and large porches.[1] The wealthier families had brick or frame-and-clapboard dwellings, orchards of peach and apple trees, large barns and stables with neatly fenced pastures and fields; the poorest still gathered wild berries and nuts in the woods to eke out a living.

The Cherokees were also developing a small class of artisans and mechanics, encouraged by the Council to supplement and ultimately to replace the hard-to-get and expensive white artisans. Spinning, sewing, and weaving as practised by most women was of course one form of this, though home industry seldom provided a surplus of cloth for the marketplace. More significant were the Cherokees who learned to be carpenters and blacksmiths, able to repair wagons, plows, and farm tools and to make spinning wheels and looms. Agent Meigs had made note of this as early as 1816 in a letter to the Secretary of War. In 1801, he said, there was only one blacksmith in the Cherokee Nation and he was a white man

[1] For an effort to define social classes in the Cherokee Nation see McLoughlin and Conser, "The Cherokees in Transition."

paid by the agency; in November 1816 there were fifteen blacksmiths in the nation, "five of them . . . Cherokees self-taught." "Many of the Indians" were now able to "pay for their own Smith work" and were eager to hire Cherokee smiths. "There are two white men and two real Cherokees [full bloods] who make spinning wheels" and who "comply with my orders for work for others. . . . The looms for weaving are nearly all made by Indians for which the price is eight dollars only apiece." "Many of them now tan their own leather; they make shoes, and there is one good saddler, a Cherokee. They have too many Silver Smiths. They make rich Hatbands, arm bands and other ornaments of dress, and silver Spurrs equal to any I ever saw." Meigs urged the Secretary to provide money to hire a tinsmith to train Cherokees to repair pots and pans for farmers' wives.[2] In the 1820s the Council passed several laws to encourage Cherokees to apprentice their sons to artisans and promising free tools to those who mastered a craft.

It would be difficult to provide precise figures for each of these economic groups. If one uses slave ownership as an indication of wealth (because all land was still owned in common), there were slightly over 200 or so Cherokee families out of 3,500 who owned one or more slaves. Only thirty to forty families owned more than ten; another thirty owned three to nine. Over 90 percent owned no slaves.[3] If one estimated wealth by the size of family farms, the wealthiest families cultivated one hundred acres or more, growing cotton, corn, and wheat; the poorest cultivated three or four acres, mostly in corn and beans; the average family worked about ten or twelve acres, often on scattered plots. When the New England missionaries arrived in 1818, they were surprised to find how little the Cherokees knew about the science of intensive farming. For example, they had never heard of the three-field system and they did nothing to replenish their soil. "The Natives already understand the art of raising corn and keeping cattle," wrote Ard Hoyt of Brainerd Mission, "but they have never experienced the advantages of [rotating] pasture, field and meadow. When they have exhausted a field by planting it with corn, they know nothing of recruiting it by sowing other grains and laying it down to grass, and for lack of this knowledge, they are either working their fields to very little profit or forsaking them to open new ones."[4] Charles Hicks,

---

[2] Return J. Meigs to William Crawford, November 4, 1816, M-271, reel 1, #1259.

[3] See Perdue, *Slavery and Cherokee Society,* p. 60.

[4] Ard Hoyt to S. A. Worcester, March 18, 1818, ABCFM. Of course, "forsaking" old fields to "open new ones" was a form of "recruiting" old land, but as the total area of Cherokee land decreased and their population increased, it became difficult to abandon old soil and cultivate other soil.

the Second Principal Chief, was equally critical of the methods of the average Cherokee farmer. In 1820 he wrote:

Most families cultivate from ten, twenty, thirty to forty acres of land without the assistance of black people: The greatest number of whom might raise plentiful crops of corn were they to get into the habit of plucking out one or two stalks in a hill in old ground. It is believed that there is not more than one-eighth or ninth part of the families but has either horses or cattle, and perhaps there is none without a stock of hogs.[5]

Many farmers let their horses, hogs, and cattle range through the canebrakes and woods to forage for themselves. Livestock that survived was generally scrawny and small.

Measurement of economic status could also be made in terms of the families that owned plows, wagons, spinning wheels, and looms, but the statistics are imprecise. Most Cherokee families had a plow and a spinning wheel; comparatively few owned wagons and looms. Over three-quarters of the Cherokees were full bloods who spoke no English. Most of these kept to themselves and did not seek to accumulate wealth. They preferred the steady routine of life and the extended kinship system of the clans. Though farmers, the men taught their sons to hunt, trap, and fish; the women taught their daughters to farm, sew, and spin. They still enjoyed their old holidays, rituals, and ball plays and went to their medicine men when they were sick, confused, or wanted a love charm. Jacob Scudder, a white trader who lived among the full bloods in Etowah from 1817 to 1831, said that the vast majority of the Cherokees he knew cultivated only four to five acres and that "their principal dependence for support is from what ground they cultivate in corn, pumpkins, potatoes and beans."

The larger portion are very poor and to persons unaccustomed to Indians, they would seem miserably so. But to me, who has resided among them fourteen years, they appear the most contented and happy people on earth. They reflect but little on the future or the past. If their wants are supplied, they are contented; if not, they exhibit but little uneasiness or regret.[6]

Scudder may have seen only the stoical side that these people wanted to present to the white man, but he was probably correct in noting the easy-going, quiet quality of their lives. Part of their simple style of life resulted from their holding on to the older values of Cherokee culture—community, sharing, harmony. They resisted the hard-driving, aggressive, acquisitive values of the wealthy Cherokees, who were trying to prove that

---

[5] Charles Hicks to Jedidiah Morse in Morse, *Report to the Secretary of War*, p. 169.

[6] Jacob Scudder to George Gilmer, September 17, 1831, WPA Project, "Cherokee Indians," ed. Mrs. E. J. Hays, part 2, p. 316, Georgia Archives, Atlanta. Scudder was writing from the predominantly full-blood town of Etowah.

they could do everything the white man could do. As Meigs had said, these Cherokees did not have a high estimate of "the advantages of being civilized"; as far as money, goods, power were concerned, "they think our enjoyments cost more than they are worth."[7] This did not mean that they rejected the advantages of iron pots, brass kettles, steel traps, or guns; nor were they averse to teaching their children to read and write in order to learn to cope with the whites with whom they had to trade. They simply preferred the leisurely friendship of life among their kin and neighbors to the bustle and anxiety of getting rich.

The rapid acculturation of the more well-off Cherokees, which won such praise from the whites and brought self-respect to those tribal leaders who had to deal regularly with the whites in order to uphold the nation's rights, brought with it internal social conflicts when new values became embodied in new laws and were enforced by a national police system. Because the full bloods were still the overwhelming majority in the Council, those who favored new ways had to convince them that change was necessary and to work hard to graft new ways to old habits. The stability and cohesion of the Cherokee Nation depended upon blending the two. It probably also required a temporizing approach to the literal enforcement of the new laws, most of which were totally alien to the experience of the average Cherokee.

The new order had a major impact upon the role of women, the structure of the family, and the kinship system of the clans. The first important break in Cherokee tradition had been the gradual erosion of clan revenge between 1797 and 1808 (although it did not die out); then the law of 1808 instituted a patriarchal concept of "children as heirs to their father's property" and the protection of "the widow's share" of her husband's estate. The new economy of the self-subsistent farm family led to the view of the husband, dominant as producer and protector, and the wife as manager of the home and children; it left little place for the traditional role of the wife's brothers as her protectors and as her ultimate source of security. Her brothers had their own wives and children as their primary responsibility. Clan relationships and responsibilities remained a shadowy form of order but in a secondary role. The most resistant aspect of family life to the white man's system was the important Cherokee tradition of women's rights to their own property and control of children. In 1819 the Council put this tradition into written form: "The improvements and labor of our people by the mother's side shall be inviolate during the time of their occupancy" of any homestead.[8]

---

[7] Return J. Meigs to Benjamin Hawkins, February 13, 1805, M-208.
[8] *Cherokee Laws*, p. 5.

This law came about in part to meet a major difficulty resulting from the removal crisis. Emigrants of Arkansas were enrolled as male "heads of family." The enrollment of a husband was sufficient under the treaty to evict his wife and children from their home even if the wife did not chose to go west. The Council's law sustained her ownership of the home. Tradition and the clan probably also sustained her right to keep her children with her, unless she had married a white man; in this case there might be a clash of interests. White husbands assumed that they had the right to their wive's property and would sell the horses, cattle, or slaves that a Cherokee wife brought with her at marriage. In 1819 the Council voted that "any white man who shall hereafter take a Cherokee woman to wife" shall be "required to marry her legally by a minister of the gospel or other authorized person after producing a license from the National Clerk . . . before he shall be entitled and admitted to the privilege of citizenship and in order to avoid imposition [on a Cherokee woman] on the part of the white man." This protected the nation from whites who used cohabitation as a means of obtaining "countryman" or "citizenship" status; it protected the Cherokee wife by making the white man responsible under his contractual concept of legal marriage. (A white man who had a wife somewhere else would be guilty of bigamy under this law.) The law further protected women's property by stating that "any white man who shall marry a Cherokee woman, the property of the woman so married shall not be subject to the disposal of her husband contrary to her consent, and any white man parting from his wife without just provocation shall forfeit and pay to his wife such sum or sums as may be adjudged to her by the National Committee and Council for said breach of marriage." It was no longer her brothers but the authority of the nation that protected a Cherokee woman who married a white.

This law may reflect the problem of the widow of Moses Melton. Melton, a white trader, moved into the nation near Muscle Shoals in 1780 and married a Cherokee. Through his friendship with Doublehead, Melton became very rich. But his marriage was not according to white law and upon his death in 1815, his brother in Tennessee came into the nation and took all his cattle, horses, slaves, and other valuable property. Mrs. Melton complained to the agent, who hired a lawyer to protect her interest in the estate, but legally she was no more than a concubine. Melton's brother and American common law did not consider a pagan woman as a common-law wife.[9]

Although laws of this kind were designed to protect the traditional status of women, they in effect sanctioned the changing status of women.

[9] Mrs. Moses Melton to Return J. Meigs, June 30, 1815, M-208.

Conservative Cherokees found the laws bureaucratic and alien. They had never been required to get a marriage license from the Council before. Hiring a lawyer to support a woman's right to her husband's property was doubly strange.

Laws governing inheritance, though they too tried to blend the old customs with new circumstances, were complex for Cherokees who did not speak or read Cherokee. Though the laws were written with good intentions, they altered traditional matrilineal concepts of inheritance. A law passed in 1825 stated that "where a person possessing property and dies inteste [sic], and having a wife and children, the property of the deceased shall be equally divided among his lawful and acknowledged children, allowing the widow an equal share with the children."[10] If there were no children, the widow was to get one-fourth of his estate and "The residue of the estate [was] to go to his nearest kin." The phrase "nearest kin" was clearly designed to permit the man's brother, or brothers, to share in the inheritance according to custom, but the complexity of giving these brothers three-fourths of the estate might be troublesome. The only way to measure three-fourths of a slave, a horse, or a large farm was to convert it into cash. And would the widow of a wealthy planter want her husband's brothers to leave her with only one-fourth of the estate? To the poor, the law mattered very little and was probably ignored. In the case of a woman of property dying intestate, the law said that "her property shall revert to her childen and husband in the same manner" as when the husband died intestate. A woman's brothers had lost the reward for their role as the ones responsible for their sister and her children; because the husband had assumed that role, he took her estate and her children. What seemed designed to protect certain important traditions was in fact subtly destroying them. The breakdown had begun as early as 1805 when wealthy Cherokee men began to ask the agent to write and witness patrilineal wills for them. It was assumed that by this act an individual could unilaterally destroy an ancient tradition.

An even more drastic revision in marriage custom took place after 1819. Cherokee custom allowed two or more wives. Until the law of 1819, white men could and did follow the same practice. Samuel Riley, the white interpreter for the agent from 1796 to 1820, had two Cherokee wives.[11] Perhaps because of missionary pressure, the Council voted in 1819 that "it shall not be lawful for any white man to have more than one wife." That same year another law stated that after that date, the Council "recommended" that Cherokee men have only one wife. Finally, in 1825,

---

[10] *Cherokee Laws*, p. 53.
[11] Return J. Meigs to John Calhoun, April 6, 1820, M-271, reel 3, #0481.

the Council prohibited any Cherokee from having more than one wife thereafter.[12] The monogamous standard of whites had become the law of the Cherokee nation. Those in the rising generation might now feel embarrassed if a parent or grandparent did not conform to the new standard.

The case of a white woman married to a Cherokee (of which there were at least seventy-three in 1826) was equally awkward. A law of 1825 required that the children of such women were "equally entitled to all the immunities and privileges enjoyed by the citizens descending from the Cherokee race by the mother's side."[13] But what was "the Cherokee race"? This law could not give a white woman clan membership. If her husband left her, who took care of her children? The law gave her children citizenship in an abstract legal sense, but citizenship traditionally meant belonging to a clan and all the privileges, protections, and responsibilities that accompanied this. Nor did the law give her citizenship. If her Cherokee husband left her, what was her status? In 1829 a law denied citizenship to childless white widows of Cherokees. The more the law meddled with tradition, trying to reconcile old and new, the more puzzling life became. Rules and regulations governing social life often produced more confusion than clarity.

Cherokee women had always had the right to practice abortion or infanticide. Limitation of family size may have been necessary to stabilize population in relation to food supply or it may have been a woman's right (and necessity) to keep her workload manageable. Women sometimes went with the men on their six-month hunting trips in winter to cook for them and prepare their pelts and skins for market. The Cherokees may have practiced infanticide chiefly on malformed children or it may have represented an effort to balance male and female children. At any rate, it shocked the missionaries. In 1826 the Council made infanticide illegal. Any woman found guilty "of committing infanticide during her . . . state of pregnancy" was to be given "fifty lashes." The same punishment was given to any person who was "accesary to such an act."[14] There is no record that this was ever enforced. It may have been passed to please the missionaries and those educated by them. Still, it set new standards of behavior and new patterns of nonconformity. How the older generation wrestled with these we do not know, but it must have caused them some uneasiness. What was formerly acceptable was now criminal.

Two laws were passed in the 1820s for the crime of rape, a crime unknown in Cherokee history. They were probably passed to protect Cherokee women against white men living in or passing through the nation.

[12] *Cherokee Laws*, pp. 10, 57.
[13] Ibid., p. 57.
[14] Ibid., p. 79.

The law of 1825 said that "any person or persons who shall lay violent hands upon any female by forcibly attempting to ravish her chastity" should receive fifty lashes and the left ear cropped for the first offense, one hundred lashes and the other ear cropped for the second, and death for the third. False accusations of rape were punishable with twenty-five stripes.[15] The concept of female "chastity" as the supreme virtue of womanhood was new to the Cherokees but fundamental for obtaining the respect of the white man, who both created the crime and set the standard. Once again, in protecting their women, the Cherokees were conforming to the whites' code of values.

With the benefits of civilization came its vices; with the Protestant ethic came disdain for idle pastimes. The combined but opposing influences of white renegades on the one hand, and white missionaries on the other led the Council to pass a series of laws in the 1820s dealing with the prevention of gambling, card playing, roulette, dice throwing, and theatrical performances. Renegades gave these activities a bad name; missionaries preached their immorality.[16] The Council also discouraged billiards by requiring a license for billiard parlors and laying a tax upon such establishments.[17] The missionaries also wished the Cherokees to outlaw ball plays and all-night heathen dances, but the Council refused to stop them, though extensive drinking and gambling took place on these occasions. Instead, the upper class tried to set social taboos against attendance, making it clear that respectable people did not attend such rowdy affairs. What had once been a source of tribal solidarity now became a source of social division.

It was not entirely due to the temperance efforts of the missionaries that limits were placed upon the use of alcohol. Most missionaries then had no objection to moderate use of alcohol, but many poor and discouraged Cherokees abused its use and some became addicted. The real problems were the arguments and violence that resulted. In 1822 the Council prohibited selling or bringing "ardent spirits" within three miles of the General Council House when the Council was sitting or within the district courthouses when the courts were sitting.[18] A Congressional Trade and Intercourse Act had prohibited whites from importing liquor into Indian nations since 1802, but in 1824 the Council reenforced this with a law of its own against the importation of liquor by whites.[19] However, the Cherokees did not prohibit their own people from importing, selling, and

15 Ibid., pp. 54, 104.
16 Ibid., pp. 26, 36, 54, 89, 96.
17 Ibid., pp. 84, 89.
18 Ibid., p. 26.
19 Ibid., p. 38.

drinking liquor. They expected Cherokees to develop the same self-control that whites had in using it.

The official lawbooks do not contain any law specifically banning the practice of witchcraft, but apparently the Council did pass a law preventing the murder of witches in the 1820s.[20] Like the laws against infanticide, there is no record of its enforcement, and there are records of the continued practice of witchcraft. Laws could not change beliefs deeply rooted in the old religion, especially in remote parts of the nation.

The missionaries were undoubtedly behind the law that prevented the Council from holding meetings on the Sabbath and requiring all stores and businesses at the capital city of New Echota to close on that day.[21] It may also have been passed out of deference to Charles Hicks and a few other chiefs who were converted to Christianity. Religious pluralism was a new fact of Cherokee life, but they tried to respect it.

The Cherokee Council wished to encourage schools. Because Cherokee parents were indulgent toward their children and did not comprehend the kind of discipline that required sitting behind a desk for long hours memorizing words in the white man's book, attendance at mission schools was irregular until the Council passed a law in 1820 making attendance compulsory once a child had enrolled.[22] If a parent withdrew a child or permitted him or her long absences, the school might expel the child and the parents would be required "to pay all expenses incurred by their children" during the time of enrollment. The law was justified on the ground that "much inconvenience and expense have devolved on the Missionaries from their scholars running away" and this was due to "the negligence on the part of the parents to take such children back to school." The schools taught the children self-discipline and the Council imposed it on the parents.

Behind the new rules lay new views of man's relationship to his environment, to his ways of making a living, and to the spiritual laws that controlled and guided human life. If nature was to be exploited in order to improve the standard of living, then hard, persistent, regular work must be taught and encouraged and private property respected. If self-interest was the chief motivation for hard work and if the rewards of private acquisition promoted the general welfare, then a competitive system

[20] Elias Boudinot, *Address to the Whites* (1826), p. 11. Boudinot wrote that "the practice of putting aged persons to death for witchcraft is abolished," but he did not say when or how. The New England missionaries reported that in 1812 a Cherokee woman saw "all her near relatives . . . slain for the supposed crime of witchcraft" and that she herself was saved only because she was pregnant (Brainerd Journal, May 28, 1822, ABCFM). Sequoyah was suspected of practicing witchcraft when he was creating the Cherokee syllabary.

[21] *Cherokee Laws*, p. 30.

[22] Ibid., p. 14.

was best for all. The values for the social system the white man brought the Cherokees were diligence, persistence, industry, frugality, fidelity to contractual obligations, and specialization. There had to be a different division of labor between man, woman and child than had formerly prevailed in the communal ethic of sharing. The rhythm of daily life had to be altered. Even the way people "told time" had to change; their diet changed; the way they cooked and dressed changed. Long before 1820, plowing a straight furrow was more important than shooting a straight arrow. Spinning and weaving were more important than cleaning and dressing deerhides. Churning butter and making cheese were more valuable skills than knowing where to find nuts and berries. Knowing how to birth calves was more important than knowing how to track deer. Knowing when to plant corn, wheat, barley, cotton, and Irish potatoes was more valuable than knowing when the fish spawned or the bear hibernated. Knowing where the nearest gristmill was and how much the miller should charge you to grind a bushel of corn was more important than knowing how to track an enemy and take his scalp. Knowing how the trader should weigh your cotton and the correct amount of money or credit he should give you for it was more important than knowing how to sing the tribal songs and do the old dances. It was all of a piece—knowing your duties and your nation's rights, knowing the white man's values and rules and putting them into your laws. Yet all these new duties, values, and rules had to be accepted and learned. Decisions had to be made about the worth of the two sets of standards. Was there nothing good in the old ways that should be preserved? Were the white man's answers to all questions right and true? The Cherokee people became very divided in their response.

How well the Cherokees lived up to their new laws is not easily measured. The district courts were busy adjudicating these problems locally after 1820, but there are no records of their proceedings or decisions. Records do exist of the Cherokee Supreme Court's cases. Basically the courts served those who engaged in accumulating property, and Anglo-Saxon forms of adjudication were used because it was essentially the white man's value system they were adjudicating. They had no such procedures and precedents, contracts and torts, in their own tradition or history.[23] Almost all recorded cases involve crimes of civil law—disputed ownership, inheritance, damages, broken contractual obligations, or debts unpaid. Proper behavior in the accumulation and transference of property was the major business of the new legal system, but it affected only those

---

[23] See Strickland, *Fire and the Spirits*, for a discussion of how the Cherokees combined older traditions into the new written laws.

with sufficient wealth to quarrel over what they had. Apparently clans and town councils still functioned at a different level of jurisdiction, providing traditional answers to traditional questions for those who preferred to live by the old norms and relationships. Little is known of the actions of these town councils except that they set the times of local festivals and dances, tried to resolve local quarrels, took stands on tribal issues, and presided over marriages. But it was an oral and ritual system. Older people and those in remote areas probably found all the regulation they needed among their local headmen, doctor/priests, and town councils. Still, they were uneasy about the implications of the many regulations established by the National Council and the new law courts.

Defining what it meant to be a Cherokee had become very difficult, just as it was now difficult to define who was a Cherokee. The removal crisis had settled the fact that a true Cherokee remained loyal to tribal ownership of the ancestral land and resided on it. But there were more subtle forms of definition with which the Council continued to wrestle. For example, the Cherokee Nation, like the United States, was multiracial. There were different kinds of Indians living among them—Catawba, Creek, Uchee, Osage; various Europeans—British, Spanish, French, American; and there was a growing body of Africans (some freedmen, some slaves). Prior to 1819 these variations were of minor importance. Thereafter, as the Cherokees sought to measure themselves by white standards, they began to make distinctions.

Concerning the white man, the problem was essentially to distinguish between the good and the bad. This could be done by laws defining behavior and by distinguishing friendly whites (usually from the east and north) from unfriendly whites (usually from the frontier around them). A few full bloods maintained that the Great Spirit meant red and white people to be separate but equal. Full bloods tended to marry full bloods. Acculturationists preferred to assert the equality of red and white by advocating intermarriage. Mixed bloods tended to marry mixed bloods or whites. A racial division arose between the full bloods and those of mixed ancestry, but it was due more to wealth, social behavior, and value differences than to purity of race.

The Cherokee attitude toward Africans underwent the most serious shift in the 1820s. Social and economic factors weighed as heavily as racial ones. According to prevailing scientific thought, the black man was biologically and intellectually the equal of red and white, all descendants of the same original man, created by the same hand, brothers under the skin. Complexion, as the Cherokees said, was an accident of climate, totally irrelevant to equal membership in the human species. But the rising cotton kingdom in the south and the growing number of slaves among the

Cherokees forced a reassessment of this judgment. The institution of slavery was not the sole issue for the Cherokees. They had enslaved captured red enemies for centuries; however, these red slaves were more often than not adopted into the tribe after some years and treated as full members.[24] In the early eighteenth century the Cherokees had captured other Indians and sold them to the English as slaves, but they had given this up by 1730. The few Africans who came to live among them before 1794 were given the same status as the remnants of the Catawbas and Uchees among them. They were eligible for adoption, intermarriage, and equal citizenship. Some English-speaking blacks were very useful as "linksters" or interpreters once they had learned Cherokee; others were useful for the skilled crafts they brought with them. But the Cherokees had no economic need for slave labor prior to 1794.

However, as the Cherokees gradually accepted the white man's style of plantation agriculture and realized how whites felt about "people of color," their attitude toward Africans changed. Most of the Presidents, Secretaries of War, federal agents, governors, generals, army officers, traders, and even missionaries whom they had to impress with their progress toward "civilization" were slaveholders. At first reluctantly and later without compunction, the Cherokees concluded that their survival as a nation depended upon their clearly distinguishing themselves from Africans. To treat blacks as equals would not raise the blacks in white eyes but would simply lower the red man. "Civilization" for the Cherokee became the adoption of the southern white attitude toward black labor. To own slaves became both a source of wealth and a source of respect. All the land that a Cherokee could cultivate or enclose was his to profit from. Since slaves were transferrable as private property and large farms and plantations could be passed on from father to son, there was no reason why Cherokees could not adopt the same life style as southern white cotton planters. Slaves were also a good investment, continually rising in value and increasing in number by natural process. The Cherokee renascence was consequently a grim imitation of the worst as well as the best in white culture.

Evidence of the equality of blacks in the Cherokee Nation in the early part of the century can be seen in the career of Jack Civills (or Sevells), a free black who lived among them from the 1780s until his death in 1805. Civills had become a Cherokee countryman by marrying a Cherokee. She evidently died or left him, and he then married a white woman. Assistant agent Lovely, a Virginian, found Civills too arrogant. "He is like all peo-

---

[24] See Perdue, *Slavery and Cherokee Society*, pp. 1–69, for a discussion of changing Cherokee attitudes toward red and black slavery.

ple of his colour, too forward," Lovely wrote in 1803; he "can't observe a due distance nor bear preferment [of others] in Society with decency; the fellow has obtained property by dint of his Industry, this with his equality with these people, appear too much for him to bear [humbly], his Indian connection creates an Idea of Indian independence and not subject to the Laws of the U. States."[25] Civills ran a tavern and trading post and both Indians and whites were sometimes in his debt. In 1804 he threatened to use force to collect a debt against a white man named Gasper Taught: "Civills was going to play the Indian," said Lovely. "I wrote to Jack informing him to take care, his complection would not do so far—of which I suppose the fellow has taken umbrage. He is certainly a spoiled Negro."[26] But there was no way that Lovely could act against Civills, who was protected by tribal law like any other Cherokee citizen. When he died in 1805, his wife took all his money.[27]

During the 1820s the Cherokee Council began to develop a special code of laws to regulate black slaves in the nation, a practice that parallleled the development of black codes in most of the surrounding states. But racial prejudice against blacks had ben growing for some time. One of the earliest recorded examples of racial consciousness among the Cherokees was in 1793 when Chief Little Turkey was explaining during the guerrilla wars why he would never ally his nation with the Spanish. He found Spaniards closer to blacks in appearance and behavior than to "real white people," he said. Spaniards were swarthy in complexion "and what few I have seen of them looked like mulattoes, and I would never have anything to say to them."[28]

By 1825 the younger generation of mission-educated Cherokee leaders, who had never known a time when blacks were treated as equals, were happy to be able to say to whites that in their nation, unlike their Seminole and Creek neighbors, "there is hardly any intermixture of Cherokee and African blood."[29] Or, as John Ridge put it in 1826, "there is a scanty instance of African mixture with the Cherokee blood, but that of the white may be as 1 to 4, occasioned by intermarriages."[30] Young Ridge wanted to indicate that Cherokees and whites were allied in the nation in the honorable status of matrimony, while whatever mixture there was of African blood had occurred illicitly between scandalous Cherokee slaveowners and their female slaves. Though Ridge and his father and

[25] W. S. Lovely to Return J. Meigs, May 17, 1803, M-208.

[26] W. S. Lovely to Return J. Meigs, April 19, 1804, M-208.

[27] James Minor to William S. Lovely, January 23, 1805, and James Minor to Return J. Meigs, January 31, 1805, M-208.

[28] ASP II, 461.

[29] ASP II, 651.

[30] John Ridge to Albert Gallatin, Payne Papers, VIII:103–104.

brothers owned slaves, they would never think to engage in such behavior. Furthermore, since the number of black slaves owned by Cherokees had increased between 1809 and 1826 from 583 to 1,277, Ridge wished the self-restraint of the Cherokee slaveowner to be respected. What little intermixture there was of red and black, he implied, had occurred long ago, before the Cherokees were an enlightened, civilized people.

To cement this state of affairs, the Cherokee Council in 1824 passed a law prohibiting "intermarriage between negro slaves and indians or whites" and setting fines for slaveowners who permitted such alliances. Any male Indian or white who married "a negro woman slave" was to be punished with 59 stripes and "any Indian [woman] or white woman marrying a negro man slave" was to be punished with 25 stripes.[31] Marrying in these cases need not mean, certainly did not mean, Christian marriage. Nothing was said in the law about marriages with freed blacks, probably because there were so few of them. The Cherokees made every effort to limit the number of freed blacks in the nation. "All free negroes coming into the Cherokee Nation" after 1824 were declared to be "intruders and shall not be allowed to reside" unless they had "a permit from the National Committee and Council."[32] (Some freed blacks may have been granted a permit on a temporary basis if they came to provide useful services as a skilled worker.)

Prior to 1819 slaves in the nation had been permitted to engage in trade or barter, but after that year this was prohibited. A Cherokee named Otter Lifter had claimed that he had bought a horse from a slave, only to find that the slave had run away from his owner, William Thompson, and the horse was Thompson's. When Thompson reclaimed the horse, he refused to refund the money Otter Lifter had paid. Otter Lifter complained to the Council, which declined to hold Thompson responsible for his slave's action and said that Otter Lifter was at fault for doing business directly with a slave instead of dealing with the slave's master. To prevent similar situations, the Council passed a law in November 1819, saying that in future "no contract or bargain entered into with any slave or slaves without the approbation of their masters shall be binding on them."[33]

A year later the Council elaborated upon this law by stating that anyone "who shall trade with any negro slave without permission from the proper owner" and who later found that he had bought stolen property was himself responsible to return that property or to pay the owner its value.[34] In addition, this law required any master who permitted his slave

[31] *Cherokee Laws*, p. 38.
[32] *Cherokee Laws*, p. 37.
[33] Ibid., p. 9.
[34] Ibid., pp. 24–25.

to purchase or sell "spirituous liquors" to pay a fine of fifteen dollars "to be collected by the Marshalls within their respective Districts." Further, "any negro" found selling liquor without his master's permission was to "receive fifteen cobbs or paddles for every such offense." This punishment was to be inflicted by "the patrolers of the settlement or neighborhood in which the offense was committed." This was the first mention in the law of neighborhood slave patrols, distinct from the lighthorse police. The law went on to encourage the creation of such patrols: "Every settlement or neighborhood shall be privileged to organize a patroling company" to assert control over the slaves in that community. The Cherokee Supreme Court ruled that any persons who aided or harbored runaway slaves were to be fined or severely whipped.[35]

The next step was to deprive slaves of the right to hold property. A law in 1824 made it illegal for "negro slaves to possess property in horses, cattle or hogs." They were given one year to dispose of such livestock and thereafter it was confiscated and sold "for the benefit of the Cherokee Nation."[36]

No law was ever passed regulating the manumission of slaves by Cherokee owners. Some slaves were freed in wills. In 1805 a slave named Paul told Meigs that he had earned $400 and bought his freedom.[37] In 1822 a Cherokee named Oowanahtekiskee bought and set free an eleven-year-old slave, stating in an affidavit, "[I] hereby claim and acknowledge the aforesaid boy to be my true begotten son."[38] Oowanahtekiskee presented this affidavit to the Council for approval; it recorded that "we do hereby receive and admit the emancipation of said Boy and will acknowledge him to be free hereafter." Several years later, a Cherokee woman, Caty Richmond, set one of her slaves free upon his paying her $150. She gave him a letter attesting to the transaction that he registered with the Supreme Court: "To all and singular to whom it may concern, Know ye that for an in the consideration of the sum of one hundred and fifty dollars received from Prince, a black man slave, we do by these presents set him free and against the claim or claims of any other person or persons."[39] How Prince had earned $150 is not revealed. In neither of the above cases was the owner required to post bond for the support or good behavior of the

---

[35] Malone, *Cherokees of the Old South*, p. 83, and Cherokee Supreme Court Docket, 1823–1835, November 1, 1824, Tennessee State Archives, Nashville.

[36] *Cherokee Laws*, p. 39.

[37] Paul Smith to Return J. Meigs, July 29, 1805, M-208, and Paul Smith to Henry Dearborn, August 18, 1805, M-271, reel 1, #0370. Smith claimed that he was seized and sold back into slavery by Doublehead despite his manumission.

[38] Payne Papers, VII, part 1, 48–49.

[39] Cherokee Supreme Court Docket, 1823–1835, January 20, 1834, Tennessee Archives, Nashville.

freedman and each was allowed to remain in the nation. Whether they were considered full or equal citizens is doubtful.

The amount of litigation in the Cherokee Council and courts over the ownership of slaves, as well as the large amount of correspondence in the agency files on the subject of slaves, indicates their economic importance. Slaves were squabbled over in inheritance disputes; they were seized by creditors; and they were loaned or rented out on contracts. It was a common practice in wealthy Cherokee families for a mother or father to give or lend a slave to a daughter when she got married, perhaps as a kind of dowry or perhaps to prevent her becoming a household drudge. Several court cases arose when husbands tried to sell such slaves; the wives successfully claimed in most cases that under Cherokee law these slaves were their personal property and not subject to the husband's disposal. Litigation also occurred when a parent wanted the slave loaned to a daughter to be returned and the daughter claimed it had been a gift; similarly when such a slave (usually they were female) had children and both the parents and their married daughter claimed them. Cherokee law, like white slave law, gave "the natural increase" of slaves to the owner of the mother. The Cherokee Supreme Court also tried cases of fraud in which slaves of "unsound" physical or mental health had been knowingly sold at the price of a healthy slave.[40]

Although agents like Meigs accused the "backward" full bloods of laziness because they preferred hunting to farming, it could have as readily been argued that wealthy slaveowning Cherokees imitated white southerners who believed that fieldwork was for blacks. One version of the Cherokee creation myth affirmed that when the Great Spirit created three kinds of man, he allotted the plow and the hoe to the black man. One wealthy Cherokee was upset when a missionary school required his son to learn the vocation of farming and made him work on the mission farm. The father accused the missionaries of making his son do "nigger's work" and offered to provide a slave to the mission to do the work allotted to his son.[41]

It was often said that Cherokees treated their slaves better than whites did. The Cherokees claimed this themselves. David Brown, one of the younger generation of educated Cherokees, wrote to the *Family Visitor* in Richmond, Virginia, in 1825: "You perceive that there are some African slaves among us. They have been from time to time bought and sold by white men. They are, however, generally well treated and they much

[40] Ibid., October 21, 1830.
[41] Robert S. Walker, *Torchlights to the Cherokees* (New York: Macmillan, 1931), p. 140, and Brainerd Journal, July 20, 1819, ABCFM.

prefer living in the nation to residence in the United States."[42] However, substantial evidence exists of Cherokee harshness toward slaves. Cherokee masters certainly did not hesitate to "cobb" or "whip" them. Runaways were cruelly punished and James Vann once tortured and then burned to death a slave who had helped a white man to rob him.[43] Several Cherokees who went west to help their brethren there fight against the Osages brought home three young Osage children as captives in 1818 and sold them to white slave traders, who treated them as blacks.[44] The Cherokees as a whole did not approve of selling other Indians as slaves and tried to prevent it. To equate red and black people in slavery was hardly in their best interest. Pathkiller told Meigs that he thought it wrong "to sell a free person for a slave . . . all nations who are free ought to enjoy the freedom which they are endowed with."[45] Nevertheless, many Cherokees, including Major Ridge, brought back Creek children captured in the Creek War and kept them as slaves. When Gideon Morgan wanted to encourage Cherokees to join in helping Jackson fight against the Seminoles in 1818, he reminded them that the Seminoles had many blacks fighting with them who could be brought home as the booty of war.[46]

When the Cherokees founded a newspaper, its columns were used to advertise for runaway slaves; David Brown was wrong to imply that only whites bought and sold slaves in the Cherokee Nation. There were Cherokee slave dealers who went to New Orleans, Savannah, and Charleston to buy slaves at auctions and bring them back for sale in the Cherokee Nation. James Vann bought many slaves for himself and others; in 1805 he bought one for the Moravian missionaries at Springplace.[47]

The complexity of racial relationships within the Cherokee Nation during the years of cultural transformation can be seen most vividly in three specific cases involved the ambiguity of being red, white, or black: the first concerned the famous Cherokee chief and warrior Chulio (Tuskingo, Shoe Boot, or The Boot); the second, the career and family of Young Wolfe; the third, the slave Chickaune. Chulio started his career as a full-blood warrior in the guerrilla forces of Dragging Canoe; later he sided with the Upper Towns against Doublehead. He fought bravely in the Creek War and became one of the most respected chiefs in the nation.

---

[42] ASP II, 651.

[43] Mrs. Jacob Wohlfahrt to Return J. Meigs, undated but included at the end of the file for 1805.

[44] Walker, *Torchlights*, pp. 74–78.

[45] Pathkiller to Return J. Meigs, September 7, 1819, M-208.

[46] Letter of Gideon Morgan's enclosed in a letter from Sam Houston to John Calhoun, July 20, 1818, M-221, reel 78, #8486.

[47] "Minutes of the Mission Conference Held in Springplace," trans. and ed. Kenneth Hamilton, *The Atlanta Historical Bulletin* (Winter 1970), p. 36.

During the course of his eventful life he had three wives, the first a Cherokee, the second a white woman, the third a black slave. During one of the last of the raids against the Kentucky frontier in the early 1790s, Chulio was in a party of Cherokees and Shawnees who raided a white settlement and captured a young white girl. Chulio bought the girl from the Shawnees and brought her home as his slave. She was about eleven years old in 1792 and her name was Clarinda Ellington. Some years later, after his Cherokee wife died, Chulio persuaded Clarinda to marry him. In 1797 some of her relatives in Kentucky, having discovered her whereabouts, came to take her back to civilization. Silas Dinsmoor, the federal agent, asked her to come to the agency to discuss the matter. Dinsmoor reported that "she refused to return to her people."[48] Six years later two relatives again appeared in the nation to "obtain her liberation." Meigs arranged an interview at the agency and asked whether she wished to return to her friends in Kentucky. By this time she had three children. Chulio was a kind husband and a wealthy one and they lived well. She agreed to return, "if I can carry my Children [with me]." Chulio would not consent to this; "if my children are taken away, I shall look on it the same as if they were dead." Clarinda then declined "going to see her friends as she cannot leave her Children." Chulio explained to Meigs "that he saved her life at the time she was taken and therefore thinks he has a right to keep her as his wife." It appeared, Meigs wrote, "that Tuskingo is a man of very considerable property."[49] A year later Clarinda decided that she would at least like to pay a visit to her relatives. Chulio was reluctant but, trusting his wife, he agreed. He bought fine new clothes for her and the children and gave them good horses and a slave to attend them. They went to Kentucky in 1804 and never returned. Clarinda died in 1807. Whether she had intended to return is doubtful. Her relatives kept her children. Chulio was distraught and felt cheated. "Being in possession of some Black people and being cross in my affections," he wrote later, "I debased myself and took one of my Black Women by the name of Daull" as his wife. "By her I have had three Children."[50]

In 1824 the oldest of Chulio's children by Daull was seventeen. As a member of the National Council, Chulio realized that the status of blacks in the nation was changing and feared that his children might not be acceptable as Cherokee citizens. He worried that at his death, his three children by Daull might be sold as slaves. He wrote a memorial to the Council explaining how he had lost his first three children (by Clarinda). He was now old "and as the time I may be called on to die is ansertain, my desire

---

[48] W. S. Lovely to Return J. Meigs, June 27, 1803, M-208.
[49] Return J. Meigs interview with Shoe Boot, October 19, 1803, M-208.
[50] Payne Papers, II:32–37.

is to have them [his children] as free Sitizens of this Nation. How can I think of them, having boan of my bone and flesh of my flesh, to be called [mere] property, and this by my imprudent Conduck. And for them and their offspring to suffer for Generations yet unborn is a thought of to[o] great Magnitude for me to remain Silent longer." The Council took pity on the old chief and on November 6, 1824, voted that it had "no objection to recognize their freedom, as well as their inheritance to the Cherokee country; but it is ordered that Shoe Boots cease begetting any more children by this said slave woman."[51] Chulio lived five more years and his black wife claimed later that in that time they had had two more children, twin sons, in 1825. Chulio's sisters, who inherited his large property, also inherited (as slaves) his twin children by Daull; they petitioned the Council in November 1829 to grant freedom and citizenship to the two four-year-old twins (they said nothing about the twins' mother). The National Council, or lower house, was willing to allow this, but the National Committee refused to concur. The boys remained the slaves of Chulio's sisters. Shortly after this, a white man appeared in the nation and claimed that Chulio had given him a deed for all his property. He took the three oldest children by Daull away with him, saying that by state law their black ancestry made them slaves for life no matter what the Council had voted. One boy, John Shoeboot, escaped and returned to the nation. Chulio's sisters brought suit for the return of the other two, but there is no evidence that their release was ever obtained.[52]

Young Wolf belonged in outlook, at least, to the new generation of self-made men. A full blood from the Lower Towns, he may have attended a mission school. In 1814, when he made his will, he wished to be very specific about what would become of the property he had accumulated. The will provides a good insight into the new ethic of the rising generation and its attitude toward slave property:

In the name of God, in men [amen], I, Young Wolf, being in real good sense at this present time, do make my last Will and Testimony, and bequeath and leave [to my] loving daughter, Ann, that Negro Woman nammed Tabb and also, to my loving Son, Dennis, a Negro man named Caesar; also I leve a yearly income for Dennis in the Turnpike Company to get equal shear [share] with the rest of the company and also leave to my loving wife, one year-old heifer and her increase . . . also one mare I let her have. . . . I leave to my son Dennis, my house and plantation and all the farming tools. If any contest should arise after my decease about my property, I leave Charles Hicks, Rattling Gourd, and the Hair to be my Executors . . . and through friendship to Elijah Hicks, I do give my brace of pis-

---

[51] Ibid.
[52] Payne Papers, VII, part 1, 46–49.

tols to him. . . . Also to my mother that raised me, I leave a Black horse, a three year old, which the Crawler has in the Army.[53]

Having disposed of his worldly goods, Young Wolf then offered a homily on success for the edification of his heirs.

By being careful and by [my] own industry, I have gathered a smart chance of property, and my first start was from my herding my brother's cattle. I receiv'd one calf which I took my start from, except my own industry and with [the] cow and calf, which I sold, I bought two sows and thirteen pigs. Some time after, I was able to purchase three mares, and the increase of them is amounted to thirty, more or less, and from that start I gathered money enough to purchase a negro woman named Tabb, also a negro named Caesar. Also I leave my loving daughter, Neecotia, one good sorrel mare and colt.

Young   ×   Wolf
His Mark

Horatio Alger or John D. Rockfeller could not have said it better. Hard work and self-reliance brought a man "a smart chance of property."

This will survived because it was contested by Young Wolf's daughter, Ann. She petitioned the National Council in 1824 to compel her mother, Jenny, to deliver bills of sale to her and her sister that would give legal ownership to them of two slave women that Jenny had permitted to work for her daughters. The Council noted that after Young Wolf's death, his widow managed his farm "with economy and propriety" and by making it "a house of entertainment for travellers" was able to accumulate "considerable money." Young Wolf evidently owed something to the abilities of his wife. Jenny Wolf's profits as an innkeeper and farmer "enabled her to purchase some negroes"; when her two oldest daughters married "and settled off to themselves," she "put into the hands of each of those daughters, a negro woman which she had bought." She intended to give these slaves to her daughters eventually, but only "after getting some of their increase for the benefit of her two youngest daughters which are not yet of age." But the older daughters, who apparently had inherited some of the business acumen of their mother, wanted "bills of sale for those negro women" in order that they might, in the words of the Council, "embrace all their increase." Having paid for the support of the slave, they thought they were entitled to some return. Furthermore, their mother had now remarried and her daughters felt she had less need of the slaves. However, the mother refused to give them up and the Council sided with the mother. It believed that the slaves had been a loan made out of "that ma-

---

[53] Payne Papers, VII, part 1, 59–61.

ternal regard which is peculiar to the trait of a fond mother" and that the daughters were now trying to take unfair advantage of it.[54]

The third illustration of racial diversity indicates the lingering commitment to the older ethic of racial equality. Some time before the Revolution, a black slave named Molly was adopted into the Deer Clan and given the name Chickaune. The adoption occurred because a white trader named Samuel Dent had married a Cherokee woman and, by his ill "usage of her in beating and otherwise mistreating of her when in a state of pregnancy," caused her death. "The Clan or tribe to whom she belonged determined to kill the said white man . . . who to appease them and satisfy said tribe [clan] did then purchase a female slave by the name of molley and brought [said] female unto the Cherokee Nation and did offer her to the Clan's remuneration for the wrongs he had done. A town council and talk was then had at Chota Old Town on Tennessee River and the said female was then and there received by [the] Deer Clan and by the authorities agreeable to the Indian Law and usage in the place of the murdered wife of the said Sam Dent, and has by herself and descendants been ever since recognized by said nation or clan as a Cherokee." Sam Dent was a very devious man however, and before giving her to the Cherokees he had evidently sold Molly to a man named Hightower in Georgia and given him a bill of sale, or so Hightower's daughter claimed in 1833. Molly Hightower, daughter of the claimant, sent agents (slave catchers) into the Cherokee Nation to apprehend Chickaune and her son, Cunestuta (or Isaac Tucker). The case came before the Cherokee Supreme Court, which ruled that the slave, Molly, had become a Cherokee, had always been treated as a Cherokee, and still retained the rights of Cherokee citizenship by virtue of her adoption into the Deer Clan, regardless of her race, complexion, or ancestry. By this same right, her son was also a Cherokee citizen. The agents of Molly Hightower had to return to Georgia without them.[55]

Thus old traditions survived among the burgeoning of new ways. Had the system of clan adoption persisted as an effective means of granting Cherokee citizenship to blacks or whites (the way formalized marriage allowed whites to attain citizenship in the nation), there would have been a simple form of emancipation available. One wonders why Chulio's sisters did not try this to save his last two children? Perhaps the Council no longer recognized the right of clans to adopt blacks? More likely the stigma associated with slavery was so great that the clan would have hesitated to adopt even Chulio's children by a black slave. By 1820 the Cher-

[54] Ibid.
[55] Cherokee Supreme Court Docket, 1823–1835, October [no day], 1832, Tennessee Archives, Nashville.

okees were freely using the term "race" in their laws and court decisions but, like whites, they still had trouble defining what they meant by it.

For example, McKenney, writing to the Secretary of War in 1825, said, "a little time only will be required, so far, at least, as it regards the Cherokees, . . . when the whole tribe will no doubt seek to place themselves under the laws of the States and by that act prepare the process for their extinction as a race."[56] On one level he was referring to the political disappearance of the Cherokee nation; on another, to the disappearance of Cherokee cultural traits; on a third, he meant that biological changes through intermarriage would end their distinction as a people. Essentially McKenney spoke here from the Enlightenment view that there were no significant differences between red and white men—yet in 1825, the problem was commonly spoken of in terms of "their race," "our race," and "the black race." Within another decade or two "the American School of Ethnology" would convince most Americans that the Enlightenment theory of racial homogeneity was wrong.[57] All men were not created biologically equal. There was a clear and ineradicable hierarchy of races with the Caucasian at the top and the Anglo-Saxon at the head of the varieties of Caucasians. The "Ethiopian race" was at the bottom. The "American race" (the Indian) was somewhere in between but rapidly dying out in its unequal competition with the superior race that was overrunning it.

In 1825, the strongest nationalist leaders among the Cherokees still held fervently to the old Washingtonian policy of Cherokee integration into the republic as soon as they reached a state of civilization equal to that of whites. In March of that year, John Ross, Charles Hicks, and George Lowrey told John Quincy Adams, the last of the Presidents to uphold the original Indian policy, that "the Cherokee, if permitted to remain peaceably and quietly in the enjoyment of their rights [on their ancestral land], the day would arrive when a distinction between their race and the American family would be imperceptible; of such change the nation can have no objection. Complexion is a subject not worthy of consideration in the effectuation of the great object—for the sake of civilization and the preservation of existence, we would willingly see the habits and customs of the aboriginal man extinguished, the sooner this takes place the [sooner] the great stumbling block, prejudice, will be removed."[58]

[56] Thomas L. McKenney to George Barbour, December 13, 1825, M-21, reel 2, pp. 298–305.

[57] For extended discussions of the development of racism in America see William Stanton, *The Leopard's Spots* (Chicago: University of Chicago Press, 1960) and George Fredrickson, *Black Image on the White Mind* (New York: Harper & Row, 1971) and Reginald Horsman, *Race and Manifest Destiny* (Cambridge: Harvard University Press, 1980).

[58] Cherokee delegation to John Quincy Adams, March 12, 1825, M-234, reel 71, #0518.

Return J. Meigs, who lived through the era of Cherokee revitalization, sensed another important aspect of the search for equality. The quality that he spoke of as "national pride" was at heart the Cherokees' rejection of their racial inferiority. Meigs blamed frontier whites for having created that sense of inferiority. "We find the Indian has also his prejudices" against whites, sometimes speaking of them as a separately created and distinctly different race. "But it does not arise from pride as ours [our prejudice] does, it arises in the Indian from his humble conception of himself and of his race, from the discovery he makes that we look down on him as an inferior being, has a tendency to make him despise himself as the offspring of an inferior race of beings. . . . These things are serious difficulties."[59] Meigs and most other government officials, no matter how well disposed, had seldom treated the Indians as equals. Caught in the tangled web of federal-state relations and the politics of east versus west, federal officials had usually adopted a smug paternalism toward them. The chief avenue left through which the Cherokees could regain self-respect became the creation of a strong national spirit of defiant independence.

One other source of self-respect opened for the Cherokees in the 1820s, although they were slow to take it. This was the spiritual power contained in Christianity, once it was divested of its stigma as "the white man's religion." If the two peoples had the same Great Spirit and if his ways of communicating with Cherokees (through their old ceremonies) had weakened, perhaps it was possible through Christianity to regain a connection with the infinite power that controlled the universe. Perhaps the white missionaries could show them a new way through which to restore that harmony between their people, their destiny, and the will of the Great Spirit whom the white men called "God." The tremendous influx of missionaries from a wide variety of denominations after 1819 opened up new possibilities for Cherokee revitalization and gave a new thrust to their renascence.

[59] Return J. Meigs to Samuel Trott, August 3, 1817, M-208.

SEVENTEEN

SEQUOYAH AND THE CHRISTIANS,

1819–1827

The Cherokees seem peculiarly partial to Guess's plan of writing. They can generally learn it in one day and in a week become writing masters and transact their business and communicate their thoughts freely and fully on religious or political subjects by writing. —The Reverend Daniel S. Butrick, February 22, 1825

Two powerful new sources of revitalization came to the Cherokees after 1820: the invention by Sequoyah of an easy way to write their own language and the spiritual message of Christianity carried to every part of the nation by dedicated preachers—some of them Cherokees. These two forces, one nationalistic and one transcending nationalism, seemed to many observers to be working in opposite directions—one moving the Cherokees back toward the old ways, the other moving them toward a revolutionary new way. But in important respects they were not competitive but complementary. Sequoyah's invention provided a new means of a self-expression among the Cherokee-speaking full-blood majority, giving them a sense of power and a stimulus to self-expression they had lacked; it helped them tremendously in overcoming feelings of inferiority and self-doubt, making them the equals of those Cherokees who had learned to speak and write English. Sequoyah's discovery played a major role in the populist movement leading up to White Path's Rebellion in 1827, when the more conservative Cherokees vigorously expressed their opposition to the speed and extent of acculturation that their leaders were forcing upon them.

Christianity offered a message of hope and personal rebirth to match their national rebirth. It opened to every individual the possibility of wiping a bad slate clean and starting over totally fresh. Christian preachers told the beleaguered and disheartened to pray to the Great Spirit and he would give them justice and courage in their struggles, personal and national. Christian theology taught that all men are spiritually equal, that all have unrealized potential, and that God will help them to achieve it. The Great Spirit gives his strength to those who feel weak, frustrated, poor, and despised. Some Cherokees realized that Christianity was not simply the white man's religion but that its true adherents constituted a chosen people regardless of their race or nation. By providing the despondent with a sense of self-worth, hope, and new possibilities, Christianity offered an important spiritual counterpart to the secular revitalization of the nationalist chiefs. The missionaries did not always preach it this way, but they brought a power beyond themselves. Pride in Sequoyah's accomplishments and the power of self-expression it gave the Cherokees matched the pride of the Christian convert at having conquered his own inner fear, his tendency to despair and self-destruction that had led some to alcoholism. Both movements seemed to provide a means of asserting greater control over themselves and their future.

Yet both movements were double-edged. Christianity threatened to divide the nation into Christian and pagan parties. Sequoyah's syllabary threatened to undermine the whole civilization program. The division between the full bloods who spoke no English and the mixed blood who spoke no Cherokee was heightened. This same division corresponded to a regional division, a class division, and a division between those who were slaveholders and those who were not. Whether the Sequoyan syllabary and the rapid spread of Christian mission activities in the 1820s would add to the cohesion of the nation or finally split it irrevocably troubled everyone.

Sequoyah's discovery of a way to write the Cherokee language in 1821–1822 was both a great impediment to missionary activity and, indirectly, a great advantage. It took the Cherokees several years before they could accept the fact that one of their own people, a Cherokee who neither spoke, read, nor wrote English, had mastered the skill that they had always assumed the Creator gave only to the white man. Some had heard that Sequoyah was at work on such a scheme and believed he must be practicing witchcraft because he was preparing to tear down a wall that the Great Spirit had from their creation placed between his white and red children. But Sequoyah was convinced that the white man had discovered the art of writing for himself and what the white man could discover for his language, the red man could discover for his.[1] Through many years of trial and error, starting first with the impossible task of designing a pictograph for every word, Sequoyah finally discovered that he could divide

---

[1] For Sequoyah's life see Grant Foreman, *Sequoyah* (Norman: University of Oklahoma, 1938); for Sequoyah's syllabary see the writings of Jack F. Kilpatrick and *New Echota Letters*, ed. Jack F. Kilpatrick and Anna Gritts Kilpatrick (Dallas: Southern Methodist University Press, 1968). Also Emmet Starr, *Early History of the Cherokees Embracing Aboriginal Customs, Religion, Laws, Folk Lore and Civilization* (Claremore, Okla.: n.p., 1917), pp. 45–55.

the Cherokee language into eighty-six syllables. He designed a symbol for each. Simply by memorizing these, anyone who could speak Cherokee could write it, whether young or old.[2]

Sequoyah's father was a white man, probably Nathaniel Gist of Virginia, who lived for several years among the Cherokees prior to the American Revolution. Sequoyah's mother called him George Gess or Guess. The liaison with Gist was temporary and Sequoyah was not raised by his father. He grew up among the full bloods in the Lower Towns, became a silversmith and blacksmith, fought well in the Creek War and, in 1819–1822, was involved in the conspiracy to sell the Lower Town area. He went to Arkansas in 1821–1822, where he probably completed his invention. Returning to the old nation, he convinced the Cherokees there that he had truly reduced their language to writing. Then he went back to live permanently in the west. When the Council finally acknowledged what he had achieved, it voted in 1824 to have a medal struck in his honor and sent him $500 in cash.[3] But the Council did not vote to adopt his form of writing as the official language of the nation; to do so would have thrown doubts on the Cherokees' commitment to civilization and eventual incorporation into white America. Whites would have interpreted such a decision as regressive—an effort to put a cultural barrier between red and white Americans. Nonetheless, for the full bloods it was a tremendous boost to nationalism and separatism. The Council did translate its laws into the Sequoyan syllabary so that the full bloods could read them and occasionally official documents were printed in that form once the nation obtained a printing press in 1828 with a font of Sequoyan type. But English always remained the official language of the nation, though only about 15 percent of the nation spoke it in 1830 and less than 10 percent could write it.

Sequoyah's system was not perfect. It lacked a means of punctuation; the symbols were complicated and easily distorted; vagaries in pronunciation (perhaps left over from the time when the nation had three or more distinct dialects) made it difficult to translate. Nonetheless, thousands of Cherokees were soon writing notes and letters to each other in Sequoyah's syllables. Written Cherokee was called "Sequoyan." "Letters in Cherokee are passing in all directions," and nothing is in "so great demand as pens, ink, and paper," wrote one missionary in January 1825.[4]

---

[2] On the difficulties of translating in the Sequoyan syllabary see Kilpatrick and Kilpatrick, eds., *New Echota Letters.*

[3] Accompanying the cash and medal were a tribute to "the great benefits of your incomparable system" that "will also serve as an index for other aboriginal tribes or nations similarly to advance in science and respectability." Its benefits "cannot be fully estimated." Payne Papers, VII, part 2, 172–73.

[4] Isaac Proctor to Jeremiah Evarts, January 25, 1825, ABCFM.

"The knowledge of Mr. Guess's Alphabet is spreading through the nation like fire among the leaves," wrote another.[5] By October 1824, the Reverend William Chamberlain of the American Board told his superiors in Boston that "a great part of the Cherokees can read and write in their own language."[6]

There was not universal pleasure among the missionaries at this. "All the scholars, as well as all the neighborhood, have become conversant with the new mode of writing," said the Reverend Isaac Proctor in 1825, and "this, no doubt, more than anything else has operated against English schools."[7] The Cherokees preferred to write in their own language rather than spending the time it took to learn English. What need was there to attend a mission school when one could easily learn to write at home? "Mr. Hicks, I am informed, thinks it will at least be the means of increasing a desire for learning among the lower class and ultimately bring more of them to a knowledge of English literature," wrote Ard Hoyt in December 1824. But who could tell. It was tremendously exhilarating to be able to express one's thoughts in one's own language and much easier than doing so in that of another people. "The Cherokees seem peculiarly partial to Guess's plan of writing," said the American Board missionary, Daniel Butrick, in February 1825. "They can generally learn it in one day and in a week become writing masters and transact their business and communicate their thoughts freely and fully on religious and political subjects by writing. They will doubtless be generally acquainted with this plan of reading and writing in the course of one year."[8] According to the prevailing standards of ethnology, they had crossed the great dividing line between a primitive (pre-literate) and a civilized (literate) society. By 1825 the majority of the Cherokees could read and write.

Although almost everyone praised Sequoyah for his great accomplishment, few whites made any effort to learn it or promote it. To write it one first had to learn Cherokee and neither the agents nor the missionaries thought this worthwhile. As the Moravian, the Reverend John Gambold, said, all schools in the Cherokee Nation should continue to teach only in English: "It is indispensably necessary for their preservation that they should learn our Language and adopt our Laws and Holy Religion. . . . The study of their language would in a great measure prove but time and labor lost. . . . it seems desirable that their Language, Customs, Manner

---

[5] William Chamberlain's Journal, October 22, 1824, ABCFM. Probably not more than two-thirds of the Cherokees learned to read and write in Sequoyah's syllabary.

[6] Ibid; see also Perdue, *Slavery and Cherokee Society*, p. 60.

[7] Isaac Proctor to Jeremiah Evarts, July 20, 1825, ABCFM.

[8] Daniel Butrick's Journal, February 22, 1823, ABCFM.

of Thinking etc. should be forgotten."[9] Some missionaries, however, like Samuel A. Worcester (nephew of Dr. Worcester) among the Congregationalists and Evan Jones among the Baptists did take the trouble to learn Cherokee and encouraged the use of the syllabary because they believed that it was the quickest way to spread Christianity. They made efforts to translate the Bible into Sequoyan. But it did not seem to bother most missionaries that their denigration of the Cherokee language and culture tended to make the full-blood children ashamed of their heritage and their parents and at the same time made the mixed bloods proud of their distinction from the "backward" members of their nation. Traditionally, shame and ridicule were the strongest means of expressing social disapproval among the Cherokees. In this case the work of the missionaries backfired.

In 1817 there were only two mission schools in the Cherokee Nation, that of the Moravians at Springplace, Georgia, and that of the Congregationalists (or Presbyterians of the American Board) at Chickamauga (Brainerd), Tennessee.[10] The Moravians were teaching thirteen students; the Congregationalists thirty-eight.[11] This constituted less than 2 percent of the school-age children.[12] Over the next two years, while the removal crisis worked itself out, no new schools were started. But in 1819 the Congregationalists founded a second school at Taloney (which they named Carmel) and a third school (with the help of a young Cherokee convert, Catherine Brown) at Creek Path.[13] The Baptist Foreign Mission Board (then in Philadelphia, later in Boston) founded a school at Valley Towns in 1819 and a second at Tinsawattee in 1821.[14] The Moravians

[9] John Gambold to Thomas McKenney, August 30, 1824, MAS.

[10] Under a Plan of Union between the Presbyterians and Congregationalists adopted in 1801, the two denominations agreed to permit church members on the frontier to adopt either a congregational or presbyterian polity. In most cases, even frontier people from Congregationalist backgrounds chose Presbyterianism. Churches with Congregationalist members who chose to identify themselves as Presbyterians were popularly known as "Presbygationalist." Congregationalist missionaries to the Cherokees joined Presbyterian Synods and their mission churches were technically Presbyterian. See Williston Walker, *A History of the Congregational Churches in the United States* (New York: The Christian Literature Co. 1897).

[11] John Gambold to Return J. Meigs, June 22, 1816, M-208, and Return J. Meigs to Samuel Trott, August 3, 1817, M-208.

[12] Return J. Meigs to Thomas McKenney, August 25, 1817, M-208; in this letter Meigs estimates the total Cherokee population in the east as 13,000 and says that perhaps 1,500 were of school age. The number of school-age children was probably two or three times that. Mission schools accepted students from five to sixteen years of age and sometimes older.

[13] Daniel Butrick to Return J. Meigs, June 19, 1820, M-208; Walker, *Torchlights*, pp. 69, 136.

[14] For a discussion of the Baptist and other early mission schools in the Cherokee Nation see McLoughlin, *Cherokees and Missionaries*.

started a second school at Oothcalogy, the town of Major Ridge, in 1821.[15] Missionary schools tended to be founded in response to local requests for them rather than according to any prearranged plan. The Moravians and Baptists never had more than two schools, but the Congregationalists continued to expand throughout the decade with schools and mission centers at Etowah (Hightower) 1823, Haweis (Turnip Mountain) 1823, Willstown (1832), Candy's Creek (1824), New Echota (1827), Amohee (1831), Red Clay (1835), and Running Water (1835). In 1822 the Methodists sent itinerant preachers to the nation and began their first school at Richard Riley's farm. Thereafter the Methodists began a system of "itinerant schools," taught for six months at a time by their circuit riders at different places along their circuits. By 1831, when the Methodists reached their peak of activity in the nation, they had seven circuits, eleven circuit riders, and six schools.

In 1828–1832, when the mission movement was at its height, all of the schools of all of the denominations probably were teaching no more than 200 to 250 of the school-age children in the nation. Moreover, school teaching proved expensive and difficult and after 1827 the mission boards demanded that more emphasis be placed on preaching than on teaching, a request the missionaries welcomed.

Because the Methodist schools were not housed in permanent buildings, they received no assistance from the fund that Congress had established in 1819 to support education among the Indians. The Education Fund was an appropriation of $10,000 annually that the Secretary of War divided up among the missionary agencies in all of the Indian nations in the United States to support schools; the bulk of this money went to the American Board of Commissioners for Foreign Missions. The Cherokee Nation received a larger proportion of this fund than any other tribe. The Georgia legislature protested against the fund in 1823 and demanded its suspension because it tended to create a permanent establishment of the Indians on its soil. However, the Congressional committee established to investigate Georgia's protest voted to sustain the fund as a benefit to the Indians and to the furtherance of the policy of civilization and integration (or incorporation).[16] The Education Fund did not provide any support, in theory, for the religious work of evangelization among the Indians that was the primary function of the missionary societies. Hence the largest proportion of missionary budgets had to be supplied by donations from the members of their churches or from local and state missionary societies organized for fund raising. To stimulate fund raising, all denomina-

---

[15] See Schwarze, *History of Moravian Missions*, pp. 156–62.
[16] ASP II, 458.

tions founded missionary journals (monthly or quarterly) and newspapers, which published reports on every mission station. Of prime importance to the subscribers were the educational progress of the Indians and their conversion to Christianity (through the founding of Indian mission churches). Statistical measurement of mission progress inevitably placed a premium on head counting—the number of children in school, the number of missionary assistants, exhorters, preachers. Only the American Board provided a seminary (in Cornwall, Connecticut) where pious natives of various nations around the world could be sent by missionaries of the Board to obtain advanced theological training to prepare themselves to become ministers to their people. The Moravians sent some of their best students to this school as well. But the Methodists and Baptists did not believe that a "learned ministry" was essential to preaching the gospel. They ordained converts who passed only minimal tests of doctrinal learning but who showed sincere and earnest faith, dedication, and preaching talent. Hence they produced more Cherokee preachers and exhorters than the other three denominations and they reaped the largest harvests in conversions.

The old debate about whether Christianization should precede education or vice versa in Indian missions had long since been resolved by doing both together. Missionaries preached to adults at their mission compounds or at various "preaching stations" around the nation and at the same time conducted schools where the young were inculcated with Christian doctrines along with their reading, writing, and arithmetic. It proved to be a much longer and harder job than most missionary boards had expected to Christianize even as "advanced" a people as the Cherokees. There were several obstacles quite apart from raising the necessary funds to send dedicated young white men and women to establish and maintain the missions. In the first place, none of the missionaries could speak Cherokee and very few of them ever learned to do so. Second, the Cherokees were more interested in having their children learn reading, writing, and arithmetic than in trying to understand (through very crude translation) the complex doctrines and dogmas of the Christian religion. Third, it took Cherokee children much longer (four to five years) to learn to read and write English than either their parents or the missionaries imagined it would and this caused great discouragement. In addition, there were the inevitable fears among many Cherokees that the missionaries were trying to take their land or had other ulterior motives; there were frictions with particular missionaries who did not hide their disdain for Cherokee manners or beliefs; and there were certain conflicts within the missions or between the missionaries and their mission boards over the best methods to be followed in their work.

Although the missionaries of some denominations did their best to hide the fact that Christians were divided into dozens of different denominations, each with its own doctrinal or ceremonial peculiarities, others flaunted the peculiarities of their denomination, hailing them as the only true doctrines or rituals and brazenly competing to win as many Cherokees as possible to their own ranks (not even scrupling to take them away from other mission churches). One of the principal reasons for the major shift in emphasis from teaching to preaching in the Cherokee Nation after 1824 was due to the highly competitive struggle for converts among the denominations. Another was that teaching was more expensive and the results were harder to document. New baptisms or admissions to churches were far more inspiring to mission donors than the number of Cherokee children who had advanced from Webster's spelling book no. 2 to spelling book no. 3. This ambition to provide statistical evidence of success and thus sustain donations contributed in the end to a reaction among the Cherokees to the more aggressive tactics of the missionaries.

At first almost all Cherokees welcomed missionaries because they thought of them as teachers of the white man's skills rather than as proselytizers for the white man's religion. Although full-blood parents sent their children to mission schools, they told the missionaries that "christianity was necessary for white people only," and that "there was nothing in [the Christian] religion, at least, that the indians could get to heaven without it."[17] If Charles Hicks wished to join the Moravian mission church, which he did in 1813, that was his private business, but it meant nothing to the nation that its Second Principal Chief had become a Christian. (Some did complain, Hicks later said, "that I was more mindful of Prayer meetings than [of] my National duties.")[18] Between 1801, when the Moravians started their mission, and 1819 they made only one other convert besides Hicks, the widow of James Vann (in 1810). In 1819, however, the Moravians were overjoyed to find that seven persons decided to join their church at Springplace. Moravian conversions continued to grow slowly but by 1830 had reached a total of only forty-five for a generation of mission work. Most of these were the parents or relatives of students who had attended their school and two-thirds of these converts were of mixed ancestry.[19] The Moravians, however, were the least aggressive of the four denominations at work among the Cherokees and never really gave up their primary emphasis on schooling and example rather than preaching. They never, for instance, sent itinerant preachers through the nation. In order to hear the Moravians preach, the Cherokees

[17] Report of the Visiting Committee, May 29, 1818, ABCFM.
[18] Charles Hicks to John Gambold, April 13, 1819, MAS.
[19] Schwarze, *History of Moravian Missions*, pp. 124–33.

had to come to their mission stations. Their church members tended to be the well-to-do who lived in the vicinity of their missions and who had concluded that belief in the Christian view of the Great Spirit was a comforting assurance that they were doing right and would obtain their rewards.

Most Cherokees, like Pathkiller, initially viewed the missionaries as benevolent white man who had come out of the goodness of their hearts to help them and their children. "It was evidence of great love," Pathkiller told the missionaries at Brainerd in 1819, "to be willing to teach and feed so many children without pay."[20] They had found that other white men demanded pay for everything they did. The missionaries, on the other hand, were pleased to find that so many Cherokees welcomed them and that they were not only more acculturated than they had expected but eager to send their children to school. Brainerd, the first American Board school, was almost overwhelmed by 119 students in 1820 and had to struggle to accept them all.

The missionaries at first supposed that the Cherokees had no organized religion of their own. They could see no regular body of priests conducting weekly services, no sacred places of worship, no rituals of regular devotion to any deity, no statues or religious idols of any kind—in short, no institutionalized religious system. One missionary told his mission board after he had been in the nation a few weeks that it was going to be a lot easier to convert the Cherokees than the Hindus or Buddhists in India because "they have not a system of false religion handed down . . . which must be overturned."[21] Even when the missionaries made inquiries through interpreters about the beliefs of the Cherokees, they could find no systematic theology behind the Indians' conceptions of the supernatural. "It is impossible to obtain any tolerable understanding of the Cherokee religion," wrote one of the Congregationalists; "I suspect . . . there was nothing among them which would be called a system of religious beliefs," or if there ever had been, he thought it had long since disappeared.[22] When they consulted sympathetic interpreters about translating the Bible and other Christian writing for their sermons or class lessons, they discovered that the Cherokee language had no words for heaven, hell, devil, grace, soul, guilt, repentance, forgiveness, conversion, salvation, evil, or sin—concepts that seemed so basic to human thought to the missionaries that their absence signified an almost subhuman ignorance. Hence the frequent missionary references to "heathen darkness," "benighted savagery," or "unenlightened paganism." One

---

[20] Brainerd Journal, January 1, 1819, ABCFM; Walker, *Torchlights*, pp. 90–92.

[21] Brainerd Journal, April 9, 1818, ABCFM.

[22] David Green, Report on Brainerd Mission, 1818–1828, dated "April, 1828," ABCFM.

Cherokee shocked a missionary by saying that Cherokees "had no expectation of anything after death, that they seldom or never bestowed any thoughts on these things, that they were not conscious of having done, said, or thought anything that was wrong or sinful."[23] The concept of afterlife to a Cherokee, insofar as they had any, according to one Cherokee, was "that in the other world they shall live in the same manner in which they live here—that they shall find there the same pleasures which they enjoy on earth; that they shall attend ball-plays and all-night dances and find various amusements in which here they take delight."[24] The distance between this world and the next was slight to the Cherokees. The spirits constantly moved back and forth and so did the dead—in dreams and visions their ancestors often came back to talk with them and they could find spiritual omens everywhere to guide or warn them. The function of their adonisgi (priests, conjurors, medicine men) was to keep in touch with these various spirits and to learn from them how to help their people. Their incantations were secret and it took some time before the missionaries learned anything about them. "The Great Spirit" merged with other spirits and took many forms, but after over a century of close contact with whites, the Cherokees understood the notion of a Creator. On the other hand, they did not always give the Creator male gender. The Great Spirit had female as well as male attributes and the earth was their Mother. The Sun was a woman and the moon her brother. One Cherokee woman, being asked her conception of God by a missionary in 1818, said "she thought there was somewhere above a good man and woman who would make people happy."[25]

The advent of numerous missionaries during the Cherokee renascence was particularly appealing to those in favor of rapid acculturation—the ambitious, the mixed bloods, the ardent nationalists. The evangelical Protestants' dynamic view of human history and their optimism about social progress made more sense to the rising generation of Cherokees than did the static world view of their own religion. Christians provided answers to their questions about human behavior and social ideals that were of practical help to these Cherokees in coping with the changes in their own lives and in providing hope in their struggle for achievement and recognition against heavy odds. White men knew things about nature that they did not know, such as how to immunize people against smallpox and how to make steam engines. "The Great Book" was not only a guide to spiritual and moral truth but the key to the white man's success in conquering so many natural obstacles—giving him the convic-

---

[23] Brainerd Journal, July 26, 1818, ABCFM.
[24] Walker, *Torchlights*, p. 27.
[25] Brainerd Journal, January 28, 1818, ABCFM.

tion that he was in control of nature and not vice versa. By adding the power of white man's religious vision and zeal to their own efforts, the believers in Cherokee revitalization believed that they had found the final key to success. Now the full scope of the white man's wisdom and power could be theirs.

The "progressive" Cherokees also shared the missionaries' view that the "backward" people of their nation needed enlightenment and improvement, both morally and intellectually. The missionaries wanted to begin by teaching the children of influential Cherokee leaders and it came as no surprise that many of these were of mixed ancestry. The missionaries also found that such students were the most persistent in keeping at their lessons, the fastest to learn, and the most eager to gain approval. Not only had their parents given them better preparation for school (speaking English in the home, encouraging them to learn their letters) but they had also given them more encouragement in school and had shown them in their own lives how advantageous it was to master the skills of the white man.

All the missionaries agreed that Cherokee children were quick and intelligent. "The general capacity of the Indian children," said Ard Hoyt after two years of teaching, "and their aptness to learn, we think is not inferior to the whites."[26] The Reverend Thomas Roberts, who taught mostly full-blood children at the Baptist school in Valley Towns, North Carolina, felt the same way: "The Cherokee children learn as fast as any Children I ever saw. They are kind, obedient, and industrious" and their "mental powers appear to be in no respect inferior to those of whites."[27] Nevertheless, almost all missionary teachers agreed that after the first month or two, the full bloods began to feel frustrated and disappointed. They asked to go home. They and their parents were discouraged at how hard it was to learn English and how long it seemed to take.

Consequently the missionaries had a disproportionately high number of mixed-blood students. "The Cherokees generally, but especially the halfbreeds, seem anxious to have their children educated," said Hoyt.[28] The Reverend Isaac Proctor, who taught at the Congregationalist mission in Etowah, noted that his school was "made up of children of half and quarter Cherokee and the children of white men with native wives."[29] The full-blood children generally seemed to be at the bottom of the class.

[26] Ard Hoyt to John Calhoun, Annual Report of Brainerd Mission, February 6, 1820, M-221, reel 85, #3323.

[27] *Baptist Christian Watchman*, March 9, 1822; see also *Latter Day Luminary*, January 8, 1822.

[28] Ard Hoyt to S. A. Worcester, September 25, 1818, ABCFM.

[29] Isaac Proctor to Jeremiah Evarts, July 28, 1827, ABCFM.

The mission schools that were established as model farms (Springplace, Brainerd, Valley Towns) devoted part of their curriculum to training Cherokee boys to be farmers and Cherokee girls to be farmers' wives. The children of wealthier, mixed-blood families had already learned much about farming before they entered school at eight or nine. Mixed-blood Cherokee girls, many of whom entered school at eleven or twelve, had already learned how to sew, cook, mend, and perform other household tasks. The table manners of the mixed-bloods were better. Because the Lancastrian method of teaching was used in almost all mission schools, the older or more advanced children taught the younger or slower children. Invariably the mixed-blood children became teachers to the full bloods.

Social differentiation gradually merged into difference in skin color. The children became painfully conscious that the students of white or mixed-blood parents were much more successful in mastering school lessons than children of full-blood parents. A kind of paternalism or patronizing attitude developed. When missionary teachers chose a pupil to set an example of correct writing, spelling, or arithmetic, the lighter-skinned pupils were always selected. When a missionary teacher asked a pupil to write a letter to a patron of the mission (in New York or Boston), explaining the progress the children were making, they might say: "I think you will be pleased to sit in our school room and see us attend our studies; you would see some tawny girls and some who are white as any children."[30] Without realizing what she was saying, even a mixed blood might express her sense of inferiority toward the white children of the missionaries in her classes: "When Miss Ames [the teacher] tells the two white girls they have done well, we [Cherokees] often say that they can do well because they are white girls." Sometimes the teacher asked a student to write about the progress of the Cherokee Nation. When she did, she might get an essay like this:

The unenlightened parts of this nation assemble for dances around a fire. Every year when the green corn, beans, etc. are large enough to eat, they dance all night and torture themselves by scratching their bodies with snake teeth before they will eat. . . . Their dishes are made by themselves of clay. . . . Many about this [mission] station are more civilized . . . and appear as well as white people.

Or:

I think that you would be pleased to hear about the improvement of the Cherokees. Many of them have large plantations and [the] greater part of them keep a

---

[30] This and the other letters from mission children cited below in Payne Papers, VIII:9-61.

number of Cattle and some have large buildings, but some live miserably; they
don't send their children to school and don't care any thing about the Sabbath.

Always the measure of perfection was the white person; the closer one
was in skin color, the closer it seemed one was to meeting that norm. The
full-blood child always had far to go and could never really catch up.

These differences in learning skills and social status were further ac-
centuated by the sermons and lectures that the missionaries required the
students to hear when they attended church services. Because the Christian religion was taught as the only true religion, all that the Cherokee
traditionalists believed was not only erroneous or false religion but "su-
perstitious," "primitive," "savage," and "benighted." All the religious
festivals, dances, and rituals were "unclean" or "polluted" customs. So
too were the medical practices of their medicine men. Daniel Butrick reported that his congregation was "very much disaffected on account of
sermons I preached on Conjuring, rain-making, etc.," but he felt obliged
nonetheless to warn them "of the folly of those heathenish practises,"
which were leading them down to hell.[31] The Reverend Isaac Proctor
preached against a medicine man named "Zacharias the aged," because he
"has lately tried to make it rain and to cure a member of the church by
conjuration. I laid before him his guilt and sin," and of course the others
in the congregation heard.[32]

Students at mission schools were forbidden to attend ball plays for fear
that they would be corrupted by the drinking, gambling and coarse language they might hear and because the players were "practically naked"
while they played. One student who was taken from school by her parents and brought back to live in a remote Lower Town wrote back to her
teachers and fellow students: "I am here amongst a wicked set of people.
. . . When I think of the poor thoughtless Cherokees going on in sin, I
cannot help blessing God that he has led me in the right path to serve
him."[33] Proctor worried about what would happen to the students from
his school when they returned home: "Can we rationally expect, Dear
Sir," he wrote to the mission board, "youths after being tolerably well
educated, would stem the current of iniquity that would come in upon
them on returning to their heathenish parents? Can they adhere to the
moral instructions given them and remain chaste and virtuous when they
would daily be obliged to hear the most impure, the most obscene con-
versations and witness the most polluting customs?"[34]

[31] Daniel Butrick to Jeremiah Evarts, May 6, 1828, ABCFM.
[32] Isaac Proctor to Jeremiah Evarts, May 10, 1827, ABCFM.
[33] Rufus K. Anderson, ed., *Memoir of Catherine Brown* (Boston, 1828), p. 39; Walker,
Torchlights, p. 181.
[34] Isaac Proctor to Jeremiah Evarts, July 28, 1827, ABCFM.

SEQUOYAH AND THE CHRISTIANS

Few of the missionaries appeared to realize the kind of social divisions they were promoting among the Cherokees. To them it was simply a matter of right and wrong, the moral and the immoral ways to think and behave. When the Reverend Daniel Butrick tried to point this out to his colleagues, he only revealed something of his own patronizing approach toward "uplifting" the "ignorant."

[I] think much of the situation of this dear people. There is a very great difference between the highest and the lowest class. The most enlightened scarcely know the depths of ignorance in which the great body of these people live nor how to get down to them so as to raise them. . . . This is the case also with many, if not most, missionaries. They will not come down far enough to take hold even of their blankets to lift them out of this horrible pit. They think they must equal [in living comfort] if not surpass the first class of Cherokees, and thus fix their marks entirely beyond the reach of all the common Indians. . . . In this way, unless peculiar caution is used, two parties will be formed which will probably be called, though falsely, the Christian and Pagan party.[35]

Butrick's prediction was all too accurate. The split between those favoring rapid acculturation and missionary expansion and those favoring retention of the old ways did produce an uprising in 1827 that reflected antimission sentiment in many aspects. Butrick was also right in saying that to label the two parties in the rebellion "Christian" and "Pagan" was inaccurate. As he tried to point out, the issue at stake was the resentment of the poorer and full-blood Cherokees against "the pride and superiority" of the rich and mixed-blood Cherokees. The missionaries did much to contribute to that resentment. Butrick also pointed out that if the mixed-blood chiefs who dominated so much of the nation's affairs "determine to support us" in such a confrontation, "they would very probably lose their authority," for the full bloods vastly outnumbered those of mixed ancestry and held the majority in the Council.

Of the four denominations that tried to spread Christianity through the nation in the 1820s, the Moravians were the least successful and the Methodists the most. As of January 1830, the United Brethren (Moravian) mission churches had 45 members; the Baptist mission churches, 90; the Congregational/Presbyterian mission churches, 167; and the Methodist mission churches, 736.[36] The missionaries did their best at the outset to play down denominational differences, but the Cherokees were quick to sense them. The missionaries were not as different in theology (the Congregationalists and Baptists were more Calvinistic, the Moravians and Methodists more Arminian) as in their religious style and in the

---

[35] Daniel Butrick's Journal, November 4, 1824, ABCFM.
[36] See *Cherokee Phoenix*, January 1, 1830 [actually 1831].

demands they placed upon those who wished to become members. The Moravians had the most strict requirements, the Methodists, the least strict. The Baptists and Congregationalists were closer to the Moravians in this respect. Strictness meant, in part, the requirements of a religious experience of salvation that the convert could describe as a work of grace by the Holy Spirit, transforming his or her heart (or soul) from sinful enmity toward God to wholehearted submission to God. It also meant a sound knowledge of the doctrinal tenets of the denomination, regular attendance at church and prayer meetings, and exemplary moral deportment. Beyond that, it meant the willingness to renounce totally all "polluting pagan customs," thereby cutting the convert off from the most basic aspects of tribal community. Even the town councils were steeped in rituals. Ball plays were forbidden, as they were to mission students, to adult Christians. To join a Methodist society (which the Methodists considered "turning toward" Christianity), the Cherokees had only to express a sincere desire to become a Christian and submit to Christian teaching.

Other factors were involved in the choices Cherokees made among the denominations. The Methodist preachers were more democratic, younger, and some of them were married to Cherokees. They had no large mission establishments but rode from village to village on horseback, sleeping in the cabins of the Cherokees, sharing their food, treating them as equals.

The other three denominations were more aloof and paternalistic. They stood apart from the Indian and sought to make him lift himself up to their level of religious and social behavior. They were slower to admit him to church and quicker to cast him out if he was guilty of some relapse into paganism or moral fault.

Joining a mission church was not the only way to appropriate the spiritual power of Christianity. Many Cherokees who were attracted to the new religion adapted it to their own needs in their own ways. They created a Cherokee form of Christianity rather than conforming to the white man's version of Christianity. Little of this was evident in the 1820s because of the tensions that developed between missionaries and traditionalists and because the Cherokees' attention was focused so strongly upon the secular reformation taking place in their social order. After 1830, however, when the missionaries began to back off, a new kind of Christianization took place under the preaching of Cherokee converts who, in their own language and style, spoke of what Christianity could mean in their lives on their terms. The work of the native ministry was not connected with specific doctrines or creeds and did not necessarily lead to church membership. The native exhorters were not, for the most part, ordained by any denomination and therefore could not administer baptism, communion, marriage, and the other rituals of denominational church life. But in the long run they were able to do more than white missionaries for the Cherokees who needed a different vision of the world and they were able to speak of this from their own experience as Cherokees. From these native preachers and from other converts, the Cherokees learned how Christianity could be a source of help and power that did not make them feel inferior to whites and that did not compel them to become just like whites. It united Cherokees and white Christians in the brotherhood of a transdenominational and interracial spiritual community. Through it they found a new order, meaning, and direction in their lives.

At this level of renewal or rebirth, Christianity became part of the Cherokee renascence. The miracle of restored unity with the Great Spirit could then combine with the miracle Sequoyah provided of written self-expression to provide them with a holistic new identity: faith within themselves and in a power beyond themselves. Thereafter the Cherokee renascence combined the secular revitalization of their nationalistic thrust and the spiritual revitalization of their religious renovation. The old religion did not die, but it began to adapt itself to new understandings of the sources of spiritual power that guided the universe and gave it meaning. The Cherokees slowly learned how to be part of the community of a wider world and yet how to see their particular ethnic destiny within it.

One way in which Christianity could be used to support nationalism was demonstrated in 1832 when the Principal Chief gave a secular sermon on a fast day he had proclaimed for the nation. In this talk he urged the Cherokees to appeal to God (or the Great Spirit) for help as a nation and drew an analogy between Satan's persecution of Job and Andew Jackson's unjust persecution of the Cherokees.[37]

Although revitalization brought a sense of tribal self-confidence, it also produced differences on internal policies. A dramatic debate began in 1824 over the necessity for further acculturation.

[37] See McLoughlin, *Cherokees and Missionaries*, pp. 338–40.

EIGHTEEN

TOO MUCH ACCULTURATION,

1824–1828

The arts of civilized life [have] been successfully introduced among [us]; [we] consider ourselves permanently settled and no inducement can ever prompt [us] to abandon [our] habitations for a distant, wild and strange clime. —Cherokee memorial to John Quincy Adams, 1824

The popular rebellion that broke out against acculturation in 1827 and that has usually been called "White Path's Rebellion" began as early as 1824. It cannot be attributed to White Path or to any particular chief. The rebellion came from the bottom up, from a widespread popular uneasiness over the policies of certain nationalist leaders. Its immediate cause was the effort of the National Council to force the adoption of a written constitution for the nation in 1827. However, there were deep-seated causes going back for almost a decade; dislike of the proliferation of new laws that seemed to have little relevance to the lives of most of the Cherokees; persistent efforts by an acculturated elite to please the missionaries by denigrating the customs and pastimes of the majority; and the increasingly aggressive evangelism of more and more missionaries who invaded every corner of the nation, denouncing traditional beliefs and practices, attacking the medicine men, dividing family against family and children against parents. At its base the rebellion was a reaction against the pace and pervasiveness of acculturation rather than against acculturation itself. It was not in any sense a rejection of nationalism or a reversion to barbarism.

The rebellion was in many respects an act of self-assertion and self-respect by the more conservative part of the nation, a mark of the new self-confidence bred by their renascence as a people—a pride of accomplishment and perseverance for which the mixed bloods and the educated took too much of the credit. The ability of the Cherokees to support themselves economically and their recognition that they had at last achieved a sense of order after years of chaos and confusion was one source of their pride. The fact that they had staved off two federal attempts to remove them totally from their homeland was another. A series of successful rejections of federal attempts to obtain more land cessions in 1822, 1823, and 1824 convinced the Cherokees that they had at last learned to hold their own against the white man. They could now speak to him as equals and command respect. Internal political reforms allowed them to speak with one voice on diplomatic matters and produced an efficient system of self-government that was superior to that of many frontier communities around them. The successful discovery of a way to write their own language evoked a new sense of their identity, history, and potential. They began to wonder whether they needed any longer to take knowledge and manners from the white missionaries and all their leadership from a handful of acculturated, well-to-do mixed bloods who claimed to speak for them in everything.

The tangible signs of Cherokee achievement were everywhere in 1824: their thriving capital at New Echota with its handsome public buildings; their well-dressed, forceful leaders; their new gristmills, sawmills, and turnpikes; their educated young man who, however supercilious toward "the backward" or "lower class" Cherokees, provided proof that a Cherokee could do all that a white man could. Some of these scholars had been to the American Board's seminary in Connecticut; they could read Latin and Greek and understood the white man's philosophy, history, theology, and political economy. One of the graduates of Cornwall Academy would, in 1828, edit their bilingual newspaper, the *Cherokee Phoenix*, for which the Council ordered fonts of type in Sequoyan as well as in English.

There were several controversies in the years 1824–1827 that made even well-educated Cherokees question how fruitful it was to continue to seek integration into a white society that discriminated against them. They wondered why, for example, having shown all that they could accomplish, were the reservees consistently denied the right to become citizens in the surrounding states? Why were Cherokees still denied the right to testify on their own behalf in white courts? Why were they told they could not lay internal taxes to support their government? Why wouldn't the War Department pay them for policing their borders? Why were they refused the funds from their own land sales to endow their own schools? Even the most sanguine Cherokees were shocked at the racial prejudice exhibited by the townspeople and Congregational clergy of Cornwall, Connecticut, toward two of their finest young men, John Ridge and Elias Boudinot, in the years 1823–1825. These two young men had gone to the American Board's academy and had fallen in love with two young white women in the town of Cornwall. When they asked these women to marry them and the women accepted, the townspeople, the local clergy, the women's relatives, and even the trustees of the academy recoiled in horror and tried strenuously to prevent the marriages. White citizens held mass meetings to denounce these "tawny" savages for their audacity. A local newspaper editor deplored the possibility that these fair young ladies would become the "squaws" of heathen barbarians. A respectable mob burned one of the couples in effigy. Worst of all, the trustees of the school (Congregational ministers and members of the American Board, whose missionaries were teaching them that red and white Christians were all brothers and sisters under the skin) not only condemned the marriages but, after they took place against their wishes, voted to close the mission school forever lest any more dark-skinned men try to marry their white-skinned women.[1] Despite all that the missionaries from New England living in the Cherokee Nation could do to deplore this behavior of their friends and superiors, these incidents cut deeply into the collective psyche of a people who had just begun to win back its self-esteem and who had accepted the missionaries from the north as its best source of hope against white injustice. It confirmed the worst fears of those suspicious of white benevolence. Why make such haste to please these people by adjusting all the new laws to their standards of morality? If northern Christians were repudiating the policy that had said intermarriage was the road to equality, if even the most brilliant, wealthy, and highly acculturated of their young people (persons dedicated to the cause of Christianity) were not respectable enough to marry white New Englanders, then what hope was there for the average Cherokee in the civilization program? The rebellion in 1827 expressed a deeply felt belief that the Cherokee people were at the point of no return. The adoption of a constitution based upon that of the United States, although it appeared to many frontier whites as the last arrogant step toward Cherokee independence, struck many ordinary Cherokees as the final surrender of their ethnic identity.

It was no coincidence that the rebellion among the Cherokees came just when white Americans were redefining their own national identity. In the 1820s Americans were shucking off the last vestiges of the Enlightenment and the classical mode that had inspired the Founding Fathers. They were adopting instead the new mode of romantic Christianity and Anglo-Saxon manifest destiny. In 1828 these Americans would raise to the Presidency the champion of the common man against aristocratic privilege—the spokesman of western expansion and untrammeled laissez-faire free enterprise. America was now ready to define its mission to lead the world to the millennium. But what Jacksonians explained as *vox populi, vox dei*, Alexis de Tocqueville was to describe in 1835 as "the tyranny of the majority."

[1] For different versions of the Cherokee marriages in Cornwall see Ralph M. Gabriel, *Elias Boudinot* (Norman: University of Oklahoma Press, 1941), pp. 57–92; Wilkins, *Cherokee Tragedy*, pp. 144–52; McLoughlin, *Cherokees and Missionaries*, pp. 187–90.

John Quincy Adams was the last President of the old school. He was committed (in theory) to the original Indian policy of George Washington. His victory over Andrew Jackson in 1824 was a fluke, the result of a three-way race in which Jackson was obviously the most popular candidate but lacked the electoral votes to win. Adams and his old Federalist school of politics were living on borrowed time from 1824 to 1828 and so were the Cherokees. A Cherokee delegation visited Adams shortly after his inauguration in March 1825, hoping to convince him to make some arrangement with the frontier states that would stop them from hounding the Cherokees to give up more land. "The crisis seems at hand," said the Cherokee deputation, "which must forever seal their doom: Civilization and preservation or dispersion and extinction awaits them. This Government [i.e., Adams's administration] is the tribunal which must pass sentence." They assured Adams that they could never be persuaded to leave their homeland voluntarily. "The arts of civilized life has been successfully introduced among them; they consider themselves permanently settled and no inducement can ever prompt them to abandon their habitations for a distant, wild and strange clime." They pointed out to Adams that although "unceasing exertions" had been made to force the Cherokees to yield their rights, "we have never as yet witnessed a single attempt made on the part of the Government to bring the Compact of 1802 with Georgia to a close by compromise." Why was it always the rights of the Indians that must yield, when their rights were equally protected by the United States Constitution? "We do sincerely hope that measures may be adopted by the United States and Georgia so as to close their compact without teasing the Cherokees for any more of their land."[2]

Yet on the same day that they were asking the new President to turn his attention to some other way of solving "the Indian question," his Secretary of War, James Barbour, instructed McKenney of the Office of Indian Affairs to be sure to ask the Cherokee delegates before they left Washington whether they were authorized by their Council "to negotiate . . . for a sale" of Cherokee land "lying within the limits of Georgia." When asked, the delegates replied politely that they were not so authorized and suggested that McKenney reread their letter of February 11, 1824, to John C. Calhoun in which they said they never intended to sell one more foot of their land.[3]

<hr />

[2] Cherokee delegation to John Quincy Adams, March 12, 1825, M-234, reel 71, #0518. Adams noted in his diary that each of the chiefs "possess fifty to a hundred thousand dollars property," which was a slight exaggeration. Wilkins, *Cherokee Tragedy*, p. 156.

[3] ASP II, 474. Cherokee delegation to Calhoun, February 11, 1824, M-234, reel 71, #0016; Cherokee delegation to Thomas McKenney, March 14, 1825, M-234, reel 71, #0524.

During the next four years, the Cherokees were subjected to the same "teasing" for land from Barbour that they had experienced from every preceding Secretary of War. President Adams and his party were in too precarious a position politically to risk alienating the voters in Georgia and other southeastern states that still had large bodies of Indians within their borders. Barbour, with Adam's support, pursued "the voluntary Indian colonization" policy that Calhoun had adopted in the last year of Monroe's administration.[4] As Monroe's Secretary of State, Adams had had no objection to Indian colonization in the west; although Congress did not fund it when requested to by Monroe and Calhoun in January 1825, Adams still believed that Indian removal was the only feasible answer to "the Indian question."[5]

The Indian colonization policy was designed to create a vast "Indian Territory" in the unsettled part of the Louisiana Territory west of Arkansas, Missouri, and Michigan. There, under close government supervision, all of the tribes east of the Mississippi were to be removed, consolidated, and provided with laws designed for their "half-civilized" state.[6] Some accused Calhoun of promoting this in order to prevent expansion by northern settlers, thereby curtailing the growth of "free" states. Under this plan, whites would be perpetually prohibited from settling west of a line from Arkansas to Canada. The Indians were to be assured that "without destroying their independence" the government would gradually "unite the several tribes under a simple but enlightened system of government and laws formed on the principles of our own, and to which, as their own people would partake in it, they would, under the influence of the contemplated improvement, at no distant day become prepared" for statehood and representation in Congress.[7] How each of the many different tribes could remain "independent" and still be consolidated under one set of laws administered by federal officials was not very clear, nor were the criteria to be met for admission as an Indian territory. Without facing the fact directly, the United States was drifting toward a form of regionalized Indian segregation. Although the Indians might become citizens and might even gain some kind of representation in Congress, they

---

[4] See Annie H. Abel, "Proposals for an Indian State, 1778–1878," *Annual Report of the American Historical Association, 1907* (Washington, D.C.: Government Printing Office, 1908), 1:90–99.

[5] Prucha, *American Indian Policy*, p. 231.

[6] Annie H. Abel, "The History of Events Resulting in Indian Consolidation West of the Mississippi," *Annual Report of the American Historical Association, 1906* (Washington, D.C.: Government Printing Office, 1908), 1:342–43; Abel, "Proposals for an Indian State," 1:90–99.

[7] Abel, "Proposals for an Indian State," 1:91, note g.

would always be segregated in one particular area and would always remain a tiny minority with little influence in national affairs.

The only virtue in Adams's colonization proposal was that it adhered to the view that removal would be voluntary. The pressure to remove voluntarily, however, became increasingly strong. The Indians were being made an offer they could not refuse. When Congress failed to authorize Monroe's request for $125,000 to inaugurate this process (starting with pressure upon the Cherokees and Creeks in Georgia), Adams, Barbour and McKenney nevertheless decided to reintroduce the bill again in the next session of Congress. McKenney was particularly eager to have it endorsed by missionaries among the Indians, in order to persuade the public that these impartial, benevolent men, who knew the Indians better than anyone else, agreed that this was the best possible solution to what was becoming a major domestic problem. If the United States was to expand westward to pursue its destiny, the Indians east of the Mississippi somehow had to be moved out of the way. The problem was to persuade a public inclined to Christian philanthropy, fidelity to treaty promises, and romantic sentimentalism that removal was the most benevolent solution possible. James Fenimore Cooper had written the first of his great Indian romances in 1823 and *The Last of the Mohicans* appeared in 1826. To the easterner, the Indian was becoming a romantic symbol of the past—a disappearing people who deserved Christian compassion and humanitarian sympathy. Politicians who yielded to the heartless demands of land speculators and frontier Indian-haters were sure to arouse righteous indignation from this segment of the public. John Quincy Adams, employing the balance pole of "benevolent colonization," tried for four years to walk the tightrope between the eastern and the western views of the Indian question. He wrote in his diary in 1825: "[Barbour] has given up the idea of incorporating the Indians into the several States where they reside. He has now substituted that of forming them all into a great territorial Government West of the Mississippi. . . . I fear there is no practicable plan by which they can be organized into one civilized, or half-civilized Government . . . but they [his cabinet] had nothing more effective to propose, and I approved it."[8]

To the Cherokees the worst part of this plan was its policy of encouraging individual emigration from each tribe whether the tribe as a whole favored the proposal or not. This would divide each tribe piecemeal, fomenting discontent to the point of total destabilization. There were always malcontents, as in the Creek Path area of the Cherokee Nation, ready (for money and other inducements) to move west. For ardent Cher-

---

[8] Abel, "Indian Consolidation, 1:316; Prucha, *American Indian Policy*, p. 231.

okee nationalists, the only possible response to Adam's colonization plan was adamant refusal. Only a firm resolve to speak and act in unity could prevent their disintegration. Over the next few years the Cherokees were to see their worst fears realized as tribe after tribe gave up and went west under inexorable government pressure and internal disunity. Those tribal nationalists who tried to hang on to their land often found it sold out from under them by a handful of self-interested chiefs.

The tribe that most immediately concerned the Cherokees was the Creek Nation, with whom they shared their long southern border. Ever since the Creek War, the Creeks had been forced to sell more and more of their land. The State of Georgia, where they owned more land and had more people than the Cherokees, was desperate to get rid of them because they were on some of its best black-soil cotton land. The Creeks were unfortunately led by a group of venal chiefs like William McIntosh who used their power to make profitable deals for themselves. Furthermore, many of the Creeks had been unsympathetic to acculturation. They had by no means kept pace with the Cherokees and in some cases had even driven out missionaries. Still divided into Upper and Lower divisions, the Creeks lacked cohesion and leadership. If the Creeks were forced to remove or to sell land on their northern border that would then separate them from the Cherokees, the Cherokee Nation would be surrounded by whites. Intruders would multiply and national stability would suffer.

Aware of this danger, some of the astute, educated young Cherokees decided in 1824 to offer political assistance to the Creeks, an effort that did not endear them to the Georgians or to the War Department. Shortly before the Creeks were to begin negotiations for a sale of their land in October 1824, the Creek council tried to follow the policy of the Cherokees. It voted that "on a deep and solemn reflection, we have with one voice [concluded] to follow the pattern of the Cherokees and on no account whatever will we consent to sell one foot of our land neither by exchange or otherwise."[9] Similarly, the Creeks had passed a law providing the death penalty to any chief who signed a treaty ceding land without the consent of the full council. When the same negotiators who had failed to move the Cherokees toward a cession that year (James Meriwether and Duncan Campbell) arrived in the Creek Nation, they reported to the Secretary of War that "for some time past the Cherokees [have] exerted a steady and officious interference in the affairs of [the Creeks]."[10] Unable to persuade the majority of the Creek council to cede its land in Georgia, Meriwether and Campbell made a fraudulent treaty with eight chiefs

[9] Debo, *Road to Disappearance*, p. 88.
[10] ASP II, 570; Wilkins, *Cherokee Tragedy*, pp. 163–80.

at Indian Springs in February 1825. The cession included millions of acres, virtually all the Creek holdings in Georgia. The Senate ratified this treaty just before John Quincy Adams took office, but when the Creeks executed Chief William McIntosh for his part in the cession and when even the federal agent protested that the treaty was unjust, Adams decided to reconsider it.[11] His was a most unusual decision and one that the people of Georgia deeply resented.

At this point the Creek Nation made a formal agreement with three Cherokees, Major Ridge, his son John, and David Vann, to assist them in their future negotiations with the United States.[12] John Quincy Adams had sent General Edmund P. Gaines to investigate the fraudulent Creek Treaty of Indian Springs. Led by Chief Opothle Yoholo, the Creeks and their new Cherokee advisors made arrangements with Gaines in July 1825 to reconsider the treaty in Washington. The Creeks asked Gaines to accept John Ridge and David Vann as voting members of their delegation, but Gaines said that the most the two Cherokees could do would be to act as secretary and scribe for the Creeks. Under this arrangement young Ridge and Vann accompanied Opothle Yoholo and the other Creek chiefs to Washington.[13]

There, Gaines recommended to Adams that the Treaty of Indian Springs should be abrogated because it was fraudulent. To assuage the anger of the Georgians, the Creeks agreed to renegotiate a proper treaty that would cede approximately the same amount of land if the government would pay a just price for it. Ridge and Vann played a crucial part in all the negotiations that followed and earned the respect of the Creeks for their skill and honesty. The government agreed to pay the Creeks a perpetual annuity of $20,000 per year, to provide a school fund, and to give them an equal tract of land in exchange on the Verdigris River in the western part of the Arkansas Territory (later Oklahoma). In addition, they negotiated an extra $217,600 for the chiefs that would cover the costs of the delegation in Washington and provide funds for restitution and emigration. The Creeks still retained over half their land in the East (now mostly in Alabama) and their northern border with the Cherokees remained almost intact. The Creeks paid Ridge and Vann $5,000 each for their services and gave Major Ridge a gift of $10,000 for his advice.[14]

When it turned out that because of faulty maps this treaty did not eliminate all Creek title to land in Georgia, Barbour began negotiations for the remaining 192,000 acres. When the Creeks refused to sell this

---

[11] Debo, *Road to Disappearance*, pp. 89–92; Wilkins, *Cherokee Tragedy*, p. 164.
[12] Wilkins, *Cherokee Tragedy*, pp. 163–65.
[13] Ibid.
[14] Wilkins, *Cherokee Tragedy*, p. 171.

land, Barbour claimed that Vann and Ridge were behind the decision. He wrote to the Principal Chief of the Creeks, Little Prince, saying, "Your Great Father fears that there may be bad men among you who advise you against his wishes. There is great reason to apprehend that John Ridge and David Vann, natives of the Cherokee Nation, are very improperly interfering in the affairs of the Creek Nation and by their Council creating and keeping up a feeling in that Nation dangerous to its peace and hostile to the best view of the Government with respect to it."[15] Such unfriendly behavior, Barbour said, was "highly disapproved of by the President and cannot be permitted." Barbour told the Creeks that failure to correct this problem would "lead to consequences that would seriously affect the tranquility and happiness of the Cherokee Nation" as well as themselves, in order to frighten the Cherokees into persuading their chiefs to force the Ridges and Vann to withdraw their services.[16] In response, the Cherokee Council voted that the Creek advisors had acted in their capacity as private citizens in this matter and had a perfect right to do so.[17]

Barbour was right that Vann and the Ridges were actively counseling their neighbors to hold out against any further cessions. John Ridge not only had drawn up the protest for the Creeks against ceding the additional 192,000 acres in Georgia but had also helped draw up a complaint for them against the abusive and corrupt behavior of their federal agent, John Crowell.[18] Moreover, the three Cherokees began efforts to help the Creeks to better consolidate their nation and centralize their government as the Cherokees had done. McKenney came to the Creek Nation in 1827 and managed to persuade Little Prince that Opothle Yoholo was plotting with the Cherokees to undermine his power as Principal Chief. Little Prince then threatened to kill John Ridge if he did not leave the nation at once and agreed with McKenney to sign a treaty ceding the last 192,000 acres of Creek land in Georgia.[19] McKenney reported to Barbour that the Creeks were "a wretched people" given to "habitual drunkenness" who, through "ignorance and weakness," had allowed these Cherokee chiefs to insinuate themselves into Creek affairs. "Conscious of their own inefficiency to manage for themselves their concerns, they have yielded to this

[15] James Barbour to Little Prince, June 23, 1827, M-21, reel 4, pp. 78–82; Thomas McKenney to John Crowell, April 26, 1827, M-21, reel 4, p. 31.

[16] James Barbour to Cherokee Council, June 25, 1827, M-21, reel 4, p. 83; Thomas McKenney to James Barbour, November 13, 1827, M-234, reel 72, #0254.

[17] John Ross to James Barbour, August 1, 1827, M-234, reel 72, #0251.

[18] Thomas McKenney to John Crowell, April 26, 1827, M-21, reel 4, p. 31; S. S. Hamilton to John Crowell, September 3, 1827, M-21, reel 4, pp. 123–24.

[19] Wilkins, *Cherokee Tragedy*, pp. 179–80; Luther Blake to Thomas McKenney, February 8, 1828, M-221, reel 107, #7024; Thomas McKenney to James Barbour, February 22, 1827, M-21, reel 3, p. 395.

state of dependence on others." He was happy to say that without such outside interference in the future, "they would submit cheerfully to be guided by the Government."[20]

John Ridge had a very different view of the controversy with McKenney, which was later published in the *Cherokee Phoenix*. He said that while he was in Washington renegotiating the Treaty of Indian Springs, certain federal officials had tried to bribe him and Vann into betraying the Creek delegation. When they refused the bribe, the government decided to deprive the Creeks of their assistance.[21]

The young Cherokee leaders later proposed to assist the Choctaws, but they discovered that the Choctaws had been warned by the War Department to have nothing to do with them. McKenney had written to them in December 1827 when efforts were about to begin to remove them to the west: "Ridge, I think, is a dangerous, meddling man. You must beware of such."[22] It proved impossible to bring about cooperation among the southeastern tribes at this critical point. The government was able to prey upon the fears of each tribe that either it would be duped by its neighbors or it would be severely punished by the government for accepting outside aid.

A new problem for the Cherokees arose in July 1826 when John Quincy Adams, at the insistence of the states of Georgia and Tennessee, urged the Cherokees to allow surveys to be made through their land for canals and horse-drawn railways.[23] The Cherokees were told of the many economic benefits that would come to them from opening such avenues of trade and employment, but the Council saw the matter as political, rather than economic.[24] It replied that after mature deliberation "and with a full sense of the great importance of internal improvements," it had nevertheless concluded that "no individual state shall be permitted to make internal improvements within the sovereign limits of the Cherokee Nation." The request would infringe upon Cherokee sovereignty and "the Cherokee Nation can never surrender" jurisdiction over any part of its soil to a state of the Union. The Cherokees dealt only with the federal government. Intrastate canals and railways, whether owned by a state or by private corporations, would set a bad precedent and weaken the Cherokees' right to rely upon the treaty power in dealing with whites.[25] To Adams and Barbour, national expansion and commerce required that the

---

[20] Thomas McKenney to James Barbour, November 29, 1827, M-21, reel 4, pp. 153–57.

[21] *Cherokee Phoenix*, April 3, 1828, and July 2, 1828.

[22] Thomas McKenney to David Folsom, December 13, 1827, M-21, reel 3, pp. 177–78.

[23] James Barbour to Hugh Montgomery, July 19, 1826, M-21, reel 3, p. 149.

[24] Hugh Montgomery to the Cherokee Council, September 26, 1827, M-208; Hugh Montgomery to Charles Hicks, December 18, 1826, M-208.

[25] Cherokee Council to Hugh Montgomery, December 18, 1826, M-208.

federal government assist the states with internal improvements. Adams believed that the Cherokees' refusal to consent to canals and railways through the nation was another example of their interference with America's national prosperity, commerce, and expansion. To the Cherokees, the division of their nation by canals and railways would ultimately destroy their national integrity; ownership and profits would go to white entrepreneurs. At the same time that Georgia and Tennessee began asking for a right of way for the Hiwassee and Coosa Canal, North Carolina persuaded a three-man commission under General John Cocke to approach the Cherokee Council "for the two-fold purpose of procuring an extinguishment" of Cherokee claims to all land within the limits of North Carolina and to obtain a right of way to build a canal connecting the Hiwassee and Connasauga rivers to aid the people of North Carolina.[26] Cocke arrived in the nation to negotiate just as the Cherokee rebellion against acculturation was reaching its climax in 1827. Never had the need for Cherokee unity been greater and yet never since Doublehead's day had they been so at odds.

While the surrounding states were becoming increasingly aggressive in their demands to obtain land and commercial privileges from the Cherokees, the missionaries were becoming more aggressive in their efforts to obtain converts. Despite the assistance that the American Board, through Dr. Samuel Worcester, had rendered to the nation in 1819 and despite the eagerness with which many Cherokees had sent their children to the Board's mission schools over the next five years, there were always many Cherokees who were skeptical about the missionaries' motives. The first signs of resentment appeared in 1821, when the rapid growth of mission stations led some local chiefs to complain that the missionaries were settling on what remained of their good land. They feared that in some devious way the missionaries' purpose was ultimately to force the removal of the nation to Arkansas so that the mission board could speculate on their land. That year Charles Hicks warned the Congregationalists at Brainerd that it was "necessary to proceed with great caution" into new areas of the nation; "the more ignorant class of the Nation," he said, was convinced "that the missionaries are about to take large tracts of land as pay for teaching the children . . . that heavy charges are [secretly] laid against the nation for the expenses of these schools, and soon the President will compel their payment in land."[27] The cynics could not believe that the students were being taught at no expense to the nation.

Hicks advised the Board to obtain approval in advance from the Council

[26] James Barbour to John Cocke, March 13, 1827, M-21, reel 3, p. 438.
[27] Brainerd Journal, August 2, 1821, ABCFM.

whenever it wished to add more white personnel at its stations. The Cherokees became uneasy when they saw great numbers of whites coming onto their land, building houses, plowing fields, and starting orchards as though they were about to settle permanently. Ard Hoyt sympathized with this fear: "When so many white people are grasping for their land, it is no wonder if the poor, uninformed Cherokees sometimes suspect that the missionaries (under cover) have the same object in view."[28] Nevertheless, as more new schools were started and the model farm at Brainerd was expanded to accommodate more students and teachers, Hicks warned Hoyt again a year later that "the people were displeased that so many persons had arrived at Brainerd; they said the intention was to build a town" of white people in their midst, just as Colonel Earle had planned to do with his iron foundry.[29]

The problem of missionary expansion was compounded by the missionaries' need to tell those who supported their work how well their funds were being spent. Accounts of mission expansion in missionary journals eventually got into the hands of the Cherokees. One article in 1822 in the *Missionary Herald*, the official journal of the American Board, annoyed the Cherokees because "it contained an estimate of mission property at Brainerd, including improvements of land to a considerable amount." Boasting to their supporters, the missionaries aroused the suspicions of the Cherokees. Hicks "said that although *he* might understand it and be satisfied" that it was done to satisfy the curiosity of those who donated money to the mission, "yet the Cherokees generally could not but consider it as a claim on the land and say, 'This is what we always told you, that these missionaries would claim the land for themselves.' "[30] When the Baptist missionaries at Valley Towns tried to take a census of the region in 1822 to determine how many Cherokee children lived near their school, the missionary superintendent reported that "the measure excited much jealousy" and he had to drop it.[31] The missionaries dared not even draw maps of the various routes they followed in their itinerant preaching: "I would endeavor to draw a map," said one missionary in 1823, "were it not for fear of continuing among the Cherokees an idea" they have "that we intend ultimately to get their land."[32] Another reported in 1824: "It appears that a very considerable number among this people have from the beginning suspected that the object of the mission

[28] Brainerd Journal, December 11, 1822, ABCFM.
[29] Jeremiah Evarts, Memo, May 9, 1822, ABCFM.
[30] Daniel Butrick to Jeremiah Evarts, January 22, 1823, ABCFM.
[31] Jeremiah Evarts, Memo, May 1, 1822, ABCFM.
[32] Daniel Butrick to Jeremiah Evarts, June 11, 1823, ABCFM.

was to obtain wealth for the missionaries."[33] Some Cherokees even suspected that Charles Hicks and other influential chiefs were enriching themselves by making special arrangements with the missionary board. When the first group of graduates from local mission schools was sent to Connecticut to obtain advanced training for the ministry at the Board's seminary in Cornwall, rumor said "that Mr. Hicks spoke well of it [Brainerd School] because he got money for everything that was done here—that the boys would be sent away among the white people and never returned—and that Mr. Hicks had a sum of money for every boy that was thus sent away."[34] Somehow the decisions being made by the newly constructed Cherokee Council of thirty-two chiefs were not being well explained to the mass of people living in the outlying areas of the nation.

Additional resentment developed when it was found that the missionaries at Brainerd were charging parents a dollar per week for room, board, and clothing for their children. Few Cherokees had ready cash in this amount and the missionaries quickly corrected the problem by charging only those parents who could afford to pay. The full bloods then began to discover how hard it was for their sons and daughters to learn to read and write when the teachers spoke no Cherokee and had to use bilingual students to help translate the lessons. Records of student enrollment at Brainerd School, the first and largest of the American Board's schools, reveal not only a sharp drop in enrollment after 1821 but an even sharper decrease in the proportion of full-blood students.[35] (See table 9.) Brainerd's enrollment increased from 38 in 1817 to a peak of 132 in 1819 and then fell to 46 in 1825. Although the full bloods constituted 75 percent of the population in the Cherokee Nation, they never made up more than 61 percent of the student body. That peak was reached in 1820; it declined thereafter to roughly 40 percent.

When the missionaries of the American Board failed to follow Hicks's advice in obtaining permission from the Council whenever they planned to bring in additional missionaries and mission assistants (blacksmiths, farmers, carpenters, and teachers) and when they failed to make periodic reports to the Council about their activities, a political quarrel erupted in 1824. The American Board was charged in the Council with deliberately flouting tribal authority. Pathkiller and The Speaker, two of the most influential older chiefs and both full bloods who did not speak English, lodged the protest. One missionary wrote in his journal: "There is now

[33] Daniel Butrick to Jeremiah Evarts, August 4, 1824, ABCFM.
[34] Brainerd Journal, June 13, 1821, ABCFM.
[35] Morey D. Rothberg, "Effectiveness of Missionary Education among the Cherokees" (seminar paper, Brown University, 1973).

TABLE 9

Mixed-Blood and Full-Blood Students at Brainerd Mission, 1817–1827

Year	Total Students	Number of Full Bloods	Number of Mixed Bloods	Percent of Full Bloods
1817	38	12	26	32%
1818	76	25	51	33%
1819	132	67	65	51%
1820	119	72	47	61%
1821	113	63	50	56%
1822	88	44	40	50%
1823	73	32	41	44%
1824	56	23	33	41%
1825	46	19	27	41%
1826	52	19	33	37%
1827	54	22	32	41%

SOURCE: Statistics compiled from archives of the American Board at Houghton Library, Harvard University, in Morey D. Rothberg, "The Effectiveness of Missionary Education among the Cherokees: The Brainerd Schools, 1817–1836" (unpublished seminar paper, Brown University, 1973).

a very powerful opposition to Missions among the Chiefs."[36] The Reverend William Chamberlain, who had succeeded Hoyt as Superintendent of the American Board's Cherokee missions, was required to appear before the Council in October to explain this breach of agreement. "Mr. Hicks is unshaken in his confidence" in the mission, Chamberlain reported to the Prudential Committee of the Board in Boston that August; "this I believe is the case with all the enlightened chiefs. But Pathkiller and the Speaker are violently opposed, and as they have great influence among the common people and the [other] unenlightened chiefs, it is very probable that there will be a very powerful opposition to the missions in the next council."[37] With the help of Major Ridge and David Brown the missionaries weathered the storm, but the suspicions did not cease.[38] In fact, the decision of the chiefs in 1824 to use money from the Cherokee National Treasury to translate the Bible into Sequoyah's syllabary may have added to the discontent. Major Ridge added fuel to the fire by trying to persuade the Council to follow the practice in state legislatures of paying a Christian chaplain to open and close Cherokee Councils with prayer.[39] A year later David Brown, a mission school graduate, made the unwarranted statement to the white public that missionary

[36] William Chamberlain's Journal, August 11, 1824, ABCFM.

[37] Ibid. and McLoughlin, *Cherokees and Missionaries*, pp. 192–95.

[38] William Chamberlain's Journal, August-October, 1824; Wilkins, *Cherokee Tragedy*, p. 160.

[39] William Chamberlain's Journal, October 26, 1824, ABCFM.

teaching had now so permeated the country that "the Christian religion is the religion of the nation."[40] This was not calculated to put the minds of the traditionalists at ease.

Another source of anti-mission sentiment among the Cherokees stemmed from the missionaries' insistence that all Cherokee medical procedures were impermissible because they were mixed with pagan superstition and "sorcery." Many Cherokees who had converted to Christianity continued to rely upon their medicine men in times of illness. But if their missionary pastor discovered this, they were subject to severe criticism and even excommunication. The pages of the missionary journals and letters in the 1820s are filled with such controversies.[41] The issue aroused great controversy whenever there was a smallpox epidemic. The missionaries and federal agent recommended preventive medicine by vaccination.[42] The Cherokees waited until people became sick and then tried in vain to exorcise it through traditional rituals.[43] Christian converts who accepted missionary advice were considered apostates. When a Moravian convert refused to allow incantations by her uncle, an adonisgi, in her home, she was driven into the woods and fled to the mission station at Springplace.[44]

After 1824 the hostility against missions mounted as the Methodist itinerants practised a new type of evangelistic activity. Not interested in schools, they did not form permanent mission stations. Following the pattern they had established in reaching the scattered settlements of the white frontier, the Methodists rode on horseback from town to town among the Cherokees, preaching wherever they could draw a crowd. The Tennessee Methodist Conference, which was in charge of frontier evangelism, decided to include the Cherokee Nation as part of its sphere of spiritual concern in 1824. Unlike the other mission agencies, the Methodists always considered the Indian nations as part of home missions rather than foreign missions. Every year after 1824 the Tennessee Conference assigned more and more missionaries to "traveling circuits" in the nation until they had covered virtually every part of it with preaching stations. A circuit rider might be assigned to preach in twenty to thirty towns over a 150-mile circuit. He would cover that circuit four times each year, preaching, baptizing, and holding camp meetings and "love feasts" until he had made sufficient converts to form a Methodist "society" or

---

[40] ASP II, 651. Brown was responsible for translating the Bible into Sequoyan; he was assisted by George Lowrey and Daniel Butrick; see Daniel Butrick to Jeremiah Evarts, June 25, 1825, ABCFM.

[41] McLoughlin, Cherokees and Missionaries, pp. 204–208.

[42] Schwarze, History of Moravian Missions, pp. 174–75.

[43] Ibid.

[44] Springplace Diary, January 9, 1824, MAS.

"class" at each point along his circuit. These societies were led by local Cherokees appointed by the circuit rider and chosen from among the most respectable, pious, and responsible of the converts in that town. The "class leaders" were not ordained, but they could lead in prayer and Bible reading and encourage the kind of piety and morality that the Methodist church discipline required of those who wanted to become members. On the white frontier, classes or societies became formalized into churches and then hired a permanent pastor. At this stage they were taken off the circuit and became self-supporting. Among the Cherokees, however, none of the societies ever advanced to that stage. Although the Methodists made many converts who were admitted as "members of classes" or societies, they had no Cherokee churches as the permanent mission stations of the other denominations did. The circuit riders had to perform all church ordinances and they were paid small salaries by the conferences.[45]

However, measured in terms of converts, the Methodist circuit riders were by far the most successful missionaries among the Cherokees. Their success was due to their simplified theology of free will, their enthusiastic style of preaching, the earnestness of their young circuit riders, and their looser concept of conversion. Whereas the Congregationalists and Baptists were Calvinists who believed that only a few of "the elect" were foreordained for salvation and the Moravians set such strict standards of pious behavior that few could meet them, the Methodists believed that salvation was open to everyone and that the willingness to say one accepted Christianity and wanted to learn more about it was sufficient to obtain baptism. Moreover, the Methodists believed that their converts could "grow in grace," that is, slowly work their way toward a better understanding of Christian teaching and toward the self-discipline that would enable them to live moral, upright lives. Methodists also allowed, as Calvinists did not, for "backsliding"; they believed that even those most anxious to be good Christians might sometimes fall into sin or error. Such "backsliders" could always repent and begin a new effort to redeem themselves. Methodism was therefore more suitable in its style and message to the needs of a people who were struggling to move from an old religion toward a new one. Methodist revival meetings or camp meetings were held out under the trees and lasted for hours or even days; they were filled with ecstatic religious exercises (speaking in tongues, jumping and shouting, whirling around, fainting or falling). Like Cherokee dances and festivals, they constituted a rhythmic bodily effort to become one with the mysterious spiritual power that filled the universe.

On the whole the other denominations disapproved of Methodist the-

---

[45] See McLoughlin, *Cherokees and Missionaries*, pp. 164–80.

TABLE 10

Cherokee Converts to Christianity by Denomination, 1800–1838

(figures listed are cumulative)

Year	Moravian (began 1800)	American Board [Congregationalist] (began 1817)	Methodist (began 1822)	Baptist (began 1819)
1800–1809	—	—	—	—
1810	1	—	—	—
1810–1817	2	—	—	—
1819	19	8	—	—
1820	19	22	—	—
1822	22	25	33	2
1823	22?	43	100	33
1824	22?	43?	289	33?
1825	35	80	309	50
1827	50	100	400	50?
1828	50?	110	675	50?
1829	45	167	763	87
1830	46	180	1028	61
1831	45	167	850	90
1832	71	167?	850?	117
1833	65	167?	936	120
1834	[missions closed]	167?	508	208
1835		167?	700	244
1838		150	[mission closed]	500

SOURCE: Figures compiled from mission reports.

NOTE: Question mark indicates no figure for that year and a holdover figure from preceding year. Declines may indicate closing of a mission, a mission moved west, or movement of Cherokees out of the mission area. Figures were not reported regularly or carefully and may include some Cherokee slaves or even whites living in the area in some cases. The figures do not include any western Cherokees. By 1838 approximately 10–12 percent of the Cherokee population were members of mission churches, a figure comparable to church membership in surrounding white settlements. For further details see William G. McLoughlin, *Cherokees and Missionaries, 1789–1839* (New Haven: Yale University Press, 1984).

ology, standards of membership, and preaching style, but they could not help being impressed by their success at saving Cherokee souls. In order to compete with them the Congregationalists and Baptists began to imitate their system of itinerant preaching. (See Table 10.) Itinerant preaching was not only more exciting (and romantic) than the tedious nature of school teaching, but it promised to capitalize upon what was assumed to be a growing interest by the Cherokees in learning about Christianity. Traveling evangelism would, as one Congregationalist missionary put it, "bring the degraded, dull Cherokees to a level with the half Cherokees" much faster than stationary preaching.[46] The Reverend Daniel Butrick,

[46] Isaac Proctor to Jeremiah Evarts, July 28, 1827, ABCFM.

one of the first Congregationalists to try the experiment (using a native interpreter, as the Methodists did), rode 3,400 miles in 1823–1824, held 171 meetings, and baptized 18 adults and 25 children.[47] He saved more souls in one year than the whole mission staff did at Brainerd. The Bible said, "Go out and bring them in," giving divine sanction to the itinerant method. Moreover, itinerancy was much less expensive than running a model farm and school.

The Baptist missionaries also drastically altered their priorities after 1826. Like the Congregationalists and Presbyterians, they had believed that civilization (i.e., education) should precede Christianization. But their vocational school at Valley Towns in the North Carolina region of the nation proved very expensive and produced very few converts. In 1827 the Boston Board required the missionary superintendent, Evan Jones, to curtail the residential, vocational school, limiting it to twenty female day students to be taught by Jones's assistants. The Baptist school at Hickory Log was to be continued only if the Cherokee parents contributed to its support. The time free from schooling was used by the missionaries to ride on horseback from place to place, preaching the gospel even in the most remote areas of the Great Smoky Mountains. Their reports of serious opposition from traditionalists and their medicine men did not deter this effort to root out paganism.[48]

The Moravians did not become itinerant preachers, though one Moravian missionary urged his denomination to follow the example of the Methodists, Baptists, and American Board, saying, "[I think] more good could be done in the itinerant plan than by the present expensive way" of schooling; "I think it is a useless expense to board [students] because other denominations are by far more diligent in diffusing religious knowledge among the natives than we are because their entire plan and system is better adapted to this country."[49]

The drastic change in missionary methods aroused a new kind of anxiety among the Cherokees, who had hitherto found that if they did not want to send their children to mission schools, they could easily ignore the whole effort of Christian imperialism. Previously they might not have liked the sympathy that their nationalist leaders so often displayed for Christianization, but it did not affect their daily lives in remote communities. After 1824, however, there was no way to escape confrontations with avid Christian proselytizing. Even the mountain villages found itinerants entering their community, starting meetings, denouncing "heathenism," and stirring up religious controversy. Inevitably some Cherokees were persuaded to join the new religion and a permanent

---

[47] Daniel Butrick to Jeremiah Evarts, September 3, 1824, ABCFM.
[48] McLoughlin, *Cherokees and Missionaries*, pp. 158–60.
[49] Henry G. Clauder, Diary, May 2 and May 10, 1829, MAB.

preaching station would be established in the area; the Christian preachers would come back regularly, their members increased and became a source of disagreement within the community as the old and new religions competed. Unlike the Cherokees, Christians enjoyed confrontations and went out of their way to force debates and stir up emotions. The old ethic of communal harmony was already badly eroded; Christian evangelistic efforts finished it, shattering the old communal consensus. To be a Cherokee now, even in one's private life, one had to stand up and fight. Nothing could be taken for granted; there were no common assumptions. Competition and theological combat now pervaded every sphere of Cherokee life. The Christian gloried in Jesus's words: "I came not to send peace but a sword . . . to set a man at variance against his father, and the daughter against her mother and the daughter-in-law against her mother-in-law."

Quarrels broke out not only within families but between conjurors and itinerant preachers and between town council members and newly formed Christian groups. Eventually, when some of the converts found that Christianity required a more total alteration in their behavior than they had originally realized, there were angry quarrels between church members and their white missionary leaders. As in many frontier white communities, the "diffusing of religious knowledge" and the deep convictions that came from new choices produced bitter arguments and the division of neighbor against neighbor. Christian converts tried to set new social and ethical norms and denounced those who failed to conform to them. The followers of the old religion had their own norms, convictions, and beliefs that they considered as sacred and divinely ordained as those of the Christians. The missionaries and their converts attacked as "wicked" and "depraved" sinners those who had more than one wife, those who drank liquor, those who gambled or went to ball plays, and those who practiced the religious ceremonies of their forefathers or Cherokee medicine. "Their conjuring is as purely heathen as almost anything to be met with on the River Ganges," said one Congregational missionary in a typical diatribe; "when conjuring they pray to almost every creature—such as white dogs, butterflies, turtles, etc. etc."[50] One missionary told a Cherokee adonisgi that all this work "was only the black waters of heathenism designed and calculated to keep their thoughts entirely from the one true God." He reported that "the people in all their wants applied only to their conjurors and these applied their petitions to some fictitious, imaginary being who had no real existence in the universe. So that the true God was neither an object of fear or reverence or gratitude." He told

[50] Isaac Proctor to Jeremiah Evarts, July 28, 1827, ABCFM.

the medicine man he must give up his system of helping people, "renounce it forever," and turn to the one true God for help.[51] Itinerant
preachers courted public debates with conjurors in order to denounce
them as wicked men who only brought harm to their communities.

Despite the rapid acculturation among mixed-blood Cherokees, the
traditional religion continued strong among the full bloods. This was especially evident whenever one of the periodic epidemics of smallpox,
measles or some other "white man's disease" swept through the nation.
During a particularly virulent outbreak of smallpox in the summer of
1824, the Congregational missionary at Carmel, Moody Hall, estimated
that "1000 will die with it." In Carmel alone, twenty-seven died. "The
Old Conjuror," Hall reported, "has appointed a great Physic dance (as in
the case of the measles), promising that all who join him shall not be afflicted with the disease."[52] The Moravians also noted the reliance upon
traditional remedies during this epidemic. "Most of the Indians believed
that this disease was spread by a monstrous serpent of the thickness of a
man and with a white head. To catch even the odor of this serpent is fatal.
Therefore the Indians sought refuge with their sorcerers. One of these
arranged a so-called 'Physic dance' at Tallony. For seven nights this dance
must be continued, the Indians drinking a tea brewed from certain herbs,
along with this exercise, while the sorcerer prays either to a great eagle
whom he pretends to see or to the black dog in the north, the white dog
in the east, the gray dog in the south and the red dog in the west. The
sorcerer's fee is seven deer hides from the community in which the dance
is held and a string of beads from each family."[53] The Congregational and
Moravian missionaries sought to expose the ignorance of the Cherokee
doctors by obtaining cow pox vaccine and urging all the Christian Indians
(and others who could be persuaded) to submit to vaccination. The Moravians reported that in their vicinity the epidemic was checked by this
method and the sorcerer discomfited.

In the town of Etowah a newly converted Cherokee, Alexander Sanders, wished to show his zeal for his new religion. In 1825, in order to
help his minister stamp out the pagan customs that were dragging his
people to hell, Sanders and some of his friends burned the town council
house to the ground. He called it "the Devil's meeting hosue" because its
meetings were opened with the old rituals and calls for dances and festivals issued from there.[54] In retaliation, the traditionalists of Etowah
threatened to burn down the mission schoolhouse. Another missionary

[51] Daniel Butrick's Journal, September 8, 1830, ABCFM.
[52] Moody Hall to Jeremiah Evarts, June 29, 1824, ABCFM.
[53] Schwarze, *History of Moravian Missions*, pp. 174–75.
[54] Moody Hall to Jeremiah Evarts, August 20, 1825, ABCFM.

was asked to withdraw from the town he preached in because his converts insisted on harassing the traditionalists. They told them they were going to hell when they died; some taunted the traditionalists by saying that the red wine taken at Christian communion was more powerful as a spiritual drink than the "black physic" taken at Cherokee religious ceremonies.[55] The headmen of one town complained to Charles Hicks that the Christianized Cherokees would no longer attend town council meetings because their religious beliefs would not permit them to participate in the rituals that opened and closed the meetings; thus the official business of the town could not be properly done.[56] Cherokee religion did not conceive of any separation between church and state; to participate in Cherokee life one participated in Cherokee religious practices. Christians, being forbidden to engage in the old practices, no longer performed their civic duties as Cherokees.

One of the more bitter controversies over the Christian values that the missionaries taught and the values of the Cherokee religion concerned the relatively benign practice of hospitality. A Cherokee was expected to welcome any visitor into his home and give him food and lodging. The missionaries called this "begging" and disliked it intensely. At first they put up with it, but as they became more sure of their position in the nation they tried to discourage it. The Reverend Moody Hall finally refused to give food to Cherokees who came to his door. He wanted the Cherokees in his community to learn the values of hard work and self-reliance. This annoyed the Cherokees and seemed inconsistent with the sermons Moody preached about how Jesus said to feed the poor and clothe the naked. One night an old Cherokee appeared at Hall's home stark naked and demanded food. Hall refused and the man burst into the room, swinging at Hall with a knife. Others present disarmed the man, but following several other incidents that Hall said displayed an intent to harm him and his wife, he hastily left the town. This pleased the traditionalists but annoyed Hall's converts. He had often told them that as a minority in their nation, they must be brave and willing to face up to the persecution of their neighbors when they joined the mission church. Now Hall had shown he lacked the courage of his own convictions.[57]

Vehement arguments sometimes took place when young converts who were licensed to preach upbraided their people in an effort to make them give up the old religion. Most of these zealous converts were young,

[55] Charles Hicks to John Cambold, June 5, 1824, MAS.

[56] See William G. McLoughlin, "Cherokee Anti-Mission Sentiment," *Ethnohistory* 21 (1974):361–70.

[57] Walker, *Torchlights*, p. 210; Jeremiah Evarts to Moody Hall, August 20, 1824, ABCFM; McLoughlin, *Cherokees and Missionaries*, p. 201.

products of the intense piety of the mission schools. By Cherokee tradition the young were required to respect their elders, to be silent before them and to heed what they said. It struck the older Cherokees as the height of bad manners for these heedless young men to denounce their elders in public for following the religion of their ancestors. One or two such itinerant exhorters were threatened with violent treatment if they returned to certain villages after such actions. On one occasion a group of traditionalists threw stones at a cabin in which an exhorter was conducting a meeting.[58]

Apart from the knife attack upon Moody Hall, no missionaries were ever attacked in the Cherokee Nation. Because of the staunch defense of missionary efforts by the nationalist chiefs, the authority of the nation was exerted to protect them. For example, the Lighthorse were sent to arrest and try the man who attacked Hall. Despite the objections of some local chiefs, the national leaders did not want to curtail itinerant preaching in any way, nor did they want the white churchgoing public to hear that there was any antagonism between the traditionalists and the missionaries. A great deal of effort was expended to cover up anti-mission incidents. Those that could not be kept secret were described as the actions of eccentric, deranged, drunken, or no-account Indians. The missionaries themselves mentioned them only in private letters. They too wished the public to believe that they were respected and successful in their work. Yet beneath the surface religious animosities intensified between 1824 and 1827. It finally broke out in the rebellion of 1827. To many it appeared that this would put an end to Cherokee revitalization and the nation would slide backward into chaos and confusion.

[58] Daniel Butrick to Jeremiah Evarts, January 15, 1828, ABCFM.

NINETEEN

REBELLION AGAINST THE
CONSTITUTION, 1827

The whole Nation here is in the greatest turmoil. The greater part wants to have the new laws abrogated and are for having the missions dissolved.... [Pagan] Dances at night are arranged and during the day they hold Council. No one trusts anyone any more. —The Reverend Johann Schmidt, missionary to the Cherokees, May 16, 1827

On October 23, 1826, the National Council voted to call a convention to meet on the following Fourth of July for the purpose of "adopting a Constitution for the future government" of the nation.[1] It nominated ten candidates from each of the eight districts and instructed the people to choose three of these to represent their district at the convention. The arguments used to support and oppose this measure in the Council have not survived, but evidently the decision was bitterly contested. In another heated session a year earlier, the Council had expelled from its membership the old and respected chief, White Path, replacing him with Elijah Hicks, the Christian son of Charles Hicks.[2] No reason for White Path's expulsion was given in the resolution that announced it, but apparently he had opposed too strenuously the centralization, rapid acculturation, and Christianization of his country. White Path was not alone in his feelings. After the vote to adopt a constitution was passed, those who agreed with him concluded that they must now band together and take a strong stand against this cultural revolution before it was frozen into the fundamental law of the land. The Cherokee renascence that its leaders were so proud of and that the philanthropists and missionaries found so heartening was becoming burdensome to many Cherokees.

The first public act of the rebellious chiefs was to call an extra-legal council at Ellijay, near Turniptown, which was White Path's town, late in February or early in March 1827. The rebellion could hardly have come

---

[1] *Cherokee Laws*, pp. 73–76.

[2] Ibid., pp. 66–67; see also James Mooney's discussion and the statement of his Cherokee informant, James Wafford, in "Myths of the Cherokees," pp. 113–114; see also Marion Starkey, *The Cherokee Nation* (New York: Knopf, 1946), pp. 104–105; Wilkins, *Cherokee Tragedy*, p. 196.

at a worse moment. In the middle of January, Pathkiller, the venerable Principal Chief, had died; two weeks later, Charles Hicks, the Second Principal Chief, died. The nation was leaderless. Both Georgia and North Carolina had just been authorized by Congress to send treaty commissioners to extract more land and the rights of way for canals through the nation. As Speaker of the Council, Major Ridge assumed leadership of the lower house; John Ross remained as President of the National Committee or upper house. John Martin became acting Treasurer of the nation. The choice of new principal chiefs required a full council, but the Council was not scheduled to meet again until October 1827.

Whether the substance or merely the desirability of a constitution had been discussed at the Council in October 1826 is not known, but the decision to call a constitutional convention culminated a series of controversies that had disturbed the internal harmony of the nation for several years. Lacking specific statements by the dissident chiefs, we can only speculate on the reasons behind their revolt. Perhaps they feared that much of the objectionable legislation passed since 1819, which so far had been only loosely enforced, would be rigorously enforced under the constitution. The dissidents clearly wanted some of these laws repealed, in any case. The most offensive laws may have been those undermining old customs (clan revenge, matrilineal inheritance, witchcraft, polygamy, infanticide) and imposing Christian morality (opposing gambling, promoting Sabbath observance, prohibiting ardent spirits "at ball plays, all night dances and other public gatherings").[3] There were certainly many who must have disliked the law of October 1826, that stated that "no person who disbelieves in the existence of the Creator and of rewards and punishments after death, shall be eligible to hold any office" nor allowed to give "testimony in any court of justice."[4] The Council had even passed an oath of office, evidently administered to some officials of the nation, that was distinctly Christian and if enforced would have excluded all traditionalists from office holding: "You do solemnly swear, by the Holy Evangelists of Almighty God, that you, as Marshall of Coosewatee district, will strictly support and observe the laws of the Cherokee Nation. . . ."[5]

Other chiefs probably objected to the expenditure of public funds for translating the Bible into Sequoyan, laws establishing a capital city with large public buildings and streets whose plots on each side were auctioned off to the highest bidders, or the laws designed to establish a seminary of

---

[3] For the law prohibiting consumption of alcohol at ball plays in 1824 see *Cherokee Laws*, p. 36.

[4] *Cherokee Laws*, p. 77.

[5] Ibid., p. 68.

higher learning. Some may have feared that the constitution would proclaim the Cherokees to be a Christian nation and thereby exclude the majority from a meaningful part in decision making or at least mark them as second-class citizens. Already the intense centralization of power had cut the number of chiefs by almost two-thirds and seriously undermined the power of the town councils in favor of the complex district courts under appointed judges. The leaders of the rebellion may well have believed that they were about to be asked to turn over the control of the nation to a highly acculturated, wealthy, English-speaking oligarchy. Chiefs had been told that they had no power to call councils even in their own towns or districts. In effect, White Path led a counterrevolution in the name of preserving the Cherokee way of life—or as much of it as it was still possible to preserve.

Those who dominated the legitimate council and wanted a written constitution modeled on that of the United States professed to be patriots and defenders of their nation's rights, but if they were to make the country into a Christian republic like the United States, would they still be Cherokees? What would be the basis of their patriotism? As Christians, assimilated to Euro-American beliefs and practices, would not their loyalties and policies lie in a different direction from that of the great majority of the Cherokee people, who spoke no English and still held to the beliefs of their forefathers? If this acculturated elite could "break" and expel White Path for voicing the concerns of the majority, if the views of people for whom White Path spoke were to be denounced with impunity by white missionaries and Christian converts (as "polluted," "ignorant," "backward" and otherwise a disgrace to the nation), then could not a constitutional government exclude from power all chiefs who held these views? The Cherokees had always believed in government by consensus, from the bottom up; but for eight years or more they had been increasingly ruled by an aristocracy from the top down. The disdain of those at the top for those at the botton was every day becoming more palpable. The average Cherokee, having won back his national self-respect over the past decade, was not willing to yield it now to a handful of acculturated Cherokees who seemed ashamed of being Cherokee.

The rebellion was not violent. No armed conflict took place; no lives were lost. None of White Path's followers accused chiefs like Ross, Ridge, Lowrey, Elijah Hicks, William Hicks, or John Martin of being traitors to the nation as Doublehead, Toochelar, and the Creek Path conspirators had been. It was not a question of selling the land of the Cherokees but of selling their souls—that is, of putting so much emphasis on saving the nation by assimilating to white patterns of behavior and thought that ordinary Cherokees no longer felt at home in their nation or knew what it stood for. White Path's movement concerned the limits of assimilation. It followed the traditional Cherokee strategy of withdrawal of the dissidents from participation in the actions of a council when they could not concur with its actions. In effect, the Ellijay council was an effort to assert a different consensus within the nation.

The revolution contained a strong religious element—a counterreformation led by Cherokee priests and medicine men who fueled the spirit of resistance to assimilation by reviving the dances and rituals of the old Cherokee order. Like the local, full-blood chiefs, the Cherokee adonisgi were facing a dire threat to their power and influence. The missionaries heard rumors of this powerful traditionalist revival, but they saw little of it; the Cherokee religion had become virtually an underground movement as Christianity had advanced. The agent, Hugh Montgomery, recorded nothing about these developments; he had lost touch completely with the Cherokees, devoting most of his time to cultivating a plantation at the agency with his slaves; he assumed that the Cherokees were now able to look out for themselves. White Path's rebellion did not appear to Montgomery to be a governmental matter (except that treaty commissioners might fish better in muddy waters) and none of the agent's reports in these years mention it. All that we know of its history comes from the confused reports and exaggerated fears of the missionaries and a few negative remarks by the acculturationists in the legally elected Council. Both sides in the rebellion were eager afterward to keep the matter hidden from the white public. It was an internal matter to be resolved by the Cherokee people.

The first extant mention of the revolt was by the Reverend Samuel Worcester, then at Brainerd. He wrote on March 29, 1827:

Since Mr. Hicks' death, a dissatisfied party have held a Council at which they are said to have had some [delegates] from every district in the nation except one (not, however, *chiefs* from all) and took it upon themselves to say what should be and what should not be, in regard to the affairs of Government, and to repeal and enact laws. They, however, took no measures to secure the execution of their laws and though perhaps the majority of the people are dissatisfied with some features of the laws, yet for want of system and energetic leaders, I presume the faction is not to be dreaded.[6]

Worcester did not say what specific laws the dissident council had legislated about, but the fact that he conceded that it represented the majority indicates the seriousness of the movement. Nor did he characterize the movement as representing only the full bloods or the poor, the "backward," or anti-mission traditionalists. He did mention that one of the

---

[6] Samuel Worcester to Jeremiah Evarts, March 29, 1827, ABCFM. Emphasis in original.

most trusted Christian converts at the mission, a full blood who had been given the name Samuel J. Mills after his conversion and who often served the mission as an interpreter, was among those who attended the rebel council "and signed their resolutions." Mills had been accused of practicing "conjuring" after his conversion, and he may have been among those disillusioned with the attitude of the Congregationalists toward the "backward" people of his nation. Worcester said that John Ross and the other leaders of the official council had dismissed the whole matter as "a noise that will end in noise only." Ross told the missionaries at Brainerd it would amount to nothing. Worcester thought "it may excite so much of a spirit of opposition to the [Cherokee] Government as to occasion serious difficulty in the excution of the laws," but he did not mention which laws nor, in March, did he mention any anti-mission activity in connection with the rebellion.

Worcester was writing from Tennessee. The Moravians, who lived much closer to Ellijay, heard a more frightening account of what was going on. To them the movement was strongly anti-missionary in its intentions and fraught with violence:

Since the death of our departed Brother Hicks, the whole Nation here is in the greatest turmoil. The greater part wants to have the new laws abrogated and are for having the missions dissolved. Hardly one in fifteen votes for the laws. . . . Dances at night are arranged and during the day, they hold Council. No one trusts anyone any more; now and again there are threats of murder. Judge Martin, who was named by the National Committee in Bro. Hicks' place as Secretary and Treasurer, is being threatened with death and with having his house burned down. . . . The negroes set fires to the houses, others are supposed to have poisoned one another. Some of the negroes run away.[7]

According to the Moravians, the rebels had named Big Tiger as their principal chief. The Moravians described him as a conjuror; he was a full blood who still wore silver arm bracelets. The Moravians were worried because John Ross, The Ridge, and the other legally elected chiefs were taking no action to put the rebellion down. The Moravians had also heard that Elijah Hicks, the Christian son of Charles Hicks, had offered to join and lead the rebels. This was a shock because Elijah Hicks was a member of the Moravian mission church.

In addition, the Moravians said that many Cherokees were having dreams and visions and making prophecies as they had done during the Ghost Dance movement of 1811–1812. Strange and remarkable events were occurring. One of these concerned "a woman [who] was delivered of three children [triplets] who brought all their teeth with them into the

---

[7] Johann Schmidt to A. Benade, May 16, 1827, MAS.

world; when the first one was born, it is supposed to have spoken and called her to account for her godless way of life."[8] In this context "godless" meant contrary to the traditional way of life. The story probably contained a symbolic message that the next generation of Cherokees would curse those who had abandoned the old religion.

To the Moravians the situation was so dangerous that they thought the forthcoming treaty negotiations might easily be manipulated by the federal commissioners in favor of a total removal, and "they [the Cherokees] will perish together with their country. . . . May God sustain them and us too."[9] They reported in May that when Alex McCoy, one of the leading nationalist chiefs, sent a letter from the legal government to "the rebellious Council" asking them to come to a conference to try to reach some agreement, one of the rebel chiefs, Rising Fawn, "who is the chief instigator among them . . . stepped on it" as a sign of contempt for their authority.[10]

The Reverend Isaac Proctor of the American Board at Carmel Mission reported on May 10 that "there is now existing in this nation a most fearful division among the Cherokee. The full Cherokees have risen up against the laws of the Nation and appear to desire their old form of Government."[11] Like the Moravians, he believed that "the old party are rather opposed to Missionaries" and he feared that the Cherokees might be about to experience the same kind of civil war that had ravaged the Creek Nation in 1813. As had Worcester and the Moravians, he recognized that "this [rebellious] party is much the largest" part of the nation. The Reverend William Chamberlain, a Congregationalist at Brainerd, wrote in May that the dissidents were in fact "the heathen party"—the full bloods—and that they were "making a grand and united effort to destroy the government and drive [true] religion and all improvements from the Nation."[12]

But apart from such vague hypotheses and rumors, there is little concrete evidence about the precise goals of the dissidents and no record of whatever votes they took against the missionaries or "the new laws." James Mooney interviewed an old Cherokee in the 1880s who recalled that "from the townhouse of Ellijay, he [White Path] preached the rejection of the new constitution, the discarding of Christianity and the white man's ways, and a return to the old tribal law and custom."[13] By the end

[8] Ibid.
[9] Ibid.
[10] Ibid.
[11] Isaac Proctor to Jeremiah Evarts, May 10, 1827, ABCFM.
[12] William Chamberlain's Journal, May 3, 1827, ABCFM.
[13] Mooney, "Myths of the Cherokees," pp. 113–14.

of May the legal government had agreed to a meeting and matters seemed sufficiently calm to permit the election of delegates to the constitutional convention. Apparently the legally elected chiefs had agreed to discuss all matters of contention prior to the convention itself but after the election of delegates.

The law that had called for the constitutional convention and that had nominated ten persons in each district to stand for election had also prescribed the manner in which the delegates were to be chosen. The election was set for "the Saturday previous to the commencement for the Courts for May Term," 1827 (the last week in May). Adult male voters were to vote orally at specified polling places for three out of the ten nominees in each district. White Path was not among the nominees nor were most of the rebel leaders. However, Kelachulee, whom Worcester identified as a rebel leader, was. Those elected to the constitutional convention were:

Chickamauga District: John Ross, John Baldrige
Chattooga District: George Lowrey, John Brown
Amohee District: Edward Gunter, Lewis Ross, Thomas Forman, Hair Conrad
Coosewatee District: John Martin, Joseph Vann, Kelachulee
Hickory Log District: James Daniel, John Duncan
Taquoee: Ooclenota, William Baling (or Boling)
Etowah: Joseph Vann, Thomas Pettit, John Beamer
Aquohee: John Timson, Situakee, Richard Walker[14]

A disproportionately high number of these were well-to-do, English-speaking mixed bloods because that was the way the nominations had been structured by the Council. It is not known whether the rebels boycotted the election (because there were so few full-blood candidates) or whether they voted for unauthorized candidates who were denied election by the authorities. Of the twenty-one delegates elected, only four were full bloods; all delegates but nine could write their names in English. The only election in which a close contest occurred was in White Path's district, where Kelachulee received the same number of votes as John Ridge. Worcester reported that Kelachulee "has been considered as the head of the opposition party." In the run-off election, he defeated the younger Ridge. Kelachulee was an aged chief, a full blood married to a full blood, a man who had long service in the Council and who had served as a delegate to meetings with the Secretary of War in Washington. All the evidence shows him to have been an ardent patriot. He spoke no English, owned no slaves, and never had anything to do with the missionar-

---

[14] *Cherokee Laws*, p. 40. It is not clear why some districts were allowed four while some had only two; each should have had three for a total of twenty-four, but only twenty-one signed the constitution.

ies. But not all those delegates who were English-speaking mixed bloods were ardent supporters of missions. Between 1824 and 1827 at least five of those elected had been described by missionaries as "quite opposed to missions" in one way or another.

Late in June, a meeting took place at New Echota between the two factions to try to work out a reconciliation. There are some brief notes of this council that show that a committee was appointed to try to resolve the main issues. After five days, it issued a long resolution that was signed by nine of the rebels: Kelachulee, Tyger (Big Tiger), Cabbin Smith, Terrapin Head, Ahchatoueh, Katchee, Frying Pan, George Miller, and Atosotokee. It stated that the signers regretted their actions that had been "calculated to produce party feelings injurious to the public welfare." The members of "the dissatisfied party" now agreed that "harmony and unanimity" should prevail "in supporting the public laws of the nation" and "that all meetings of opposition be discouraged." They also agreed that the rebels would petition the lawful council regarding any of the laws that they "considered unwholesome." In short, they agreed to end the rebellion and to work for reform within the legal system. It is perhaps significant that three of those mentioned in other sources as leading figures in the rebellion did not sign this agreement: White Path, Rising Fawn, and Drowning Bear. Furthermore, the Moravians reported that this reconciliation council was only sparsely attended and that in their opinion "the prospects [were] bad" for reconciliation of the two factions.[15] The Congregationalists, however, believed that "the tumult of the people in this nation" had ended.[16]

General Cocke came to New Echota early in June to observe the constitutional convention and to lay the groundwork for his treaty negotiations in the fall. Cocke learned that the council of reconciliation "adjourned without settling their business amicably and that some of the old Indians are very much dissatisfied and intend to raise opposition to their new mode of Government by Constitution."[17] According to his source, the whole rebellion stemmed from the arrogant behavior of the mixed bloods over the preceding six or eight years: "the mixed bloods are now, and have been for some time, at the head of affairs and passed laws so contrary to ancient customs that the native Indian is ready to revolt."[18] Evidently to deter further rebellion, those attending the reconciliation council at New Echota voted "that every leader of an extra [illegal] coun-

[15] Johann Schmidt to Theodore Schulz, July 2, 1827, MAS.
[16] Ard Hoyt to Jeremiah Evarts, July 16, 1827, ABCFM.
[17] John Cocke's Journal, July 18, 1827, M-234, reel 72, #0248.
[18] John Cocke's Journal, July 1, 1827, M-234, reel 72, #0245.

cil should be punished with a hundred lashes," which seems to indicate that they expected further trouble.[19]

The constitutional convention met, as scheduled, on July 4, 1827. John Ross was elected president and Alex McCoy, clerk. Ross probably presented a draft copy at the first session that was then debated and amended over the next three weeks.[20] There are no extant minutes of the convention nor any comments on its actions by those who attended, but from internal evidence it is possible to suggest some of the issues that may have been controversial and some that may have been written in such a way as to alleviate the worst fears of the rebels. The draft of the constitution was obviously designed as the capstone of Cherokee nationalism and of the Cherokee renascence—a Cherokee version of the American Constitution to suit Cherokee needs. The drafters wished to demonstrate to the world that politically—as a nation—the Cherokees were now fully civilized and republicanized and that they were fully capable of self-government according to the same kinds of laws and legal system that white Americans adopted in a Western territory prior to statehood. As such, the convention hoped to show that the Cherokees had nothing to gain and much to lose by being sent to the West under any "colonization" scheme that would place them under some "modified" form of republican laws suitable to "half-savage" people. The convention also wanted to demonstrate that the Cherokee way of life was now perfectly compatible with Christianity and that its people were open to the same kind of development to become a Christian nation as the rest of the United States. However, much of the wording about religion was so ambiguous that adherents to the old Cherokee religion could not claim that their ways were in any respect proscribed or that Christianity was the preferred religion of the nation. The preamble, however, went further toward acknowledging the deity than the American Constitution.

We, the Representatives of the People of the Cherokee Nation, in Convention assembled, in order to establish justice, ensure tranquility, promote our common welfare, and secure to ourselves and our posterity the blessing of liberty; acknowledging with humility and gratitude the goodness of the Sovereign Ruler of the Universe in offering us an opportunity so favorable to the design and imploring his aid and direction in its accomplishment, do ordain and establish this Constitution for the Government of the Cherokee Nation.[21]

In adapting the American Constitution to the Cherokee situation, one of the most important issues was to define their territorial boundaries.

[19] Johann Schmidt to Schulz, July 18, 1827, MAS.

[20] For a comparison of the Cherokee constitution with the United States Constitution see Strickland, *Fire and the Spirits*, pp. 65–66.

[21] This and the quotations below from the Cherokee constitution are taken from *Cherokee Laws*, pp. 118–25.

Hence Article I spelled these out very specifically and stated that the land within those boundaries was "solemnly guaranteed and reserved forever to the Cherokee Nation by the treaties concluded with the United States" and that they "shall forever hereafter remain unalterably the same." This was, of course, the heart of the matter, for if this Indian nation was not to be subject to diminution by further cessions or by the ultimate incorporation of the people as individuals into the United States (i.e., the denationalization of the Cherokee Nation), the Cherokees had subverted the whole intention of George Washington's Indian policy. The Cherokees argued that Washington's policy was not of their making but that they had for thirty years tried to live up to it. They could also demonstrate that since 1808 the federal government had been trying to alter that policy through its removal and exchange program. In addition they could argue that within the past five years the states in which they lived were frank in their demands for total extinction of Cherokee land claims within their boundaries and seemed determined to subvert the Cherokees' treaties with the federal government by one means or another. Finally, they could argue with equal force that with the adoption of the colonization plan by Monroe and Adams, the chief executives themselves had altered Washington's original policy, leaving only the shred of "voluntary" removal. The next obvious step was forced removal. The Cherokee constitution was an effort to prevent that and to assert their choice (while they still had one) to remain forever where they were under the original Washingtonian grant of self-government.

Section 2 of Article I asserted the national sovereignty of the Cherokee people and affirmed the traditional Cherokee principle of communal ownership of the land:

The sovereignty and jurisdiction of this Government shall extend over the country within the boundaries above described, and the lands therein are and shall remain the common property of the nation; but the improvements made thereon, and in possession of the citizens of the nation, are the exclusive and indefeasible property of the citizens respectively who made or may rightfully be in possession of them.

Moreover, no citizen had the right to dispose of his or her improvements "to the United States, individual states, nor to individual citizens thereof." Citizenship in the Cherokee Nation meant residence within the constitution's prescribed boundaries. Any citizens who moved outside these boundaries to Arkansas or who accepted reserves "and became citizens of any other Government, all their rights and privileges as citizens of the nation shall cease." Presumably the chiefs and councils elected by the Arkansas Cherokees constituted a separate government. Clearly, under the Cherokee constitution, any who might emigrate to Arkansas did

not automatically carry with them a proportionate share of their homeland for exchange purposes.

Article II divided the government into three "distinct Departments:
the Legislature, Executive and the Judicial." Article III defined the powers
of the legislature or "General Council"; the National Committee (or upper branch) was to be made up of two elected members from each of the
eight electoral districts; the National Council (or lower house) was to
consist of three members from each district. Qualifications did not differ
for the two branches. Article III also defined the qualifications for voting,
making explicit the sexual and racial qualifications that had already
evolved in practice. Women, for example, had had no rights in council affairs for twenty years. Voting rights were now limited to "all free male
citizens (excepting Negroes and descendants of white and Indian men by
negro women who may have been set free) who shall have attained the
age of eighteen years." The Cherokees were determined to follow the
practice of the southern states in defining as "Negro" any person who had
a drop of black blood. Office holding was similarly limited, but full citizenship was granted to those of mixed white-and-Cherokee ancestry regardless of any official form of marriage (Christian or secular)—in itself
a concession to traditionalism.

No person shall be eligible to a seat in the General Council but a free Cherokee
male citizen who shall have attained to the age of twenty-five years; the descendants of Cherokee men by all free women except [of] the African race, whose parents may be or have been living together as man and wife according to the customs and laws of this nation, shall be entitled to all the rights and privileges of
this nation as well as the posterity of Cherokee women by all free men. No person
who is of a negro or mulatto parentage, either by the father or mother's side shall
be eligible to hold any office of profit, honor or trust under this government.

The Cherokee Nation was a slaveholding state. On the one hand, traditionalists may have been pleased that white men were excluded from office, on the other, they may have disliked the elimination of women's participation in councils and may have been offended by the implicit
assumption that the father, not the mother, was the official source of parentage, which indicated the abandonment of the matrilineal clan kinship
system. The disfranchisement of women (who in earlier times had the
right to some participation in town and national councils) seems to have
aroused no reaction among the Cherokee women. Except for the women's
petition of 1818, there is no evidence of female participation in the governing process after 1794 (although Stone Carrier had taken two women
in his delegation to Washington in 1808). Probably women retained their

traditional authority in clan affairs, but clans were nowhere mentioned in the constitution.

A significant reversal of the American Constitution provided that all money or appropriation bills must originate in the upper house, a decision that had its roots in 1813, when the National Committee ordered the federal agent turn over all national income to it.

Article IV defined the duties and qualifications of the Principal Chief and Assistant Principal Chief. They were to be elected for four-year terms by the General Council—a significant shift from the tradition of life tenure. "No person except a natural born citizen shall be eligible to the office of Principal Chief," and he must be over thirty-five years old. A distinctive feature of the Cherokee constitution (though not unlike the "cabinet" of the American Chief Executive) was the creation of a Council of Advisors. They were to be elected by the legislature "to advise the Principal Chiefs." The two chiefs and three counselors constituted an executive body with power to act when the council was not in session (but their acts had to be reviewed and ratified by the Council). Now that the National Committee was, strictly speaking, the Senate of the legislature, it was not clear how it would function between legislative sessions. That the counselors may have been created as roles for old chiefs not elected to the Council is indicated by the requirement that when unanimity was lacking the opposing positions of counselors in any executive committee decision were to be written and considered by the Council when it reviewed the actions of that body.

The National Treasurer was to be elected by the legislature and to give bond with sureties. He could draw no money from the National Treasury "but by warrant from the Principal Chief and in consequence of appropriations made by law."

Article V defined the official duties of the judges of the supreme, circuit, and district courts much as they had already been defined in previous legislation. They were to be "appointed by a joint vote of each House of the General Council" and must be over thirty years old. Retirement was mandatory at seventy.

Article VI contained what amounted to the Anglo-Saxon Bill of Rights, guaranteeing a jury trial, due process of law, "free exercise of religious worship," and freedom "from unreasonable seizures and searches." Nothing was said about freedom of speech or freedom of the press, but this was not an oversight. The nation was in the process of establishing a national newspaper (its first edition appeared in February 1828), with an editor appointed by the Principal Chief and removable by him. Because this paper was paid for by national funds and distributed at no charge and because it was to represent the official position of the nation, it was not designed to be open to dissident positions that would divide and confuse the people. The existence of other newspapers or other forms of free expression was not prohibited, but having just been through a rebellion, those who drafted the constitution did not want to encourage such behavior. This was to cause problems for the editor of the *Cherokee Phoenix* in the difficult years ahead.[22]

Article VI also dealt with education. Its phraseology resembled Article III of the constitution of Massachusetts. The parallel is interesting because Massachusetts at that time still had a religious establishment with entaglements between church and state as well as between religion and education. Because the missionary schools included religious instruction and were supported by money appropriated by Congress and because in the near future the Cherokees hoped to have their own national school fund that might in part support mission schools, it was necessary to explain in this article the relationships involved: "Religion, morality and knowledge being necessary to good government, the preservation of liberty and the happiness of mankind, schools and the means of education shall forever be encouraged in this Nation." The constitution did not specifically say that public taxes might be levied for the support of schools or for mission activities, but this was left an open possibility; the relationship between religion, education, and good government was articulated. The rebel faction may not have liked the implications of this.

Probably even more annoying to conservative Cherokees was the section in Article VI stating that "no person who denies the being of a God or a future state of rewards and punishments shall hold any office in the civil department of this Nation." This was strangely at odds with the oath of office specified in Article III of the constitution: "I, A.B., do solemnly swear (or affirm, as the case may be) that I have not obtained my election by bribery, threats, or any undue and unlawful means used by myself or others . . . and that I will bear true faith and allegiance [to the nation and its constitution]." Ostensibly this was designed (as were the oaths in most American state constitutions) to exclude atheists, but unless the word "God" in Article VI was translated as "Great Spirit," it could have caused difficulty for believers in the traditional religion. However, there is no indication that it was ever interpreted to exclude those who adhered to the old religion.

Another section of this grab-bag article lifted a clause from many early American state constitutions excluding ministers of the Gospel from holding office on the grounds that they were "by profession, dedicated to

---

[22] See Theda Perdue, ed., *Cherokee Editor: The Writings of Elias Boudinot* (Knoxville: University of Tennessee Press, 1983), pp. 25–26; Boudinot was fired as editor in 1832 because he represented a minority view that advocated signing a treaty of removal.

the service of God and to the care of souls and ought not to be diverted from the great duty of their function" by entering politics. This too may have been a concession to the fears of conservatives over the rising number of Christian converts and exhorters under the auspices of the various mission agencies. However, this article was never enforced and in later years some notable Cherokee preachers did hold high office, such as Jesse Bushyhead, Young Wolf, Turtle Fields, John Timson, and Stephen Foreman.

The constitution ended with an article permitting amendments with the vote of "two-thirds of each House" provided that the amendment passed in two separate and successive sessions (a provision also contained in the Massachusetts constitution).

Judged as a measure of Cherokee political maturation, the constitution was a sound and workable document. It grew out of a generation of political experience. In most respects it simply codified existing statutes and legal practices. Its chief virtue was that it did not directly challenge the old customs beyond those reforms that had already been enacted by the Council. Most Cherokees probably saw the document for what it was— an ideological statement to head off the vigorous efforts to remove them or take their land. It did not really alter their current structure or behavior in any significant way. Neither, of course, did it place any brake upon rapid acculturation.

The constitution was originally designed to go into effect at once, but apparently when the chiefs discovered what an uproar it aroused in the neighboring states (Governor Troup of Georgia angrily sent a copy of it to President Adams demanding his denunciation of it), the nation's leaders felt that it would be judicious to wait for Adams's reactions. The Georgians expected him to declare it null and void; the Cherokees expected him to approve it. Adams took seven months to find a way out. When the National Council met in October 1827, it elected interim chiefs to replace Pathkiller and Charles Hicks and announced that permanent replacements would be chosen under the constitution the following year. The fact that John Ross was not chosen as acting chief may indicate some displeasure with him. Instead the Council elected William Hicks, the brother of Charles Hicks, as interim Principal Chief; Ross became Second Principal Chief and Elijah Hicks, President of the National Committee.

While the Council was meeting at New Echota in October, General Cocke and two other treaty commissioners sent them a message from the federal agency in Hiwassee stating that they wished the Council to come there to discuss important business. The Council replied, as it had in 1822, that it declined to attend a meeting concerned only with the business of asking it to cede more land. "The Cherokee Nation has no more land to dispose of" they said, and "we cannot accede to your propositions."[23] Cocke was unwilling to come to New Echota and therefore he and the other commissioners returned home without holding any negotiations. In his report to the Secretary of War, Cocke blamed the Cherokees for assuming that they now had "a separate, independent government not amenable or subject to that of the United States."[24] The Cherokees had insisted in their letter to Cocke that they were unwilling "to part with our home—the land of our birth" simply for the "aggrandisement" of the states of Georgia and North Carolina on whose behalf Cocke had come to bargain for Cherokee land.

Though Cocke had been provided with funds for "inducing" well-disposed chiefs to sign a treaty, none of the rebels associated with White Path came to Hiwassee to accommodate him. Nonetheless, Cocke reported to the Secretary of War that in his opinion "two-thirds of them are willing to cede their whole country and remove to the west of the Mississippi."[25] He blamed the impasse upon the mixed-blood elite, who had intimidated "the real Indians." There is no evidence for this. In fact, over the next decade the full-blood conservatives proved far more determined to remain in their homeland than many of the mixed-blood elite. However, White Path's rebellion helped to provide frontier whites with an excuse to persist in seeking Cherokee removal; they said they were acting in the interests of the full bloods against the monopoly of power held by the mixed bloods.

Concerted efforts by White Path and his friends to curtail the rapid pace of acculturation ceased after 1827, but there were continued outbursts of resistance to missionary expansion as long as the Cherokees remained in the East. In fact, only two days after the constitutional convention ended in July 1827, the Reverend Johann Schmidt of Springplace wrote that "adversaries of the Gospel are not lacking"; "in the Chatooga District," he said, "old Drowning Bear . . . [still] tries to convince everyone that the teaching of the white people is not suitable for Indians."[26] In April 1828, Dr. Elizur Butler, medical missionary for the Congregationalists, reported that the traditionalists near Haweis mission sometimes "threaten our lives but more frequently [threaten] to whip us" for continuing to proselytize in their towns.[27] Two months later, a Cherokee convert who frequently exhorted for the Congregationalists was preach-

---

[23] John Cocke's Report on Cherokee Negotiations, August 15–October 11, 1827, M-234, reel 72, #0267–0298.

[24] Ibid.

[25] Ibid.

[26] Johann Schmidt to Schulz, July 30, 1827, MAS.

[27] Elizur Butler to Jeremiah Evarts, April 7, 1828, ABCFM.

ing twenty miles from Haweis when he was "stoned" by a crowd amidst "considerable disturbance."[28] Even after the Council voted in November to fine ten dollars "any person or persons [who] shall interrupt by misbehaviour any congregation of Cherokee or white citizens assembled at any place for the purpose of Divine worship," such outbursts continued.[29] In September 1830, the Reverend Daniel Butrick of the American Board reported that at the town of Running Water some Cherokees threatened to meet him with loaded guns if he appeared to keep a preaching appointment. He came anyway. Those opposed did not attack him.[30] In the years 1836–1838 a new revival of the Cherokee religion frightened many of the missionaries. But open rebellion by any large number of Cherokee conservatives did not occur again in the east.

While Adams and the War Department mulled over their copies of the Cherokee constitution, the Cherokees engaged in their first public political campaign as various candidates vied for election to the National Council, which would ultimately ratify the new fundamental law. The *Cherokee Phoenix* began publication in February 1828 and in its pages various candidates offered their views on how the government should operate under the new constitution. In addition, the editor of the *Phoenix* printed several letters addressed to him expressing the views of various citizens on the issues facing the nation. Because the paper was printed in both English and Sequoyan, the non-English-speaking Cherokees could participate in this debate and become conversant with the issues. In its way, the Cherokee Nation was embarking on its own version of Jacksonian democracy. The common man had a new sense that he was part of the political process that for so long had been dominated by the elite.

As a national paper, subsidized by the National Treasury, the *Phoenix* took no side in the debate. Its editor, Elias Boudinot (Buck Watie or Oowatie), was a nephew of Major Ridge, educated at the Moravian school at Springhouse and the Cornwall Seminary. Married to a white woman and officially engaged in helping the Reverend Samuel Worcester translate the Bible into Cherokee for the American Board, Boudinot was a conscientious editor, thoroughly devoted to the process of acculturation and Christianization. He had overcome his hurt pride at the racial prejudice demonstrated by the whites in Cornwall over his marrying Harriet Gold. In 1826 he had gone on a speaking tour for the nation to raise funds for

[28] Elizur Butler to Jeremiah Evarts, June 5, 1828, ABCFM. Actually the cabin in which he was preaching was stoned, not the preacher.

[29] *Cherokee Laws*, p. 107. This law also prescribed 39 lashes for any Negro who interrupted a Christian meeting, but it is doubtful whether slaves were active in White Path's Rebellion.

[30] Daniel Butrick's Journal, September 8, 1830, ABCFM.

the printing press and the national academy. The address he gave in Philadelphia, New York, Boston, and other places was printed in pamphlet form, the first work by a Cherokee to be printed. In it he explained the Cherokees' progress and looked forward to the day when they might be allowed full equality as citizens to share in the rising glory of the United States. Like John Ridge, David Vann, and David Brown, he was among those bright young leaders of the rising generation who were determined to prove that they could meet every test the whites held up for them and earn their respect despite their "complexion." Under Boudinot's editorship, the *Cherokee Phoenix* proved to be a remarkable force both in attracting white support for the nation (copies were sent to many ministers and missionary societies throughout the United States and were exchanged with other newspapers) as well as keeping the Cherokee people informed of the efforts of the state and federal politicians to obtain Cherokee land. A year after it started publication it added to its name the words *and Indian Advocate* to indicate that the Cherokees saw themselves as the spokesmen for all the Indian nations in the fight against Indian removal.[31]

In the months before the election of August 1828 the chief issue debated in the nation was what qualifications for office a candidate should have. More specifically, the issue was how to balance the interests of the 75 percent of the population who were non-English-speaking, traditionalist, full bloods against the 25 percent (or less) who spoke English and understood the complex problems of dealing with white society. A democratic society required proportional representation, but national survival seemed to indicate the need for rule by the aristocracy of talent, wealth, and experience. Since 1810 the two principal chiefs had been representatives of these two segments of Cherokee society; the Principal Chief represented the full blood majority while the bilingual Second Principal Chief attended to most of the diplomatic relationships with white officials. Similarly, the National Committee consistently contained a majority of bilingual, well-to-do mixed bloods because its principal activities concerned relations with federal officials. The full bloods had their power in the National Council, or lower house, which dealt with local affairs. But was this division of labor necessary or advisable now that the nation had reached such an advanced position of economic and political sophistication? Could the full bloods who spoke no English and understood little of the economic complexities of a market economy serve effectively under the new constitution? Or had their rebellion indicated that they were so disaffected, that they found the new ways so alien and offensive, that

[31] Perdue, *Cherokee Editor*, p. 18.

they would obstruct or distort the nation's development (as the acculturated Cherokees defined it) and jeopardize its security?

In May 1828, a letter addressing these issues appeared in the *Phoenix*
signed "Utaletah" (the author's identity was not otherwise given). Utaletah argued that "unity" was the overriding necessity for the nation. The
Cherokees must combine with "one object, the preservation of ourselves
as a free and sovereign people, observing strictly our relations with the
United States with whom alone we are connected by solemn treaties."
There were many who did not understand the complexity of their situation. "The art of legislation is little understood by a majority of the nation," Utaletah wrote. Would it not be best, therefore, to select candidates
for the National Committee who were "men of education and good
knowledge of the affairs of our nation," while the National Council, or
lower house, "should be composed of full blooded Cherokees known for
their love of country, the land of their forefathers, and also celebrated for
their good natural sense, justice and firmness."

Our nation as a political body has reached an important crisis, and bids fair for
rapid progress in the path of civilization, the arts and sciences; while at the same
time we can say with no ordinary degree of exultation, that agriculture is gradually gaining an ascendancy amongst us equalled by no other Indian Tribe.[32]

Utaletah favored continuing the development of the nation as it had
evolved under the system of the past twenty years, but he wished to assure the full bloods of an equal voice in decision making.

Elijah Hicks, the thirty-year-old son of Charles Hicks and brother-in-
law of John Ross, wrote a letter to the *Phoenix* in July that took the view
that the nation needed leadership chiefly from the well-educated. He was
himself of that group. "I shall support strenuously the election of a Principal Chief who shall be a learned man." He hoped none would try to perpetuate "the past custom of placing an unlearned person in that department." He would find it "humiliating" to have the nation led now by a
Cherokee who spoke no English and understood nothing of the complex
ways of the modern world; such a man would lack "competency to perform all the business connected with the office" and become "dependent
on others" for advice, as Pathkiller had been dependent on Elijah's father.
The chief of the Cherokees should not have to conduct official business
through the use of an interpreter. "If it is our object to place useful men
in our offices," then "our advanced situation requires a learned man at
the head of our government."[33]

On the other hand, Hicks appealed to the anti-mission sentiment of the

[32] *Cherokee Phoenix*, May 6, 1828.
[33] *Cherokee Phoenix*, July 21, 1828.

conservatives by expressing serious criticism of the twelve mission stations with their "splended establishments on the choicest of lands" that
now existed in the nation and that seemed bound to increase in number
and size. "We have permitted them to settle on our land without a special
understanding of the duration of time for their continuance." It was time
to obtain some specific contractual agreements with the various mission
boards to establish inspection of mission work and to regulate their activities. Of course, the best kinds of persons to undertake this delicate work
would be those who understood the nature and purpose of education.

A letter from John Huss, a full blood formerly known as "The Spirit"
or "Captain Spirit" but rechristened after his conversion by the Congregationalists, appeared in the *Phoenix* opposing the view that "the National Committee should be composed of men acquainted with letters and
the Council of full Indians."[34] This "would be a great evil, for it would
appear like creating a division among the people." It was well known, he
said, that the poor and uneducated feel that "those who talk English are
overbearing. Dissensions will soon follow if such a course is pursued." In
his opinion both the upper and lower houses "should be mixed" with
English-speaking and non-English-speaking representatives so that they
would have to learn to work together. "Our Chiefs and legislators have
made for us a Constitution. If we be of one mind in the support of this
Constitution, the inhabitants of Georgia will not take away our land . . .
if we be divided into parties, we shall be liable to lose our territory." He
realized that some did not like the new constitution, but he thought it had
strengthened the nation. "Wherever a people preserve a regular system
of government, that community is firmly established. So let it be with us
Cherokees." The great mistake of the Arkansas Cherokees was that they
had wandered off from their brethen and were "like a lost people." The
division of the Cherokees into east and west had occurred "for want of a
regular system of government." Now the eastern Cherokees had a regular system and they should use it to prevent further divisions.

Major Ridge wrote a letter urging those who were uncertain about the
new form of government to participate in it and help to guide it. As a non-
English-speaking chief he sympathized with those who had doubts and
believed that "to elect hastily such men as will be too speedy imitators of
white people would not be well." He knew that many were worried over
the new ways because they did not understand them. "It is not right to
proceed hastily and from laws which the people do not understand. If a
child beginning to walk attempts to run, he soon falls and cries. And if a

---

[34] *Cherokee Phoenix*, July 2, 1828. Huss could not write English so Boudinot must have
translated this. For Huss see Walker, *Torchlights*, p. 128. Huss was ordained as a Cherokee
evangelist by the Congregationalist missionaries in 1824.

man working in the field does not perform his work thoroughly, he goes over much ground indeed but the field which he has passed over is still full of weeds." He did not favor turning the nation over to educated men who would rush into assimilation; some balance had to be kept with those who respected the old ways and wished to move more slowly. The nation was well aware that it was in a critical position. More federal negotiators had been appointed to meet with them in October. They needed to bridge the gap between the eager young acculturationists and the worried followers of White Path and Rising Fawn.[35]

In order to assure the white public that their country was stable and that their democratic system was functioning smoothly, the chiefs asked some of the missionaries to serve as supervisors and poll watchers when the election took place in August 1828. One of these wrote: "I was present at one of the Precincts at the late Cherokee State Election and was astonished to see so much order and regularity. There was nothing of that intrigue or unfairness which is to be seen at the elections in the civilized States."[36] The rebels did not create any fuss. White Path himself ran for election from his district and won. (Kelachulaee had died in February 1828.) Several Christian converts were also elected. The Reverend Isaac Proctor said that of the forty persons elected "more than one-fifth are pious"—meaning churchgoers.[37] Less than one-tenth of the Cherokees were Christians at this time. The list of those elected shows that most of those who had led the nation for the preceding ten years received a vote of confidence.

At its first meeting in October, the new Council ratified the constitution and then elected John Ross, First Principal Chief; George Lowrey, Second Principal Chief; Lewis Ross, President of the National Committee; Going Snake, Speaker of the Council; John Martin, Chief Justice of the Supreme Court; Alex McCoy, clerk of the lower house; and William Shorey Coody, clerk of the upper house. Major Ridge and William Hicks were chosed as counselors to the chiefs. On the whole, the National Committee continued to be predominantly those of experience, of mixed ancestry, wealthy, and English-speaking while the National Council was predominantly non-English-speaking and full blood.

To discourage any further rebellions, the Council ratified the decision of the reconciliation council in June 1827, punishing those who organized "unlawful meetings with intent to create factions . . . or to encourage rebellion" with 100 lashes.[38] However, probably also as a result of agree-

---

[35] *Cherokee Phoenix*, June 24, 1828.

[36] Isaac Proctor to Jeremiah Evarts, September 3, 1828, ABCFM.

[37] Ibid. Proctor did not identify the nine who were "pious."

[38] *Cherokee Laws*, p. 117. Apparently no one was ever punished for this.

ments reached at that council, the Council agreed in October to take up the problem of missionary expansion and regulation. William Hicks and John Ross had addressed a joint message to the Council on October 13 in which they made a number of recommendations for action. One suggestion was the establishment of a visiting committee to supervise the various mission schools.[39] The Council engaged in an extensive debate on this matter. John Gunter introduced a motion to require all members of the mission staffs "to obtain permits" just as white traders and artisans had to do.[40] In the past the Council had requested the missionaries to ask its permission before bringing in new personnel, but the missionaries had ignored this. The Tennessee Methodist Conference never bothered to ask permission when it expanded its traveling circuits year after year. All the mission boards had blithely assumed that they had a perfect right to increase their mission staffs and activities more or less at will. Gunter argued that this was "inconsistent" with the right of the nation to regulate all activities by whites within its borders.

Gunter's motion was opposed by Richard Taylor and Joseph Vann (of Coosewatee) who "argued on the blessing of education and the good which has been produced by mission establishments." From the intensity of this debate it is clear that the rebels had not been silenced, although they were abiding by their agreement to seek reform within the constitutional system. Following the debate, the Council voted to undertake a full investigation of all the missionary agencies in order to determine what privileges they did and did not have within the nation. In addition, the Council appointed two committees to visit all the schools in the nation (private and missionary) "once a year and to report to the General Council annually on the number of scholars, progress of education, etc."[41] The Council thereby assumed the power to administer the nation's educational system. They expected soon to have a national academy of their own and if the War Department would ever fulfill its agreement to sell the Cherokee education tract and provide an endowment fund for education, the nation expected to have sufficient funds to create its own common schools to complement the existing mission schools.

Early in the spring of 1828, John Quincy Adams had finally reacted officially to the Cherokee constitution. Secretary of War Barbour wrote to Montgomery on March 23, instructing him to call the chiefs together and inform them that as far as President Adams was concerned, their constitution had not altered their relationship with the United States. Or, as he

[39] *Cherokee Phoenix*, October 22, 1828.
[40] Payne Papers, VII:91–92. This is one of the few surviving records of a debate in the Cherokee National Council.
[41] *Cherokee Laws*, p. 94.

put it, their new form of government would "not be recognized as changing any one of the relations under which they stood to the General Government." Adams stated that the constitution "cannot be considered in any other light than as regulations of a purely municipal character."[42] This was meant to assure the State of Georgia and others concerned that Adams did not acknowledge that the Cherokees had, by adopting a constitution, established their independence as a sovereign state.

Despite its negative tone, the Cherokees were happy with this response. John Ross wished to put the same face on the matter: "The constitution," he said, "is not considered in any respect to change the relationship which the Nation sustains with the government of the United States; it was adopted with no view to set up independence unwarranted by the Treaties with the United States."[43] Its purpose was to assert the nation's right to self-government within the treaty obligations through which the United States had agreed to protect its borders against the individual states of the Union. Ross was well aware that Andrew Jackson and the western states believed that Indian treaty relationships with the federal government were the great stumbling block to Indian removal. Only an assertion of states' rights against and above those of the federal government could ultimately attain the goal of those favoring total compulsory removal. The Cherokees had now maneuvered white America into a corner. To drive the Cherokees off their homeland, the whites would have to subvert their own Constitution.

This had already become clear in February 1827 when the State of Georgia directly confronted President Adams with its claim that it was sovereign over Indian land within its own boundaries and dared him to call out the United States Army when Georgia flouted a treaty made with the Creek Nation. By a treaty ceding Creek land in Georgia, the Creeks in Georgia had been given a certain period of time within which to remove themselves (either to western Arkansas or to what remained of their land in Alabama). During that period no whites were to enter the ceded area. However, the Georgians could not wait to start surveying it for sale. When Governor Troup ignored the treaty and sent the state surveyors into the Creek Nation in January 1827, the Creeks complained to Adams and Adams protested to Troup. When Troup refused to heed Adams's warnings to withdraw the surveyors immediately, Adams announced his intention of sending the army to prevent "encroachment upon the territories secured by a solemn treaty to the Indians." He said he would use "all the force committed [to him as Chief Executive] for that

[42] Hugh Montgomery to James Barbour, April 17, 1828, M-234, reel 72, #0547.
[43] John Ross to John Cocke, in Cocke's journal of the treaty negotiations, August 15–October 11, 1827, M-234, reel 72, #0267.

purpose."[44] To this threatened use of federal force against a sovereign state, the Congressman from Mississippi (a state equally eager to assume the sovereign right to remove the Choctaws from its land) said that "if the bayonets of the General Government should on this account [protecting Indian rights] be turned against any of the States," the Georgians "would speedily find its friends rallying around it."[45] Adams was saved from this crisis by the speedy completion of Georgia's survey and the withdrawal of its surveyors before he got around to instructing the army to eject them.[46]

In December 1827, Georgia's legislature passed a resolution affirming that it was sovereign over the Cherokee land within its border. It did this to show that Adams had not won the confrontation. After 1828, the question of states' rights became a burning issue for white Americans in several different ways. One concerned the status of Indian nations within state boundaries; another, the right of the federal government to lay and collect tariff duties; and the third, the supremacy of treaty rights over state sovereignty. The Cherokees became one of the focal points of this complex national debate. In a sense, the Cherokees had seized the initiative in 1827 by asserting their right to a self-governing constitution. The states needed a popular referendum to regain the initiative. Jackson's election provided it. White Americans moved toward a populist form of democracy at the precise moment that White Path's populist movement collapsed among the Cherokees, but how well the United States Constitution would fare under Jacksonian democracy was yet to be seen.

[44] George Troup to John Quincy Adams, February 17, 1827, M-221, reel 105, #6051; John Quincy Adams to James Barbour, February 24, 1827, M-221, reel 105, #5606; see also Dale Van Every, *Disinherited* (New York: William Morrow, 1966), p. 100 and Ulrich B. Phillips, "Georgia and States' Rights," *Annual Report of the American Historical Association, 1901* (Washington, D.C., 1885), 2:60–62.

[45] Van Every, *Disinherited*, p. 102.

[46] The best account of this confirmation between Adams and Georgia is contained in Green, *Politics of Indian Removal*, pp. 132–35.

TWENTY

THE REMOVAL CRISIS
OF 1828

*The lands in question belong to Georgia. She must
and will have them. —Resolution of the Georgia
legislature, December 1827*

When the Cherokees refused to discuss with treaty commissioners either a land cession in Georgia or permission for Georgia to build canals through their nation in October 1827 and when it became clear that John Quincy Adams had no intention of doing anything about the Cherokee constitution, the Georgians decided it was time to take matters into their own hands. To vent their anger and to provide the people of the United States with a new and simple remedy for the Indian question, the resolutions passed by Georgia in December 1827 were designed to explain to the Cherokees exactly what their status was within the boundaries of that state. The first of these resolutions stated that "the absolute title to the lands in controversy is in Georgia," and "she may rightfully possess herself of them when, and by what means, she pleases." "We are aware that the Cherokee Indians talk extravagantly of their devotion to the land of their fathers," said the legislators, and Georgia was well aware that "they have gone very far toward convincing the General Government that negotiations with them in view of procuring their relinquishment of title to the Georgia lands will be hopeless," but such was not the case. The intransigence of the Cherokees would change "if the General Government will change its policy toward them and apprise them of the nature and extent of the Georgia title to those lands and what will be the probable consequence of their remaining refractory." However, if the Federal (i.e., "General") government was unwilling to act, then Georgia's government could and would. The Federal General government was to be allowed just one more chance to fulfill its sacred obligation under the Compact of 1802 and it was given a deadline to meet this ultimatum.[1]

[1] Report of the Georgia Legislature, December 19, 1827, M-234, reel 72, #0432; see also Phillips, "Georgia and States Rights," pp. 71–72; Wilkins, *Cherokee Tragedy*, pp. 71–72; Van Every, *Disinherited*, p. 103.

Asserting that "the policy which has been pursued by the United States toward the Cherokee Indians has not been in good faith toward Georgia," the legislators demanded that the government once again reopen frank and serious "negotiations with the Cherokee Indians upon this subject" and explain to them that Georgia would magnanimously allot one-sixth of the Cherokee area within Georgia to those Cherokees who chose to reside on their farms as personal reserves (to be held as their private property under state law). Georgia would not rescind the law denying Indians the right to testify in its courts and, although the resolutions did not say so, these Cherokee citizens of Georgia would have only the precarious status of freed slaves.[2]

Finally, Georgia's resolutions of 1827 stated that if the Cherokees failed to cooperate in this final effort to extinguish their title to all their land within the boundaries of Georgia, the state would exercise its sovereign power by "taking possession of, and extending our authority and laws over, the whole of the lands in controversy." Let there be no mistake: "The lands in question *belong* to Georgia. She *must* and *will* have them." Georgians had fought and died in the Revolution to free their land from the British and their Indian allies; they had temporarily yielded their rights in the land to allow the federal government to treat with the Indians until the west was free of foreign influence; they had given their western territory (now Alabama and Mississippi) to the federal government in exchange for a solemn promise to extinguish all Indian titles within Georgia as soon as reasonably possible. A quarter of a century had gone by. The Creek War and the War of 1812 had been fought and more of Georgia's blood had been shed. "Georgia has the right to extend her authority and laws over her whole territory and to coerce obedience to them from all description of people be they white, red or black." (The term "white" in the last phrase was a veiled reference to the missionaries, whom the Georgians suspected of encouraging the Cherokees to believe that the land was theirs and that the federal government would permanently protect their right to it.)[3]

The resolutions were received with wild enthusiasm by virtually all the citizens of Georgia. Three years earlier, Hugh Montgomery had explained these strong feelings to the War Department: "The prevailing idea in Georgia, especially among the lower class, is that they are the Rightful owners of the soil and that the Indians are mere Tenants at will; indeed, sir, there is only one point on which all Parties, both high and low, in Georgia agree, and that is that they all want the Indian Lands!"[4] Al-

[2] Ibid.
[3] Ibid. Emphasis in original.
[4] Hugh Montgomery to Thomas McKenney, April 23, M-234, reel 71, #0595.

though he was Federal agent to the Cherokees, Montgomery was a Georgian and knew whereof he spoke.

Yielding to the electoral winds of constitutional doctrine blowing from the west, John Quincy Adams instructed his Secretary of War to sound out the Cherokees once again "on the subject of ceding their land or any portion of it within the limits of Georgia."[5] Barbour relayed the message to Montgomery and one day when John Ross was at the agency, Montgomery read the letter to him. Ross looked at him silently for some time and then remarked grimly that "he supposed that the Government took it for granted that the Indians were not in earnest."[6]

Two months before this incident, McKenney had managed to work out a treaty with the Arkansas Cherokees that he believed would solve the government's dilemma. If Adams would only press home the advantage that this treaty gave him, McKenney believed, he might yet solve the Indian question before the election in November. The need for this treaty arose from the failure of the government to fulfill properly and completely the promises it had made to the Cherokees who had emigrated to the West in 1817–1819. They had been promised perpetual ownership of a tract of land in Arkansas equal to their proportionate share of the eastern part of the nation. But the exact amount of land was still in question because of incomplete surveys of the land ceded by the eastern Cherokees in 1817 and 1819. Moreover, in 1818, President Monroe had promised that those in Arkansas would be given "a western outlet"; now not only were white men crowding in on the Cherokees' eastern border in Arkansas but the whites had gotten around behind them and blocked the possibility of an outlet to the west. However, the citizens of Arkansas Territory seemed as determined to try to move the western Cherokees totally out of their boundaries as the citizens of Georgia were to remove the eastern Cherokees. John C. Calhoun had suggested in 1825, just before Monroe left office, that the Arkansas Cherokees should seriously consider moving further west, but they had refused. They had sent delegations to Washington in 1826 and 1827 to try to get their boundaries firmly settled, to have their outlet surveyed, and to obtain the removal of white intruders on their land, but nothing had been done for them. They had not yet even been fully reimbursed for the costs of their removal.[7]

In April 1828 their delegation was still bargaining with Barbour in Washington about these matters. Barbour told them that Monroe had not promised them a western outlet, but McKenney was able to confirm their

---

[5] Thomas McKenney to Hugh Montgomery, July 22, 1828, M-21, reel 5, pp. 47-48.

[6] Hugh Montgomery to Peter B. Porter, August 26, 1828, M-234, reel 72, #0605.

[7] See Royce, *Cherokee Nation of Indians*, pp. 114–24; Thomas McKenney to James Barbour, December 5, 1825, M-21, reel 2, p. 312.

claim.[8] Neither Barbour nor Adams wanted to remove the white settlers in Arkansas who now blocked such an outlet. McKenney's alternative was to press for their removal further west under the new colonization plan. The western delegates knew that a treaty agreeing to leave Arkansas in exchange for lands farther west would be opposed by the chiefs and people who had sent them. They pointed out that they had not been authorized by their people to make any new treaties; they had come simply to obtain the full implementation of the old treaties. The Arkansas Cherokees had passed the same kind of law adopted by the eastern Cherokees authorizing the death penalty for any chiefs who ceded land without the authorization of the full Council. The delegates included George Guess, James Rogers, Thomas Maw, Thomas Graves, George Morris (or Marris), John Looney, J. W. Flory, and Black Fox. When they asked why McKenney could not simply have their present tract surveyed (including the outlet) and remove the white intruders, McKenney said that the surveys of the eastern Cherokee cessions of 1817 and 1819 were not yet completed so that he was not sure precisely how much land they were entitled to in Arkansas. He estimated, however, that they would be entitled to 3,917,784 acres. The delegation felt that much more than that was due to them. For six weeks in April and May McKenney wrangled with the delegates, holding out to them the promise of a tract of seven million acres further west plus the outlet, if they agreed to move again. He said otherwise they would have to wait until the eastern surveys were completed. He also threatened that the government might never be able to give them their outlet if they did not take it on these terms, because soon too many whites would have settled west of them. Frustrated and worn out, the delegates finally yielded on the condition that whatever they agreed to would be valid only when ratified by the full council in Arkansas. On May 6, 1828, they signed a treaty that McKenney assured Adams would lead to the removal of the eastern Cherokees as well as settle the problems of those in the west.[9] Adams submitted it for ratification by the Senate without waiting for the Cherokee council in Arkansas to consider it.

Ostensibly this treaty concerned only the problems of the Cherokees in Arkansas; no delegates from the eastern Cherokees were present at the signing of the treaty, nor were they informed of its negotiation or asked to ratify it. Its principal clauses called for a grant to the western Cherokees of seven million acres along the headwaters of the Arkansas River in what is now the northeastern corner of Oklahoma (but was then the western part of Arkansas Territory), plus the award of an outlet (or strip

[8] Thomas McKenney to James Barbour, April 12, 1828, M-21, reel 4, p. 401.
[9] Royce, *Cherokee Nation of Indians*, pp. 118–20, and Cherokee Treaty, May 6, 1828, M-21, reel 4, p. 430.

of land) fifty-five miles wide extending from this area due west to the United States border with Mexico. They were also to receive a grant of $50,000 outright for the land they now occupied in Arkansas and $2,000 per year for three years to help them resettle farther west on the new tract. In addition, the government agreed to reimburse each Cherokee in Arkansas for the appraised value of the improvements he had made on the land there. The treaty included a promise that this new seven-million-acre tract would remain the land of the Cherokees "forever."[10]

The most important point of this treaty for McKenney and Adams and ultimately for the eastern Cherokees was a clause that the westerners had very little real interest in. They had not objected, however, when McKenney suggested its insertion. Article 8 stated that in order "that their Brothers yet remaining in the States may be induced to join them" in their new tract, it was agreed "on the part of the United States that each Head of family" now residing in the east, "who may desire to remove West, shall be given, on enrolling himself for emigration, a good Rifle, a Blanket, a Kettle, and five pounds of tobacco" as "just compensation for the property he may abandon" in the eastern nation. Furthermore, "the cost of emigration" was to be "borne by the United States" as well as the cost of "provisions for twelve months after their arrival" in the new tract.[11] McKenney told the western Cherokees that he had to include this clause because he was giving them a much larger tract than their numbers entitled them to and further emigration would help him to justify the treaty. Furthermore, he pointed out, with every new emigrant the westerners would be entitled to a larger proportion of the annuity paid to the nation each year (it being assumed that the Cherokees were still one nation and that this sum was perennially open to revision, claims that the eastern Cherokees would not have concurred in). McKenney's cleverest trick, one he considered particularly astute considering the pressures the Georgians were placing on Adams, was to promise that every head of family among the eastern Cherokees who took four persons with him to the new tract and who "migrated from within the chartered limits of the State of Georgia" would be paid $50 (or $10 per individual if there were over five in the family) upon his arrival in the new tract.

President Adams was delighted with the treaty and immediately authorized Montgomery to make this new opportunity for emigration

---

[10] Cherokee Treaty, May 6, 1828, M-21, reel 4, p. 430; Thomas McKenney to George Graham, May 28, 1828, M-21, reel 4, p. 471; Royce, *Cherokee Nation of Indians*, pp. 118–20; and Berlin B. Chapman, "How the Cherokees Obtained the Outlet," *Chronicles of Oklahoma* 15 (1937): 30–41.

[11] Cherokee Treaty, May 6, 1828, M-21, reel 4, p. 430.

known to the eastern Cherokees and to start enrolling emigrants.[12] Montgomery was to take special care to induce emigration from the Georgia area because "the obligation of the United States in the compact with Georgia created [the] obligations which led to such a treaty."[13] But the only way the treaty of 1828 could fulfill that compact was under the assumption, not stated in the treaty, that for each emigrant an equivalent proportion of Cherokee land in the Georgia area would be ceded. If enough emigrants could be enrolled, the Cherokees in the east would be told that they must cede all of their land in Georgia. "Much is expected of you," McKenney told Montgomery, for on the agent's ability to induce a large scale emigration depended Adams's response to the Georgia resolutions and perhaps his reelection.

Adams was so pleased with this arrangement that he authorized McKenney to pay $500 each to James Rogers and Thomas Maw of the western delegation to return home by way of the eastern nation, where they were to spend several weeks or more as secret agents of the government, inducing their friends and relatives to enroll for emigration.[14] In explaining this to Montgomery, McKenney warned him that much of Rogers's and Maw's success "will depend upon keeping the object of [their] visit a secret."

Thus out of Adams's desperation and McKenney's artifice the Cherokees were faced with their third removal crisis in the summer of 1828. They soon became aware of the treaty and obtained a copy. The editor of the *Phoenix* printed it in full in July and wrote a blistering editorial. "If our emigration is to be effected, we had rather that a treaty was made with us directly." The government could hardly expect their cooperation with a treaty made behind their backs.[15] The National Committee then appointed a group of chiefs to travel throughout the nation explaining the treaty and urging resistance to it. This committee visited every town and village, arguing that no one should place any reliance whatsoever on the government's promises of assistance to them in emigrating or in their securing a permanent home in the west. They had only to remember the false promises made to those who had removed in 1809–1810 and in 1817–1819; they had only to look at the sad plight of their brethren who had settled in western Arkansas under firm promises of government protection and now they were being forced to give up all their improvements and move farther west.[16] Boudinot emphasized this in his editorial in the *Phoenix*:

[12] Thomas McKenney to Hugh Montgomery, May 27, 1828, M-21, reel 4, p. 465.
[13] Ibid.
[14] Ibid.
[15] *Cherokee Phoenix*, July 21, 1828.
[16] Ibid., March 4, 1829; Wilkins, *Cherokee Tragedy*, pp. 199–200.

Thus has it happened to the Cherokees in Arkansas to whom a beautiful talk was given promising peace and happiness and now, scarcely ten years are passed, and they [the whites] have become weary of them. But those to whom this delusive promise was first made do not now remember it. Glass and Tutsalah [Toochelar] now sleep. I pity those Cherokees who have gone from us. Our wandering blood will be extinguished far away from us. But let us learn. Let us hold fast to the country which we yet retain. Let us direct our efforts to agriculture and to the increase of wealth and to the promotion of knowledge.

His editorial declared that the history of the western Cherokees was "proof of the uselessness of this emigration scheme." As for the inducements McKenney offered to promote removal, Boudinot declared them "trifling"—an insult to the Cherokees: "A blanket has lost its former value with us; so has the rifle and the kettle, and the mention of five pounds of tobacco in a treaty where the interest of a nation of Indians is supposed to be concerned looks to us too much like jesting."[17]

The treaty seemed to be a major coup for Adams in the battle to get around the stubbornness of the Cherokee Council. The people of Arkansas were pleased to have the Cherokees in their territory removed farther west. Georgia's congressional delegation supported McKenney's suggestion that the $50,000 that Congress had recently appropriated to try one more negotiation for land with the Cherokee Council should be now applied to promoting the emigration plan in the treaty.[18] The white Americans who favored moving all the Indians to an "Indian Territory" were pleased that the eastern Cherokees might be the avant-garde of this program to rid the east of all Indians.[19] McKenney boasted to the Reverend Thomas Stuart of Mississippi: "Indians I have found out, are only children, and can be properly managed only by being treated as such."[20]

Unfortunately for the eastern Cherokees, there was another shortage of food during the summer of 1828 and heavy rains that spring had produced flooding that had held up the planting and thus delayed the summer corn harvest. A white trader in the Georgia area, Jacob Scudder, told Montgomery in August that the Cherokees in his region were "literally starving." Many of them were so demoralized by harassment from Georgia's intruders who constantly stole their livestock that they had not bothered to plant anything. They were "living on Tarapin and Frogs," Scudder said and "a very great portion of the Indians in that quarter will go" west.[21]

McKenney prepared for a great exodus. He ordered blankets and ket-

---

[17] *Cherokee Phoenix*, July 9, 1828.
[18] Thomas McKenney to Peter Porter, July 9, 1828, M-21, reel 5, p. 16.
[19] James Barbour to William McLean, April 29, 1828, M-21, reel 4, p. 423.
[20] Thomas McKenney to Thomas Stuart, April 14, 1828, M-21, reel 4, p. 406.
[21] Hugh Montgomery to Peter B. Porter, August 7, 1828, M-234, reel 72, #0594.

tles from Joseph Lopez Dias in New York City and 500 rifles from Henry Derringer in Philadelphia for those who would enroll. He told Montgomery to make contracts for flatboats, keelboats, and provisions to move the emigrants down the Tennessee and up the Arkansas River to their new home.[22] The federal agent to the Indians in Arkansas, Colonel Edward W. Duval, was instructed to have supplies ready at a depot in the new tract to assist the emigrants when they arrived. To assist Rogers and Maw in their clandestine efforts to promote enrollment, McKenney printed copies of the resolves passed by the Georgia legislature in December 1827 and told them to distribute these as evidence of the futility of trying to hold on to their land in the east. These reprints were to be employed, McKenney said, "not as threats to intimidate individuals but as inducements rather for them to accede to the wishes of the General Government."[23]

In June 1828 Adams had replaced James Barbour as Secretary of War with Peter B. Porter, a general from New York State. Porter had been a war hawk in 1812 and a bitter opponent of Tecumseh. He had no doubt that total removal of all the Indians east of the Mississippi was both necessary and desirable. His appointment was an effort to convince the western states that Adams was wholeheartedly behind the colonization plan. Porter gave full support to McKenney's effort to promote emigration among the Cherokees and assured the Georgia Congressmen that they need not continue to push for a treaty with the eastern Cherokees for total extinction of Cherokee title to land in their state because "the machinery for the accomplishment of the same object was contrived in, and has been set in motion under, the late Treaty with the Cherokees of Arkansas."[24]

McKenney had talked with the Georgia Congressmen; he told Porter that they preferred "the mode which the provision in the Treaty and the instructions under it provides" to the choice of appointing new treaty commissioners who would probably face another humiliating refusal. "Those Indians," McKenney said, "are no longer to be treated in the usual mode of entering into compacts under the treaty form." This had proved ineffective and that was why he had taken other means.[25]

In July, Congressman James C. Mitchell of Tennessee wrote to the War Department asking why the important task of stimulating emigration among the Cherokees had been left solely to the resident agent. Mitchell

[22] Thomas McKenney to Peter Porter, July 26, 1828, M-21, reel 5, p. 52; Thomas McKenney to Joseph Dias, August 4, 1828, M-21, reel 5, p. 74; Thomas McKenney to Hugh Montgomery, November 26, 1828, M-21, reel 5, p. 205.

[23] Thomas McKenney to Hugh Montgomery, July 22, 1828, M-21, reel 5, pp. 47–48.

[24] Thomas McKenney to Peter Porter, July 9, 1828, M-21, reel 5, pp. 32–33; Thomas McKenney to J. C. Mitchell, July 10, 1828, M-21, reel 5, pp. 34–35.

[25] Thomas McKenney to Peter Porter, July 9, 1828, M-21, reel 5, pp. 32–33.

was not aware of the secret assistance Montgomery had from Rogers and Maw and wanted special agents appointed to assist Montgomery (as McMinn had assisted Meigs in 1817–1819). Furthermore, Mitchell thought it unfair for the government to provide a cash bonus only to Cherokees who emigrated from Georgia. The same bonus should be offered to those who would leave Tennessee.[26] McKenney's prime concern was Georgia's claims and he did not want anything to compete with them; he declined Mitchell's suggestion. He had to admit however, that Rogers and Maw in their first few months among the eastern Cherokees had not been very effective. In the first place, they had not been able to keep their mission secret for long. When it became known, they met so much resistance that they became demoralized and McKenney heard that they were using their subsistence funds to keep themselves in whiskey. After corresponding about this with Montgomery, he told him that he should accompany Rogers and Maw in order to keep an eye on them and urge them to greater efforts.[27] He reminded Porter that Montgomery had been appointed federal agent to the Cherokees at the request of Georgia's politicians: he "is the chosen agent of Georgia, and if there be a failure, no blame can attach to the Executive."[28]

Montgomery was unhappy that Porter had ruled that no remuneration would be given to any emigrant for any crops left in his fields when he departed or for any of his horses, cattle, hogs, chickens, sheep, or other livestock that he did not want to transport west. The emigrant was "to sell on his own account" any stocks or crops he wished to leave and get the best terms he could. Under the circumstances the emigrant was at some disadvantage in trying to obtain profitable terms from Cherokee neighbors who opposed his going and white buyers who would take advantage of his need for cash.[29]

Although Montgomery had been optimistic in June about the success of the plan, by the end of August he was disappointed with the results. "I must confess," he wrote to McKenney on August 26, "that the prospects is not at this time very propicious." He blamed this on the successful efforts of the Council to counteract the program. "All the influential part of the nation [have worked] to discourage the poorer class from inrolling and even threatening those who are engaged in it. I feel but little will be

[26] Thomas McKenney to J. C. Mitchell, July 10, 1828, M-21, reel 5, pp. 34–35; Thomas McKenney to J. C. Mitchell, August 23, 1828, reel 5, pp. 94–96.

[27] Hugh Montgomery to Peter B. Porter, July 3, 1828, M-234, reel 72, #0572; Hugh Montgomery to Peter B. Porter, August 7, 1828, M-234, reel 72, #0594; Thomas McKenney to Peter Porter, July 26, 1828, M-21, reel 5, pp. 54–55; Thomas McKenney to Hugh Montgomery, August 26, 1828, M-21, reel 5, p. 101.

[28] Thomas McKenney to Peter Porter, July 26, 1828, M-21, reel 5, pp. 54–55.

[29] Thomas McKenney to Hugh Montgomery, August 2, 1828, M-21, reel 5, p. 73.

done this year.''[30] During the fall and winter, teams of Cherokee chiefs led by Major Ridge, John Ross, and John Ridge again rode on horseback around the nation opposing emigration and speaking against the folly of trusting the government's promises. The *Cherokee Phoenix* also kept up steady opposition to enrollment.[31] The National Committee assigned three influential Cherokees (George Sanders, Samuel Graves, and Thomas Foreman) to dog the steps of Rogers, Maw, and Montgomery through the nation and give public answers to every statement they made.[32]

In the course of these public debates, feeling ran high against the Arkansas Cherokees for having allowed this problem to arise and then for lending two of their people to promote it. Thomas Foreman told a throng at Coosewatee in September that Rogers and Maw belonged to a body of traitors who in 1817 ''had sold this country and were [now] come to persuade the Indians [still here] to give it up.''[33] Montgomery reported that Foreman, Sanders, and Graves had also privately warned Rogers and Maw that they had better return to Arkansas for ''their lives were in danger'' and the Council could not be responsible for what might happen to them.[34]

The only parts of the nation in which enrollment had any success were around Creek Path and Wills Valley in the Lower Towns and near the federal agency in eastern Tennessee. According to Montgomery, however, those who were most eager to emigrate were white men with Cherokee wives or the sons of such marriages. Moreover, most of these people expected bribes: ''I believe many white men who married into the nation and some of the halfbreeds are expecting something like douceurs for breaking the ice'' and leading the movement west, Montgomery told McKenney in October.[35] ''I find (and they know it too) that on the former ocation [of removal, 1817–1819] money was dealt out liberally [by McMinn], indeed thousands in a week, to individuals (many of whom never went) with a view to their acts and example opperating on others. This may have been right then, but now we feel the effects of it, and this example and the hopes of Reservations, opporate more injuriously [against us] than all the influence of the chiefs. Many of the best informed halfbreeds say they expect better terms and will therefore wait.''

[30] Hugh Montgomery to Peter B. Porter, August 26, 1828, M-234, reel 72, #0605.
[31] *Cherokee Phoenix*, September 3, 1828.
[32] Hugh Montgomery to Peter B. Porter, September 26, 1828, reel 72, #0616.
[33] Ibid.
[34] Ibid.
[35] Hugh Montgomery to Peter B. Porter, October 2, 1828, M-234, reel 72, #0621.

In short, the only persons willing to go west or to enroll expected to be paid handsomely for it.

Toward the end of October, 1828, a violent quarrel occurred between Rogers and two Cherokees named James Spears and Archy Foreman. According to Montgomery, Spears and Foreman walked into a tavern where Rogers was drinking and "without speaking a single word to him, struck him on the head with a rock supposed to weigh near four pound." When Rogers staggered to his feet and asked why Spears had hit him, Spears simply hit him again.[36] Montgomery was outraged and feared that this would intimidate any Cherokee from enrolling thereafter. He ordered the arrest of Spears and Foreman; Foreman escaped but Spears was taken to prison. Foreman was thought to be planning a similar assault upon Maw. "The hostility" had caused some enrollees to have second thoughts, Montgomery said. Unless the government provided armed protection to those who wanted to go west, such violence would put "an end to emigration here."[37]

As Principal Chief, John Ross provided money to free Spears on bail and told Montgomery that he had no right to interfere in a quarrel between two Cherokees.[38] Spears's assault, he said, was not related to the emigration program at all; it was the result of a personal quarrel between him and Rogers over a matter of family property. Montgomery had arrested Spears because Rogers was an official agent of the War Department and in his opinion Rogers had been injured while acting in the line of duty. The Cherokee Council supported Ross's interpretation and protested that Montgomery had exceeded his authority in "arresting an Indian for whipping another Indian" in a private matter.[39] The Council said at the same time "We do hereby protest against the Arkansas Cherokees interfering or intermeddling with the concerns of our citizens" and trying "to seduce any of our citizens away from this country." The Council also told Montgomery it would accept no responsibility if such insidious actions aroused some patriotic Cherokees to retaliate.[40] Montgomery responded that "no dishonorable steps have or will be taken to induce any of the Cherokees to enroll," but he said he knew that many poor Cherokees wanted to go and he thought they were hesitant because "they were afraid of the Big Men at the New Town [New Echota]." The

---

[36] Hugh Montgomery to Peter B. Porter, October 31, 1828, M-234, reel 72, #0639; Gideon Morgan to Thomas McKenney, October 24, 1828, M-234, reel 72, #0630.

[37] Hugh Montgomery to Peter B. Porter, October 31, 1828, M-234, reel 72, #0639.

[38] Cherokee Council to Hugh Montgomery, November 21, 1828, M-234, reel 72, #0659; Hugh Montgomery to Cherokee Council, November 24, 1828, M-234, reel 72, #0663.

[39] Cherokee Council to Hugh Montgomery, November 21, 1828, M-234, reel 72, #0659.

[40] Ibid.

government would not tolerate any effort to intimidate these poor Cherokees, he told the Council.[41]

McKenney was equally incensed by the attack on Rogers. He told Porter that the Cherokees had displayed "a fixed purpose by threats and otherwise to keep their people from emigrating. The remedy is the presense of an armed force near or upon the borders of these people for the protection of such as may desire to remove."[42] Porter agreed to send troops to the Cherokee border in Georgia and told Montgomery to go ahead and press the suit against Spears for assaulting Rogers. The American public was led to believe, however, that the troops were sent in connection with problems over Creek removal in the southern part of Georgia.

A second serious check upon emigrant enrollment came on November 12, 1828, when the *Phoenix* printed a letter from the clerk of the Arkansas Cherokee council, William Thornton, stating that the Cherokees in Arkansas were so angry with the delegates who had made the treaty in May forcing their own removal that they had deposed them from office and repudiated the treaty. Thornton wished to inform the eastern Cherokees that the westerners would not encourage emigration from the east to their territory: "I understand that two of our people are in your nation hunting emigrants to this nation. . . . we don't approve of this, and I hope they will not be countenanced. That part of the Delegation that has arrived [here from Washington] are all broke[n] and silenced forever and the others [Rogers and Maw] will fare the same" when they return. The whole delegation "have acted with fraud and deception" Thornton said.[43]

On October 31, Montgomery reported that six months of emigration efforts had resulted in almost total failure. "We have on the [enrollment] register but eleven persons and four or five of them have no family." Most of these "want a part of the price of their improvement before they go to releve them from debt."[44] This was a far cry from the thousands McKenney had expected and prepared for. The Cherokees seemed to have successfully resisted the third attempt to remove them. That fall both their Council and the council of the western Cherokees voted to send delegations to Washington to put an end to the problems raised by McKenney's treaty.

When Porter made his report on Indian affairs to President Adams in

---

[41] Hugh Montgomery to Cherokee Council, November 24, 1828, M-234, reel 72, #0663.

[42] Thomas McKenney to Peter Porter, December 1, 1828, M-21, reel 5, p. 214.

[43] *Cherokee Phoenix*, November 12, 1828; the letter from Thornton is dated September 28, 1828. See also Templeton W. Ross to Peter Porter, September 28, 1828, M-234, reel 72, #0667.

[44] Hugh Montgomery to Thomas McKenney, October 31, 1828, M-234, reel 72, #0639.

November 1828, he fully endorsed removal of all Indian tribes "into a colony consisting of distinct tribes or communities but placed contiguous to each other and connected by general laws which shall reach the whole. Let the lands be apportioned among families and individuals in severalty"; administrators and superintendents should "assist them in forming and administering a code of laws adapted to [their] state of civilization." The most surprising part of Porter's report was an attack upon the missionaries and missionary schools supported by the Education Fund. Mission schools had created, he said, a group of "half-educated" Indians who "finding no outlet for their intellectual skills and attainments among their degraded people," either became useless drunkards or "obnoxious" troublemakers. As for the missionaries, Porter said, they were little more than "agents [who] are operating, more secretly to be sure, but not with less zeal and effect, to prevent such emigration" and thus to thwart the benevolent intentions of the government. He explained that their reason for wanting to prevent Indian removal was because "missionaries and teachers with their families . . . having acquired principally by the aid of this [Civilization] fund, very comfortable establishments [east of the Mississippi], are unwilling to be deprived of them by the removal of the Indians."[45]

President Adams, in his report to Congress on the Indians on December 2, noted that "we have been far more successful in the acquisition of their lands than in imparting to them the principles, or inspiring them with the spirit, of civilization." This to him was proof of the failure of the original Indian policy of George Washington and his successors. He saw no good deriving from the Education Fund that was designed to carry out the policy. Although the Cherokees might have been cited as an exception to this evaluation, Adams had no difficulty explaining why they too should be removed as part of the colonization plan: "When we have had the rare good fortune of teaching them the arts of civilization and the doctrines of Christianity, we have unexpectedly found them forming in the midst of ourselves, communities claiming to be independent of ours and rivals of sovereignty within the territories of our Union."[46] The more successfully an Indian nation acculturated itself, the more dangerous it became to American expansionism. The Cherokee renascence might have been hailed by Adams as a remarkable achievement for the Indians as well as the crowning success of America's philanthropic civilization program. Instead, he portrayed it as a grievous failure.

Congress did not pass the proposal for Indian colonization that Adams

[45] *Cherokee Phoenix*, January 7, 1829.
[46] Prucha, *American Indian Policy*, pp. 232-33.

and Porter introduced in January 1829, because Adams was by then a lame-duck President. Andrew Jackson had been elected in November 1828 and everyone knew that when he was inaugurated on March 4, he would have his own plan for removing the Indians. What that plan would be was predictable. The State of Georgia in effect provided the basis for it in a series of laws its legislature passed toward the end of December, when it was clear that McKenney's emigration plan was a flop. Georgia's program for the Indians was not really new. Return J. Meigs had proposed it as early as 1811 and several times thereafter. However, it was unworkable so long as the Presidents of the United States believed that treaties were the supreme law of the land and that under their treaties the Indians had the right to refuse to cede land or remove to the west. Given this, there was no way the government could coerce them. Georgia's detailed law of December 1828 was based on the assumption that under Andrew Jackson these previous presidential assumptions would cease to apply. Treaty obligations and even the Trade and Intercourse Acts would be abandoned.

The Georgia law stated that the terms outlined in it would not take effect until June 1, 1830 (presumably to give the Cherokees two years to remove to the west if they did not like what the new policy had in store for them). The law then asserted that "all laws of this state . . . are extended over" the territory claimed by Indians [Creeks and Cherokees] within Georgia's boundaries. That land was to be surveyed within the next two years by the State of Georgia and divided into counties. "After the first day of June, 1830," all Indians still residing in those areas "shall be liable and subject to such laws and regulations as the legislature may hereafter prescribe." When this happened, "all laws, usages, customs made, established and enforced in the said territory by the said Cherokee Indians be, and the same are hereby on and after June 1, 1830, declared null and void." On that date Cherokee tribal existence in the east would cease. All the laws, the constitution, the court system, as well as the old unwritten customs of the Cherokee Nation (such as tribal ownership of land) would be null and void. Cherokees would thenceforth be subject to the same laws as other Georgians except that, being savages, heathens, and people of color, "no Indian or descendant of an Indian residing with the Creek or Cherokee nations of Indians shall be deemed a competent witness or party to any suit in any court created by the constitution or laws of this state to which a white man may be a party."[47]

Georgia's action was part of the same states' rights feeling that asserted itself in South Carolina over the Tariff of Abominations and that (following Calhoun's South Carolina Exposition that year) led to the nullifica-

[47] Peters, *Case of the Cherokee Nation*, pp. 281–282.

tion of the tariff. Nationalistic feelings, it seemed, had inspired not only the United States and the Cherokees and the Creeks but also the southern states. James W. Moore, Congressman for Georgia, in denouncing the Cherokee constitution, had said that "sovereignty over soil is the attribute of States, and it can never be affirmed of tribes living in savage condition."[48] Georgia, however, was in a civilized condition and "Georgia," Governor Troup said, "must be sovereign upon her own soil, within her chartered limits; she has made no surrender of her territorial sovereignty and jurisdiction by entering into the Union."[49]

The Cherokees had feared the worst when they learned that Jackson had been elected. The editor of the *Phoenix* said in the issue of December 10, 1828, that it was now certain Jackson would be the next President. The voice of the white electorate had spoken and, by their majority opinion, the fate of the Indian seemed sealed. Thus "republican tyranny expells" the Indian from his homeland.[50]

The Cherokee delegation that came to Washington in January 1829 to discuss McKenney's treaty realized that the matter was now out of Adams's hands and decided to stay on in the city until Jackson was inaugurated and talk to him. It surprised them that Adams had nothing to say about Georgia's open defiance of the Constitution and its treaty power. To make matters worse, the State of Alabama had followed Georgia's example in January and had said that it too planned to extend its jurisdiction over all the Indian lands within its borders.[51] A few days after Jackson's inaugural, the Cherokee went to speak with his Secretary of War, John Eaton. Their first question was what reaction President Jackson would have toward the laws passed by Georgia in "defiance of the Laws of the United States and the most solemn treaties existing" between the Cherokees and the government. They were told they would have to wait for Jackson himself to answer that; he did so in April when he instructed Eaton to tell the Cherokee delegates that the federal government would never assert its authority against the sovereign power of the State of Georgia with regard to the land or the people within its borders. Did the Cherokees really expect otherwise, Eaton asked? Did they think the government would

step forward to arrest the constitutional act of an independent State exercised within her own limits? Should this be done and Georgia persist in the maintenance of her rights and authority the consequence might be that the act would prove injurious to us and, in all probability, ruinous to you. The sword might be

[48] Van Every, *Disinherited*, pp. 119.
[49] ASP II, 743.
[50] *Cherokee Phoenix*, December 10, 1828.
[51] Green, *Politics of Indian Removal*, pp. 145-147.

looked to as the arbiter in such interference. But this can never be done. The President cannot and will not beguile you with such expectation. The arms of this country can never be employed to stay any state of the Union from those legitimate powers which attach and belong to their sovereign character.[52]

Eaton went on to explain to the Cherokee delegates that this being the unalterable political reality, the President advised them to remove as soon as possible to the seven-million-acre tract that had been designated for them in the treaty of May 6, 1828. The Cherokees in Arkansas, he reminded them, had already accepted this choice when their council withdrew its initial objection to the treaty in January 1829. The western Cherokees were already in the process of removing to the new tract and the eastern Cherokees should do likewise.

Eaton then drew the State of Tennessee into the effort to remove the Cherokees on the terms that its Congressman, James Mitchell, had suggested to McKenney the preceding summer. Realizing that Rogers, Maw, and Montgomery had been ineffective in pushing the emigration plan, Eaton appointed two new secret agents. These were Governor William Carroll of Tennessee and General John Coffee, Jackson's old friend. Eaton called this a mission of mercy in his letter to Carroll in May 1829:

A crisis in our Indian Affairs has arrived. Strong indications are seen of this in the circumstances of the Legislatures of Georgia and Alabama extending their laws over the Indians within their respective limits; these acts, it is reasonable to presume, will be followed by the other States interested in those portions of their soil now in the occupancy of the Indians. In the right to exercise such jurisdiction, the Executive of the United States fully concurs and this has been officially announced to the Cherokee Indians.[53]

Therefore, Eaton continued, the President wished to ask Carroll if he would "undertake to enlighten the Cherokee and Creeks" on the necessity of emigration. "In your progress through their Country, it would be well to ascertain, if you can do so without disclosing the purpose of the Executive" in appointing them, whether or not the Cherokees manifested "a willingness to negotiate for a cession" of their land under these new circumstances. The President, though upholding the rights of the states to assume control over Indian land, nevertheless wished to be helpful to the Indians in this situation. If they were to cede their land to the federal government, he would be able to pay them for it and to assist them in moving west; surely that was preferable to coming under the jurisdiction of Georgia and Alabama. "The President views the Indians as the Children of the Government. He sees what is best for them." Carroll's mis-

[52] James Eaton to Cherokee delegation, April 18, 1829, M-21, reel 5, pp. 408–410.
[53] John Eaton to William Carroll, May 30, 1829, M-21, reel 5, p. 456.

sion was really "a work of mercy," Eaton said, because in his view, there was "no doubt, however, but the mass of these people would be glad to emigrate, and there is as little doubt but that they are kept from this exercise of their choice by their Chiefs and other interested and influential men amongst them [the missionaries] who, tenacious of their authority and their power, and unwilling to forego their gainful positions, keep them under the ban of their dictation." Carroll's task was to work on the self-interest of the well-disposed in order to assist "the real Indians" against their chiefs. Bribery, he implied, might be in order. "It becomes therefore a matter of necessity, if the General Government would benefit these people, that it move upon them in the line of their own prejudices and, by the adoption of any proper means, break the power that is warring with their best interest." In Carroll's private talks with those influential chiefs who were disposed to emigrate (or to encourage others to migrate), Eaton told Carroll that "offers to them of extensive reservations in fee simple and other rewards" should be made that would "it is hoped, result in obtaining their acquiescence" to a total cession of Cherokee land in the east. "Go to them as a friend," Eaton urged; "enlarge on their corporate degradation as a people and the total impossibility of their ever attaining to higher privileges while they retain their present relations to a people who seek to get rid of them."

The Cherokees never saw this letter, but they knew well enough what was in store for them. They had bested John Quincy Adams's effort to remove them in 1828, but now their fourth removal crisis was at hand. This time they had very few means to withstand it. Probably the missionaries in the field would help, but the mission boards that employed them were cautious about entering politics. Perhaps out of humanitarian interests the churchgoing public could be aroused to defend the Constitution of the United States and the nation's pledged honor in Indian treaties. But the vast majority of the public had already spoken in favor of Jackson. In the end, the Cherokees found only one real source of power that might take their side, the Supreme Court of the United States. It was still led by that old Federalist appointee and arch foe of Andrew Jackson, John Marshall of Virginia. Perhaps from him they would obtain a validation of their sovereignty.

TWENTY-ONE

THE MISSIONARIES AND THE SUPREME
COURT, 1829–1833

We believe no one can now remain neutral . . . each individual in America must either be for the Indians or against them. —Cherokee Phoenix and Indian Advocate, January 1, 1831

The Cherokees' fourth removal crisis began in April 1829 when Jackson's Secretary of War, John Eaton, gave new life to Thomas McKenney's moribund treaty of 1828 with the western Cherokees. Georgia's ultimatum to Adams and the Cherokees and Jackson's forceful support for it brought a new and different kind of pressure to bear upon the Cherokees. The new administration was prepared to make good on the threats of withdrawing federal protection of treaty rights, threats that had been made before but never acted on. Jackson and his Secretary of War did all they could to impress the Cherokees with the hopelessness of their situation. Without federal protection they would be at the mercy of the state governments and the frontier whites.

Jackson's first step had been to stimulate enrollment for emigration under the treaty of 1828 by appointing Carroll and Coffee as secret federal agents to work among the Cherokees. At the same time, Jackson prepared a removal bill for Congress that was designed to provide money for land cessions—ostensibly to ease the difficulty of removal for each tribe east of the Mississippi by providing money, in exchange for land, with which to start over in the west on new land to be assigned to them. The removal bill applied to all Indians in the east, but the Cherokees became the *cause célèbre* in Jackson's removal effort. As long as the Cherokees successfully resisted removal, the plan was in jeopardy. To bolster his position, Jackson portrayed himself as the Indians' best friend. Their enemies, he said, were their wealthy half-breed leaders, their misguided missionaries, and the relentless (but understandable) demands of the white westerners for more land. Jackson's aim was to convince those voters who sympathized with the Indians and who did not want to force them to leave their homelands that his removal policy offered a more benign and helpful option than the one Georgia and Alabama presented or the one the Cherokees wanted. Georgia's plan to denationalize them and put them in a class with freed blacks would destroy the Indians, Jackson said. The Cherokees' plan to create separate Indian sovereignties within the existing states was unconstitutional. He claimed to see no reasonable alternative to removal and exchange of lands.

The problem for the Cherokees was to convince the public that it was not in America's or the Indians' best interest to allow compulsory removal and that under federal treaty protection they could best survive and thrive where they were. Removal would destroy a generation of intense Indian and white effort to civilize and Christianize the Indians. If forced to go west, they would have to abandon homes, farms, schools, churches, and all other improvements and start these efforts all over again in the wilderness. This would be very expensive to themselves and to the taxpayers. The only persons who would profit from this Draconian measure would be white land speculators and cotton planters in a few southern states and their equivalents in the old northwest. The Cherokees tried to demonstrate to the average white citizen that, furthermore, Jackson was in effect subverting the United States Constitution by upholding states' rights over treaty rights (the supreme law of the land).

In the end, most Americans chose to believe what they wanted to believe: namely, that white America was a benevolent society, that American expansion was predestined by God for the good of mankind, and that although removal was harsh and expensive, it represented the only hope for Indian survival. Americans chose to believe it was necessary "in the nature of things."[1] Indian removal was no one's fault, really; the Indians were so far behind in human progress and ability that they would need generations to catch up. Removal would give them more time for this. A certain amount of Indian comfort and rights must be sacrificed to the white man's mission to expand, to cultivate the earth and develop its resources. Being optimists, the Americans convinced themselves that the Indians would be all right once they got used to the idea of starting over again in the west. White Americans constantly moved west and started over and improved their lot; the Indians could do the same. Of course, someday the westward movement of the white frontier would catch up with the Indians in their new homes, but presumably by then they would be ready for integration. Meanwhile, of course, the American government would and should do all it could to help the Indians: the government would buy their eastern lands, pay for their transportation west, send agents there to help them adjust; the missionary societies would

[1] See Brian W. Dippie, *The Vanishing American* (Middletown, Conn.: Wesleyan University Press, 1982).

continue to educate and Christianize them there. With a little effort by the Indians themselves, everything would work out in the long run.

One of the chief obstacles the Cherokees faced in trying to overcome these rationalizations for removal was that some Indian tribes were indeed suffering badly in the east. Some of these, like the Potawatomies, the Miamis, and the Kickapoos voluntarily went west; they believed that it could hardly be any worse for them there. These were small tribes of a few hundred families living in New York, Ohio, Indiana, and Michigan, who had been given very tiny tracts of land, who were surrounded and constantly harassed by whites, and whose communities lacked leadership and coherence; they had no possibility of becoming self-sufficient. Unlike the Cherokees, they had become demoralized, split into factions, and mired in poverty, debt, and alcoholism. Their future was indeed as hopeless as Jackson portrayed it.

But the situation was very different for the five large southeastern tribes. They still owned considerable valuable soil; they had made steady progress toward economic self-sufficiency and political stability; with continued assistance they could survive and prosper where they were. For these Indians, the so-called five civilized tribes, the Cherokees became the spokesmen. If an exception were made for them, the Indians might yet be able to find their place in the destiny of the new nation. Cherokee success would give hope to the other tribes that all was not lost.

Having overcome their internal crisis over acculturation, the Cherokees in 1828 had elected an extremely able and experienced group of men to lead them under their new constitution. The success of their renascence provided their people with considerable confidence and unity. The less acculturated believed that their leaders would allow them to retain as much of their traditional way of life as they wanted. Three times they had faced removal threats and with each victory they had gained more strength. When their delegation, headed by Principal Chief John Ross, returned from Washington in the spring of 1829, it met with the National Council to plan its response to Georgia and Jackson. Their survival required efforts on two fronts: the protection of their own borders from white intruders and the defeat of Jackson's removal bill in Congress.

Jackson's support of Georgia's assertion of state sovereignty over Indian land encouraged white settlers to intrude into the Cherokee Nation; the Council's repeated requests to the federal agent to remove these intruders met with no response. The administration wanted the Cherokees to see just how vulnerable they were to white oppression without federal support. Fate dealt the Cherokees a cruel blow when gold was discovered in several streams along the nation's southeastern border with Georgia, particularly on the Chestatee River. The discovery was made sometime during the spring of 1829, but the amount of gold available was not then known. As prospectors poured in and discovered that there was apparently a great deal of it easily obtainable by panning, a gold rush started that brought hordes of whites and Indians to the gold regions along the Chestatee River near Dahlonega and then spread to nearby areas. Had the federal government protected their borders and had the Cherokees been allowed to mine their own mineral resources, the nation would have suddenly entered an era of tremendous prosperity and growth. Under the circumstances, the gold rush only added to their instability and the disruption of civil order.[2] Many white Americans could not believe that God intended such riches to be left to those they viewed as savage pagans.

In August 1829, John Eaton instructed Hugh Montgomery that removal of the white intruders on Cherokee land was now the duty of Georgia and not of the federal government because the sovereign state of Georgia now had preeminent authority within its own borders.[3] A month later, the Cherokee Council decided to take matters into its own hands. They were most worried at that time about an area in the southeast corner of the nation near Beaver Dam and Cedar Creek, where a large number of intruders were building cabins, clearing land, and sowing crops (though no gold had been found in this area). If the Cherokees could, by a show of authority, drive off these settlers, that might discourage others. Major Ridge was authorized to gather a lighthorse patrol and eject eighteen families of Georgians from their unauthorized farms in this area. In January 1830, Ridge and thirty armed Cherokees rode to Beaver Dam. They politely but firmly ordered the white families to leave and then burned their cabins, destroyed their crops, and tore down their fences.[4] The intruders left resentfully but did not go far; soon after Ridge and his troops had gone, they returned. They discovered four of Ridge's men in

[2] Mooney, *Historical Sketch*, p. 110; Starkey, *The Cherokee Nation*, pp. 110–114. Accounts vary as to precisely when the Cherokees discovered gold and when the whites in Georgia found out about it. See also Hugh Montgomery to John Forsyth, July 12, 1828, Georgia Archives, Atlanta. Montgomery writes: "On the subject of gold diggers, the last accounts give the number at from four to seven thousand. Their morrals [sic] are as bad as it is possible for you to conceive; you can suppose the gamblers, swindlers, debauchers and profane Blackguards all collected from six or seven states without either law or any other power to prevent them from giving full vent to their vicious propensities, or think of Sodom before the arival [sic] of the distroying angils—and you have some faint idea of the morals of the place."

[3] John Eaton to Hugh Montgomery, August 18, 1829, M-21, reel 6, p. 69; John Ross to John Eaton, September 3, 1829, M-221, reel 100, #8539. In addition to ejecting white families and burning their dwellings in Beaver Dam, Major Ridge and his regulators also did the same in Vann's Valley, Terrapin Creek, and Cedar Town. J. B. Pendleton to George Gilmer, February 7, 1830, Georgia Archives, Atlanta.

[4] Wilkins, *Cherokee Tragedy*, pp. 204–205; Starkey, *The Cherokee Nation*, p. 114. See Allen Fambrough to George Gilmer, February 8, 1830, Georgia Archives, Atlanta.

one of the deserted cabins, drinking whiskey they had found. A gang of twenty-five whites assaulted the four Cherokees and beat them so badly that one of them died from his injuries. To try any of these intruders for murder was impossible. In fact, the other three battered Cherokees were themselves placed in prison in Georgia by those who had assaulted them. The Georgians were so angry at the Cherokee effort to remove their citizens from "Georgia's land" (though within Cherokee treaty boundaries) that Governor George Gilmer demanded that Jackson retaliate against this unjustifiable assertion of Indian authority.[5] Neither the state nor the federal government was sure at this point who was responsible for the Cherokees.

Meanwhile, so many whites had settled in the gold mining region of the Cherokee nation that fighting between them and the Cherokee residents was constant. The Council estimated that $1,500 to $2,000 worth of gold rightfully belonging to the Cherokee Nation was being extracted every day. Cherokees who went to the gold regions near Dahlonga were robbed and driven out by whites. Whites quarreled among themselves over the best sites for digging and panning. Agent Montgomery said he had no troops and no authorization to try to maintain order. The Council sent a protest to John Eaton in March 1830 stating that their agent simply "stands here with folded arms, as it were, merely to witness the rights of the Cherokees invaded and trampled under foot with impunity."[6] Georgia's legislature passed a resolution that the mineral resources within the Cherokee Nation belonged to the State of Georgia because Indians were only tenants on the land; Georgia forbade Indians to extract any gold.[7] Ultimately, out of fairness to those Georgia citizens who would soon become owners of this land when it was surveyed and given away by lottery, Governor Gilmer prohibited whites from extracting gold and requested Jackson to send troops to clear these areas, which he did.

After June, Georgia created its own police force to patrol the Cherokee area. Known as the Georgia Guard, it was essentially a private security force under militia officers. The state gave the Guard orders to maintain law and order in the Cherokee lands within the borders of the state, but the state accepted no responsibility for the actions of the Guard. Individuals who complained of the behavior of the Guard (as some missionaries eventually did) were told that they would have to bring a private suit against the individual guardsman involved.[8] Although the official orders

---

[5] George Gilmer to John Eaton, February 5, 1830, M-234, reel 74, #0132.

[6] Cherokee Council to John Eaton, March 3, 1830, M-234, reel 74, #0096.

[7] George Gilmer to Yelverton P. Ring, June [no day] 1830, M-221, reel 100, #8773.

[8] Mooney, *Historical Sketch*, p. 111; George Gilmer to John Howard, *Methodist Christian Advocate and Zion's Herald*, September 30, 1831.

to the Guard instructed them to protect both Cherokees and whites, in fact the Guard rightly understood its job to be one of harassing the Cherokees and siding with white intruders in any dispute. Over the next few years the Guard arrested missionaries who obstructed Georgia's will, arrested John Ross (and seized all his papers), arrested a newspaper reporter who had come to interview Ross (and seized his papers), and confiscated the Cherokee printing press and all its type. In day-to-day affairs the Georgia Guard became a prime source of Cherokee destabilization from 1830 to 1835.[9]

In January 1830, Congressmen from Tennessee (at Georgia's request) had introduced Jackson's Removal Bill. The Cherokees rested their hopes for ending the removal crisis upon defeating this bill. In addition to their own memorials against its passage, the Cherokees were delighted to find that many philanthropic white citizens around the nation were also submitting petitions against it. Quaker groups from Pennsylvania were particularly active in this work, as were church and missionary societies in New York and New England. Editorial writers in secular newspapers also alerted the public to the controversial aspects of the bill.[10]

Passage of the Removal Bill in 1830 became the test of whether Jackson had a mandate to reverse American Indian policy. His bill would institute what was tantamount to compulsory removal of all Indians east of the Mississippi. McKenney, at the Office of Indian Affairs, having spent all of the $50,000 appropriated by Congress to treat with the Cherokees in 1828 in his futile effort to stimulate Cherokee emigration, now supported Jackson's bill as ardently as he had supported President Adams's colonization bill. The Removal Bill authorized the Secretary of War to negotiate the removal of every tribe in the Mississippi Valley and committed Congress to providing the funds to reimburse the tribes for land they ceded in the east and several millions more to transport them to an Indian territory in the west.

Jackson provided his rationale for the bill in a message to Congress on December 8, 1829. The Constitution, he said, "declares that no new State shall be formed or erected within the jurisdiction of any other State without the consent of its legislature. If the General Government is not permitted to tolerate the erection of a confederate State within the territory of one of the members of this Union against her consent, much less could it allow a foreign and independent government to establish itself there." The Indian nations were "foreign and independent governments" under

[9] See John Howard Payne, *Letter to My Countrymen*, ed. Clemens de Baillou (Athens, Ga.: University of Georgia Press, 1961).

[10] Starkey, *The Cherokee Nation*, pp. 120–22; Ronald N. Satz, *American Indian Policy in the Jacksonian Era* (Lincoln: University of Nebraska Press, 1975), p. 20.

the treaty system, but treaties that had promised them permanent self-government within their present boundaries were without a doubt, in Jackson's opinion, unconstitutional. The temerity of the Cherokees in establishing their own constitution was the prime example of the folly of the original Indian policy. "Actuated by this view of the subject," Jackson said, "I informed the Indians inhabiting parts of Georgia and Alabama, that their attempt to establish an independent government would not be countenanced by the Executive of the United States and advised them to emigrate beyond the Mississippi or submit to the laws of those States."[11] In order to allow for their orderly emigration, he now asked for money from Congress and the authority to negotiate cessions of all Indian land in the east to reimburse the federal government and states for the cost of helping the Indians remove.

The debate over the bill took place in April and May. At times Congress was so evenly divided that votes on key amendments resulted in ties. The Cherokees were happy to find that "their friends at the north" were strongly opposed to the bill. The leaders of the American Board of Commissioners for Foreign Missions, most of whom lived in Boston, were particularly helpful to their cause; the secretary of the Board, Jeremiah Evarts, spent considerable time in Washington lobbying against the bill. Perhaps the most effective service rendered by Evarts was his publication of a series of articles that were widely reprinted under the pseudonym "William Penn" and later appeared in book form (copies of which were given to every Congressman). Evarts's articles were carefully researched and documented; they provided powerful arguments in favor of the treaty rights of the Indians, the authority of the federal government over Indian affairs, and the progress the Indians had made toward the goal of civilization and incorporation as equal citizens.[12]

Evarts's position was supported by the most influential spokesmen of the National Republican Party (soon to become the Whig Party) in Congress, including Henry Clay, Daniel Webster, Theodore J. Frelinghuysen, and Davy Crockett. Carefully read, their speeches do not display strong faith in the progress or equality of the Indians, but they contained strong arguments against Jackson's policy toward them. Jacksonian political leaders maintained throughout that opposition to the Removal Bill was essentially founded on party lines rather than on principles. Judging from congressional voting patterns, the struggle seems to have been between western and eastern states. To assist the Democrats, the Reverend Isaac McCoy, a Baptist missionary to the Potawatomi Indians of Indiana, was

[11] Van Every, *Disinherited*, p. 112. See also Francis Paul Prucha, "Andrew Jackson's Indian Policy," *Journal of American History* 56 (June 1969):527–39.

[12] Prucha, ed., *Cherokee Removal*, pp. 4–27.

persuaded to inform Congress why he and most of the members of his denomination supported the bill.[13] McCoy had in fact persuaded the Triennial Convention of Baptists throughout the nation to support Adams's colonization plan in 1827 and had written a book in favor of the idea. In the winter and spring of 1830 Congressman Lumpkin of Georgia, chairman of the House Committee on Indian Affairs, used McCoy to drum up petitions from religious leaders supporting the removal bill and to respond to petitions opposing the bill. McCoy noted in his memoirs that almost all of the petitions received by Congress in opposition to removal cited the progress of the Cherokees as the principal argument for allowing the Indians to remain where they were. McCoy had never visited the Cherokee Nation but he considered them the exception that proved the rule. McKenney helped support the bill by organizing a group of Dutch Reformed ministers in New York City to work for it. He told Jackson privately that all the members of the group were strong supporters of the Democratic Party.[14]

The Cherokees were sorry to see the divisions in the missionary ranks that McCoy and McKenney managed to create, but they felt that the Congregationalists in Massachusetts, the Presbyterians in New Jersey, and the Quakers in Pennsylvania were more powerful and effective in their support than the Baptists and Dutch Reformed ministers who constituted Jackson's chief religious support. The most effective leader of the Whig opposition in Congress was Senator Theodore J. Frelinghuysen, a Presbyterian from New Jersey and formerly one of the directors of the American Board. He centered his attention upon the compulsory aspect of Jackson's policy. Although the bill itself left it up to each Indian tribe whether it would sign a removal treaty or whether it would accept the jurisdiction of the state government where it lived, Frelinghuysen made two important points about these cruel alternatives. First, he pointed out that in Georgia and the other southeastern states, denationalized Indians would become second-class citizens under state jurisdiction, which was hardly a viable option: "Do the obligations of justice change with the color of the skin?" he asked. "Is it one of the prerogatives of the white man that he may disregard the dictates of moral principles when an Indian shall be concerned?" George Washington and the Founding Fathers had inaugurated the original Indian policy of integration, he said, because in 1776 they "contended for the very rights and privileges that our Indian neighbors now implore us to protect and preserve to them." Were the free

---

[13] For McCoy's position see McLoughlin, *Cherokees and Missionaries*, pp. 273–77.

[14] See James Van Hoeven, "Salvation and Indian Removal" (Ph.D. diss., Vanderbilt University, 1972), pp. 113–44 and Francis Paul Prucha, "Thomas L. McKenney and the New York Indian Board," *Mississippi Valley Historical Review* 48 (1962):625–55.

white citizens of the United States to "turn traitors to our principles" because the Indian's skin was a different shade? Frelinghuysen concluded his speech by saying that the arguments of the Jacksonians simply boiled down to "how shall we most plausibly break our faith."[15]

Frelinghuysen's second argument addressed the claim of Jackson that his Removal Bill was a benevolent act to help the Indians out of a dilemma forced upon them by the sovereignty of the states. Senator (later President) James Buchanan, speaking for the Democrats, had noted that there was apparently some "misapprehension of the bill and of its purpose" among the friends of the Indians. "It was commonly believed," he said, "that the Indians were to be removed from the Southern States by force; and nothing was further from the intention of Congress or the State of Georgia."[16] But there was force involved, Frelinghuysen said; the question was only what kind of force. Jackson admitted that the Georgians were harassing the Indians, but he wished to portray himself as their savior. To call his bluff Frelinghuysen introduced an amendment to the Removal Bill that made its supporters face up to the government's responsibility for state harassment. This amendment stated, "that until the said tribes or nations shall choose to remove, as by this act is contemplated, they shall be protected in their present possessions and in the enjoyment of all their rights or territory, and government as heretofore exercised and enjoyed, from all interruptions and encroachments."[17] The amendment asked Jackson to provide federal troops to keep out intruders and maintain law and order in all the Indian nations, as by treaty and the Trade and Intercourse Acts they were required to do, until any tribe voluntarily agreed to remove. No Indian nation could survive white harassment without federal protection. As the Cherokees and the other southeastern tribes had discovered, once federal troop protection was withdrawn, life became intolerable both on and within their borders. Neither property, life, nor limb was safe from the kind of whites who encroached upon them. Nevertheless Frelinghuysen's amendment was defeated. The combined votes of the southern and western Senators were greater than those of the New England and mid-Atlantic states. In the end, white Americans chose not to see what they were doing and how they were doing it.[18]

On May 26, 1830, the Removal Bill came up for its final vote. New

[15] Van Every, *Disinherited*, p. 115.
[16] Ibid., p. 113.
[17] Ibid., p. 117.
[18] Alexis de Tocqueville, touring America during the removal crisis, wrote of the political attitude toward the Indians, "it is impossible to destroy men with more respect for the laws of humanity" (Dippie, *The Vanishing American*, p. 70).

England's Senators voted 11 to 1 against it; southern Senators voted 18 to 0 for it. In the House, the southerners voted 60 to 15 in favor; New Englanders voted 28 to 9 against it. Those from the northwest were more evenly divided but voted 23 to 17 in favor.[19] Jackson signed the bill on May 28 and three days later Georgia asserted its authority over 192,000 acres of Creek land left in that state and 4,600,000 acres of Cherokee land, including their capital city of New Echota, the homes of John Ross, Major Ridge, and many other members of the Council, and six missionary stations (three of the American Board, one of the Baptists, and the two run by the Moravians).[20] Thereafter, as far as the Georgians were concerned, the Cherokee Nation did not exist. Its Council was forbidden to meet; all Cherokee courts were closed; its laws and its police were not allowed to function. Three hundred and twenty Georgia surveyors immediately entered the nation to begin dividing it into tracts of 160 acres each to be given away to white citizens by lottery (the gold field region was so valuable that lottery tracts here were limited to 40 acres). Hundreds of white Georgians followed the surveyors into the region (under the protection of the Georgia Guard), eager to locate the best farms, plantations, millsites, missionary stations, ferries, and taverns so that they could speculate how to obtain them for themselves. Although the Georgia law stated that all Cherokees would be given a tract of land, subsequent revisions made it clear that they would get only the land that no white citizen wanted. Furthermore, as experience with the reserve system had shown, sooner or later most of the Cherokees would be forced off or cheated out of whatever land they received. Having no right to defend themselves in the Georgia courts, there was no way they could defend their property. Soon after the lottery began handing out tracts in October 1830, Georgia's citizens were forcefully moving Cherokees out of their homes and off of their farms.[21]

John Ross became the leader of Cherokee resistance, ably supported by his brother Lewis and virtually all of the elected chiefs and local headmen. The crisis produced a tremendous spirit of solidarity in the nation. Everyone realized this was a life-or-death struggle for their national homeland.

[19] Van Every, *Disinherited*, pp. 117, 120.

[20] McLoughlin, *Cherokees and Missionaries*, pp. 300–320. There were two Moravian mission stations (Springplace and Oochgelogy), three American Board stations (Carmel, Haweis, and Hightower—Worcester's station at New Echota had no school or church), and one Baptist station (with a church at Tinsawatee and a school in the nearby town of Hickory Log) within the boundaries of Georgia.

[21] Georgia at first promised that Cherokees could retain the 160-acre tract on which they lived and farmed after it had been surveyed by the state, but white intruders and the Georgia Guard tended to dispossess Cherokee families at will in the effort to harass the entire tribe into removing to the West.

Ross wished to continue to hold Council meetings at New Echota after June 1, 1830, despite Georgia's assertion of its jurisdiction, but the Council persuaded him that it would be wiser to move the seat of government temporarily to a Cherokee town in Tennessee called Red Clay, just across the border from Georgia. Tennessee and North Carolina had not yet joined Georgia and Alabama in exercising their sovereignty over the Cherokee land within their borders, though both eventually did so. While Cherokee Councils met thereafter in Red Clay, the Cherokees in Georgia and Alabama continued to live as best they could on their farms. They obeyed their own laws and chiefs and continued to hope that the Council would find some solution to their mounting problems.

The Council authorized Ross to hire white lawyers to assist them in the increasing number of cases involving Cherokees arrested by the Georgia Guard for interfering with Georgia's authority or engaging in disputes with white intruders. The two most important lawyers for the Cherokees were William Wirt, former Attorney General of the United States and soon to be a candidate for President against Jackson on the Anti-Masonic Party ticket, and John Sergeant, who ran for Vice President with Henry Clay in 1832. Almost at once the Cherokees encountered difficulty raising money to pay these lawyers. John Eaton decided that after 1830 no Cherokee Nation existed in the east; hence there was no Cherokee Treasury or Treasurer to whom the government could pay its share of the tribal annuity. His solution was to divide the $6,666.66 in the annuity by the total of 14,500 Cherokees and to issue instructions through the federal agent that each Cherokee head of family could apply to the agent for his 45-cent share and the shares of his family members.[22] Ross and the Council protested against this and persuaded the great majority of Cherokees to boycott the process of dissipating their funds. For five years the government kept the annuities in escrow in a Nashville bank while the Cherokees ran deeper and deeper into debt.[23] Eaton's decision was an obvious form of harassment designed to prevent the Cherokees from effectively governing their nation and bringing their test cases to court. Just because the Cherokee Nation had ceased to be recognized by Georgia and Alabama did not mean that it had cased to exist in Tennessee and North Carolina.

The first opportunity for a test case occurred in the fall of 1830 when

[22] Royce, *Cherokee Nation of Indians*, p. 113.

[23] Montgomery reported that only 3 percent of the Cherokees came to the agency to ask for their share of the annuity in 1830–1831. He paid out a total of $325. Some of those who came to him asked for food rather than money. He also claimed that some Cherokees who broke the boycott were whipped for it by tribal patriots. See his translation of an article on the subject published in Sequoyan, August 4, 1831, M-234, reel 74, #0618.

Georgia arrested a Cherokee named Corn Tassell (or George Tassel) for the murder of another Cherokee. He was arrested by the Georgia Guard, tried, and condemned to death. Wirt applied to the federal court to free Corn Tassell on a writ of error on the ground that Georgia had no jurisdiction over a crime that, under the treaty power, was within the self-governing police rights of the Cherokee Nation. Had the Supreme Court adjudicated this case, it might have ruled Georgia's laws unconstitutional and returned the Cherokee Council to control over their land in Georgia and Alabama. The authorities in Georgia, fearing this, executed Corn Tassell before any federal court could make a ruling, thereby making the issue moot.[24]

Next Wirt sought an injunction against Georgia's laws for infringing the sovereignty of the Cherokee Nation under federal treaties. This case reached the Supreme Court early in 1831 and on March 3, 1831, the Court ruled in *Cherokee Nation* v. *Georgia* that the Cherokees had no right to bring such a suit because they did not qualify as an independent foreign nation.[25] The Cherokee Nation, John Marshall said in the Court's first formal effort to define the exact nature of Indian tribes within the United States, was "a domestic, dependent nation." It had no standing in the Court and its suit was thrown out.

Although this case failed to stop Georgia, John Ross and the Council were pleased by the Court's definition of the Cherokees as "a domestic nation," for at least that indicated the Cherokees were not simply "tenants at will" of the states in which they resided. Ross had the decision printed and distributed so that the Cherokees could see that they had established for themselves a clear legal status as "a nation"—though what the rights of a "domestic, dependent nation" were was yet to be defined.

John Marshall let it be known privately that he sympathized with the constitutional argument of the Cherokees on the supremacy of the treaty clause to states' rights, but he said their lawyers must find a better means to bring this matter before the Court.[26] The Georgians had provided the opportunity for this by passing a law in December 1829 that was designed to drive the missionaries out of the Cherokee Nation. Not only had the missionaries to the Cherokees been under attack for some time by westerners for their role in civilizing the Indians, but the federal Education Fund of 1819 itself had been denounced by Georgia as contrary to the Compact of 1802. In June 1830, Eaton curtailed all grants from this fund

---

[24] Grant Foreman, *Indian Removal* (Norman: University of Oklahoma Press, 1932), pp. 233–35; Phillips, "Georgia and States Rights," pp. 75–76.

[25] Satz, *American Indian Policy*, pp. 44–46; Peters, *Case of the Cherokee Nation*, pp. 2–224.

[26] Phillips, "Georgia and States Rights," pp. 77–78.

to mission schools east of the Mississippi because the administration's policy henceforth was to support only Indian education that took place in the territory set aside for Indians in the west. However, Eaton let it be known that his real aim was to support Georgia in its effort to rid the Cherokees of missionary assistance: "The Government by its funds," he said, "should not extend encouragement and assistance to those who, thinking upon this subject, employ their efforts to prevent removals."[27] No doubt the American Board's lobbying efforts against the Removal Bill were the principal cause for this action, but the Georgians themselves were convinced that individual missionaries within the Cherokee Nation were providing political advice and moral assistance to those resisting removal.

The most convincing evidence for this was a statement issued by seven of the nine Methodist missionaries who were itinerating among the Cherokees. These missionaries had met at the Chatooga camp meeting ground in the Cherokee Nation in September 1829 and, after a rousing revival meeting, issued a set of resolutions that were later published in a Methodist newspaper, the *Christian Advocate*, printed in New York City. The resolution was designed to arouse denominational and public support for the Cherokees and opposition to the efforts to force them to sign a removal treaty. The seven missionaries claimed to speak for the two absent circuit riders as well as themselves when they said: "It is the unanimous opinon of this board of missionaries that a removal of the Cherokees to the west of the Mississippi would, in all probability, be ruinous to the best interests of the nation." Furthermore, they denied the charges made by Jackson, Eaton, Montgomery, and other government officials that the Cherokees were "under the controlling influence of the principal men of the nation" and that the missionaries opposed removal "merely in order the more effectually to extend our missionary operation here." Asserting that the great body of the Cherokee people "is firmly resolved not to remove," they called for "the sympathy and religious interposition of the Christian community in these United States, together with all true and faithful friends of humanity and justice" on behalf of the oppressed Cherokees.[28]

The Cherokees were heartened by this and the editor of the *Phoenix* published an editorial asking the missionaries of the other denominations to add their support: "Must their mouths be muzzled because they are embassadors of religion?"[29] The Reverend Samuel Worcester had then called for a meeting of all the missionaries of all the denominations to

---

[27] Prucha, *American Indian Policy*, p. 246.

[28] McLoughlin, *Cherokees and Missionaries*, pp. 289–92.

[29] *Cherokee Phoenix*, October 1, 1830.

meet at his home in New Echota early in December to sign a similar manifesto. The meeting (after a short postponement) was attended by nine members of the Americans Board Missions, two Moravians, one Baptist, and one of the Methodists who had signed the September resolves. Their manifesto was signed on December 29, 1830. The missionaries said that although, as missionaries, they did not give direct advice or counsel to the Cherokees in political affairs, nevertheless as individuals they had the right to express their opinions when asked by Cherokees. Furthermore, they felt they had the right to say that removal of the Cherokees was not in the best interest of that people. Like the Methodists, the missionaries of the other denominations insisted that the Cherokees were by no means intimidated by their "halfbreed" leaders but that their leaders clearly represented the will of "the whole mass of the Cherokee people." The majority of Cherokees were "totally averse to a removal." They were a democratic republic, the missionaries noted, and "the disposal of office is in the hands of the people"; no man could possibly remain long in office "in opposition to the will of the people." Although it was true that "Indians of mixed blood" dominated the upper house, they did so because of their experience. Two-thirds of the members of the lower house of the Cherokee legislature were full bloods and without their concurrence no action was possible in the nation. The missionaries then stated the "facts" of the tremendous improvement that had taken place in the social, economic, and political order of the Cherokees over the past thirty-five years. As persons laboring to "aid them in their progress, we cannot do otherwise than earnestly deprecate any measure which threatens to arrest it." In their view, the removal of this nation was to be "deprecated" because it could only serve "to retard, if not totally to arrest their progress in religion, civilization, learning and the useful arts." The whole Indian removal policy of the Jackson Administration was "not merely of a political but of a moral nature, inasmuch as it involves the maintenance or violation of the faith of our country."[30]

The editor of the *Cherokee Phoenix* issued an "extra" edition containing the entire manifesto on January 1, 1831, two days after the meeting. In addition an editorial by Elias Boudinot said: "We believe no one can not remain neutral . . . each individual in America must either be for the Indians or against them."[31]

A week before the missionaries had met to issue this statement, the legislature of Georgia had passed a law requiring all white men living within the area formerly claimed by the Cherokees in Georgia to take an

[30] Ibid., January 1, 1830 [actually 1831].
[31] Ibid.

441

oath of allegiance to obey the laws of the State of Georgia. Whites were given until March 1, 1831, to sign the oath or to remove outside Georgia's boundaries.[32] Copies of this law were sent in January to each of the thirty-two missionaries residing in the Cherokee Nation as well as to white traders, mechanics, innkeepers, millwrights, and other whites there. The legislature had little doubt that those doing business in the nation would take the oath, for most of them were residents of Georgia and the surrounding states. But they knew that the missionaries, especially those from the northern states, might decline to do so. If they did sign, they would of course be bound to submit to the laws of Georgia or face imprisonment. If they did not take the oath, they would have to leave or be subject to imprisonment—assuming, of course, that the law was constitutional.

Here at last might be a case that could be brought before the United States Supreme Court, if some missionary was willing to risk imprisonment by disobeying it. The one Baptist missionary living within the boundaries of Georgia, Duncan O'Briant, was a native of Georgia and supported by the funds of the Sarepta Baptist Missionary Society of Georgia. Unlike the Reverend Evan Jones in Valley Towns, North Carolina, who was supported by the Baptist Foreign Missionary Board in Boston, O'Briant had not signed the manifesto in Worcester's home and had no intention of opposing removal. In fact, he not only signed the oath of allegiance to Georgia but helped to persuade the members of his missionary church at Tinsawattee to enroll for emigration under the treaty of 1828. He and his church members departed for the west March 30, 1832.[33]

Of the nine Methodist missionaries in the nation, only two lived in Georgia. However, all of those who had signed the Chatooga resolves had been severely censured by their mission board in Tennessee for meddling in politics and had been instructed to steer clear of politics thereafter.[34] The Moravians at Springplace and Oothcaloga wrote to their mission board in Salem, North Carolina, for advice. Their board confirmed their own view that they should neither sign the oath nor engage in civil disobedience. Their only alternative was to close their two mission stations and move to Tennessee, where they tried to continue to look after their converts.[35]

---

[32] Phillips, "Georgia and States Rights," p. 73. The law requiring an oath of all whites within the Chreokee Nation was passed by Georgia on December 22, 1830, but the missionaries were not aware of it when they wrote their manifesto a week later.

[33] McLoughlin, *Cherokees and Missionaries*, pp. 279–82.

[34] Ibid., pp. 293–94.

[35] Ibid., pp. 284–88.

There were five male members of the American Board missions living in Georgia (women missionaries were exempted in the law from signing the oath): Samuel A. Worcester, Elizur Butler, Daniel S. Butrick, Isaac Proctor, and John Thompson. They too wrote to the Board for advice, but added their position that they could not sign the oath nor could they yield their right to preach the gospel to the heathen. Therefore, they wished to bring a test case by risking imprisonment "for righteousness sake." The American Board in Boston, fully in sympathy with their position, said that they must make their decisions as individuals but that the Board would provide legal help for any who were arrested and wished to bring a test case before the Supreme Court. Soon after this, three of the five had second thoughts. They felt that missionaries should not interfere with "That which is Caesar's" and noted that the Bible ordered all Christians to "obey the powers that be for they are ordained of God." If the President of the United States supported Georgia's position, then Georgia was "the powers that be" and must be obeyed. Since they could not in conscience sign the oath, they would move out of the state and continue to minister to their flock by itinerating (which in their view was not residence).[36] This left two missionaries, the Reverend Samuel Worcester at New Echota and the medical missionary, Dr. Elizur Butler, at Haweis, to bring the case. Having refused to sign the oath, they were arrested by the Georgia Guard on July 7 and, under very rough treatment, taken to Lawrenceville, Georgia, for trial. The court found them guilty and sentenced them to four years at hard labor on September 8, 1831. Their lawyers, paid by the Board, immediately appealed to the Supreme Court.[37]

During the weeks between March 1 and July 7 the Georgia Guard had been particularly hard upon a number of missionaries who at first declined to sign the oath. It had arrested and temporarily imprisoned at least five missionaries, two of them Methodists, at different times. Ultimately all but Worcester and Butler escaped conviction, but the news of these arrests and the news that ministers of God had been dragged through the forests tied to the horses of the Guards, rudely cursed, shoved, and made to sleep with chains around them on jail floors shocked and horrified Protestants across the country. Even ministerial associations and presbyteries in the South that were strongly in support of Georgia and Jackson were moved to protest against such actions. The Cherokees believed that now the Georgians had gone too far and that white voters would finally realize the kind of unscrupulous, lawless, godless people with whom the Indians had to deal on the frontier. Public opinion, they believed, would at last

[36] Ibid., p. 260.
[37] See Edwin A. Miles, "After John Marshall's Decision," *Journal of Southern History* 39 (1973): 520–44; McLoughlin, *Cherokees and Missionaries*, p. 262.

turn against Jackson and force him to modify his policy, at least in their particular case.

On March 3, 1832, after the two Congregationalist missionaries had been in prison for eight months, John Marshall finally rendered the decision of the Supreme Court in *Worcester* v. *Georgia*. The arrest of the missionaries, Marshall said, was illegal because Georgia had no authority to execute its laws within an Indian nation protected under the treaty clause of the Constitution. "The Cherokee Nation . . . is a distinct community, occupying its own territory . . . in which the law of Georgia can have no right to enter but with the assent of the Cherokees. . . . The Act of the State of Georgia [in arresting and imprisoning the defendants] . . . is consequently void."[38]

The Cherokees had at last been vindicated. Georgia's arguments for states' rights and Jackson's defense of them were declared unconstitutional by the highest authority in the land. The Cherokees could have asked for no more. In principle, their cause was settled. But principle was not the ruling power in this situation. The voice of the people was the voice of God; it had spoken in favor of Andrew Jackson and it continued to speak in his support. The State of Georgia refused to release its prisoners when the lawyers appeared with Marshall's decision. Jackson was angry, but he had no intention of changing his mind. In his opinion the Supreme Court was only one of several branches of government that could interpret the Constitution; Congress and the Chief Executive could also do so. All were sworn to uphold the Constitution as they saw it. In his own veto messages he had told the Congress when it had acted unconstitutionally. He believed that his judgment on the Cherokee case was as good as John Marshall's. If the people did not agree with him, they could refuse to reelect him. The Court, with its appointed life tenure, spoke only for itself. It was not responsible to the people and in this case, in Jackson's opinion, it had acted against the best interest of the people.

The American Board consulted with its lawyers and discovered that there was one more step that must be taken. Jackson had to be faced technically with the fact that Georgia would not execute the Court's decision. This required the lawyers to go back to Marshall and obtain a writ from him that would ask the Chief Executive to see that the Court's order was carried out. Jackson would then be unable to remain silent (as he had so far). He would either have to compel Georgia to release the missionaries or to defy the Court and the Constitution. The lawyers could not return to Marshall for the writ until January 1833, when the Court reconvened.

---

[38] Satz, *American Indian Policy*, pp. 47-53; Wilkins, *Cherokee Tragedy*, p. 228; McLoughlin, *Cherokees and Missionaries*, p. 264.

Meanwhile the two American Board missionaries who had brought the case remained at hard labor in the Georgia penitentiary.

In the months between March 1832 and January 1833 many new circumstances intervened against the Cherokees. First, Jackson's Whig enemies forced him to veto a bill to recharter the Bank of the United States, a decision that was a grave miscalculation. The veto was highly popular among the common people; they considered the bank an oppressive tool of the eastern, monied aristocracy. Then in July 1832, Congress passed a new tariff law, again over the vehement objection of South Carolina, which threatened to nullify it; and the sovereign state of South Carolina fully expected the other southern agricultural states to join it in this action. The states too, it seemed, had the power to interpret the Constitution.

In one respect the nullification threat placed Jackson in a dilemma. It seemed to be simply another example of states' rights aggression against the federal union. If he were to enforce the tariff against South Carolina, as he wished to do, would he not have to act with equal force against Georgia's assertion of states' rights? On the other hand, if he could isolate South Carolina by granting Georgia's claims, might he not thereby prevent Georgia and other southern states that wanted Indian removal from joining in the nullification movement? Jackson's reelection in 1832 seemed to place the popular will once again in his hands.

South Carolina, not to be intimidated, voted on November 24 to declare the new tariff null and void within its borders as of February 1, 1833. In order for Jackson to use his popular power to bring South Carolina into line, he would first have to come to some agreement with Georgia. But were Marshall to face him with the task of releasing the missionaries, he would be on the horns of the dilemma. If he ignored Marshall's order, he would be hard put to take a strong stand against South Carolina for defying federal authority while he was allowing Georgia to do so. If he enforced Marshall's order against Georgia, he might well drive that state as well as other southern states toward nullification and precipitate a major national crisis. It was perhaps possible to argue that Georgia was acting only on a matter of internal concern while South Carolina was acting in direct defiance of Congress, but this was not a strong position from which to unite the country behind federal supremacy.

Suddenly the two missionaries in Milledgeville Penitentiary found themselves the focus of national attention. Only they could get Jackson and the country off the hook and save the nation from civil war. Or so they were told by a steady stream of distinguished southern visitors to the prison, all of whom begged them to tell their lawyers not to carry an appeal to Marshall. Governor Lumpkin of Georgia invited Worcester's and Butler's wives to meet with him and then to visit their husbands to persuade them to put the safety of the Union ahead of their own cause. Lumpkin let it be known that if the two missionaries would simply request a pardon, he would grant it without implying that they had done any wrong but had merely acted out of conscience. The Prudential Committee of the American Board met in executive session on December 25, 1832, to decide what advice it should send to its two missionaries.

The Board voted to advise them not to make the final appeal to Marshall; by the time their letter reached the prison, Worcester and Butler had already reached the same conclusion. They would sacrifice the Cherokees to save the Union. They instructed their lawyers not to carry an appeal to Marshall and their case was over.

Instead, on January 8, 1833, they wrote to Governor Lumpkin saying that they had withdrawn their suit lest it "might be attended with consequences injurious to our beloved country"; that is, it might force a confrontation between the federal government and Georgia that would push Georgia onto the side of South Carolina and nullification. Lumpkin forced the missionaries to ask for "magnanimity" from the state and then, publicizing their request as an admission of guilt, he told the warden to release them on January 14. Two days later, Andrew Jackson, freed from embarrassment over the Cherokee question, presented Congress with his Force Bill to obtain the power to use the army and navy, if necessary, to force South Carolina to obey the federal government. Georgia, its success against the Cherokees now ensured, offered no support for South Carolina; nor did any other southern state.[39] On January 21, South Carolina suspended its nullification proclamation, hoping that Congress would pass a more moderate tariff. When Congress did so in March, South Carolina, having no support from other southern states, agreed to pay the tariff. The nation, Whigs and Democrats alike, united in praise of the strong executive who had saved the Union from secession and civil war.

The Cherokees had lost their last hope. For them the worst blow was that the American Board, having written to advise Worcester and Butler to withdraw their final appeal to Marshal, sent another letter to John Ross on December 27, 1832, advising him that further resistance was useless and that he should try to persuade his nation to make the best bargain it could with Jackson for its land and then remove to the west.[40] When

---

[39] Miles, "After John Marshall," p. 541. According to Ulrich Phillips, however, the majority of voters in Georgia were never in favor of South Carolina's position on nullificaton. Phillips, "Georgia and States Rights," pp. 78–82, 113.

[40] William Wisner to Samuel Worcester, December 26, 1832, ABCFM; David Green to John Ross, December 27, 1832, John Ross Papers, Gilcrease Institute, Tulsa, Oklahoma;

Worcester returned to New Echota, he was convinced that he had made the right decision and agreed with his Board that the Cherokees should give up. For the past eighteen months, the Cherokees had treated him as a heroic martyr; now they became decidedly cool toward him and toward all missionaries. From this point on, they realized, they were on their own. There was no body of white men they could rely upon for help.

Further progress for the Cherokee renascence had to wait as the nation devoted all of its energy and resources to the single end of political survival in the east. This desperate struggle rested on the forlorn hope of a presidential victory for the Whig Party in 1836.

Samuel Worcester to David Greene, January 23, 1833, ABCFM; Lucy Butler to David Greene, June 23, 1833, ABCFM. Lucy Butler said that Ross and the Cherokees were very upset over "the change of sentiment among the friends of the Cherokees." Ross had hoped they would be as stubborn about opposing Jackson's policy as the National Council was. The American Board had conceded to Jackson too hastily, he thought.

447

THE END OF THE CHEROKEE
RENASCENCE, 1833

We have been made to drink the bitter cup of humiliation; treated like dogs; our lives, our liberties, the sport of whitemen; our country and the graves of our Father torn from us. . . . We find ourselves fugitives, vagrants in our own country. —*John Ross, Chief of the Cherokees*

The first Cherokee renascence ended on January 8, 1833, if any precise date can be picked. Some, of course, would argue that if the passage of the Removal Bill in May 1830 had not made certain their defeat, the reelection of Jackson in November 1832 certainly did. The precise date is not important.

Probably it is not fair to place the blame for the fate of the Cherokee Nation on the two missionaries who capitulated to Georgia after having sacrificed so much to help the Cherokees. Had they persisted in asking John Marshall to make Jackson execute the Court's decision, Jackson would have found reasons to refuse and the voters would have supported him. The missionaries, like the Cherokees, were pawns in a much larger game. Who can say precisely why the Age of Reason with its faith that all men are created equal gave way between 1789 and 1833 to the Age of Romanticism with its conviction that the United States was "a white man's country"? The capitulation of the missionaries was merely symbolic of that shift. Still, when even these staunch allies yielded, the Cherokees were left with no organized or active support for their cause among white Americans, and alone they could not hope to succeed.

As early as March 1832, Senator Frelinghuysen and Associate Justice John McLean of the Supreme Court, two of the leading national figures in the fight for Cherokee rights, had told John Ridge that Jackson's refusal to accept Marshall's decision meant that removal could not be stopped.[1] It remains questionable how deep the commitment to defend Indian rights was among Whig politicians. If Henry Clay had been elected in 1836, he would hardly have been able to hold back the expansionist clamor to remove these "inferior people" from the path of progress. As Secretary of State in 1825, Clay had expressed to John Quincy Adams his

[1] Wilkins, *Cherokee Tragedy*, pp. 230–31, 243.

448

doubts about Indian survival. Adams wrote in his diary that Clay told him

that it was impossible to civilize Indians; that there never was a fullblooded Indian who took to civilization. It was not in their nature. He believed they were destined to extinction, and, although he would never use or countenance inhumanity towards them, he did not think them, as a race, worth preserving. He considered them as essentially inferior to the Anglo-Saxon race which were now taking their place on this continent. They were not an improvable breed, and their disappearance from the human family would be no great loss to the world.[2]

Jackson probably spoke for the overwhelming majority of white voters when he said, after his second election, that the Indian question was a racial question:

It is to be hoped that those portions of two of the Southern tribes [Cherokees and Seminoles] . . . will realize the necessity of emigration and will speedily resort to it. . . . Those tribes cannot exist surrounded by our settlements and in continued contact with our citizens. . . . They have neither the intelligence, the industry, the moral habits, nor the desire of improvement which are essential to any favorable change in their condition. Established in the midst of another and superior race and without appreciating the causes of their inferiority or seeking to control them, they must necessarily yield to the force of circumstances and ere long disappear.[3]

Whether the racial superiority of the Anglo-Saxon was considered biologically innate or whether Indian inferiority rested on cultural habits resistant to change was irrelevant. Ethnocentricity was as effective as racism in dooming the Indians to second-class citizenship.

By 1833 a party had developed within the Cherokee Nation that favored removal on the best possible terms. John Ridge spoke for this group when he said in February 1833: "I hope we shall attempt to establish [ourselves] somewhere else," for "we can't be a nation here."[4] John Ross, who led the anti-removal party, continued to believe that if they couldn't be a nation where they were, they couldn't be a nation anywhere. Ross was right. The kind of nation that the Cherokees later became in the west was far different from what they had worked so hard to be in the east.

Much has been written and is still to be written about the Removal

---

[2] Quoted in Richard Drinnon, *Facing West*, pp. 179–80.

[3] Andrew Jackson, Message to Congress, December 3, 1833, Congressional Serial House Documents, Twenty-third Congress, *American State Papers*, vol. 234, p. 14. Jackson was speaking here in terms of an older, ethnocentric argument for racial superiority rather than in terms of the new biological argument, though the two positions were slowly shading into each other. His statement implies that the Indians had it in their power to improve themselves, but they refused to do it because they were so habituated to their old ways. Using this concept of permanent racial inferiority placed the blame squarely upon the Indians by implying they had the free will to change but simply would not exercise it.

[4] Wilkins, *Cherokee Tragedy*, p. 243.

Party among the Cherokees and the fatal and fraudulent treaty that its leaders signed at New Echota with Jackson's emissary, the Reverend John F. Schermerhorn, in December 1835.[5] In that treaty, a small minority of chiefs agreed to cede all their homeland for five million dollars and other commitments to assist them in reestablishing themselves in what is now northeastern Oklahoma. This pro-removal faction was not made up of full bloods wanting to retain their old hunting ways far from the oppressive whites, nor were they the worst members of the mixed-blood class in the nation. These were some of its best, most dedicated, patriotic leaders—Major Ridge, Elias Boudinot, John Ridge, William Hicks, Stand Watie, David Vann, Andrew Ross, and William S. Coody. In their opinion, the effort to remain in the east after 1833 was causing more suffering than it was worth. They believed that John Ross's stubborn refusal to face up to reality was only hurting the people who trusted him. In a sense they were right, but they sacrificed principle for practicality.

Speaking for the signers of the Removal Treaty in 1835, Elias Boudinot confirmed much of what the dissidents in White Path's Rebellion had feared: the educated, young leaders of the nation had gotten too far ahead of their people and yet still claimed the right to speak for them. As Boudinot put it, "if one hundred persons are ignorant of their true situation and are so completely blinded as not to see the destruction that awaits them, we can see strong reasons to justify the actions of a minority of fifty persons to do what the majority *would do* if they understood their condition."[6] However, the signers of this treaty were not as fifty out of one hundred; they were a tiny minority of 75 out of 15,000. Even after the Removal Treaty was signed, fewer than 2,000 Cherokees deserted the stubborn Ross in the cruel years betwen 1835 and 1838. White Path himself remained with Ross and died with thousands of other Cherokees in the forced emigration in 1838–1839. Close to 1,000 Cherokee full bloods in the Great Smoky Mountains fled to secret hideaways and were never rounded up by the United States troops; their descendants still remain in North Carolina.

It can be argued that, phoenix-like, the Cherokees once again rose from the ashes of defeat after 1839. They put down new roots in their allotted corner of the west and made that part of "the Great American Desert" bloom like the rose. They built good homes and farms and prospered. However, this second renascence was unlike the first. It lacked that simple, buoyant idealism and hope, that ebullient expectancy of successful

---

[5] The best account of the "Treaty Party" and the signing of the Removal Treaty in 1835 is contained in Wilkins, *Cherokee Tragedy*, pp. 254–78.

[6] Elias Boudinot, *Letters and Other Papers Relating to Cherokee Affairs*, in *Cherokee Editor*, ed. Perdue, p. 162.

participation as equals in the future destiny of the republic that had inspired them prior to 1833. In a totally different environment, with the stinging memory of their betrayals and humiliations, the optimistic spirit of their first renascence was replaced by a more hard-headed, grim reliance upon self-interest. The Cherokees knew they would not share in the rising greatness of the United States.

The full-blood conservatives, although they had displayed less eagerness before 1833 to emulate the white man, suffered more from the alien environment. They missed the ancient hills, valleys, rivers, and springs of their ancestral land; they could not find in the West that rapport with nature or that healing power in its alien flora and fauna that had sustained their spirits and bodies in the East. The herbs and roots upon which their adonisgi relied for their medicine could not be found. An uprooted people, physically and emotionally, they did not thrive culturally in the new soil.

For another generation they cultivated the new land as best they could, but they knew that their days of self-government were numbered. Worse than the deepening disdain of white Americans, however, was the bitter enmity that poisoned their internal relationships. Three of the signers of the Removed Treaty of New Echota were assassinated in June 1839 (Boudinot, Major Ridge, and John Ridge) for breaking the law against selling tribal land without the approval of the people in full council. A terrible civil war ensued for the next seven years in which the Removal Party and the "old settlers" (those who had emigrated between 1794 and 1835) struggled for control of the nation against the far more numerous Ross Party who came west in 1838–1839. The brief second renascence of the Cherokee Nation in the years 1846 to 1860 ended with the Civil War. After struggling to avoid involvement in "the white man's war," the Cherokees split again, half joining the Confederate States of America, half joining the United States. Twice in one generation, Cherokee fought against Cherokee. Whatever was left of their ancient tradition of government by consensus and the old ethic of harmony died forever in 1833.

This is not to say that the Cherokee people or their culture died. The Cherokees are more numerous today than ever. And cultures do not die; they simply develop in new ways. The search for a self-governing Cherokee state within the United States was just one phase in the continuing evolution of Cherokee culture. It was, however, a remarkable phase, and the failure of that renascence has cast a heavy shadow. The Cherokees did their best in the years 1794 to 1833 to realize Jefferson's promise that "We shall all be Americans." The failure was not theirs.

BIBLIOGRAPHY

I have relied primarily on the records of Indian affairs in the National Archives, first-hand accounts by missionaries, and materials in state archives. The National Archives have now placed on microfilm most of their records relating to Indian Affairs and the Office of the Secretary of War. A list of the most important of these microfilm series for this study, indicating the abbreviations used for annotation, is given at the beginning of the book. The most important missionary archives are those of the Moravians (or United Brethren) in Bethlehem, Pennsylvania, and Winston-Salem, North Carolina; the American Board of Commissioners for Foreign Missions at Houghton Library, Harvard University; the Presbyterian Historical Society, in Philadelphia; the American Baptist Historical Society in Rochester, New York; the Dargan-Carver Memorial Library of the United Methodists in Nashville, Tennessee; and the Garrett Evangelical Seminary in Evanston, Illinois.

The state archives in Nashville, Tennessee; Atlanta, Georgia; and Raleigh, North Carolina have been very helpful in providing the perspective of the frontier states that surrounded the Cherokee Nation in the years covered by this study. Important Cherokee archives include the Gilcrease Institute, Tulsa, Oklahoma (where the John Ross Papers and Grant Foreman Papers are located) and the Cherokee Museum at Qualla, North Carolina. Other important sources of materials relating to the Cherokee Indians include the Silas Dinsmoor Papers, the John Howard Payne Papers, and the Ayer Collection at the Newberry Library, Chicago; the Oklahoma Historical Society, in Oklahoma City; the Western Collection of the University of Oklahoma, Norman; the Worcester-Robertson Papers and the Schleppy Collection at Tulsa University; and the Daniel Parker Papers at the Pennsylvania Historical Society, Philadelphia. I have also made extensive use of the editions of the *Cherokee Phoenix* at the American Antiquarian Society in Worcester, Massachusetts.

Bibliographic resources on the Indians of North America are becoming more numerous and valuable. For this study I have particularly made use of James P. Ronda and James Axtell, *Indian Missions: A Critical Bibliography* (Bloomington: Indiana University Press, 1978); Raymond D. Fogelson, *The Cherokees: A Critical Bibliography* (Bloomington: Indi-

453

ana University Press, 1978); the bibliography contained in Charles Hudson, *The Southeastern Indians* (Knoxville: University of Tennessee Press, 1976); and the bibliography in the new edition of Thurman Wilkins, *Cherokee Tragedy* (Norman: University of Oklahoma Press, 1985).

A major and accessible source of of primary documents relating to Indian Affairs that is particularly rich with respect to the Cherokees is *American State Papers: Indian Affairs*, vols. I and II, *Documents, Legislative and Executive of the Congress of the United States*, edited by Walter Lowrie, Walter S. Franklin, and Matthew St. Clair Clark (Washington, D.C.: Gales and Seaton, 1832, 1834).

I. PRIMARY SOURCES

Adair, James. *History of the American Indians*. Edited by Samuel C. Williams. 1775. Reprint. New York: Johnson, 1969.

Bartram, William. "Observations on the Creek and Cherokee Indians." *American Ethnological Society Transactions* 3 (1853):1–81.

Boudinot, Elias. *An Address Delivered to the Whites*. Philadelphia, 1826.

Cherokee Nation. *Laws of the Cherokee Nation*. Tahlequah, Cherokee Nation, 1952.

Evarts, Jeremiah. *Essays on the Present Crisis*. Boston, 1829.

Gilmer, George R. *Sketches of Some of the First Settlers of Upper Georgia*. New York: Appleton, 1855. Reprint. Americus, Georgia, 1926.

Hawkins, Benjamin. *A Sketch of the Creek Country*. Publications of the Georgia Historical Society, vol. 3 (1938).

Lumpkin, Wilson. *The Removal of the Cherokee Indians*. Wormsloe, Georgia, 1907.

McCoy, Isaac. *History of Baptist Indian Missions*. Washington, 1840. Reprint. New York: Johnson, 1970.

McKenney, Thomas L., and James Hall. *History of the Indian Tribes*. Philadelphia, 1836.

Morse, Jedidiah. *A Report to the Secretary of War*. New Haven, Conn., 1822.

Owen, Narcissa. *Memoirs*. Washington, D.C., 1907.

Peters, Richard. *The Case of the Cherokee Nation against the State of Georgia*. Philadelphia, 1831.

Ross, William P. *Life and Times of Hon. Wm. P. Ross*. Fort Smith, Ark., 1893.

Stuart, John A. *A Sketch of the Cherokee and Choctaw Indians*. Little Rock, 1837.

Timberlake, Henry. *Memoirs*. Edited by Samuel C. Williams. 1765. Reprint. Marietta, Ga., 1948.

II. CHEROKEE CULTURE

Bloom, Leonard. "The Acculturation of the Eastern Cherokee: HIstorical Aspects." *North Carolina Historical Review* 19 (October 1942):328–58.

Brown, John P. *Old Frontiers*. Kingsport, Tenn.: Southern Publishers, 1938.

Butrick, Daniel. *Cherokee Antiquities*. Vinita, I.T.: Indian Chieftain Publishers, 1884.

Fenton, William N., and John Gulick, eds. "Symposium on Cherokee and Iroquois Culture." Smithsonian Institution, Bureau of American Ethnology *Bulletin* 180. Washington, D.C.: Government Printing Office, 1961.

Fogelson, Raymond D. "The Cherokee Ballgame Cycle." *Ethnomusicology* 15 (1971):327–28.

———. "On the Varieties of Indian History." *Journal of Ethnic Studies* 2 (1974):105–112.

Fogelson, Raymond D., and Richard N. Adams, eds. *The Anthropology of Power*. New York: Academic Press, 1977.

Gearing, Fred O. *Priests and Warriors*. American Anthropological Association Memoir 93. Menasha, Wis.: American Anthropological Association, 1962.

Gilbert, William H., Jr. "The Eastern Cherokees." Smithsonian Institution, Bureau of American Ethnology *Bulletin* 133. Washington, D.C.: Government Printing Office, 1943.

Hudson, Charles M. *The Southeastern Indians*. Knoxville: University of Tennessee Press, 1976.

———, ed. *Four Centuries of Southern Indians*. Athens: University of Georgia Press, 1975.

Hultkrantz, Åke. *Belief and Worship in Native North America*. Syracuse: University of Syracuse Press, 1981.

Kilpatrick, Jack F. *Sequoyah, of Earth and Intellect*. Austin: Encino Press, 1965.

———, ed. "The Wahnenauhi Manuscript." Smithsonian Institution, Bureau of American Ethnology *Bulletin* 196. Washington, D.C.: Government Printing Office, 1966.

Kilpatrick, Jack F. and Anna Gritts Kilpatrick, eds. *New Echota Letters*. Dallas: Southern Methodist University Press, 1968.

———. *The Shadow of Sequoya*. Norman: University of Oklahoma Press, 1965.

Loomis, A. W. *Scenes in the Indian Country*. Philadelphia: Philadelphia Presbyterian Board, 1859.

Mooney, James. "The Cherokee Ball Play." *American Anthropologist*, o.s., 3 (1890):105–132.

———. *Historical Sketch of the Cherokee*. Chicago: Aldine Publishing Co., 1975.

———. "The Sacred Formulas of the Cherokees." Smithsonian Institution, Bureau of American Ethnology *7th Annual Report, 1885–88*. Washington, D.C.: Government Printing Office, 1891.

———. "Myths of the Cherokees." Smithsonian Institution, Bureau of American Ethnology *19th Annual Report, 1897-98*, part 1. Washington, D.C.: Government Printing Office, 1900.

———. "The Ghost Dance Religion." Smithsonian Institution, Bureau of American Ethnology *14th Annual Report, 1892–93*, part 2. Washington, D.C.: Government Printing Office, 1896.

Reid, John Philip. *A Law of Blood*. New York: New York University Press, 1970.
———. *A Better Kind of Hatchet*. University Park: Pennsylvania State University Press, 1976.
Spicer, Edward H. *Perspectives in American Indian Culture Change*. Chicago: University of Chicago Press, 1961.
Strickland, Rennard. *Fire and the Spirits*. Norman: University of Oklahoma Press, 1975.
Swanton, John R. "The Indians of the Southeastern United States." Smithsonian Institution, Bureau of American Ethnology *Bulletin* 137. Washington, D.C.: Government Printing Office, 1946.
Wilms, Douglas C. "Cherokee Settlement Patterns." *Southeastern Geographer* 14 (1974):46–53.
———. "Cherokee Indian Land Use in Georgia, 1800–1838." Ph.D. dissertation, University of Georgia, 1973.

III. AMERICAN INDIAN POLICY

Abel, Annie H. "The History of Events Resulting in Indian Consolidation West of the Mississippi." *Annual Report of the American Historical Association, 1906*. Vol. 1. Washington, D.C.: Government Printing Office, 1908.
———. "Proposals for an Indian State, 1778–1878." *Annual Report of the American Historical Association, 1907*. Vol. 1. Washington, D.C.: Government Printing Office, 1908.
Dippie, Brian W. *The Vanishing American*. Middletown, Conn.: Wesleyan University Press, 1982.
Green, Michael D. *The Politics of Indian Removal: Creek Government and Society in Crisis*. Lincoln: Nebraska University Press, 1982.
Harmon, George D. "Benjamin Hawkins and the Federal Factory System." *North Carolina Historical Review* 9 (1932):138–52.
———. *Sixty Years of Indian Affairs*. Chapel Hill: University of North Carolina Press, 1941.
Horsman, Reginald. *Expansionism and American Indian Policy, 1783–1812*. East Lansing: Michigan State University Press, 1967.
———. *Race and Manifest Destiny*. Cambridge: Harvard University Press, 1981.
McCoy, Isaac. *Remarks on the Practicability of Indian Reform*. 2d ed. New York. 1829.
Miles, Edwin A. "After John Marshall's Decision." *Journal of Southern History* 39 (1973):520–44.
Phillips, Ulrich B. "Georgia and States' Rights." *Annual Report of the American Historical Association, 1901*. Washington, D.C.: Government Printing Office, 1902.
Prucha, Francis Paul. *American Indian Policy in the Formative Years*. Cambridge: Harvard University Press, 1962.

———. "Andrew Jackson's Indian Policy: A Reassessment." *Journal of American History* 66, no. 3 (December 1969):527–39.

———. *The Great Father: The United States Government and the American Indians.* 2 vols. Lincoln: University of Nebraska Press, 1984.

Prucha, Francis Paul, ed. *Cherokee Removal: The 'William Penn' Essays and Other Writings by Jeremiah Evarts.* Knoxville: University of Tennessee Press, 1981.

Royce, Charles C. "The Cherokee Nation of Indians, A Narrative of their Official Relations with the Colonial and Federal Governments." Smithsonian Institution, Bureau of American Ethnology *5th Annual Report, 1883–1884.* Washington, D.C.: Government Printing Office, 1887. Reprint. Chicago: Aldine Publishing Co., 1975.

Satz, Ronald N. *American Indian Policy in the Jacksonian Era.* Lincoln: University of Nebraska Press, 1975.

Sheehan, Bernard. *Seeds of Extinction.* Chapel Hill: University of North Carolina Press, 1973.

Viola, Herman J. *Thomas L. McKenney, Architect of America's Indian Policy, 1816–1830.* Chicago: Swallow Press, 1974.

IV. CHEROKEE HISTORY, 1700–1840

Abel, Annie H. "The Cherokee Negotiations of 1822–1823." *Smith College Studies in History* 1 (July 1916).

Brown, John P. *Old Frontiers.* Kingsport, Tenn.: Southern Publishers, 1938.

Conser, Walter H., Jr. "John Ross and the Cherokee Resistance Campaign, 1833–1838." *Journal of Southern History* 44 (May 1978):191–212.

Corkran, David H. *The Cherokee Frontier, 1740–1762.* Norman: University of Oklahoma Press, 1962.

Cotterill, Robert S. *The Southern Indians.* Norman: University of Oklahoma Press, 1954.

Dale, Edward E., and Gaston L. Litton, eds. *Cherokee Cavaliers.* Norman: University of Oklahoma Press, 1939.

Debo, Angie. *And Still the Waters Run: The Betrayal of the Five Civilized Tribes.* 1940. Rev. ed., Princeton: Princeton University Press, 1972.

———. *The Rise and Fall of the Choctaw Republic.* Norman: University of Oklahoma Press, 1934.

———. *The Road to Disappearance.* Norman: University of Oklahoma Press, 1941.

DeRosier, Arthur H., Jr. *The Removal of the Choctaw Indians.* Knoxville: University of Tennessee Press, 1970.

Drinnon, Richard. *Facing West: The Metaphysics of Indian-Hating and Empire-Building.* Minneapolis: University of Minnesota Press, 1980.

Eaton, Rachel. *John Ross and the Cherokee Indians.* Chicago: n.p., 1921.

Foreman, Grant. *Indian Removal.* Norman: University of Oklahoma Press, 1932.

————. *Sequoyah*. Norman: University of Oklahoma Press, 1938.

Gabriel, Ralph H. *Elias Boudinot*. Norman: University of Oklahoma Press, 1941.

Gibson, Arrell M. *The Chickasaws*. Norman: University of Oklahoma Press, 1971.

Goodwin, Gary. *Cherokees in Transition*. Chicago: University of Chicago, Dept. of Geography, 1977.

Govan, Gilbert E., and James W. Livingood. *The Chattanooga Country, 1540–1951*. New York: E. P. Dutton, 1951.

Halliburton, Rudi, Jr. *Red over Black*. Westport, Conn.: Greenwood Press, 1977.

Haywood, John. *Civil and Political History of Tennessee*. Nashville, 1821.

King, Duane, ed. *The Cherokee Indian Nation*. Knoxville: University of Tennessee Press, 1979.

Littlefield, Daniel F., Jr. *Africans and Creeks*. Westport, Connecticut. Greenwood Press, 1979.

McKenney, Thomas L. and James Hall. *Biographical Sketches and Anecdotes of Ninety-Five of 120 Principal Chiefs from the Indian Tribes of North America*. Washington, D.C.: U.S. Department of Interior, 1967.

McLoughlin, William G. "Cherokee Anti-Mission Sentiment." *Ethnohistory* 21 (1974):361-70.

————. *The Cherokee Ghost Dance and Other Essays on the Southeastern Indians*. Macon, Ga.: Mercer University Press, 1984.

————. *Cherokees and Missionaries, 1789–1839*. New Haven: Yale University Press, 1984.

————. "Experiment in Cherokee Citizenship." *American Quarterly* 33 (1981):3–25.

————. "A Note on African Sources of American Indian Racial Myths." *Journal of American Folklore* 89 (1976):331–35.

————. Thomas Jefferson and the Beginning of Cherokee Nationalism." *William and Mary Quarterly*, 3d ser., 32 (October 1975):562–80.

McLoughlin, William G. and Walter H. Conser, Jr. "The Cherokees in Transition." *Journal of American History* 64 (1977):678–703.

Malone, Henry T. *Cherokees of the Old South*. Athens: University of Georgia Press, 1956.

Moulton, Gary. *John Ross, Cherokee Chief*. Athens: University of Georgia Press, 1978.

Perdue, Theda, ed. *Cherokee Editor: The Writings of Elias Boudinot*. Knoxville: University of Tennessee Press, 1983.

————. *Slavery and the Evolution of Cherokee Society, 1540–1866*. Knoxville: University of Tennessee Press, 1979.

Pound, Merritt B. *Benjamin Hawkins, Indian Agent*. Athens: University of Georgia Press, 1951.

Rogin, Michael P. *Fathers and Children: Andrew Jackson and the Subjugation of the American Indians*. New York: Knopf, 1975.

Royce, Charles C. *The Cherokee Nation of Indians*. 1887. Reprint. Chicago: Aldine, 1975.

Starkey, Marion. *The Cherokee Nation*. New York: Knopf, 1946.

Starr, Emett. *Early History of the Cherokees Embracing Aboriginal Customs, Religion, Laws, Folk Lore and Civilization* (Claremore, Okla.: n.p., 1917.

––––––. *History of the Cherokee Indians and Their Legends*. Oklahoma City: Warden, 1922.

Traveller Bird. *Tell Them They Lie: The Sequoyah Myth*. Los Angeles: Western-lore Publishers, 1971.

Van Every, Dale. *Disinherited*. New York: William Morrow, 1966.

Wardell, Morris. *A Political History of the Cherokee Nation, 1838–1907*. Norman: University of Oklahoma Press, 1938.

Woodward, Grace. The Cherokees. Norman: University of Oklahoma Press, 1963.

Young, Mary E. "Indian Removal." In *Indians of the Lower South*. Edited by John Mahon. Pensacola: Gulf Coast History and Humanities Conference, 1975.

––––––. *Redskins, Ruffle Shirts and Red Necks*. Norman: University of Oklahoma Press, 1961.

––––––. "Women, Civilization and the Indian Question," in *Clio Was a Woman: Studies in the History of American Women*. Edited by Mabel E. Deutrich and Virginia C. Purdy. Washington, D.C.: Howard University Press, 1980.

V. MISSIONARY HISTORIES

A. General

Beaver, R. Pierce. *Church, State and the American Indians*. St. Louis: Concordia, 1966.

Berkhofer, Robert F., Jr. *Salvation and the Savage*. New York: Atheneum, 1976.

Bowden, Henry W. *American Indians and Christian Missions*. Chicago: University of Chicago Press, 1981.

B. Denominational

Anderson, Rufus K., ed. *Memoirs of Catherine Brown*. Boston, 1828.

Andrew II, John A. *Rebuilding the Christian Commonwealth*. Lexington: University of Kentucky Press, 1976.

Bangs, Nathan. *An Authentic History of the Missions under the Care of the Missionary Society of the Methodist Episcopal Church*. New York, 1832.

Barclay, Wade C. *History of Methodist Missions*. 2 vols. New York: Board of Missions of the Methodist Church, 1949–50.

Bass, Althea. *Cherokee Messenger*. Norman: University Oklahoma Press, 1936.

Bass, Dorothy C. "Gideon Blackburn's Mission to the Cherokees." *Journal of Presbyterian History* 52 (Fall 1974):203–226.

Coleman, Michael C. "Not Race but Grace: Presbyterian Missionaries and American Indians, 1837–1893." *Journal of American History* 7 (June 1980):41–60.

Faust, Harold S. "The Growth of Presbyterian Missions to the American Indians." *Journal of the Presbyterian Historical Society* 22 (1944):82–123.

Fries, Adelaide L., trans. and ed. "Records of the Moravians in North Carolina."

Publications of the North Carolina Historical Commission. Vols. 23, 24, 25, 27. Raleigh, N.C., 1943, 1947, 1954.

Hamilton, Kenneth G., trans. and ed. "Minutes of the Mission Conference Held in Springplace." *The Atlanta Historical Bulletin* (Winter 1970):9–87.

———, trans. and ed. "Minutes of the Mission Conference Held in Springplace." *The Atlanta Historical Bulletin* (Spring 1971):31–59.

Harrell, David E. *Quest for a Christian America*. Nashville: Bethany Press, 1965.

John, Isabelle G. *Handbook of Methodist Missions*. Nashville, 1893.

Lazenby, Marion E. *History of Methodism in Alabama and West Florida*. N.p., 1960.

McCoy, Isaac. *History of Baptist Indian Missions*. Washington, D.C., 1840.

McFerrin, John B. *History of Methodism in Tennessee*. Nashville: Southern Methodist Publishing House, 1879.

Malone, Henry T. "The Early Nineteenth Century Missionaries in the Cherokee Country." *Tennessee Historical Quarterly* 10 (June 1951):127–39.

Moffitt, James W. "Early Baptist Missionary Work among the Cherokee." *The East Tennessee Historical Society's Publications* 12 (1940):16–27.

Moseley, J. Edward. *Disciples of Christ in Georgia*. St. Louis: Bethany Press, 1954.

Mudge, Enoch. "History of the Missions of the Methodist Episcopal Church." In *History of American Missions to the Heathen*. Worcester, Mass.: Spooner & Howard, 1840.

Peacock, Mary T. "Methodist Mission Work among the Cherokee Indians before Removal." *Methodist History* 3 (1965):20–39.

———. *The Circuit Riders and Those Who Followed*. Chattanooga: Hudson Printing Co., 1957.

Phillips, Clifton J. *Protestant America and the Pagan World*. Cambridge: Harvard University Press, 1969.

Routh, Eugene C. "Early Missionaries to the Cherokees." *Chronicles of Oklahoma* 15 (December 1937):449–65.

Schultz, George A. *An Indian Canaan*. Norman: University of Oklahoma Press, 1972.

Schwarze, Edmund. *History of the Moravian Missions among the Southern Indian Tribes of the United States*. Bethlehem, Penn.: Times Publishing Co., 1923.

Strong, William E. *The Story of the American Board*. Boston: Pilgrim Press, 1910.

Tracy, Joseph. *History of American Missions to the Heathen*. Worcester, Mass., 1840.

Walker, Robert S. *Torchlights to the Cherokees*. New York: Macmillan, 1931.

Washburn, Cephas. *Reminiscences of the Indians*. Richmond: Presbyterian Committee of Publication, 1969.

West, Anson G. *History of Methodism in Alabama*. Nashville, 1893.

INDEX

abortion. *See* infanticide

acculturation. *See* Cherokees, acculturation of

Adair, Edward, 20, 75

Adams, John, 46, 47, 77

Adams, John Quincy, 348, 369, 411, 413, 414, 415, 448–49; and Cherokee constitution, 401, 408–409; effort to remove Cherokees (1828–1829), 416–29; and Indian colonization, 370, 371, 372, 373, 375, 376

adonisgi. *See* Cherokees, adonisgi

Afro-Americans, 337–38, 348. *See also* slaves and slavery

agents, federal Indian, 34–57, 110. *See also* Hawkins, Benjamin; Lewis, Thomas; McMinn, Joseph; Meigs, Return J.; Montgomery, Hugh; Shaw, Leonard

agriculture. *See* Cherokees, agriculture and farming of

Alabama (territory and state), 7, 20, 22, 58, 186, 187, 194–95, 198–201, 206, 208, 214, 247; Cherokee reserves in, 275; detribalizes Cherokees, 425

American Board of Commissioners for Foreign Missions. *See* missionaries, American Board

American Revolution, 3, 19–20, 21

American school of ethnology, 348

annuity. *See* Cherokees, annuities of

anti-mission sentiment, 376–87, 388–91, 392–93, 396, 402–403, 430, 441–47. *See also* Ghost Dance movement; White Path's Rebellion

Arkansas (territory and state), 56, 80, 94, 128, 130, 209

Arkansas, Cherokee settlements in, 80, 94, 128, 130, 135, 153, 160, 162–64, 170, 209, 211, 217–20, 225, 228, 261–68

Arkansas, removal of Cherokees to, in 1808–1810: 128–37, 147–67; in 1817–1819: 222–57; in 1828–1829: 222–57, 413–28. *See also* Creek Path conspiracy

Arkansas River, 152, 153, 219, 235

Armistead, Captain A. B., 121

Armstrong, John, 190, 195, 197

Army garrisons, 121, 128, 179, 280, 309

artisans and mechanics in Cherokee Nation, 36, 66, 72, 83, 171, 175, 290–91, 327–28

Augusta, Georgia, 64

Augusta-Nashville Turnpike ("Georgia Road"), 77–90, 92–93, 121, 127

Autowe, 102

backsliding, 381

Badger, The, 20

Badger's Son, 61, 126, 158

Baldridge, John, 210

ball plays, 15, 33, 64, 120, 362

Baptists. *See* missionaries

Barbour, James, 318, 369, 370, 373, 374, 375, 413, 414

Bark, The, 210, 211

Benge, John, 210

Big Bear, The, 115, 175, 182

Big Tiger, 392, 395

Big Warrior, 188, 190

Blackburn, Rev. Gideon, 74–75, 141–42, 248. *See also* missionaries, Presbyterian

Black Fox, 59, 60, 87, 88, 99, 100, 103, 105, 109, 111, 115, 116, 118, 122, 125, 130, 137, 138, 139; death of, 190; deposed, 145, 147; reinstated, 156, 157

blacks. *See* Afro-Americans; slaves and slavery

Blair, James, 181, 304

blood revenge. *See* clan revenge

Bloody Fellow, 20, 22, 24, 25, 60, 61

Blount, Gov. William, 23–24, 40, 60, 61

Blount, Gov. Willie, 166, 167, 320

Bold Hunter, 63

Bone Polisher, 120

Boone, Daniel, 18

Boot, The. *See* Chulio

Boudinot, Elias (Buck Watie), 277, 288, 367–86, 403, 416–17, 441, 450–51

Bowl, The, 159, 166

461

LIBRARY OF CONGRESS
CATALOGING-IN-PUBLICATION DATA

McLoughlin, William Gerald.
Cherokee renascence in the New Republic.

Bibliography: p.
Includes index.
1. Cherokee Indians—History.   2. Cherokee Indians—Government
relations—History.   I. Title.
E99.C5M4 1986   975'.00497   86–42843
ISBN 0–691–04741–3 (alk. paper)

William G. McLoughlin is Professor of History at Brown University.
He is the author of numerous works, including *Cherokees
and Missionaries* (Yale).